WAR IN THE SHALLOWS

U.S. NAVY COASTAL AND
RIVERINE WARFARE IN VIETNAM
1965–1968

John Darrell Sherwood

Naval History and Heritage Command
Department of the Navy
Washington, DC
2015

Published by
Naval History and Heritage Command
805 Kidder Breese Street SE
Washington Navy Yard, DC 20374-5060
www.history.navy.mil

Book Design by Jamie Harvey

Front cover caption: A "Tango" boat steams down the Long Tau River.

AN UNCOMMON VALOR SERIES
REPRINT EDITION
January 2016

Use of ISBN

This is the official U.S. Government edition of this publication and is herein identified to certify its authenticity. Use of 978-0-945274-76-6 is for the U.S. Government Publishing Office editions only. The Superintendent of Documents of the U.S. Government Publishing Office requests that any reprinted edition clearly be labeled a copy of the authentic work with a new ISBN.

In accordance with the Superintendent of Documents proviso above, this is an unabridged reprint edition of *War in the Shallows,* and provided with a new ISBN:

ISBN-13: 978-1523488766
ISBN-10: 152348876X

CONTENTS

Preface vii
Acknowledgments xv

CHAPTER 1
Early Years 1
    Origins of the Vietnam Navy and the Naval Advisory Group 5
    Establishment of the Coastal Force 13
    River Force 17
    Sea Force 19
    Vietnam Navy in the 1963 Coup 21
    Barrier Patrols and the Bucklew Report 24
    Navy SEALs in Vietnam 28
    The Vung Ro Incident 31
    End of Tour 36

CHAPTER 2
Coastal Warfare, 1965–1966 39
    First Patrols 43
    Vietnam Navy in Crisis: 1965 45
    American Role Expands 52
    Coast Guard Support for Market Time 57
    Arrival of the PCFs 66
    Tale of Two Swift Boats 72
    Postscript: The Arnheiter Affair 80

CHAPTER 3

War on the Rivers: Game Warden, 1966–1967 89
    Origins of Game Warden 92
    LCPLs in the Rung Sat 97
    Operation Jackstay 98
    The PBR Story 104
    Basing and Base Life. 111
    YRBM-16 Mining 119
    Seawolves 123
    Naval Intelligence Liaison Officers 130
    Civic Action 133
    PBR Combat Experiences 135
    War Escalates on the Rivers 153

CHAPTER 4

Mobile Riverine Force 161
    Origins, Training, and Command Relationships. 166
    Boats of the Mobile Riverine Force 175
    Afloat and Ashore Bases 182
    Operational Tactics and Rules of Engagement 191
    Initial Operations 200
    Coronado V: Rach Ba Rai 207
    Coronado IX: Rach Ruong 215

CHAPTER 5

War on the Coast, 1967 221
    Market Time SITREP 225
    Vietnam Navy and Market Time. 229
    Market Time Naval Gunfire Support 231
    Fog of War 236
    Point Welcome Incident. 237
    More Friendly Fire Attacks 240
    Asheville-class Patrol Gunboats. 243
    Trawler Intercepts. 248
    Demise of Coastal Group 16. 258
    PSYOP and Civic Action 261
    PSYOP Mission: 6 December 1967 267

CHAPTER 6
Tet, 1968 275
    The Man at the Center of the Storm 276
    Storm Clouds. 280
    My Tho 285
    Ben Tre 292
    Vinh Long 300
    Can Tho 308
    Postscript: Task Force Clearwater during Tet 312

Conclusion 319

Acronyms and Abbreviations. 325
Bibliography. 331
Endnotes 343
Index 407

PREFACE

More than 174,000 sailors served in South Vietnam between 1960 and 1972.[1] At the height of the U.S. Navy's involvement in South Vietnam, the Navy's coastal and riverine forces included more than 30,000 sailors and over 350 patrol vessels ranging in size from riverboats to destroyers.[2] Naval Forces Vietnam, the Navy's major South Vietnam command, also operated minesweepers, floating barracks and maintenance ships, a fleet of maritime patrol aircraft, and helicopter gunships. Shore facilities included one of the largest and finest ports in the world, Cam Ranh Bay, as well as many smaller bases spread out along the 1,200-mile coastline of South Vietnam and its major rivers.

Besides being large and resources-intensive, the Navy's war in South Vietnam was a stark departure from the oceanic or "blue water" operations that characterized much of the U.S. Navy's 20th-century history. The capital ships of the "brown water" (riverine) and "green water" (coastal) navy were not battleships, ballistic missile submarines, or aircraft carriers but small boats, many of which were converted World War II-era landing craft or modified commercial craft. Vietnam was a decidedly low-tech, manpower intensive operation—an anathema to a navy focused on fleet operations and cutting edge technology. The story of how the U.S. Navy shifted gears during the Vietnam War, constructed three inshore task forces from scratch, and adapted to a form of warfare not experienced since the Civil War is the subject of this work.

While many books have been written about the U.S. Army and U.S. Marine Corps in Vietnam, the Navy has received less attention. What little has been written consists mainly of memoirs written by veterans. The best general account of this chapter of the Navy's history is Thomas Cutler's *Brown Water, Black Berets: Coastal and Riverine Warfare in Vietnam* (1988). Cutler, a veteran of the River Patrol Force, wrote an imminently readable account based mainly on interviews with sailors from the period. The book is a fine piece of work on the subject, but the history was not meant to be a definitive one. Commander Richard L. Schreadley served as a historian with the Naval Forces Vietnam staff in 1969 and later wrote an overview of the Navy's involvement in the war, entitled *From the Rivers to the Sea: The U.S. Navy in Vietnam* (1992) with several chapters devoted to coastal and riverine operations. Based mainly on his personal files from his tour in Vietnam, the book suffers from a lack of documentation on many operations covered and is journalistic in its style. It is also too broad brush of a treatment, covering the entire naval enterprise in Vietnam (including Seventh Fleet operations and amphibious readiness), to offer extensive insight on riverine and coastal warfare.

The Naval History Division and the Naval Historical Center, predecessor organizations to the Naval History and Heritage Command, published two official histories of the Navy during the Vietnam War: Edwin Bickford Hooper, Dean C. Allard, and Oscar P. Fitzgerald, *The United States Navy and the Vietnam Conflict*, vol.1, *Setting the Stage to 1959* (1976); and Edward J. Marolda and Oscar P. Fitzgerald, vol. 2, *From Military Assistance to Combat, 1959–1965* (1986). Although much more comprehensive and better documented than the Schreadley book, these volumes only cover the period through 1965. U.S. Navy in-country operations, which began in 1965 with Operation Market Time, receive brief treatment in volume 2.

Edward J. Marolda, the former senior historian at the Naval History and Heritage Command, wrote an illustrated history of the Navy in Vietnam titled *By Sea, Air, and Land: An Illustrated History of the U.S. Navy and the War in Southeast Asia* (1994) that includes many pictures of the Navy in South Vietnam and short textual descriptions of major operations. R. Blake Dunnavent's, *Brown Water Warfare: The U.S. Navy in Riverine Warfare and the Emergence of a Tactical Doctrine, 1775–1970* (2003) traces the Navy's involvement in brown water operations from the American Revolution through 1970, but it devotes only a single chapter to Vietnam. Alex Larzelere's *The Coast Guard at War, Vietnam, 1965–1975* (1997) and Paul Scotti's *Coast Guard Action in Vietnam: Stories of Those Who Served* (2000) collectively offer a comprehensive account of the Coast Guard in South Vietnam, but U.S. Navy operations are covered tangentially and only in so far as they related to Coast Guard missions.

In short, no scholarly work focusing solely on U.S. Navy coastal and riverine warfare in Vietnam from 1965 to 1968 exists. Relying heavily on recently declassified documents held by the Naval History and Heritage Command, this book represents the first comprehensive scholarly attempt to piece together the operational history of the U.S. Navy in South Vietnam from the first coastal patrols in 1965 through the 1968 Tet Offensive. The U.S. Navy invested many resources to the in-country war: in addition to vast amounts of equipment purchased and expended, the three shallow-water task forces lost 457 sailors during the war, and many others were wounded.[3] This book seeks to understand what kind of return the U.S. Navy received for this investment and sacrifice. How did the Navy's coastal and riverine force affect the overall allied effort in Vietnam? How did the Navy's operational tactics evolve over the period? How did the Navy quickly develop an inshore capability and adapt to the unpredicted combat situation in Vietnam? Was Vietnam a triumph for naval arms or a travesty or something in the middle? In the 2004 presidential campaign, Senator John Kerry made much of his experiences in Swift boats in Vietnam, but did these small boats and others like them have a measurable impact on the struggle? These are some of the central questions this book addresses.

The impact of the Vietnam War on the Navy's sailors is another important theme of this book. Who were the men who fought in the shallows and how did they differ from traditional sailors with the Seventh Fleet and other blue water units? Was there something unique about the culture of the brown and green water Navy? Did these forces represent an elite force as many memoirists have implied?[4] To help answer these questions, more than 125 veterans were interviewed. Whenever possible, their stories are woven into the narrative to expose the human side of the Navy in South Vietnam. Material from these interviews also serves to drive the narrative, making it accessible to readers more accustomed to biography than traditional operational history based solely on documents. After-action reports, usually written in the driest language by staff officers removed from the action, only offer one picture of a battle—a picture often factually accurate but lacking *Sturm und Drang* (storm and stress). These reports do not reveal the thoughts of a sailor fighting for his life on a lightly armed small boat or the fabric of his daily life on patrol or at his base, ashore or afloat. Oral histories, when used in combination with documents, provide a necessary tool for reconstructing the world of the shallow water sailor. They offer a glimpse of the humanity behind the hardware rarely seen in message traffic or action reports. To ensure authenticity the spelling and punctuation in the original quotations have been maintained, and the treatment of measurements remain true to their sources.

If the Navy's World War II historical narrative was dominated by admirals such as Chester Nimitz, William Halsey, and Raymond Spruance, the Vietnam narrative consists of many smaller tales told by junior officers and petty officers. In Vietnam, lower ranking personnel played a larger role in combat decision making than ever before in U.S. Navy history. In both the River Patrol Force and the Mobile Riverine Force (MRF), petty officers often commanded the major fighting unit of conflict—the small boat. Even in the Coastal Surveillance Force, only one junior officer typically rode on a Swift boat, which meant that ordinary sailors performed many significant jobs held by officers on larger vessels. By delving into the social backgrounds of enlisted boat captains and their crews, this book strives to highlight the fact that these ordinary men possessed "agency," or the capacity to act independently and control events.

Junior officers (those below the rank of lieutenant commander, O-4) also receive extensive attention in this volume. These men played a vital role in the conflict, commanding not only small boats but also larger formations, including river patrol sections and river assault divisions. Most volunteered for duty in Vietnam despite warnings that such assignments might not be career-enhancing. In the 1960s there was no clear-cut career path for a small boat officer. Promotion boards, for the most part, did not believe that service on small boats in Vietnam better prepared officers for larger surface commands than did traditional division assignments on oceangoing ships. Most junior officers volunteered for assignment in South Vietnam out of a sense of adventure and for the opportunity for independent command responsibility at a young age. Many were reservists who received their commissions from Reserve Officer Training Corps (ROTC) programs on college campuses or the Navy's Officer Candidate School in Newport, Rhode Island, and expected to serve in the Navy for a short period of time before returning to civilian life. Living, working, and fighting in close proximity with sailors on small boats allowed them to form close bonds with enlisted men—bonding experienced much less often by junior officers on ships where there was much more physical and psychological distance between officers and enlisted men.

As a group, the young lieutenants and enlisted boat captains of the inshore task forces in South Vietnam were the face of the United States Navy as far as the local populace was concerned. Their interactions with civilians during boat searches, civic actions missions, and at shore bases often proved critical in America's attempts to "win the hearts and minds" of the people of the Mekong Delta, the Rung Sat swamp, and the coastal areas of South Vietnam. Finally, these men possessed command autonomy found in few other places in the U.S. Navy. Once they left their bases, these junior officers and petty officers faced a myriad of life or death decisions with regard to small unit tactics, about the use of force, and even about how to react to sea states, tides, and weather. It was not a job for the faint of heart, and while not every boat captain lived up to the challenge, the vast majority succeeded admirably. The willingness of American officers and petty officers to sail into harm's way on the smallest of craft and aggressively prosecute their mission in a highly professional manner often stunned the enemy and led to some surprising victories.

The naval war in South Vietnam consisted of many small unit actions punctuated by only a small number of larger operations. In this war, a "major" operation would be a trawler intercept by the Coastal Surveillance Force or an amphibious operation by the Mobile Riverine Force involving more than one battalion of Army troops. With the exception of the Tet Offensive, there were no actions comparable to even mid-sized World War II operations. Nevertheless, *War in the Shallows* makes an effort to cover in detail most of the large U.S. Navy operations that occurred during the 1965 to 1968 period. For smaller actions this book delves only into battles or incidents that illuminate key trends and themes. Several sections of chapters 2 and 6 cover special topics that do not fit neatly into the general narrative but still relate to the major themes of book: inshore warfare and the unique experiences of sailors fighting in South Vietnam.

War in the Shallows begins with an analysis of the naval situation in South Vietnam from 1950 to 1965—the so-called advisory period. This contextual section seeks to explain why the Vietnam Navy (VNN) failed to effectively stem the flow of supplies from North Vietnam to South Vietnam and why the U.S. Navy by 1965 felt compelled to directly intervene in the conflict to solve the seaborne infiltration problem. The book makes a special effort to analyze the nature of the Navy's advisory role, the plight of Navy advisors, and why they were unable to build up the VNN fast enough to meet the growing Communist threat. The acquisition of new ships was only one aspect of the VNN's challenges. Other problems were structural and related to its youthful and inexperienced officer corps, a lack of well-trained noncommissioned officers, the poor morale of its enlisted force, inadequate training and maintenance facilities, the politicization of the South Vietnamese armed forces, and budgetary woes. Even if more U.S. advisors had been able to speak to their counterparts in Vietnamese, it is doubtful that they could have helped this fledgling service overcome its obstacles in the early 1960s.

The book then turns to the first large-scale U.S. Navy coastal interdiction campaign in Vietnam—Operation Market Time. The American role in seaborne interdiction off the coast of South Vietnam began with a handful of larger surface combatants acting in a surveillance-only role and expanded into a multilayered blockade comprising a task force (TF 115) of 5,000 personnel and 126 craft from two services—the U.S. Navy and its partner, the U.S. Coast Guard. The U.S. Navy's war in South Vietnam is often thought of as primarily a brown water war in the rivers, but the coastal interdiction effort, in many respects, was more significant. It was far more successful as an interdiction program than the riverine war and also the longest, most sustained U.S. Navy operation in the waters of South Vietnam. Market Time had a rapid impact on the Communist supply effort, making it exceedingly difficult for North Vietnam to employ the large trawlers and oceangoing junks to resupply its forces in South Vietnam. The operation depended on both small surface units, such as the Navy's iconic Swift boat and the Coast Guard's 82-foot cutters, and a sophisticated network of land, sea, and air radars linked to surface units via a sophisticated command and control system. As the Cuban missile crisis had demonstrated in 1962, the blockade was one of the Navy's strongest suits, and the Vietnam effort was no exception. Operation Market Time proved so successful that by 1967 some of its assets began to be used for other purposes such as naval gunfire support, civic action, and even patrolling larger rivers. Although the operation never had the resources to stop small wooden-hulled boats such as junks and sampans from breaking the blockade, it virtually eliminated infiltration by larger, steel-hulled ships.

Like Market Time before it, Operation Game Warden developed largely in response to the deficiencies of the Vietnam Navy. The River Patrol Force (Task Force 116) began as a river patrol on the Long Tau River, the busy shipping channel running from Saigon to the South China Sea, and soon expanded to include the entire Mekong Delta. At its height in 1968, TF 116 contained five divisions, each with 20 PBRs (patrol boats, river), spread out across the vast Mekong Delta, the Rung Sat swamp, and in I Corps on the Cua Viet and Perfume rivers. Some of the PBRs operated from dry land bases and others from floating bases such landing ship tanks (LSTs) and landing ship docks (LSDs). The River Patrol Force began as a constabulary tasked mainly with searching water traffic for contraband and checking papers of civilians traveling on the rivers but quickly evolved into a mobile strike force intent upon attacking Viet Cong (VC) positions and disrupting river crossings. As an interdiction operation, Game Warden had only a limited effect in halting the spread of enemy supplies on the waterways of the Mekong Delta, but as a direct action force, it succeeded in frustrating numerous Viet Cong river crossings, disrupting large-scale enemy troop movements, and securing the major rivers in the delta for commerce. The River Patrol force also proved invaluable as a roving cavalry for the allies during the 1968 Tet Offensive, providing several beleaguered outposts in the delta with valuable gunfire support, especially during the early days of the offensive.

The Mobile Riverine Force (Task Force 117) was an amphibious riverine strike force designed to operate with the U.S. Army's 9th Infantry Division to search out and destroy large formations of the Viet Cong operating in the Mekong Delta. In 1968 at its height, it consisted of over 1,600 sailors organized into four squadrons, with each squadron further divided into two river assault divisions. Each division contained up to 40 converted landing craft ranging from heavily armed monitors and armored troop carriers to minesweepers and command and control boats. After explaining the concept of the MRF and its bases and technology, *War in the Shallows* examines major assault operations from early 1967 to the Tet Offensive in January 1968. In several of these engagements, large elements of Viet Cong were successfully located and engaged but often at a hefty price in terms of casualties. Although the MRF's armored riverine craft could withstand most small-caliber rifle and machine-gun fire, they were much more vulnerable to antitank rockets employed by the Viet Cong in considerable numbers during the late 1960s. What did not prove vulnerable were the strong bonds that developed between the Army and Navy personnel assigned to this unique fighting force. Through shared danger and hardships, the Army and Navy elements of the MRF overcame command and control challenges, cultural differences, and other challenges to become a close-knit and lethal fighting force.

On 31 January 1968, the Viet Cong units attacked nearly every major city and town in the Mekong Delta. At the time of the attacks, the Mobile Riverine Force and the River Patrol Force were among the few combat units in the area prepared to respond. Tet showcased the mobility, firepower, and shock effect of brown water forces in a way no earlier battle had done. How these riverine forces assisted in blunting the offensive and recapturing the Mekong Delta is the final story told in this book. It represents one of the Navy's finest hours, but one never before fully analyzed. In particular, this section closely examines the battles for the most significant cities and towns in the delta, including My Tho, Ben Tre, Vinh Long, and Can Tho, and in so doing explains how the ability of the Navy to bring firepower and ground troops to besieged towns throughout the delta quite literally saved this area during the Tet Offensive.

Tet represents the end of this book for several reasons. First, it stands out as the high-water mark of the Navy's coastal and riverine war in Southeast Asia. The Navy's in-country strength peaked in September 1968 at 38,083 men. By the end of 1970, that number had dropped to 16,757. After Tet, the Navy accelerated the process of turning over its responsibilities and equipment to the Vietnam Navy. By June 1969 the Mobile Riverine Force ceased to exist, and much of the equipment and patrol sectors of the other task forces had been turned over to the Vietnamese. In September 1970, the Vietnamese navy took charge of the inner barrier and assumed control of Task Force 115's remaining Swift boats and *Point*-class cutters. In December 1970, the River Patrol Force was disestablished, and its 293 PBRs turned over to the VNN.[5] After Tet, the Navy also shifted its strategic emphasis from the coasts and the lower and middle Mekong Delta to areas near the Cambodian border. This new strategy, known as SEALORDS (Southeast Asia Lake, Ocean, River, and Delta Strategy), involved fusing elements from all three task forces to create new infiltration barriers. The SEALORDS campaign and Vietnamization are certainly important chapters in the Navy's history in Vietnam, but they are too large in scope to cover effectively in this volume and deserve separate book-length treatments.

War in the Shallows is both an operational and a social history of the Navy's three riverine and coastal task forces during the 1965–1968 "American" phase of the Vietnam War. Because this story is intimately tied to the history of the Vietnam Navy and the Naval Advisory Group's efforts to create an effective indigenous naval force, the VNN and the U.S. Navy advisors who worked with it receive some attention in this book, as do the coastguardsmen who participated in Operation Market Time. SEAL and light helicopter support for riverine operations are examined in sections of chapters 1 and 3, respectfully. Naval Support Activity operations are addressed sporadically throughout the book in terms of basing and logistics for the coastal and riverine navy. A few Navy units that operated extensively in South Vietnam are absent from this volume. They include but are not limited to Seabees, Navy medical personnel, Sea Dragon naval gunfire support, and amphibious operations along the coast of South Vietnam in support of the Marines in I Corps. These units performed invaluable work for the Navy, but this volume's primary focus is on the operations of the Navy's three inshore task forces in Vietnam

ACKNOWLEDGMENTS

Central goals of the Naval History and Heritage Command (NHHC) are to advance knowledge of the U.S. Navy through historical research and writing and to serve as the Navy's institutional memory. This book never could have achieved these ends without the support of so many members of the command. I am very privileged to work for NHHC and, by extension, the U.S. Navy. With that said, the conclusions and interpretations in this book are mine alone and do not necessarily reflect the views of the U.S. Navy, the Department of Defense, or any other agency of the federal government.

I am indebted to NHHC's leadership, especially its directors, for making this book possible. Retired Rear Admiral Paul Tobin, who served as director from 2005 to 2008, approved the initial project proposal for this book. As a former flag lieutenant for Commander, Naval Forces Vietnam Robert Salzer, he offered unique insights about the Vietnam War. When retired Rear Admiral Jay DeLoach became director of NHHC in 2008, he recognized that inshore and riverine warfare would be crucial for the Navy in the new century. Admiral DeLoach not only embraced this work but also dug deep in his budget to come up with funds for a research trip to Vietnam. More recently, Captain Henry "Jerry" Hendrix, Mr. James Kuhn (acting), and Samuel J. Cox, USN (Ret.) were instrumental in ushering the book through its final production and in securing the funding to publish the work. I am deeply indebted to these leaders for their support.

In Vietnam, naval intelligence liaison officers (NILOS) often provided critical, actionable intelligence to riverine and coastal forces. For this project, my NILOS were NHHC's able staff of librarians and archivists, who always kept an eye peeled for books and documents of interest to me. Curtis Utz, the director of NHHC's Operational Archives answered numerous questions about records from a practitioner's perspective. Longtime archives staff member John Hodges served as my chief guide to the facility's voluminous collections, and this book benefited tremendously from many hours spent with John hunting down obscure tidbits of knowledge buried in the collections. Robert Hanshew was instrumental in helping me with photo research, both at NHHC and at the National Archives. Other archivists who assisted with me include Tracey Caldwell, David Colamaria, Lisa Crunk, Greg Ellis, Dale "Joe" Gordon, John Greco, Kristina Henderson, Dan Jones, Tim Pettit, Barbara Posner, Jonathan Roscoe, Honey St. Dennis, Tracy Wilson, and Laura Waayers. Glenn Helm, the director of the Navy Department Library (NDL), aided and assisted this project in myriad ways. A Vietnam scholar in his own right, Glenn shared personal papers with me and critiqued excerpts of the manuscript. Other librarians who provide extensive reference support include Linda Edwards, Davis Elliott, James "Allen" Knectmann, Alexandra McCallen, Young Park, and Tonya Simpson. The Navy is truly fortunate to possess the NDL, one of the largest repositories of military knowledge in the world and a true national treasure.

Federal historians, librarians, and archivists are a close-knit community always willing to help colleagues in other agencies. I am fortunate indeed to be a member of this fraternity. Nate Patch, a military records specialist at the National Archives, helped me on numerous occasions to track down documents and photographs related to the project. Thomas Lauria of the Air Force Historical Research Agency (AFHRA) scanned and emailed me valuable material related to the *Point Welcome* and PCF-19 incidents. Steven Paget and Lieutenant Colonel Jens Robertson, USAF, of AFHRA also helped me reconstruct these fratricide incidents using the Thor database, the Air Force's project to document every bomb it has deployed since World War I. John Carland of the State Department History Office and the author of the official Army Vietnam history *Stemming the Tide, May 1965 to October 1966 Combat Operations*, answered numerous research questions. Clarence R. "Dick" Anderegg, the director of the Air Force History Support Office and a Vietnam veteran who flew 170 combat missions during the war, fielded a variety of Air Force history-related questions. The Coast Guard History Office opened its doors on multiple occasions to my interns and me and assisted me with my research. My thanks go out to the director of that office, Robert Browning, and his staff: Chris Havern and Scott Price. James Willbanks of the Army Command and Staff College participated in a useful panel on the Tet Offensive with me at the U.S. Naval Academy, and this book has benefited from his scholarship on Tet, 1968. Eric Villard of the U.S. Army Center of Military History (CMH) allowed me to copy his working files on the operations of the U.S. Army 9th Infantry Division in the Mobile Riverine Force, including after-action reports and oral histories with key Army personnel from the unit. On a day-to-day level, Mark Reardon, also of CMH, was never too busy to answer numerous reference questions on the Army in Vietnam. Finally, this book has been greatly informed by CMH's vast scholarship on the Vietnam War, which is often cited and provided important contextual knowledge.

Other government officials and government contractors who assisted me include Peter Swartz, an analyst with the Center for Naval Analyses and a former COMNAVFORV staff officer. Peter provided numerous personal files on the war, helped me locate veterans, and answered a variety of questions about the war. Al Jensen, a declassification contractor with the Joint Chiefs of Staff, answered questions about JCS materials held by NHHC. Suzanne Spray and YN1 Antonio Diggs of the Navy Department Board of Decorations and Medals shared files on James Elliot Williams. Finally, Jeffrey Grey, a professor at the Australian Defence Forces Academy and the author of Australia's official naval history of the Vietnam War, reviewed the manuscript and offered many valuable suggestions for improving it.

From the project's inception, I strove to include stories from Navy and Coast Guard veterans. Tracking down an individual sailor who served on a particular boat during a specific action for an interview could be a daunting task. Unlike officers, who occasionally can be located through such organizations as the Navy League, the Military Officers Association, and the Naval Academy Alumni Association, former enlisted sailors often "drop off the grid" after leaving the Navy. Fortunately for this project, several reunion associations and unit web pages proved instrumental in finding these unsung heroes. They include Albert Moore of the Mobile Riverine Association; Raul Herrera of Coastal Squadron 1; Paul Scotti, the author of *Coast Guard Action in Vietnam*; James Steffes, the author of *Swift Boat Down*; and Fred McDavitt of the Gamewardens Association. Chief Steffes shared his book files with me on the sinking of PCF-19 and read an excerpt from the book about the incident. Lieutenant McDavitt read numerous excerpts and answered a barrage of questions about riverine warfare in Vietnam throughout the project. He has been an important "sounding board" for me on Game Warden issues. Master Chief Signalman Roderick Davis, a former boat captain with River Section 532, and Gunner's Mate (Guns) 3rd Class Paul Cagle served a similar function with the enlisted force. Captain Do Kiem, a former Vietnam Navy officer and the author of *Counterpart: A South Vietnamese Naval Officer's War*, answered questions throughout the project on the Vietnam Navy. Other veterans who have shared personal files or photographs or helped me track down other veterans include Alexander Balian, Max Branscomb, Edward Bergin, David Butler, Richard Cragg, Robert Fuscaldo, John Green, Arthur Ismay, Charles Lloyd, Charles Mosher, Edwin "Larry" Oswald, Frank Spatt, Stephen Sumrall, Stephen Ulmer, Ray Verhasselt, and James "Larry" Weatherall. As the project lengthened, I appreciated the words of encouragement these veterans and others provided me in person, over the phone, and by email.

In 2008, I traveled to Vietnam to interview former Viet Cong. My thanks go to two Navy veterans who accompanied me there and assisted in the effort: Lieutenant John Donovan and Master Chief Davis. I also am grateful for the support of the following Vietnamese who helped arrange interviews: Luu Van Phi of the Tien Giang Province People's Committee; General Nguyen Huu Vi, the head of Ben Tre Veteran's Association; Nguyen Van Phong, the former second deputy of the People's Committee for Tien Giang Province; and his son Phuc Minh. Nguyen Huy Son provided us with translation services in Vietnam. In the United States, Serena Le Whitener has assisted throughout the project in translating Vietnamese documents and teaching me some of the nuances of the language.

The American veterans who shared their stories with me are the cornerstone of this book and represent a living link to the Navy's past. I cannot thank them enough for their interviews, which often dredged up painful memories. The names of veterans who participated in interviews are mentioned in the bibliography, footnotes, and text. Approximately one third of the interviews I conducted are not cited in the book, mainly because the actions discussed did not make it into the final narrative. Their stories, nevertheless, provided me with valuable background and context on the war and naval operations. All interviews will become part of the Navy's growing oral history collection.

Editors transform manuscripts into books, and NHHC has been fortunate to possess five of the best in the federal government: Debra Barker, Andrea Connell, Caitlin Conway, Sandy Doyle, and Wendy Sauvageot. All have been involved with this project on a variety of levels. Ms. Doyle, the book's main editor, worked hard to streamline and develop certain sections. This book benefited greatly from her many years of experience editing books on the history of the Vietnam War. Ms. Debra Barker did a masterful job with the final editing and production phases of the book.

One could not ask for a better community of scholars than that found in the NHHC histories branch. Branch members during this project included Regina Akers, Jeffrey Barlow, Charles Brodine, Dennis Conrad, Robert Cressman, Justin "Lance" Eldridge, Mark Evans, Tim Frank, Christine Hughes, Kevin Hurst, Karl Rubis, Michael Rouland, and Chris Warren. The support and assistance of all these individuals at various points in the project have been invaluable. So too has been the support of various interns who have worked for me over the years, including Patricia Boh, Mark Keller, Thibaut Bousquet, Kristen Krammer, Sophie Stewart, and Katherine Balch.

Gary Weir, the head of the Contemporary History Branch from 1996 to 2006, originally encouraged me to write on this subject and has supported the project for its duration. His vision of a branch dedicated to analytical history and primary source research has guided all of my writings since I joined the branch in 1997. Other branch and deputy branch chiefs who have supported the project include Michael Crawford, Kristina Giannotta, Tim Francis, Randy Papadopoulos, and Robert Schneller. Division and deputy division heads include Greg Martin, Commander Robert Moss, and Sharon Baker. NHHC deputy directors and chiefs of staff include Commander Jeffrey Barta, Captain Wando Biskaduros, Captain Jeffrey Gaffney, James Kuhn, and Captain Michael McDaniel. All of these managers have lent a helping hand at crucial points during the project and secured valuable resources for the endeavor.

A driving force behind NHHC's efforts to document and write the history of the Navy in Vietnam is Edward Marolda, who served as the NHHC senior historian, the acting director, and a government contractor. The author of seven published books on the Navy in Vietnam, he stands out as a leading authority on the subject, and his advice and support throughout the project and the access he gave me to his personal files have been invaluable. Dr. Marolda also reviewed the finished manuscript and offered suggestions designed to improve the work even further—nearly every one of which was followed.

Thanks go to my wife, Darina, for helping me with some statistics related to the project and for enduring all the nights and weekends I spent working on this book.

Finally, thank you to those who fought for the U.S. Navy, its sister services, and allies in the shallows of Vietnam. This is your story and your book. Your service and sacrifice will never be forgotten. I am honored to tell your story and analyze the impact you made on the war.

CHAPTER 1

Early Years

On 13 August 1964 at 0500, Lieutenant Harold "Dale" Meyerkord loaded his M1 carbine with a clip of tracer rounds. In the event of an ambush, the U.S. naval advisor would use the tracers to mark targets for heavier caliber guns on his Vietnam Navy (VNN) monitor to take out. Several days earlier while flying as a passenger in a Cessna L-19 aircraft, Meyerkord had discovered Viet Cong activity on the Mang Thit River in Vinh Long Province. The Viet Cong were using fish traps to block river traffic, stop boats, and demand taxes from area residents. His unit, River Assault Group (RAG) 23, planned to send seven boats and 60 Civil Guard troops to break up the enemy position. It had been eight months since government naval forces patrolled this small waterway, and Meyerkord and his VNN counterpart, Lieutenant Hoa, expected action.[1]

RAG 23's 19 boats operated out of Vinh Long and regularly patrolled three of the Mekong Delta's provinces: Vinh Long, Vinh Binh, and Kien Hoa. As an assault force, the RAG could transport up to 400 infantrymen into the wetlands areas of the delta on converted landing craft. It also possessed various patrol boats and armored craft, capable of carrying mortars, 40- and 20-millimeter (mm) guns, and machine guns. The RAG, therefore, could not only move an assault force to a target but provide naval gunfire support as well as command and control, logistic, and medical support for sustained combat operations.[2]

For Meyerkord, service with RAG 23 represented an opportunity to participate in operations not witnessed by many U.S. Navy officers since the Yangtze River patrol in the early decades of the 20th century. Meyerkord joined the U.S. Naval Reserve in 1960 shortly after graduating from the University of Missouri at Columbia with a bachelor's degree in political science. After serving on the cruiser *Los Angeles* (CA-35) and the destroyer *Duncan* (DD-874), he volunteered for duty as an advisor in Southeast Asia because, as he wrote in a letter to his mother, "a lot is going on there that will eventually change the world."[3]

Lieutenant Harold "Dale" Meyerkord served as a naval advisor in South Vietnam from 13 July 1964 until his death on 16 March 1965.

One of the key advantages of advisor duty was the heavy responsibility placed upon junior officers by the chain of command. Meyerkord, who lived and worked with the RAG in Vinh Long far away from his superiors in Saigon, had great latitude in his personal schedule and duties. He devoted much of his time to training Vietnamese personnel at Vinh Long but also participated in combat operations. Chief Eugene Barney, one of Meyerkord's enlisted sailors, later told a reporter that most officers he had served under "wait for someone else to tell 'em what to do. But this one's different. He goes out visiting the village councils and hamlet chiefs. He tells them about the RAG and that we can provide heavy firepower and bring in troops against the Cong; that they can evacuate them if necessary and bring in medical supplies. Nobody told him to do that. He just does things on his own."[4] A high-spirited 27-year-old, Meyerkord often wore an Australian bush hat on patrols and went by the call sign "Hornblower" after the fictitious British naval officer in C. S. Forester's novels. He also authorized RAG 23 boats to fly the "Jolly Roger" because "River Rats love to fly the skull and cross bones in combat."[5]

By 0830 the assault force reached Tra On, a town 20 miles downstream from Can Tho. Lieutenant Hoa and Meyerkord conferred with the local chief about Viet Cong activity in the area. The chief reported none, and the unit continued up the Mang Thit toward Tam Binh. "The river is very narrow, really just a canal," Meyerkord recalled, "and because our command post is on an open deck of the monitor we are very vulnerable to small arms fire."[6] The command monitor was a 56.2-foot-long landing craft, mechanized (LCM) 6 armed with one 40mm and two 20mm guns, an 81mm mortar, and a .50-caliber machine gun. The boat carried a lot of firepower but was a slow, lumbering vessel with a top speed of just eight knots. Accompanying it approximately 100 yards[7] in front of the troop transports were two STCAN/FOMs—36-foot patrol craft equipped with one .50- and two .30-caliber machine guns manufactured by *Services Techniques des Construction et Armes Navales/France Outre Mer* [Technical Services and Construction of Naval Weapons/Overseas France].[8]

By the time the unit reached Tam Binh at 1030, the troops and sailors were "tense and fatigued."[9] The district chief informed Lieutenant Hoa that the Viet Cong had been stopping

A South Vietnamese STCAN/FOM was a French-designed and -built 36-foot vessel used by the Vietnam Navy for river patrol, fire support, and minesweeping.

river traffic north of the town and demanding taxes as high as 20,000 piasters for large junks. At 1120, five minutes after the force got under way on the Mang Thit, the Viet Cong opened fire on the two STCAN/FOMs, and the patrol craft returned fire with machine guns. The monitor moved in to support the STCAN/FOMs, and Meyerkord was soon directing 40mm fire with tracer rounds from his carbine. In the meantime, the LCMs and the landing craft, vehicle, personnel (LCVPs) landed troops to the south of the enemy position. The Viet Cong withdrew into a dense thicket of sugar cane. Two dead or wounded Viet Cong had to be carried away by their comrades. By 1200 the RAG had lost contact with the enemy. The RAG continued north along the Mang Thit, removed the fish traps, and by 1830 was safely in Vinh Long with no losses sustained. In his report of the incident, Meyerkord wrote that the main lesson learned was that "troops carried with RAG deployments have great potential to damage the Viet Cong. Some canal banks have belonged to the Viet Cong for years."[10]

Another unwritten lesson was that strong leadership rendered by U.S. Navy advisors and their Vietnamese counterparts could produce tangible results in the delta if these forces could only live up to their "potential."[11] The VNN, however, never did live up to its potential and, as a result, the U.S. Navy became gradually more enmeshed in the war in South Vietnam, first on the coasts and then the rivers. The development of the VNN and the establishment of the U.S. Naval Advisory Group (NAG) in Vietnam were intimately connected. Both grew in fits

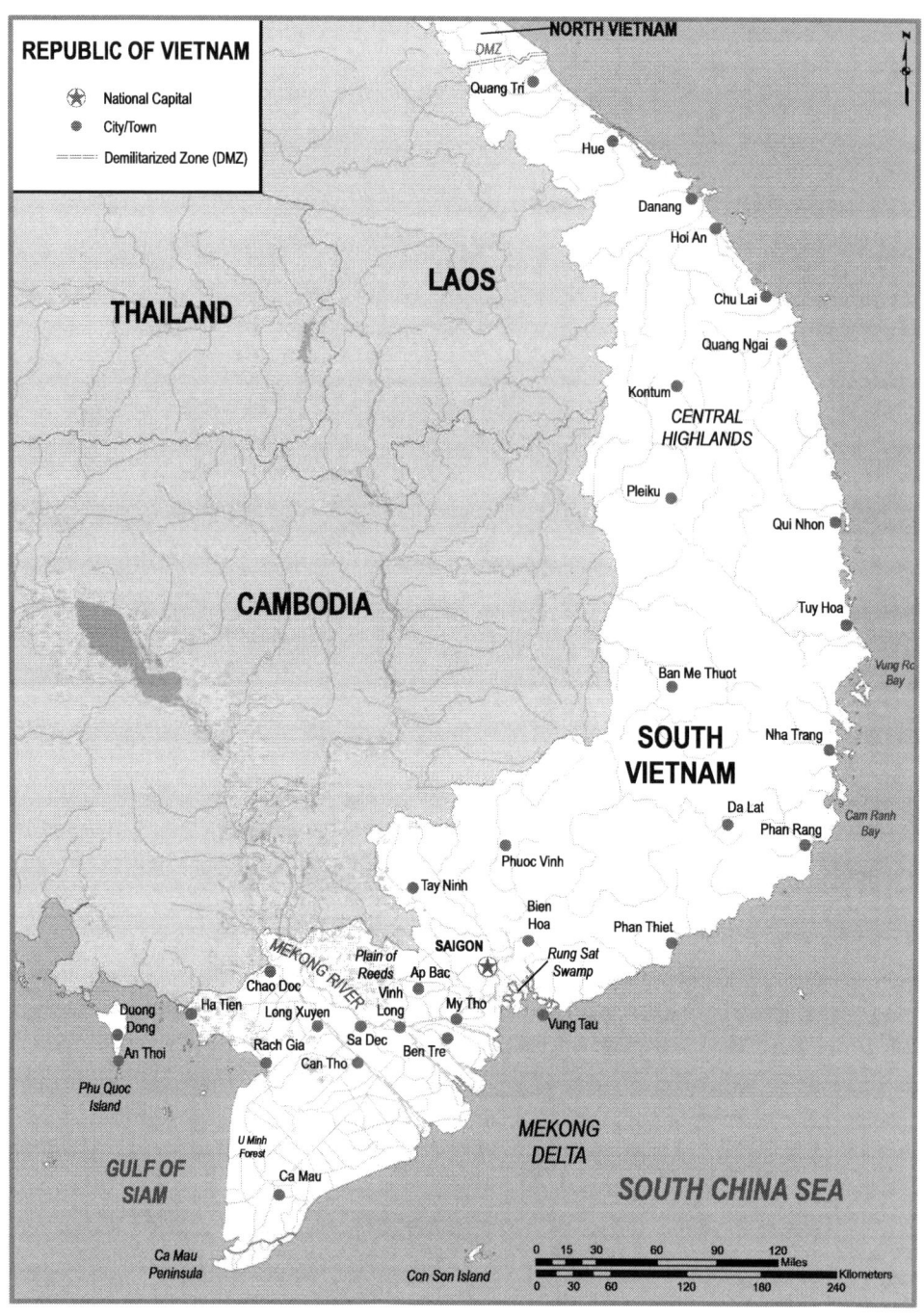

South Vietnam.

and starts during the 1950s, and the problems the VNN encountered in its development would have a direct bearing on the U.S. Navy mission in Vietnam.

Neither the French in the beginning nor the Army of the Republic of Vietnam (ARVN) after 1954 envisioned a strong, independent sea service for Vietnam. Consequently, the VNN struggled during its early years for financial support from the South Vietnamese government. The fact that it would later back President Ngo Dinh Diem in the ill-fated 1963 coup assured that this trend would continue through the Americanization of the war in 1965 and beyond. Despite the heroic efforts of advisors like Meyerkord and their Vietnamese counterparts, the VNN's inherent institutional weaknesses prevented it from becoming an effective force during its early years. At the same time, the need for a strong seaborne counterinfiltration program increased dramatically between 1962 and 1964. During these years, the number of Viet Cong doubled to over 51,000, and Hanoi relied increasingly on oceangoing junks and trawlers to supply this burgeoning force in the South.[12] With the VNN in disarray, American military planners in Saigon would demand a stronger U.S. naval presence to protect the coasts from seaborne infiltration.

Origins of the Vietnam Navy and the Naval Advisory Group

In 1946, fighting broke out between Viet Minh guerrilla forces under Ho Chi Minh and French units in Haiphong. The war would last until 1954 and would end with Vietnam being partitioned into two countries and the demise of French colonialism in Southeast Asia. In the middle of this war, in September 1950 Washington established the Military Assistance Advisory Group (MAAG) in Indochina to administer foreign military aid in the region. That fall the first American naval advisors arrived in Saigon and began overseeing the transfer to the French of aircraft carriers, aircraft, and amphibious vessels. During the early 1950s the U.S. military assistance effort focused more on helping the French defeat the Viet Minh insurgency than on developing the capability of indigenous Vietnamese armed forces. Paris insisted that local troops be led by French officers and noncommissioned officers and viewed a truly independent Vietnamese military as a threat to its colonial interests.[13]

The subject of an independent navy for Vietnam first arose in the Franco–Vietnamese military agreement of 1949, which called for the French to provide a group of indigenous Vietnamese sailors for a riverine force and to furnish basic and advanced training for it. Much to the dismay of Vietnamese navy advocates, the overall French commander, General Jean de Lattre de Tassigny, viewed the agreement with skepticism from the start. He wanted to create a single Vietnamese armed service and did not want a separate navy. Vice Admiral Paul Ortoli, the commander of French Naval Forces Far East, also had reservations. He feared that such a naval force would interfere with the recruitment of Vietnamese for the French navy in Indochina.[14]

Little progress was made on the issue until November 1951 when construction began on a recruit training center at Nha Trang.[15] Early in 1952, Paris accepted a proposal by Admiral Ortoli to organize two VNN *dinassauts*, transfer three auxiliary motor minesweepers (YMSs) to the Vietnamese, and create a VNN naval staff. *Dinassaut* stands for *division d'infanterie navale d'assaut* or roughly translated, "naval assault division."[16] The French created the first *dinassaut* in 1945 from a collection of 14 landing craft purchased from the British and modified with additional armor and armament. The *dinassaut* was designed to quickly transport two companies of infantry (approximately 400 men) to flash points in the Red River Delta region and then provide organic gunfire support and logistics for these forces once they engaged with the enemy.[17] During the First Indochina War *dinassauts* scored a number of spectacular successes. In spring 1951 *Dinassaut Trois* helped repel an attack on the French forces at Yen Cu Ha, a town located a few miles south of Ninh Binh. A support landing ship (large) (LSSL), which arrived just as the enemy entered the town, fired a 76mm round at a watchtower where the Viet Minh had centered its defense. Viet Minh resistance soon crumbled, and the French were successful, capturing 55 enemy troops in the watchtower.[18] Writing later about the war, historian Bernard Fall stated, "*dinassauts* may have been one of the few worthwhile contributions of the Indochina War to military knowledge."[19]

The Vietnam Navy established its first *dinassaut* at Can Tho on 10 April 1953. Later renamed river assault groups, the Can Tho *dinassaut* originally consisted of one command LCM, two standard LCMs, and LCVPs. These boats, although acquired from the French, were almost all of U.S. origin. Most were former World War II–era amphibious craft modified for riverine operations.

A Vietnamese Navy LCM monitor conversion armed with a .50-caliber machine gun, 20mm and 40mm cannons, and an 81mm mortar, 31 August 1964.

In June 1953 the VNN activated another *dinassaut* at Vinh Long. Although the original two VNN *dinassauts* were partially manned by French cadres and under French command, the craft flew the Vietnamese flag.[20] During the First Indochina War, the VNN suffered from manning problems caused by French reluctance to spare Vietnamese recruits for the new force and difficulties in recruiting sailors with the technical skills to operate naval craft.[21] By July 1952 the VNN had recruited only 350 Vietnamese apprentice seamen. "As 1953 drew to a close, it was painfully evident that the VNN had progressed very little in the course of four years," wrote Marine Lieutenant Colonel Victor J. Croizat, a U.S. military advisor who served in Indochina from 1954 to 1956. "Its small size made it appear inconsequential in the military budget so it was largely ignored by the Vietnamese government."[22]

When the First Indochina War ended in summer 1954, the VNN had 131 officers and 1,358 sailors. Its operating forces consisted of four *dinassauts*, two escort ships (600-ton), two coastal patrol ships, two medium landing ships (LSMs), three YMSs, two LSSLs, four landing craft, utility (LCU), 16 coastal patrol boats, and three LCU repair craft.[23] Initially, France and the United States shared responsibility for training the VNN via a combined Training Relations Instruction Mission (TRIM). Established in December 1954, TRIM originally consisted of five French and five American officers (three Army, one Navy, and one Air Force), but would grow to 109 men (33 U.S. and 76 French) by February 1955. TRIM called for a navy with the following capabilities:

- Limited amphibious operations
- River and coastal patrol
- Minesweeping
- Naval gunfire support
- Logistical support for military forces.[24]

Many years passed before these ambitions were fully realized. Lieutenant Colonel Croizat complained, "the Vietnamese Army dominated the general staff, where there was little interest in a Navy." The French also had far more influence than the Americans had during this period because they provided all logistic support, manned the Saigon Naval Shipyard, and held all the ships and river craft scheduled for transfer to the Vietnamese under the terms of the 1954 Geneva Agreement on the Cessation of Hostilities in Vietnam. Although the agreement expressly forbade the introduction of additional arms to Vietnam, it allowed for the replacement of military equipment "destroyed, damaged, worn out or used up after the cessation of hostilities."[25]

The Geneva Agreement divided Vietnam into two zones: Communist North Vietnam and pro–Western South Vietnam. The 17th parallel formed the line of demarcation between the two areas, which eventually solidified into separate countries after a planned national election in 1956 failed to materialize. As the French military began departing Vietnam following the agreement, the situation began to change for the South Vietnamese armed forces and the VNN. On 12 February 1955, the U.S. Military Assistance Advisory Group took over responsibility from the French for training the South Vietnamese military, and in May 1955 the French formally transferred command of the four Vietnamese *dinassauts* to the senior officer of the new

VNN, Lieutenant Commander Le Quang My. Shortly after this transfer, relations began to sour between My and the French over financial issues. The French accused My of misappropriating funds, a claim he denied. Hence in July 1955, rather than relinquish control of the entire VNN to My, the French opted to hand it over to Army Brigadier General Tran Van Don on 1 July 1955—a move that pleased many in the powerful Army of the Republic of Vietnam but devastated the navy's officer corps. Fortunately for the new naval force, President Diem terminated General Don's command on 20 August 1955 and allowed My to resume control of the VNN. According to Croizat, My deserved the post because he had effectively led several riverine operations in May and June and had "done well."[26]

In its early days, the Republic of Vietnam was not a cohesive nation but a loose coalition of competing groups and sects. President Diem sought to control the sects through a divide-and-conquer strategy, offering some sect leaders money and government positions in exchange for political support and putting down others by force. The Binh Xuyen, one of the most powerful sects, proved to be the most difficult to subdue. Its leader, a colorful gangster named Bay Vinh, controlled a loose militia of 25,000 men and supported the organization with revenue earned from gambling and prostitution rings.[27] In late March 1955 the Binh Xuyen, working in conjunction with two other sects, began a series of armed uprisings in towns near Saigon and on the Ca Mau Peninsula at the southern tip of Vietnam. In the capital itself, the Binh Xuyen attacked the national army headquarters, the central police compound, and even fired shells into the presidential palace. Diem mobilized 40 infantry battalions and reestablished control of Saigon on 10 May.[28] Croizat, who had recently moved into a new home in Saigon on 24 April with his wife and children, vividly recalled the uprising. "As we sat down to our first dinner of canned chicken noodle soup, because firefights had kept the cook from getting to the market, the transformer down the street was blown up and the lights and ceiling fans went out. We continued our meal by candlelight against a background of small arms fire, the explosion of an occasional mortar round, and the clamor of ambulances bringing wounded to the hospital across the street. The children found it all exciting; Meda and I were grateful for the scotch."[29]

Once driven from Saigon, the Binh Xuyen fled to the Rung Sat swamp south of Saigon. Known as the "Forest of the Assassins," this 400-square-mile wetland area was a no-man's land and a traditional hideout for pirates and criminals. Its maze of rivers, streams, and canals, along with its mangrove forests and dense tropical vegetation, made it an ideal operating base for insurgents. It would dominate riverine operations in Vietnam for many years to come.[30] In September 1955, Diem initiated joint army-navy attacks against 1,500 Binh Xuyen militiamen holding out in the Rung Sat. Four VNN *dinassauts* participated in the operation, cutting off supplies of food, water, and ammunition to the enemy, and then landing Army and Marine Corps units. Confronting a closing perimeter, most of the Binh Xuyen force surrendered on 21 September 1955. It was the first major test for the new navy, and the young service's success in the effort greatly impressed President Diem.[31]

Aerial view of a section of the Rung Sat swamp.

The departure of the last French troops and advisors from Vietnam in April 1956 ushered in a new phase for the VNN. Americans would now take the lead role in training and advising this new force. Admiral Herbert G. Hopwood, Commander in Chief, Pacific Fleet (CINCPACFLT), reported after a 1959 trip to Southeast Asia that he was "favorably impressed with the Vietnam Navy, its ships, craft and facilities," but all was not what it appeared on the surface. The VNN still lacked the necessary trained personnel and maintenance facilities to operate a modern naval force. Social and cultural differences between American naval advisors and their Vietnamese counterparts often exacerbated the situation, and the small number of naval personnel assigned to the Military Assistance Advisory Group made matters even worse. By spring 1958, only 78 American sailors and marines served with the MAAG and the Temporary Equipment Recovery Mission (the group in charge of transferring military equipment from the French to the South Vietnamese).[32] Furthermore, American advisors were forbidden from going along on operational missions with their Vietnamese counterparts until May 1959, when North Vietnam formally initiated an armed struggle to overthrow the Diem government of the Republic of Vietnam.[33]

The frustrations many young U.S. Navy advisors felt about the VNN can be seen in a 1962 end-of-tour report submitted by Lieutenant (j.g.) Harold V. Smith, who served as an advisor with RAG 21 based at My Tho. Smith complained about the poor quality of the VNN's senior leadership and how its bad example trickled down to the lowest ranks. "The junior officers could not count on the support of their seniors and feared reprimand for actions which would display individual initiative," Smith wrote. "As a result the only tasks accomplished were those for which specific orders had been issued." It was not uncommon for officers and enlisted sailors to be involved in areas "in which they had no experience or responsibility," and VNN training at every level was "poor." For example, graduates of the Radioman School could not line up a transmitter or load an antenna, and enginemen lacked basic knowledge of boat engine operation and maintenance. Smith concluded that the VNN required major personnel reforms to correct such "deficiencies."[34]

Another advisor from the same period, Lieutenant (j.g.) Charles G. Stowers, blamed the VNN's problems on its position within the Republic of Vietnam Armed Forces (RVNAF) as well as the quality of its leadership. In his end-of-tour report he noted, "The VN Navy (River Forces) has been hampered because of the organization of the Armed Forces, allowing the Army to run all operations." Stowers contended that the ARVN perceived the navy as nothing but a taxi service for infantry and did not understand that riverine craft could take an active role in denying the enemy the use of canals and rivers and interdicting supplies. "The sailors take a dim view of being the lackey boy" of the army, Stowers explained. His report argued that naval officers should be involved at all levels of amphibious operations, from planning to execution, and that a combined effort (ARVN and VNN) should be "instigated to control the waterways which are highways of the Viet Cong."

With regard to its personnel, Stowers, like Smith, reported that VNN junior officers lacked initiative and would not commit themselves or their forces without explicit orders from higher headquarters. There was little an advisor could do to change the situation. As Stowers wrote, "It is impossible to think that an advisor can step into a foreign country and begin advising in a game where the American has very little idea of the rules (customs, ideology, philosophy of the native's thinking)." The advisor, after all, is only in Vietnam for a short time, but the VNN officer "is there for the rest of his life."[35]

Lieutenant Do Kiem, a VNN officer and a graduate of the prestigious French Naval Academy in Brest, explained the situation from the perspective of a Vietnamese. When he welcomed his first U.S. Navy advisor on board HQ-331, a landing ship, infantry (large) (LSIL), Do Kiem, as well as the American, Lieutenant Wayne Valin, had no idea of formal advisory duties. "I'm here to help," Valin kept telling Do Kiem, but since he spoke neither Vietnamese nor French, his effectiveness on HQ-331 was limited. Eventually, the advisor settled into a predictable routine. He would ask Do Kiem about the plan of the day each morning, "plod around the ship for a few hours, writing things down in his notebook," and then retire to his stateroom after lunch to sleep. Once Do Kiem woke him up to meet President Diem, but he grumbled about having his sleep interrupted, and after that Do Kiem just let him "snore."

Do Kiem's next advisor, Lieutenant Jack Quimby, was the polar opposite of Valin. He never slept and constantly prowled around the ship, looking for violations. If a man failed to wash his hands after using the toilet, Quimby wrote him up. What this American failed to understand was that most of Do Kiem's crew had never seen a toilet before entering the service and had no understanding of the proper hygiene to follow after using one. The navy issued the former peasants two uniforms when they joined the service but did not pay them enough money to purchase replacements. It took all of Do Kiem's efforts just to maintain his aging 158-foot-long vessel and teach his men how to properly operate it in a combat situation. He had no time for issues such as the cleanliness of his crew.[36]

Lieutenant Commander Ho Van Ky Thoai, the commander of the Second Coastal Zone, experienced a similar form of cultural misunderstanding with his counterpart, Lieutenant Commander Harvey P. Rodgers. A 1952 graduate of the U.S. Merchant Marine Academy from Smithtown, New York, Rodgers was a hard-charging officer (he would later play a key role in the capture of a North Vietnamese trawler at Vung Ro Bay in 1965), who early on in his tour displayed typical American ignorance and arrogance in dealing with the Vietnamese and their customs. When one of Rodgers' junior officers hit a Vietnamese sailor with his jeep and then took off, Thoai confronted Rodgers who brushed him off, saying, "I have nothing to do with the matter; it's now in the hands of the MPs [military police]." After Rodgers learned that a group of VNN sailors intended to shoot the guilty officer, however, he went to Thoai and begged him to "do something about it." Thoai requested that the junior officer visit the injured sailor in the hospital, apologize, and give him a small gift of two oranges. The sailor, who suffered a broken leg, accepted the act of contrition and did not seek any other form of compensation, either legal or monetary. Had Rodgers better understood the Vietnamese, he would have urged his subordinate to admit to his crime and apologize instead of simply referring the matter to the military police.[37]

The cultural gap between the Vietnamese and the U.S. Navy is epitomized by a report by Captain Joseph B. Drachnik about his experiences in Vietnam, first as the chief of Navy Section, MAAG, from December 1961 to February 1962 and then as head of the naval component of Military Assistance Command, Vietnam (MACV) from February 1962 to January 1964.[38] In it, he exhibited extreme frustration and borderline racist attitudes about his counterparts. He attributed the poor management of the VNN to the "low general intelligence" of its officers. "They seem to lack the ability to recognize the fundamentals of a situation or to do something constructive about known problems," he wrote. "There is a great deal of naivety in their thinking, their attitudes, and their approach to problems. . . . They learn rapidly but show poor judgment." The chief task of the U.S. advisor, Drachnik believed, was to keep his VNN counterparts "on the track" and "to guide and direct their efforts towards the desired goals." The Vietnamese, according to Drachnik, were "incapable" of planning operations and solving complex problems. They required advisors "where ingenuity of any type is needed." The condescending tone of this report suggests that Drachnik's frustration with the VNN had reached a boiling point by the time he left Vietnam, but were his observations accurate?[39]

One of the U.S. Navy's most effective managers of the time, Drachnik attended the University of California at Berkeley prior to entering the U.S. Naval Academy in 1939. Upon graduation from Annapolis in 1942, he joined the destroyer minesweeper *Zane* (DMS-14) in the South Pacific one day before the Guadalcanal landing.[40] He saw action in that operation and later during the occupation of New Georgia–Rendova and Vangunu. After attending gunnery school in the states, he served on the destroyer *Allen M. Sumner* (DD-692) from 1944 to 1947. During the early Cold War period, he worked in a variety of staff jobs and as gunnery officer for the cruiser *Des Moines* (CA-134). He commanded the high-speed transport *Liddle* (APD-60) from March 1953 to March 1954 and the radar picket destroyer *Benner* (DDR-807) from August 1959 to October 1961. Vietnam was still a backwater command when he accepted the post of senior naval advisor in November 1961, but Drachnik believed that the country would soon become a central front in America's struggle with communism and that this assignment would pave the way to flag rank. During his term as senior naval advisor in Vietnam, which lasted to January 1964, the VNN fleet doubled in size, and Drachnik helped set up training programs for the influx of new sailors. In collaboration with his Vietnamese counterparts, he also planned and directed the construction of over 564 junks for the VNN's Coastal Surveillance Force. Admiral George W. Anderson Jr., Chief of Naval Operations (CNO), visited Vietnam in the summer of 1962 and reported that Drachnik was doing an outstanding job. Drachnik also became good friends with the head of the VNN for much of this period, Ho Tan Quyen. In a later oral history, Drachnik described his counterpart as "young, brilliant, and hard-charging. He thought just the way I did, and shared the same goal—to win the war!"[41]

Drachnik pinned much of his hopes for the VNN's future on Quyen, but as he and many other advisors soon realized, the VNN simply did not possess enough men like Quyen to make the overall enterprise a success.[42] More often than not, VNN officers lacked the education, training, and motivation to command even rudimentary naval vessels, and American advisors rarely hesitated to highlight these deficiencies in their reports. Captain Phillip H. Bucklew, an officer who interviewed numerous U.S. Navy personnel in 1964, described the plight of the advisor in the following terms: "Those guys were not out there as advisors; they were out there as missionaries. They were the most frustrated men I have ever encountered in the military."[43]

Left to right: Captain Joseph Drachnik, Chief, Navy Section, Military Assistance Advisory Group Vietnam from 1961 to 1964; Lieutenant Wesley Hoch, the Fourth Coastal District advisor; Captain William Hardcastle, Commander, Naval Forces Vietnam from 1964 to 1965; and an unidentified naval officer. The men are inspecting a Coastal Force quarters at An Thoi, October 1964.

Establishment of the Coastal Force

Between 1959 and 1964, the Vietnam Navy grew from a force of 5,000 men to over 8,000, and its flotilla doubled to 244 ships and boats of various sizes. Functionally, VNN forces were divided into three operational forces: the Sea Force, the Coastal Force, and the River Force. As their titles suggest, these three operating forces were defined by geography (the ocean, the coast, and the rivers), but only the Sea Force and the River Force were manned by professional servicemen. The Coastal Force, perhaps the most crucial of the three for interdiction, was designed from keel up as a militia or coast guard auxiliary similar in some respects to the South Vietnamese Civil Guard and Civil Defense Corps (or later, the Regional and Popular forces).[44]

The genesis of the Coastal Force dates to April 1960, when Admiral Harry D. Felt, Commander in Chief, U.S. Pacific Command (CINCPAC), recommended that the VNN assume a larger role in curbing the flow of enemy supplies coming into South Vietnam from the sea. Partly because of this recommendation, President Diem established the Coastal Force, often referred to as the "junk force," as an autonomous unit directly under South Vietnam's Department of State for National Defense.[45] The force did not become an official branch of the Vietnam Navy until 1965. The idea of a coastal force as a paramilitary unit fit in well with the Kennedy administration's belief that self-defense units represented one of the best means of fighting the Communist insurgency. Consequently, the administration ordered the Defense Department to support the new force by funding the construction of 501 junks by South Vietnamese shipyards.

The original plan for the Coastal Force, written by Commander Quyen, called for 420 sailing junks and 63 motorized junks, manned by 2,200 civilian irregulars drawn from local fishing villages, to patrol the inshore coastal waters up to five miles from the coast. Quyen hoped that his force would blend in naturally with coastal fishing junks, allowing his units to keep their true identity secret until they drew up to a suspect junk for a search and boarding mission. The plan called for creating 21 junk divisions (also known as coastal divisions), each with 23 junks. Every division would patrol a 30-mile stretch of the South Vietnamese coastline, and their operations would be coordinated by radio from coastal command surveillance centers. Coastal divisions, in turn, reported to one of four VNN coastal districts. These districts were headquartered in Danang (I), Nha Trang (II), Vung Tau (III), and An Thoi (IV), and each district commander controlled all naval forces operating within his district. On 16 October 1963, the advisory team persuaded the Vietnamese navy to create four naval zone commands, from the 1st Naval Zone in the north to the 4th Naval Zone in the Gulf of Thailand. Thereafter, an overall commander whose area of responsibility now corresponded with that of an army corps commander controlled operations of the Sea Force, River Force, and Coastal Force in a particular zone.[46]

By the end of 1963, the junk force had grown to 632 junks and 3,700 civilian crewmembers. From its inception, however, problems beset the fledgling organization. Recruiting sailors for the new force proved more difficult than expected. Vietnamese fishermen made an adequate living from the sea during this period and had little interest in joining the junk force.[47] The

Sailing junks from the Coastal Force on patrol, May 1962.

VNN instead recruited urban peasants and refugees from the north. With no seafaring tradition, these northerners were prone to leave or desert the service at first opportunity. Enlistments rarely kept up with attrition, which averaged over 106 sailors per month during 1963–1964.[48]

Desertion and absent-without-leave rates also were high due to the deplorable conditions under which these men served. "When it rains, they are wet—no rain gear is provided," wrote the Fourth Coastal District advisor, Lieutenant Commander Wesley A. Hoch, in his end-of-tour report. "At night it is cold for no warm clothing or blankets are provided. Many have no food or cooking utensils for none are provided. In most cases, these men return from patrol to a base that consists of a few straw huts so over-crowded that there is no room for them." In a February 1963 survey of the men in the Fourth Coastal District, Hoch and his VNN counterpart, Lieutenant Tran Binh Sang, found that over 500 of the 657 men on duty in the unit had not received any pay in the past six months, and none had ever received any formal training. "Many men on the junks at this time had never fired a gun or been on a junk before," Hoch wrote. "Needless to say, morale was non-existent and approximately 50 men per week were deserting."[49] A 1964 study by the Naval Advisory Group Saigon confirmed these observations, stating that the root cause of the problem was poor pay and benefits for junk force sailors.[50]

Not only were these men paid meager wages, but commands rarely received funds for messing, berthing, and basic medical care for the sailors. In a medical survey of Junk Division 33 in 1963, one advisor found that over 50 percent of the junkmen had some type of treatable disease. Many illnesses resulted from unsanitary water because his coastal division lacked funds for water treatment tablets (iodine). Only 30 percent of the junkmen had received a tetanus shot and just 15 percent, regular doses of chloroquine, a malaria prophylaxes.[51]

Wooden junks required much more maintenance than planned because they were prone to infestations of marine worms and rot. A VNN/USN survey conducted in May 1964 found that 174 junks were sidelined for repairs, and 64 others were beyond repair.[52] In Lieutenant Commander Hoch's zone, 98 of the 121 junks were out of commission because of maintenance problems when he first arrived. For his first six months Hoch spent an inordinate amount of time "talking, report writing, and beating around the bush" until finally in July 1963 repair funds came through. He and his VNN counterpart then had to set up repair facilities from scratch. Initially, the Fourth Coastal Zone began repairing junks at Song Ong Doc using imported contractors. Soon after get-

Junk force sailor with a Thompson submachine gun, May 1962.

ting the maintenance facilities operational, workers began abandoning the site because of threats from the Viet Cong and nonpayment of wages by the naval zone. Sang and Hoch ultimately had to hire another contractor at Doung Don and Kien Giang (Rach Gia) to "patch up" the junks.[53] The Vietnamese government deserved much of the blame for these problems because it tended to fund continued expansion of the force at the expense of maintenance for existing units, but lack of regular preventative maintenance on the part of the naval units was also to blame.[54]

Operationally, the work of the junk force was not only tedious but dangerous. Motorized Viet Cong junks often out-sailed and out-gunned the force's many sailing junks; their wooden hulls offered little protection from enemy bullets. In the shallow waters of canals and tributaries, junks often could not follow the smaller enemy sampans. Several attempts to augment the junk patrols with Vietnamese air force surveillance aircraft foundered because of the unavailability of aircraft and communications difficulties between aircraft and junks.[55]

The operational challenges confronting the junk force were illustrated by the experiences of Lieutenant Dallas Walton Shawkey, a U.S. advisor assigned to the Second Coastal District at Cam Ranh Bay. Early in the morning of 19 August 1963, Shawkey and a force of eight junks set sail for Vinh Hy, a village suspected of harboring 25 Viet Cong. The command junk fired twelve

57mm rounds into the village, and the other junks peppered the place with their .30-caliber machine guns. The junks then moved toward the beach to disembark a shore party. Just as the first junk was about to touch shore, an estimated 10–20 enemy troops opened fire with M1 rifles, but none was seen by either Shawkey or his counterpart, Lieutenant Thinh. One bullet penetrated the hull of Shawkey's boat and hit the advisor, a 1957 graduate of the University of Pennsylvania. A Vietnamese corpsman attended the advisor while the junk force withdrew. The after-action report stated that the "retirement was required because of the scattered and unknown positions of the VC" [Viet Cong] even though the "junk force units had both numerical and fire power superiority."[56] *Nam Du* (HQ-607), a motor gunboat standing by offshore, transported Shawkey to Nha Trang two hours away where he was medivaced by helicopter to a U.S. Army field hospital for further treatment.

Shawkey survived the encounter, but the event highlighted the dangers faced by advisors operating at great distances from advanced medical care. To encourage the Vietnamese gunners to return fire, Shawkey and Thinh remained on deck when the enemy opened fire, but such exposure made them highly vulnerable. Lieutenant Billy D. Graham, a navy officer who wrote the after-action report of the incident, concluded that in the future advisors should not wear khaki uniforms and ought to remain out of sight as much as possible because their presence "could well draw enemy fire."[57] Lightly armed wooden boats may have functioned well for surveillance, but direct action against an armed adversary often proved beyond the capability of this force.[58]

In spite of its many problems, the junk force generated impressive statistics. During 1963 alone, the Coastal Force and the Sea Force, a deepwater force of larger vessels, checked 127,000 junks and 353,000 fishermen. Additionally, the Coastal Force detained 2,500 Viet Cong suspects, and the Sea Force, another 500.[59] Yet even with all the so-called progress reported, enemy infiltration of men and material to the South appeared to be on the rise. In January 1963 between three and four hundred main force Viet Cong soldiers defended a radio transmitter against a superior force of ARVN troops and civil guardsmen near Ap Bac, a Mekong Delta hamlet 40 miles southwest of Saigon. Before withdrawing, the Viet Cong downed five helicopters, put out of action several M113 armored personnel carriers, killed 80 ARVN troops, and wounded another 109. While Communist losses may have exceeded 100, the battle demonstrated that the enemy had the firepower, the supplies and ammunition, the troop numbers, and the discipline to inflict tough blows on battalion-size ARVN units.[60]

During 1963 the North Vietnamese navy's 125th Sea Transportation Unit (formally Group 759) hauled an estimated 800 tons of supplies south in small steel-hulled trawlers. These trawlers often sailed south under the flag of the People's Republic of China, and then on dark nights offloaded their supplies to junks. Neither the larger motor gunboats (PGMs) of the Sea Force nor the junks of the Coastal Force detected any of these trawlers in 1963—a significant failure on the part of the VNN, especially given its recent growth.[61] From 1961 to 1963, the Vietnam Navy had grown from 3,200 to 6,000 men. The Coastal Force alone went from 80 junks to 644, and the Sea Force acquired 30 vessels of various types. As for the River Force, it deployed its sixth RAG in 1962 and by September 1963 had grown to 1,224 men and 208 boats.[62] VNN senior leaders were clearly more focused on growth than operations during this period, and this inattention to the "day-to-day" aspects of running the navy not only hurt morale in the junior officer corps but undermined military effectiveness.

Lieutenant Tran Binh Sang, the commander of the Fourth Coastal Zone, best summarized the situation at the lower echelons. In a report to the VNN Chief of Naval Operations, he wrote, "I am confronted with such a deplorable and hopeless situation, of which no champion of optimism could endure." Although Sang, according to his American counterpart, did his best to inspire his men and conduct combat operations, ultimately the stresses of handling constant personnel, maintenance, and logistic problems defeated the man. In August 1963 Sang was hospitalized with bleeding ulcers and never returned to the zone.[63]

River Force
With its professional sailors and heavily armed and armored boats, the River Force should have performed significantly better than the junks and civilian irregulars of the Coastal Force, but by 1963 it too was suffering from many of the same problems: low morale, lack of properly trained personnel, maintenance setbacks, and poor leadership.

Control of the force by the ARVN III Corps commander was partly to blame. The ARVN perceived the River Force as nothing more than an armed ferry service for the army and rarely employed it for combined armed assaults. Instead, ARVN generals tended to use helicopters to

A fully loaded Vietnam Navy LCM, circa 1966.

insert troops into combat zones and relied on the RAGs for hauling supplies and troops to and from already secured areas and bases. Lieutenant Charles Patrick Ragan, an advisor attached to RAG 22, reported that from December 1963 to April 1964, his RAG had participated in only two major operations. "At no other time have all the boats been assigned a mission," he lamented.[64] The army also did not allow navy officers to assist in planning operations. This situation produced disastrous results in several ferrying operations between March and April 1962. In one case, three LCMs transporting troops under a bridge north of Saigon had to wait ten hours until the tide was low enough to clear the bridge. In another, a convoy of four LCMs, four LCVPs, and four STCAN/FOMs waited nine hours at an enemy-erected barricade that army engineers had failed to clear prior to the operation.[65]

The River Force also suffered from maintenance problems nearly as severe as those of the junk force. Basic preventative maintenance was virtually nonexistent, and equipment failures such as inoperative radios, faulty ordnance, fouled ramp winches, leaking fuel tanks, and discharged batteries often went unreported.[66] Between March and June 1962 alone, the River Force lost three boats due to maintenance problems and improper handling: one LCVP swamped, another sank at the pier, and an LCM sank because of a leak.[67] Up until January 1963, when a boat skipper-training program was implemented, boat captains often took to the rivers with little or no formal training, in either maintenance issues or boat handling.[68] Lieutenant Ragan witnessed a boat sinking at the pier and petty officers simply milling about because they had neither the will nor the training to prevent it.[69]

Poor naval leadership from the top down to the lowest levels was at the core of the River Force's subpar operational readiness. Lieutenant Commander Ray C. Nieman wrote in a report sent to Drachnik that the River Force has "the upper hand against the Viet Cong in almost every situation [but is not] winning the war" because of a "lack of strong aggressive determined leaders."[70] Lieutenant Commander Richard Chesebrough, the senior River Force advisor, echoed this sentiment: "the most critical problem is the lack of initiative and leadership being displayed by Commander River Force and his subordinates."[71] Lieutenant Ragan noted that sailors occasionally slept while on watch in his RAG but could not be disciplined unless caught in the act by an officer from their boat. "Junior officers assigned to a RAG staff," he explained, "insist that it is not within their authority, let alone responsibility, to correct poor practices or conditions unless they are specifically directed." Junior officers viewed their duties in the narrowest terms possible and showed little or no initiative. Ragan complained that they also acted in a careless manner in combat zones. Force protection measures were lax, and sailors tended to treat the war as a nine-to-five job. "I have seen more than half of the two RAGs anchored near Ben Luc Bridge during the afternoon siesta when not one sentry was posted, leaving the boats exposed to swimmer attack or floating mines."[72]

A fundamental problem with the River Force was that it performed only a very limited interdiction roll during this period. Its major mission was to support ARVN troops in the Mekong. A group appointed by MACV in October 1963 prepared a study of infiltration on inland waterways and along the coast and concluded that "Cambodia's broad Mekong River system, flowing generally from north to south, represents the most convenient channels for Communist supplies destined for the VC in Southern Vietnam." Captain Drachnik, however, resisted attempts by the MACV staff to broaden the mandate of the River Force to include interdiction, believing that the VC relied more on coastal junks to transport supplies than river sampans.[73] It would not be until the formation of the U.S. Navy's Task Force 116 in December 1965 that the allies would make a concerted effort to stop the enemy logistics flow on the Mekong Delta's inland waterways.

Sea Force

At the beginning of 1959, the Sea Force consisted of 16 patrol boats, minesweepers, and landing craft.[74] By 1963, it had doubled in size to 32 hulls. New additions to the fleet included ten PGMs, two LSMs, three tank landing ships (LSTs), one self-propelled gasoline barge (YOG), 12 motor launch minesweepers (MLMSs), and two fleet minesweepers (MSFs). Built in the United States, the 101-foot-long PGM could steam up to 16.4 knots and was equipped with radar and a variety of guns, including a 40mm and two twin 20mm mounts. It was an ideal ship for coastal patrol: fast, maneuverable, well-armed, and relatively easy to maintain. The additional U.S. Navy landing craft gave the VNN the capability to haul over 10,000 tons of cargo a month. With its large ships and new equipment, the Sea Force was the pride of the VNN. It not only attracted the most talented sailors and officers but was the larger of two professional operating forces with 2,000 men assigned to it by the end of 1963 (the River Force by comparison consisted of 1,200 officers and men).[75]

The Sea Force had three basic responsibilities: minesweeping, logistic and amphibious support, and coastal patrol. Since the Viet Cong did not use mines in the coastal region during this period, the minesweeping flotilla of the Sea Force devoted most of its efforts to training and, by the end of 1963, the MLMSs were being considered for modification into inland patrol units. Logistic support proved more vital to the war effort, and Sea Force landing ships often supplied Army units along the coast when VC saboteurs cut the rail lines. The force also conducted coastal amphibious operations on occasion. In January 1963, for example, a flotilla of landing craft, along with RAG 22, two junk divisions, and two battalions of Vietnamese marines participated in an amphibious assault in An Xuyen Province. The major assault on 3 January encountered no resistance, but several smaller actions saw light combat. By 27 January the combined force had killed an estimated 40 Viet Cong and wounded another 660. Friendly losses included five killed and 28 wounded.[76]

Despite the influx of new equipment during the early 1960s, the Sea Force did not have the resources to adequately stop infiltration by sea. An analysis of the situation in 1961 by the U.S. Naval Attaché stated, "there is too much coastline, too many junks, too few patrol craft, and inadequate authority to prevent junks from doing almost as they please."[77] Despite its higher status within the VNN, the Sea Force suffered from many of the same ills plaguing the other naval forces. PGMs commissioned in 1963 were sidelined after less than a year of service because of the VNN's failure to order adequate spare parts.[78] Shipboard maintenance also was deplorable. As Sea Force advisor Lieutenant J. O. Richter Jr., United States Naval Reserve (USNR), explained in his end-of-tour report, "Presently there exists an attitude of 'let the shipyard fix it' when installed equipment fails rather than have the ship's own sailors attempt repairs."[79] Another advisor, Lieutenant Charles W. Long, USNR, echoed these sentiments: "It was the attitude of at least three commanding officers that almost all mechanical and electrical work should be accomplished by the shipyard."[80]

Commander Do Kiem and his wife, Thom Thi Le.

Crews also were not paid a living wage, which lowered morale and encouraged desertion. "It has been my experience," wrote Commander Aaron A. Levine, "that the average naval officer's wife is required to take on work in order to support the family and enlisted personnel are in even worse shape."[81] Do Kiem's wife, Thom Thi Le, worked as a telegraph clerk for Shell Oil for much of his VNN career to help pay the bills and, even with a second income, things were tight. "VNN salaries were not high enough to meet the basic needs of officers and their families," explained Do Kiem. Later in the war, some officers engaged in black market activities to supplement their meager wages.[82]

Inadequate food and medical care created additional problems for crews. "Medical care across the board is lacking and most of the troops that I have seen in the field are undernourished and completely lacking in vitamin diet," noted Commander Levine. Ship captains could barely feed their men on the money allotted for food, and when patrols were extended, ships occasionally ran out of food.[83] The poor sanitary conditions on many of the ships further exacerbated the situation. Chief Barney, after being savaged by bed bugs one evening, refused to sleep in berthing spaces and instead opted to sleep on the open deck during overnight patrols.[84] "Heads, wardrooms, and crew compartments are unsat from a sanitary point of view," complained Levine, and these conditions resulted in a sharp increase in amoebic dysentery among crews and advisors.

As in the case of the River Force, poor leadership lay at the core of many of the Sea Force's problems. "The VNN is lacking in dynamic leadership up and down the line," wrote Levine. "This is evident in the high desertion rate, poor material condition of ships, low standard of cleanliness and in the high percentage of commanding officers indicating a lack of consideration for the troops."[85] However, to blame the Sea Force officers for all the ills ignores the structural problems confronting this nascent naval force. Many VNN commanding officers simply were not getting enough resources from the Vietnamese government to run their ships properly. Everything from food to spare parts was in constant short supply. Under these circumstances, even the best officers had difficulty meeting American standards of excellence. To prepare for a training exercise in the Philippines, Do Kiem and his men gave their LSIL a fresh coat of paint and worked weeks on the engine plant. They then endured a rough weeklong voyage across the South China Sea with the ship tilting 45 degrees to port and starboard along the way. When the battered and tired crew finally steamed into Subic Bay, they were not allowed to tie up at the pier until a U.S. Navy team inspected the ship. After finding rats in the hold, the inspection team quarantined the ship. Pronounced unfit for training, the LSIL had to turn around "and sail home through waves of shame."[86]

Vietnam Navy in the 1963 Coup

In 1963 the VNN had a reputation of loyalty to President Ngo Dinh Diem. During the early days of the republic, it had backed Diem against the Binh Xuyen and other rebel sects. When a disgruntled colonel and three battalions of paratroopers staged an unsuccessful coup in November 1960, the navy again stood by Diem and his government. Two years later in February 1962, a pair of Vietnamese Air Force (VNAF) AD-6 Skyraiders bombed the presidential palace and made strafing runs on the shipyard and police headquarters. Navy ships anchored in the Saigon River went to general quarters, and *Huong Giang* (HQ-404) shot down one of the aircraft. Impressed by the navy's loyalty during the episode, Diem promoted Ho Tan Quyen to captain.[87]

With a navy of just 6,000 men in 1963, Quyen had no chance of defeating a coup by ARVN, which numbered over 196,000 troops, but in a factional struggle, he could ally his forces with those defending the government just as the VNN had done in earlier coups.[88] To thwart such a move, the 1963 coup plotters, led by two ARVN generals (Doung Van Minh and Tran Van Don) co-opted Lieutenant Commander Thuong Ngoc Luc, a RAG commander and a trusted subordinate of Quyen's, to capture the CNO and lock him up. Luc, with Lieutenant Nguyen Kim Giang, visited Quyen on his birthday, Saturday, 1 November 1963. The three men then proceeded in the CNO's vehicle to a birthday party with Quyen driving, Luc in the passenger's seat, and a co-conspirator, Lieutenant Giang, in the backseat. Luc initially tried to convince Quyen to join the plot, but when he rebuffed the offer, Luc drew a knife and stabbed Quyen in the chest. Quyen let go of the steering wheel

A smiling President Ngo Dinh Diem on a Vietnam Navy vessel observes an operation near Saigon with Vietnamese and foreign military, undated.

and tried to use a judo move to seize the knife. In the ensuing struggle, Luc's left hand was cut, and the car careened off the road into a water-filled culvert. Giang ended the fight by firing three shots into Quyen's head. Luc and Giang then loaded the CNO's corpse into a second car driven by Luc's driver, and dumped it at the Phu Tho rubber plantation.[89]

By 1340, the coup was in full swing. Rebel troops began attacking pro-Diem units throughout Saigon. Brandishing a .45-caliber pistol, Luc returned to the navy headquarters with a group of ARVN soldiers and ordered the naval officers there to lock down the armories. He and some of the troops then entered the headquarters building, rounded up various naval staff personnel, and loaded them at gunpoint into a coastal minesweeper (MSC-116). While other ARVN troops entered and secured the shipyard, Luc made several calls to Major General Duong Van Minh and to an unidentified U.S. naval officer. He informed the American that he had no desire to become CNO or deputy CNO, and told him that he had recommended Commander Chung Tan Cang, the River Force commander, for the job.[90]

Commander Ho Tan Quyen with Rear Admiral Alfred G. Ward, Commander, Cruiser Division 1, on board *Toledo* (CA-133), 27 October 1959. Quyen was assassinated on 1 November 1963.

Captain Drachnik, the senior naval advisor, was at home eating lunch when he first got word that "something funny was going on." His deputy informed him that some of his advisors had been incarcerated and that the CNO might be dead. "There was no doubt in my mind," recalled Drachnik, "that this was a very bad thing for the country. All of the work I'd put in for two years was eroded when Quyen was killed."[91] As early as May 1962, Drachnik knew that internal divisions existed in the Vietnam Navy and that some officers were actively petitioning politicians and generals on the Joint General Staff (JGS) to replace Quyen, but he had no idea that two trusted subordinates would go so far as to kill the CNO—on his birthday no less. A few months prior, Quyen had even gone out of the way to save Luc's career after the young officer had been accused of mishandling navy funds. Quyen's relationship with Luc extended back to their midshipmen days at the Nha Trang Naval Academy, and the two men had been "very close friends" up to the day of the coup according to several VNN officers who knew both men.[92]

Despite the confusion and despair caused by Quyen's murder, some VNN officers did attempt to defend the Diem regime. Lieutenant Commander Dinh Manh Hung, the Sea Force commander, took to the Saigon River in the LST *Cam Ranh* (HQ-500), along with five other ships. Lieutenant Do Kiem commanded one of those vessels—the submarine chaser *Van Don* (HQ-06)—and was eating lunch in his wardroom when the coup began. Seeing ARVN troops holding the naval headquarters at gunpoint, Do Kiem ordered his ship to fire warning shots at the headquarters. The ship's 20mm guns unleashed red tracer rounds on the coconut palms lining the base, sending the ARVN troops scurrying for cover. After a few minutes, Do Kiem called a cease-fire and evaluated the situation. VNN Chief of Staff Bang Cao Thang soon emerged from the main headquarters building with his hands in the air, followed by three ARVN soldiers. Thang warned Do Kiem not to shoot but did not tell him what was happening.[93]

Shortly thereafter, a flight of two A-1H Skyraiders made a pass over the area. Three explosions followed, and HQ-500 started firing, followed by four other Sea Force ships in the river, including Do Kiem's boat. The JGS had apparently ordered an air strike on the River Force headquarters building in an effort to convince the VNN leadership to join the coup. Gunfire from the ships downed one of the planes, and the other disengaged from the attack and returned to base.[94] Things quieted down after the attack, and Do Kiem and other Sea Force skippers tried to piece together events from scattered radio reports.[95]

Late in the afternoon, Commander Cang arrived at the naval headquarters to assume control of the situation. He sent out an LCVP to each warship anchored in the channel, ordering its skipper to board the craft and return to the headquarters for a meeting. "Don't go, sir," Do Kiem's sergeant at arms pleaded. "They'll kill you."[96] Do Kiem left his ship anyway and was soon joined by six other ship captains in a large conference room. Cang and Luc sat at the head of the table drinking beer. Slightly intoxicated and scowling, Luc announced that Ngo Diem was no longer in power and that a revolutionary council, led by Major General Minh, had assumed control of the government. After the meeting, Do Kiem and most other junior officers were allowed to return to their ships. The more senior officers in the room and on the headquarters staff were interrogated, restricted, or placed in custody.[97]

The coup came as a complete surprise to the VNN. Once senior leaders were killed or captured, opposition among junior officers and enlisted evaporated. "In an environment where the government is unstable," Drachnik observed, "it's very hard for military officers to know what to do in a coup situation."[98] In the end, doing nothing proved easier for most than taking action. Nevertheless, because of the former CNO's support of Diem and the strong initial stand by the Sea Force, it would take several months before the new army-dominated revolutionary government gained a semblance of trust and confidence in the VNN, and then only after it had purged many senior leaders from the VNN's ranks. In January 1964 that government, run by Major General Minh, was overthrown in another coup led by a 37-year-old ARVN major general named Nguyen Khanh, who in turn fell 8 February 1964. Several governments and purges later, a group of "young Turks" led by Air Vice Marshall Nguyen Cao Ky and ARVN General Nguyen Van Thieu assumed control of the government and ran the country until 1975.[99]

For the VNN as a whole, the 1963 coup and subsequent turbulence in the government devastated morale and robbed it of its most talented and effective leader, Ho Tan Quyen. The rapid succession of politically inept military juntas also diverted attention from the more important mission of fighting the Viet Cong and underscored to the officer corps the inherent fragility of the Republic of Vietnam. Lieutenant Commander Thoai, Quyen's Second Coastal Zone commander, believed that the 1963 coup was the beginning of the end of the Vietnam Navy and the republic. Thoai, who was briefly arrested during the episode, served under a dark cloud for years after the event because he had briefly worked as a naval aide to President Diem early in his career. Thoai reacted to these suspicions by working hard. "I loved the Navy and wanted to continue to serve."[100] Many of Thoai's subordinates did not share his feelings. They tended to slack off, knowing that their commanders would be replaced in the next regime change. "I had a hard time to keep them in line," lamented Thoai. "We lost time and confidence." Lieutenant F. T. Lazarchick, a Sea Force advisor, noted that before the coup commanding officers "seem to have been assigned for their professional knowledge, leadership, and seafaring experience." After the coup, personnel changes led to an increase in "young and inexperienced commanding officers. Approximately fifty percent are very poor shiphandlers."[101]

Barrier Patrols and the Bucklew Report

The U.S. Navy made its first attempt to directly assist the VNN with interdiction in December 1961. Seeking to catch infiltrators near the border with North Vietnam, the U.S. Navy stationed four of its ocean minesweepers (MSOs) five miles south of the 17th parallel. For the next several months, these ships, along with two VNN submarine chasers (PCs), sailed on an east-west track in close proximity to the border. The MSOs of Minesweeper Division 73 were not allowed to stop any ships but, by using radar and visual surveillance, they could locate suspicious vessels and then direct VNN ships to intercept them. Martin SP-5B Marlin seaplanes based in Taiwan, which patrolled the waters between the northern coast of South Vietnam and the Paracel Islands, aided these surface vessels. Although this first coastal interdiction effort yielded few suspects, at a Pacific commanders meeting in January 1962 Secretary of Defense Robert S. McNamara insisted on continuing them. McNamara hoped that material in captured junks would yield concrete evidence of North Vietnam's direct support of the insurgency in the south.[102]

In February 1962, the destroyer escorts *Edmonds* (DE-406) and *Walton* (DE-361) replaced the MSOs along the 17th parallel and added a patrol in the Gulf of Thailand called the "Gulf of Siam Patrol" to stop infiltration from Cambodia. Because of their higher speed and better seaworthiness, each destroyer escort could perform the work of two MSOs.[103] Despite the deployment of these assets, the patrols did not yield much in the way of tangible results. From reports of seizures received as of March 1962, Vice Admiral William A. Schoech, Commander Seventh Fleet, concluded that "there has been no concrete evidence of massive or even significant infiltration," and that it "must be concluded that the patrols have not been effective in capturing infiltrators if significant infiltration is taking place." In the same message, Schoech noted that the VNN was not capable of conducting effective patrols at the time without U.S. assistance because of its "poor state of training and material readiness, lack of forceful leadership in some ships, and need for additional experience at sea by all SVN [South Vietnam] ships."[104]

In May the U.S. Navy halted the Gulf of Siam Patrol because there was no evidence of infiltration in the area.[105] Two months later Admiral Felt terminated the northern patrol for

Esteem (MSO-438), an ocean minesweeper (nonmagnetic), patrolled the outer infiltration barrier with other ships of her class.

the same reason. While the barrier patrols uncovered little evidence that North Vietnam was supplying the Viet Cong via the sea, they did serve as a useful training exercise for the VNN. U.S. Navy personnel took the opportunity to train the Vietnamese in tactics, communications, and gunnery. According to a report written by Task Group (TG) 72.7, this training "unquestionably" improved "the state of readiness of the SVN ships." However, the joint patrols also revealed many deficiencies and may have sowed the seeds of dependency for this still-young navy. "Some officers of the Vietnamese Navy," the report stated, "have privately opined that USN participation in and supervision of the patrol so saps the initiative of the VNN officers on patrol as to cancel any training or motivational advantages achieved."[106]

As soon as the joint patrols ceased, Communist infiltration skyrocketed. Using steel-hulled ships, the North Vietnamese Navy delivered 3,600 tons of weapons to the Viet Cong during 1964—nearly three times the amount sent by sea in 1962 and 1963 combined. More supplies were in transit by sea in 1964 than had moved down the overland Ho Chi Minh Trail during the entire war to date.[107] In an attempt to solve the infiltration conundrum, Admiral Felt commissioned a study of the problem in January 1964 by a survey team of nine men led by Rear Admiral Paul Savage, commander of the Amphibious Training Command, U.S. Pacific Fleet. When Savage became ill, Captain Bucklew, the commander of Naval Operations Support Group, U.S. Pacific Fleet, took command of the team. He turned out to be a perfect choice for the assignment.[108]

A pioneering special warfare officer, Bucklew possessed an adventuresome spirit and firsthand knowledge of a naval advisor's role. The son of a streetcar motorman from Columbus, Ohio,

Bucklew was born on 18 December 1914, and at the age of 16 lied about his age and enlisted in the U.S. Naval Reserve, where he enjoyed summer cruises on the Great Lakes as well as the pay. He applied to the Naval Academy but failed the admissions test and instead ended up at Xavier University on a football scholarship. After graduation in 1934 Bucklew played for the Columbus Bulldogs of the American Football League and later for the Cleveland Rams.[109]

When World War II broke out, the Navy recalled him to duty and assigned him to Norfolk, Virginia, as a physical education instructor. He quickly was bored with shore duty and volunteered for a more adventurous assignment with the "Scouts and Raiders." The scouts surveyed beaches during the days before an invasion and then guided Army troops ashore on D-Day. On his first assignment in North Africa, German aircraft torpedoed his transport ship (*Leedstown* [AP-73]) off the coast of Algeria on 9 November 1942. He survived the attack and went on to lead a scout raider team that surveyed the Salerno beaches in Sicily. During that invasion, he received a Navy Cross for guiding the initial assault teams to the beach under heavy enemy fire. In 1944 he received a second Navy Cross during the Normandy invasion by repeatedly guiding boats to the beach despite stiff currents and heavy fire. He also picked up wounded and fired his boat's rockets in support of the first wave of Duplex Drive tanks.[110] At the end of 1944, the Navy sent Bucklew to China to survey locations for potential Allied invasions. Working with local guerrillas and disguised as a coolie, he set out by foot from Kunming to survey beaches in southern China for intelligence purposes.[111]

Bucklew left the Navy in 1946 and returned to Xavier to coach football. A year later the service recalled him to duty to teach Naval Reserve Officer Training Corps (NROTC) at Columbia University. From 1951 to 1956, he commanded Beach Jumper Unit 2 at Little Creek, Virginia, and then departed for Korea to become an advisor to the director of naval intelligence for the South Korean navy. In this position, he learned a great deal about the plight of the naval advisor. He discovered that advisors often worked with officers of higher rank but with less experience than their U.S. counterparts. "Their militaries were built rapidly under the stress of war," and many of their officers were "Johnny-come-latelys." The tendency of many American officers was to "look down on their counterparts and always push American weaponry, doctrine, and training," he explained. Bucklew, however, tried to understand the situation from the other side.[112] Rather than press his counterpart Captain Kim Se Won to develop a sophisticated radio communications network with his agents in North Korea, he accepted the existing carrier-pigeon system and even signed off on a budgetary request for birdseed. When his U.S. chain of command complained that the South Korean navy was not doing enough to prevent the infiltration of North Korean agents along the coast by fishermen, Bucklew went out on a patrol boat to observe the situation firsthand. He noticed that during the spring rockfish season, thousands of unmarked fishing boats, both from the North and South, plied the coastline, and that there was no way that the South Korean navy could possibly inspect every vessel for enemy agents or contraband.[113] In 1964 Bucklew would encounter similar situations in South Vietnam where there were simply too many civilian craft plying the coastal waters for naval forces to search effectively.

The Korean experience left Bucklew deeply skeptical of the Navy's advisory system. "An advisor would spend about 6 months [of his one year tour] trying to find out what his job is and the next six months thinking about going home," he noted in an oral history. "If it is a hardship country and they are separated from their families, they are not happy in the first place and may spend as little time as possible with their counterparts." It takes a special type of officer to thrive in the advisor role—someone with an appreciation of foreign cultures and a strong sense of adventure. For Bucklew, a better system would have utilized volunteers, trained them adequately in the foreign language of the host country, and then sent them away on two- to three- year assignments.[114]

After Korea, Bucklew became head of the intelligence section for Amphibious Training Command Coronado and, in 1961, a staff intelligence officer for Amphibious Group 1. The following year he supervised a secret beach survey of South Vietnam by an underwater demolition team (UDT). In 1963 he took command of a new organization responsible for Navy counterinsurgency, guerrilla, and special warfare operations in the Pacific called Naval Support Group Pacific.[115] It was with this command that he traveled to Vietnam to study the problem of infiltration. He spent the first few weeks of the assignment at Pearl Harbor, attending meetings with the CINCPAC staff. Toward the end of his stay, Admiral Felt explained the rationale for the mission: "I want to know what is going on out there; I want to know why all I get are messages of success but meanwhile we're getting the hell kicked out of us and I want to know why?"

Bucklew's group traveled throughout South Vietnam, interviewing advisors at the lowest levels. "It became my firm belief that these men best knew the problems but were not often listened to," Bucklew recalled. "We wanted their opinion. Most of it stemmed from lack of communication and lack of supplies, and some were in very sad situations." One young advisor he met even resorted to contacting his aunt, Republican Senator Margaret Chase Smith of Maine, and pleading with her directly for supplies. Senator Smith purchased medicines and supplies with her own money and shipped them to her nephew's unit.[116]

In another instance, just after dark Bucklew was riding a Vietnamese gunboat on the Mekong when they heard considerable gunfire along the shore. Bucklew went to the bridge and asked the VNN officer if he planned to assist the ARVN unit engaged with the enemy. The officer told him it was none of his business. The VNN was completely independent of the army and rarely coordinated with the shore troops.[117] Another problem he encountered was the navy's difficulty in determining friend from foe. "The entire war was fought by night throughout Vietnam. They came by night and they left by night. It was hit and run and they received a lot of support from the local hamlets. There was no way in the world you could tell friend from foe. They dress alike, looked alike, spoke alike. And as we said with the fishing boats in Korea, you can only identify friend from foe when they start firing at you."[118]

The Bucklew Report, which came out in February 1965, proved prophetic; nearly all of Bucklew's predictions turned out to be correct. The report concluded that the communist supply system ran "from North Vietnam, via Laos and Cambodia, with delivery accomplished via the

Ho Chi Minh trail, via major rivers, and by a combination of man-carried and inland waterborne transfers." Control of the rivers, especially the Mekong, Bassac, and related waterways, was essential to stemming the flow of enemy supplies. A coastal surveillance force was also necessary to prevent seaborne infiltration, even though no "hard evidence existed" that large amounts of material were being infiltrated by sea. The Coastal Force, he argued, needed additional patrol craft and junks to adequately patrol the entire 1,200-mile coastline of South Vietnam, but the coastal quarantine would fail without additional operations to seal-off riverine traffic, especially along the Cambodian border.[119]

To secure the rivers, he advocated a system of fixed and mobile check points on bridges, major canals, and waterway junctions manned by trained military or paramilitary personnel. Personnel attached to these outposts would search suspicious vessels as they passed through the control points. Irregular river patrols operating in conjunction with the mobile checkpoints would keep the enemy off-balance and further disrupt the enemy supply system. The six VNN river assault groups would be used to raid Viet Cong landing sites, way stations, supply depots, and assembly points on the rivers. Vietnamese Marines would initiate clear and hold operations via amphibious assaults. Halting river infiltration also depended heavily on other security measures advocated in the report. These included a beefed up customs service and a system of 260 land checkpoints throughout the country manned by police, civil guard, and self defense corps personnel. "Control of banks or shoreline must be accomplished prior to the establishment of effective river traffic control," the report noted. It also depended on a barrier patrol at sea near the 17th parallel by the Sea Force and a coastal quarantine by the 632 junks of the Coastal Force.[120]

While Bucklew strongly believed that most of the enemy's personnel and munitions entered into South Vietnam from Cambodia by land routes and along the rivers, he stopped short of advocating direct U.S. Navy intervention, especially on the rivers. "There were many of our top level people who were determined that the Navy would never become involved in muddy-water operations," and he did not want his report to ruffle too many feathers. The study's primary goal was to gain more resources for the VNN and bolster the U.S. Navy's advisory efforts in Vietnam. It would take several more years for the U.S. Navy to fully comprehend the importance of South Vietnam's rivers and to develop forces capable of effectively combating the problem—namely Task Forces 116 and 117. For the next several years, the focus of Navy planners would be on coastal surveillance.[121]

Navy SEALs in Vietnam

Some of the very earliest groups of naval advisors in Vietnam were Navy SEAL teams. Founded in 1962, the SEALs drew nearly all of their original members from underwater demolition teams.[122] On 1 January 1962, SEAL Team 1 was activated on the West Coast at the Naval Amphibious Base Coronado, California, and SEAL Team 2 on the East Coast at the Naval Amphibious Base Little Creek, Virginia.[123] As head of the Naval Support Group Pacific during the early 1960s, Captain Bucklew had a direct hand in developing the early SEAL community and is often referred to as the "founding father of the SEALs."[124]

Initially, the mission of the SEAL was twofold: to develop a specialized capability for sabotage, demolition, and other clandestine activities conducted in and from restricted waters, rivers, and canals; and to conduct training of selected indigenous personnel in a wide variety of skills for use in naval clandestine operations. Early SEAL training consisted of a 25-week Basic Underwater Demolition/SEAL course, plus three weeks of parachute training followed by specialized training in such fields as battlefield medicine, small arms, riverboats, land navigation, and hand-to-hand combat. The object of the extensive and grueling training regimen was to produce a small group of elite Navy warriors capable of attacking installations behind enemy lines; landing and recovering guerrillas, Special Forces, and downed aviators; and training indigenous forces in similar combat methods. SEALs have the capability of operating from land, aircraft, small boats, and even submarines.[125]

The first deployment of SEALs to Vietnam occurred in July 1962, when a pilot group of three officers and 15 enlisted sailors arrived at Danang. During the 1962–1964 advisory period, SEALs trained the *Biet Hai* commandos (Coastal Force specialists in reconnaissance, sabotage, and guerrilla warfare) and regular Vietnam Navy UDT members, known as *Lien Doc Nguoi Nhia* (LDNN). SEAL teams also conducted hydrographic surveys along the South Vietnamese coast.[126] In December 1965, SEALs began conducting extensive direct-action missions in the waterways of the Rung Sat Special Zone (RSSZ) and the Mekong Delta while still serving as advisors to various indigenous Special Forces units, including the LDNN and provincial reconnaissance units (PRUs).

The average SEAL mission lasted six hours and was carried out by the smallest operational SEAL contingent of the period—a squad of seven SEALs (one officer and six enlisted) plus two indigenous personnel. The most common types of missions were observation patrols, ambushes, and body snatches. In a patrol, SEALs would move along an area where Viet Cong were suspected to operate until enemy troops were spotted. The SEALs would then observe and gather intelligence about VC movements or, if the conditions were right, set up an impromptu ambush. Ambushes from specific locations were another common mission. Some of the most successful operations were body snatches, whereupon SEALs acting on local intelligence would kill or capture a Viet Cong leader. Other missions involved leading indigenous commandos on raids against VC units and rescuing downed aviators.[127] According to a Center for Naval Analyses study of Game Warden published shortly after the war, "about 90 percent of the SEAL effort was devoted to gathering intelligence."[128] Arguably, without the intelligence gathered by SEALs, the riverine forces would have taken heavier casualties and been much less effective in thwarting river crossings.

By mid-1968, the 211-man SEAL Team 1 had four to five platoons operating in Vietnam, and SEAL Team 2, another three platoons. Each 14-man platoon contained 12 enlisted men and two officers organized into two squads. SEAL platoons were headquartered at Danang,

Nha Be, and Can Tho but operated throughout the country and especially in the Mekong Delta and RSSZ. SEALs not serving as advisors fell under the command of Task Force 116 (Operation Game Warden), whose river patrol boats (PBRs) and Navy UH-1B Iroquois helicopters often provided transportation and fire support for SEAL operations. The SEALs also operated their own fleet of small boats, including Boston Whalers, SEAL team assault boats, 26-foot-long armored trimarans, landing craft, and even Vietnamese sampans.[129]

The SEALs suffered their first combat casualty in Vietnam on 19 August 1966 during a reconnaissance patrol against enemy bunkers southeast of Nha Be. Radarman 2nd Class Billy Machen, a 28-year-old SEAL from Dallas, Texas, and a member of SEAL Team 1, was in the point position when he spotted several Viet Cong. Rather than diving for cover, Machen opened fire, forcing the enemy to trigger its ambush prematurely. Machen's actions alerted his teammates, giving them time to take cover and egress from the scene, but he ended up sacrificing his own life to save the others. Less than two months later in October 1966, two SEAL squads were transiting a small river in the RSSZ on an LCM 3 when a mortar round struck the boat, wounding 16 of the 19 men on board. Despite these casualties, the squad engaged the enemy position immediately, killing 40 Viet Cong in the process. As these two incidents reveal, SEALs represented a special breed of warrior. Per capita, the SEALs received more combat decorations than nearly any other Navy unit of the war. Awards earned by individual SEALs included two Medals of Honor and six Navy Crosses.[130]

As PBRs began deploying to the Mekong Delta during the spring of 1966, the SEAL platoons began participating in more operations in support of U.S. naval forces in South Vietnam. In 1966 alone, SEAL Team 1 gathered troves of intelligence for TF 116 and also killed 86 Viet Cong, destroyed 21 sampans, and captured 521,000 pounds of rice.[131] In 1967, SEALs initiated four-day surveillance operations in enemy territory, demonstrating that they could operate for extended periods without external support. SEALs also proved instrumental in disrupting Viet Cong attempts to mine water traffic on the Long Tau shipping channel. On 21 September, Alpha platoon of SEAL Team 1 ambushed a sapper squad preparing to plant a mine on the river, killing or wounding seven elite Viet Cong sappers and capturing all of their mine-laying equipment. Intelligence gained from surveillance patrols and captured documents allowed SEAL Team 1 platoons to prosecute eight successful ambushes toward the end of 1967. Overall in 1967, SEAL Team 1 platoons killed 60 Viet Cong, captured 24, sunk 23 sampans, and destroyed 27 base camps. SEAL Team 1 losses included four killed and 26 wounded.[132]

In 1967, SEAL Team 2 also racked up an impressive record, killing 163 Viet Cong and capturing another 98, in exchange for 19 SEALs wounded. The SEAL Team 2 command history stated that classified information obtained by the unit in one mission "was of extreme high value to military planners and was considered one of the major intelligence coups of the Vietnam conflict."[133]

During the 1968 Tet Offensive, SEALs successfully defended many Navy shore facilities spread out in the Mekong Delta and in several cases proved instrumental in defending provincial capitals. At My Tho, SEAL Team 2 members fought off a sustained attack on the PBR billeting area against fantastic odds (see chapter 6). SEAL Team 1 defended other U.S. installations, rallied ARVN defenders, provided counter-sniper support, and called in air and artillery strikes on enemy targets.[134] During the Viet Cong attack on Chau Doc (also known as Chau Phu), a town bordering Cambodia in the upper Mekong Delta, members of SEAL Team 2, together with a small PRU force led by Army Special Forces Staff Sergeant Drew Dix and a handful of PBRs, succeeded in liberating the provincial capital in a vicious battle against an enemy force of two battalions.[135]

Overall, 49 U.S. Navy SEALs lost their lives in Vietnam. None was captured.[136] SEAL intelligence proved instrumental for Game Warden operations, resulted in many significant ambushes, and thwarted river crossings. SEALs also achieved one of the highest kill ratios of any combat unit during the war and were successful in helping to destroy Viet Cong leaders in the Mekong Delta, especially during 1968–1970. From June 1969–April 1970, SEALs in the delta conducted 1,192 missions resulting in 581 Viet Cong killed and 193 captured.[137] Draftsman 1st Class Harry Humphries explained the success of SEALs in this way: "Because of our technique of operating, the ferocity of how we did our job, and the tactics we used, we were very much like the VC themselves, only better. We were much more aggressive."[138]

The Vung Ro Incident

The catalyst for renewed direct U.S. Navy participation in coastal interdiction was the discovery on 16 February 1965 of a North Vietnamese steel-hulled supply trawler at Vung Ro Bay in central Vietnam. The ship, filled with arms and ammunition, verified that infiltration of supplies by sea was indeed taking place, and that the Viet Cong were planning more large-scale operations in the South. The finding prompted General William C. Westmoreland, the MACV commander, to hold a conference in Saigon to develop a combined USN/VNN force to counter directly such infiltration in the future.[139]

The North Vietnam Navy's Group 125 had been supplying its southern cadres by steel-hulled ships since 1963 and, by January of 1965, was shipping up to 400 tons a month of material to secret supply depots in South Vietnam. Ship 145 was a 130-foot-long diesel-powered trawler capable of transporting up to 100 tons. Originally bound for Cochinchina, it altered course on 15 February after receiving reports of danger in the original unloading area. It arrived at Vung Ro in central Vietnam at 0300 on the 16th and began unloading supplies and weapons at a dock hidden by rocks. By daybreak the ship still had not finished disgorging its shipments, so its captain decided to stay put and finish the operation after nightfall.[140]

That same morning, U.S. Army 1st Lieutenant James S. Bowers took off from Qui Nhon in a UH-1B Huey on a medical rescue mission. Flying south along the coast, he passed by Vung Ro at 1030. As the helicopter banked around Cap Varella, he glanced down at a tree-covered island and noticed slight movement. Looking closer at the island, he realized that it was not an island but a ship covered in tree foliage. Bowers made note of the ship's location on his map and telephoned Lieutenant Commander Rodgers, the senior naval advisor for the II Corps area, after completing his mission. Rodgers immediately requested an air strike from the VNAF and then flew out in an observation plane to investigate the situation in person with two other naval advisors. He arrived at Vung Ro at 1425 and just in time to watch the third wave of VNAF A-1 Skyraiders capsize the trawler, and a fourth hit a nearby supply camp.[141]

Meanwhile, the South Vietnamese Second Coastal Zone commander, Lieutenant Commander Thoai, requested the services of VNN divers, arranged for a company of troops from the 23rd ARVN Division to be transported into the area by the LSM *Tien Giang* (HQ-405), and ordered additional air strikes. Thoai planned to recover useful intelligence material and then blow up the ship and its cargo with demolition charges. The VNAF, however, failed to provide the air strikes, and Thoai's plan to land troops was thwarted by the Phu Yen province chief, who refused to send soldiers under his command because he considered the area too strongly defended to be taken by one company.[142] This delay gave the Viet Cong time to attempt to blow up the ship with a one-ton charge, but the charge only managed to break the vessel into two parts. Viet Cong troops then began unloading the cargo and hiding it in nearby caves.[143] The next morning, on the 17th, the VNAF struck the area, and HQ-405 made two attempts to enter the bay with a team of VNN divers. Enemy fire drove the LSM back both times.[144]

To improve coordination between the services, the Military Assistance Command Vietnam sent its director of operations, Army Brigadier General William E. DePuy, to Nha Trang on the 18th to develop a plan to secure the area. A World War II veteran of Normandy who would later help rebuild and transform the U.S. Army after Vietnam as the first head of its Training and Doctrine Command, DePuy was one of the Army's brightest and most effective generals. At the planning conference attended by representatives from the ARVN and the VNN, he arranged for a two-battalion blocking force from the ARVN 23rd Division to seal off Vung Ro along Route 1. An ARVN company would then move along the shore towards the trawler from Deo Ca, and a Special Forces company would attempt an amphibious landing from HQ-405. Naval gunfire support and additional air strikes would further support the operation.[145]

While the conference was taking place, the patrol escort (HQ-08) arrived at Vung Ro and raked the trawler with gunfire. The escort encountered no opposition and withdrew at 1420.[146] The next day, a submarine chaser (HQ-04) arrived at Vung Ro with 15 Vietnamese LDNN frogmen and the team's advisor, Lieutenant Franklin W. Anderson. Shortly after 0800, HQ-04, HQ-08, and an LSM (HQ-405) moved into the landing area, and two VNAF aircraft commenced a napalm attack on the beach. Most of the napalm landed in the water, and the flotilla turned away after taking some rifle and machine-gun fire and suffering five casualties (one killed and four wounded). At 1025, the flotilla made a second landing attempt but turned away at long range. The VNN later decorated Lieutenant Tran Van Triet, the commanding officer of HQ-04, for this action, but Lieutenant Commander Rodgers, who was at the scene, labeled both attempts as "feeble" in his after-action report. The withdrawals were "extremely cautious given the firepower capability of the opposing forces."[147] Lieutenant Commander Thoai described the situation differently. While admitting that the commander of HQ-405 initially showed reluctance to land in the face of fire,

Thoai claimed the commander, at his urgings, ultimately pressed on and made the landing despite taking casualties. "I saw the man killed; he was firing HQ-405's 20-millimeter and he got shot. They were close so I could see it." Thoai also saw the boatswain's mate on HQ-04 get shot and collapse right in front of Triet, yet this lieutenant pressed on with the attack.[148]

At 1100, the LDNN team finally landed and began moving off the beach under sniper fire. By 1515, it had secured the areas and divers began searching the wreck for intelligence material. Later in the afternoon, HQ-405 delivered an ARVN company and a Special Forces team to the area as reinforcements, but all forces withdrew back to the LSM at 1930. The Special Forces commander reported that he could not hold the beachhead overnight and that very little cargo remained so another landing would not be necessary. He also claimed a body count of 18 Viet Cong killed in action. American enlisted advisors who accompanied the unit had a different story. They reported only four enemy killed in action and over 1,000 cases of ammo and many weapons still at a dump on shore.[149]

Throughout the night Rodgers, who was on HQ-08, urged his counterpart, Thoai, to make another landing, but the VNN officer refused, claiming he would be held accountable if the landing failed. The VNN chief of staff, Lieutenant Commander Tran Binh Sang, who was also on board HQ-08, concurred with Thoai's decision. Rodgers later blamed Thoai's intransigence "on a hope for cancellation of the operation rather than any evidence of significant numbers of enemy troops."[150] In a later oral history, Thoai argued that the supplies were on top of a steep mountain and hard to reach. He wanted to destroy those stores with naval gunfire rather than risk taking more casualties in a tricky night operation. "For three days and four nights," he later explained, "I hadn't eaten anything; I didn't sleep. I was always on the bridge, and was very tired and nervous because I was in command of the whole amphibious operation. The advisor was responsible to the U.S. Navy, not to me, so he did not understand."[151]

After a flurry of messages back and forth to higher headquarters, Thoai finally agreed to land the troops at 0215 on the 20th after receiving an order directly from President Khanh. Backed by heavy fire from supporting vessels and unwanted flares, the force landed at 0545. Night blindness from the flares prevented troops from moving to the dump until 0635. When they finally reached the area, the Special Forces troops began stealing the medical supplies. Rodgers requested that the Special Forces commander stop the looting and order his troops to move the captured goods to the beach. The commander disregarded the guidance. Rodgers then radioed Thoai and asked him to take corrective measures. At Thoai's urging, the Special Forces troops finally began moving material at 0835.[152] A survey of the captured supplies revealed 1,000,000 rounds of small arms ammunition, 2,000 rounds of 82mm mortar ammunition, 500 antitank grenades, 500 rounds of 57mm recoilless rifle ammunition, 1,000 rounds of 75mm recoilless rifle ammunition, and over 3,000 small arms among other war materials. There were also indications that previous large deliveries of supplies had been made in the area. The VNN displayed the cache to a group of journalists as well as members of the International Control Commission on 21 February.[153]

On the 23rd, a VNN flotilla landed troops at the Cap Varella peninsula for a mop up operation.[154] Another LSM, HQ-406, was unable to beach because of an uncharted sandbar and had to be guided to an alternative spot by a spotting plane. The water there was still too deep and the troops had to be offloaded by junks. During the afternoon, several firefights occurred, and a 57mm round fired by ARVN troops detonated a Viet Cong ammunition dump in the area. By 1100 on the 24th, the area was considered secure, and by 1230 the task force was under way to Nha Trang.[155]

The Vung Ro incident did more than demonstrate that North Vietnam was shipping large amounts of military supplies to the south by sea; it also revealed many problems within the VNN. Not only did a 130-foot long steel-hulled freighter manage to slip through VNN's coastal patrols, but it took the VNN (with ARVN and VNAF support) over four days to secure the area and seize the ship's goods. Vice Admiral Paul P. Blackburn, Commander Seventh Fleet in 1965, noted that the VNN was "very young. They were equipped to run 2–3 patrol boats and that was about it. They had some wonderful guys but also some peasants from the rice paddies who didn't know nothing."[156] The junk force, which bore the brunt of the coastal quarantine program, was in even worse shape. According to the Bucklew Report, its personnel were "by and large, illiterate," operating "under the most difficult living conditions and on an extremely austere basis." In addition to suffering nearly constant maintenance problems, the force's inadequate wooden junks could not pursue the faster motorized junks, not to mention steel trawlers like Ship 145. Many of the Junk Division bases also were situated in VC-dominated areas with little or no local security forces. Lines of communication within the force were "almost negligible."[157] At the time, the VNN coastal interdiction needed exactly what the U.S. Navy had to offer—modern ships equipped with the latest radar and communications equipment, along with ample air support and highly motivated, well-trained crews to man them.[158]

To come up with tangible solutions to the coastal infiltration problem, General Westmoreland held a meeting at the Naval Advisory Group headquarters in Saigon with representatives from Seventh Fleet, CINCPACFLT, the Naval Advisory Group, and other services to develop a plan for a joint USN–VNN infiltration force. He told the attendees "he needed help from all the resources in the . . . area in order to beat the VC military machine and to inspire or shame the Vietnamese, particularly the [navy], into doing a better job, since they were about the worst of the three services in VN."[159] The resulting plan called for a U.S. Navy sea and aircraft patrol that would concentrate on locating oceangoing shipping like the steel-hulled trawler discovered at Vung Ro. U.S. forces, consisting of destroyers, minesweepers, and shore-based SP-2H Neptune maritime patrol aircraft, would track suspicious contacts and vector VNN ships to board and search them.[160] U.S. surface units would be stationed at the 17th parallel and along eight patrol areas along the coast, each averaging 108 nautical miles in length and 35–40 nautical miles in depth.[161] One destroyer, four minesweepers, two SP-2s, three single-engine aircraft, and two photoreconnaissance aircraft would patrol each area.

The role of the VNN Sea Force was to board, search, and, if necessary, seize trawlers tracked and identified in each patrol zone by U.S. Navy assets. Smaller coastal traffic would be detected, seized, or destroyed exclusively by VNN gunboats, and the junk force would concentrate on boarding and inspecting smaller junks and sampans. Sixteen patrol ships and 100 junks would patrol each area. Naval Advisory Group personnel would form the link between the Seventh Fleet and the Vietnam Navy, and 250 new officer and enlisted billets were requested to meet the demands of the new operation. Under the plan, the NAG would provide 101 U.S. advisors to the junk force (one for each underway patrol group), 30 Sea Force ship riders, and 75 personnel to man a surveillance operations center in Saigon and the five surveillance centers along the coast 24 hours a day. The NAG also requested communications equipment for all VNN ships, as well as for junk patrols and junk shore bases.[162]

The plan was designed to inspire the VNN to increase the quality and quantity of their searches by augmenting it with a conventional patrol force consisting of modern U.S. ships and aircraft equipped with the latest surveillance technology. These reinforcements, the Naval Advisory Group hoped, would prevent many (if not all) large, steel-hulled trawlers from infiltrating South Vietnam's coast. VNN ship-riders on U.S. vessels would also learn a great deal about the operational techniques of the world's most advanced and sophisticated Navy, and the new communications system installed on VNN vessels would improve overall coordination within the fleet.

The new counterinfiltration plan, which became known as Market Time, was not without shortcomings. Some were relatively easy to fix. Destroyers and minesweepers, for example, ended up being too big for the job and were replaced by smaller ships. The rules of engagement

Nguyen Doc Bong (HQ-231), a 250-foot Vietnam Navy gunboat. Crewed by six officers and 65 enlisted sailors, the ship could reach speeds of up to 16.5 knots, circa later 1960s. In World War II, the boat served with the U.S. Navy as LSSL-129.

were changed in May 1965 to allow U.S. ships to "stop, search, and seize vessels not clearly engaged in innocent passage."[163] Others proved more intractable. Although Market Time forces would eventually patrol parts of the Bassac, Cua Dai, and Co Chien Rivers, the initial concept ignored the issue of infiltration along the smaller waterways of the delta. Lieutenant M. L. McGuire, a very insightful young advisor in the Third Naval Zone, summarized the situation well in his 1965 end-of-tour report. "There is a very detrimental fixation on 100+ ton metal hull vessels due to the Vung Ro incident. The current infiltration if indeed it exists is via sampans and/or junks. The war will be won from in-country through bottom up efforts. RAG groups and their ops appear to be poor cousins—a rather significant miscalculation."[164] It would take the U.S. Navy over a year to establish a separate river control operation called Game Warden to fully deal with the threat McGuire and Bucklew outlined. While Market Time would succeed brilliantly in stemming the flow of coastal infiltration, ultimately the waterborne interdiction war would be won or lost on the rivers.

Finally, the plan partially Americanized the infiltration battle without solving any of the VNN's fundamental problems. These included:

- shoddy or nonexistent maintenance
- poor morale in the enlisted force caused by low pay and deplorable living conditions
- a young, inexperienced officer corps devastated by the loss of Quyen and the corruption and politicization of the South Vietnamese armed forces
- inadequate maintenance and training facilities
- few experienced petty officers—the backbone of a good navy
- a dysfunctional coastal force composed of wooden junks manned by illiterate peasants
- U.S. advisors without enough language and cultural training to provide a proper mentorship role.

Writing about the Vietnamese army during this period, historian Ronald Spector summarized the situation by quoting an expression commonly heard in Vietnam: "You can't make somethin' out of nothin'."[165] The same could be said about the VNN. No U.S. Navy intervention could succeed without uplifting its ally and ultimately preparing it to fight fully the battle on its own.

End of Tour

Captain William H. Hardcastle Jr., chief of the U.S. Naval Advisory Group in 1965, believed that the ideal advisor had to be a "co-equal" leader with his Vietnamese counterpart and be in the forefront of all operations. The naval advisor to a RAG was expected to act not only as diplomat but also to set an example as a leader when under fire. "Should an advisor flinch under such fire, or show signs of nervousness, or momentary indecision," wrote Hardcastle, "it would be immediately noted by the Vietnamese River Force personnel, and the advisor's effectiveness would be diminished." Lieutenant Meyerkord exemplified these virtues. By spring 1965, he had been involved in more than 30 combat operations in which he had come under direct fire. In several of these actions, he performed well above and beyond the call of duty.[166]

On 13 January 1965, he and his counterpart, the recently promoted Lieutenant Commander Hoa, led a group of three LCMs, six LCVPs, four STCAN/FOMs, a monitor, and a River Force commandament (an altered LCM designed to serve as a command ship) down the 45- to 60-foot-wide Long Ho Canal that linked Vinh Long to Ba Ke. RAG 23's mission was to carry the 1st Battalion of the 13th ARVN Regiment and search the canal for enemy activity. About 1,000 yards down the canal, a small force of Viet Cong fired on the lead boat with a 60mm mortar and Browning automatic rifles, forcing the small boat to run aground. The second boat retreated and informed Meyerkord and Hoa that wounded were trapped in the grounded small craft. Disregarding his own safety, Meyerkord jumped into the second boat and proceeded to the beached lead boat. While under constant fire from both sides of the canal, he administered first aid to the wounded Vietnamese and helped evacuate them to safety. ARVN troops then landed north of the ambush site, and the VC squad broke contact and retreated. Casualties included three VNN and three Viet Cong wounded and two Viet Cong killed.[167] Meyerkord's efforts to save the Vietnamese sailors without regard to his own safety made him much loved within the navy. Army Major Oscar H. Padgett, the 13th Regiment's senior advisor, praised Meyerkord as an advisor "without peer. His rapport with his counterpart was the best I have seen since serving as an advisor in Vietnam."[168]

A little over a week later on 24 January, Meyerkord again excelled in a combat situation. The night before, a Viet Cong company had attacked an outpost in the Duc Ton district of Vinh Long Province, and RAG 23's mission was to relieve the garrison with a company of Regional Forces (RF) troops. As it headed down a narrow canal to the outpost, Viet Cong dug-in along the banks ambushed Hoa's small flotilla. A .30-caliber machine gun round struck Hoa in the leg and incapacitated the officer. Meyerkord, although wounded in the foot shortly thereafter by a piece of shrapnel, assumed command and ordered the small flotilla of one monitor, four STCAN/FOMs, and one LCM to retreat. After regrouping his forces, Meyerkord ordered a devastating counterattack, killing 15 enemy troops in the process. After an hour-long battle, the Viet Cong were in full retreat.[169] Though it was not his war, Meyerkord fought each battle to his utmost, and the Vietnamese, as one enlisted advisor noted, accepted him "as one of their own."[170]

On the day of his last mission, 16 March 1965, Meyerkord was scheduled to appear at the Naval Advisory Group headquarters to receive a Bronze Star. Early that day, Meyerkord contacted Captain Hardcastle's office and asked to be excused from the ceremony, explaining that he wanted to accompany his counterpart on a mission against a suspected VC position near Vinh Long.[171] Later that day he and Hoa were again leading a flotilla down a small canal. The flotilla turned a bend and was caught in a fusillade of enemy fire. Chief Eugene Barney seized his 12-gauge shotgun and took cover with an Army advisor behind a bench. Meyerkord remained in the exposed deckhouse and returned fire with his pistol. After a bullet slammed into his stomach, he cried out, "I'm hit," and collapsed on the deckhouse but continued firing. Barney got up, grabbed Meyerkord in a bear hug, and attempted to get him to safety. A round hit Meyerkord in the chin and another struck Barney's back. Both men collapsed onto the deck of the commandament. Barney, who would later receive a Bronze Star for his heroism that day, was flown by helicopter from Vinh Long to the Third Field Hospital near Saigon and then back to the United States where he would spend the next six months recovering from his wound at the Balboa Naval Hospital in San Diego. Meyerkord was not as fortunate. He died by the time the commandament reached Vinh Long a few hours later.[172]

Meyerkord was one of the first U.S. Navy officers killed in Southeast Asia, and his death marked the end of the advisory phase of the war and the beginning of an era of direct military intervention by conventional naval warriors. The advisory effort continued and expanded exponentially during the war, but it was not until the Navy began its accelerated turnover to the Vietnamese in 1969 that these men would once again command center stage. The Navy ultimately awarded Meyerkord a Navy Cross and named a frigate (FF 1058) after him, but the greatest honor bestowed upon him came from the fond memories of his comrades. In support of the Navy Cross citation, Chief Engineman Ralph J. Gentile wrote, "Meyerkord was more than just a naval advisor; he was everything a Naval Officer should be and more . . . The officers and men of the Vietnamese Army and Navy from this area will never forget Lt. Meyerkord, everywhere he went, villages or district towns, he was welcomed and respected, not because he was an American but because of his knowledge of the situation and his courage under fire which was often."[173]

The U.S. Navy lost one of its best riverine fighters when Meyerkord died. As Meyerkord's Army counterpart, Oscar Padgett, phrased it, "If you send the best over here, you're going to lose the best."[174] Hardcastle was less positive about the situation: "All of our advisors didn't have the same degree of initiative; nor did all of them have the same type of counterpart; and some of the Vietnamese naval people were not at all aggressive."[175] American commanders were losing patience with the VNN in 1965 and demanding American solutions to the problem of infiltration. Market Time would be the first step toward full-scale U.S. naval involvement in South Vietnam.

CHAPTER 2

Coastal Warfare, 1965–1966

Late in the evening of 9 May 1966, the Coast Guard patrol boat *Point Grey* (WPB-82324) bobbed up and down in eight-foot-high seas off the eastern coast of the Ca Mau Peninsula, the southernmost tip of South Vietnam. The boat's commanding officer, Lieutenant (j.g.) Charles B. Mosher, was trying to sleep after learning that his four-day Market Time patrol was extended for two more days. At 2200, the watch stander in the pilothouse spotted fires on the beach and reported the situation to Mosher. The young officer wondered why anyone would burn fires in the rain. He decided to remain in the area throughout the night. A 1963 graduate of the Coast Guard Academy from Jackson, Michigan, Mosher had experienced hurricanes in the Gulf of Mexico as the commander of a 95-foot cutter before shipping off to Vietnam, and foul weather and heavy seas did not intimidate him.

At 0100 on 10 May, *Point Grey* picked up a radar contact on what appeared to be a large steel-hulled vessel. Ten minutes later, she closed on the contact and flashed a challenge with her signal light. The contact, a 110-foot-long unmarked coastal freighter riding low in the water without lights, did not respond but slowed down and started to maneuver on different courses. "We thought she was lost," Mosher explained. Since the seas were too rough to attempt a boarding, *Point Grey* took up a position inshore of the contact and maintained surveillance "for what seemed like eternity." An hour later *Point Grey* fired illumination mortar rounds to try to get the trawler to stop. "I didn't want to open fire on her," recalled Mosher. "We thought she was Nationalist Chinese." Mosher could see people walking on the deck but decided to wait until daylight to board.

As dawn approached the seas calmed, and Mosher decided to make a boarding attempt. The trawler was 400 yards from the shore and appeared to be drifting. When the cutter approached, fire erupted from the mangrove tree lined beach. "Firing was coming from three locations," Mosher said, "I don't think we took any hits. Most of the splashes were short of us." *Point Grey* withdrew to a position 1,500 yards from shore and made three firing passes on the shoreline with her .50-caliber machine guns and 81mm mortar. The radar picket escort *Brister* (DER-327) and the minesweeper *Vireo* (MSC-205) arrived later in the morning, but shallow water prevented these larger ships from getting near the shore.

The tide and sea conditions continued to work against boarding operations, carrying the trawler to within 100 yards of the shore. Mosher went aboard *Brister* for a conference with other officers at the scene. Although the American vessels could easily have destroyed the trawler from a distance with gunfire, the intelligence value of potential documents and arms on board convinced the group to attempt a boarding. The officers decided that *Point Grey* would go in, covering itself as best as it could, and crewmembers would try to board the vessel. If the water proved too shallow for the WPB to approach the vessel, a motorized whaleboat from *Brister* would make an attempt with *Point Grey* providing cover fire.

At 1325, three Air Force F-100 Super Sabers napalmed and strafed the shoreline. *Point Grey* made her approach an hour later. Martin J. Kelleher, a husky gunner's mate 1st class from New England with 15 years of Coast Guard experience, prepared to clear the deck of anyone lying in wait with grenades. He was part of a four–man boarding team hunkered down in the cutter's starboard bow. Major Gillespie, an Army officer catching a ride to An Thoi after inspecting defenses at a remote junk force base, manned the forward .50-caliber gun.[1] The cutter got within 200 yards of the shore, and the Viet Cong opened up with small arms and automatic weapons. After a round struck Gillespie in the leg, Kelleher jumped up and took over the machine gun. Mosher then pulled the throttles full astern to back out of the fire. His propellers struck mud, and black smoke surged from the aft exhausts as he struggled to control the WPB. "When I got her back to where she was floating, I twisted the ship around to get the port guns firing."

In the meantime, *Point Grey*'s Vietnamese liaison petty officer was struck in the shoulder while delivering ammunition to the forward gun. A crewmember pulled him below for first aid. Kelleher, whose gun had run out of bullets, looked around for his loader, Commissaryman 2nd Class William N. Kepler. He found Kepler on the deck clutching a leg wound. Kelleher pulled him up and told him to get off the bow. Kelleher then attempted to reload the forward .50 caliber, but the ammunition belt twisted and the gun jammed. Not wanting to give up the fight, he continued firing at the enemy with a submachine gun.

Gillespie too was eager to return fire. With a tourniquet on his leg, he took over a starboard quarter .50-caliber gun. "He was mad as hell," recalled Mosher. "He expended seven belts of ammunition on the enemy, expertly walking the rounds up the beach to the enemy positions in the tree line." When Mosher looked over his shoulder, he noticed that the motorized whaleboat from *Brister* was retreating and decided to do likewise, evacuate the wounded, and assess the damage. "Our bridge was pretty well shot up. We had hits in the superstructure and a few through the hull." All the wounded survived the attack, and Kepler became the first coastguardsman wounded in the Vietnam War.

Throughout the afternoon, surface and air units pounded the beach with fire to thwart any Viet Cong attempt to unload the trawler. By 1700 the vessel had shifted to within 50 yards of the

Lieutenant (j.g.) Charles B. Mosher, USCG, left, and Commissaryman 2nd Class William N. Kepler, USCG, shake hands shortly after Kepler received the Purple Heart for a wound sustained on 10 May 1966 in actions against a North Vietnamese trawler.

shore, making a night boarding impossible. The decision was made to destroy the vessel at 1726. *Brister* put 37 rounds into the ship with her 3-inch 50-caliber guns, causing several secondary explosions. *Vireo* contributed with 20mm fire, and the cutters *Point Grey* and *Point Cypress* (WPB-82326) lobbed 81mm mortar rounds at the target. The trawler burned until 2030 that night.

Salvage operations on 12 and 13 May by Harbor Clearance Team 1 later recovered six crew-served weapons and approximately 15 tons of ammunition, including 120mm mortar ammunition manufactured in the People's Republic of China. It was the first evidence that this type of ammunition was being used in the Mekong Delta region. A Viet Cong doctor captured on the Ca Mau Peninsula later stated that the 110-foot trawler had sailed from Haiphong south through the South China Sea and west to the Ca Mau Peninsula. Mosher's decision to loiter in the area despite strong winds and heavy seas resulted in the first successful intercept of a steel-hulled trawler in South Vietnam since the Vung Ro seizure in 1965. For his heroism that day, the mild-mannered Mosher received the Silver Star.[2]

In 1964 the Viet Cong began launching a series of large-scale military operations in South Vietnam. Reacting to this increased threat and the aggression demonstrated by the North Vietnamese Navy during the August 1964 Gulf of Tonkin incident, President Johnson sharply escalated America's involvement in the war by initiating a bombing campaign against North Vietnam and sending 3,500 U.S. marines to South Vietnam. Operation Market Time, established in March 1965 to curb the infiltration of steel-hulled trawlers similar to the one intercepted by *Point Grey*, represented the first significant Navy foray into coastal warfare in South Vietnam. Within a year, the operation would for the most part succeed in its major goal of stopping the larger, steel-hulled infiltrators from reaching the shores of South Vietnam. Market Time's multiple layers of aircraft, patrol vessels, and surveillance centers on the shore would make it virtually impossible for the North Vietnamese to slip these larger vessels through the net. There were simply too many types of radar scanning the coastal waters of South Vietnam to make supply with metal-hulled ships viable.

Market Time, however, proved less successful in stopping steel-hulled ships bound for ports in "neutral" Cambodia. If these ships stayed in international waters, allied forces could not search them. Consequently, North Vietnam could ship arms and supplies to Sihanoukville in Cambodia with relative impunity. From there, the contraband could be driven to the border by truck and then moved into South Vietnam by sampan via the Mekong River or its tributaries. Except in rare situations, Market Time units did not venture very far up the rivers in 1966, and when they did they became very vulnerable to ambushes from the shoreline. Not until the establishment of Operation Game Warden in May 1966 did American forces make a concerted effort to extend its counterinfiltration effort to the middle and upper Mekong Delta, and it wasn't until Operation SEALORDS in late 1968 that Market Time and Game Warden units became integrated into a single interdiction campaign—an idea originally recommended by Captain Phillip Bucklew in February 1964.[3]

Market Time was also less successful in countering small coastal infiltrators such as wooden junks. On any given day, 4,000 junks plied the waters off the coast of Vietnam. Most were peasant fishermen trying to eke out a meager living from the waters of the South China Sea, but a select few were blockade runners. Since Market Time forces could not search every junk, separating friend from foe depended on Vietnamese language ability and cultural knowledge—skills in short supply on most American Market Time vessels. In fact to search junks, Market Time relied heavily on the VNN junk force—a force often outgunned and outclassed by the enemy.

Although the VNN was an important partner in Market Time, Vietnamese officers resented the gradual takeover of the naval war in South Vietnam by the U.S. Navy and often felt like a junior partner in the endeavor. The Navy's goal throughout the war was always to help the VNN fight better, but when it failed to reach necessary operational benchmarks, beginning in 1965 the Navy began edging the VNN out of certain operations. This trend would continue until the 1968 SEALORDS operation when Vice Admiral Elmo R. Zumwalt Jr., the new COMNAVFORV, began making a more conscious effort to place the Vietnam Navy in the forefront of operations. One of the great ironies of Operation Market Time was that while it was implemented because the shortcomings of the VNN in stopping large infiltrators, in the end it would depend heavily on the VNN to fill in gaps in the barrier system. No matter how much the Military Assistance Command attempted to aid and augment the young navy, it was a VNN fight, one in which the South Vietnamese had to actively participate to win.

First Patrols

The 1,200-mile coastline of South Vietnam was a blockade-runner's delight. Pockmarked with a multitude of bays, harbors, coves, and river mouths and punctuated by numerous islands offshore, the coastline runs from the 17th parallel to the tip of the Ca Mau Peninsula and then doubles back along the Gulf of Thailand to the Cambodian border. Near the 17th parallel, rice fields could be found along the coast, followed by the Annamite Mountains in the central portion of the country. The southern Mekong Delta area consisted of rice paddies, palm jungle, canals and waterways, as well as numerous stretches of mangrove swamp. Mud flats, in some instances, extended miles out to sea from the swampy delta shores. As one CINCPACFLT report noted, "It is a coast designed for pirates or smugglers—or infiltrators—with every mile a dozen good places to hide or unload or simply beach and duck into the jungle."[4]

As originally established, the Market Time coastal surveillance force had neither the resources nor the authority under the rules of engagement to seal off completely the coasts of South Vietnam from potential infiltrators. The initial Market Time concept envisioned assigning only larger ships and surveillance aircraft to the patrol. These units would track vessels along the coasts and report any suspicious contacts to the Vietnam Navy for further investigation. During the early days of Market Time, only VNN crews had the authority to board, search, or seize suspect vessels, and then only within the 12-mile territorial waters of South Vietnam. The U.S. role was limited to tracking and reporting suspicious contacts. At first designated as Task Force 71, Market Time came under the Seventh Fleet command, which controlled all naval surface, amphibious, and air forces operating off the coast of both North and South Vietnam, and was for most of the war the Navy's principal actor in the conflict. In July 1965 control of the coastal surveillance force shifted to the Naval Advisory Group Vietnam. Not until April 1966 would the U.S. Navy stand up a separate organization, Naval Forces Vietnam, to command small craft operating in coastal and riverine waters of South Vietnam.[5]

From March to June 1965, Task Force 71 averaged 15 ships—primarily destroyers and minesweepers. A minimum of three U.S. warships patrolled the 40-mile-long, 10-mile-wide barrier seaward of the 17th parallel, and at least one U.S ship patrolled each of eight patrol areas along the Vietnamese coast. American ships focused their attention on trawlers and larger craft approaching the coast more or less perpendicularly and relied on the VNN to intercept junks and small craft.[6] The first U.S. ships to participate in Market Time were the destroyers *Higbee* (DD-806) and *Black* (DD-666), which began patrolling on 11 March 1965.[7]

P-2 aircraft based at Tan Son Nhut air base in Saigon and P-3s based at Sangley Field in the Philippines augmented the efforts of surface combatants. These aircraft flew daily patrols from Vung Tau to the demilitarized zone (DMZ). An additional patrol of two EC-121s patrolled the sea space between the 17th parallel and to within 50 miles of Hainan Island, China. On 10 May 1965 the seaplane tender *Currituck* (AV-7) established a P-5 seadrome at Con Son Island in the southern part of the country to further bolster the air surveillance effort. The technical capabilities of some of these surveillance aircraft were impressive even by modern standards. The P-2 had a range of 4,350 miles and could patrol areas of the coast for ten hours at a stretch. Its radar, the APS20, had a 200-mile range. As one P-2 pilot explained, "It was so effective that almost no ships were spotted visually."[8] In only a handful of cases did surface ship radar initially detect steel-hulled infiltrators. Junks, however, were another story.[9]

The experience of the destroyer *Jenkins* (DD-447) in April 1965 revealed the challenges that these smaller craft posed for the Market Time effort. Assigned to an area south of Danang, the destroyer averaged one to two junk contacts per hour. Vietnamese junks had a wide variety of hull designs and propulsion systems, making them very difficult to categorize, but most of *Jenkins*' junk contacts were at least 50 feet long.[10] If she could, the destroyer would get within 50 feet of the target and file a report on the junk's markings, deck cargo, crew, and course. Within a few minutes, *Jenkins* would pull away and resume her patrol, her men unsure of what lay in a junk's shelter, cargo, or bilges. It would be up to the VNN to board and search vessels deemed suspicious.[11]

Destroyer *Jenkins* (DD-447), shown here en route to Manila, participated in early surveillance patrols along the coast of South Vietnam in 1965.

Between 28 March and 17 April 1965 Task Force 71 reported 14,962 junks in its area of operation. Forty percent of these were within three miles of the South Vietnamese coast, and the remaining 60 percent between three and 40 miles from the coastline. The VNN inspected 2.5 percent of the former contacts, and 7 percent of the latter. Clearly, the VNN Coastal Force could not keep up with the flow of contacts being reported by TF 71 units. Of the 530 junks assigned to Market Time from the Coastal Force, only 33.7 percent were utilized in patrols during this same period, and only half of the 44 assigned Sea Force ships participated.[12] In a report to the CNO, Vice Admiral Paul P. Blackburn, the Seventh Fleet commander, summarized the situation as follows: "The VNN Coastal and Sea Forces effort in Market Time Operations has degenerated to the point where it is effectively non-existent.... We must recognize that this US/VNN anti-infiltration chain is no stronger than its weakest link."[13]

Vietnam Navy in Crisis: 1965

On 13 June 1965, Lieutenant John Warren Chidsey began his first patrol on *Tien Moi* (HQ-601) as naval advisor and ship rider. Although this 101-foot motor gunboat was only a year old at the time, Chidsey could not believe its physical state. "She was absolutely filthy from stem to stern," noted the 1959 Naval Academy graduate from Rochester, New York. "There were cockroaches all over the place. Food and garbage were lying on the deck, sailors were strewn all over the place, and no one was in uniform." Most of the crew wore nothing but underwear and rubber shower sandals. The ship's Decca 303 radar was inoperative and one of its engines, broken. Even if the PGM managed to locate a suspicious contact visually, it could only achieve a top speed of six knots in calm seas, making it impossible to catch most blockade-runners, which were capable of speeds of up to eight knots. During his first three-day patrol, Chidsey contacted various Market Time ships for information about suspicious contacts, but the commander of HQ-601, Lieutenant (j.g.) Thi, refused to pursue any leads. "He didn't want to mix it up with anybody," Chidsey wrote in his after-action report. "He just wanted to go up and do his three days and come back to Danang."[14]

Back at port, Chidsey spent every waking hour trying to repair the ship. He arranged for a U.S. Navy electronics technician (ET) to work on the radar but could never get the ship and the ET together long enough to accomplish the repairs. "The attitude of the ship's company," he later explained, "was 'let the Americans fix it or the Saigon [Naval] Shipyard will take care of it.'" Just obtaining basic supplies such as fuel and ammunition posed serious challenges for HQ-601. When a Vietnamese shore officer started hoarding lubricating oil, Chidsey had to resort to asking *Floyd County* (LST-762) for two 55-gallon drums of this basic necessity.

From 13 June to 7 July 1965 HQ-601 searched only 19 fishing vessels and arrested just one man for failure to provide proper identification. Chidsey tried to stay on the bridge as much as possible to cajole his Vietnamese counterparts to pursue their Market Time mission more aggressively, but to little or no avail. "Throughout the period the ship patrolled at a speed of 4–6 knots and would not alter course to search junks which did not happen close aboard." The monotony of life on the ship was occasionally broken up by a request for shore bombardment, but even these missions could be botched by the careless attitude of the Vietnamese. On 3 July, HQ-601 received a request for gunfire support from Junk Division 14 near Hoi An, a town 30 kilometers south of Danang. The PGM neither established radio contact with the junk division nor employed spotters in junks or aircraft. It simply laid down harassment fire in a quarter mile area. No targets were designated and the results of the mission unknown. "It is felt by this advisor," wrote Chidsey in an after-action report, "that the practice of shooting up a village that might harbor VC . . . is wasteful of ammunition and an unnecessary hazard to Vietnamese nationals and non-combatants."[15]

Chidsey began his tour as a ship rider full of vigor, ready to sail into dangerous waters and do great things for the Navy. After 145 days at sea with HQ-601, Chidsey was a physical wreck. He had worked in an environment where soap was rarely used for washing or cleaning dishes, sailors regularly defecated over the side of the ship, blood from slaughtered chickens covered the fantail, and the cook cleaned toilets as a collateral duty. Having suffered from dysentery nearly every day of his tour, Chidsey ultimately ended up at Station Hospital Saigon with intestinal disease. Stress also took its toll. Along with stomach treatments, the doctor on board *Floyd County* had to prescribe him sedatives to calm his nerves. "I simply had to keep my patience with these people. I knew that if I lost my patience one minute and made an unguarded remark that I would upset any possible good that I could have done. So I would take tranquilizers, mainly to control my own temper."[16]

Chidsey ultimately recovered from his medical problems and went on to receive a Bronze Star with Combat V for heroism during a gunfire support mission with another Sea Force ship, LSSL-228, in January 1966. Still, his service as an advisor was quite a revelation for this ambitious young officer. The isolated nature of the assignment, the poor sanitary conditions, and the lack of aggressiveness of the crew could challenge even the most optimistic and effective U.S. Navy officer.[17] Sea Force advisor Lieutenant Gordon Abercrombie wrote in his end-of-tour report,

> [W]ith rare exception, patrol units took a lackadaisical approach to their mission. Specifically they spent approximately 40% of deployed time in coastal ports; when at sea they often found it convenient to anchor at night. Surveillance of commercial shipping and small craft was non-existent in the case of the former and minimal in the later. . . . The Vietnamese Navy with rare exception is controlled and staffed by friendly, competent, non-professionals who have no pride in their organization. In this respect they are typical of an apparent national trait which dictates care of personal property and neglect of that belonging to others, indulgence of personal ambition and lack of sacrifice to a group cause. I foresee very little improvement in the VNN as long as this attitude is prevalent.[18]

With 44 ships and over 2,731 men, the Sea Force should have been the pride of the Vietnam Navy and a vital partner in Operation Market Time.[19] However, the readiness and employment of the Sea Force never lived up to American expectations in 1965. Planners had hoped for 75 percent of the Sea Force to be ready for sea duty at any given time and 55 percent of the fleet to be actively employed in Market Time patrols, but readiness generally hovered 3–4 percent below that target, and employment 5 percent below. Simply put, many VNN officers lacked the will to properly maintain their ships and vigilantly patrol the coast. In January, two SP-2 aircraft surveyed the entire South Vietnamese coast and observed over 50 percent of the Sea Force at anchor. During one flight the Deputy VNN CNO for Operations, riding on the aircraft, spotted six of the seven Sea Force ships in the Gulf of Thailand at anchor.[20] Echoing the sentiments of Chidsey and Abercrombie, Lieutenant D. M. Bennett wrote in his end-of-tour report, "The advisor in Vietnam is dealing with a highly personal, politically oriented group of individuals, masquerading as a Navy. The efforts of the advisors are complicated by the general unconcern of most Vietnamese. Unconcern for their navy, for their country and for each other seems to be the dominant fact of life."[21]

As wretched as the Sea Force's situation appeared in 1965, the state of the coastal junk force was worse. Although this force patrolled the vital inner barrier of the Market Time blockade and was responsible for controlling vast stretches of the coastline, it was in many respects the weakest link in the chain. On average, less than 40 percent of the force was on patrol at any given time with the remaining 60 percent either undergoing repairs or inoperative due to manpower shortages, base defense requirements, or lack of aggressiveness. North of Vung Tau, the Viet Cong controlled approximately 142 miles of the 591-mile coastline and south of that town, 300 miles of the 400-mile coast. In many instances the Coastal Force bases were little more than government islands in a sea of hostile territory.[22]

At the beginning of 1965, the Coastal Force consisted of 526 junks assigned to 28 Coastal Force divisions spread out along the entire coast of South Vietnam. The force included 81 command, 90 motor-sail, 121 motor-only, and 234 sail-only junks. The command junks were relatively capable vessels. Armed with one .50-caliber and two .30-caliber machine guns, these 54-foot junks could reach a maximum speed of 12 knots—more than adequate to intercept similar vessels used by the Viet Cong. The 31-foot sail-only junks, on the other hand, were more of a liability than an asset. Their small three- to five-man crews carried nothing but small arms and had no hope of stopping motorized blockade runners. Beginning in 1964 the Naval Advisory Group recommended that all of these junks be stricken from the fleet; 134 were retired during 1965, with the remainder scheduled to go in early 1966.[23]

To replace them, the Saigon Naval Shipyard built 90 "Yabuta" junks during 1965. Mr. Yabuta, a Japanese engineer at the Saigon Naval Shipyard in 1961, originally designed the 57-foot junk. Armed with a .30-caliber machine gun, it featured a 110-horsepower diesel engine capable of generating ten knots of speed and was built entirely out of fiberglass, which obviated the need to treat the hulls for wood-boring Teredo worms. Wooden junks, by contrast, needed to have their hulls scraped, blow-torched, and resealed every three months to prevent them from looking like Swiss cheese. As one advisor remarked, "We've probably lost more junks to that damn

U.S. Navy advisors on a Coastal Force Command Junk, October 1964.

worm than to the VC."[24] The U.S. Military Assistance Program provided funds for building materials and engines, and the Vietnamese paid the wages of the shipyard laborers who built the junks.[25] Captain Hardcastle viewed the Yabuta junk as one of his crowning achievements: "You get the Vietnamese in on the ground roots of planning. Let them have a part of it, and if they believe in it, they are going to succeed and they are very capable."[26] Unfortunately for the Naval Advisory Group, the program fell far short of Hardcastle's expectations.

After the first Yabutas were completed, output slowed significantly. In 1966 the Saigon Naval Shipyard built only nine junks and in 1967, just 15. Production went from three junks a week in 1965 to one every five weeks in 1967. Overhauls of larger VNN ships dropped by 50 percent, and delays averaged 43 days. Close to ten skilled workers departed the shipyard each month, mainly to pursue higher paying jobs in private industry. Private construction firms lured these workers away with salaries, on average, three times higher than what the government had paid them.[27]

The shortcomings of the junk force, as well as its dangerous mission, are evident in the experiences of Lieutenant Norman G. Mosher (no relationship to Charles), who served as a Coastal Force advisor from August 1964 to August 1965. Born in 1935, Mosher grew up in Marblehead, Massachusetts, and graduated from Boston University in 1957. He entered the Navy by way of Officer Candidate School at Newport, Rhode Island, and after serving as a first lieutenant and

A Yabuta junk near Vung Tau, April 1966.

weapons officer on board *Power* (DD-839) and then teaching NROTC at Purdue University, he volunteered for duty in Vietnam. He was assigned as the senior advisor to the Third Coastal Zone—a unit consisting of 91 junks and 1,000 men and responsible for patrolling a 200 mile stretch of coastline. Assisting him were two U.S. Navy officers and five sailors. During his tour Mosher had to contend with a variety of challenges: an inadequate logistics system, deficient seafaring skills among VNN officers and men, lack of repair capability, and inadequate support from the Army of the Republic of Vietnam. "Underlying these deficiencies," he wrote in his end-of-tour report, "has been the one characteristic of the military, without which it cannot hope to improve, and that is the absence of discipline." He was especially struck by the poor quality of his Vietnamese counterpart. "My counterpart was a graduate of the General Line School at Monterey; he graduated second in his class at the Vietnamese Naval Academy; he took command of a PCE in Philadelphia and steamed her successfully to Vietnam, yet he is still a poor seaman" who "never insisted on good seamanship within his command."[28]

Consequently, Mosher often found himself leading more than advising, especially when under fire. In all, he participated in 22 combat patrols and fought in six combat operations. On the night of 13 December 1964, while patrolling with units of Junk Division 33, he received word that a Popular Force post in the Hoa Thuan district of Vinh Binh Province was under attack from guerrillas and in danger of being overrun. While the junkmen opened fire on the Viet Cong with a 60mm mortar, Mosher and 12 Vietnamese sailors landed and attacked the flank of the enemy with automatic weapons and grenades, forcing the VC to withdraw in confusion.

In another instance, on 22 November 1964 Mosher learned that his counterpart had run a 24-foot-long patrol boat aground somewhere off the coast of Kien Hoa Province in the Mekong Delta. He persuaded an off-duty helicopter pilot to fly him over the area until he located the boat on a sandbar. Noting that a VC force was in the tree line on the beach, apparently waiting for the tide to recede in order to reach the stranded boat, Mosher requested close air support from an A1E while his helicopter landed on the sandbar to evacuate weapons and men. Realizing the task would take a while, Mosher ordered the helicopter to take off while he stayed with the boat and helped to dismantle the guns. Despite being in imminent danger of a Viet Cong assault and under fire from the beach continuously, Mosher remained on the sandbar until all the weapons and crew were evacuated.

A fishing junk passes behind Lieutenant Norman G. Mosher, a U.S. Navy advisor with Coastal Division 33, February 1965. Junk Force advisors like Mosher worked in isolated, often very dangerous locations.

On 12 January 1965 Mosher participated in a combined operation that involved transporting two companies of ground troops by junk to Long Son Island in the Phuoc Tuy Province. An advance element was supposed to secure the beach for the Vietnamese marines; however, this element landed at the wrong beach. To secure the actual landing zone, Mosher persuaded his counterpart to accompany him on a beach reconnaissance. While on the beach, the two men drove off a small party of Viet Cong tax collectors and secured the beach for the marines, who landed in time to successfully rendezvous with the rest of their battalion.

For this action and others, the Navy awarded Mosher a Legion of Merit with Combat V. "His courage under fire and aggressiveness in operations," the citation stated, "was inspirational to the paramilitary with whom he worked. His concern for the welfare of the junkmen and his willingness to share their austere way of life greatly increased their effectiveness while he was with them." Typical of many advisors, though, Mosher did not see his service as exceptional. "I am not all certain that the Third Coastal Zone is better for my having been there," he wrote in his end-of-tour report, "but I am sure that the increased advisory effort plus the commitment of U.S. manned units within the zone will improve Vietnamese performance." Mosher believed that the only way for advisors to be effective was to suffer the same hardships and danger as the Vietnamese. "Undoubtedly, some will be lost, others will be heroes, a few will have their health impaired as a result of this duty but it must be accepted if we hope to win the war by influencing the Vietnamese."[29]

Others were less optimistic. According to junk force advisor Robert K. Reilly, "The junkman, contrary to popular opinion, is not a good sailor. He does not like to go to sea and in order to avoid extended periods at sea (over one day) will resort to lies regarding sickness, approaching storms, the sea state, lack of food, water, fuel, and the material condition of the junk. Junkmen have been known to purposefully cripple their boats in order to return to the beach."[30] A February 1965 Naval Advisory Group staff study concluded that the "deficiencies in anti-infiltration naval patrols by the Vietnamese Navy have been many." It listed the major shortcomings as lack of aggressiveness, lack of coordination with other forces, and poor leadership.[31] Even Rear Admiral Chung Tan Cang, the VNN CNO, admitted that the Coastal Force was in a state of crisis during this time: "The junk force itself had many problems."[32] General Westmoreland concurred: "The Coastal Force is considered the weakest link in the patrol effort."[33]

The general political turmoil in South Vietnam was one of the root causes of the VNN's malaise. The position of nearly every senior officer in the VNN was directly tied to the political fortunes of their patrons. As governments changed so too did the leaders of major VNN commands. This frequent turnover of top level personnel undermined morale further down the chain of command and compelled junior officers to pay close attention to shifting political alliances. The situation was made worse by various other rivalries within VNN, including those between officers born in North Vietnam and South Vietnam, between Christians and Buddhists, and the various VNN force components. After the death of Quyen in 1964, northerners in particular lost much of their status within the VNN. Rear Admiral Cang, a southerner with strong ties to Prime Minister Nguyen Khanh, tended to favor southerners when it came to personnel assignments and promotions. According to Do Kiem, southerners were "getting chief of staff positions, while the Navy's northern officers found themselves stuck on semi-permanent sea duty."[34] Cang also undermined the authority of the various force commanders. Before the Diem coup, force commanders acted as separate "mandarins" with considerable control of their ships, personnel, and budgets. Although as the former River Force commander Cang had benefited from the old system, once in power as CNO, he attempted to concentrate power within his office and establish a system of personal loyalty among the officer corps to him alone. The situation came to a head in April 1965, shortly after Cang's patron, Khanh, was deposed by General Nguyen Van Thieu, General Nguyen Van Cao, and Air Marshal Nguyen Cao Ky on 21 February 1965.[35]

Led by the operating force commanders and with the support of Air Marshal Ky, a handful of young officers, mostly from the North, barred the entrance to the Saigon naval headquarters and prevented Cang from entering the base. They accused Cang of graft and demanded his removal. Cang had graduated from the Vietnamese Merchant Marine Academy and was thought to be getting kickbacks from corrupt merchant ship captains, but the charges were never proven. Bang Cao Thang, the Saigon Naval Shipyard commander and a key planner in the mutiny, later confessed that the underlying reasons of the mutiny were Cang's favoritism of southerners and his relationship with the recently ousted General Khanh.

Both sides in the dispute strove to avoid bloodshed. "We didn't want Navy people shooting at each other," explained Thang.[36] Likewise, Rear Admiral Cang insisted that he "could have easily taken control of the Navy, but that would have resulted in some loss of life." Still, the situation was tense. At one point Thuong Ngoc Luc, the man who had stabbed Quyen in 1963, tried to persuade the mutineers to back down. With his hand on his sidearm and three sailors behind him with M14 rifles, Do Kiem, one of the mutineers, met with Luc but refused to back down. "I'll remember it," Luc remarked and then did an about face and left the scene.[37] After a three-day standoff, Cang agreed to become commandant of the Armed Forces Staff College at Da Lat and, after much wrangling, a group of key commanders and staff officers, by secret ballot, elected Captain Tran Van Phan, another southerner, as the new CNO. Soon after his appointment, Phan ordered four of the mutineers (the three force commanders and the Saigon Naval Shipyard commander) to be placed under house arrest but was soon informed by Premier Phan Huy Quat that charges against them had been rescinded.[38]

A period of great turmoil followed. The Vietnam Navy doubled in size from 8,000 to 16,000 personnel while at the same time experiencing continued turnover in the officer corps because of the mutiny and political instability in the government. A June 1965 Naval Advisory Group staff study lamented, "loyalty to persons, rather than loyalty to service or country was the norm. Not only were direct orders seldom given, but when given are often reluctantly followed up. The syndrome was apparently one of insecurity born of inexperience and uncertain position. In this environment, apathy, direct disobedience of orders and lack of aggressive pursuit of the war effort were common, though by no means rampant."[39] Ultimately, some of the problems with the Coastal Force were alleviated by integrating it into the regular navy in July 1965, but the sorry state of the service as a whole continued throughout 1965. General William Westmoreland in an April message to Commander Seventh Fleet noted "the lack of responsiveness and substandard patrol effort on the part of the VNN," and concluded, "no breakthrough is expected in these areas. . . . Current political and command situation with the VNN has resulted in a wait and see attitude. The adverse effect on morale has been severe."[40]

American Role Expands

As American confidence in the VNN reached a new nadir in April, Secretary of Defense Robert McNamara and Secretary of the Navy Paul H. Nitze decided to increase greatly the U.S. Navy mission in South Vietnam by deploying patrol craft, fast (PCF) Swift boats, manned with American crews, for close-in coastal patrol. The Swift boat was a 50-foot, all-welded aluminum craft

A Swift boat (PCF-38) near Cat Lo, Vietnam, 15 April 1966.

manufactured by Stewart Seacraft of Berwick, Louisiana. Originally designed to transport crews to offshore oilrigs in the Gulf of Mexico, the Swift boat's shallow 3.5-foot draft and high-speed of 28 knots made it an ideal boat for coastal patrol. Captain William Hardcastle estimated that one Swift boat could do the job of ten motorized junks. The Swift's radar could detect smaller wood-hulled vessels up to 2.5 miles away, and its twin .50-caliber machine-gun tub and piggy-backed 81mm mortar/.50-caliber machine gun gave these boats more than enough firepower to handle junks, and even larger steel-hulled infiltrators. A typical crew consisted of an officer in charge and four sailors: a radarman, boatswain's mate, gunner's mate, and an engineman. On 23 April 1965 the Navy ordered 20 of these boats, and by October they were patrolling the waters of South Vietnam.[41]

In mid-April, Secretary Nitze also requested assistance from the Coast Guard, which agreed to assign 17 *Point*-class WPBs to Vietnam. At 82 feet in length and with a displacement of 65 tons, the WPB was larger than the Swift boat and had better endurance and seaworthiness. It also had air-conditioning, making it much more habitable in the tropical Vietnamese climate than the non-air-conditioned Swift boat. While the Swift was designed for 24–36 hour patrols, the WPB could easily patrol for four days or even longer. Built at the Coast Guard's Curtis Bay shipyard near Baltimore, Maryland, the WPB was a simple and highly reliable small patrol boat. Transom exhausts eliminated the need for bulky smokestacks. From its bridge, one had a 360-degree view of the deck and could control the engineering plant, talk on the radio, and read key navigation equipment. Four people could run the boat effectively, but the requirement for long patrols in Vietnam meant that most of the cutters carried two officers and nine coastguardsmen, allowing for two watches. Built for foul weather, the WBP performed much better than the Swifts during the monsoon season and could operate amid 35-knot winds and 15–20 foot seas. The WPB's chief drawbacks when compared to the PCF were its slower 18-knot speed and larger 5.5-foot draft, but its 660-horsepower twin screws proved reliable in operation and easy to maintain. The WBP's power plant also allowed for a 3-knot creep speed, which was ideal for conserving fuel on long patrols. Armament consisted of four .50-caliber machine guns and one piggybacked 81mm mortar/.50-caliber machine gun.[42]

Beginning 11 May 1965 the South Vietnamese government granted formal approval for U.S. units to "stop, search, and seize vessels not clearly engaged in innocent passage inside the three mile territorial limits of South Vietnam and in a contiguous zone extending 12 miles offshore."[43] Vessels outside the 12-mile limit could be searched if reasonably thought to be South Vietnamese, even if the vessels were flying a foreign flag.[44] These new rules of engagement combined with smaller patrol craft capable of close-in patrols in shallow waters transformed the U.S. Navy role from that of a passive tracker of infiltrators to a full combatant with equal powers as the VNN within South Vietnamese waters. In another big boost for the operation, Secretary McNamara announced on 30 April 1965 the transfer of Market Time patrols from Task Force 71, a Seventh Fleet command, to Task Force 115, which would fall under the chief of the Naval Advisory Group. The transfer, which took place on 31 July 1965, expanded the mission of the Naval Advisory Group from advising the VNN to planning, executing, and leading combined combat operations. Concurrent with this announcement, Rear Admiral Norvell Gardiner "Bub" Ward became the first Navy flag officer to be assigned to Vietnam when he relieved Hardcastle as chief of the Naval Advisory Group on 10 May 1965.[45]

Ward would have a major impact on the role of the Navy in South Vietnam. He oversaw not only the expansion of Market Time but also the creation of two additional U.S. task forces: a river patrol force (TF 116) and a riverine amphibious assault force (TF 117). By the end of his tour in September 1967, the naval war in South Vietnam would become fully "Americanized" with U.S. patrol craft and sailors taking the lead in fighting along the rivers and coasts of Vietnam.

A 1935 Naval Academy graduate, Ward served in submarines in the Pacific during World War II and saw extensive combat on *Gato* (SS-212) in 1943 and *Guardfish* (SS-217) in 1944. During *Guardfish*'s eighth war patrol in June and July 1944, Ward pressed home six attacks against a well-escorted Japanese merchant convoy, sinking four ships in the process. For his heroism during this 56-hour-long engagement, he received a Navy Cross. During the Korean War he commanded *Yarnall* (DD-541), a World War II–era *Fletcher*-class destroyer that performed gunfire support and other missions. Ward's most significant assignment before Vietnam

Rear Admiral Norvell G. Ward discusses Market Time operations with staff in the operations center of *Krishna* (ARL-38), December 1965. From May 1965 to April 1966, Admiral Ward served as Chief Naval Advisory Group, U.S. Military Assistance Command. From April 1966 to April 1967, he was the Commander U.S. Naval Forces Vietnam; Chief Naval Advisory Group; Naval Component Commander, U.S. Military Assistance Command Vietnam.

was command of the first squadron of Polaris missile-armed, nuclear-propelled submarines (SSBNs) from 1958 to 1961. As head of Submarine Squadron 14, he had responsibility for one of the most critical elements of America's strategic arsenal during the height of the Cold War.[46]

From 1961 to 1965, he worked in the Pentagon for the Navy Staff and learned a great deal about the inner workings of the military headquarters and the relationship between military and civilian officials in Washington. His success in the Pentagon paved the way for his promotion to rear admiral in 1963 and consideration for high-level command. His first choice was command of an amphibious readiness group based in San Diego, but events in Vietnam changed his plans. The Navy needed a flag officer to command Seventh Fleet ships chopped to the Naval Advisory Group, and "people started pointing the finger" in Ward's direction.

Ward arrived in Saigon during a time of tremendous upheaval. The Viet Cong had just bombed the U.S. Embassy and would engage in several other spectacular attacks during the year, including bombings at the My Canh Cafe and the Metropole Hotel. The Vietnam Navy had recently experienced a mutiny, and the South Vietnamese government was in turmoil. When Air Vice Marshal Nguyen Cao Ky took over as prime minister on 19 June 1965, he became the

55

eighth leader of South Vietnam since the assassination of Diem in 1963. Ward's first priority as the new chief of the Naval Advisory Group was to assess the state of the VNN, improve its performance, and "avoid doing anything which would permit it to go downhill."[47]

During his first six weeks in Vietnam, he visited nearly every unit in the VNN to get a firsthand look at their bases and talk with advisors in the field. "One thing became readily apparent to me that for a period of weeks, the Vietnamese Navy, with the exception of the coastal force and river assault groups, had been dormant. They were not doing a thing.... The Vietnamese Navy, with all its problems, sat back and let us take over the Market Time patrol offshore."[48]

Another thing that struck Ward during his tour of VNN ships and shore facilities was the vulnerability of some remote junk bases to Viet Cong attack. On 9 July, Junk Division 15 located just north of Chu Lai became the first Coastal Force base to be overrun by the Viet Cong. In the early morning hours, an estimated force of 200 enemy troops attacked the position, killing over 20 Vietnamese sailors and two U.S. Navy advisors, Boatswain's Mate 1st Class Leon C. Stein and Lieutenant William L. Brown.[49] John Chidsey, a classmate of Brown's at the Naval Academy, visited the base the next day to retrieve the dead bodies. On the battlefield, Chidsey searched in vain for Brown's 1959 Naval Academy class ring. "I had just had a few drinks with him in Danang a few days before the attack and he had his ring then. He was hit on the left side with the full blast of probably a 57mm mortar and had numerous .30-caliber injuries. Stein had similar wounds." In his report, Chidsey claimed that the front gate of the base had been deliberately left open during the night of the attack.[50]

Junk force sailors hold general quarters at Coastal Division 15 in the village of Ky Ha, South Vietnam, 8 August 1964. The division's base was the first Coastal Force base overrun by the Viet Cong on 9 July 1965.

The attack on Coastal Division 15 revealed the extent of the Viet Cong's control of the coastline. Before the attack, Ward had sought to bolster the prestige of the 3,444-man Coastal Force by integrating it into the regular Navy; after the attack, he pressed his VNN counterpart to recruit an additional 874 sailors for base defense and secured a grant of $35,000 from the Secretary of Defense to purchase arms for base security. Making meaningful reforms of the VNN, however, would not be easy.[51] He found his counterpart, Captain Tran Van Phan, to be weak and pliable. "Most everything I would suggest to him, he'd say, 'Yes, sir. Yes, sir, do it right away.' And then nothing would get done. I believe he realized that he had no control over the Navy."[52] After a month dealing with Phan and realizing that the navy was "almost worthless" with him in command, Ward petitioned General Westmoreland to replace him, but it would take over a year for the America's top officer to persuade the South Vietnamese government to install a new CNO.[53]

With the VNN in turmoil, Ward leaned hard on the Market Time force to fill the void. He divided Task Force 115 operations into nine patrol areas, 30–40 miles deep and 80–120 miles long, stretching from the 17th parallel in the north along the coast to the Brevie Line (the maritime border between Vietnam and Cambodia) in the Gulf of Thailand. Normally, each patrol area was the responsibility of a radar picket escort or, if sufficient DERs were not available, an ocean minesweeper. These ships, along with aircraft, patrolled the outer infiltration barrier, 15–40 miles from the coast. VNN Sea Force ships covered the middle barrier, 10–15 miles from the coast, and the inner barrier (within 12 miles of the coast) consisting of inshore waters was the responsibility of Coastal Force junks and, as they became available, WPBs and Swifts. Five Coastal Surveillance Centers (Danang, Qui Nhon, Nha Trang, Vung Tao, and An Thoi) coordinated the U.S. Navy and VNN patrol units.[54] By August 1965, TF 115 comprised eight large U.S. Navy vessels (DERs, MSOs, and MSCs), 11 Coast Guard WPBs, 15 VNN Sea Force ships, and 215 junks.[55]

Coast Guard Support for Market Time

The first inshore boats to begin patrols in South Vietnam were the Coast Guard *Point*-class WPBs. The 245-man Coast Guard force in Vietnam was designated Coast Guard Squadron 1 and led by Commander James A. Hodgman, United States Coast Guard (USCG). The unit was further divided into Division 11 based at An Thoi near the Cambodian border and Division 12 at Danang. Merchant ships transported the first group of these cutters to the Philippines in June 1965 and, after a month of training and exercises, eight WPBs of Coast Guard Division 12, still painted in Coast Guard white, made an uneventful crossing to Danang. Eight days later, nine cutters from Coast Guard Division 11 and their escort ship, *Floyd County*, had an entirely different experience. Thirty-knot winds and 15-foot seas battered the small cutters. Gunner's Mate 1st Class Martin J. Kelleher of *Point Grey* remembered the trip well. At one point, he attempted to take a shower and nearly ended up in sick bay. "We took a violent roll and I grabbed that rail and it came off in my hand and I fell backwards and hit that soap dish and it came unglued and gouged my back. . . . I'll tell you it was mean."[56] Hodgman described the transit as the "longest and roughest trip any of the personnel had taken in this type of boat."[57]

Led by *Point Marone* (WPB-82331), Coast Guard Division 11 cutters depart Subic Bay Naval Base for Vietnam, 17 July 1965.

That all the WPBs survived such a punishing five-day transit intact and were able to begin Market Time patrols just 24 hours after arriving in Vietnam was a testament to the seaworthiness of these small boats and the toughness of their Coast Guard crews.[58] Because they had greater endurance and range than the Swifts, Ward assigned these boats to the 17th parallel and the Gulf of Thailand. "WPBs were much better for patrolling along the coasts than the Swifts were," Ward later stated in an oral history.[59]

The first major Coast Guard engagements occurred in the Gulf of Thailand, an alluvial plain with numerous rocky islands and the larger island of Phu Quoc off the coast of Cambodia. The nine cutters of Coast Guard Division 11 arrived in the area on 30 July 1965. Except for a handful of American naval advisors, the only other U.S. Navy operational unit in the area was a DER or MSO on patrol offshore. VNN units assigned to the Fourth Coastal Zone included seven coastal groups, with approximately 20 junks each, and three larger patrol craft of the Sea Force. Anchored just offshore of Phu Quoc Island, *Floyd County* served as a repair and logistics ship, as well as a floating base, until 17 September when the landing craft repair ship *Krishna* (ARL-38) arrived. *Krishna* could perform almost any type of cutter maintenance short of dry-docking,

Point Glover (WPB-82307).

including engine overhauls and replacements. It also contained an operations center, complete with six voice operator positions, status boards, and surface and air plots.[60]

By mid-September, Coast Guard Division 11 had been deployed in the Gulf of Thailand for six weeks with no evidence of infiltration. The situation took a dramatic turn in the early hours of the 19th. At 0100, *Point Glover* (WPB-82307) on patrol just north of the Balua Islands picked up a contact five miles west of Nui Bai. Lieutenant Robert T. Nelson, a native of Liverpool, Ohio, and a 1958 graduate of the Coast Guard Academy, commanded the cutter. Nelson, who eventually rose to become the vice commandant of the Coast Guard in 1992, confessed later that he initially harbored a few doubts about the mission in Vietnam.[61] "As we sailed into Vietnam, I asked myself, 'Are we really prepared to do this? Do we have any idea what we are going to face?'" After a month and half of patrolling the Gulf of Thailand, his confidence in his boat and crew increased, but he still was not "overly impressed we were going to be successful."[62]

Point Glover illuminated the junk with its spotlight when it came within 100 yards of the vessel and signaled for it to come alongside. The 20-foot motorized junk continued running erratically, at one point even bumping into the cutter.[63] "I think it was accidental," claims Nelson, "He bounced off and started running away."[64] Several coastguardsmen fired Thompson submachine guns at the junk's engine, hoping to disable it. No fire was returned, and the junk's crew soon began jumping over the side.[65] *Point Glover* then came alongside the now empty, sinking vessel and towed it to the beach. Searchers later found six small arms and 480 rounds of ammunition on the junk. They also captured a prisoner on the beach. A later salvage effort conducted by *Krishna* (ARL-38) uncovered two more weapons, two bodies, and 10,000 piasters of currency.[66]

Twenty-one hours later, on the night of 19 September, *Point Marone* (WPB-82331) made contact with a 40-foot motorized junk south of the *Isles des Pirates*, a small chain of islands between Phu Quoc Island and the mainland. The cutter fired warning shots across the junk's bow, but it refused to slow down and its crew began attacking the cutter with small arms fire, grenades, and what appeared to be floating mines. *Point Marone* returned fire with her .50-caliber machine gun until all firing from the junk ceased and it went dead in the water. *Point Glover* soon arrived and illuminated the area with her spotlight. Both WPBs then opened fire on the water after seeing three swimmers approaching the cutters. In all, three swimmers and another six Viet Cong on the junk were killed in the engagement. *Point Glover* tried to take the junk under tow, but it soon sank.

South Vietnamese Regional Forces later captured a wounded Viet Cong who managed to escape from the junk that had engaged *Point Glover*. He confirmed that both junks on that day were on supply missions from Phu Quoc Island. During both actions on the 19th, Coast Guard units sustained no damage or casualties. In his diary, Commander Hodgman wrote, "Engagements at point blank range with no warning in the middle of the night are experiences few sailors encounter in this day. The officers and men performed well under fire. I am proud of them."[67]

Coast Guard WPBs not only intercepted junks but also proved very useful for special operations insertions and naval gunfire support. On 26 September, *Point Comfort* (WPB-82317) and *Point Grey* delivered a raiding party of 32 Civilian Irregular Defense Group (CIDG) troops, along with several Vietnamese and American Special Forces soldiers, to a position 200 yards offshore from a beach at the south end of Phu Quoc Island. At 0500, the raiders headed to shore on two inflatable rafts while the cutters stood by at a position 1,000 yards from the beach. Six and a half hours later the raiding party was ambushed while crossing the Hon Mot River. The lead man, U.S. Army Staff Sergeant James Elmer Pruit, was hit first and died immediately. Trapped by fire from the other side of the stream and a nearby island, the surviving American advisor called *Point Comfort* for gunfire support. The cutter silenced the fire coming from Hon Mot Island with seven 81mm rounds and then moved close to the island to cover *Point Grey*, which launched its Boston Whaler to evacuate the wounded and dead. The evacuation was successful, but *Point Comfort* got a little too close to shore and struck a rock with her port shaft. Operating on just one shaft, the cutter, soon joined by *Point Marone*, provided cover fire for the remaining raiding party, which egressed from the area in rubber rafts.[68]

Less than a month later, the Coast Guard again demonstrated its prowess in gunfire support. When a South Vietnamese Popular Force outpost south of Ha Tien came under attack on 20 October, *Point Clear* (WPB-82315), patrolling nearby, moved into firing position. Trapped in a bunker, the militiamen expended their last tracer rounds to point out targets for the cutter. *Point*

Clear fired its .50-caliber guns until they turned red but failed to stop the attack. In complete desperation, the government forces threw hand grenades at the Viet Cong and told *Point Clear* to lay down 81mm mortar rounds where the grenades exploded. "This is not a recommended course of action except in extremis," Hodgman later wrote, but "it proved extremely effective this time."[69] Captain William E. Angel, an Army Special Forces advisor who visited the outpost the next day, claimed that the "81mm HE [high explosive] and illuminating fire in addition to .50-caliber MG fire was in my opinion the turning point of the VC attack."[70]

The most critical job performed by the WPBs was in halting the infiltration of steel-hulled trawlers into South Vietnam. During the spring of 1966, the Viet Cong made two significant infiltration attempts with trawlers near the Ca Mau Peninsula—the 10 May *Point Grey* intercept described earlier and another on 20 June by *Point League* (WPB-82304). With the exception of a few government-controlled population centers, the region was under Viet Cong control, making offloading relatively simple for the enemy. U.S. Market Time assets in the area consisted of two PCFs and two WPBs patrolling the inner barrier and two DERs, two MSCs, and an MSO on outer barrier. Coastal Force junks, air patrols by Navy SP2Hs, and *Floyd County*, which served as a support ship, augmented these assets.[71]

At 1545 on the 19th, an SP2H from Patrol Squadron (VP) 2 detected and photographed a trawler 80 miles east of Con Son Island. The plane's crew believed on the initial pass that it was an infiltrator based on its unusual course and the fact that its sailors were not fishing or working. On the third pass, the trawler crew began working with fishnets. The SP2 filed a spot report alerting vessels in the area of the contact and then tracked and photographed the suspicious vessel for the next hour and a half.[72]

An SP-2H Neptune Market Time surveillance patrol south of Vung Tau, April 1967.

Engineman 2nd Class Daniel R. Vaughan, manning the radar that night on *Point League*, got a radar contact on the trawler at 0245 on the 20th. Steaming at ten knots, the trawler was less than eight miles away at the mouth of the Co Chien River.[73] Lieutenant (j.g.) Stephen T. Ulmer, a 24-year-old from Coral Gables, Florida, commanded *Point League*. As a kid, Ulmer had enjoyed watching *Victory at Sea* and always dreamed of serving the country on a ship. After failing to gain admission to the Naval Academy, he accepted an offer from the Coast Guard Academy and graduated in 1963. His first assignment out of school was as an ensign on the high-endurance cutter *Ingram* (WHEC-35). There he qualified as officer-on-deck and became a skilled gunnery officer on the ship's 5-inch gun. In 1966 he deployed to Vietnam as the executive officer on *Point Gammon* (WPB-82328), a Coast Guard Division 12 boat based in Danang. Ulmer spent eight months on *Point Gammon* and after a four-month stint as an operations officer with Division 12, he volunteered to extend his deployment to become an officer in charge of his own WPB. In June, Ulmer took command of *Point League*. Nicknamed "Point Loser," the cutter had not seen any combat since arriving in Vietnam four months earlier and had a reputation for being the least aggressive boat in Coast Guard Division 13. This status would dramatically change on Ulmer's first patrol with the boat.[74]

Lieutenant Stephen T. Ulmer, USCG, six months after his return from Vietnam, 1967.

Ulmer informed the Vung Tau Coastal Surveillance Center of the contact as the WPB closed on the trawler. When he got within visual range of the trawler, now closing on the coast at a speed of six knots, Ulmer challenged the ship by flashing his signal light four times. At 600 yards, he illuminated the trawler with a searchlight and discovered a 99-foot steel-hulled vessel with a 40-foot junk alongside it. Ulmer ordered Gunner's Mate (Guns) 2nd Class Albert J. Wright Jr. to fire warning shots across the bow of the suspect. The trawler stopped momentarily and then increased speed to 12 knots and headed to the mouth of the Co Chien River. *Point League* fired two more bursts of .50-caliber fire across the bow, and the trawler returned fire with .50-caliber incendiary rounds. Several slammed into *Point League*'s pilothouse. A piece of shrapnel hit Lieutenant (j.g.) Neil Markle, the executive officer, in the head, knocking him flat on the deck. Another round grazed Wright's ankle.[75]

Temporarily blinded by the flashes from the rounds, Ulmer handed the radio mic to his Vietnamese liaison officer, Ensign Tung. "Tell Coastal Surveillance that we are engaged in a firefight and that we would report additional details once things had calmed down," he told the young officer. In careful English, Tung said, "Sorry, we are busy. Call back later." Tung then placed the mic upside down in an empty coffee mug because at five feet two inches he was too short to reach the bracket mounted above the window of the pilothouse. The coffee cup activated the transmit button, giving everyone on the circuit a riveting firsthand audio account of the battle for the next 45 minutes.[76]

The trawler headed to shore, exchanging gunfire with *Point League*, and grounded in shoal water 100 yards from the beach. *Point League* fired three 8 mm mortar flares to illuminate the area and then made three gunnery passes at 1,400 yards, blasting the stricken trawler with .50-caliber and high explosive mortar rounds. As helicopter gunships and other air support began arriving in the area at 0600, Ulmer decided to move *Point League* closer to the trawler for a closer investigation and immediately came under intense fire from the shore.[77] "They were firing from behind every sand dune. We could see muzzle flashes and splashes in the water," Ulmer said.[78] He had his gunners return fire as they withdrew to safer waters to replenish their ammunition. A pair of Air Force F-100 Super Saber jets swept down and pounded the enemy with their eight 20mm Pontiac M39 automatic cannons—a terrifying weapon cable of firing 1,500 rounds a minute. "It appeared that the vessel was hit several times and an explosion rocked the vessel at 0615," Ulmer later reported. A fire also broke out on the trawler.[79]

After forcing a steel-hulled trawler aground, *Point League* (WPB-82304) stands off as the trawler burns, 20 June 1966. Salvage teams ultimately recovered 100 tons of contraband from the vessel.

The cutter *Point Slocum* (WPB-82313), which had arrived on scene at 0520, made several firing passes on the beach while *Point League* replenished her ammunition from *Point Hudson* (WPB-82322). "On all passes we received automatic weapons fire and on the final pass we drew three or four rounds of recoilless rifle or mortar fire," wrote Lieutenant (j.g.) B. Foster Thomson III, the officer in charge of *Point Slocum,* in his after-action report. One round hit the powder bags for the high explosive mortar rounds, spraying Chief Boatswain's Mate Bruce D. Davis with burning powder and shrapnel but only causing minor wounds. Helicopter gunships supported the cutter by laying down additional suppression fire on the beach.[80]

At 0715, *Haverfield* (DER-393) arrived, and the embarked commanding officer of Escort Squadron 5, Commander Orlie G. Baird, assumed the role of on-scene commander of a flotilla that now included three Coast Guard cutters plus the destroyer *John A. Boyle* (DD-755) and units from VNN Coastal Group 35 and River Assault Group 23.[81] Surface and air attacks continued on the Viet Cong beach. For Ulmer, the highlight of the morning was watching an Air Force AC-47 gunship hose down the beach with its ten .30-caliber machine guns and three 7.62mm General Electric miniguns, each capable of firing 6,000 rounds per minute. "It looked like a downpour in the water around the ship," he said.[82]

At 1000, a volunteer damage control party consisting of sailors from the WPBs, *Haverfield*, and the VNN units approached the burning trawler in two coastal group junks. As ammunition cooked off from the wreck and bullets from occasional small arms fire buzzed around them, the party doused the flames with hoses connected to portable seawater pumps. *Point League*

The Coast Guard cutter *Point Slocum* (WPB-82313).

The hulk of the trawler intercepted and damaged by *Point League* burns, 20 June 1966.

attempted to tow the trawler to deeper water, but when the towline broke, the attempt was aborted. At 1105, *Point Slocum* moved in to assist the firefighters followed by an LCVP and an LCM from dock landing ship *Tortuga* (LSD-26) carrying more damage control personnel.

By 1315, fires were under control, and elements of the ARVN 21st Division had landed on the beach and established a defensive perimeter. *Point League* then made a second attempt to tow the trawler away from the beach but was soon interrupted in its efforts by LSIL-225, which moved alongside the cutter. Ignoring warnings to stay away, VNN sailors, according to Ulmer, "poured across our decks and grabbed souvenirs from the vessel like a woman's bargain sale." Finally heading Ulmer's pleadings, LSIL-225 moved away, and *Point League* made another futile effort to tow the trawler.[83] A VNN LCM tried as well but ended up running over its own towline and fouling a screw.

A small fleet of VNN and U.S. Navy vessels remained overnight to guard the trawler. "The sea was lit up like Christmas with many ships (who all claimed the prize) and the sky was ablaze with flashing lights," Ulmer wrote in his after-action report.[84] The next day sailors from Harbor Clearance Teams 1 and 3 found the trawler listing 20 degrees to port with at least eight holes in the deck and starboard side from 81mm rounds and numerous smaller holes from machine-gun fire. The salvage teams used pumps to remove water from the ship and began offloading the cargo. At 1200, LSSL-226, a VNN ship, finally pulled the trawler free and towed it to Saigon. It arrived at the VNN shipyard on the morning of 23 June.[85]

Salvage teams ultimately recovered over 100 tons of cargo from the 99-foot trawler. The weapons were mainly Chinese-manufactured with some Soviet and North Korean weapons. Included in the haul were seven 82mm mortars, 316 automatic rifles, 21 light machine guns, 20 75mm recoilless rifles, 25 40mm rocket launchers, and 222,880 7.62mm rounds (the standard round for the AK-47 rifle), as well as numerous other ammunition. Intelligence officers concluded that the large quantity of sophisticated arms indicated that the cargo was intended for units stationed well beyond the local area. This was the most significant trawler intercept since the Vung Ro incident and the second major trawler intercept by Coast Guard cutters. From July 1965 to December 1971, Market Time forces destroyed or captured ten enemy trawlers. Coast Guard cutters played a major role in nine of these intercepts. Historian Paul Scotti argues, "the Coast Guard's experience in long, wearisome rescue searches gave them an advantage in maintaining alertness during patrol monotony." This author believes that it had as much to do with the endurance and range of the WPB as it did with the fine crews that manned them. As suspected infiltrators closed on the Vietnamese coastline, WPBs were statistically more likely to be called in to intercept the ships rather than were PCFs, which had shorter patrols and a more limited range.[86]

The night after the engagement, Stephen Ulmer offloaded his two wounded men to *Tortuga* for treatment of minor injuries and received some ice cream for the rest of his crew. He then dropped Commander Baird off at *Haverfield*. At 0200 on the 21st, he finally sat down to write his after-action report, and the next thing he remembered was being medically evacuated to Vung Tau. Doctors later told him that he had passed out from exhaustion, but his vitals were fine and he soon returned to duty. It was not until 1970 that Ulmer was diagnosed with a mild form of epilepsy called "petit mal." Apparently, the stress of battle had induced his first documented seizure.[87] The Coast Guard would later award him a Silver Star for the trawler intercept, and Vietnamese head of state, Nguyen Van Thieu, would personally confer him with a Vietnamese Cross of Gallantry. Although the events of June 1966 forever changed Ulmer's life and may have propelled him to high rank in the Coast Guard, this pious young man never lost track of his true calling. At the change of command ceremony for his last command (Coast Guard Base, Mayport, Florida), he told his men, "I have attempted to fulfill my duty to my Commander in Chief, the President of the United States, as a commissioned Coast Guard officer; but I have received a commission from the Supreme Commander in Chief, the Lord Jesus Christ, to serve Him as a pastor; therefore, I must obey." Ulmer lived up to this promise by attending Dallas Theological Seminary and later becoming an ordained Baptist minister.

Arrival of the PCFs

In September 1965 representatives from CINCPAC, MACV, CINCPACFLT, OPNAV, and the Naval Advisory Group met in Saigon to examine the infiltration problem. The study that resulted, known as the Long Range Plan for the U.S. Naval Effort in Vietnam, made a variety of recommendations that included increasing the offshore patrol from 9 to 14 ships on station, doubling patrol aircraft coverage and placing four aircraft in the air at all times, increasing the number of PCFs from 54 to 84 and the number of WPBs from 17 to 26, and initiating an extensive river patrol requiring a total of 120 river patrol craft.[88]

Written by Captain Carey E. Landis of the CINCPAC staff, the study envisioned a much larger role for the U.S. Navy in South Vietnam than what had been originally planned when TF 115 was established earlier in the year. Specifically, it called for a beefed up coastal patrol force to provide "24-hour surveillance with sufficient numbers of craft to allow a large visit and search effort in the high density junk areas" and for the creation of an entirely new American task force to patrol the rivers.[89] Unlike the Coast Guard, which adapted relatively quickly to the environment in Vietnam, the Navy had only limited experience in inshore and riverine operations, and the first PCF crews to fight in Vietnam would suffer greatly from this knowledge deficit.[90]

Using the Landis study as an organizational template, Rear Admiral Ward established Boat Squadron 1 on 1 October 1965 as the umbrella unit for the Swifts and then divided his forces into five separate divisions based at locations recommended by the study: Divisions 101 at An Thoi, 102 at Danang, 103 at Cat Lo, 104 at Cam Ranh Bay, and 105 at Qui Nhon.[91] An Thoi, Cam Ranh Bay, and Danang became the major repair and support complexes with complete Swift boat repair facilities as well as berthing, messing, and medical services for crews. Cat Lo and Qui Nhon were utilized as intermediate support bases with berthing and messing facilities along with the capability to make minor repairs to hulls, machinery, electronics, and communications equipment.[92] The initial plan called for the major bases to support 19 Swift boats each and the intermediate ones, 14.[93] The Landis study assumed that PCF crews would only be able to patrol 12 hours because of the physical strain of operating small boats in rough seas, but patrols ended up being 24 hours or longer. "They envisioned the crew working very hard," noted a senior officer on Ward's staff. "And indeed they did."[94] The first Swifts (PCF-3 and PCF-4) arrived at An Thoi on 30 October 1965. Thirty hours later they went on patrol with *Point Comfort* and *Point Garnet* (WPB-82310). By May 1966, 20 additional PCFs had arrived in Vietnam, and by November 1966 all 84 PCFs were on station.[95]

To lead Boat Squadron 1, Ward chose as his flag secretary, Commander Arthur P. Ismay. A native of Tuckahoe, New York, and a 1951 graduate of the U.S. Naval Academy, Ismay had more small boat experience than most officers of his year group. As a young officer, he had commanded *Spoonbill* (MSC-202), a 144-foot-long coastal minesweeper. He also had served as the executive officer of the minesweeper *Ruddy* (AM-380) and the radar picket escort *Otterstetter* (DER-244). Later in his career, he commanded the Secretary of the Navy's VIP yacht *Sequoia* (AG-23) and hosted President John F. Kennedy's last birthday party in May 1963.[96] In addition to these assignments, Ismay had combat experience from his time as the assistant main propulsion officer on *Philip* (DD-498), a *Fletcher*-class destroyer that participated in naval gunfire support missions during the Korean War. Ismay, however, believed that his best preparation for the assignment was sailing competitively at the U.S. Naval Academy. "Competitive sailing

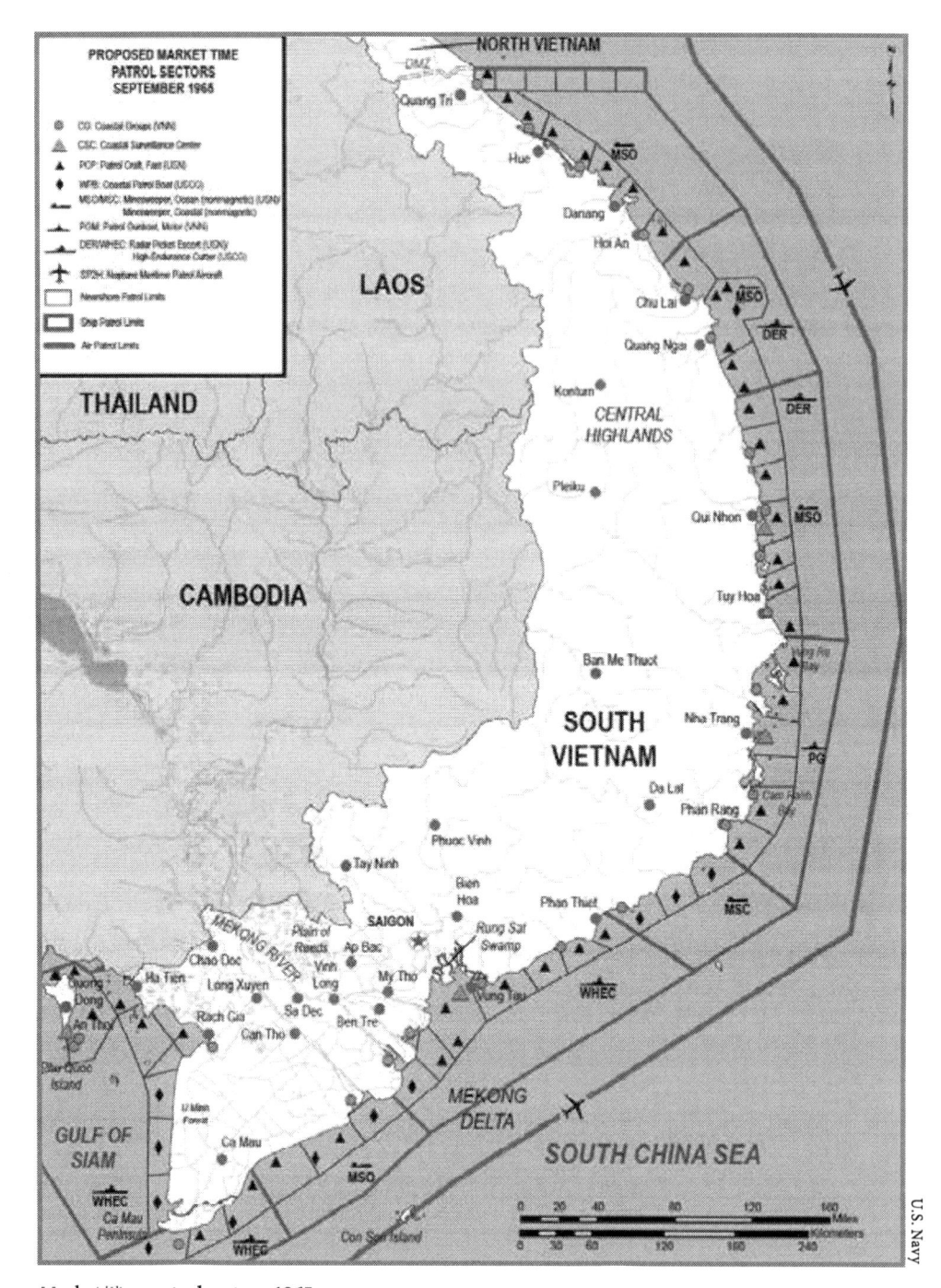

Market Time patrol sectors, 1965.

really tuned me in to the influence of tides, currents, and winds, which helped an awful lot in understanding what happens when maneuvering a small boat on the water."[97]

Ismay was on the bow wave of a massive buildup of American naval forces in Vietnam, and things did not always run smoothly. Training at Coronado, California, was initially haphazard and disorganized. "They were not able to cope with the large number of people who suddenly appeared in Coronado to train," and as a result some of the early crews only received a two-week crash course on the PCF. "We didn't develop any hard doctrine until we actually had the first boats in operation in An Thoi," explained Ismay. "This I did personally with the division commander and the first two skippers on the line. On each of our patrols the division commander rode one PCF and I rode the other one. We developed the doctrine during the first ten days."[98] The situation persisted throughout 1965 and into 1966. In a January 1966 letter to the commander of the Amphibious Training Command, Ismay complained, "the training of PCF crews has been deficient in knowledge of Market Time operational requirements and knowledge of boats." Crews arrived in Vietnam with almost no training in such fundamentals as radio procedures, simple engineering and electrical systems, the rules of engagement, and gunnery doctrine.[99]

Ismay had to contend with inadequately prepared crews and with boats that did not always live up to the challenges of duty in Southeast Asia. As he put it, "getting the PCFs prepared for

PCF Swift boats of Division 101 underway in the Gulf of Thailand off Phu Quoc Island. The Swift boat's shallow 3.5-foot draft and high speed of 28 knots made it an ideal craft for coastal patrol in Vietnam, December 1965.

combat was a challenge."[100] The Navy initially modified the Stewart crew boat by gutting the main cabin, cutting a hole in the pilothouse roof for a twin, ring-mounted .50-caliber machine gun, and mounting a combination 81mm mortar/.50-caliber machine gun aft on a strengthened deck. Once deployed, the Swifts would require even more modifications. The radar console had to be moved from the main cabin to the pilothouse, and the air intake needed to be elevated to handle rough sea conditions.[101]

The Swift's poor seaworthiness proved a particular challenge to Ismay and his men. Because its bridge was so far forward and its bow so low, the boat tended to nose into waves and take on water. Six-foot waves could sink a Swift, and even moderate sea states posed a challenge. Lieutenant Frank P. Hamilton, riding a Swift from An Thoi to Rach Gia, experienced a rough ride in nonmonsoon conditions with winds gusting only to 15 knots and seas at a moderate three feet. Although the skipper of his PCF reduced speed to six knots, "water began washing up over the pilothouse and entering from the canopy." As Hamilton reported, "Finally after severe pounding even at this reduced speed, the forward hatch on the forecastle broke open and flooded. We had to come to a complete stop and bail out the hatch. The captain radioed and received permission to return to An Thoi. During the entire period while we were traveling everyone was holding on the best way possible, and two Vietnamese passengers and two crewmembers of the boat got seasick."[102]

During the monsoon season, PCFs often negotiated even rougher sea states. Lieutenant Gary Blinn, who commanded PCF-97 in 1967, claimed that if you cranked the boat up to 20 knots in 4-foot-high seas, the shock on the spine and knees was like jumping off a picnic table every three seconds for hours at a time. After a 24-hour patrol during the monsoon season, "the crews would climb off the boat as tenderly as if they were 80 years old. Soaking wet. Sprained backs, aching necks, headaches, and discs that screamed in pain. Swollen feet. The worst were knees. They felt as if they had endured a 24-hour football game." Crews often had no desire to eat. They just wanted to sleep and take "some aspirin washed down with a couple of beers."[103]

Several PCFs were lost in heavy seas, but in most cases the crews survived.[104] One of the most deadly weather-related accidents occurred on 15 November 1966. While entering Hue River in heavy seas, PCF-22 lost a man overboard. PCF-77 maneuvered to assist in rescue operations. Just after recovering the PCF-22 sailor, a rogue wave flipped PCF-77 end over end. Most of the crew, including the rescued, escaped through the port pilothouse door, but Radioman 3rd Class Bruce A. Timmons ended up trapped in the after compartment. Chief Machinery Repairman Willy S. Baker forced his way into the compartment to try and rescue his shipmate, but the boat sank keel up in 13 feet of water one and a half minutes later, killing him, Timmons, and another sailor, Boatswain's Mate 3rd Class Harry G. Brock.[105]

Housing the PCF crews at remote bases also posed a challenge. Crews at An Thoi lived on *Krishna* initially but soon moved ashore into tents, where they were subject to frequent VC attacks.[106] According to one officer living there, "They'd fire a few rifle shots or maybe a mortar round into the camp every once in a while just to harass us and keep us up. We'd then man base

Cat Lo base, Vietnam, 1967.

defense positions with hand-me-down World War II weapons."[107] At Danang, Swift crews had to "carve out for themselves" living spaces and a mess hall on large covered lighter *YFNB-21*, which sat tied to a pier in the harbor, because the larger, more comfortable support ship, *YR-71*, was filled to capacity with personnel from Coast Guard Division 12.[108] In 1965, Cam Ranh Bay, soon to become one of the largest naval bases in the world, was just a beach. The first sailors to arrive there lived in tents, bathed in the ocean, and dug their own latrines just like marines. Coastal Division 104 sailors had the best deal—they lived in a hotel in nearby Vung Tau until barracks could be constructed at Cat Lo, a village renowned for producing a pungent Nuoc Mam sauce but lacking in such basics as potable water and adequate dry land for new construction. The Navy took close to three years to dredge enough landfill from the Long Tau riverbed to complete the facility, which by that time was supporting over 627 personnel.[109]

Typically, boats would leave their bases at staggered times during the morning or the evening for patrols and, when they reached a patrol area, commence searching sampans, junks, and any other vessels in the area. Crews could not search every boat, so officers in charge used their own judgment in deciding which vessels to search. If a boat had no hatches or over decking, crews might release it after a quick inspection of documents, but if a larger junk was found after dark in curfew areas, the crew approached with great caution and thoroughly searched the junk. Any suspicious cargo or personnel were turned over to the Vietnamese. A PCF could make many patrols without ever running across a suspicious contact; thus, Market Time duty could be quite mundane.

"We searched about 20 fishing boats on an average day, sometimes more, sometimes less," recalled Lieutenant Charles Lloyd, the office in charge of PCF-4. SEAL instructors at Coronado had told Lloyd to hog-tie Vietnamese before searching their boats, but once in-country he soon found this approach impractical. "When you have to search 20 boats a day, this is not going to work. First of all, you would tick everyone off and turn people who weren't VC into VC."[110] Lloyd's boat did not carry a liaison officer, so he communicated with the Vietnamese via crude hand signals. As the war progressed, VNN liaison petty officers helped bridge the language gap, but even this system was far from perfect.

"We were only partially confident that they translated the wild stories of the locals accurately back to us, but that was to be understood," claimed Blinn, "They often avoided conflict" and filtered information. Although Swifties often found routine searches to be tedious, Blinn enjoyed the work. "We would shout, '*Dung lai* [stop],' at the fishermen. They would stop and show us that they had nothing to hide. No gun running. No trouble." Blinn's crew would then trade cans of C-rations for fresh fish and joke a bit with young kids. "Life was good. Poor, honest people. They didn't even make a dollar a day in this country. Yet the kids were happy." Blinn particularly enjoyed patrolling at sunrise when the morning temperature was 70 degrees and listening to Armed Forces Radio. "All in all, life was good. I had never felt so *alive*." However, it was not always that way for him. "Some missions were dangerous; some were a piece of cake. The hardest part was telling which was which. Often what appeared to be a routine mission, proved dangerous." This was certainly the case for the crew of PCF-4—the first Swift lost in combat in Vietnam.[111]

Tale of Two Swift Boats

On Valentine's Day, 1966, PCF-4 was completing a two-day patrol in the Gulf of Thailand. The crew had not seen any action since arriving at An Thoi in late October 1965, and after many hours of monotonous junk searches under the hot Vietnamese sun, the crew was bored, half-asleep, and not thinking straight. Lieutenant Lloyd spotted a VC flag attached to a bamboo pole sticking out of the water about 250 yards from a beach midway between Ha Tien and Rach Gia. "I wanted to throw some grenades at it, back off, and get them to shoot so we would have something to shoot at," said Lloyd, a native of Steubenville, Ohio, and a 1959 graduate of Wheeling Jesuit College in Wheeling, West Virginia. "We were just trying to get some action going and this was not the way to do it."[112] Before he ordered the boat forward, Lloyd consulted his crew. "We all, without question, told him that we should take it down," claimed Radioman 3rd Class Robert R. Johnson.[113]

As the PCF steamed toward the flag, one of the crew threw three grenades and, when nothing happened, the Swift eased up alongside the flag to cut it down. At that moment a command-detonated mine blew up underneath the boat. The blast struck the underbelly of the boat, causing the main deck to buckle upwards and killing three crewmembers instantly: Engineman 2nd Class Jack Charles Rodriguez, Boatswain's Mate 2nd Class Tommy Edward Hill, and Gunner's Mate (Guns) 2nd Class Dayton Luther Rudisill. All were standing on the starboard side of the boat except Hill, who had the con, and Rudisill, who was manning the twin .50 mount. The boat then settled to the bottom in 10-foot-deep water.[114]

Lloyd, who was standing next to the flag when the mine went off, was propelled into the water by the force of the blast. When his head came up and he saw his PCF, Lloyd's first thought was, "Oh my God! This is a disaster." Despite suffering shrapnel wounds in both legs, he managed to paddle to the boat with his hands in the shallow water. "One boot was pointing one way and the other, the other way." The first person Lloyd saw was Johnson, his radioman, attending to a severely wounded seaman, David J. Boyle. After being told by Johnson that the radio was dead, Lloyd ordered him to get Boyle into a life raft and move away from the boat.[115]

Shortly thereafter, three junks from Coastal Group 43, under the command of Petty Officer 1st Class Sam Mu Tong, arrived at the scene and immediately came under small arms and machine-gun fire from a platoon-size force of Viet Cong dug in along the shoreline.[116] Seven Viet Cong were swimming toward the PCF-4 wreck when Petty Officer 3rd Class Nguyen Quang Hoang and Seaman Nguyen Duong maneuvered one of the junks close to the stricken vessel in an attempt to draw enemy fire and protect the survivors. Armed only with World War II-vintage M1 Garand rifles, the two VNN sailors killed three VC swimmers and forced the others to withdraw. Another junk manned by Petty Officer 3rd Class Duong Thuong and Seaman Huynh Hong Son then pulled up to the life raft and hauled Johnson and Boyle onto the boat. With fire still coming from the shore, Thoung, joined by Petty Officer Lam Van Phat and Seaman Huynh Van from a third junk, saw Lloyd clinging to PCF-4 and jumped in the water to help the injured officer clamber into to the junk.[117]

Once on board, Lloyd's first thought was to call in a medical evacuation for Boyle. The junk had an old PRC-10 radio, but it worked, and Lloyd soon placed a mayday call. Lieutenant Gilliam Dunn, a naval advisor based at Rach Gia, answered the call and requested support from an Army helicopter unit in the area. Once the helicopter located PCF-4, Dunn, his counterpart Dai-uy Dang, an Army medic, and a Navy chief jumped into a 15-foot inflatable Zodiac and headed to the scene in building seas. Soaked to the skin, Dunn's group made it to the junk and began rendering medical attention to the crew. Boyle was dead with no pulse, so Dunn next examined Lloyd who had a fractured femur and was slipping in and out of consciousness. Johnson suffered from severe swelling of the right knee and a contusion of the right calf but did not appear to have life-threatening injuries.[118]

Dunn requested a helicopter evacuation for all three men, but the aircraft only managed to pick up Johnson because the junk was pitching so erratically in heavy seas. PCF-3 transported Lloyd to the aid station at Rach Gia. During that trip Dunn and the medic noticed that Lloyd's right leg was swelling under a bandage applied by the Vietnamese. After removing the dressing, they discovered a ruptured artery and applied a tourniquet, thereby saving the officer's life. Lloyd

The mostly submerged hull of PCF-4 lies to the left of the bow of an LCM. In the background, naval gunfire from nearby U.S. Navy and Coast Guard vessels rakes possible Viet Cong sniper positions, February 1966.

would spend the next 15 months in hospitals in the Far East and the United States before being medically discharged from service. His injuries included multiple compound fractures in both legs and a ruptured main artery in his right leg that refused to heal properly. It burst several times during his convalescence due to severe infections, causing numerous complications and rendering the leg virtually useless.[119] Johnson fared better. After spending two months in the naval hospital at Yokosuka, Japan, and three months on limited duty at the Yokosuka naval base, he returned to Vietnam and worked on the staff of Coastal Squadron 1 as a radioman from July 1966 to July 1967.[120]

Throughout the night U.S. and Vietnamese units guarded the remains of PCF-4, often exchanging fire with the Viet Cong platoon still dug in along the shoreline. On 15 February, LCM (8) from Rach Gia managed to drag the sunken hulk to a point 2,000 yards from the beach, and on the 16th, *Krishna* arrived and began salvage operations. First, divers focused on recovering the remains of the three sailors. Crews then lifted PCF-4 from the bottom and shipped the wreck to the Ship Repair Facility, Subic Bay, for analysis. Information obtained from PCF-4 ultimately helped the Navy improve future hull designs against mining.[121] "We learned a lot from that episode," Commander Ismay said. "In hindsight, we did not know enough about booby traps to insert it into training ahead of time."

After the explosion, instruction on booby traps became a fundamental part of the Coronado syllabus, and training there improved markedly.[122] Gary Blinn, who attended the two-week course late in 1966, learned every inch of the boat from radios to guns. Crews learned how to repair everything from a damaged steering mechanism or a broken radio. "After a morning of lectures on subjects like diesel mechanics, we would then practice in the afternoon on an actual GM diesel," explained the 1966 Naval Academy graduate from Norfolk, Nebraska. Blinn particularly enjoyed language training taught "by a young and pretty Vietnamese girl" and gunnery practice at a nearby island. In the end, however, he admitted that no amount of training could adequately prepare him for the rigors of war. "It was hard to truly believe that what we were doing in sunny California would be the same as our life in-country." The instructors, who were by then mostly Swift boat veterans with a year's experience in Vietnam, "simply couldn't express to us what we would encounter. The things that *really* mattered. They didn't socialize with us. They looked at us with sad, vacant eyes."[123] From the loss of PCF-4 and the death of four of its six crew members, they understood implicitly how vulnerable the unarmored Swifts boats were to attack from the shore and that some of their pupils might not survive their tour in Vietnam.

The issue was again underscored a few months later in the Rung Sat Special Zone. In the spring of 1966, this area became a major focus of MACV's efforts to root out Viet Cong sanctuaries near Saigon. Beginning with Operation Jackstay in March, U.S. Marine Corps, U.S. Navy, and VNN units engaged in a series of amphibious assaults designed to seek out and destroy VC base areas in the 400-square-mile Rung Sat swamp.[124] VNN river assault groups and Swift boats provided security for the landing forces as well as naval gunfire support. For the Navy, these operations represented its first major foray into the rivers of the Mekong Delta and, while they did not result in very many enemy deaths, they fulfilled their main objective of disrupting VC operations in the Rung Sat, primarily by capturing weapons and supply caches and destroying VC facilities. They also demonstrated MACV's ability to strike at the enemy in a place the Viet Cong originally believed was beyond the control of allied forces.

On 22 May, PCF-41 was patrolling the Dinh Ba River, 20 miles south, southeast of Saigon in support of Operation Lexington III, an amphibious and helicopter assault operation conducted by elements of the U.S. Army's 1st Infantry Division.[125] In command of the boat was Lieutenant (j.g.) Alexander Balian—a highly gifted young officer from a prominent Armenian-American family in Los Angeles. Throughout his childhood, Alexander had been groomed by his father to take over the family business—a supermarket chain and an ice cream factory. An adventurous type by nature, Balian instead chose to join the Navy after graduating from UCLA with a degree in business administration. His first assignment after attending Officer Candidate School in Newport, Rhode Island, was as a personnel officer on board *Kearsarge* (CVS 33). Captain Charles Paul Muckenthaler Jr., the commanding officer of this support aircraft carrier, wrote in Balian's fitness report that "he not only accepts responsibility, but seeks it. A mere mention of a job to be done is his cue to 'grab the ball and run'. . . . He could well become an outstanding candidate for early command at sea.'"[126] This prophecy became a reality in 1965 when Balian volunteered for Boat Squadron 1 and subsequently took command of a Swift boat when he arrived in Vietnam April 1966.[127]

Balian was at the aft controls of his PCF, keeping an eye out for movement along the shore as dusk approached. Inside the pilothouse, Raleigh Godley, a 36-year-old boatswain's mate (BM) 2nd class, manned the conn, and on his left stood Radioman (RM) 3rd Class Robert Lee Kiem looking at the shoreline through binoculars. Engineman 3rd Class Charlie Barham sat in the twin .50-caliber turret above the pilothouse and Gunner's Mate (Guns) (GMG) 2nd Class Glenn Greene manned the .50-caliber/81mm gun aft, with Seaman (SN) Ralph Powers serving as loader. Coast Guard Warrant Officer George Fenlin was a volunteer rider along for a little excitement.[128]

A few days before Balian had volunteered for this operation—a two-day patrol on a tributary of the Long Tau called the Dinh Ba River. PCF-41 was proceeding north and just rounding a bend in the river when a 105mm, fin-stabilized round fired from a Chinese rocket launcher slammed into the pilothouse.[129] Within seconds of the initial hit, a mine exploded near the PCF, causing additional damage to the boat's bottom.[130] The rocket explosion in the pilothouse instantly killed BM2 Godley, a 16-year Navy veteran from Lawson, Missouri, with a wife and four children. The force of the blast hurled Kiem out of the pilothouse onto the catwalk that ran along the side of the PCF. Despite suffering from shock and shrapnel wounds in his thigh, Kiem stumbled back into what remained of the pilothouse. He found Godley's body on the deck. Kiem reached for the wheel but could not find it—it had disappeared in the blast. As the boat raced down the river out of control, Kiem called out, "Controls shot out. Godley's hit." Lieutenant (j.g.) Balian grabbed the aft wheel and tried to gain control as another rocket just missed the boat, showering the crew with spray.[131]

Powers, who had also been knocked to the deck by the blast, got up and began firing at the shoreline with the aft .50-caliber gun. Despite suffering from minor shrapnel wounds and having his .45-caliber pistol knocked out of the holster by an enemy bullet, Powers continued to put rounds on the beach. "I didn't realize I had been hit until much later on in the fighting. I just kept thinking I had to get as much fire into enemy positions as possible."[132]

EN3 Barham, manning the forward turret, managed to fire 100 rounds before both guns jammed. He recalled that there were at least three machine-gun positions on the shore and "in between them there was about 15 or 20 yards of beach that was nothing but muzzle flash—small arms." When he saw that the boat was out of control, he jumped out of the turret and headed for the aft controls just as the boat rammed the bank of the river. Careening down river at high speed, the boat slammed bow first into a river bend 200 yards upstream from the enemy position.[133]

Powers and GMG2 Greene worked the aft mortar and .50-caliber until they ran out of ammo, while Balian fired an AR-15, and Fenlin, an M79 grenade launcher. Kiem tried the radio to seek help but to no avail because it had been damaged in the initial blast. He soon had to place a tourniquet around his leg or risk passing out from lack of blood. Balian tried to signal passing aircraft with the 8-inch searchlight. None spotted him, so he decided that his only course of action left was to abandon the boat since they were rapidly running out of ammunition. The crew gathered up the crypto codes, the charts, and the log. They then blasted the electronics with an AR-15 and destroyed the engines with thermite grenades. Under a dark evening sky, they placed all of their small arms, along with the crypto, charts, and log, in a life raft and then stripped into their skivvies and entered silently into the water. Because of his wounds, RM3 Kiem was placed on top of the raft by SN Powers and Balian. There was no room on the raft for Godley's body, so it was left behind.

The plan was to have the crew cling to the raft and drift downriver past the enemy positions. It was not an easy task. The crew battled strong currents for an hour and then hit a school of Portuguese man-of-war (*Physalia physalis*). Waves of pain spread through their tired bodies as arms and legs were stung, but the men could not yell or scream for fear of giving away their position to the enemy. Several of the crew went into mild shock and needed to be held close to the raft while they recovered. The raft drifted into a second school and once again the crew gasped with pain. Later the raft tipped over, and all weapons and equipment were lost. During the entire two-mile trip, SN Powers and Balian refused to rest and insisted on aiding other wounded sailors and reassuring the men that everything would be all right. The Navy later awarded both men Silver Star medals for gallantry and intrepidity in action.

After two hours and 45 minutes in the water, the sailors heard the sound of PCF-37. Barham held up his rifle and the PCF's radar picked up the metal gun barrel and the raft. PCF-37 transferred Kiem to Dong Hoa village for helicopter medical evacuation. The remaining

Commander Arthur Ismay, left, the commander of Boat Squadron 1, speaks to crewmembers of PCF-41 at the U.S. Army 36th Evacuation Field Hospital, Vung Tau, South Vietnam, after presenting them with Purple Heart medals. In the picture are Engineman 3rd Class Charles Barham, Seaman Ralph E. Powers, and Lieutenant (j.g.) Alexander George Balian.

crewmembers were taken to the U.S. Army's 36th Evacuation Field Hospital near Vung Tau for treatment of shock and minor injuries.[134]

Helicopter fire teams then went into the area to prevent the Viet Cong from stripping PCF-41. A six-boat VNN reaction force from River Assault Group 22 with a U.S. Navy SEAL team left Nha Be at 2300. When they arrived at the scene four hours later, they found PCF-41 heeled over to port about 45 degrees and about 80 percent submerged. The reaction force recovered Godley's remains along with the forward .50-caliber guns, the starlight scope, and some munitions. One of the VNN vessels attempted to tow the boat from the sandbar where it had grounded, but bottom damage from the mine explosion caused the PCF to sink midstream in 25 feet of water. The reaction force marked the spot of the sinking and withdrew from the area. The next day a salvage team of seven SEAL divers, along with seven RAG 22 boats and a Regional Forces company, returned to the scene. The search failed to locate PCF-41, but the RF company made contact with the enemy on the north bank of the river and, in a resulting action, killed four Viet Cong and captured several small arms and a B-50 antitank rocket launcher. The B-50 was the first captured in South Vietnam. The weapon has an effective range of 250 yards and fires a 105mm rocket capable of penetrating eight inches of hardened steel.[135]

B50 Rocket.

The loss of two PCFs in just two months revealed the vulnerability of these unarmored patrol craft to mines and rocket attacks. By the end of 1966 a line of demarcation was drawn across the mouth of each river, and PCFs were not permitted to cross into rivers without special consent or unless involved in hot pursuit. In August 1966 the Naval Research Laboratory commissioned a study to explore the feasibility of installing enough armor on the PCF to give it limited protection against .30- and .50-caliber machine guns and 57mm rockets. The study, conducted by Westwood Research, concluded that the armor protection would have reduced the speed of the PCF considerably and so the effort was abandoned.[136]

The study also severely criticized the PCF's lack of seaworthiness, noting that three PCFs (14, 76, and 77) sank in rough seas during the course of the war. "The Swift boat performed well during nine months of the year," concluded the Westwood study, "but for the remaining three months during high seas the craft was virtually useless for the tasks it was assigned. The PCF was almost completely ineffective in seas greater than five feet in height, and those seas occur frequently in some coastal sectors during the monsoon seasons"[137] The PCFs often had to abandon their patrol sectors and seek shelter from the monsoons. Rear Admiral Ward was so disappointed in the performance of the PCFs that he later regretted his decision to purchase them. "Because of those sea conditions off the coast, I regretted not getting larger ones," he said.[138] Ward instead relied heavily on Coast Guard WPBs to patrol areas most affected by monsoons—yet another reason why most of the major steel-hulled intercepts were made by these boats and not by the Swifts.

Despite the problems associated with the PCFs, Market Time as a whole proved generally effective in curbing infiltration by steel-hulled trawlers. In the end, the stronger elements of the barrier compensated for the weaker ones. Perhaps the greatest unsung heroes of the barrier patrol were the patrol aircraft that performed long, often very dull search missions over the South China Sea. Of the 17 trawlers attempting to infiltrate before 1970, aircraft initially detected all but two.[139] It was difficult indeed for any large steel-hulled ship to slip through Market Time's powerful net of airborne radars, and those that did would inevitably be picked up by a galaxy of shipboard radars. Historian Mark Moyar, who examined North Vietnamese naval records, concluded, "Market Time swiftly brought Hanoi's maritime infiltration operations to ruin, as if the stopper had been pulled and all of South Vietnam's coastal waters had gone down the drain." He based this assessment on Communist records, which indicated that between February 1962 and February 1965 North Vietnamese navy trawlers made 89 trips to South Vietnam and succeeded in delivering their cargoes on 86 occasions. By comparison, from the beginning of Market Time in March 1965 to the end of the war in April 1975, North Vietnam would make only 80 supply voyages, and of this number only 14 would reach their destination.[140]

Market Time was much less successful in stemming the flow of supplies coming into the country on smaller wooden-hulled junks. The Center for Naval Analyses found that in 1966 U.S. Market Time forces searched only about 15 percent of the junks they detected at sea and that the probability of discovering a wooden-hull infiltrator from outside South Vietnam among thousands of junks that plied the waters off South Vietnam on any given week was extremely low. "Considering such a large junk population," the report stated, "the likelihood of detection by a random selection process is quite small and can further be reduced by action such as: movement at night when visibility and boarding rates are reduced, transiting in areas too shallow for coastal surveillance ships, and transiting when nearby patrol vessels are observed boarding other junks."[141] Although the largest wooden junks only carried about five tons of supplies—far less than the 100 tons carried by the average trawler—the quantity of junks that made it through the barrier on a daily basis made them as serious a threat as blockade runners. Rivers were another weak link in the operation. Market Time had little impact on supplies moving along rivers and smaller waterways of the Mekong Delta, especially those coming in along rivers from Cambodia. Not until the establishment of a separate river control operation in May 1966 would the U.S. Navy begin to undermine the Communist logistics operation in the rivers and canals of the Mekong Delta.

From February 1965 until 1968, the U.S. Navy's role in Vietnam mushroomed while the VNN began to take a secondary role. The trend would continue as the Navy developed a river patrol force and later a riverine assault force. While the Navy's technology was highly successful in interdicting the larger ships, it could not win the war against infiltration unless it also stemmed the flow of supplies on smaller boats. Accomplishing this end with limited means required the resources of the Vietnam Navy, especially its language and cultural skills. Based on subtle design differences, paint jobs, and even sailing techniques, a Vietnamese junk force sailor born and raised in a local area knew immediately which junks were harmless fishermen and which ones were Viet Cong. If a junk needed to be boarded, this same sailor could immediately tell if a junk crew was Viet Cong based on the accents, dress, and the mannerisms. Thousands of hours spent searching junks might have been spared through better utilization of the Coastal Force, but the rapid Americanization of the war pushed the very forces needed to win the effort to the sidelines. To his credit, Rear Admiral Ward understood implicitly how significant the VNN was toward winning the infiltration battle and made improving the force a top priority of his command. At the same time, he also had to make a serious dent in infiltration to satisfy General Westmoreland, a man who completely lacked confidence in the VNN. At a time when the operational effectiveness of the VNN was at a nadir, Ward had few choices but to look to his own Navy to jumpstart the infiltration campaign. Only after MACV became committed to turning the war back over to the Vietnamese after the Tet Offensive in 1968 would the U.S. Navy again be able to forge a more even-keeled partnership with its VNN counterparts.

Postscript: The Arnheiter Affair

On 22 December 1965, Lieutenant Commander Marcus Aurelius Arnheiter assumed command of *Vance* (DER-387) at Pearl Harbor. *Vance* was a World War II–era radar picket escort ship being used by the Navy for Market Time operations. During his change of command speech,

Vance (DER-387), 26 November 1968.

Arnheiter promised the crew action, excitement, and drama. The crew listened stoically, but those who had already served on the Market Time patrol took it with a grain of salt, knowing that the ship would be lucky to fire a shot in anger. Symbolizing his desire to sail "into harm's way" like his hero John Paul Jones, Arnheiter ordered Lieutenant (j.g.) Louis A. Belmonte, the ship's first lieutenant, to purchase a speedboat for tactical as well as recreational purposes. Arnheiter intended to use the boat mainly for junk searches and for scouting out enemy positions on the shore but purchased it with $950 of recreational funds in violation of Navy policy. Just before the ship's departure from Hawaii on Christmas Day, he allowed his wife to serve brandy-laced eggnog to various officers on duty that day in violation of the Navy's longstanding prohibition against alcohol consumption on board ship. Belmonte and other officers were concerned by their new skipper's willingness to flaunt rules but, eager to make a good first impression, they decided not to challenge him.[142]

Upon assuming command, Arnheiter began making major changes immediately to improve the military bearing of the crew. He instituted daily personnel inspections and prohibited sailors from drinking coffee on the bridge. He also clamped down on his wardroom. If he or any of his officers committed major or minor errors anywhere on the ship, they would be compelled to deposit a fine of 25 cents into a so-called boner box. Arnheiter used the proceeds to purchase cigars for the wardroom. The new policy that drew the most resentment from his wardroom, however, and ultimately helped spark a judge advocate general (JAG) investigation of the ship, was Arnheiter's directive that all hands except those on watch would be required to convene on the fantail for moral guidance every Sunday. The meetings, which were supposed to be nonreligious in nature, included prayers and religious hymns. Lieutenant (j.g.) William T. Generous Jr., the operations officer and a devout Catholic, took offense to these "church calls," initially expressing his objections in a memorandum to Arnheiter. After Arnheiter refused to excuse him from the meetings, he sent a letter to the squadron chaplain in Hawaii complaining of the commander's "infringement" on his "constitutional rights."[143]

This letter and other reports of "irregularities" on *Vance* soon found their way to Commander Donald F. Milligan, Commander Escort Squadron 7, who then initiated an investigation of the ship. Ninety-nine days after taking command of *Vance*, Arnheiter was relieved for cause. In a fleet of 880 warships, such occurrences were not unusual. What was extraordinary about this case was the amount of negative publicity it generated for the Navy, not only in the media but also in the halls of Congress. Unlike most other commanding officers relieved of their command, Arnheiter did not sail away quietly. Rather, he exposed private details about the U.S. Navy and its personnel in a way not experienced by the service since the so-called Revolt of the Admirals in the late 1940s or the controversy surrounding Hyman Rickover's promotion to rear admiral in 1953.[144] Familiar with the inner-workings of public affairs, Arnheiter hoped that going public with his arguments could rehabilitate his career. Instead, his actions brought additional dishonor to himself and raised a host of questions about the fitness of the Navy's officer corps and the service's performance in the war in Southeast Asia. The story of how a single Market Time commander keelhauled the Navy remains one of the greatest scandals of the Vietnam War period.

Born and raised in the New York area, Arnheiter graduated from the U.S. Naval Academy in 1952 near the bottom of his class (628 out of a class of 783). He served as the assistant navigator on the battleship *Iowa* (BB-61) from 1952 to 1954 and received an average evaluation from his first commanding officer. After attending electronics school and graduating last in a class of 39 students, he became the electronics officer on the destroyer *Fiske* (DDR-842) where he ran afoul of the commanding officer, Commander James B. Sweeny. Determined to drum Arnheiter out of the service, Sweeny wrote in a fitness report that he "will never make a naval officer" because of a variety of deficiencies, including "an inability to admit mistakes, lack of common sense, selfishness, poor judgment, and a compulsive tendency to concentrate his energies on minor details rather than his major duties." Because of this poor performance review, Arnheiter was passed over for promotion to lieutenant despite the fact that there was a 96.7 percent selection rate for that officer grade in 1955.[145]

Rather than resign from the service, he persevered, serving as the gunnery officer on *Coolbaugh* (DE-217) and the operations officer on *Abbot* (DD-629). His fitness reports improved, and he subsequently was promoted to lieutenant in 1956. From 1960 to 1963 Arnheiter worked in the Navy's Briefing and Progress Analysis shop in the Pentagon where he excelled in writing press releases about various Navy programs for popular newspapers and magazines and even published a novel, *Shadow of Peril* (about the activities of a Soviet submarine off the East Coast), under the pseudonym Aleksandr I. Zhdanov. He was promoted to lieutenant commander and secured an assignment as an operations officer on a destroyer—the first step towards command at sea.[146]

From May 1963 to March 1964, he served as the operations officer on guided missile frigate *Worden* (DLG-18) and then became the executive officer of *Ingersoll* (DD-652), serving with that destroyer until May 1965. His fitness report for *Ingersoll* claimed that he performed brilliantly, and was the "best DD XO [executive officer] in the fleet." Due in part to this fitness report and a decent review in his next assignment on the staff of Cruiser Destroyer Flotilla 9, Arnheiter successfully screened for command at sea, but only by the narrowest margins (two of three panel members voted against giving Arnheiter a ship). Only Captain Richard G. Alexander, a personal friend, voted in his favor. Alexander also managed to secure him a place on a list of officers who might be given command on an "emergency" basis. Hence, when *Vance*, a ship on an emergency wartime deployment, needed a new commander in late 1965, Alexander had the authority to cut orders for Arnheiter to assume command.[147]

Once at sea Arnheiter began exhibiting a variety of eccentricities. Over lengthy meals in the wardroom, he regaled his officers with tales from naval history while smoking cigars (purchased at the wardroom's expense) and eating canned pears smothered with his favorite liquor, Cherry Heering. He took particular pleasure in compelling his officers to give impromptu speeches on topics of his choice during Toastmaster nights. Arnheiter's high-jinx style extended to shore leave. At a dining-in ceremony held at a local officers' club in Guam, he encouraged his officers to steal a coffee pot and silver candelabras from the club and to siphon gasoline from vehicles on the base for the ship's speedboat. In Bangkok, he spent $550 of recreational funds on hotel accommodations for officers and chief petty officers, steak dinners for the crew, and additional candelabras for the wardroom without seeking permission from the ship's Welfare and Recreational Committee.[148]

On 20 January 1966 *Vance* reported for duty to commander, task force (CTF) 115, relieving *Finch* (DER-328) at Qui Nhon. The main duties of DERs in Market Time at this stage of the war consisted of screening water traffic for Viet Cong infiltrators and material in the outer Market Time barrier. DERs also provided logistical support to PCFs and WPBs working the inner barrier. It was mundane work but necessary for the success of the blockade. On 28 January he ordered his ship to hug the coastline, hoping to draw fire. If fired upon, *Vance* had full authority to return fire under existing rules of engagement. *Vance*, however, did not have authorization to move beyond its assigned patrol sector to the inshore barrier, nor was naval gunfire part of *Vance*'s regularly assigned duties in this sector. To cover his tracks, Arnheiter directed that a false position report be sent to Coastal Surveillance Center Qui Nhon over the objections of the executive officer, Lieutenant Ray S. Hardy Jr.[149]

The next day Arnheiter had *Vance* again sail close the shoreline near Point Kim Bong, hoping to engage in a gunfire mission. *Mason* (DD-852) was operating in the same area nearby and on two occasions requested *Vance* to stop fouling its range. Late in the afternoon, *Vance* requested permission from a spotter plane to fire at some bunkers in sand dunes not far from friendly troops. The spotter was unable to observe any fire from the beach or see the bunkers but confirmed the request anyway. Arnheiter immediately ordered his gunners to lay down 17 rounds on the "emplacements"—a reckless move given the presence of both American and South Vietnamese troops in the vicinity. Even more irresponsible was a mission he executed on 30 January in the same area. As *Vance* closed to within 1,000 yards of the beach, Arnheiter told the bridge that he had observed fire coming from the beach. All witnesses, including Lieutenant Hardy, denied seeing anything. "They are shooting at us," Arnheiter yelled. He then ordered the ship to return fire. *Vance* fired a total of 65 rounds of 3-inch munitions and 600 rounds of .50- caliber at a target no one else on the ship could see. The JAG Manual Investigation later concluded that Arnheiter disregarded the rules of engagement in both this case and the mission on 29 January, and castigated him for neglecting "his primary mission of patrol for several days in Market Time Area 3 in order to manufacture gunfire support missions."[150]

Arnheiter's lack of judgment manifested itself in other ways as well. In one instance, he left a group of sailors in the whaleboat for two hours without cover in Xuan Dai Bay while *Vance* steamed ten miles away to intercept a possible Viet Cong junk. On several other occasions, he ordered *Vance* to tow the speedboat and whaleboat, with sailors embarked, under hazardous conditions and at unsafe speeds. Once while his men were searching a junk, he shot at a sea snake, spooking the boarding crew and nearly causing them to open fire on innocent civilians. On 6 February 1966 he gave away candy from the ship's store to Vietnamese refugees on a junk and then told the supply officer to process a false survey for candy, which Arnheiter signed. On 26 February *Vance* received a message from its squadron commander requesting a list of certain diesel spare parts on board. The engineering officer prepared the required report, but Arnheiter refused to release it. Instead, he told the officer to reduce the quantities and thus forced the submission of a false report on items that were in critical supply. By involving his officers in deceitful acts, he undermined their integrity and fueled resentment against him.[151]

On 28 February Lieutenant George W. Dando, a chaplain, paid *Vance* a visit while she was on patrol in Market Time Area 3. While on the ship, he heard numerous complaints from the men about Arnheiter and the ship's low morale. When Dando later tried to discuss the situation with Arnheiter, he reported that the skipper "did not appear stable." As the evidence began to mount against Arnheiter's fitness for command, Commander Milligan decided to act. Although Milligan was concerned about the compulsory moral guidance sessions and poor morale on the ship, he was even more worried about complaints he was receiving from other destroyer commanders about the unauthorized naval gunfire missions. After informing his chain of command of the situation, Milligan notified Arnheiter by a message that he was "hereby detached" from *Vance* and that he was to "proceed immediately and report to the destroyer tender *Dixie* (AD-14) for temporary duty." The next day Rear Admiral Thomas S. King, Commander Cruiser Destroyer Flotilla 3, ordered Captain Ward W. Witter, the commander of Destroyer Squadron 11, to conduct an informal JAG Manual Investigation into the affair. In all, 30 witnesses, including every officer from *Vance*, testified under oath during the next three days. Arnheiter was present with counsel throughout and often exercised his right to confront witnesses and cross-examine them.[152]

On 27 April, Witter submitted a 413-page, single-spaced report to Rear Admiral King. The report included 40 "findings of fact" about irregular practices occurring on Vance during Arnheiter's tenure as commander. The most significant were submitting false position reports, engaging in unauthorized gunfire support missions contrary to the rules of engagement, submitting a fraudulent survey report, violating Navy alcohol regulations, and injecting "religious overtones" in mandatory moral guidance lectures for the crew. In the investigation's recommendations, Witter concluded that Arnheiter was a "poor leader," that his removal from command be sustained, and that he "not be assigned command in the future, either ashore or afloat." Factors that contributed to his lack of fitness as a ship commander included "insensitivity," a failure to "see black from white" and "extremely poor judgment."[153]

With the investigation complete, Arnheiter was assigned to Commander, Cruiser-Destroyer Force Pacific staff based in San Diego. While there he made a very favorable impression upon his new boss, Rear Admiral Walter H. Baumberger, who eventually proposed that Arnheiter be reassigned to command another destroyer escort.[154] Vice Admiral Benedict Joseph Semmes Jr., Chief of Personnel, disagreed. On 9 September 1966 Semmes approved the detachment for cause and directed that papers be filed in Arnheiter's personnel jacket.[155] This action sealed Arnheiter's fate in terms of ever receiving a Navy command, and on 25 September 1967 he was passed over for promotion.[156]

Rather than accept Semmes's September 1966 decision and move on with his life, Arnheiter initiated a lengthy appeals process. In a February 1967 letter to Secretary of the Navy Paul R. Ignatius, he forwarded charges of mutiny against Lieutenants Hardy and Generous and recommended a full-scale court of inquiry and/or a general court martial. Because Arnheiter's letter presented no new evidence against his former subordinates, the secretary rejected the appeal and dismissed the accusations.[157]

Arnheiter refused to yield. Now assigned to the staff of Commander Western Sea Frontier at Treasure Island, California, he began talking to journalists.[158] Many of the articles subsequently written about the case portrayed it as a generational clash between Arnheiter, who stood for traditional naval values of the 1950s, and a "collegiate" young wardroom more accustomed to the anti-establishment, countercultural mores of the late 1960s.[159]

Arnheiter also solicited support from active duty and retired officers. His most strident advocate in this category was his former detailer, Richard Alexander. Now a captain and the prospective commander of the battleship *New Jersey* (BB-62), Alexander did an end run around his chain of command and pleaded Arnheiter's case directly to members of Congress. On 7 November 1967 he distributed a 27-page memorandum to 15 members of Congress, stating that Arnheiter was indeed a "competent commander" and that his career was derailed by the "unfounded allegations of disloyal subordinates who succeeded in stampeding naval authorities into taking unjustified summary action against him." Alexander claimed that Arnheiter deserved redress because the case had ramifications for "every commanding officer in the service." That same day he presented new evidence to Secretary Ignatius consisting of a mock "Plan of the Day" and a "Familygram" lampooning Arnheiter's command. The Judge Advocate General's Office reopened the files on the case, paying close attention to the actions of Generous and Hardy but, after a lengthy investigation, concluded that the "new evidence" did not warrant a court of inquiry. On 24 November, Secretary Ignatius reaffirmed the decision and stated that the case was hereby closed.[160]

Still, the affair would not die. Arnheiter continued to send papers and rebuttals to officers in the Pentagon, congressional members, the media, retired flag officers, and anyone else who might lend him a sympathetic ear. The Secretary of the Navy and other leaders were not just upset by Arnheiter's behavior but with other officers who openly supported him, especially Captain Alexander. After the captain submitted his written defense of Arnheiter to members of Congress, Admiral Thomas H. Moorer, Chief of Naval Operations, summoned him to his office and reprimanded him for taking such action without consulting his chain of command and for publicly criticizing several junior officers under Arnheiter's command. Shortly after the meeting, Admiral Moorer received and accepted a written request from Alexander for reassignment for "personal reasons."[161]

Congressman Paul Y. Resnick (D-NY) held three days of ad hoc hearings on the issue from 7 to 10 May 1968. Resnick contended that the main point in the case of Lieutenant Commander Arnheiter was not whether he was fit to command a ship, but whether a group of dissident subordinate officers could get rid of a commanding officer they disliked by writing unofficial letters about him behind his back.[162] Arnheiter, Alexander, a medical officer from *Ingersoll*, and two enlisted men testified, but no new evidence was introduced. Upon conclusion of the hearings, Resnick demanded that Secretary Ignatius resign.[163]

Following the hearings, a slew of articles critical of the Navy were published. An editorial in the *Denver Post* called the Navy's handling of the case "arbitrary" and demanded a court of inquiry.[164] The *Virginian-Pilot* warned that every skipper "may be undermined from below and abandoned from above."[165] Jack Anderson of the *Washington Post* accused the Navy of suppressing details of the case and covering up the truth to protect the brass.[166] "The Navy is suffering a leadership crisis," he wrote in one editorial, in which "desk-bound admirals at the Pentagon have put loyalty to each other above loyalty to the Navy and the nation."[167]

One of the Navy's most effective weapons in countering this negative publicity was a *New York Times* reporter named Neil Sheehan. Sheehan had spent three years in Vietnam working as a war correspondent before becoming the *New York Times* Pentagon correspondent in 1966 and its White House correspondent in 1968. Known for being generally critical in his appraisal of the armed forces in Vietnam, Sheehan was an unlikely ally for the Navy, but in stark contrast to many journalists who covered the fracas, he interviewed not only Arnheiter but most of the officers who had served on *Vance* with him and many crewmembers as well. Sheehan also obtained and read a copy of the JAG Manual Investigation and other documents related to the case. What he learned about Arnheiter surprised him. Far from being a victim of a wardroom conspiracy, Arnheiter came across as hypocritical, delusional, and narcissistic. In a long exposé on the affair published in August 1968 in the *New York Times Magazine*, Sheehan wrote that the crew told of a "paranoid captain, a real-life Queeg" who "violated Navy regulations and the orders of his superiors whenever it suited him and tried to run a private war."[168] The article, and later a book published about the incident by Sheehan in 1971, corroborated nearly every charge leveled against him in the Witter investigation. It also affirmed that the Navy's removal of Arnheiter from command was both necessary and proper.[169] After Sheehan's compelling article appeared in print, media interest in the Arnheiter case waned, and by the middle of 1969 only a few Arnheiter defenders still demanded a court of inquiry.[170]

In the end the Arnheiter case revealed how a single officer who understood public relations could deeply embarrass the Navy by enlisting the support of the fourth estate. In portraying himself as an Alfred Dreyfus unfairly condemned by a self-serving Navy bureaucracy, Arnheiter was able to convince many journalists that the Navy suffered from a profound leadership crisis. Unlike Sheehan, who conducted exhaustive research on the case, most members of the media were more interested in stirring up controversy than analyzing the merits of the case. That the Navy failed to effectively contain Arnheiter's media blitz reflected poorly on its public affairs division and the Washington headquarters leadership. From their experiences with Rickover, Navy leaders should have known how much damage an officer could inflict on the service by going public and contained the damage earlier by informing journalists about the facts of the case.

The Arnheiter affair also cast an unfavorable light on Operation Market Time and the entire role of the U.S. Navy in Vietnam. It revealed an operational environment where a ship commander bored with fruitless junk searches recklessly endangered the lives of allied forces and his crew in unauthorized missions. Arnheiter's emphasis on spit and polish and his wardroom antics also lent credence to the notion that the Navy was not engaged in a *real* war in Southeast Asia and that America was wasting resources on a bloodless and ineffective interdiction campaign. Finally, it painted the most unflattering picture imaginable of the caliber of Navy leadership in Vietnam. How did an officer with obvious personal shortcomings slip through the Navy's careful screening process to secure a ship command in wartime? Was the Navy scraping the bottom of the barrel to staff its command billets in Vietnam? Did all ship commanders treat their men as poorly as Arnheiter did? These were just some of the many questions raised by the case that potentially undermined public support for the Navy and its Market Time operations in Vietnam.[171]

CHAPTER 3

War on the Rivers: Game Warden, 1966–1967

Fred McDavitt was typical of many officers who ended up fighting on the rivers of Vietnam. A noncareerist, McDavitt grew up in a traditional middle-class family from the Cleveland area, graduated from a liberal arts college (Monmouth College in Illinois), joined the Navy to avoid being drafted into the Army, and ended up volunteering for Vietnam out of a sense of adventure and patriotism. Before the war he served as a communications watch officer on the attack aircraft carrier *Oriskany* (CVA-34) for three years, but he found the work dull and left the Navy. Missing the camaraderie of shipboard life, he reenlisted three months later and joined *King* (DLG-10) as the communications officer. The ship deployed to Vietnam, and one day McDavitt witnessed *Nasty*-class fast patrol boats refueling from his ship. "I had read about PT 109 a year earlier and became totally enamored with those boats." He soon volunteered to be an officer in charge of a *Nasty* boat but, as fate would have it, the Navy assigned him to command a PBR unit instead.[1]

As a 26-year-old lieutenant, McDavitt arrived in Vietnam in March 1966 and assumed command of River Section 531 based in My Tho, a provincial capital on the Mekong River 70 kilometers from Saigon. His unit consisted of four officers, 56 sailors, and ten PBRs. Its mission was to conduct patrols, establish and enforce curfews, and prevent Viet Cong infiltration, movement, and resupply in its area of operations—a 40-mile stretch of the Mekong River.[2] During its first months of operation, the unit established a night curfew in its sector and devoted much time to searching sampans and junks and checking IDs along the river.

When McDavitt arrived in My Tho, basing arrangements for his unit were still being sorted out. Lieutenant Ray Zogg of Naval Support Activity Saigon, Detachment My Tho, quickly found housing for the river section in the Hotel Victory, an old French villa that had served as a "comfort station" for Japanese troops during World War II and after that as a girl's school. The building had no air-conditioning, but it did offer the men relatively decent rooms with large windows and cold showers supplied by a large rainwater collection tank on the roof.

Lieutenant Fred McDavitt, the officer in charge of River Section 531, searching a junk with a two-boat PBR patrol. To his right is the rear .50-caliber machine gun of a PBR, June 1966.

In the foreground of this overhead view of My Tho, an LCM (6) is being used as a makeshift pier for U.S. Navy PBRs transiting to other bases. My Tho–based PBRs were berthed at the Vietnam Navy River Assault Group 27 base, which is to the right just outside the frame, December 1966.

McDavitt's next concern was tropical clothing for the men—many of whom had arrived in marine winter utility uniforms. Lieutenant Constantine "Charlie" Varelas, his "cumshaw expert," soon traded bottles of Johnny Walker Black Label scotch for green jungle fatigues from the U.S. Air Force and jungle boots from the U.S. Army.[3] To McDavitt's great frustration, though, he could never find 60 of the same type of hat, so when he noticed some of his men wearing black berets they had purchased in town, he went out and with his own money purchased every beret he could find for his section, even though they were not officially authorized.[4]

Food proved to be the biggest challenge. "When we first got there, Lieutenant Zogg was buying food from the local market, and just about everyone came down with chronic diarrhea or dysentery. An Army doctor finally made a call to the base and issued us tetracycline and told us to keep taking the pills until they killed all the bacteria."[5] Between survival school and dysentery, McDavitt lost 20 pounds during the first few months of 1966.

Much of the work on the river involved routine patrolling and sampan and junk searches but, on occasion, McDavitt had an opportunity to set up ambushes. One of his earliest occurred on 23 July 1966. A naval intelligence liaison officer told him that the Viet Cong might attempt to cross the Cua Tieu River 15 miles east of My Tho—an area outside of the river section's normal operating area. McDavitt headed out that evening with a patrol of four PBRs.

When the PBRs arrived at the probable crossing point, the engines were cut and the two boats drifted silently. At 2123, McDavitt, in PBR-110, heard an engine astern of his boat, and ordered PBR-105, commanded by Boatswain's Mate 1st Class James Elliot Williams, to investigate. Williams, a salty, heavyset 35-year-old petty officer from South Carolina, closed on the 25-foot sampan, illuminated it with a spotlight, and then yelled through a bullhorn, "*Lai day* [come here]." Two of the occupants stood up and fired on Williams's boat with AK-47 rifles. PBR-105 responded with machine gun and small arms fire, killing six of the Viet Cong outright and forcing the remaining three to abandon the junk and swim to the north bank of the river. A Vietnamese liaison sailor in PBR-103 then used a bullhorn to appeal to the Viet Cong to surrender. PBRs -103 and -105 opened fire on the men as they emerged on the beach, killing one Viet Cong and seriously wounding another.

A salvage of the sampan later found documents revealing Viet Cong taxation methods and persons who had been contributing to the Communist cause, along with a rifle and several bombs.[6] Williams, McDavitt, and the patrol officer in PBR-103, Chief Radioman Donald Ray Williams, each received the Bronze Star with Combat Distinguishing Device as well as the Vietnamese Cross of Gallantry with Bronze Star for the action. The event also convinced McDavitt to qualify BM1 James Elliot Williams as a patrol officer. He was the first sailor below the rank of chief petty officer in River Section 531 to command a two-boat patrol. "I took more guff about that than anything I have ever done" recalled McDavitt. "The officers didn't care, but the chiefs were incensed!" McDavitt held his ground. "I did this because I learned in this action that James Elliot Williams was better under fire than all of the officers and chiefs in the unit. He was quicker to react under fire than the rest of us. He had a command sense. He knew what was going on and was able to get the big picture very fast and bring it all together."[7] Williams, in short, had what aviators call "situational awareness"— the ability to think ahead rapidly and clearly in time and space.

Williams was also extremely lucky not only to have had a commanding officer who recognized his potential, but also to have fought most of his battles as a predator rather than as prey. Too often in Game Warden actions, it was the other way around with devastating results. A recoilless rifle round or an accurate burst of machine gun fire from a hidden emplacement could easily disable a fiberglass PBR, and sailors in these boats were virtually defenseless against even small arms and grenades. For every BM1 Williams thwarting an enemy crossing, there was a Radioman 2nd Class Terrence Jay Freund being killed by an enemy machine gun, or a Lieutenant Don Witt, by a recoilless rifle round.

Game Warden sailors, in short, paid a steep price for what in the end were only modest interdiction gains on the waterways of Vietnam during 1966–1967. The River Patrol Force never became big enough to fully prevent infiltration along the rivers. There were simply too many small boats on too many waterways for the relatively small PBR force to effectively search and control. The River Patrol Force had more success in thwarting the crossings of larger Viet Cong units on the larger rivers; keeping the major riverways in the delta and the Rung Sat Special Zone open to commercial shipping; enforcing curfews; supporting U.S. Special Forces, especially SEAL attacks against key Viet Cong leaders; and extending government control in the IV Corps Tactical Zone. Whenever the enemy did stand and fight, the ability of the PBRs to rapidly move to the scene of hostilities and provide fire support often allowed small numbers of allied troops to prevail against larger numbers of Viet Cong. This was especially true during the Tet Offensive, where PBR fire support proved instrumental during several major battles in the delta. Over time, the devastating effects of ambushes on Game Warden river craft would be mitigated through more effective use of airpower (especially attack helicopters), but duty in PBRs would remain a dangerous one throughout the war, and the men who wore the black berets often exceeded all expectations with their small–boat handling skills, heroism, and aggressiveness.

Origins of Game Warden

Like Market Time before it, Game Warden developed largely in response to the deficiencies of the Vietnam Navy. By the summer of 1965, it had become painfully evident to the Navy leadership that the VNN's River Force was incapable of effectively controlling the waterways of the Mekong Delta and the Rung Sat Special Zone (RSSZ). Six million people—nearly 40 percent of South Vietnam's population—lived in this hot, humid watery region south of Saigon. This rich tableland of mud also produced most of the country's rice, and its 3,000 nautical miles of waterways afforded farmers with a highly efficient means of transporting crops to market. The fact that the Viet Cong could operate battalion-size units in this area with near impunity, establish bases, and levy taxes and supplies from the local populace revealed the extent of the problem. As Commander Sayre A. Swartztrauber, a former commander of

Aerial view of the Mekong Delta landscape, undated.

River Squadron 5, wrote in *U.S. Naval Institute Proceedings*, the VNN "lacked the leadership, resources, and training to dislodge the Viet Cong and reestablish the necessary government control" of the Mekong and the RSSZ.[8]

At the beginning of 1965, the VNN River Force consisted of six RAGs and two river transport groups. Unlike Operation Game Warden, which would be designed exclusively as a river patrol force, the River Force served a dual purpose: to patrol the rivers and to conduct offensive amphibious operations with Vietnamese troops. However, its boats—mainly an amalgam of modified landing craft—were better suited for assaults than patrols. A typical RAG of 250 men and 19 small boats could support a landing force of up to 500 men for periods lasting 14 days or more.[9] Its landing craft could not only transport a large number of troops but also provide organic gunfire support for landings. Although many of the RAG boats were heavily armed and armored, all were slow moving and cumbersome on the rivers. LCM (6) monitors, for instance, traveled no faster than nine knots—too slow to catch a fast-moving motorized sampan or enforce curfews.[10]

As the direct descendent of the French *dinassauts*, the River Force historically had been the most aggressive branch of the VNN. During the 1950s, RAGs were instrumental in putting down the Binh Xuyen sect in the RSSZ (see chapter 1). A decade later the force was still chalking up combat successes. On 24 December 1964, RAG units carrying ARVN troops launched an amphibious operation against a Viet Cong supply base near the mouth of the Soirap River, resulting in the seizure of 600 kilograms of rice, ten sampans, and a motorized junk.[11] In January 1965, RAG 22 saved a Vietnamese Ranger unit from being overrun in the Long An Province. Its river craft halted a VC assault with mortar and machine-gun fire and then evacuated the Rangers across a river just as the enemy commenced a second assault. During the four-hour-long engagement, 72 Viet Cong were killed and another 130 wounded.[12] On 7 February 1965, River Force units rescued a Regional Forces outpost at My Loi in My Tho Province. An estimated 70 Viet Cong had overrun the post, sinking one Regional Forces LCVP and capturing three other craft and a large cache of weapons. The River Force retook the post and recovered all captured boats and weapons with no losses. During September 1965, RAGs launched 17 combined operations with the ARVN and engaged in 23 fire support missions, killing 164 Viet Cong while losing just four vessels.[13]

Despite these tangible successes, the River Force in 1965 was plagued with many of the same problems affecting the other VNN operating forces. The April 1965 mutiny against Admiral Chung Tan Cang (see chapter 2), in particular, left the force bitterly divided. As a former River Force commander, Cang had developed a large personal following within the RAG units, and the mutiny against him shattered morale. After the coup, many River Force officers assumed an unaggressive posture and in some cases refused outright to carry out orders from the new leadership.[14]

One of these men was Lieutenant Khanh Quang Do, commander of the newly organized RAG 27. Prior to the mutiny, Khanh had developed an elaborate plan to avoid combat by keeping his new RAG in Saigon for extended training. When Commander Do Quy Hop, the River Force commander, rejected his proposed training schedule, Khanh attempted to stall the deployment of his unit to My Tho in other ways. He first refused to release his LCM (8)s to the shipyard for the installation of armor. When Admiral Cang finally ordered him to do so, Khanh then failed to assign a coxswain to pilot test runs of the modified boats. According to Commander Charles Z. Hanus, the senior River Force advisor, Khanh was "disrespectful and discourteous to all advisors," and "made no secret of the fact that he holds a position of favor with the Admiral [Cang] and frequently goes to him without permission of the River Force Commander." Once Cang was ousted, Khanh refused to take orders from the new acting River Force commander. The brazen young lieutenant also regularly engaged in graft by utilizing his boats to escort commercial barges in the Saigon area and charging barge owners 15,000 piasters per trip.[15] Khanh was eventually relieved of his command on 19 June, nearly two months after the coup, and his unit was finally commissioned as the VNN's seventh RAG at My Tho on 1 July.[16]

The Khanh affair was an extreme manifestation of problems afflicting the VNN, but it was in no way unique. An undated Naval Advisory Group analysis of all end-of-tour reports submitted during the period concluded that "some sort of command is going to have to be instituted in the VNN that actually commands. There is a tendency on the part of senior U.S. officers to regard an advisor on every ship as the answer to all the problems. But this isn't so. Until there is some system in the VNN where the C.O. is made to do his job, the advisory effort has gone as far as it is going to go."[17] Major Ardath C. Smith Jr., the senior advisor in the Rung Sat concurred, "Time and time again I have seen junior officers fail to carry out the orders of their seniors and even tell them No to their face. Yet, no follow-up action or punishment is initiated."[18]

In a January 1966 study of VNN force structure requirements for the Naval Advisory Group, Lieutenant Robert J. Powers noted that the VNN's "instability and reduced effectiveness" could be traced to two issues: rapid expansion and the bureaucratic turmoil caused by the two mutinies and multiple reorganizations.[19] Between 1964 and 1966 authorized VNN billets jumped from 7,149 to 15,491 sailors. In July 1965 nearly 17 percent of the force (2,008 out of 11,962 sailors) was either in training or awaiting training. Since the Nha Trang and Cam Ranh Bay training centers could produce only 1,200 sailors every two months, many prospective sailors were compelled to perform "coolie-style" hard labor until a slot opened up. Once they graduated from basic training, there were few officers to lead them. In 1965 the officer shortfall stood at 268 men. The naval academy at Nha Trang could only produce 90 ensigns per year at most to make up for this deficit. The Naval Advisory Group staff estimated that it would take the academy four years at least to catch up. Clearly, with its existing training facilities, the Vietnam Navy simply could not keep up with the expansion demands being placed upon it.[20]

Emblematic of the VNN's problems were the losses suffered by RAG 22. Between June and November 1965, ten of its craft were mined and 181 of its force of 250 sailors killed or wounded. The worst attack occurred on 18 November 1965 when a large mine exploded in a convoy, sinking one LCM (6) and severely damaging another, along with two LCVPs. A track record of careless watches and lax security contributed to the RAG's vulnerability, as did a commanding officer who failed to take measures to improve the situation.[21]

As early as August 1965, the Naval Advisory Group had recognized deficiencies in the River Force and commissioned a short study to explore the idea of U.S. Navy participation in river patrols. The study concluded that the VNN did not have sufficient assets to patrol the rivers and also launch amphibious assaults. Moreover, the force was structured more for assaults than patrols. To effectively patrol the waterways, a naval force needed fast boats equipped with radar and good communications equipment. The study recommended that the U.S. Navy develop such a force to cover 500 miles of major rivers, check traffic during the day, and establish a delta-wide curfew at night.[22]

Between 2 and 18 September 1965, representatives from CINCPAC, CINCPACFLT, MACV, Office of the Chief of Naval Operations (OPNAV), and the Naval Advisory Group Vietnam met in Saigon, primarily to review the progress of Market Time (see chapter 2), but also to consider the issue of riverine infiltration. In the end, it recommended the establishment of an extensive

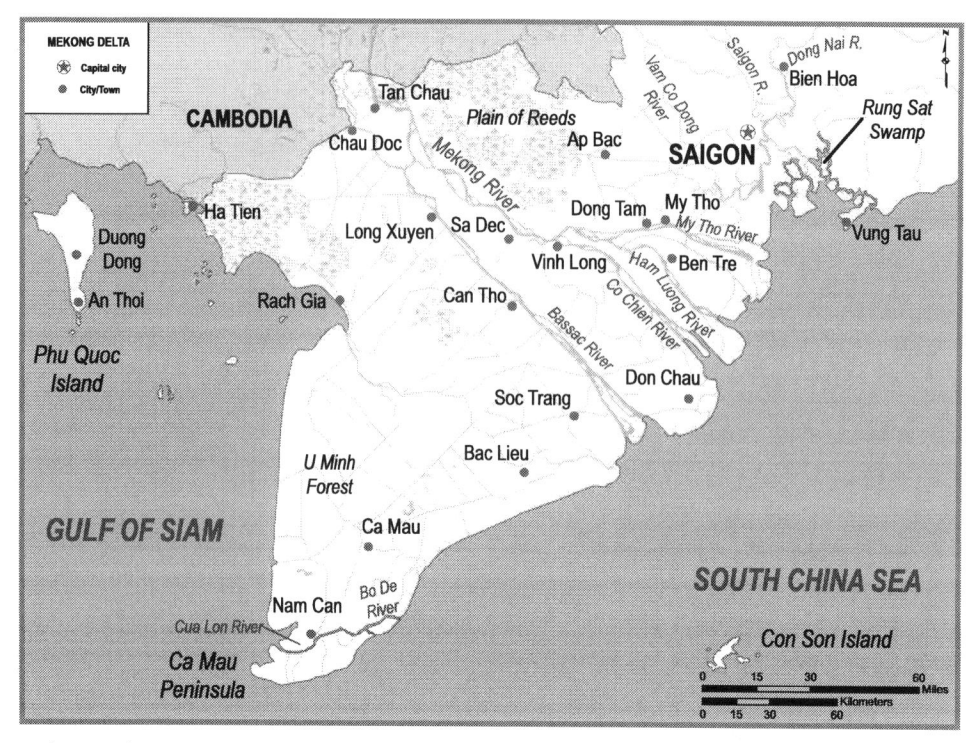

Mekong Delta.

river patrol with 120 river patrol craft.[23] On 18 December the U.S. Navy established Task Force 116 (River Patrol Force) to participate in Operation Game Warden, a combined U.S. Navy/VNN operation to deny enemy movement and resupply on the major rivers of the Mekong Delta and the RSSZ. TF 116 would come under the operational control of the Naval Advisory Group but would be separate from Market Time (TF 115). The original Game Warden concept called for groups of ten patrol boats to operate from a mixture of LSTs and shore bases. Initially, planners organized the force into two task groups: the Delta River Patrol Group (TG 116.1) located in the Mekong Delta and the Rung Sat Patrol Group (TG 116.2) located in the RSSZ. Forty boats were assigned to TG 116.2 and eight to TG 116.1. The original mission of Game Warden as promulgated in its February 1966 operation order was to prevent Communist exploitation of the waterways by:

- Patrolling the major inland rivers
- Searching suspicious craft
- Enforcing curfews
- Keeping the main shipping channel into Saigon open by patrolling and minesweeping in the Long Tau River.

It was hoped that these actions would counter enemy movement and resupply efforts in the Delta and RSSZ as well as prevent the Viet Cong from taxing the local populace.[24]

LCPLs in the Rung Sat

By the end of 1965 the 400 square-mile Rung Sat swamp had emerged as a significant haven for the Viet Cong. Its tropical jungles, mangrove swamps, miles of small waterways, and lack of road infrastructure made it an ideal base for the Viet Cong, which established arms factories, rest and training camps, and medical facilities there during the early 1960s. Control of the swamp also gave the Communists a base area within striking distance of Saigon just 20 miles to the north and threatened the flow of supplies to the capital along the Long Tau River, the primary deep–draft shipping route to Saigon. Throughout 1964 and 1965 the Viet Cong had extended its control in the area, taking over Regional Forces outposts one by one.[25] By the end of 1965 they controlled all but a small strip of villages on the South China Sea coast, and the situation had become dire. The Viet Cong only had to disable a single merchant ship in the narrow Long Tau River to block this thoroughfare. The salvage and removal of such a large vessel might have closed the waterway for weeks. As a November 1965 confidential MACV Fact Sheet warned, "The VC operations and influence in the RSSZ must be checked and eventually eliminated in order to return this vital territory back to RVN control."[26]

As a stopgap, Rear Admiral Ward ordered four 36-foot-long LCPL (landing craft personnel, large) patrol boats, based in Saigon, to begin boarding and searching suspicious sampans and junks in the RSSZ. In command of this first U.S. Navy river patrol was the 1960 U.S. Naval Academy graduate Lieutenant Kenneth Logan MacLeod III. A submariner by training like Ward, MacLeod was tapped for the job after writing a feasibility study for the Naval Advisory Group on the use of LCPLs as river patrol craft.[27]

LCPL on the Saigon River, October 1965. These 36-foot-long patrol boats provided security for the Saigon shipping channel prior to the arrival of the PBRs.

MacLeod had been promised new boats but received a bunch of hand-me-downs, which his sailors had to completely refurbish. They repaired old engines, mounted a variety of weapons on the boats, and repainted the hulls, adding shark's teeth and eyes on the bow. "MacLeod's Navy" patrolled the Rung Sat from September 1965 to April 1966, coming under fire over 20 times. "Until we came along the Viet Cong had uncontested control over the place," noted MacLeod in an interview with journalist Paul Dean of the *Arizona Republic*, but the place was not without challenges. "It's a goddamned maze! Nothing but rivers and streams and canals laced together through thick forests of mangrove. Half of it is swamp; the rest is islands, lots of them. There are no roads to speak of. The Vietnamese Army's got enough sense not even to think about going in there, so they turned it over to the VNN, but they haven't got the assets to set up any kind of meaningful deterrence."[28] MacLeod's Navy did not change the equation much, but it did provide a patrol presence in the Rung Sat and demonstrated the Navy's growing commitment to riverine warfare. A few lessons were also learned from the experience—namely that Game Warden would need a boat much faster than the 13-knot LCPL to effectively interdict Viet Cong motorized sampans.[29] It also needed one with more protection for the crew. As Chester C. Stanley Jr., a gunner's mate on one of the boats put it, "You were kind of naked on her. I was shooting the .50-caliber gun on the bow and it just had a small gun shield, and after we got done with the shootout there were bullet holes in my pants."[30]

Operation Jackstay

On 26 February 1966, the Viet Cong ambushed the SS *Lorinda*, a 346-foot-long Panamanian coastal freighter, on the Long Tau River 18 miles south of Saigon. Seven 57mm recoilless rifle rounds struck the ship's hull and another four hit the superstructure, wounding six of the crew, including the pilot and the master, and causing the freighter to run aground. Although the ship was soon refloated and moving again toward Saigon, this attack highlighted the vulnerability of the Long Tau channel in the Rung Sat. Neither the Regional Forces based in the few towns still under government control nor the VNN river assault group in Nha Be actively engaged the Viet Cong in this "Forest of the Assassins." As a consequence, MACV decided that a large-scale U.S. amphibious raid in the area would be necessary to ease enemy pressure on the shipping channel.[31]

In March, a newly regrouped U.S. Marine Corps battalion landing team (1st Battalion, 5th Marines) became available for the operation, along with a variety of amphibious warfare ships, including amphibious assault ship *Princeton* (LPH-5), attack transport *Pickaway* (APA-222), *Alamo* (LSD-33), *Belle Grove* (LSD-2), and attack cargo ship *Merrick* (AKA-97). Lending firepower to the force would be the carrier *Hancock* (CVA-19), the guided-missile destroyer *Robison* (DDG-12), and Air Force B-52s based in Guam. PCFs and WPBs from Market Time, along with LCPLs from the Rung Sat patrol force, would provide blockade support. This assemblage represented a significant show of U.S. might, but planners nevertheless understood implicitly that a single marine battalion landing team would not be able to root out enemy activity in the

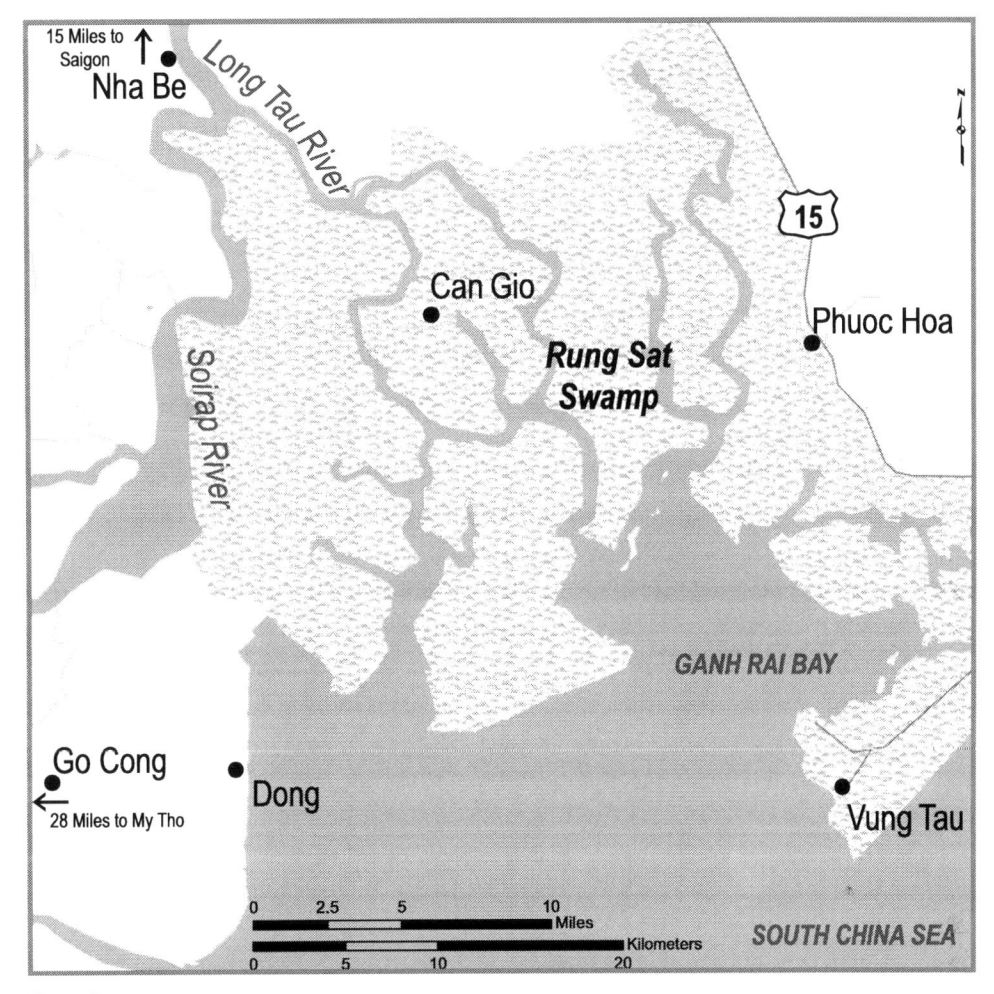

Rung Sat.

400 square miles of waterways, mangrove swamps, and Nipa Palm jungle of the RSSZ. At most, they hoped to disrupt Viet Cong operations and demonstrate that this vital Viet Cong rear area was no longer invulnerable to penetration.[32]

Three officers ran the operation. Captain John D. Westervelt commanded the amphibious task force (Amphibious Squadron One /Amphibious Ready Group); Captain John T. Shepherd, the Naval Advisory Group forces, including elements of TF 115; and Colonel J. R. Burnett, USMC, the Marine Special Landing Force. Phase 1 of the operation called for an amphibious assault on the Long Thanh Peninsula where much of the Rung Sat's population lived (5,000 of the estimated 15,000 people of the region). Once marines secured the peninsula and cut the Viet Cong off from potential support from the villages, Phase 2 would commence against suspected VC base areas deeper into the Rung Sat.[33]

The attack began on the morning of 26 March with a bombardment from *Robison* and aircraft from *Hancock*. A company-size force of marines then landed from surface craft near Dong Hoa on the western end of the peninsula. Two companies followed in helicopters, landing on the center and eastern end of the peninsula, respectively. Except for some sporadic sniper fire, no resistance was met. On one beach, marines discovered the body of a villager with a sign posted near it that read: "All soldiers: do not follow the U.S. Army. The booby traps are used to kill the Americans. The soldiers who kill U.S. Army love their country."[34] During the first night of operations, the marines established surveillance points in various parts of the swamp with 21 four–man reconnaissance teams. The Viet Cong lobbed grenades at one of the teams, killing two marines and instigating a brief firefight that killed three enemy troops.[35]

Because the PBRs were not yet available, Jackstay relied heavily on Market Time forces to prevent the reinforcement and resupply of Viet Cong forces by way of the rivers. Six PCFs and nine WPBs patrolled the major waterways, which included the Long Tau, the Dong Tranh, and the Soirap Rivers. Lieutenant (j.g.) James C. Thorell participated in the first of these patrols on the Soirap River on 26 and 27 March 1966 in command of PCF-31. It was his and his crew's first patrol in Vietnam, and they had been on the river for 30 hours of what should have been a 24-hour patrol when the enemy opened fire from both banks, about a mile inland from Can Gio on the Long Thanh Peninsula. The river was so narrow at the point of ambush that shrapnel from hand-thrown grenades hit the boat.

Thorell, a Naval Academy Class of 1963 graduate from Stuttgart, Arkansas, was stepping down from the pilothouse into the cabin at the start of the action to get a much-needed cup of coffee when his boat was hit. "When the fireworks went off," recalled Thorell, "the first thing I did was grab my M16 and fire a shot through an open window in the cabin. And the damn thing jammed. And I pulled back, slammed it to the ground and at that point a .50-caliber round went right through the window that I had been firing out of and clear through the boat." Thorell then noticed that Boatswain's Mate 2nd Class Robert P. Heinz Jr., who had been manning the con at the moment of the attack, was hit and lay slumped on the deck of the pilothouse. A .30-caliber round had penetrated Heinz's flak jacket, hit a rib, and lodged against his liver.

The boat was headed straight for the bank, so Thorell leapt into the pilothouse and with his left hand, swung the PCF so it was headed upriver. He applied the throttle, grabbed the radio, and in a calm Arkansas drawl, he reported his situation: "Lettuce, this is spinach. We are under heavy attack. Request immediate assistance." Meanwhile, Gunner's Mate 2nd Class Michael D. Crawford pounded away at the shoreline from the twin .50-caliber gun turret above the pilothouse, and a quick-thinking engineman second class named Alton R. Gunter moved to the stern to man the 81mm mortar. "Gunter was hit a couple of times on his helmet. He had a little shrapnel in both arms and some minor flesh wounds as well. He got knocked off his feet once and maybe twice on the way back to the mortar," explained Thorell. Gunter emptied the .50-caliber first and then started firing white phosphorus (WP) rounds from the 81mm mortar. Intense white smoke and burning flakes of phosphorus rained down on the enemy, finally silencing their guns. Although wounded by shrapnel, Gunter, a 25-year-old sailor from Alabaster, Alabama, kept right on firing. "What I did was mostly instinctive," he later told a reporter. "I was so scared. I don't even remember reloading."

Thorell then turned his attentions to Heinz. "When I saw that Heinz had some very dark blood coming from his side, I got on the radio and within about 5–10 minutes I had a medevac helicopter on the way. I had to beach the boat on a sandbar so the helicopter could land. That probably saved Heinz's life." Heinz spent five months convalescing in a hospital and then volunteered to return to Vietnam. When his detailer asked him where he wished to serve, he responded, "I want to go back wherever Mr. Thorell is." A record–holding long-jump champion from his Naval Academy days, Thorell had never had a bullet fired at him in anger before the engagement, nor had he even patrolled a river in Vietnam, but through his calm actions that day, he saved his boat and spared Heinz from almost certain death. The boat maintenance staff at Cat Lo later counted 121 bullet holes in PCF-31's hull. Thorell recommended Gunter for a Silver Star but declined a combat decoration for himself, telling Commander Ismay, "I was just doing my job." The Navy later awarded Gunter a Silver Star. He was the first sailor to receive America's third highest decoration for gallantry during the war.[36]

Phase 2 of Jackstay began on the 28 March, first with an unopposed marine landing a mile and a half up the Soirap River, followed by a deeper thrust up the Vam Sat River three days later. Considered a vital supply route for the enemy, the Vam Sat linked a major Viet Cong headquarters complex deep in the interior of the Rung Sat to the Soirap River. To soften the area, aircraft from *Hancock* dropped over 15 tons of bombs and fired numerous rockets and 20mm rounds at suspected enemy positions along the river. Next, *Henry County* (LST-824) and *Washoe County* (LST-1165) laid down a barrage of 40mm and 3-inch fire. Finally, Marine Ontos self–propelled antitank vehicles stationed on the deck of *Henry County* fired 69 rounds at any Viet Cong who might be waiting to ambush the task force at the mouth of the river. Each Ontos (Greek for "The Thing") mounted six 106mm recoilless rifles, each capable of firing "beehive" rounds packed full of small steel darts known as flechettes. One beehive could turn any human within a 50-foot radius of impact into ground meat. It was a truly devastating weapon.[37]

Beginning at dawn on the 31st, a 24-boat armada consisting of U.S Navy landing craft filled with marines and augmented by VNN river assault boats wound its way up the Vam Sat. Overhead, Army helicopters provided reconnaissance and air support. Like the other Jackstay landings, little resistance was encountered. The Viet Cong detonated a mine near the convoy about 1.5 miles from the Soirap and then opened up with small arms fire, but no one was injured and no boats damaged. The convoy responded with 40mm from a monitor and machine guns from other boats. Marines also joined fray, coming out of the well decks of the LCMs and opening fire with small arms. The convoy offloaded two companies of marines along both sides of the Ba Giong River at 0930. After a two-hour search, the marines discovered an arms-manufacturing facility, along with 18 carbines and 1,000 grenades.[38]

LCMs during Operation Jackstay, March 1966.

The Vam Sat operation was the first of four major river penetrations of the Rung Sat by allied forces. Like the 31 March operation, several of the other landings uncovered enemy base areas and supplies, but none encountered serious resistance. When Jackstay concluded on 6 April, the final enemy body count stood at 63 killed in action.[39] During the two-week operation, aircraft from *Hancock* and later *Kitty Hawk* flew 410 attack sorties, *Robison* expended 1,633 rounds of 5-inch naval gunfire, and *Washoe County* and *Henry County* supported marine landings with over 5,231 rounds from their 3-inch and 40mm guns. Army helicopters, Air Force B-52, and riverine craft pulverized the area with additional ordnance. Marines on the ground destroyed several important enemy facilities, including arms factories, training camps, a headquarters complex, and a hospital. The hospital complex alone contained 25 buildings. All the buildings were connected by raised log walkways.[40] Large amounts of rice and supplies were also captured, including 60,000 rounds of ammunition and 300 pounds of gunpowder. As Captain Westervelt reported in a press release on the operation, "The size of the VC installations suggests that they were used as a base for support of operations elsewhere in-country in addition to activities in the Rung Sat. The destruction of these facilities certainly reduced the immediate VC war making potential."[41] True to Westervelt's words, Viet Cong activity in the Rung Sat did indeed wane after Jackstay and continued to decline after Game Warden patrols were implemented on 10 April 1966, although no amount of patrolling could end the mine threat on the Long Tau or completely eradicate VC activity on the rivers.

Like the ubiquitous water hyacinth (*Eichhornia crassipes*) that floated on the waterways and clogged the engine intakes of river craft, the Viet Cong infestation in the area would not be easily eradicated.

Jackstay was the first full-scale U.S. amphibious operation of the Vietnam War carried out in a river delta and the most southerly marine landing of the war. The operation also tested many concepts that would become standard for U.S. forces as the war progressed—namely river assaults, river patrol, and the integration of airpower, ground power, and naval power in a riverine environment. The operation proved that with a reasonable investment in technology and firepower, the Navy could challenge the enemy's control of the rivers of South Vietnam, at least temporarily. PCFs and LCPLs of the blockading force probed all the large rivers in the RSSZ with some going as far as Nha Be. They operated 24 hours a day and almost certainly prevented the enemy from making crossings and transits and laying mines. The use of Army UH-1s in the operation revealed that helicopters could operate from LSTs and provide near-constant air cover for river patrols operating deep in the jungle. Eventually the Navy would form its own light helicopter attack squadron (HAL-3) to operate with the river forces. The Navy also would develop a river assault force later in 1966 to conduct search and destroy operations with ground troops in the delta. Like the Vam Sat convoy, the new Mobile Riverine Force (MRF) would contain a variety of troop carriers, along with monitors, command vessels, and support boats.

As in any difficult test, Jackstay also exposed some of the challenges that lie ahead. Extreme heat, dampness, and humidity, for example, proved as much of a hazard as enemy bullets. In all, the marines tallied 55 cases of heat prostration, 35 of immersion foot, and 25 of cellulitis during the operation.[42] By comparison, Viet Cong weapons only killed five Americans and wounded 31.[43] Another shortcoming was the vulnerability of some of the river patrol boats, especially the slow ones, to enemy fire. The relatively slow-moving LCPLs came under fire 17 times during Jackstay and, if it were not for the skillful handling of their crews and the constant presence of naval gunfire support from *Robison,* several of these slow-moving 36-footers would certainly have been lost. The faster Swift boats proved less vulnerable, but their deeper draft meant that they could not penetrate every waterway. *Belle Grove* contained 30 new PBRs, but the new crews did not have enough experience to participate directly in Jackstay, although some did take orientation patrols on Swift boats. As they cruised up the rivers of the RSSZ, these men would take comfort in the Navy's choice for a new river patrol craft—a choice that put a premium on shallow draft and speed. On the delta rivers speed was life, and in this regard the new PBR would not disappoint. *Belle Grove* delivered the first 11 PBRs to Vung Tau, South Vietnam in February 1966 and, after a testing and shakedown period lasting until mid-April, the PBRs began patrolling the Long Tau River as part of River Patrol Section 541. By July 1966, 72 PBRs were operating in South Vietnam throughout the Rung Sat and Mekong Delta from afloat and land bases, including Nha Be, Cat Lo, My Tho, and Binh Thuy (near Can Tho).[44]

Belle Grove (LSD-2).

The PBR Story

The PBR's life began at Hatteras Yacht Company in New Bern, North Carolina, in the spring 1965. Responding to a request for a 30-foot patrol boat, Hatteras' president, Willis Slane, proposed a 28-foot fiberglass hull powered by water-jet pumps. Water jets would allow the new boat to operate in extremely shallow water. Enthusiastic about the proposal, the Bureau of Ships asked for a prototype. Slane, who had flown transports over the Hump for the Army Air Forces during World War II, gave it his all. Working 24-hour days, his team of builders and suppliers produced a working prototype in just two weeks. Powered by jet pumps manufactured by Indiana Gear Works and fitted with a wooden deck and a speedboat style windshield, the boat achieved speeds of up to 30.5 knots. Sadly, Mr. Slane did not live to see his creation showcased. The night before the demonstration, he died of a heart attack. Sarah Phillips, a long-time employee, had warned her boss to slow down, but Slane, who suffered from diabetes, ignored these warnings, ultimately working himself to death to transform his vision into a working prototype.[45]

Impressed with his boat, the Navy asked for bids for a patrol boat similar to Slane's beloved prototype. The boats had to achieve speeds of 25 to 30 knots, draw just nine inches of water while cruising, and accommodate a crew of four along with extensive equipment and weaponry, including a twin .50-caliber machine gun in an armored turret forward and a .30-caliber gun (later replaced by a .50-caliber) aft. Making matters even more challenging for the vender, the Navy requested 120 boats in less than six months. United Boatbuilders of Bellingham, Washington, won the contract with the lowest bid. Unlike Hatteras, which was primarily a builder of recreational boats, United had extensive experience working with the Navy, having previously

A Uniflight pleasure craft and a PBR steam side by side. Both boats shared the same 31-foot fiberglass hull and were constructed in Bellingham, Washington. The PBR typified the ability of American manufacturers of the period to quickly develop specialized equipment for the military based on off-the-shelf technology.

built boats ranging from 15 to 52 feet under Navy contract. The eventual Mark I design incorporated United's 31-foot fiberglass cruiser hull along with a completely new, Navy-designed superstructure. Twin General Motors' 216-horsepower diesel engines powered the boat's water-jet propulsion system, and Raytheon Pathfinder 1900N radar provided enhanced navigation and target acquisition capability. Fully loaded, the boat weighed 14,600 pounds and could reach speeds of up to 25.7 knots—slower than the Hatteras prototype but within the Navy's specifications for a 25–30-knot boat. The original boats cost $75,000 each ($547,000 in 2014 dollars).[46]

The beauty of the PBR design was its innovative application of off-the-shelf technology to a military role. The commercially manufactured Styrofoam-filled fiberglass hull, for example, would prove remarkably durable in combat. Unlike metal, it did not rust or corrode and was strong enough to withstand beaching. It was also relatively easy to repair. But most remarkable, shaped warheads often failed to trigger on the hulls: lacking a solid target to detonate, they tended to penetrate and exit the boat's hull without exploding.[47]

The PBR's jet propulsion system allowed the boat to travel on virtually any waterway in the delta and perform maneuvers impossible for the traditional, propeller-driven boats. A PBR could run over a sandbar or beach itself on dry land without damaging the propulsion system and could stop or turn 180 degrees in its own length.[48] Lieutenant Peter A. Huchthausen, a PBR officer in charge based in My Tho, developed a begrudging respect for the boat's newfangled capabilities during training at Mare Island, California. "A PBR handled so well at high-speed that the slightest touch of the helm caused immediate and violent reaction. At slow speeds it was an obstinate beast. Successfully handling the PBR at lower speeds required the coxswain to

This late-model Mark I boat (PBR-130) on the trailer features four finned underwater exhaust pipes for quiet running and two water jet nozzles with gates, shown here in the up position for forward motion. If they were in the down position, covering the nozzle discharge opening, the closed gate would cause water to shoot under the boat, resulting in reversing the boat's motion.

turn the helm exactly the opposite than would be done on a normal boat because of the reverse effect of the nozzles.... Nevertheless, the ardent small-craft handler could learn in short order to set these bundles of energy smartly alongside a pier, even against the strong river current."[49] One of Seaman Jerry Hammel's favorite tricks to play with his PBR was to spin it around on a single axis like a top. "You could hurt somebody if you did not tell them ahead of time what you were going to do. You could throw them off the boat."[50]

The PBR, though, was not immune to problems. Fully loaded, the Mark I PBR ultimately drew one foot 10.5 inches of water—far more than the nine inches planners had originally requested. The Mark I boats deployed to Vietnam never attained the trial speed of 25 knots. The GM engines, almost uniformly, could not reach speeds greater than 2600–2650rpm (rotations per minute) compared with the trial speed of 2700rpm. Many crews exacerbated the problem by carrying extra engine oil, water, and ammunition.[51] "The boats were way slower than advertised," lamented Fred McDavitt. "If a crew added a couple extra boxes of .50-cal ammo or carried the patrol officer and/ or a Vietnamese policeman, the boat could barely achieve speeds above 12 knots." At the heart of the PBR's shortfalls were the Jacuzzi pumps, which greatly reduced the efficiency of the GM engines—so much so that with screws instead of water jets, one Uniflight representative told Fred McDavitt, the boat probably would have achieved speeds in excess of 40 knots.[52]

To make the boats lighter, some crews removed engine covers and other unessential equipment. BM1 Williams often went out on patrol with just three-quarters of a tank of fuel and a minimum ammunition load, figuring that if his boat got into a real jam, the HAL-3 Seawolves could back him up with their helicopters' extra firepower. Engineman Fireman (ENFN) Clem Alderson, a young River Section 531 sailor from Washington State, increased the maximum speed of Williams' 105 boat and several others to 30 knots by shimming the governors of the engines so they could run as high as 3,200rpm as opposed to the 2,800 maximum rate set by the factory.[53] Alderson also grafted triangular shaped wedges to the underside of the hull about three quarters of the way aft so that at about 12 knots the boats would "jump" up on the step and achieve speeds up to 25 knots.[54] "Alderson had a surgeon's touch," explained McDavitt, "but no matter how fast your PBR could go, it couldn't outrun a bullet. Speed, such as it was at 30 knots, provided a false sense of security."[55]

Other problems with the Mark I models included drive shafts that did not stand up well to the rigors of Southeast Asia and fiberglass hulls that were easily damaged during sampan and junk searches.[56] The hulls also developed leaks from pinhole cracks, as well as bullet holes, which caused water to seep into the Styrofoam between the fiberglass layers and slow the boats down.[57] To rectify the problem, the boats had to be removed from the water and quarter-inch holes drilled in the keel to allow the water to drain. These holes, in turn, had to be patched with fiberglass.[58]

Finally, just about every PBR crew complained about the constant need to clean clogged jet pump intakes. The screen over the intake had sharp blades, which cut up most of the water hyacinth and other plants before they entered the pumps, but what little got through this filter

A river patrol boat (PBR) near Cat Lo, 13 April 1966.

could wreak havoc on the propulsion system. When an intake clogged during a high-speed run, the PBR would make an unexpected U-turn known as a "flying 180," occasionally sending equipment and crewmembers tumbling off the boat.[59] To prevent such mishaps, boat captains had their crews clean the intakes once or twice per patrol, depending on the amount of flotsam on the river. Seaman Jere Beery vividly remembered the unpleasant duty: "The intakes are on the bottom of the PBR and I would have to strip naked, jump in, go underneath the boat, and clean them." On occasion, a live snake would be caught in an intake. According to Lieutenant Robert P. Fuscaldo, "some of those snakes were pretty angry. We used to try and lift the cover off the pumps and push them out with a broom handle, but sometimes that didn't work and you had to go underneath and pull them out, so it was interesting."[60]

Despite these issues, the boat generally performed better than expected given how hastily they were procured. As one Naval Ship Systems Command report explained, the PBR "was not built to current U.S. Navy standards," nor was it subjected to an "adequate test and evaluation period." Not surprisingly, a few bugs arose once it deployed in combat, but most were resolved expeditiously in theater.[61] Author Tom Cutler, a veteran of the riverine forces, phrased it more eloquently: "Born in an atmosphere of urgency and tested under actual combat conditions, the PBR could have been a disaster. Instead, it proved to be a fierce little combatant that accomplished its mission."[62] More than anything else, the PBR demonstrated that off-the-shelf technology could be adapted for military use when circumstances demanded it.

In the blue-water oriented Navy of the Cold War, the PBR was a unique vessel in other ways as well. In contrast to the average *Essex*-class carrier of the period, with a crew of more than

2,600 men, the average PBR carried just four men: a boat captain, an engineman, a gunner's mate, and a seaman. Initially, boat captains were junior officers and chief petty officers, but as the war progressed, a select group of first- and second-class petty officers also was given the opportunity to command these boats. In no other Navy command or ship were enlisted sailors given so much responsibility. Every crewmember cross-trained to perform every role on the boat, and during combat everyone was a gunner. For enlisted men accustomed to performing highly specialized work on large ships, the jack-of-all-trades nature of the PBR experience made them feel like sailors of yesteryear, and the danger of the rivers led many to think of themselves as a an elite group—a status unofficially conferred by the black berets they adopted as part of their uniform. "It was a unique experience to be on a 31-foot boat in the middle of a country where everyone wanted to kill you," recalled Jere Beery. "You really develop a since of camaraderie." Beery's African-American shipmate, Seaman Harold Sherman, claimed many years later that it was the only assignment in his entire Navy career where he did not experience some form of racism.[63] McDavitt agreed that PBR service was unique but challenged its "elite" status. "A lot of people ended up in riverine warfare who had been 'volunteered' from other commands," he said. "We were no different from any other ship in the Navy."[64]

Patrols lasted up to 18 hours and covered distances of up to 35 miles from a base. For chow, sailors subsisted mainly on canned rations heated on the engine manifolds.[65] To liven up the menu, some crews purchased kerosene camp stoves to prepare seafood and vegetables purchased from the locals. Eating Vietnamese food, however, was not without risk. Bacteria on unwashed produce could easily send a sailor running to the stern of the boat to defecate. Signalman 2nd Class Roderick Davis of River Section 512 described this act, known as "hanging ten," as practically an Olympic event. "One had to step over the transom, drop trou, squat down on the flat stern board, hold on while hanging out, and finally, wipe while holding on precariously with one hand. Thence step back inboard. It took courage, skill, and balance and you could get points at the end of the exercise for a good dismount."[66] For the PBR sailor, privacy was the first casualty of war.

PBRs generally patrolled in two-boat sections. The main mission of the patrols during the day was inspecting river craft for contraband and checking IDs. One PBR would approach a contact at an angle, which allowed all weapons to concentrate on the target, and the crew would conduct the search while the other PBR stood at a distance to provide cover. All searches were to be conducted midstream as far from the shoreline as possible. Between 2100 and 0600, the patrols enforced night curfews and on occasion ambushed Viet Cong river crossings. Interdiction, in short, was the major objective of Task Force 116. The February 1966 Game Warden Operation Order stated that PBRs would not participate in shore assaults with the VNN River Force, nor would they normally conduct patrols in waterways and canals off the major rivers. If ambushed from the shore, the operation order advised PBRs to make a speedy withdrawal. "River Patrol Force Boats," it noted, "are not designed, armed, or armored to stand and fight against superior firepower in the manner of VNN RAG craft." Air strikes or artillery support could always be called in against the target following a tactical withdrawal.[67]

Stern view of a PBR searching a sampan.

The initial rules of engagement as promulgated in the February 1966 operation order allowed PBRs to stop any South Vietnam–flagged vessel (or one with no flag) to demand identification or search the vessel. Since PBRs did not have time to search every sampan and junk on a river, they often randomly chose their quarry. If a sampan failed to heed orders to come to, warning shots could be fired, but a sampan could not be engaged directly until its occupants fired first on the PBR. The staff officers who devised the operation order understood the counterinsurgency nature of the Game Warden mission and wanted to avoid alienating the local populace through the use of excessive force.[68] Nevertheless, the inherent conservatism of these rules of engagement often put the PBR crews at a distinct disadvantage in combat. As Peter Huchthausen wrote, they "gave the enemy the luxury of choosing when and where to engage," and whittled away "our advantage in firepower . . . to an easy parity with the Viet Cong."[69]

Bored with the endless searches of sampans and junks, some PBR sailors sought out firefights either by setting up night ambushes or by venturing up some of the smaller rivers and canals in the delta. Signalman 1st Class Chester B. Smith, a boat captain and patrol officer with River Section 531, explicitly favored night patrols because of the curfew. "We had full authority on the river after sunset," he said in an interview. "If we saw something moving, we could go after it. You could not necessarily shoot them, but you could go after them because they were fair game. The philosophy was that if you could get them in a compromising situation, they would want to shoot. If they did, we could then return fire. There was nothing there that could outrun us unless they had a tremendous jump on us."[70] On occasion, this type of aggressiveness led to spectacular successes, but tragedies also occurred when some patrol officers were too bold. On large rivers the PBR's maneuverability and firepower made them difficult targets, but in narrow canals or near the shore, the advantage rapidly shifted to the enemy. As critical as some sailors were of the TF 116 Operation Order, it was designed to minimize risk and maximize the impact of the River Patrol in stopping infiltration.

Basing and Base Life

Unlike blue water warships, which are essentially self-contained villages at sea, PBRs required extensive bases for berthing, messing, and other personnel services for its sailors, as well as maintenance and logistics support for the boats. As originally conceived, Game Warden was allocated eight shore bases and three LST floating bases. The LSTs were to be stationed at key river mouths, and the shore bases were established at the following locations: Cat Lo, Chau Doc, Binh Thuy (Can Tho), Long Xuyen, My Tho, Nha Be, Sa Dec, Tan Chau, and Vinh Long. During the early days of the operation, the LSTs provided the best basing solution for the force, but as the shore bases developed better facilities, fixed bases became more desirable.

In 1966 the Navy brought four World War II–era LSTs—*Jennings County* (LST-846), *Harnett County* (LST-821), *Garrett County* (LST-786), and *Hunterdon County* (LST-838)—out of mothballs and modified them for brown water operations. The Pacific Repair Shop increased the communications suite of *Jennings County* fourfold by building an entirely new level to the superstructure. It also added a ten–ton cargo boom for handling PBRs, a helicopter landing area with lighting for night operations, and 18 new air-conditioning units to make the ship more habitable in the hot Southeast Asia weather. Dockworkers sandblasted and recoated the ship's entire exterior, including the underwater sections, overhauled the engineering plant, and completely modernized the galley, mess decks, and laundry facilities. Built during World War II by the American Bridge Company in Ambridge, Pennsylvania, and named after Jennings County, Indiana, this venerable old LST was completely transformed from a rust bucket to a modern sea base in a little over six months. Recommissioned on 11 June 1966 in San Francisco, she became the first ship specifically configured for PBR support missions to join the fleet.[71]

Commander Don Sheppard, who served on various LSTs as the commander of River Division 51 in 1967, had fond memories: "The air-conditioned interior of the "T" and its routine happenings, such as the sounding of bells to indicate the half hours and the boatswain's pipe call for reports, and for sweepers [clean-up] and for meals, were pleasant to hear. This, with the myriad of other things that denoted life on a U.S. ship were a tonic to me." But he also recognized that these 328-foot-long ships could get pretty busy carrying a full crew complement of 111 sailors plus the PBR and helicopter crews and maintenance personnel. "No one slept easily or very often," he added. "The boats were coming and going at all hours of the day and night.

Harnett County (LST-821) with PBRs tied to it.

The noisy take-offs and landings of the two-helo gunships shattered the silence. Meals were available at all hours. The PBRs were always under repair, being gingerly lifted by crane in and out of the well decks."[72]

While the LSTs were being modernized in the United States, other ships filled in as Game Warden support ships, including the landing ship docks *Belle Grove* (LSD-2), *Comstock* (LSD-19), and *Tortuga* (LSD-26). *Tortuga*, named for a group of desert islands 60 miles west of Key West, commenced Game Warden operations in April 1966. Not only did she provide basing for ten PBRs of River Section 512 and two UH-1B helicopters from the Army's 145th Aviation Battalion, but she also engaged in search and rescue and even in civic action missions. On 26 June 1966 she coordinated a sea and air rescue mission on a stormy night for the crew of a Coastal Force junk that sank in heavy seas off the Mekong Delta. As part of Project Handclasp, *Tortuga* delivered soap, toothbrushes, toothpaste, food, medical supplies, fishing gear, and candy (for children) directly to villages in the delta.[73]

Because Game Warden LSTs often possessed more firepower than most other friendly units in their area of operation, these ships soon became a vital source of gunfire support. When friendly units discovered that *Hunterdon County* had eight 40mm naval guns, for example, she started to receive all sorts of requests for naval gunfire. During the month of July 1967, she fired 200 rounds of 40mm into an area where a helicopter had reported fire, and another 430 rounds during a combined operation against a Viet Cong training site.[74] Overall, between November 1966 and September 1968, the four Game Warden LSTs, in addition to originating nearly 6,400 PBR patrols and conducting over 11,000 helicopter launches and recoveries, engaged in 475 separate naval gunfire support missions.[75]

As capable as the modernized LSTs were as motherships, shore bases eventually became the preferred basing solution for the PBRs. In 1967 Commander Sayre A. Swartztrauber, the commander of River Squadron 5 described the differences: "LSTs were overcrowded to begin with, having been outfitted with just about everything one could fit into a ship with little room for berthing, stowage, or repair facilities. The bases ashore, on the other hand, had room to develop and expand—for workshops, for stowage, and for creature comforts."[76]

Shore bases also put the PBR sailors in closer proximity to the Vietnamese people. For a select few, this intimacy allowed them to improve their Vietnamese language skills, develop friendships, and gain a better understanding of the local area in which they fought. Others never left the base. Most, however, enjoyed the opportunity to eat a meal at a local restaurant, drink a Number 33 beer, have a uniform altered by a Vietnamese tailor, or just escape from the pressures of war by soaking in the fabric of daily life—the sights and smells of the local marketplace, fishermen mending their nets, or young women bicycling in their fashionable ao dais. Seaman Jerry Hammel, who served half his tour on *Hunterdon County* and the other half at My Tho, explained the situation this way. "I preferred My Tho because I liked to come in at night, go downtown and hang out and try to lead some type of normal life. I was bored on the ship."[77]

Game Warden established its first land bases at Cat Lo and Nha Be bordering the RSSZ; My Tho on the My Tho River; Vinh Long on the Co Chien; Long Xuyen and Binh Thuy (Can Tho) on the Bassac; and Sa Dec on the upper My Tho. The locations were chosen partly because Vietnamese naval and military forces already had preexisting facilities at each of them. All but Sa Dec contained a Vietnamese river assault group. Strategically, the bases, along with LSTs stationed at river mouths, provided excellent coverage of the central and northern delta and RSSZ, and each one could be easily reached by air or water, thereby simplifying logistics.[78] However, there were no bases in the deep southern delta around Ca Mau and in the upper delta along the Cambodian border during this period. Service Force, U.S. Pacific Fleet (SERVPAC) built and operated the shore facilities for the brown water Navy and administered them via subordinate units known as Naval Support Activity detachments.

At some bases, sailors lived in local hotels rented out by the Navy to serve as makeshift barracks. Bearing some resemblance to the hotel where the prostitute Sadie Thompson entertained sailors on the island of Pago Pago in the 1928 film *Sadie Thompson*, the Hotel Kin Tinh served as the enlisted barracks for PBRs stationed at Long Xuyen on the Bassac River. The hotel contained bedrooms with large windows and balconies, a dining facility, and a club that showed movies every other night. Established in July 1966, Long Xuyen emerged as the largest PBR base in March 1967, and bristled with first-rate facilities, including a villa for officers' quarters, an administrative building, an armory, a boat repair shop, an electronics shop, and a supply warehouse. Ironically, the 20 PBRs stationed here did not achieve enough contacts with the enemy to justify the facility, and just one month later in April 1967 SERVPAC disestablished the base and transferred most of its assets to Tan Chau.[79]

While living conditions at some of the Navy's inshore facilities in the delta were comfortable, most were quite primitive. Sa Dec started out as a tent city on the edge of a soccer field until the Seabees could erect screened- and louvered-walled tropical barracks called hootches.[80] Lieutenant Fuscaldo, who was based at Sa Dec in early 1967, remembered Seabees dumping truckload after truckload of gravel onto the soccer field to shore up the ground. He also had fond memories of drinking Pabst Blue Ribbon beer at the club and eating locally baked bread. "We had a Vietnamese baker who had worked for the French ambassador who made the most incredible bread you have ever had in your life. Army observation pilots would land on the road there just to eat some of this bread."[81]

The base at Nha Be presented the Service Force with some its biggest challenges. Located in a swampy area ten miles southeast of Saigon where the Long Tau River joins the Soirap in the RSSZ, Nha Be had no available real estate in early 1966. Support facilities initially had to be crammed into the VNN RAG base there, compelling sailors to live in a tent city constructed in an area prone to flooding. Rather than complain, the men adapted to their soggy environs by building raised floors for the tents and walkways with dunnage scavenged from supply ships. Vice Admiral Edwin B. Hooper, the commander of Service Force U. S. Pacific Fleet, visited the facility in 1966 and left thoroughly impressed by the morale of sailors there. "The more severe the sacrifices, the prouder the men seemed to be of their performance."[82]

Sa Dec PBR base, 10 February 1967.

Nha Be base, 1968.

The Navy eventually secured a site for a permanent base in May 1966 on a point of land near the RAG base, and an extensive reclamation process was begun to transform the marshy peninsula into a viable base. Dredging and filling in the area took seven months, and construction, another seven. When completed in the summer of 1967, Nha Be supported over 500 Navy personnel and contained five enlisted and officers' quarters, a mess hall, maintenance and repair shops, three 1,000-barrel fuel tanks, an administrative building, a communications space, warehouses, and a small boat pier. Yet problems existed there for the remainder of the war. Potable water had to be shipped in by truck and barged from Saigon after an attempt to dig a deepwater well hit rock at 485 feet.[83]

One of the greatest advantages of dry land bases over floating ones was the opportunity for PBR sailors to interact with local people. Unlike many U.S. Army bases in Vietnam, which were built far from surrounding communities in highly fortified compounds, Navy inshore bases often formed an integral part of the Vietnamese towns. All that separated the My Tho base from the town was an 8-foot concrete wall topped by barbed wire. Sailors leaving the compound were a short stroll away from shopping and restaurants in the heart of the town. Lieutenant (j.g.) John J. Donovan Jr., a patrol officer at My Tho from Milton, Massachusetts,

Lieutenant (j.g.) John J. Donovan Jr., a patrol officer with River Section 531, with two unidentified South Vietnamese personnel.

enjoyed immersing himself in the Vietnamese culture there. He used to eat at local restaurants regularly with his Vietnamese interpreter, Nguyen Minh, who would also introduce him to local women. "I received a lot of intelligence from Minh and other Vietnamese friends that I never got when I was stationed on an LST." One night, he was walking down a street with Minh, who told him not to stare at five Vietnamese men of military age hanging out on a street corner. "They are VC," he said. Apparently up until the Tet Offensive, My Tho also served as a Viet Cong rest and relaxation (R&R) center.[84] Jerry Hammel took no chances when going into My Tho at night. "We had to always watch our back. I carried a Thompson Machine Gun, plus my M16, plus a .45 . . . like American Express, you never leave home without 'em."[85]

Fred McDavitt taught English to Vietnamese during his off-hours. "It all began when the director of public safety in My Tho told me there were people in town interested in learning English and learning about America." McDavitt held his firsts classes in a thatched roof hut. "Whenever it rained, we had to hold an umbrella over the blackboard." Eventually, he raised enough money to build a brick building with a tin roof. He also enlisted other My Tho–based sailors, including Jim Howell, Charlie Varelas, and Don Witt, as teachers. By the end of his tour, he had mentored over 125 Vietnamese in rudimentary English. Fighting and teaching left McDavitt with little time to himself, but it was worth it. He found the experience personally rewarding and believed that it helped convince many locals of the value of the Navy mission at My Tho.[86]

Lieutenant Fuscaldo, the officer in charge of River Division 532 based at My Tho from October 1967 to June of 1968, actively encouraged his men to form friendships with the Vietnamese. "We always tried to get to know the Vietnamese and treat them with respect. It was not totally

Signalmen 2nd Class Roderick C. Davis volunteered for three consecutive tours in Vietnam in various PBR assignments from 1966 to 1968 and a fourth tour as a naval advisor in 1969. He was one of the few Game Warden sailors to develop some fluency in the Vietnamese language.

altruistic. That way they were not always against you and a lot of times they would help you. The number of times a river person would tell us not to go someplace because the VC had set up an ambush was amazing." One of Fuscaldo's chief links to the Vietnamese was Signalman 1st Class Roderick C. Davis, who used to walk around My Tho talking to any Vietnamese who would listen to him. Gradually through hard work and dogged determination, this 23-year-old from Virginia Beach learned enough Vietnamese to become proficient as an interpreter. "Unlike some of the Vietnamese interpreters, Davis knew exactly the point I was trying to convey to locals," explained Fuscaldo.[87] Davis also gained a lot of inside information from the Vietnamese with whom he socialized in town. "I got good intel from a friend who owned a local tailor shop." For a time he also dated the madam of one of the local bordellos. "I was 23 and she was in her mid-30s. Rumor had it that her husband was out with the VC and hadn't been back for years. I said to myself, 'Good, that's another way I will get 'em.'" After the war he returned to My Tho and tracked down his old flame. He was shocked at what he discovered. In a small, decrepit apartment stood a bald, older woman, with few teeth, whom he barely recognized. The woman proudly displayed six certificates from the Communist Party praising her work during the war. Apparently, Davis' main intelligence source had been a double agent.[88]

Davis was not the only one to get involved with prostitutes in My Tho. Seaman Jerry Hammel, another My Tho–based sailor, also admitted to seeing local women. "I had a girlfriend. She was a bar girl. We all had girlfriends. We got some intelligence from the girls, as well as from the mama-sans."[89] Fuscaldo allowed his men to have Vietnamese girlfriends up to a point. "I did not want it to get too destructive."[90]

Like prostitution, booze was another temptation for sailors living ashore. "We had a lot of problems with alcohol," claimed Donovan. "Crews on the cover boats, which sort of hung out while the lead boat searched craft, could get away with drinking on patrol. It was not uncommon for these guys to take beers and other alcoholic beverages out on patrol. I had petty officers reporting with alcohol on their breaths, and some guys had to be turned back because they were drunk. I did my best to try and cover up for these guys, who were senior petty officers, and get them out of there. They just couldn't handle the combat stress."[91] Engineman 3rd Class Rodney Dean "Weasel" Morgan of River Section 532 also complained about alcohol use by his shipmates, especially higher rank enlisted. "At the time it was pretty hard to be in the Navy and not drink to excess. If you got above an E-5 and you were not an alcoholic, something was wrong. On my boat [PBR-144] anyone showing up for patrol drunk was given a corner of the boat to sleep it off. I always hoped that the miscreant would get badly sunburned as punishment for his irresponsibility. Drunkenness was a real pain in the ass."[92]

Jere Beery, a sailor with River Section 511, enjoyed playing his guitar and drinking at a local bar in Binh Thuy. "It was a lenient environment, and we had our share of drinkers, but as long as you did not get belligerent and violent or cause a problem you could get as drunk as you wanted."[93] In an era of the three-martini lunch, the notion of drinking a few beers every day after duty did not represent aberrant behavior. "Alcohol was cheap, but I don't remember it being a problem," recalled Engineman 3rd Class Steve Watson, who also served at Binh Thuy. "I drank my fair share of it but certainly did not go out on patrol drunk. It would be suicidal to do that."[94] Lieutenant Lowell Webb, the officer in charge of River Section 532 from April through September 1967, concurred. During his time there most of the drinking was kept within the compound at an all-hands club. "The club just had beer and no hard liquor. I don't recall alcoholism being a problem with the crews."[95] Radioman 1st Class Frank R. Spatt admitted that some of the sailors in River Section 531 drank a lot, but most avoided alcohol if they had a patrol the next day. "When you came back from patrol, you were dog tired," he explained. "After you did your debrief and updated your charts, cleaned the boat and the guns, you hit that crappy little half salt/half fresh water shower and then hit the rack."[96] Alcohol consumption, in short, varied from one individual to the next but did not generally pose a problem during patrols. For those with a fondness for drink, however, easy access to cheap booze, both in towns and on bases, combined with the stresses of war could transform a social drinker into an alcoholic during the course of a deployment. Officers, for the most part, turned a blind eye to the issue unless a sailor turned up drunk for a mission.

YRBM-16 Mining

YRBM-16 was a former 261-foot-long lighter *YFNB-21* converted into a repair, berthing, and messing barge (non-self-propelled) in the spring of 1967 and assigned to Vietnam as a Game Warden support vessel. It contained four diesel generators for power but had no propulsion system and had to be towed from one location to the next by a tugboat. *YRBM-16* could support up to 300 Naval Support Activity and Game Warden sailors along with 21 PBRs. It contained a state of the art tactical operations center as well as maintenance shops, berthing areas, a large sick bay, a laundry facility, a barber shop, radio room, and messes—all the services of a decent-size shore base.[97] Lieutenant Edwin "Larry" Oswald, who served on the YRBM as a Naval Support Activity supply officer, described it as a "destroyer tender" for small boats. Its maintenance facilities and machine shop could perform extensive maintenance on the boats while the crews enjoyed hot showers, home-cooked meals, and air-conditioned sleeping quarters.[98] The barge's water purification system could produce over 15,000 gallons of fresh water a day, allowing sailors to take showers any time they wished with no time limits imposed for hot water.[99]

The Navy employed several repair, berthing, and messing barges during the course of the war, including *YRBM-16*, which was mined on Thanksgiving evening, 1967. This image shows *YRBM-21*, a Game Warden support vessel.

Not surprisingly, many sailors loved the barge. "Off-patrol routine on the *YRBM-16* was the easy life," wrote Lieutenant Wynn A. Goldsmith of River Section 534 in his memoir. "Air-conditioned sleeping quarters and a more comfortable rack than I'd had aboard the minesweeper. Good Navy chow served in a wardroom setting, complete with individualized napkin rings for the white linen napkins. Movies in the wardroom after evening chow with plenty of fresh coffee." Goldsmith particularly appreciated the "beer barge." Alcohol was forbidden on U.S. Navy ships, but the YRBM got around this regulation by allowing the crew to drink beer with an alcohol content of 3.2 percent on the pontoon platform (AMMI barge) used for loading and unloading PBRs. According to Goldsmith and several others interviewed, "On Sunday afternoons steaks and lobster tails were grilled outside. Beer drinkers like me could then feast while downing suds and listening to good ol' rock 'n' roll music in the waning tropical skies. If you could forget about the war all around you, you could really savor the fact that it was a great life in the tropics."[100]

Security for the barge consisted of four 81mm mortars and twelve .50-caliber machine guns. At all times sentries, armed with M14 rifles, manned watch stations fore and aft, looking for anything suspicious moving along the river. "We got pretty good with those weapons," explained Electronics Technician (Radar) 3rd Class John Hendrickson, "If you even saw a coconut floating on the river, you shot at it."[101] When the YRBM arrived in-country, these watchstanders would lob concussion grenades into the river at irregular intervals to deter swimmers but the practice was soon abandoned by the commanding officer, Lieutenant Commander Villard Blevins Jr. A prior enlisted sailor from Washington State, Blevins decided to halt the practice because several officers complained that the grenade explosions reverberating off the hull were preventing them from getting any rest.[102] At YRBM's first base, Tan Chau, mine netting was installed around the ship as an added security measure, but when the barge was moved to Ben Tre, no netting was employed. At the junction of the Ben Tre Canal, the Ham Luong River is over a mile wide with swift currents. A ship anchored in the middle of the river at this spot, Blevins believed, should have been relatively safe from a swimmer attack.

What neither Blevins nor higher-ups in Saigon anticipated was an attack by frogmen with skills equivalent to Navy UDTs. During the war the Navy trained VNN frogmen, known as the LDNN, at Coronado, and several crewmembers suspected that it was one of those guys who blew up the ship. "We knew that because of where the charges were placed, where they were in relation to the waterline, and so forth," claimed Lieutenant Oswald, who helped oversee *YRBM-16*'s overhaul in Japan after the attack. "Whoever did this was damned good. These mines had been placed with tremendous precision."[103] A search party from the 7th ARVN Division later found 500 meters of electrical wire, rubber floats, and two vehicle batteries near the site of the mining. Intelligence sources revealed that the sappers, along with a company of Viet Cong, had moved into the area on 23 November 1967. Several local civilians ostensibly "friendly" to the government of South Vietnam saw the special unit but did not inform the government or U.S. forces because the Viet Cong threatened to behead any who left their houses.[104]

On Thanksgiving night the *YRBM-16* mess went all out to produce a quality holiday meal. That night's menu featured shrimp cocktail, cream of tomato soup, fresh salad, baked ham, roasted tom turkey, cornbread oyster dressing, corn O'Brien, yams, green peas with mushrooms, homemade rolls, pumpkin pie, mincemeat pie, and fruit cake. "We had a great Thanksgiving dinner," recalled Communications Yeoman (CYN) 3rd Class Jerome "Jerry" Wojciechowski, "It was the whole nine yards. A lot of guys, especially PBR sailors, went to the beer barge and got blasted afterwards, but I had to stand midwatch, so I refrained."[105] Gunner's Mate (Guns) 3rd Class Joseph Slavish and Electronics Technician Radar (ETR) 3rd Class Hendrickson also confirmed that several PBR guys got "blasted."[106]

Satiated by the special meal and in some cases inebriated from alcohol, most of the crew had long since retired for the night when the attack occurred at 0115 on 24 November 1967.[107] At that moment, a water mine exploded, creating a gaping 18-by-17-by-9-foot hole in the ship's hull below the waterline on the starboard side abreast the mast. The blast penetrated parts of a fuel tank, the ship's engineering space, and a berthing area for enlisted sailors. Fire fed by fuel from the ruptured tank aided by the explosion of acetylene bottles quickly gutted the engineering and nearby shop spaces. The explosion also buckled the after portion of the superstructure deck, completely destroying PBR-116, which was atop the superstructure for repairs. Immediately after the explosion, water began pouring into the berthing area, and several other compartments and the stern of the ship began sinking, eventually settling nine feet into the river until she became buoyant.[108]

CYN3 Wojciechowski was sitting in the radio room when the blast occurred. "I was rocking back in my chair by the radio consul when the whole ship lifted up out of the water and then settled back down again. I fell over backwards. I knew right off the bat that it was not a good thing. I sounded general quarters with the horn and then reported the attack to the MACV compound at Ben Tre."[109]

Hendrickson was sleeping in the crew berthing space when the event occurred. "The next thing I know I was on the deck [floor] with four sailors on top of me." Hendrickson quickly put on a pair of dungarees and headed to the mess deck. Thinking it was a mortar attack he grabbed his flak jacket and an 81mm mortar round and tried to take it to one of the guns. When he got to the O-1 level, the deck was so slick with diesel fuel and oil that he tripped and fell on his back. "No telling where the mortar round went." Hendrickson eventually evacuated to Dong Tam by a Mike boat. "That was the longest ride of my life. I thought we were going to get it at any minute. The Army was real good to us giving us smokes, drinks, etc., and I recall staying there until dawn."[110]

Ensign Dick Strandberg, an officer with River Section 522, was in the officers' bunk space forward on the ship when the mining occurred. "The explosion blew us out of our racks. Smoke filled the rooms and passageways." Strandberg and other officers in those spaces made their way topside and immediately noticed flames shooting high into the sky from the area near the blast aft of the ship. "A whole crowd of us ended up slipping our way down one of the ramps to a Mike boat. That's how we survived." Other River Section 522 sailors made it to the mess deck, where they evacuated on PBRs. Others were not so lucky. Some of the interior space nearest the blast site served as the River Section 522 enlisted berthing area. The blast caused an air-conditioning duct to break loose and block a ladder leading out of the area. One sailor became trapped under the duct and died. Others drowned because they could not get around the obstruction before water flooded the compartment. Some sailors never woke up because they were so inebriated from the festivities of the night before. "They passed out at night and the next day they were in heaven," explained Wojciechowski, who would have been sleeping in that compartment had he not been standing radio watch.[111] In all, five PBR sailors from that berthing area died in the attack.[112]

Another sailor who died was Electronic Technician (Communications) 3rd Class Robert Lyndon Gray from the ship's company. When the general quarters sounded, Gray immediately went to his battle station on the crow's nest—a lookout 40–50 feet above the waterline atop the main mast used mainly for artillery spotting. Smoke from the burning diesel tanks soon enveloped the tower, making life very uncomfortable for Gray. At one point, he attempted to contact the officer of the deck that night and the barge's operation officer, Lieutenant (j.g.) Moore, and request permission to come down. Moore denied the request, thinking that there might be targets on the shore that Gray could spot. "Can you see anything?" Moore repeatedly asked Gray.[113]

As the mast began to heat up from the burning diesel, Gray tried to climb down the ladder but hot metal soon burned through his hands, forcing him to jump. Gunner's Mate (Guns) 3rd Class Joseph M. Slavish, a member of the ship's company, was the first to reach Gray on the deck. He hoisted Gray over his shoulders and struggled to get him into an LCM. A secondary explosion hurled Slavish to the deck and peppered his leg with shrapnel, but this tough gunner's mate kept going and eventually made it to the LCM with his severely wounded shipmate. "I collapsed and woke up in a field hospital," explained Slavish. Gray was transported to a burn unit in Tokyo, where he later succumbed to his wounds.[114]

Many on the crew later blamed Moore's orders to remain on watch for Gray's death. "After the explosions, there was no one firing at us. They kept Bob up there too long, and he died a horrible death," lamented Hendrickson.[115] Lieutenant Oswald happened to meet Moore in Saigon not long after the attack and remembered how traumatized the officer was from the event. "He was pale and seemed almost in a daze. He had trouble forming sentences. The crew wanted to kill him and probably would have had the Navy not transferred him to the Naval Support Activity (NSA) Saigon compound soon after the incident. People somehow believed that if Moore had been doing his job, they would have seen these frogmen."[116]

Many of the crew were also disappointed with Lieutenant Commander Blevins' performance. "We were on fire and appeared to be sinking and it was turning into a Chinese fire drill. First the order to abandon ship then belay that," explained Hendrickson, "and then another abandon ship order—this time for real." Rather than departing the ship last as seafaring tradition demands, Blevins was one of the first to leave the barge after issuing the second abandon ship order. He sat next to Wojciechowski on an LCM (6) nervously smoking Chesterfield cigarettes as his ship burned.[117] Other sailors blamed Blevins for lax force protection measures prior to the attack, especially the lack of mine nets around the ship and the prohibition imposed on sentries against using concussion grenades to ward off swimmer attacks.

The men most responsible for preventing the barge from sinking were Boatswain's Mate Chief Michael P. Quigley and Lieutenant Jim Dykes, the commander of River Section 522. Quigley rallied the crew and fought the fires until flames forced him to abandon ship. His calm presence in the chaotic environment inspired many to try to save the barge. Dykes ordered several of his PBRs to begin immediately pumping foam into the fire, using portable fire pumps. He sent others to Ben Tre to fetch more foam and equipment to fight the fires. According to Goldsmith, "if not for the work of Jim Dykes, *YRBM-16* would have been totally destroyed."[118]

Dyke's and Quigley's actions alone, however, did not save the barge. Many others were also were involved. The Army had firefighting supplies rapidly airlifted to Ben Tre by Army aircraft as well as Navy helicopters from HAL-3. *Hunterdon County*, which had been operating 30 miles away at the mouth of Ham Luong, arrived at the scene at 0330, and began assisting with the fire-fighting efforts. For the remainder of the 24th, LSVPs from *Hunterdon County* shuttled relief fire-fighting teams and equipment to the YRBM, provided fuel and ammunition for the homeless PBRs of River Section 522, and berthing, food, and clothing for the displaced YRBM crew.[119]

Damage control parties finally extinguished the fires and brought flooding under control by 1600 on the 24th. The next day the YRBM was towed to Dong Tam for temporary repairs. The fleet (oceangoing) tug *Abnaki* (ATF 96) then picked her up on 27 December and began towing her to Sasebo, Japan. En route she encountered heavy seas, which tore off her sea patch and forced her to put in to Kaohsiung for more emergency repairs from 6 to 19 January. On 24 January, *YRBM-16* finally arrived at Sasebo, again partially flooded, but still salvageable.[120] Lieutenant Oswald remembered meeting the YRBM at Sasebo and being completely aghast by what he saw. As he stood on the pier gazing at the craft, he thought, "How the hell did they tow this thing to Sasebo? It was just blown all to hell." When he entered the ship, he looked up and noticed that the I-beams were "warped to the point that they looked like pretzels." He was also shocked to discover human remains still on the ship during his initial inspection: "We found parts of a guy's foot. We found most of a scalp. The smell was god awful."[121] In all, the blast killed seven sailors and wounded 14. It was one the biggest tragedies to befall the brown water Navy during the course of the entire war. Despite the tremendous damage, the Sasebo repair yard overhauled the ship in less than eight months and, by August 1968, *YRBM-16* was back in action in Vietnam.[122] The ship proudly served as a U.S. Navy brown–water support vessel from September 1968 until September 1971, when she was turned over to the Vietnam Navy and renamed HQ-9612.[123]

Seawolves

The single biggest danger confronting riverine forces in South Vietnam was ambush. Helicopters, with their ability to see around river bends and over dikes and rows of trees, quickly emerged as one of the brown water Navy's most effective defenses against this ever-present danger. Since 1962, the Army had been deploying UH-1 Iroquois helicopter gunships, the so-called Hueys, in Vietnam to protect its infantry formations in the field, clear landing zones, and cover medevacs. The Navy's association with these gunships began in 1966 and would continue throughout the war. It would serve as an ideal, if not indispensable, fire support platform for riverine and SEAL operations on the rivers of South Vietnam.

The Navy's first experience with helicopters in the light attack role occurred in March 1966. During Operation Jackstay, two U.S. Army UH-1 fire teams were temporarily assigned to support the first American river assault operation of the war. One element operated from *Belle Grove*, and another from Vung Tau.[124] After Jackstay, the Army UH-1s continued to operate with Navy riverine forces until July 1966, when eight pilots from Navy Helicopter Combat Support Squadron (HC) 1 took over this gunship support role.[125] Knowing that Army helicopter support for Navy riverine operations was temporary, Rear Admiral Ward convinced the Office of the Deputy Chief of Naval Operations for Air Warfare (OP-05) to contribute pilots for the new program, and General Westmoreland secured UH-1B helicopters from the Army for the new unit.[126] The Army also agreed to provide training, higher echelon maintenance, and spare parts for the helicopters.[127] HC-1 would form part of the Navy's River Patrol Force (TF 116).

To provide effective coverage for all PBR forces operating in the Mekong Delta and the Rung Sat Special Zone, the unit was divided into detachments spread across the southern part of South Vietnam, mainly in the IV Corps Tactical Zone. Initially, detachments were based at

A U.S. Navy UH-1B Iroquois flies low cover over PBRs on the Cho Gao Canal in the Mekong Delta in April 1968. The "Seawolves" of Light Helicopter Attack Squadron 3, or HAL-3, were on-call 24 hours a day to provide air support for riverine units in South Vietnam.

Tan Son Nhut, Bien Hoa, Vinh Long, and Soc Trang.[128] From these dry land bases, two gunships at a time would rotate out to floating bases—LSDs initially, but later LSTs and YRBMs. Each detachment contained two helicopters, eight pilots, eight aircrew, and eight ground support personnel.[129] Crews took turns standing alert for 24-hour shifts, thereby offering the PBRs nonstop air support, both day and night, in all TF 116 areas of operation.

The original gunship plan called for staging helicopters on LSTs anchored at the mouth of major rivers, but strong tides and heavy swells in these areas soon convinced the TF 116 leadership to move the LSTs to calmer waters upriver. The squadron crew enjoyed the air-conditioned berthing and superior Navy chow on LSTs, but the small flight decks made operating from these landing craft a tricky proposition. A second aircraft could not land on an LST flight pad until the first helicopter's main rotor had completely stopped. This caused some "anxious moments" when aircraft returned from missions with limited fuel. Land bases offered more operating space and better access to Army maintenance facilities, which were often collocated on the bases, but had less desirable berthing and messing. As fixed positions often situated in or near Viet Cong territory, land bases also came under frequent mortar and rocket-propelled grenade (RPG) attack. During the Tet Offensive, some of the fiercest fighting in the Mekong Delta occurred at the Navy helicopter base area at Vinh Long (see chapter 6).[130]

During the early period, training for Navy gunship pilots, all of whom were volunteers, consisted of SERE (search, evasion, resistance, and escape) training and a personal weapons and physical training course. Pilots then shipped off to Vietnam for UH-1 familiarization training provided by the Army at Tan Son Nhut Air Force Base in Saigon followed by more specialized on-the-job training with the Army's 197th Armed Helicopter Company. HC-1 pilots initially flew operational missions as copilots with Army pilots until they were deemed competent enough to become helicopter aircraft commanders. One of the great strengths that Navy pilots brought to Vietnam was superb instrument training and familiarity flying at night and in bad weather. In time, the Seawolves' competency in night attack would eclipse that of many comparable Army units.[131]

Garrett County (LST-786) anchored on the Co Chien River with PBRs next to her and a Navy UH-1B helicopter on the deck.

The hand-me-down Army UH-1Bs flown by HC-1 were long in flight hours but rugged and dependable aircraft, well suited to the combat environment of the Mekong River Delta. Manufactured by Bell Helicopter Company of Fort Worth, Texas, the UH-1B was powered by a single, 1,000-horsepower turbine engine and had a maximum cruising speed of 138 miles per hour. The aircraft carried a crew of four: a pilot, copilot, door gunner, and crew chief (who also served as the second door gunner).[132] "Navalizing" these aircraft involved adding M60 door guns and a radar altimeter. The Game Warden support ships at the time had only rudimentary flight decks and landing aids, so the radar altimeter was a particularly important addition, especially for night and bad weather operations.

Door guns for the helicopters originally were suspended with bungee cords, but after several overly enthusiastic door gunners accidentally shot holes into various parts of the aircraft, pintle mounts with stops were installed. External armament consisted of four electronically controlled, flex-mounted M60 machine guns (two on each side) fired by the copilot. These guns could turn a total of 80 degrees on the horizontal plane, and elevate 10 degrees and depress 85 degrees vertically. Two rocket pods, each housing seven 2.75-inch folding-fin aerial rockets, were mounted on each side of the aircraft. Pilots normally fired the rockets and appreciated their firepower and versatility. High-explosive rockets came with proximity fuzes and could be used effectively against vehicles; the white phosphorus rounds were ideal for starting fires; and flechette munitions, each packed with 2,400 one-inch-long steel projectiles, could devastate a formation of enemy troops. In addition to these weapons, individual crewmembers carried a variety of personal weapons ranging from M16 rifles to hand grenades.[133]

An often overlooked advantage of the helicopters was their communications suite. Each carried UHF, VHF, and FM radios, allowing a pilot or copilot to talk with troops on the ground, tactical operations centers, support ships, Special Forces, air forces, and other units. In some instances, a flight team lead (FTL) would assume the role of "on-scene commander" because he was the only battlefield manager capable of communicating with all units in the multidimensional battle space.[134]

On 1 April 1967, the four Vietnam-based detachments of HC-1 became HAL-3 at a commissioning ceremony held at Vung Tau, and HC-1 detachments 29, 27, 25, and 21 became HAL-3 detachments 1, 2, 3, and 4, respectively. Vung Tau became the administrative headquarters for the new unit, which nicknamed itself the "Seawolves." By August 1967, HAL-3 had grown to eight two-helicopter detachments based at Vung Tau, Binh Thuy, Dong Tam, Vinh Long, Nha Be, and on LSTs anchored on the Ham Luong, Co Chien, and Bassac Rivers.[135] In May 1968, HAL-3 became one of the Navy's largest squadrons with in-country strength of 103 officers, 330 enlisted aircrewmen, and 433 enlisted ground support sailors.[136] Beginning in May 1968, full captains commanded the unit.[137]

As the unit grew and matured, so too did training. In 1967 the Navy arranged a more extensive UH-1 gunship course for Vietnam-bound attack helicopter pilots at Fort Benning, Georgia, and later in 1968 at Fort Rucker, Alabama.[138] Enlisted crewmembers, most of whom also volunteered for the assignment, received their training in either the United States or Vietnam, depending on time and circumstances. Many eventually received aerial gunnery and basic helicopter maintenance training at Fort Rucker.[139] Daniel E. Kelly, an enlisted door gunner, described the rigorous nature of crew training he received in Vietnam in his memoir on the Seawolves. Training at Vung Tau consisted of spending a week in each of the maintenance shops learning about aircraft maintenance and 50 hours of in-flight gunnery training. "You didn't get thrown in, handed an M60 machine gun, and told to go for it," he wrote. "You had to be good, and everyone had to know that, under fire, you would perform well and not get any good guys killed." It was the final audition into a special fraternity, and gunnery skill was not the only criterion for the job. "It was very important that the team like you, because the job was a team effort. It was also a brotherhood. There was no room for out-of-control egos."[140]

From its inception the Seawolves were designed as a quick-reaction force. Two ship formations would stand alert for 24-hour shifts and respond to close air support requests up to 50 miles away from their base. Requests could come at any time of day or night, in fair weather or foul. Some missions lasted no longer than five minutes, and others could stretch on for over an hour. As soon as a unit completed a mission, all crewmembers (including the pilot and copilot) worked furiously to reload and refuel the aircraft, sometimes in a "hot" mode with the engine running. "If a safety officer would have seen us in those days he would have shut us down," explained one pilot. "We often fueled and armed the aircraft as it sat their wobbling on the skids while the rotor blades turned."[141]

When not standing alert, aircrews performed maintenance on aircraft and participated in base security operations at land bases, including manning guard posts and doing revetment sweeps. "We really never had any time off," recalled Lieutenant Commander Allen Weseleskey. Army colleagues at Vinh Long often requested that Weseleskey fill in as a copilot on Army helicopters when not pulling alerts with HAL-3, Detachment Vinh Long.[142] If he had any spare time at all, pilot Al Billings would work out, play cribbage, or water ski with the SEALs on the Nha Be River.[143] Daniel Kelly spent much of his free time in the hanger, helping maintenance crews.[144]

HC-1, and later HAL-3, fell under the command of Task Force 116 and was originally deployed to support PBR operations, but in time these gunships found themselves supporting Task Force 117 operations and even Army forces. Like a wartime emergency service, Navy pilots responded to any call for help. A HAL-3 detachment officer in charge who served in 1967–1968 estimated that 44 percent of his missions were related to TF 116 assets, 20 percent to Mobile Riverine Force operations, and 36 percent to other missions, such as requests for fire support from Army advisors and Army Special Forces units.[145] By 1967 the Seawolves' repertoire not only included close air support but also troop insertions for SEALs and Army Special Forces, medical evacuations, and even civic action missions. As historian and former naval aviator Richard Knott wrote, "Under no circumstances would they allow friendly personnel, on water or on ground, be killed or captured by the enemy if they could possibly do anything about it."[146] The Seawolves code demanded that if any American or ARVN unit needed help, they would do everything they could to assist.[147] This was one reason why the U.S. Army so readily supported the organization with maintenance and supplies. In an era of intense interservice rivalry, the Seawolves were a true purple (joint forces) outfit.

Lieutenant Commander Weseleskey epitomized this ethos. The son of a Russian immigrant coal miner from the Pittsburgh area, Weseleskey fought nearly as many battles as a youth as he would later fight in Vietnam. He first fought with his father, an alcoholic and a gambler, until his father kicked him out of his house as a teenager. He then fought to survive by sleeping on the porches of kindly neighbors and working part-time in the hearth department of a steel mill while also attending high school. He achieved high enough marks in school to attend college. A skilled tuba player for the Springdale, Pennsylvania, band, Weseleskey finally got a break in his junior year of high school. The band director managed to secure him a full scholarship to Valley Forge Military Academy (VFMA) in Wayne, Pennsylvania. His late admission meant he had to endure plebe hazing as a senior, but after his hardscrabble childhood, he was well-conditioned to endure the suffering: he not only successfully matriculated from the VFMA high school program but earned a two-year associate degree there as well. In July 1955, Weseleskey entered the Navy as a naval aviation cadet in fulfillment of a life-long dream to become a pilot.[148]

After receiving a Reserve commission and wings, Weseleskey started out in the AD-5N Skyraider, deploying first to the Western Pacific with Attack Squadron (All-Weather) VA (AW)-35 on *Hancock* (CVA-19) in 1957. The highlight of that tour was flying patrols in southern Taiwan during the 1958 Taiwan Strait conflict shortly after the Communist Chinese began shelling Quemoy and Matsu islands. Following this tour, in November 1958 Weseleskey volunteered for helicopter training because he believed it would enhance his marketability as a commercial pilot if the Navy ever compelled him to separate from the service early. Recognizing his talents, the Navy not only admitted him to pilot school but ultimately gave him a regular commission and a promotion to lieutenant in September 1960, thereby solidifying his status as a career naval officer. His work as a helicopter pilot began as a rescue pilot, flying the HUP, HO4S, HUK, and SH-3A helicopters, and deploying on *Hancock* again and later to Guam and Norfolk. During the early 1960s, he also received his bachelor's degree in political science from the Naval Postgraduate School in Monterey.

Always a warrior at heart, Weseleskey volunteered for HAL-3 in 1967. Now a lieutenant commander, he began his tour as the officer in charge of Detachment 1 at Vung Tau, but clashes over supply issues with Commander Robert W. Spencer, the HAL-3 commanding officer, eventually led to his being relieved of detachment command. Short of pilots, Spencer sent Weseleskey to Vinh Long to serve as a FTL rather than transferring him back to the states. At Vinh Long, Wesleskey ended up in the thick of one of the most desperate battles of the Tet Offensive (see chapter 6).[149] The Tet attacks at the base gradually calmed down, but the demand for Seawolves' close air support did not diminish as allied forces continued to skirmish with enemy forces throughout the spring of 1968.

On 9 March, Weseleskey's two-ship flight was scrambled to provide air support for an ARVN battalion ambushed not far from Cao Lanh near the Cambodian border. En route to the battle, Weseleskey was informed that an American advisor had been severely wounded. Army First Lieutenant Jack Jacobs was with two companies of ARVN troops on a mission to halt infiltration from Cambodia when his unit was ambushed by a well-prepared enemy position. A mortar round fell just a few feet away from him, leaving him blind in one eye and turning his face into a bloody mess. Jacobs quickly assessed the situation and realized he needed to act or everyone would be killed. He ordered his unit to withdraw to a safer position and then began dragging several wounded comrades to safety. After moving 13 soldiers from the kill zone, he got on the radio to call for air support.[150]

A VNAF flight of AD Skyraiders made one pass but retreated from the scene after taking several hits from large caliber machine guns. Jacobs then managed to achieve contact with the two Seawolves en route to the scene.

"We're in hurtsville," he told Weseleskey. "We can't seem to get any air support. We're all wounded and I cannot see with one eye."

"Roger, we're coming in to get you," Wesleskey replied.

"No way, man. It's too hot."

"It's my choice. I'm going to get you."

In strict adherence to the unwritten Seawolves' code of honor, Weseleskey refused to back down. Since he could not tell exactly who was friendly and who was not, he ordered his flight to make one low pass over the target to draw some fire and attempt to suppress it with rockets and M60s. "That maybe was a foolish approach," he later admitted. Both aircraft were hit in the run with the trailing ship suffering the most damage. Its pilot, Lieutenant (j.g.) Harold W. Guinn Jr., received a bullet wound in his right calf, and one of the door gunners took a hit in the hand, losing several fingers. Weseleskey asked the other aircraft's copilot if he could still fly the aircraft, which was streaming hydraulic fluid. The pilot told him he could fly it okay, and Weseleskey ordered him to go home.[151]

"You mean you're not coming with me," the copilot asked.

"No I'm not coming with you," Weseleskey replied. "I'm going back to get these guys. Now go home."

Weseleskey made several more passes over Jacobs, trying to land, but he kept receiving heavy fire. After ordering his own copilot to continue to prosecute the mission even if he was killed, he got his bird down to "sand blower" level, just a few feet off the ground, and flew into a makeshift landing zone established by the ARVN. As soon as his plane skidded to a stop, ARVN troops swarmed it, trying to escape the battle. "I told my gunners to shoo them away and if necessary, shoot 'em." Once the two Americans were safely on board, Weseleskey lifted the aircraft to see if he could take an additional casualty. Sensing he had enough power, he had his crew pull the severely wounded Vietnamese battalion commander on board. He then dragged the helicopter along the ground in a running translational lift to get it airborne and fired all his remaining rockets at a row of trees in front of him, trying to cut down tree branches so he could safely clear the tree line. The aircraft knocked down branches as it struggled to achieve enough lift to clear the trees, but everyone made it out alive, and Weseleskey was soon en route to Dong Tam to drop off the wounded, refuel, and re-arm.

Weseleskey ultimately received a Navy Cross for the mission. His was one of five Navy Crosses, 31 Silver Stars, 219 Distinguished Flying Crosses, 156 Purple Hearts, and 101 Bronze Stars awarded to HAL-3 sailors during the course of the war. One of the most decorated units in naval history, HAL-3 also received the Presidential Unit and the Navy Unit citations. The Presidential Unit Citation noted that the "decisiveness" of the Seawolves' helicopter fire support during the Tet period in particular was a "classic example of the professional naval response to a dangerous enemy threat" and that its actions, along with those of the PBRs, devastated the enemy force, relieved beleaguered enemy outposts, established control on the main rivers, and provided moral strength to the indigenous forces and civilian populace."[152]

Naval Intelligence Liaison Officers

Naval intelligence liaison officers served throughout the war as a critical intelligence source for naval forces operating in South Vietnam. NILOs were assigned to each coastal and riverine area advisory staff and also to select province or sector advisory staffs. The job of the NILO was to collect intelligence of naval interest within his geographic area of responsibility, coordinate with other allied intelligence assets, and disseminate the information to U.S. naval forces in South Vietnam. By 1967 NILOs could be found in approximately half of all South Vietnamese provinces, and by the end of the war approximately 150 officers had served in these billets.[153]

While every NILO's tour was unique depending on the period and place of service, Lieutenant (j.g.) Nicholas Carbone's experience at Lam Son on the Saigon River from May 1969 to May 1970 reveals some of the typical work many of these officers performed on a daily basis. Carbone lived in the advisor compound at the base of the 5th ARVN Division. His basic duties included collecting intelligence on Viet Cong activity in his area and then briefing PBR crews every day on the enemy situation in their patrol sectors. Carbone worked closely with local Army intelligence officers, civilian intelligence personnel, and Vietnamese naval intelligence officers to collect the information he needed for his briefings. He gleaned some of his information from translations of captured documents and transcripts of POW and Chieu Hoi interrogations. Other information he collected himself by flying as an observer in light U.S. Army and U.S. Air Force aircraft such as the O-1 and L-19 and by personally interrogating prisoners. Although Carbone had received three months of Vietnamese language training at the Defense Language Institute in Monterey, California, prior to his departure, he never gained proficiency in the language and relied heavily on his VNN counterpart, Lieutenant Choung, for translation assistance during interrogations.[154]

As Carbone's experience illustrates, NILOs often had to be creative and resourceful to gather useful, actionable intelligence for local naval forces operating in the area. Except for an occasional Boston Whaler or Jeep, the Navy did not provide its intelligence officers with aircraft, boats, or vehicles. Consequently, NILOs depended on local operational forces for transportation to and from the field. In addition to providing useful intelligence, trips to operational areas, whether on aircraft or water, demonstrated a NILO's willingness to take personal risks and helped forge better relations between him and the operators. Most NILOs volunteered for assignment to Vietnam, so very few shied away from going on PBR or Swift boat patrols.

Captain Earl "Rex" Rectanus, COMNAVFORV Assistance Chief of Staff for Intelligence during the late 1960s, encouraged NILOs to develop several separate skill sets. First, they needed to be able to collate and analyze field intelligence from a wide variety of disparate sources. As Rectanus later explained in an oral history, "these Lt (jg) officers knew very little about the Navy (small unit operations), the VNN, the craft of intelligence, [and] the intelligence field environment" of various U.S. and a South Vietnamese intelligence entities operating in their local area, but they developed this knowledge very quickly and became highly proficient in analyzing enemy ground movements in their respective areas.[155]

The second skill set involved developing intelligence from their sources and creating an agent network. This was done by talking to local villagers, performing their own reconnaissance, and interrogating local prisoners captured by SEALs and other local forces.[156] Lieutenant Gene Koral, a My Tho-based NILO in 1966 recruited agents during MEDCAP (Medical Civic Action Program) missions in Dinh Tuong Province. He also solicited information from a Vietnamese contract worker with USAID (U.S. Agency for International Development) who traveled extensively throughout the delta and talked frequently to local merchants about the Viet Cong situation in the area. However, his best piece of intelligence came from South Vietnamese military sources. On 23 July 1966, acting on information from RAG 27 and the 7th ARVN Division, the NILO revealed the location of a VC tax collection team to River Section 531, which promptly hunted down and killed the two-man team and captured their sampan and weapons. According to Fred McDavitt, who participated in the mission, "When we returned to My Tho and tied up at the 27th RAG pier, the VN Navy personnel were wide-eyed. We never received real time intel from the 27th RAG or the 7th ARVN Division again."[157]

In addition to running agents and gleaning information from allies, most NILOs regularly performed reconnaissance of their operational areas in light aircraft. Lieutenant Albert G. Hallowell, a Fourth Coastal Zone NILO, died in a plane crash on 6 October 1966 in Kien Hoa Province while conducting such a mission.[158] On 15 November 1969, Lieutenant (j.g.) John "Jack" Graf, the Third Coastal Zone NILO, was flying as an observer in an Army OV-1C Mohawk 19 miles southeast of Phu Vinh when the plane was hit by enemy ground fire. The pilot, Army Captain Robert White, and Graf ejected and were soon surrounded and captured by local Viet Cong. According to White's debrief after the war, the two men were moved to several Viet Cong POW camps until Graf's escape on 26 or 27 January 1970. Graf's remains have never been recovered, and he is presumed dead.[159] Lieutenant Peter B. Decker, who served as the NILO at Duc Hoa from 1969 to 1970, flew visual reconnaissance missions every afternoon at 1630 over the

Vam Co Dong River and the Plain of Reeds in the Mekong River Delta near Cambodia. Decker observed that while flying at 1,500 feet looking for the enemy, "heavy machine gun fire when the FAC [forward air controller] was up-sun from the gun could really blow your whole day."[160]

Lieutenant Frederick A. Olds, who served as the Fourth Riverine intelligence officer at Can Tho from May 1966 to May 1967, explained in a 2009 interview how the entire NILO intelligence gathering, analysis, and dissemination system came together. For him, the first step in the process was to examine written and verbal intelligence information ranging from U.S. Army, U.S. Air Force, and VNN sources at IV Corps headquarters. He would compare this information with his own intelligence gleaned from prisoner interrogations and a network of informants (mainly fishermen paid to report on Viet Cong activity on the rivers). After sifting through his voluminous data, he would develop a list of suspected Viet Cong crossing points and then task an Army aircraft equipped with side-looking airborne radar (SLAR) and "Red Haze" infrared equipment to fly over these areas at night. The SLAR picked up movement on the water, and the "Red Haze" equipment could see cooking fires. Once he triangulated on the most likely crossing point, he flew visual reconnaissance over the area in an O-1, taking numerous photos. The photos often yielded additional evidence of Viet Cong activity and proved useful as visual aids in the next stage of the process: the briefing. Only after Olds believed that he possessed actionable intelligence would he alert PBR patrol officers and/or SEAL commanding officers of a suspected crossing site. Furthermore, to demonstrate he was willing to "eat what he cooked," he often accompanied the PBRs on these ambush operations.[161] According to his Bronze Star citation, intelligence developed by Olds resulted in over "200 Viet Cong killed in action, as well as many weapons, ammunition, documents, and other enemy war material confiscated."[162]

It took Olds seven months to establish an effective intelligence collection and analysis operation at Can Tho, which eventually included a small intelligence operation and analysis center, a CONEX (Container Express) intermodel shipping container for storing classified data, a holding cell, and an interrogation room. Worried that the Vietnamese would mistreat his prisoners, Olds insisted on holding his most important catches in his own cell and would pay for prisoner food from his personal funds. "I would play psychological games with the prisoners, but I never laid a hand on them or tortured them." Olds supplemented his own interrogation information with information gained from other U.S. government and allied intelligence assets in the area.[163]

Naval officers like Fred Olds, John Graf, Peter Decker, and Nicholas Carbone remain unsung heroes of the naval war in Vietnam. These men worked in the shadows, often at grave personal risk, to provide PBR crews, SEALs, and others with useful intelligence. As Rectanus explained in his oral history, the Navy had only modest experience running intelligence operations on the ground prior to the Vietnam War, and NILOs, through great resourcefulness and courage, filled a significant void during the war by developing unique methodologies to collect and analyze intelligence at the local level.[164] A critical element in their success was the ability to build personal relationships with other intelligence components and nearby operating forces. The willingness of NILOs to get out into the field and collect their own field intelligence is symbolized by the sacrifices of the three NILOs killed in the line of duty in Vietnam: two of the deaths (Graf and Hallowell) involved reconnaissance flights over enemy territory, and the third, Lieutenant Kenneth W. Tapscott, resulted from a rocket attack on a PBR patrol.[165] "Being a NILO was not about sitting in an office in some Federal Center and working on SPOTREPS from submarines or aircraft," recalled Lieutenant Robert C. Doyle, a NILO based at Ben Tre, it's "down-and-dirty, nitty gritty intelligence gathering in the field."[166]

Civic Action

In addition to engaging in direct combat with the enemy, enforcing curfews, and inspecting river traffic for contraband, Game Warden personnel participated in numerous humanitarian operations known during this period as civic action and medical civic action program missions. By the numbers, the scale of this type of activity was impressive. In September 1967 alone, COMNAVFORV units in South Vietnam built two bridges, a dispensary, 24 family homes, and two schools for local Vietnamese. Navy doctors, dentists, nurses, and corpsmen performed 24,860 medical treatments—including 4,510 dental exams and 54 surgeries—on Vietnamese civilians. Other sailors distributed thousands of pounds of goods to the local populace, including 97,300 pounds of cement, 75,950 pounds of food, and 163,000 board feet of lumber. Still others taught 26 classes in personal hygiene and 110 English classes.[167] These missions not only fostered better relations between Task Force 116 and the civilian populace but often yielded valuable intelligence, helped convince locals to support the government cause, and improved sailor morale by allowing them to engage with civilians in a humanitarian capacity.

The Seabees contributed more than any other Navy unit to civic action because of their unique construction capabilities. Most of the schools, hospitals, bridges, roads, power plants, and other large structures donated by the Navy to the Vietnamese were built by Seabees, known informally as the "Navy's Peace Corps in the Delta." In June 1967, for example, Seabee Team 1009 at Vinh Long built a 26-foot-long bridge, began work on a second 90-foot structure, hauled 310 cubic yards of rock to surface 1,500 feet of road, and completed various construction projects at the provincial hospital and the orphanage.[168] Seabee Team 1011 resurfaced the marketplace at An Duc, a hamlet seven miles southeast of Vinh Long. When Lieutenant (j.g.) Thomas E. Brisbane, a young Seabee from Denver, Colorado, arrived at the town with his 12-man team, he found the marketplace to be a simple, dirt square between the houses and the river. To prevent it from becoming a mud bath during rains, he had his men work with villagers to lay a concrete floor, complete with drainage ditches. Not only did Brisbane give the village a more sanitary place to buy and sell food and other goods, but he helped train villagers in modern construction techniques and invited the most promising tradesmen to the Seabee compound in Vinh Long for additional training. "The people are weak on equipment training," he told a Navy journalist, "and one of our main short-range aims is to train mechanics."[169]

Civic action, though, was not limited to Seabees alone. Riverine units, because of their unique access to isolated communities in the delta, were often at the front lines of Navy civic action projects. In May 1967, Delta River Patrol Group (TG 116.1) units provided medical treatment to 1,337 Vietnamese, evacuated another 120 to local hospitals, and distributed 250 pounds of Bulgar wheat, 150 pounds of medical supplies, and 100 pounds of soap to various villages and hamlets in its area of operation.[170] Medical personnel from *Jennings County*, stationed on the Co Chien River, treated 1,100 civilian patients ashore on MEDCAP missions in August 1967. During these same missions, the LST also distributed 1,200 pounds of clothing, 400 pounds of soap, and 3,000 board feet of lumber in the form of empty ammunition crates, spare parts crates, and pallets. After discovering a young boy severely wounded by a stray U.S. Army mortar round in Dong Hoa village, *Jennings County* sailors raised 15,000 piasters (roughly $197 in 1967 dollars) for skin-graft operations at the famous Grall Hospital in Saigon to restore the use of the child's leg. For the village of Hung My, the site of VNN Coastal Group 35 headquarters, sailors from the ship prepared a down-home American barbeque, complete with hamburgers, hot dogs, macaroni salad, cookies, beer, and soft drinks for over 1,000 local people.[171]

At Long Xuyen, civic action became a way of life for the men of River Sections 522 and 523. A group of sailors from the support detachment and PBR crews established an English language school. Originally planned for 65 students, the school nearly tripled in size to 180 in just a few weeks of operation. Students were split into three groups (beginners, intermediates, and advanced), and classes were held three days a week for each skill level. Sailors from the unit also rebuilt five homes destroyed by floodwaters, delivered many pounds of food to local villages, and participated in weekly MEDCAPS, which became so popular with locals that the river section sailors raised money to hire a Vietnamese nurse and purchase an ambulance for the community. "Once we get rolling," stated Lieutenant Ken Anderson, the officer in charge of the Naval Support Activity detachment at Long Xuyen, "we hope to put the ambulance on the mike boat and hold daily sick call up and down the rivers in our operating area."[172]

At My Tho, Lieutenant Peter Huchthausen's PBR medically evacuated a young girl named Nguyen Thi Lung, who had been wounded in the leg by mortar fire, to the local provincial hospital, where doctors amputated her limb. Huchthausen and his men visited her in the hospital nearly every day, bringing gifts to raise her spirits. Roderick Davis often acted as translator during these visits. The men became so attached to Lung that they arranged for her to be fitted for a prosthetic leg in Saigon and paid for her to attend a local Catholic boarding school. During the 1968 Tet Offensive, the Viet Cong overran the school, killing 47 students. Huchthausen, then stationed at Sa Dec as commander of River Section 513, lost contact with Lung and feared the worst. Eighteen years later in 1980, Lung sent a letter to the U.S. Embassy in Thailand, asking for help getting out of Vietnam. In it was a photo of her and Huchthausen. The embassy published the photo in several newspapers around the Far East, and eventually a 1962 Naval Academy classmate of Peter's named Ted Schaeffer recognized the man in the photo and immediately sent a cable off to Belgrade, Yugoslavia, where Huchthausen was serving as the U.S. Naval Attaché. Peter and his wife eventually sponsored Lung under the Orderly Departure Program to come to the United States.[173] The Huchthausens, with help from the United States Catholic Conference

Department of Migration and Refugee Services, paid the relocation expenses for her and her daughter, housed them temporarily, and found Lung a job as a seamstress. Four years later in 1984, Lung arrived in Washington, DC, to begin a new life in America.[174]

Civic action and MEDCAPs, in short, were more than just charity efforts designed to win the hearts and minds of the locals; they were also a true calling for people like Huchthausen and many others like them. "A big part of my interest was running MEDCAPs and winning the hearts and minds of the people," recalled Lieutenant John Donovan of River Section 531. Donovan became heavily involved in Operation Cleft Lip, which arranged for children suffering from harelips and cleft palates to receive specialized treatment in Saigon. "These kids had been ostracized because they were deformed. It was incredibly fulfilling to help these kids—it was an amazing transformation. They came back to their villages looking normal."[175] Civic action missions also served to put a human face on the war for sailors often hardened by the stresses of combat. As Robert Fuscaldo put it, "When people are getting shot, it is easy to lose your guideposts. Getting to know the people helped the sailors stay grounded in what they were doing."[176]

PBR Combat Experiences

RM2 Terry J. Freund

When Terrence "Terry" J. Freund was just four years old, he helped save a drowning boy in Lake Delton, Wisconsin, by alerting the boy's mother, who promptly rescued the lad. Quick thinking on Terry's part spared the child from almost certain death. These same instincts would later save his PBR crew years later in Vietnam. In 1966 Freund was on his second Navy enlistment, having joined the Navy in 1959 after dropping out of Sheboygan High School. Neither a student nor an athlete, Freund found his niche in the Navy as a radioman second class. According to his shipmate, Engineman 3rd Class Steve Watson, "He was a squared away sailor whose clothes were always clean, and who was always happy, and proud to be a sailor."[177]

On the afternoon of 26 October, Freund was manning the forward .50-caliber guns of PBR-40 on the Bassac River near An Lac Thon Village in Ba Xuyen Province, South Vietnam. EN3 Watson was coxswain, Gunner's Mate (Guns) 3rd Class William A. Ratliff manned the aft .50-caliber, and Boatswain's Mate 1st Class Carl Anderson served as the boat captain. Also on board was a Vietnamese National Policeman, Do Van Thien, and Lieutenant Norman B. Howell, the patrol officer in charge of the two-boat patrol, comprising PBRs 40 and 34 from River Section 511 based in Binh Thuy (Can Tho). The patrol had spent most of the daylight patrol searching sampans at various checkpoints. Nothing out of the ordinary occurred until shortly after 1400, when the crew of PBR 40 observed a 20-foot-long sampan coming out of a canal with three men aboard. According to Watson, "they had on peasant clothes, but they did not look like farmers." Howell said, "Let's check that one," and he pointed to the sampan.[178]

When hailed, the sampan refused to come alongside, and the patrol gave chase. After a couple of warning shots were fired, the PBRs opened up on the sampan as it beached, setting the craft on fire. The three men leapt from the sampan and dove into some underbrush as other Viet Cong in multiple foxholes along the beach returned fire against the PBRs. Without further orders, Freund began to rake the enemy positions with fire from his twin .50 mount, temporarily silencing enemy opposition on shore. GMG3 Ratliff, with Do Van Thien, attempted to board the sampan and seize it for intelligence purposes. Intense enemy fire soon forced the two men to jump into the water. PBR-40 then swooped in and extracted them as Freund and others hammered away at the shore positions with their guns. "I saw Freund jerk back and I thought, 'what the hell happened to him?'" recalled Watson. Little did Watson realize at the time, but an enemy machine gun round had just buried itself deep in Freund's chest. "Are you okay?" Howell asked. "I'm okay," Freund replied as he trained his guns on the enemy machine-gun position. Weak and in excruciating pain, Freund fired on the position until he slumped over his guns. Faint from loss of blood and in shock, Freund roused himself, went to get more ammunition, and reloaded his guns. He continued to fire over half the bullets in his tray until he succumbed to his wound.[179]

Howell then ordered both boats to withdraw, and Watson went forward to check on Freund while Anderson took over the helm. "He was lying down in the bow of the PBR and he was dead." Freund subsequently received the Navy Cross for heroism. The citation states "Freund's determined and accurate covering fire, delivered while mortally wounded, enabled his boat, without further loss of life or damage, to be extricated from the peril in which it had been placed in order to rescue two shipmates." Watson had a different take on the action. "We should have never chased the sampan but we did. We should have let it go. We were making up the rules as we went along." After the ambush, it took two Army helicopter gunships and Vietnam Navy RAG boats, equipped with 40mm cannons, to neutralize fully the enemy soldiers who killed Freund.[180]

As the Freund episode reveals, combat for Game Warden crews often came unexpectedly and violently. Viet Cong ambushes, generally from the shore, were responsible for most Game Warden deaths. Plastic-hulled boats were simply not designed to stand and fight against enemy soldiers attacking from bunkers and trenches on the shoreline. As Watson argued and the Game Warden Operation Order dictated, when confronted with superior firepower from the shore, the best course of action was to back off and call in air support. Patrol officers, though, often refused to back down. Like John Paul Jones and David Glasgow Farragut before them, these men relished the opportunity to engage the enemy, especially after endless days of routine searches on hot and muggy weather conditions of the delta. Few sailors epitomized the aggressiveness and risk-taking nature of many of the brown water Navy patrol officers than Signalman 1st Class Chester Smith and BM1 James Elliot Williams.

SM1 Chester Smith

Growing up in Celina in western Ohio, SM1 Smith was a rambunctious kid, uninterested in school or academic achievement. "I was more interested in seeing the world than going to school." Few in this town of 5,000, the county seat for Mercer County, would have predicted that this high school dropout would become one of the most decorated riverine warriors of the conflict and eventually retire from the Navy as a captain. Like many American youths of the period, Chet found his calling in the U.S. Navy, and the Navy in turn helped him cultivate talents he never knew he possessed.[181]

Smith joined the Navy in 1954 at the age of 18. After attending boot camp at Great Lakes, Illinois, he entered Radioman A School but soon dropped out "because school was not why I joined the Navy." Instead, he served on the miscellaneous auxiliary ship *Timmerman* (AG-152) as an unrated sailor in the deck division. *Timmerman* was a former *Gearing*-class destroyer re-designated in 1954 as a miscellaneous auxiliary ship and used by the Navy to test and evaluate engineering equipment. Smith spent most of his one-year tour with this ship maintaining the ship's hull and performing other menial work with the deck force. His next assignment was with the radar picket destroyer *Kenneth D. Bailey* (DDR-713). During his 1956–1959 tour, the ship supported the 1958 U.S. intervention in Lebanon and visited numerous Mediterranean ports. It was in this assignment that Smith began to take a shine to Navy life. He enjoyed traveling around the Mediterranean and his new job as a signalman, a rating he struck for during this tour. "I loved being a signalman. It was open air and I got to see messages before anyone else."[182]

From 1959 to 1961, Smith served as a signalman on the destroyer *Hugh Purvis* (DD-709), which spent most of the year in the Boston Naval Shipyard undergoing a fleet rehabilitation and modernization overhaul.[183] He then joined Pearl Harbor's smallest commissioned naval vessel, the auxiliary fleet tug *Sunnadin* (ATA 197), and served there from 1961 to 1964. At only 143 feet long and carrying a crew of between 30 and 45 sailors, *Sunnadin* was a far cry from the larger destroyers Smith had served on, but he loved the assignment despite how rough this pug-nosed little vessel sailed (tugs are notorious for a bumpy, rough ride in heavy seas). "You could count on every member of the crew to do his job. We were very close knit."[184]

His next assignments in security at the Naval Supply Center in Oakland, California, and Naval Station Treasure Island, San Francisco, convinced him that shore duty was not for him. Seeking to recapture the camaraderie of serving on a small vessel, he volunteered for small-boat duty in Vietnam and in early 1966 became a plank owner with River Patrol Section 531 based in the central Mekong Delta at My Tho. "We were the first U.S. Navy boats to arrive in the area so the enemy had no idea what to expect. We had the element of surprise."[185] Upon meeting Smith for the first time, Fred McDavitt, the commanding officer of the unit, was immediately impressed with him. "He was a quiet guy, but I could see the intensity burning just below the surface." Smith's military bearing also impressed McDavitt. "Smith was a tall, slender muscular sailor who looked impressive in any uniform he wore from dress blues to jungle greens."

McDavitt, however, hesitated at first in appointing Smith as a boat captain because he did not initially believe that signalmen had enough boat handling skills to perform the role. A shortage of boatswain's mates soon compelled him to look to other ratings for these command assignments, and Smith's extensive seagoing experience and aggressive attitude made him a good pick. After passing the requisite tests, Smith took command of PBR-98. According to McDavitt, Smith acquired most of his leadership skills on the job. "He had to learn by critiquing his own performance after firefights, discussing tactical pros and cons after large firefights with his fellow PBR boat captains. He spent several months as 'cover boat' for a two-boat patrol where he learned the skills of not only protecting his own PBR and crew but also providing supporting fire for the 'lead boat' and taking the tactical lead if communications were lost due to battle damage to the lead boat. Being boat captain of the cover boat is a tedious role 90 percent of the time and is mixed with sheer terror the other 10 percent of the time when the enemy ambushes the lead boat and its very survival depends on the quick and correct action of the cover boat, a role that SM1 Smith easily mastered."

Not content to remain a boat captain, Smith sought to win a coveted slot as a patrol officer, a billet traditionally reserved for commissioned officers and chief petty officers. Through hard work, skill, and determination, he eventually passed all the tests and hurdles required for the slot, thereby becoming only the second 1st class petty officer of the unit (the first was Williams) to achieve this position. As a patrol officer, Smith was responsible for a two-boat patrol and had full authority to initiate combat against the enemy and to call in air and artillery support when needed. As McDavitt noted in an evaluation of Smith, "his ability to take charge of a situation and quickly bring order out of the chaos of battle made him an asset in any combat situation in which he found himself. He was admired by the members of his crew and garnered their devoted loyalty."[186]

In early December 1966, Smith had just returned to Vietnam from emergency leave. His father had died suddenly and Smith traveled to the United States for 30 days to take care of his affairs. Back in Vietnam he was eager to reenter the fray and prove his metal as a patrol officer. On 2 December he received shrapnel wounds in the buttocks while on a patrol near My Tho, but that did not slow him down even a beat.[187] According to McDavitt, Smith was an "intense competitor who very much wanted to engage the enemy on his own terms as a patrol officer."[188]

On a routine patrol on the morning of 11 December, Smith succeeded. His two-boat patrol was west of My Tho when he spotted a sampan carrying two green uniformed occupants heading out of a canal near Thoi Son Island. When PBR-98 and the cover boat, PBR-106, turned toward the sampan, it retreated up the canal. Smith's next decision violated two River Patrol Section 531 standing operating procedures. No PBR was supposed to enter narrow canals and especially not when the tide was going out. There were good reasons for this policy. On a small canal, a PBR often cannot turn around, which meant its only escape was to back out. Narrow canals also do not allow for effective gun angles. Without proper standoff distance between a PBR and a canal bank, a PBR cannot depress its guns low enough to hit an enemy soldier firing from a bunker on the bank of the canal. Low tides exacerbated this problem and made it more likely that a PBR would run aground. Well aware of these hazards, Smith decided to pursue his prey anyway.[189] Similar to aviators, riverine warriors often had to "hang it out" to score victories against the ever-elusive Viet Cong. They had to trust their instincts and situational awareness to help them prevail against often-heavy odds. Smith was willing to take a calculated risk to achieve a potential combat victory, confident that the shallow draft, high speed, and small size of his PBRs would allow his patrol to succeed in the engagement. "I understood the importance of safety, but we were there to do a job," Smith later explained.[190]

As the PBRs entered the canal in pursuit, they soon found another group of Viet Cong in a second sampan and began taking fire from this group. Smith's forward gunner quickly dispatched these troops and the two other Viet Cong in the first sampan. Seeing elements of the VC 263rd Main Force Battalion preparing to embark in 40 sampans along the bank, Smith's patrol continued up the canal and soon began taking heavy fire from both banks. Smith refused to back down and instead ordered his PBRs to continue up the canal. The PBRs killed six soldiers in sampans and caused other Viet Cong to flee from positions on the banks. At one point, PBR-98 began firing on a hut with .50-caliber and M79 rounds, setting the structure on fire and causing a huge secondary explosion. "It was apparently an ammo bunker," noted Smith in his after-action report. When PBRs -103 and -110 arrived, they began towing away captured sampans while Smith's units spotted for a helicopter fire team from HAL-3. Smith's section stayed in the canal 45 more minutes, directing the helicopters to various targets in the area and, after the helicopters left, the section killed three additional Viet Cong attempting to cross the canal ahead of them. To egress the area, Smith's boat had to slide over a sandbar at the mouth of the canal—something one could do with a shallow-draft water jet at flank speed and a maneuver the unit had experimented with recently with 6–10-foot sandbars. He also engaged in a duel with several snipers in trees—two of whom were killed.[191]

Overall, 15 Viet Cong were killed, 28 sampans sunk, 12 damaged, and three were captured during the engagement. The next day, General William Westmoreland sent the following message to Admiral Ward:

> PBRs 98 and 106 were right on the job on the morning of 11 December, resulting in a fine victory against the enemy at Dinh Tuong. Attack by PBRs and light fire team disrupted large VC force and was an outstanding example of success of Game Warden. Please pass on my hearty congratulations to all concerned. Westmoreland sends.[192]

For his "daringly aggressive actions, outstanding initiative, extraordinary courage, and gallant leadership" during the engagement, Smith later received America's second highest award for gallantry, the Navy Cross.[193] With this decoration, he became the second most decorated sailor in one of the most storied Navy units of the war. After the war Smith stayed in the Navy, eventually becoming a warrant officer and then a limited duty officer. In October 1975 he served as the executive officer of the salvage ship *Grapple* (ARS 7) and briefly commanded the vessel during its decommissioning. He later served as the executive officer of the salvage ship *Reclaimer* (ARS 42) and, from September 1979 to November 1981, commanded the fleet ocean tug *Moctobi* (ATF 105). Smith retired from the Navy as a captain in 1993 after 40 years of service.[194]

BM1 James Elliot Williams and the Halloween Massacre

For the Navy, BM1 Williams is a larger than life figure. Not only was he one of the most decorated enlisted men in the history of the service, but in many respects, he epitomizes everything a sailor warrior ought to be—an enlisted boatswain's mate whose actions demonstrated that in close combat, the sailor can be as tough and lethal as the best marine or soldier.[195] The Navy honored Williams by naming a ship after him, the guided missile destroyer *James E. Williams* (DDG-95).[196] Who was James Elliot Williams? Was he the "Popeye the sailor man" of mythology, an ordinary sailor just doing his job, a glory seeker, or someone altogether different? Because his aggressive style of enlisted leadership set the tone for the entire Game Warden task force, his persona deserves special attention.

Born on 13 June 1930 in Rock Hill, South Carolina, Williams grew up in nearby Darlington.[197] His father, Roy Franklin Williams, worked as an investigator with the South Carolina Law Enforcement Division (SLED). A tough taskmaster, Roy had hoped that Elliot, as James was known as a child, would attend college and have a professional career, but Elliot had other ideas. At age ten, he remembered seeing an uncle wearing the Navy "Crackerjack" uniform and from that moment onward set his sights on a naval career. "It was the prettiest uniform I'd ever seen."[198]

Boatswain's Mate 1st Class James Elliot Williams was awarded the Medal of Honor by President Lyndon B. Johnson in May 1968.

Bored with school, Elliot first attempted to join the Navy at 16 but was told he was too young. Not one to take no for an answer, he convinced his father to help him get in. His father begrudgingly agreed and asked a friend, who was a county clerk, to alter Elliot's birth certificate so he could enlist a year early.[199] Williams attended boot camp in San Diego in 1947 and later in the year joined the deck force of the tank landing ship *Sedgwick County* (LST-1123) based in San Diego. During his time on board, the ship rarely left her mooring, and Williams spent most of his time painting the deck with large swabs.[200] Disappointed he had not been given the opportunity to sail the seven seas, Williams left the Navy after his enlistment ended in August 1950 but reenlisted three months later to avoid being recalled involuntarily because of hostilities in Korea.[201]

During his second enlistment, Williams served as a boatswain's mate seaman on the destroyer *Douglas H. Fox* (DD-779). Recommissioned in November 1950, *Fox* spent the first 14 months of the war on the East Coast of the United States before deploying to Korea on 22 January 1952. From March until June 1952 the destroyer participated in numerous fire support missions against supply points, gun emplacements, and Communist troops on the Korean peninsula. On several occasions she received counterbattery fire, and on one occasion she was hit on the port side by a shell, which injured three men but caused no significant damage to the ship. During her 1952 combat tour, *Fox* fired over 8,500 rounds of 5-inch ammunition at shore targets.[202]

In addition to gunfire support missions, the ship also attempted to enforce the United Nations blockade by employing its motor whaleboats to stop and search sampans moving up and down the coastline. During these missions the six men of Whaleboat Detail 1, led by Lieutenant (j.g.) William K. Doran, captured 114 North Koreans and 26 enemy sampans. In Vietnam, Williams enjoyed exaggerating a bit when telling sea stories and would occasionally claim to have participated in these exploits. The records, however, tell a different story. They indicate that Williams served not in Detail 1, but rather in Detail 2 led by Lieutenant Robert C. Rumbaugh. Detail 2 participated in only one mission on one day, 3 May 1952, and even that patrol was cut short by intense fog.[203]

During his second enlistment Williams decided to make a career out of the Navy and began paying greater attention to his military bearing. "I had the sharpest damn knife and the shiniest shoes in the Navy. That's what I was taught. That's what I believed in, being a good sailor."[204] While on *Thomaston* (LSD-28), Williams once received 60 hours of extra duty just for "giving an officer a funny look." He believed punishments like this one were what made him a good sailor. "It learnt you a lot of discipline. No it wasn't fair. It's a form of training. That's what keeps the military going."[205] For his entire life Williams contended that humility was a core virtue of military service. Writing to a former shipmate after the war, he noted that joining the military is "one of the greatest things" you can do because "when one is humiliated by life, one goes on to do great things."[206]

After Korea, he served on several ships, including guided missile light cruiser *Little Rock* (CLG-4), oiler *Chuckawan* (AO-100), repair ship *Amphion* (AR-13), and cargo ship *Alcor* (AK-259), working as a boatswain's mate and a master at arms.[207] When he wasn't at sea, Williams attended Navy schools, including the Advanced Damage Control School in Charleston, South Carolina, and the Career Appraisal School in Bainbridge, Maryland.

Despite this impressive background and many years of service at sea, Elliot had trouble advancing beyond the rank of petty officer first class (E-6). Many of his shipmates believed that his lack of formal education made it difficult for him to pass the chief's test, which he took and failed on several occasions before his Vietnam deployment. Some even suggested that he may have been illiterate. In truth, Williams was an avid reader and a huge fan of author Louis L'Amour. With his ability to read, along with some coaching or correspondence courses, Williams should have been able to pass the chief's test, which was a multiple-choice exam but, for whatever reason, he never achieved a score high enough to advance before the war. Williams' lack of upper level high school math may have made it hard for him to score highly on test sections pertaining to cargo handling, rigging, and navigation. Since the test was graded on a curve, the relative talent of other petty officers taking the exam also might have been a factor.[208]

After 19 years in the service with little hope of advancement, Williams contemplated getting out of the service and entering a career in law enforcement. He had a wife and five children to feed and Navy pay for a first class petty officer could be stretched only so far. His family had

Left to right: Lieutenant Fred McDavitt and Boatswain's Mate 1st Class James E. Williams stand at attention waiting to receive the Vietnamese Cross of Gallantry with Bronze Star for action behind enemy lines on 23 July 1966. They also received U.S. Bronze Stars for the same action. In the background just left of the flagpole is Quartermaster 1st Class Terrel E. Carter who would later be killed on patrol with Williams on 15 January 1967.

long-standing connections with Senator Strom Thurmond, and he knew he could parley those connections into a job with SLED, or even a federal law enforcement agency. In the end, however, Williams chose to stay in the Navy. More than anything else, he wanted see combat and believed that the new riverine force represented an opportunity for him not only to fulfill this dream but to lead men in battle as a boat captain. "He had delusions of grandeur and wanted to be in command of a combat unit," McDavitt later revealed. "Fortunately for all of us, he was as good as he thought he was."[209]

As one of the original members of River Section 531, Williams, or "Willy" as he asked his shipmates to call him in Vietnam, quickly made a name for himself on the river.[210] The July 1966 Bronze Star incident (discussed at the beginning of the chapter), in particular, showed his true metal. "When you get fired at during an ambush, even if it is not the first time, you can't believe this happening to you," McDavitt said. "You often have no frame of reference and the first reaction to fire is paralysis and extreme fear. However, a good combat leader can break through the fear of his troops by calmly talking to them and telling them what to do. Williams had this skill."[211]

Signalman 1st Class Chester Smith, a boat captain who often went on patrol with Williams, concurred. "Willie was a sage gentleman. He was the guy who had good advice for us because he was in Korea and most of us were fairly young compared to Willy."[212]

After patrols he would hold court with his men at the horseshoe pit, offering advice and gambling incessantly. "He would wager a bet on anything, even two ants crossing the road," according to McDavitt. "He didn't make big bets, but he loved betting on horses or anything else with the longest odds. He brought that philosophy to the rivers." Williams was hardly a reckless gambler, but he did take many calculated risks. To tweak more speed out of PBR-105, he removed some of the ceramic armor and often carried less ammunition and fuel than other PBRs. On patrol, he particularly liked situations where there were large concentrations of enemy troops on riverbanks and large numbers of watercraft ferrying them across. Whereas other patrol officers might stay out of range and call in reinforcements, Williams would immediately make a single firing run, getting as close as possible to the shore to survey the situation. Only then would he move out of range and call in helicopter support. When the Seawolves arrived, he would recommence his runs into the kill zone to assist the helicopters in finding the enemy positions. "While this may sound foolish on Williams' part," explained McDavitt, "his line of thinking went something like this: When the helos were in the air, the VC paid more attention to them than to the PBRs because the helos had more firepower, better visibility, and were faster than the PBRs. So while the VC were tracking and shooting at the helos, Williams was using the opportunity to shoot at the VC positions, usually without taking return fire."[213] By contrast, he often ignored lesser threats. His normal reaction to a solitary sniper was to move his boats out of range. "There was good reason for this approach," said McDavitt. "On some occasions, when PBR patrols went storming in to deal with what they thought was a single sniper, they found themselves face to face with a big time VC ambush."[214]

Williams's biggest gamble took place on 31 October 1966. River Section 531 had received solid intelligence that a 1,000-man North Vietnamese regiment on the north side of the Mekong River might attempt a crossing near My Tho and that a Viet Cong unit of unknown size (probably between 200 and 900 troops) was south of the river to provide security for the crossing. Late in the afternoon of Halloween, Williams was leading a two-boat patrol on the Mekong River ten miles west of My Tho. His crewmembers for that patrol were Seaman Rubin G. Binder, Seaman Harry L. Stump, and Engineman Fireman John W. "Clem" Alderson. PBR-107 was commanded by Signalman 2nd Class Thomas A. Poling and crewed by Boatswain's Mate 3rd class Andrew J. Eichner, Gunner's Mate (Guns) Leroy G. Bragg, and Fireman Leonard Lee Sheppard.[215]

Williams spotted a small motorized sampan crossing the river from north to south, and steered the boat toward the target. As he closed, a man in the sampan fired two shots from a rifle at PBR-105. Rather than backing off and waiting for air support to arrive, Williams charged ahead while Binder, the forward gunner, unleashed rounds from the twin .50-caliber. Binder, a 21-year-old Jewish kid from Brooklyn, New York, was not the type of sailor one might expect Williams, a good old boy from the South, to hand pick for his crew, but Williams chose Binder because he behaved well under fire and was a highly skilled gunner. During the course of the war Binder participated in 59 firefights with the enemy, mostly with Williams, and he earned nine awards, including two Bronze Stars and a Purple Heart.

Once Binder began firing, the sampan reversed course and evaded across a flooded rice paddy on Ngo Hiep Island and into the Nam Thon River. When a second sampan emerged, Williams turned his attentions toward it. Bullets from PBR-105's guns struck down two enemy soldiers as they attempted to dive into the river. The tide was high and the view to the north across Ngo Hiep Island was unobstructed. Williams could still see the first sampan heading east on the Nam Thon and concluded that this sampan might be part of the larger force his patrol had been hunting. Rolling the dice, Williams opted to pursue the craft and perform a reconnaissance of the Nam Thon. This was a "gutsy move given the narrowness of the river and the prospects of large numbers of enemy forces in the region," according to McDavitt, but Williams was betting that surprise would be on his side. Before taking off in pursuit, he advised McDavitt at the Naval Tactical Operations Center (TOC) in My Tho of his plans and requested helicopter fire support. "Williams may have been a gambler," McDavitt later noted, "but he also had a supersized portion of common sense. That's why he did not receive the Medal of Honor posthumously." Air support would later prove critical during the course of the battle.[216]

As they entered the Nam Thon River, heavy fire erupted from eight positions on the north bank. Williams ordered his units to suppress the fire and continue into the narrow inlet into which the sampan had evaded. There he discovered two large junks, each containing approximately 20 enemy soldiers. Behind the junks were eight sampans carrying more soldiers (about 8–10 per craft). More enemy soldiers manned 12 machine-gun positions along the riverbank. Seeing this large force, Williams swung the PBRs away from the kill zone but continued engaging the enemy with the machine guns from a safer distance. Frequently, Williams exposed himself to direct the attack and encouraged his men to fight, but as the return fire became more accurate, he realized that he would have to withdraw to save the unit. It was now dusk and visibility was decreasing. Williams knew that he would have a tough time exiting to the east past several fully alerted enemy positions. At the same time, he noticed additional movement to the west. Hearing the approach of a Seawolves' helicopter fire team, he gambled again, opting to disengage west to investigate the situation there.

Passing an unnamed island on the Nam Thon, Williams surprised the bulk of the enemy's forces, a flotilla estimated to contain 50 sampans and seven junks. Many of the craft were nestled deep into the foliage, neatly hidden but still afloat in the high tide. Having recently been abandoned, some had not been tied down properly and were adrift bobbing up and down. Rather than turning around and retreating east, Williams engaged this second force, figuring that surprise was on his side. The enemy could be heard shouting in confusion as they retreated into the foliage. With the enemy in complete disarray, PBRs 105 and 107 systematically sank all seven junks and 25 sampans and damaged most of the remaining craft. As soon as the enemy began to recover and return fire, Williams withdrew his force to the eastern part of the unnamed island to await helicopters.[217]

Darkness shrouded the scene as the helicopters arrived on station, but Williams remained undeterred. He reentered the channel once again to pinpoint additional targets for the Seawolves. The enemy, having regrouped, returned fire from over 40 positions on the shore, but the helicopters suppressed much of it, saving Williams' unit and permitting an orderly withdrawal. "I want y'all to go in there and have a field day on them guys," he purportedly told the Seawolves' team lead, Lieutenant Commander Joseph B. Howard. "You guys showed us plenty of guts," the pilot replied.[218] The helicopter destroyed two large junks and silenced most of the fire from the shoreline. Seeing the enemy fleeing the scene once again, Williams ordered the two PBRs to come about, switch on their spotlights, and eliminate the enemy troops as they tried to run away from the area. Four additional PBRs arrived by then and began salvaging sampans and junks for further investigation.[219]

The battle ended nearly three hours after it began, and Williams and the other PBRs headed back to My Tho with three captured enemy junks and three sampans in tow. The patrol emerged from the battle with several bullet holes in the hulls of the boats but suffered no casualties other than some minor shrapnel wounds. Later intelligence reports estimated that Williams and his men had thwarted a battalion-size river crossing, killing over 50 troops, and sinking 28 sampans and six junks. Another 25 sampans were damaged.[220]

Williams later told his son Michael that he believed that these numbers were inflated: "I did not personally kill all the people and boats mentioned in the citation." Williams instead insisted that friendly fire (red on red) caused much of the damage that day: "They were shooting from opposite banks with machine guns and RPGs and hitting each other rather than us." He also credited his team more than himself for the victory. "It takes a team to win any battle, not an individual." It remains unclear to this day how many enemy casualties resulted from friendly fire and how many were felled by American fire. Whatever the case may be, the Halloween Massacre, as it came to be known, represented the biggest PBR action of the war involving a single patrol—one for which Williams ultimately received a Medal of Honor.[221]

Williams not only took risks to kill the enemy but also gambled to save American lives. In January 1967 *Jamaica Bay*, the world's fourth largest dredge, was working on the Mekong River at Dong Tam, sucking alluvial silt out of a basin for use as landfill for a new 600-acre U.S. Army base. During the predawn hours of 9 January, while most of the crew of American contractors slept, a team of Viet Cong swimmers crawled into the vessel through its large dredge pipe and placed at least two mines below the waterline on either side of the hull of the $3 million craft. The resulting blasts killed three crewmembers, tore large holes on both quarters of the hull, and transformed the deck into distorted mass of metal. The dredge came to rest at the river bottom in 25 feet of water in a position 100 yards east of the Dong Tam entrance channel and began listing. Williams heard the explosion while on patrol a half mile west of the site and headed for the wreck. He first picked up two survivors still on board and transferred them to a tug. He then searched the debris-clogged water with PBR-105's spotlight, finding five more crewmembers, which he also took to a tug.

Returning to *Jamaica Bay*, Williams heard tapping from the hull, which was mostly submerged by this point. He and Binder stripped to the waist and dove into the murky water. They swam to the side of the dredge and shouted, trying desperately to locate the man. An older American contractor known as "Pops" responded, telling them he was trapped in a compartment. "Hang on," Williams told him, "We'll get you out." Williams and Binder swam underwater and searched with their hands for an opening to the compartment where the man was trapped. Finally, they found a closed hatch four feet underwater but obstructed by pipes. They hailed the tug, which soon pulled the pipes way with a rope. He and Binder dove back under and tried to open the hatch. No luck. It had been damaged by the blast. There was no time to get the tug to pull it open, so they mustered all their energy for one more attempt. Miraculously, the hatch came free, and Binder entered the completely darkened compartment. He found Pops clinging to a beam with water nearly up to his nose. He grabbed the man and then swam back to the surface. Both Williams and Binder received a Navy and Marine Corps Medal for saving Pops and seven other men that day.[222]

It took salvage crews over a month to refloat *Jamaica Bay*. Divers had to make underwater repairs to the hull in near zero visibility conditions and contend with swift currents and occasional sniper fire. Finally, on 8 March, *Jamaica Bay* was refloated, but just four days later while being towed to Vung Tau, she encountered a storm near the mouth of the Mekong. Eight-foot swells cracked seams in the hull and loosened a door patch amidships, eventually causing the ship to capsize and sink in 36 feet of water. There was no loss of life, but further salvage efforts were deemed impracticable.[223]

After heroics like this incident and the one on 31 October, many sailors would have been content to play it safe and just kill time until their tours ended. Not Williams. He embarked on each patrol intent upon achieving contact with the enemy. In most engagements his aggressiveness prevailed, but on 15 January 1967 the odds caught up to him. At 1545 that day, PBRs -105 and -103 received a report from a Vietnamese outpost that Viet Cong with heavy weapons were crossing the Nam Thon channel north of Ngo Hiep Island. Williams notified the ARVN 7th Division's TOC and then proceeded to the crossing area. As the boats approached the area, and Williams noted two heavily loaded sampans in the channel, his patrol came under intense fire from both banks and the sampans. He ordered his boats to pull back and then called for artillery and air support. A Cessna L-19 spotter aircraft swooped in and started marking enemy positions with smoke markers. The patrol, in turn, lit up the marked areas with .50-caliber fire. Artillery and air strikes followed. PBRs 105 and 103, joined by 104 and 96, entered the channel under cover provided by Army helicopter gunships to investigate the sampans, which had beached during the engagement. It was this decision that cost Williams the life of one of his closest shipmates, Quartermaster 1st Class Terrel E. Carter, the boat captain of Williams' cover boat and a frequent cribbage partner. "I think Daddy would have traded all of his medals in exchange for Carter's life," his son Michael said in an interview. "The event haunted him his entire life." Williams once admonished Patricia Oladeinde, a reporter for *All Hands* magazine, for asking him too many questions about his decorations. "You gotta stop and think about your shipmates. That's what makes you a great person and a great leader—taking care of each other."

Blistering fire from the shoreline erupted as soon as the PBRs drove into the channel and, before they could retreat, Murphy's Law entered—PBR-96's intakes clogged, forcing the three other boats to remain in the kill zone providing cover while the crew worked desperately to clear the pumps. During the subsequent firefight, a bullet struck Carter in the head. Two other Americans were also wounded, including Williams, who received a round in the deltoid muscle of his left arm.[224]

Although Williams rarely mentioned it later, the Navy awarded him a Navy Cross for his leadership that day. The citation claims his patrol successfully interdicted a crossing attempt of three heavy-weapons companies totaling nearly 400 men, killed 16 enemy troops, wounded 20 others, and destroyed nine enemy watercraft. For Williams, the event was a defeat because he lost a shipmate. This loss coupled with his growing disillusionment over the Vietnam War and his problems making chief convinced him to leave the service after his Vietnam tour ended.

Williams was particularly concerned with the growing tendency of the Viet Cong to use civilian villages as cover for ambushes, making it very difficult for American forces to return fire effectively, especially since the rules of engagement required PBRs to "display sound judgment in replying to fire from the vicinity of populated areas to ensure that unnecessary civilian casualties do not occur."[225] He was also dismayed by the lack of support River Section 531 was receiving from its Vietnamese counterparts. When Williams and others discovered a large crossing or congregation of enemy troops, the My Tho-based VNN unit, RAG 27, was often slow to provide support.[226] According to Captain Paul N. Gray, who assumed command of Task Force 116 in 1967, the VNN river assault groups by this time were not interested in directly confronting the Viet Cong. Their main concern was escorting barges moving supplies from Saigon to the outposts in the delta. They were quite content to let TF 116 "go out and shoot up" the Viet Cong.[227]

Finally, Williams was angered by his failure to make chief. He had failed the E-7 test multiple times, but he thought that his performance in combat in Vietnam might convince the Navy to give him a waiver and promote him. Shortly after being awarded the Medal of Honor, Williams took the test one last time. He knew he failed. The Navy offered him a promotion anyway but with one caveat—he had to serve as a recruiter for a couple of years. "Nah, I've had enough," he reportedly told the detailer. After the war he went on to become a U.S. Marshal, ultimately rising to become U.S. Marshal for the State of South Carolina. On 9 July 1975, Secretary of the Navy J. William Middendorf II appointed Boatswain's Mate 1st Class Williams as honorary chief petty officer in recognition of his Vietnam service. Honorary appointment carried with it all the rights, responsibilities, authority, and duties of a chief petty officer with the exception of entitlement to pay and allowances of the higher grade.[228]

The spirit of Williams lived on in his protégés—young sailors and officers who sought out direct combat with the enemy troops and loathed the more mundane police work PBRs performed most days on the rivers. Eager for action, many of these men preferred to engage enemy ground troops rather than perform the core missions of TF 116: enforcing the curfew, searching sampans, and conducting surveillance. Such boldness may have worked for Williams and the early riverine warriors, but by spring 1967 the enemy better understood PBR tactics and had become increasingly more effective in setting up ambushes. They expected the Americans to act aggressively and planned accordingly.[229] Using populated areas as cover, building elaborate bunkers on the shorelines, and relying heavily on recoilless rifles and larger caliber machine guns, the enemy slowly started to challenge the River Patrol Force's control of some of the narrower channels and canals.

Ambushed: Don Witt, Mike Devlin, and the End of the Williams Era

On the wet, soggy evening of 23 May 1967, twelve sailors crowded into a small office at My Tho and reviewed the mission plan for the day's patrol. Lieutenant Charles "Don" Witt, who had recently replaced McDavitt as the commanding officer of River Section 531, would be the patrol officer that day. In his briefing he noted that sandbars had been shifting on the Ham Luong. For the past five days, the Viet Cong had been moving men and supplies to an area of highly fortified bunkers on the Ham Luong. Witt told the men that he was going to take his patrol on a reconnaissance of those emplacements. "I recommended that he not go up to that area and instead stick to the main river," recalled John Donovan, "but Witt just shrugged his shoulder and said he would go anyway. My last words to him were, 'Don, you have a wife and kids.'" Witt's position as River Section commander did not allow him to get out on the rivers often, so he tried to make every patrol count. "Every time he went out, he wanted to make something happen," explained Donovan.

A Class of 1959 Naval Academy graduate from Lubbock, Texas, Witt was an energetic 31-year-old officer with youthful good looks and a boyish grin. He had heard about all the decorations that Williams and other sailors of River Section 531 had received and arrived at My Tho determined to win some for himself. "If my tour hadn't run up in April 1967," Commander Morton E. Toole, the commanding officer of River Division 53, later admitted, "I would have had to have put some type of leash on him to restrain his obvious exuberance and quest for glory. Witt was very headstrong and seemed to have his own ideas about how the war would be fought after he took over. He listened with great impatience about the lessons that we had learned on the river."

McDavitt spent several weeks with Witt, trying to transition him to the new job and was not impressed either. "He felt his training at Mare Island was the equivalent of my combat experience on the rivers." McDavitt had to politely remind him that no training in the world can "simulate being under fire and seeing the guy next to you having his head blown off." Witt felt his career was lagging behind those of his Naval Academy classmates and saw Vietnam as an opportunity to improve his promotion prospects. "Witt said, on several occasions, that he would do everything in his power to get the Medal of Honor." For McDavitt, who attended a traditional college, such competitiveness was foolish, especially since it risked getting sailors killed in the process.

As the men got into jeeps for a short ride to the docks, one sailor hesitated. Ivan Travnicek, a yeoman third class working in the River Section 531 headquarters, had volunteered to go on the patrol as a tag-along.

> I liked going on patrols for the camaraderie, but there was something wrong with this patrol. I couldn't identify the source of my unease. Perhaps it was because I was an unnecessary afterthought to the mission. Maybe it was because the weather was nasty. Or perhaps it was one of those precognitive warnings that enter the subconsciousness and cause a fateful decision to be made.[230]

Since the patrol was completely optional for him, Travnicek made an excuse about the weather and told Witt he was staying behind to catch up on paperwork. Witt released him. Seaman Mike Devlin also harbored serious doubts about the mission. "I thought Lieutenant Witt was a cowboy. The atmosphere was not good." Unlike the front office yeoman, however, Devlin could not opt out of the patrol. As a member of PBR-101's permanent crew, Devlin could only be released due to serious illness. Failure to make a patrol would have been grounds for a captain's mast or even court martial. More significantly, it would have meant letting his shipmates down.

The son of an enlisted Army military policeman, Mike Devlin was born in 1945 in the Republic of Panama and grew up in the New York City environs. Mike attended elementary school in Manhattan and Hoboken, and two years of high school in Clifton, New Jersey. School did not go well for him. Either because of an undiagnosed learning disability or problems at home, he never learned to read or write. "I had difficulties as a kid," Devlin recalled. "My father had issues with alcohol and responsibility. I joined the Navy because I really didn't have a sense of who I was or a direction." If Witt knew exactly what he wanted in life and how to get it, Devlin was the opposite—a lost soul from a disadvantaged background who drifted into the Navy for lack of other alternatives.

In 1965 Devlin had to take the Armed Forces Qualification Test three times before the Navy finally admitted him. Despite his illiteracy, the Navy initially wanted to put him on a track to become a yeoman—an enlisted career field that placed great emphasis on reading and writing skills. Once the Navy discovered he was illiterate, they transferred him to the deck force, traditionally a place where the least educated sailors served. On his first ship, major communications relay ship *Annapolis* (AGMR-1), he spent most of his time painting and cleaning the deck of this former World War II escort carrier converted in 1963 to serve as a communications major relay ship.

After a year with *Annapolis*, Devlin volunteered for duty with small boats in Vietnam because he found life on a big ship boring. "We were out at sea 90 days at a time and I found it hard being confined and doing the same thing over and over again." After training in San Diego, Devlin arrived in My Tho in May 1967. Once assigned to PBR-101, Seaman Devlin generally served as either the forward, mid, or aft gunner. In the weeks leading up to this patrol his boat had been shot at twice on the river, so he knew he could perform "okay" under fire. "One boatswain's mate told me that if I froze, he'd shoot me and throw me overboard. It made quite an impression on me—I never froze!"[231]

The Ham Luong River was two hours' steaming distance from My Tho, so the patrol left base at 2200 to be on station by midnight. Devlin served as the after .50-caliber gunner. Electronics Technician Radar 2nd Class Roy L. Castleberry from Marietta, Georgia, on his second Vietnam tour, was the boat captain and manned the con. Witt had personally chosen to ride with Castleberry because he had served in a similar role with Williams in PBR-105 and was a seasoned combat veteran. The rest of the crew did not have much experience. Seaman Michael C. Quinn, a young sailor from San Angelo, Texas, had just arrived in-country and was assigned the M60 amidships. Controversy exists over the positions of the remaining crew. Most official documents state that Engineman Fireman Terry F. Leazer was in the forward .50- caliber gun tub, and Witt was in the coxswain's flat with Castleberry. However, some veterans dispute this official version of events. Jim Schlosser, a police advisor who saw the boat soon after the attack, claimed that Witt was in the forward gun tub, a position he often favored because he enjoyed firing the guns.

Seaman Mike Devlin single handily drove PBR-101 back to My Tho after the rest of the crew was killed in an ambush on the Ham Luong River on 24 May 1967.

In the very early hours of the 24th, PBR-101 ran aground on a sandbar going into the Ham Luong from the Mekong. Sandbars at the mouths of rivers shift constantly, and Castleberry, who had just come back from leave, was unfamiliar with these recent changes. PBR-101 sat on that bar until the tide came in at 0530 while PBR-106 loitered in the area, trying its best to provide cover for the stranded vessel. The two boats drifted on the river until the curfew ended and the morning river traffic commenced. At 0700, PBR-101 inspected a water taxi that emerged from behind an island. The river was 1,500 meters wide at that point. "The four people on the water taxi were very nervous and wanted to get away from us as soon as possible," recalled Devlin. When the sampan finally did pull away at 0720, PBR-101 was idling and not at general quarters. The Viet Cong hit the PBR first with a recoilless rifle round. The concussion from the blast pushed Devlin knee first into the deck, and some shrapnel sliced into his head.

When I got my senses and returned fire, I noticed that the boat was veering to shoreline and that no one was alive. I saw Lieutenant Witt behind the coxswain. Both his limbs were hanging by a thread.... There was nothing left of his front. I then went into the cockpit and I was still catching a lot of shit [fire from the shoreline]. I picked up Castleberry and he fell apart in my hands. He was completely gone.[232]

Devlin removed Castleberry's remains from the coxswain's position and placed them next to Witt. He then pulled back on the left throttle and swung the boat towards the center of the river. Using the throttles to steer the boat, Devlin maneuvered the boat away from the kill zone. The initial recoilless rifle round claimed Witt, Leazer, and Castleberry, and subsequent machine-gun fire killed Quinn at the M60 position amidships.

As for the other boat, PBR-106, it had followed PBR-101 into the kill zone, firing furiously at shore positions until it too took a hit from a recoilless rifle round. The round exploded amidships, decapitating Troung Huong Chau, an accompanying Vietnamese Maritime Police officer, lacerating the thumb of Gunner's Mate 3rd Class Daniel Paul Artman, who was manning the M60, and sending shrapnel into the chest and arms of Engineman 3rd Class Warren G. Bolen, who was on the after .50-caliber gun. Gunner's Mate 2nd Class Gary Stouffer, the boat captain, escaped injury and managed to maneuver the boat at high speed out of the kill zone while Gunner's Mate (Guns) Seaman Charles A. Davidson Jr. expended nearly all of his ammunition in the forward turret at targets on the shoreline. During the egress Davidson radioed PBR-101, telling it that they had been "hit bad." Without any call sign, Devlin replied, "I'm all alone." Upon hearing this transmission, two other PBRs (-110 and -104) sped toward the scene, but PBR-110 suffered engine trouble, compelling it to proceed on just one engine.

At 0740, PBR-104 rendezvoused with PBRs -106 and -101, and the three units proceeded to Ben Tre, about 35 minutes away, to evacuate the wounded and the dead. Lieutenant (j.g.) Donovan had just come off patrol when the fight erupted and was immediately summoned to the My Tho TOC. "There was lots of confusion and shock," he recalled. "Nothing like this had ever happened." It was the deadliest ambush to date for Operation Game Warden.

Donovan would later call for an investigation into Witt's decision to take the PBRs into the area. The TF 116 Operations Order specifically stated that except in self-defense TF 116 units "may not initiate any attack on ground forces or watercraft without specific authority of CTG 116.1 or CTG 116.2." River Division 53 rejected the recommendation, but it did not confer a heroism award on Witt for that patrol. Posthumously, Witt would receive a Silver Star for another action on 19 May 1967 and the Navy Commendation Medal with Combat V for his service as officer in charge of River Section 531 from March to May 1967.[233] On a subtle level, the decision not to confer a valor award on Witt for the 24 May action may have been an admission by the chain of command that he showed poor judgment that day because the other sailors on his boat, killed in similar circumstances, received valor awards for the action. Castleberry and Quinn received Bronze Stars with Combat V. Devlin ultimately received a Silver Star.[234]

When the boats got to the MACV compound at Ben Tre, Devlin suffered a breakdown of sorts. He did not want anyone but American military personnel handling his dead shipmates—a proud tradition in the U.S. armed forces but impractical under the circumstances because there were no American soldiers or sailors available for grave detail. "I would not let any of the ARVNs on the boat. I was yelling and screaming at them and finally someone came on the boat and told me to get off the boat and get medical treatment." Jim Schlosser finally was called in to supervise the removal of the bodies and help clean the blood off the boats. Schlosser first removed the wallets, rings, and other valuables from the bodies and then placed them in an ambulance for transfer to Ben Tre Hospital, where they were eventually turned over to American military authorities. Schlosser had recently gone on patrol with Witt and vividly recalled removing his body from the forward gun tub. He also remembered pulling the headless body of Officer Chau from the 106 boat. "I had personally trained Chau and had attended his wedding. He was a gung ho young policeman and I was deeply saddened by his loss. I'll never forget seeing one of my other officers retrieving Chau's head and bringing it to the hospital in a bucket."

Devlin's shrapnel wounds did not seem serious at the time, so he was back on the river in three days. "I had bad headaches for a while and still have ringing in my ears from the attack." Diagnosed with PTSD (post-traumatic stress disorder) after the war, Devlin was scared to go on the river afterwards but did not want to "embarrass myself or my country by avoiding patrols." Shipmates at My Tho did what they could to keep him off patrols where they expected heavy contact. He was "psychologically damaged," explained Donovan, "but the guys looked up to him and tried to protect him." Devlin managed to endure the remainder of his tour by self-medicating. "I drank three bottles of Jack Daniels a week when I wasn't on patrol." After the war he stayed in the Navy for a while, working for a time as a mess cook for a Navy fighter squadron based in Key West, and then he got out of the service. "From the time of the attack until ten years later," claimed Devlin, "I was an alcoholic." He bounced around the country, trying to put his life together, often not leaving his various residences for days at a time and occasionally getting into fights. One day in 1977, he walked into the Bergen County Adult Learning Center in Hackensack, New Jersey. "I was so beyond myself. Between the war and not being able to get a job, I was down in the dumps." Devlin spoke to the head administrator there.

"What do you want?" he asked.

"I wanna learn how to read and write so I can function in this frickin world."

"If you work with me, I'll teach you."

The center ended up building a new literacy program to help Devlin and many others in the region. For Mike, it was a turning point. He went on to attend college at New York's Fashion Institute of Technology and as of the date of this publication works as a supervisor who coordinates sales for seven stores of a New Jersey grocery chain. "There have been so many people who have really extended themselves to give me helping hand. The war hurt me in many ways, but at my darkest moments there was always someone there to help."[235]

War Escalates on the Rivers

The Witt patrol revealed how the dangers on the river gradually increased over time as the enemy developed new tactics to combat PBR patrols. For much of its first year of operations, Game Warden scored major successes against the enemy and suffered few casualties. In fact, Task Force 116 did not lose its first sailor until 11 September 1966, when an entrenched Viet Cong gunner killed Boatswain's Mate 3rd Class Charles A. Baker on the Co Chien River 26 miles southeast of Vinh Long.[236] Game Warden did not lose an officer until 3 December 1966, when Lieutenant (j.g.) Henry I. Klein died on the lower Bassac River from a hail of automatic weapons fire.[237]

The reasons for the low casualty rate in 1966 remain a matter of speculation, but evidence from the American side suggests that the Viet Cong were initially surprised and intimidated by the new River Patrol Force and aggressive operators such as Williams and many others. Accustomed to fighting the slow, predictable, and often timid VNN boats, the Viet Cong were shocked by the speed and firepower of the PBRs and the willingness of patrol officers to operate on the narrowest of canals. It took time to develop effective countermeasures, but when they finally did, the PBRs began to suffer mightily.

While studying the tactics of the new River Patrol Force, the Viet Cong did not halt all operations against the allies. Rather, they focused more effort on attacking civilian vessels. In addition to the *Jamaica Bay* mining in January 1967, the enemy succeeded in mining the cargo ship *Eastern Mariner*, of Panamanian registry, on 26 May 1966, and the Military Sea Transportation Service ship *Baton Rouge Victory* on 23 August 1966. Damage to *Eastern Mariner* was slight, but *Baton Rouge Victory* had to be beached to avoid blocking the critical Long Tau River channel after a mine tore a 16-by-45-foot hole in the port side of the ship. In all, seven members of the crew perished in the engine room from the mine explosion. The *Baton Rouge Victory* attack resulted in the single largest loss of life suffered by the American merchant marines from enemy action during the war.[238]

Beginning in summer 1966 the enemy expanded its attacks to minesweepers. Since June 1966 Mine Squadron 11, Detachment Alpha, had been keeping the major shipping channels in the Rung Sat clear of mines using minesweeping boats (MSBs). The MSB was a 57-foot-long, wooden-hulled boat lightly armed with one .50-caliber machine gun, four .30-caliber machine guns, and a Honeywell 40mm grenade launcher. Equipped with surface radars and minesweeping gear for clearing explosives from the waterways, MSBs generally carried a crew of six and had a maximum speed of 11 knots.[239] Typically, they made several daily sweeps of the Long Tau shipping channel, traveling slowly at between five and seven knots. Although these boats were designed to sweep shallow water areas such as bays and rivers, their slow speed and lack of armor and armament made them particularly vulnerable to ambushes. "If you looked at an MSB casually, it looked sort of like a pleasure boat or a fishing trawler," explained Seaman Ken Carlstrom, an MSB-45 crewmember.[240] The boat was not designed to operate in the high threat environment of the delta, but the men of Mine Squadron 11 persevered nonetheless, living up to the Navy minesweeping community's motto "Wooden ships, iron men" and earning the Navy's first Presidential Unit Citation of the war.[241]

Viet Cong mine.

On 29 August 1966, MSB-54, while conducting a chain drag sweep of the river, struck an underwater mine. The Viet Cong then opened up on the boat with automatic weapons. The force of the blast knocked down Boatswain's Mate 1st Class William W. Johnson, the petty officer in charge, but he managed to regain his feet, direct machine-gun fire against the enemy positions, and maneuver the boat to safety while other sailors below decks worked furiously to patch and shore up holes in the two forward compartments, which were rapidly flooding. The quick response of the crew prevented the MSB from sinking. No one was injured in the attack.[242]

Two months later on 1 November, this same boat was ambushed again while making a chain sweep on the Long Tau River. In this type of sweep, an MSB towed a chain equipped with spikes on the end of it along the bottom of the river. The spikes were designed to dig into the river bottom and cut any detonation wires buried in the silt and mud. In this incident, the Viet Cong planted a command-detonated mine near the shoreline where they knew MSBs liked to operate rather than in the main shipping channel. The mine exploded near MSB's bow, causing it to slowly sink. The Viet Cong fired on the stricken craft with a 57mm recoilless rifle and small arms. MSB-49, which was operating on the opposite bank, returned fire against an estimated 18 enemy soldiers situated in 11 foxholes on the shoreline. While still under fire, it then moved in and picked up two MSB-54 crewmembers in the water and another two who had managed to swim ashore. All of the survivors were wounded, and two men perished: Seaman Apprentice Thomas M. Moore and Engineman 2nd Class George R. Weaver. MSB-54, later salvaged and towed to the Saigon Naval Shipyard, was the first MSB lost to mining during the war.[243]

On 15 February 1967 at 0655, the Viet Cong ambushed two U.S. minesweepers on the Long Tau five miles downstream from Nha Be as they made a chain drag sweep of the shipping channel. Three 75mm recoilless rifle rounds struck MSB-49, completely disabling the vessel and wounding all six of its crew. Two 75mm rounds also hit her companion sweeper, MSB-51, wounding another three sailors, including the patrol officer in charge. Despite these losses and heavy automatic weapons fire still coming from both shorelines, MSB-51 managed to push the sinking MSB-49 to a beach outside of the kill zone. Still under fire, the three uninjured crewmembers of MSB-51 removed all weapons from MSB-49 and evacuated the wounded. During the evacuation Seaman Rodney H. Rickli, a 20-year-old crewmember from Fond Du Lac, Wisconsin, died from a gunshot wound in the chest he had received during the action. MSB-49 was successfully salvaged the next day.

A little over three hours after the attack on MSB-49, Viet Cong sappers triggered a command-detonated mine under MSB-45 on the same river. According to Signalman 2nd Class Thomas Wasmund, who witnessed the mining from MSB-22 (accompanying boat), the mine pitched MSB-45 into the air and broke it in two. Seaman Carlstrom, who was manning the bow .30-caliber, remembered being shot out of the boat like a cannonball. "By the time I was in the air, I was nearly unconscious. And when I came to I remember the masts of the boat came down on top of me under the water. I was probably two seconds away from giving up getting to the surface. I kept swallowing diesel fuel and dirty water. My hands are sweating just talking about it." Carlstrom eventually clawed his way to the surface and clung to a piece of wood until he was rescued by MSB-22, which braved strong enemy fire from the shoreline to retrieve the MSB-45 crewmembers. In addition to Carlstrom, Boatswain's Mate 2nd Class Patrick T. Welch (the petty officer in charge of the boat), Engineman 2nd Class Lonnie J. Treat, and Boatswain's Mate 3rd Class Thomas J. Crain were injured seriously enough in the attack to require hospitalization, and Damage Controlman 3rd Class Gary C. Paddock, a 19-year-old from Marysville, Washington, died, either from drowning or concussion.[244]

Only a few hours after these events, heavy fire from the shoreline of the Long Tau channel blasted MSBs -32 and -51, 11 miles southeast of Nha Be, with two rounds hitting MSB-51 in the stack and sweep winch. The minesweepers and their PBR escorts quickly reversed course upstream. Twelve minutes later the enemy again fired on this force, wounding four U.S. sailors. Two helicopters of the Long Tau helicopter fire team quickly responded to the ambush and firing ceased. Following the 15 February attacks, Mine Squadron 11 had to send two additional MSBs from Long Beach to Nha Be to replace Detachment Alpha's loss of MSBs 45 and 49. The ambushes also convinced Army and Navy leadership to initiate amphibious operations in the RSSZ with the newly formed Mobile Riverine Force.[245]

U.S. Navy minesweeper MSB-21 moves down the Long Tau River in Vietnam. In February 1967, five MSBs were attacked in a single day on this busy shipping channel.

Overall, the minesweeping force suffered dearly to keep the Long Tau channel open in 1966, but its sacrifices did yield some significant dividends. According to historian Edward Marolda, "allied mine warfare forces began to turn the tide on the enemy's river interdiction effort during the latter part of 1967 and 1968." In June 1967 the allies developed a sweep plan that almost doubled the miles covered by its minesweeping forces. The following month the first of six U.S. landing craft motorized minesweepers joined the force. The new craft had steel hulls for better crew protection, twin screws for enhanced maneuverability, and improved sweep gear. As a result of tests conducted by the Navy's Research and Development Unit Vietnam, remotely controlled minesweeping craft designed to reduce the risk to personnel soon entered service. From the relative safety of MSR river minesweepers (formerly ASPBs), crews remotely operated the drone craft. The employment of these specialized craft increased the effectiveness and limited the casualties of mine warfare forces during this period of heavy combat on the rivers, and in the end the Viet Cong were unable to shut down the Long Tau channel or the port of Saigon.[246] After February 1967 no MSBs were sunk in ambushes, and Mine Squadron (MINRON) 11 Detachment Alpha suffered no killed in action for the remainder of the war. In fact, by 1967 the Military Sea Transportation Service was supplying General Westmoreland with enough food, ammunition, and other supplies by water to allow him to initiate big unit actions, such as *Attelboro, Cedar Falls,* and *Junction City.*

Beginning in March 1967 the Viet Cong employed increasingly lethal weapons and tactics against the PBRs. Using Soviet-manufactured M1891 rifles equipped with 3.5 power telescopic sights, trained Viet Cong snipers began hitting targets on the river up to 600 meters away. On 2 March a Viet Cong sniper fired two rounds at a River Section 511 PBR patrol in the vicinity of Can Tho, hitting Engineman Fireman Charles M. Dunn in the leg and knee. On the 18th, Fire Control Technician Seaman Apprentice William R. Dennis III was hit in the head and killed from a range 500–600 meters away on a dark night. On the 11th, a patrol from River Section 531 was checking an 80-foot junk on the My Tho River seven miles southwest of My Tho when a sniper fired two rounds at PBR-96. Lieutenant (j.g.) David George Kearney, a 24-year-old from Pittsburgh, took a round through the back. Another bullet wounded Seaman Rene Garcia in the lower jaw. The patrol returned fire with its .50-caliber guns and departed from the scene to evacuate Kearney and Garcia. Radioman 1st Class Frank R. Spatt, the patrol officer that day, was in the bowels of the junk looking for contraband when the attack occurred. "I heard a couple of small shots, you know, 'pow, pow,' and then I heard our fifties going off. I came flying out of there and jumped on the boat and saw Kearney laying face down on the deck, and my coxswain Rene Garcia standing there in a state of shock with blood running down his face." With the help of reconstructive surgery, Garcia eventually recovered from his wounds, but Kearney died before the medevac helicopter arrived. According to Spatt, Kearney was doing a familiarization ride that day in preparation for duty as a tactical operations center officer. "He did not feel the PBR guys would have confidence in him as a radio controller unless they knew him personally and felt he had some personal familiarity with the rivers," explained Spatt. "He had only been in Vietnam a few days before his death." In the seven days following the PBR-96 incident, the Viet Cong initiated nine additional sniper attacks on Game Warden forces, leading Captain Robert A. Dowd, the staff intelligence officer for COMNAVFORV, to conclude in a Game Warden Weekly Intelligence Summary that a "new VC tactic seems to be developing using well-trained snipers with top-grade weapons," and that if the trend continued "PBR crews would be hard-pressed to effectively combat" these new tactics.[247]

As attacks against Game Warden units began to increase, a new task force commander entered the fray. On 31 March 1967, Captain Paul Gray relieved Captain Burton B. Witham as the commander of Task Force 116. Known as the "Bald Eagle" because of his lack of hair, Gray graduated from the Naval Academy in 1941 and saw action in World War II as the gunnery officer of the battleship *South Dakota* (BB-57) during the battle of Santa Cruz Islands and the naval battle of Guadalcanal. At the age of 26, he left the surface Navy to attend flight school, graduating with his wings in 1943 and later seeing more action at the end of World War II as the commanding officer of Bomber Squadron 92 on aircraft carrier *Lexington* (CV-16). It was in the Korean War as the commander of Fighter Squadron (VF) 94, however, that Gray solidified his reputation as a naval aviation legend. On one occasion he landed a Skyraider with 59 holes on *Essex* (CV-9) and then walked away from the plane "as if he had no nerves in his body," wrote author James A. Michener, who was on the ship at the time covering the war as a correspondent. On three other occasions, battle damage forced him to ditch his plane in the icy waters of the Sea of Japan. After the third ditching, a Navy cook wrote on his traditional "welcome home" wardroom cake: "Cut it out!"[248]

As the new CTF 116, Gray brought some his aggressive aviator spirit to the rivers. He insisted that all of his staff officers go on PBR patrols and qualify as patrol officers. He also initiated operations designed to achieve contact with the enemy. "Our best intelligence was a reaction," he explained in an oral history, "If we could get shot at some place, we'd immediately take a look and see what's going on. If we continued to get shot at, then we'd bring everything we had to take them on."[249]

In April he initiated a major operation in the Vinh Long and Vinh Binh provinces designed to ensnare and destroy the Viet Cong's 306th Main Force Battalion. Elements of the ARVN 9th Division launched a series of amphibious assaults in the area while PBRs provided reconnaissance, mobile firepower, and blocking forces for the operation. In the end the operation destroyed three junks and captured 32 abandoned sampans but did not achieve much contact with the Viet Cong. Lieutenant Commander Donald D. Sheppard, who participated in these operations as the commander of River Division 51, criticized the ARVN for the lackluster results. "Did the ARVN respect our power?" wrote Sheppard in a memoir. "Did they realize now what a potent force the PBRs were? Fuck no! The entire operation proved nothing."[250] Lieutenant (j.g.) Wynn Goldsmith, a patrol officer in the operation, concurred. "To me they [the ARVN troops] looked like a disorganized mob of teenagers made to dress up for some sort of play war. The noncommissioned officers wore bright yellow or orange scarves around their necks and were shouting things to the grunts in the singsong Vietnamese language, but the troops were ignoring them. They wanted to hunker down on their haunches and put their fingers in their ears to silence the loud explosions from nearby."[251] Gray blamed the situation more on the Viet Cong than on the South Vietnamese. "We'd try sweeps from now and then when I was in the CTF 116, and go down and really take on an area that we knew had a lot of Viet Cong there. But, by the time we'd do anything, usually they were gone."[252]

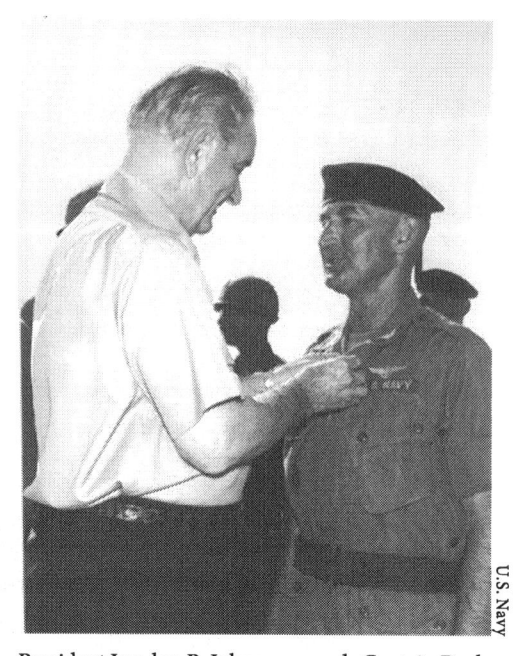

President Lyndon B. Johnson awards Captain Paul N. Gray the Silver Star. Captain Gray commanded TF-116 from March 1967 to March 1968 and received the Silver Star for his leadership during an action that occurred on 9 May 1967.

On 9 May, in a smaller sweep near Tan Dinh Island on the Bassac River, Gray did achieve contact. The 10-kilometer-long island was being used as a way station and rest area for the enemy and, during the days leading up to the attack, friendly units had been fired upon several times in the area. In an attempt to stamp out Viet Cong activity on the island, Gray personally led a small force of river boats, supported by SEALs and helicopters, down a channel less than 50 meters in width at many points. During the operation the patrol encountered heavy fire from several well-bunkered emplacements, and from an LCM Gray directed return fire, at one time even manning a grenade launcher. Gray and his forces made two sweeps of the narrow channel during the two-hour fight, the results of which included six Viet Cong killed in action and one junk and six sampans destroyed.[253]

Boldness on the 9th may have yielded a small victory for TF 116, but the Witt ambush at the end of the month quickly eclipsed this success. On a front page editorial in *The Jackstaff News*, the bulletin for U.S. Naval Forces Vietnam, Gray described the event as "the greatest disaster in the history of Game Warden operations," and vowed to "strike back and hurt the responsible enemy."[254] In truth, he admitted after the war, the enemy proved extremely hard to find and kill, especially in the first six months of 1967. They operated more like a "criminal paramilitary," he stated, than an organized military force, striking the PBRs in places and times of their own choosing. By 1967 the enemy was also becoming much more careful about troop and supply movements, making it much more difficult for Game Warden forces to score the kind of successes Williams achieved during the early days of the operation. "The Viet Cong are cautious and patient," Gray wrote in his end-of-tour report, and "willing to wait many hours at their staging areas along canal banks before crossing."[255] An Army report written by the IV Corps advisor in 1968 confirmed these observations, noting that when Game Warden PBRs initially began operating in early 1966, frequent engagements with VC watercraft resulted in heavy enemy losses, but by the end of 1967 such incidents became much less frequent due to the Viet Cong's reduced use of the major rivers for transportation of insurgents and supplies.[256] Despite Gray's frustrations over lack of contact with the enemy, PBRs appeared to be succeeding in reducing enemy activity on the main rivers.

Gray also believed that the riverine blockade was ineffectual and that there was simply too much traffic on the river for the Navy's small force of PBRs to control. "I could go from the mouth of the Bassac all the way into Cambodia and never get stopped." Gray argued that the U.S. forces were too spread out and unfocused to cause much damage to the enemy. "We were acting more as a highway patrol, trying to win hearts and minds." For him, the only way the Game Warden force could have been successful would have been by taking the war to enemy sanctuaries in Cambodia such as Sihanoukville—a strategy not employed until later in the war.[257]

Gray was correct is pointing out the ineffectiveness of maintaining waterborne interdiction barriers in the lower and middle delta and the RSZZ without also covering the waterways in the upper delta near the Cambodian border, but he failed to point out that Game Warden was achieving successes in other areas during this period. A 1976 Center for Naval Analysis (CNA) study concluded that Game Warden interrupted enemy movement on the major delta rivers and prevented the Viet Cong from closing inland shipping routes. Metrics from the operation tend to support this conclusion.[258] In November 1966 Game Warden PBR forces boarded 16,263 sampans and junks, detained 588 suspects, and destroyed 120 junks, 29 structures, and 45 huts in over 76 separate firefights. Enemy casualties claimed included 68 killed and 154 wounded in exchange for two friendly personnel killed and another ten wounded. One year later in November 1967, these forces boarded 37,568 watercraft, detained 356 suspects, and destroyed 102 sampans, 149 structures, and 25 bunkers in 46 separated firefights. Enemy killed stood at 227 and wounded at 68, in exchange for seven friendly forces killed and 45 wounded.[259] It would be hard to argue that an effort of this magnitude was not having a significant impact on the enemy in the Mekong Delta and RSSZ.

What is less difficult to argue is that the job of the PBR sailor became more dangerous as the war progressed and the Viet Cong developed new tactics. As the Witt patrol graphically illustrated, Game Warden paid a price in American blood for its real or imagined successes. By February 1968, 40 Task Force 116 sailors had been killed and another 412 wounded. However, these numbers pale in comparison to the losses suffered by the ground force during the same period. Taken in a larger context, Game Warden was a very cost-effective means of imposing government control on the labyrinth of waterways in southern Vietnam. Its boats were cheap, modified fiberglass cabin cruisers equipped with surplus weapons from World War II, and its sailors were volunteers from a variety of ratings with no specialized (A school equivalent) small-boat training other than what they received in Coronado prior to their deployment. Unlike the destroyer or carrier forces, which had decades of experience to hone doctrine, technology, and training, the brown water forces had almost zero of the above prior to onset of Market Time and Game Warden. By 1967, however, this improvised, makeshift force was effectively denying the Viet Cong use of the main rivers in the delta and RSSZ, ensuring the free flow of commerce on these watery interstates, imposing a curfew, reacting to intelligence, eliminating Viet Cong tax collection efforts and other activities, stopping major crossings, and destroying a significant amount of enemy material—a major accomplishment given the Navy's relatively modest investment in the endeavor.

CHAPTER 4

Mobile Riverine Force

Boatswain's Mate 2nd Class David K. Butler is a soft-spoken retired police officer from Cooperstown, New York. He doesn't like to talk about his naval service in Vietnam, nor does he attend veterans' reunions. Drawing disability compensation for complications related to wartime wounds and Parkinson's disease connected to Agent Orange exposure, Butler has had a difficult life, but he doesn't complain, "I made it out alive; others were not so lucky."[1]

From an early age, Butler dreamed of joining the Navy. Inspired by his father, who had served as an officer on an oiler during World War II and saw action in the Atlantic against German U-boats, Butler entered the Navy in his junior year of high school at the age of 17. He attended boot camp at Great Lakes in 1961 followed by small-boat handling school in Little Creek, Virginia. As a kid growing up in Fort Lauderdale, Florida, Butler spent a lot of time in his family's 25-foot powerboat exploring the intercoastal waterway and was an experienced small-boat handler before entering the Navy. As a sailor, he quickly qualified as a coxswain with responsibility for a 55-foot landing craft and three crewmembers. This experience convinced him to strike for boatswain's mate.[2]

In 1966 Butler was an assault boat coxswain with Assault Craft Unit 2 based in Little Creek when the call came for volunteers for a new unit called River Flotilla 1. The Navy was looking for specific rates (gunner's mate, engineman, and boatswain's mate), and although Butler had no burning desire to go to Vietnam, he volunteered anyway. "I was a qualified guy and considered myself to be a team player." The Navy needed him, so he went.[3]

On 11 July 1967, Butler was the coxswain of Monitor 112-1, a 55-foot-long landing craft converted into a floating tank, complete with heavy armor and multiple cannons and machine guns. The monitor was the lead boat in a riverine operation deep in VC-controlled territory. His flotilla consisted of eight armored troop carriers (ATCs), two minesweepers, a command and control boat, and a second monitor. Each ATC carried 40 combat troops from the 2d Brigade of

View from below of an 81mm mortar on a monitor, 23 May 1968.

the U.S. Army's 9th Infantry Division. The unit and its three companies of soldiers left its floating mother ship, self-propelled barracks ship *Benewah* (APB-35), at 0615 to commence operations in the Can Giuoc district of Long An Province.[4] The convoy landed troops at various positions and then took stations to block escape routes. Throughout the day company-size units were frequently embarked and relanded elsewhere in a series of leapfrogging movements. During one of these movements, the enemy detonated a claymore mine just as ATC 112-4 dropped its ramp, wounding seven sailors and four soldiers.[5] Simultaneously, the two monitors in the unit began receiving small-arms and recoilless-rifle fire. The monitors responded with all of their firepower, including 20mm and 40mm cannons, .50- and .30-caliber machine guns, and 81mm mortars. Air and artillery strikes were also called in.

During this initial action, Butler alternated between the 81mm mortar and a .50-caliber machine gun mounted nearby it. "I put many rounds into the jungle. I did it because I was scared and I wanted to kill them before they killed us. If you weren't scared, you weren't there." When a group of Viet Cong emerged from a hole and started running away from the monitor, Butler and a seaman named Abernathy caught them in a fierce crossfire, taking out five troops in a single barrage. "I remember cutting one Viet Cong's American-manufactured Springfield sniper rifle in half with a .50-caliber round." During the battle a pair of Navy A-4 Skyhawks arrived on scene. Butler looked overhead and saw one of the planes dropping a 750-pound bomb, and the other, napalm. "It was a bright sunny day, and one of the pilots came so close to us that I could see his face shield. He gave us the thumbs up, released his load of napalm, and shot straight up into the air. The yellow and orange of the napalm looked so pretty against the royal blue sky. That was one of the coolest things I have ever seen in my life." The air strikes silenced the enemy fire, and Butler and his shipmates began to relax. "We were all somewhere between tears and laughter. Emotions would flow freely once you found out you were alive. I went out and got the remains of the Springfield rifle, and someone took a picture of me near a dead VC as I recovered the rifle."[6]

Following the air strike, Company A of the 4th Battalion, 47th Infantry made contact with an enemy unit on the Xom Cau Creek. The two monitors (112-1 and 112-2) went 100 yards up the narrow stream to provide cover fire. While the monitors fired, two ATCs landed Company B on the east bank of the creek. The flotilla then began sweeping south to support the troops. Companies A and B continued to leapfrog south along the east and west banks of the Xom Cau, Kinh Dong, and Song Doung Le supported by other boats in the operation.[7] At 1758, Butler's unit came to a very narrow part of the Xom Cau. Lieutenant Norman L. Wells, the commander of River Assault Division 112, was riding in Monitor 112-1 with Butler. He noticed on the right bank of this narrow stream a platoon of Army troops pinned down and "getting clobbered." Wells, the son of a career foreign service officer and a 1962 graduate of Tufts University, ordered the unit to go 100 yards down the stream and provide fire support for the beleaguered unit. "I ordered the 40mm to rake that area," explained Wells, "We raked it pretty good and then moved up another 50 meters or so."[8]

Monitor 112-1 also began taking return fire from the port side. "There was so much smoke from all the guns on the boat shooting that I could hardly breathe," Butler explained. "They told us to move up the river quickly. The hardest thing I had to do was turn up those throttles because it meant going deeper into harm's way." At one point, a Viet Cong emerged from a hootch and fired at the monitor with a rifle. A crewmember shot back with an M79 grenade launcher, hitting the man squarely in the chest. "Scratch one VC," Wells announced dryly on the internal radio system.[9]

By this time, Monitor 112-1 had been fighting off and on for almost seven hours

Sailor fires an M79 grenade launcher from a river assault boat, 23 September 1967.

and fatigue was setting in. Butler, standing ankle deep in spent .30-caliber bullet casings, was doing his best to continue steering the boat. Seeing Butler getting tired, Boatswain's Mate Chief Howard M. Bannister, a 38-year-old boat captain from Delbarton, West Virginia, came up through a hatch from the mortar pit and said, "Do you want some water?" Butler said yes, and the chief replied, "I'll take the wheel and you go down and take the gun in the mortar pit." On Monitor 112-1, crewmembers often alternated positions during long patrols, and Butler had a lot of experience firing the mortar. Butler moved down the ladder to the mortar pit and was taking a drink from a 5-gallon water jug when he sensed some movement out of the corner of his eye. A Viet Cong soldier had emerged from a spider hole with an antitank rocket launcher. An expert rifleman, Butler grabbed an M16 and told Seaman David Parker, who was standing by his side, "I am going to get that bastard." As Butler waited for the soldier to emerge again, a B40 antitank rocket fired by another Viet Cong came right over his shoulder and slammed into the conning station, killing Bannister instantly and wounding six others with shrapnel.[10] Lieutenant Wells, who was standing at the rear of the monitor between the two gun mounts, said it hit the slit of the conning tower at a slight right angle, striking Bannister in the chest. "It was a good shot, a lucky shot."[11]

The Viet Cong then opened up on the monitor with small arms. "All hell broke loose," recalled Butler, "So I grabbed a .50-caliber machine gun and poured fire everywhere. All of a sudden a second rocket round hit somewhere on the boat and that one knocked the crap out of me."[12] Hit by shrapnel in the right leg and buttocks, Butler fell down to the deck and ended up with his head under the 40mm mount. "The big 40mm was going boom, boom, boom, and these spent brass shell casings were coming down on me. Of course my helmet had been blown off, and I was trying to protect my head. My arms were burning from the casings. I was trying to move out from under the gun and I remember moving my arm across the deck and sloshing through a puddle of blood. I yelled to the guy in the gun mount, 'What's my leg look like.' And he responded, 'What leg?'" The sailor could not make out the shape of Butler's leg. He could only see blood and exposed tissue.[13]

Lieutenant Wells, who had been wounded in the face with shrapnel and was having difficulty seeing, ordered the monitor to make a three-point turn and reverse course. Straddling Bannister's lifeless body, Seaman Thomas E. Stover, who had taken over the helm following the attack, struggled to nudge the bow into the bank and turn the large boat around in the narrow river. Butler, still lying on the deck, heard the bottom of the craft scraping the mud and the screaming of the engine, but he could not move and worried about passing out and dying from loss of blood.

Due in no small part to the bravery of Stover and the other able-bodied survivors of the attack, Monitor 112-1 made it back to a staging area where Butler and Wells could be evacuated by helicopter to an Army hospital. At the evacuation site, Monitor 112-2 came alongside Monitor 112-1 to assist with the wounded. Boatswain's Mate 2nd Class Robert E. Davis, a young, enthusiastic sailor from Connecticut who always had been eager to engage the enemy, was transformed by what he saw. "Do you still want to go up the river now?" his superior officer, Lieutenant Richard A. Citarella, sardonically asked. Davis said nothing. "It was the realization that this was for real and that a person doing my job had just gotten killed. This was the first time in my life I was speechless. I had nothing to say." From that point forward, Davis understood that the war was not about personal glory. "We were there to do a job and it was a hard job."[14]

At the Army 93rd Evacuation Hospital in Long Binh, nurses and medics prepped Butler for a leg operation. They first took away all of his gear (including a .38-caliber pistol, a sheath knife, and some M16 magazines) and then cut away all his clothes and gave him several IVs. In the triage, Wells walked over to Butler's gurney, put his hand on Butler's shoulder, and said, "You're going to be okay." The next thing Butler remembered was being wheeled into an air-conditioned operating room and thinking, "This is good." He fell asleep and awoke the next day. He would spend three weeks at Long Binh before being transferred to Japan and then to Portsmouth Naval Hospital for ten months of recovery. The doctors were able to save his right leg, but severe nerve damage in the leg compelled the Navy to medically discharge him soon after his release.[15] As for Wells, once doctors determined that his eyesight was not permanently damaged, he was back out on patrol in 24 hours. Bannister was not so lucky. Just five days after his 38th birthday, the chief became the first Mobile Riverine Force sailor killed in action during the Vietnam War. His death would usher in one of the bloodiest chapters of the Navy's experience on the rivers of Vietnam. In all, 115 Task Force 117 sailors and 2,624 soldiers from the 9th Infantry Division were killed in action during the conflict.[16] The Viet Cong, however, suffered far greater casualties. The MRF kept enemy forces in the delta on the defensive and allowed MACV to focus more resources in other areas of the country, secured the vital and populous "bread basket" of South Vietnam, and provided essential backup to the three ARVN divisions there. In many respects, it served as the cornerstone for General William Westmoreland's southern flank.

MACV created the Mobile Riverine Force in 1966 to conduct operations in the Mekong Delta in support of General Westmoreland's strategy of employing American units to search out and destroy enemy formations and base areas throughout the country. The 186 assault craft of the MRF's naval component, which ultimately became Task Force 117, were responsible for transporting elements of the U.S. Army's 9th Infantry Division to and from assault zones in the Mekong Delta and providing fire support for the troops while they operated in the rice paddies and jungles. Originally, planners believed that heavily armed armored assault craft would minimize casualties and allow the MRF to operate with near impunity. But as fate would have it, the Viet Cong began equipping its troops with armor-piercing weaponry. These weapons, the B40 in particular, would make it much more dangerous for TF 117 to operate than planners had originally envisioned.[17] The B40 was a Vietnamese-manufactured warhead designed to be fired from the RPG-2 shoulder-fired antitank weapon. The rocket had a 40mm stem and an 80mm shell that extended beyond the smooth barrel of the launcher. With an effective range of 150 meters, the B40 system was lightweight, highly reliable, and required minimal training to operate. Its blowback system virtually eliminated recoil, while the shaped hollow charge warhead concentrated its force in a narrow direction, creating a jet of superheated metal capable of penetrating the armor of 1950s-era main battle tanks and all types of light armored vehicles. The B50 system was similar to the B40 except for its 50mm stem and launch tube, which extended the weapon's effective range beyond 150 meters. For the men of the TF 117, these rockets were the most feared ordnance in the VC inventory.[18]

Despite the losses these weapons would inflict, the successes of river assault tactics usually outweighed the costs. The MRF could operate in a watery world inaccessible to all other means except helicopters, which were always in short supply during this period. For much of 1967, the MRF also boasted a 15 to 1 kill ratio.[19] Finally, the MRF in General Westmoreland's words, "saved the Delta" during the 1968 Tet Offensive, and several of its river assault division earned Presidential Unit Citations.[20]

Origins, Training, and Command Relationships

The Mekong Delta was in many respects the most significant piece of real estate in the Republic of Vietnam. More than a third of the country's 17 million people lived in its 16 provinces and 40,000-square kilometers of rice paddies and jungle. The area also produced more than 75 percent of the country's food. As a "rice bowl" alone, it merited the attention of military planners, but given that it was also a Communist stronghold and cradle of the insurgency in the South, planners made it even more of a priority. Communist guerrillas had been active there since the 1930s, and the delta could lay claim to some of the most pro-Communist provinces in South Vietnam. By 1967 American advisors estimated that the Viet Cong had over 50,000 troops in the delta—45 percent of total insurgent strength in South Vietnam.

Against this insurgent force, South Vietnam's IV Corps commander, Major General Nguyen Van Manh, fielded a force of 30,000 regular troops and close to 100,000 Regional and Popular forces. IV Corps also included six Vietnam Navy river assault groups, each capable of

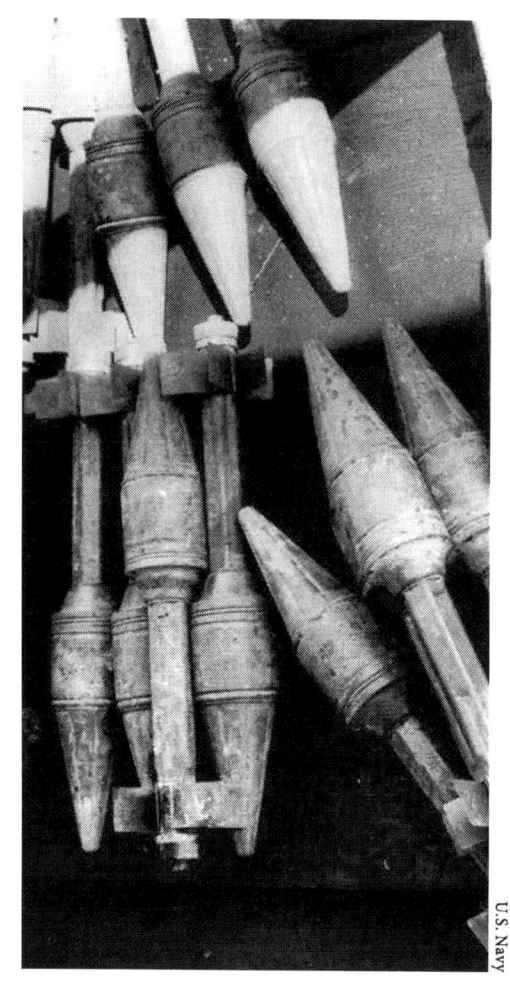

Designed as antitank weapons, these rockets were employed with great effectiveness by the Viet Cong against the armored boats of the Mobile Riverine Force, January 1967.

U.S. Navy

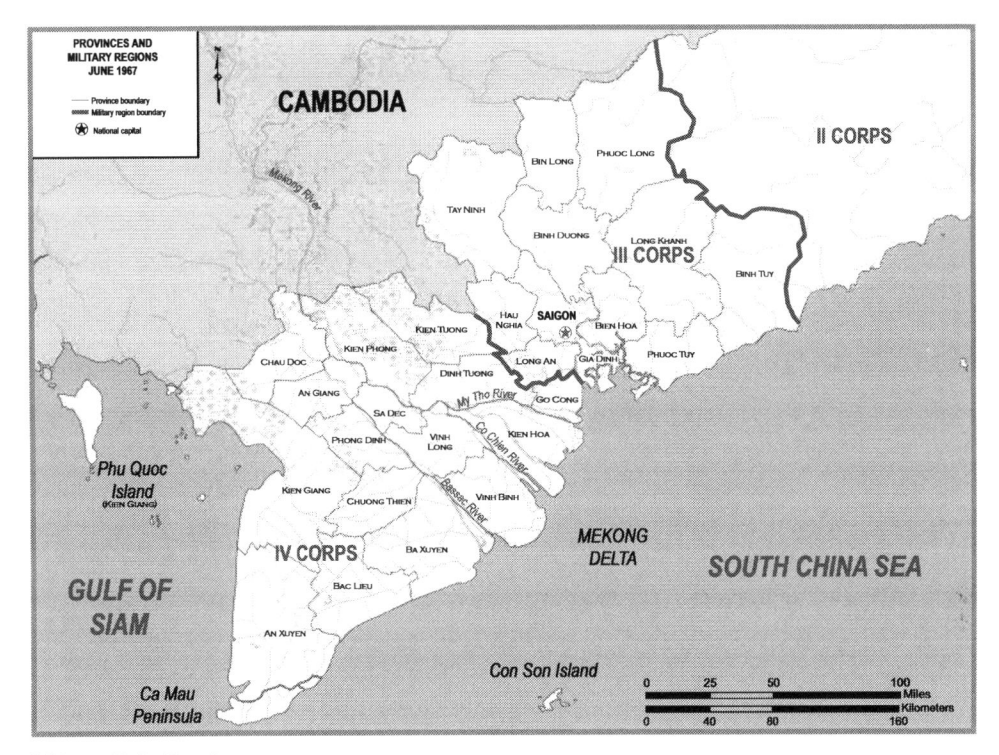

Mekong Delta Provinces.

transporting a battalion of infantry troops. With such a large force, Manh should have been able to quell the insurgency but, according to U.S. Army historian George MacGarrigle, "By 1967 the best Saigon could claim was a stalemate." Manh devoted a good deal of his resources to securing the main towns and keeping Route 4, the main highway in the delta, secure. That meant the Viet Cong controlled much of the rural countryside, especially at night when South Vietnamese forces tended to remain in their bases and outposts. As Colonel William B. Fulton, the first commander of the MRF's Army component, later wrote, "far from being totally cleared of Communist forces, in 1966 the delta was more than ever under Viet Cong control." For much of this period, the enemy spread terror throughout the countryside by initiating up to 1,000 small-scale attacks per month on government outposts, watchtowers, and isolated villages. On several occasions the Viet Cong forcibly relocated the populations of entire hamlets. VC agents also siphoned off much of the country's rice production in the delta through illegal taxation: in 1963, four million metric tons of rice reached markets in Saigon; by 1966, this number had dwindled to three million tons, compelling South Vietnam to make up the deficit with imports.[21]

Recognizing that something needed to be done, General Westmoreland decided in late 1965 that American troops would be introduced in the area to cut off enemy main force units (which were operating mainly in I, II, and III Corps Tactical Zones) from the bread basket of

South Vietnam.[22] "My conviction," he stated in a 1966 message to CINCPAC, "is that enemy access to Delta resources must be terminated without delay."[23] He therefore directed his staff to prepare a plan for stationing a force, known initially as the Z Division, in the delta. In examining the alluvial plain riddled with 6,400 kilometers of navigable streams and waterways, planners quickly realized they would need a flotilla of landing craft to transport soldiers around the area. They also discovered that the area offered few suitable areas of dry land for bases. Nearly every scrap of land was densely populated, and building almost anywhere would require uprooting hundreds of people. Thus, planners turned to the concept of floating barracks ships. From their deliberations evolved the Mekong Delta Mobile Afloat Force (MDMAF) concept.

As initially configured, the MDMAF, renamed the Mekong Delta Mobile Riverine Force, or MRF, would consist of a Mobile Riverine Base (MRB), based on a larger river, to accommodate a brigade of troops and provide maintenance and logistics support for river assault operations. Smaller troop carriers, monitors, assault support patrol boats, and command boats would in turn launch attacks from this floating base against targets located near smaller waterways. Additionally, one land base, known as Dong Tam, would be created eight kilometers from My Tho to house an additional brigade.[24]

The basic mission of the MRF's Navy component, which eventually became known as River Assault Force, or Task Force 117, was to conduct river assault missions in conjunction with the Army. This task involved transporting Army troops from their bases afloat and on shore to areas of operation, providing gunfire support for the troops once they had landed, and then picking them up once the operations concluded. TF 117 forces also provided blocking forces in support of ground operations and waterborne security patrols for MRF bases, suppressed ambushes with naval gunfire, conducted mine countermeasures operations, and established floating medical aid stations for Army troops and medevac services as needed. TF 117 base units provided messing, berthing, and hospital facilities for all embarked personnel (both Army and Navy) as well as maintenance and repair support for all equipment. It was a tall order for a Navy with only a year's worth of experience in the rivers of Vietnam.[25]

In February 1966, the 2d Brigade, 9th Infantry Division, was activated at Fort Riley, Kansas, for deployment to Vietnam as part of the MRF. It consisted of 2,120 men organized into three infantry battalions and one artillery battalion. The unit received 24 weeks of training prior to deployment. The training emphasized basic and small-unit infantry combat training but did not specifically deal with riverine operations because, according to the 2d Brigade commander, Colonel William Fulton, "Too little was known about riverine warfare to incorporate it fully into training" at that time.[26] Even if more had been known, it is doubtful that the tight deployment schedule would have permitted it. "The training was terribly abbreviated and the haste was almost indecent," explained Major Lucien "Blackie" Bolduc, who commanded the 3d Battalion, 47th Infantry during 1966–1967. Most of Bolduc's men came straight out of reception centers, which compelled him to devote the first eight weeks to basic combat training followed by another eight weeks of advanced combat training. This left him with only eight weeks for small-unit training at the squad, platoon, and company level. Compounding training difficulties was the Army's introduction of the new M16 rifle, which forced Bolduc to spend additional valuable training hours transitioning his men from the M14 to the M16.[27]

Navy training commenced in October 1966 and consisted of an 11-week course in boat handling, gunnery, first aid, radios, basic engine mechanics, and a myriad of other skills sailors needed had to learn to operate small boats on rivers. Initially, the Naval Amphibious Base, Coronado, California, administered the course. In March 1966, it transferred to the San Francisco Bay Naval Shipyard at Mare Island, California, because this location in the Sacramento River delta contained sloughs and waterways similar in some respects to the riverine environment of the Mekong Delta. On 30 January 1967 this new training center was commissioned as the Naval Inshore Operations Training Center (NIOTC).[28]

The quality of training varied considerably depending on when a sailor entered the course. Sailors who trained for MRF duty in 1966 and 1967 had a vastly different experience from those who entered the program later in war. Lieutenant Alan Breininger, who trained at Coronado in 1966 and returned to NIOTC as an instructor in October 1968, criticized his initial training as "unrealistic." Few instructors had combat experience, and the LCM (6)s that he trained in were different from the heavily modified LCMs that he eventually fought in during the war—"the training boats were lighter and handled differently, and visibility without the gun turrets was very different." Breininger also complained that he only received training on the .50-caliber machine gun and 20mm cannon during heavy weapons training off of San Clemente Island even though he was destined to serve on monitors, which also had 40mm guns and 81mm mortars. Initially, he explained, "it was a thrown-together operation with very little funding." When he returned as an instructor in 1968, however, the situation had changed dramatically. Riverine veterans now taught gunnery and boat handling, and the training was much more realistic, especially the last five days when sailors went out on 24-hour mock operations in the Sacramento River delta and experienced ambushes and sabotage similar in some respects to what they would later encounter in the Mekong Delta.[29]

No matter when a sailor attended the school, most praised the physical training they received.[30] "PT was conducted by SEALs, and we did about 10 miles a day of running," recalled Radioman Seaman David Raybell. "It was very intense."[31] Butler concurred, "I don't think I was ever in better physical condition."[32] Almost universally, they also found the interdisciplinary nature of training to be highly effective. As Engineman Fireman Larry D. Rodgers described it, "We cross trained in a variety of other disciplines (hospital corpsman, navigation, coxswain, gunner's mate, and radioman). I learned stuff in training that I would have never learned in the fleet. I learned how to tear down, clean, and put back together an assortment of weapons—40mm and 20mm cannon, the .50-caliber machine gun, the M16 rifle, and the .45-caliber pistol. I also learned how to operate a tactical radio and gained some real good knowledge in basic first aid."[33] Michael Harris, a radioman on an ATC in 1968, appreciated the mock ambush training. Getting shot at in a training boat by .50-caliber blanks and dummy rockets "helped us with the reality of what we were going to face. But again, once you're there, it's a whole new on-the-job learning experience."[34]

The heart and soul of NIOTC training was gunnery. No skill was more important for the MRF, and every TF 117 sailor had to be able to competently fire any weapon on the ATC plus a variety of small arms. Electrician's Mate Lester Schneider fondly remembered firing round after round of .50-caliber and 20mm munitions at a gunnery range near San Clemente Island. Harris also found weapons training to be "pretty intense."[35] Lieutenant (j.g.) Walter F. Lineberger III, the chief of staff for River Assault Division 91 in late 1968, was amazed by the gunnery abilities of enlisted NIOTC graduates. "One of my 40mm gunners, a guy named William Zachmann, could launch an ice box target into the air with a well-placed round and then hit the box again as it fell to the ground. Another guy fresh out of NIOTC spotted three VC on a distant riverbank one day, grabbed an M16, and dropped all three in a matter seconds." Lineberger, who served with the MRF during 1968–1969, also praised NIOTC for its ability to transform civilians into warriors. "Some of the guys coming from the States had long hair, wore beads, and displayed peace symbols. I thought they were going to get us killed, but all it took was one firefight and these people were instantly turned into killers. It was an amazing transformation! It was scary. They were so well trained—a real testament to NIOTC. What a bunch of tough guys. The ability of the human spirit to adapt to circumstances was amazing."[36]

Harris concurred: "We adapted extremely well. I mean, you had a job to do and you had a machine gun and ammunition and you knew how to tear it apart, and the rest was just practical experience. When you got in an ambush you operated the gun." Harris also noted that by early 1968 many of the NIOTC instructors had served with the MRF and had a lot of practical experience on the rivers.

> Because they had been there, we trusted them, and I mean if you ever wanted to be attentive in your life, that's the time to be attentive because these men were conveying stuff that could save our lives and save the lives of others.... I remember one instructor addressed the class and said, "Look at the man next to you, on each side. Some of you are going to be wounded; some of you are going to be killed"; and he was right. We got over there and there were wounded and killed in our own class, many of them.[37]

Besides gunnery, the segment of training perhaps most responsible for imbuing sailors with a warrior ethos was SERE training (usually conducted at Warner Springs, California, or Whidbey Island, Washington). Some sailors resented the harsh treatment they received at SERE, but others looked at it as part of the mental and physical conditioning process required for combat. Part of SERE training involved living off the land with just a survival knife, eating berries, small mammals, and whatever else could be scrounged. The other part was POW training in a mock prison camp, complete with barbed wire, watchtowers, and guards dressed in Soviet uniforms. According to Gunner's Mate (Guns) 3rd Class John L. Green Jr., "SERE was a wonderful experience. They'd strip you down in your underwear and put a hood over your head, and ropes around your neck and march you through cold, muddy fields. They'd take you into horse stalls and throw freezing water at your face and you would lose your breath under the hood. They'd put you in coffins. I was in a coffin next to the senior ranking POW officer (a pilot). Each coffin had a little drill-hole where they could observe your face. The coffins were only meant for a 5-foot 6-inch person and I am 6 feet 4 inches. Your entire body would fall asleep from your armpits to your toes."[38] Michael Harris thought that the main purpose of the course was to teach students how to survive in unexpected circumstances and the importance of maintaining discipline in stressful circumstances. "I spent 12 hours in the box and I'm pretty claustrophobic. I would just sing to myself and try to stay sane, really."[39] Even the MRF chaplains had to endure the rigors of SERE. Padre Raymond Johnson recalled being beaten, thrown in the box until his legs lost circulation, made to do endless push-ups, and interrogated. "I wouldn't have made it through the program had I not been in pretty good athletic shape."[40]

Continual harassment and lack of food and sleep affected different people in different ways. SERE trainers tried to induce severe stress in a sailor by various means and then evaluate how each person reacted. Some handled the stress magnificently. Recalling his weeks at SERE, Gunner's Mate (Guns) 2nd Class Chester C. Stanley derisively dismissed it as just another unpleasant training exercise: "I got water boarded, ate squirrels, and was told by interrogators that my sister was a whore. This made me chuckle. I ain't got no sister. I got two brothers."[41] Lieutenant Edwin Oswald, on the other hand, had an entirely different experience: "SERE is where I pretty much got crushed. It changed my life. In a lot of ways, SERE is harder to talk about than the combat." According to Oswald, it was a tradition at SERE for the enlisted camp guards to pick the "newest, the youngest, the least-senior officer and hammer his ass." As a young supply officer, Oswald became a perfect target for this treatment. "We got dunked in ice. We got locked in a coffin-like box. We got shocked with cattle prods. I got my teeth examined with a cattle prod. It hurt, but I just rolled up and went inside." What truly disturbed Oswald were the psychological games the instructors played on him and several other junior officers. After being duped into reading propaganda in front of a camera, he felt like a complete failure. "What it did to a guy like me was make me reexamine my conscience." At the beginning of the training, an instructor had said, "Gentlemen, SERE is not here to build character, it's to reveal character." And Oswald believed him. When that same instructor put him in front of the class at the end of training and announced that he was a traitor, every positive feeling he had about himself evaporated. "I was destroyed. I think if I would have had access to a gun that night I probably would have killed myself."[42]

The relatively long length of training allowed boat captains and officers to evaluate individual sailors and experiment with different crew combinations. "I wanted each boat to be able to function independently," claimed Lieutenant Norman Wells.[43] "I also wanted people to get along. I depended heavily on Chief Bannister in putting together the crews and creating the best teams." Breininger made a point of getting to know all the boat captains in his river division and many of the sailors as well.[44] Lieutenant Commander Francis E. "Dusty" Rhodes, the commander of River Assault Squadron 11, handpicked Chester Stanley to be the 40mm gunner on his command monitor. "We hit it off well because we had both been junk force advisors," said Stanley. "He called me his gunner."[45]

In August 1966, Captain Wade C. Wells was named the Navy component commander of the MRF and the head of River Assault Flotilla (RIVFLOT) 1. A native of Georgia and a 1937 graduate of the Georgia Institute of Technology, Wells was on the light cruiser *Helena* (CL-50) during the Pearl Harbor attack in 1941 and later saw combat in the Pacific during World War II on the light cruisers *Cleveland* (CL-55) and *Vincennes* (CL-64). From January 1951 to July 1952, he commanded *Tingey* (DD-539), a *Fletcher*-class destroyer recommissioned for service in Korea. Under Wells' command, *Tingey* operated off Wonsan providing gunfire support for United Nations ground troops, conducted antimining and shore bombardment patrols off Hungnam, and supported South Korean commando raids. Before taking over RIVFLOT 1, he had been the operations officer for Naval Defense Force Eastern Pacific.[46] As a hard-nosed "tin can" sailor, Wells had a reputation for raising his voice and using profanity, but he was also a good administrator who had a knack for getting the job done and securing much needed equipment and supplies for the MRF.[47] Navy Chaplain Raymond W. Johnson, who knew the commodore well, described him as follows: "he was a rocks-and-shoals, hardcore piece of leather, but underneath it all was a soft, mellow soul."[48]

Captain Wade C. Wells, the first commander of Task Force 117.

Wells contended that the MRF should act as a separate force independent of 9th Infantry Division control, and that it should operate exclusively in the IV Corps Tactical Zone under COMNAVFORV. Westmoreland disagreed. Since the 9th played a significant role in the defense of Saigon's outer ring, the MACV commander insisted that the 2d Brigade remain under division control, so that in the event of an attack on the capital it could immediately deploy to Long An Province and the Rung Sat.[49] As a consequence, he decided in December 1966 to place U.S. Army forces conducting riverine operations under the 9th Infantry Division commander, who would exercise control via Wells' Army counterpart, Colonel Fulton, the commanding officer of the

2d Brigade. U.S. Navy riverine forces would be under the operational control of the COMNAVFORV (Rear Admiral Ward), who would exercise this control through COMRIVFLOT 1 Wells (who later became Commander Task Force 117). MACV also dictated that riverine operations could take place in both the IV and III Corps zones. This command arrangement as promulgated in MACV Planning Directive Number 12-66 meant that in practical terms each service in the MRF would retain command of its own forces. Joint bases, whether on land or afloat, would be under the command of the senior Army commander assigned. When the MRF weighed anchor, the Navy component commander would assume control until the movement was over. During combat a similar arrangement prevailed. Troops in landing craft would be under Navy control while in transit, but as soon as the troops landed, the Army commander would regain control. Upon reembarking, the troops would once again fall under Navy control until they returned to a base (whether ashore or afloat), whereupon they would again fall under Army command.[50]

Wells initially resented having the commanding general of the 9th Division assign missions to the MRF, but a meeting between him and Major General George S. Eckhardt, the 9th Infantry Division commander, in April 1967 smoothed ruffled feathers, and Wells agreed to accept MACV Planning Directive Number 12-66. There would be no single commander of the Mobile Riverine Force. Any differences that arose in this "two-headed" command would be resolved through cooperation, coordination, liaison, and good judgment at all levels of the Army and Navy chains of command: Wells via COMNAVFORV and Fulton via the 9th Division commander, followed in turn by the II Field Force commander. In the event that a dispute could not be settled at any level of the respective Army and Navy command chains, the ultimate arbiter would be General Westmoreland himself.[51]

Initially, the MRF commodore also took exception to sharing a command with an officer with less time in grade. As he got to know his Army counterpart, Colonel Fulton, however, his attitude changed. Like Wells, Fulton was a Reserve Officer Training Corps (ROTC) graduate and a veteran of World War II. After graduating from the University of California at Berkeley in 1942, Fulton was commissioned as a second lieutenant and went on to fight as a company officer with the 91st Division in Italy during World War II. After the war, he served as a staff officer in Headquarters European Command and later with Army Forces Far East in Japan during the Korean War. Before assuming command of the 2d Brigade, 9th Infantry Division, he was teaching at the U.S. Army War College in Carlisle Barracks, Pennsylvania.[52]

When Fulton, a mild-mannered northern Californian, first met Wells at Coronado, he returned to Fort Riley "fighting mad" because he could not get Wells to "budge" on nearly any issue. Once in Vietnam, the two officers would often square off in heated arguments, but in the end both men always managed to iron out their differences locally without resorting to their respective chains of command—a testament to the mutual respect they had for one another as officers. Lieutenant Colonel James S. G. Turner, a marine assigned to the 2d Brigade as riverine advisor, claimed the shared command arrangement worked well specifically because no service was in overall control of the MRF: "The fact that the two are co-equal, and that there is this pressure to reach agreement within the force, has prevented the hardening of positions and has resulted in an active spirit of cooperation in solving problems which probably would not have existed had there been a common superior to which problems could be referred for resolution."[53]

Wells particularly enjoyed working behind the scenes to solve problems for Fulton, who often accompanied his troops into battle. Wells came up with the idea of using pontoon barges to embark and disembark troops, and he transformed several troop carriers into floating medical aid stations. He also was instrumental in developing a logistical support concept for both the Army and Navy components of the force to secure virtually everything the MRF needed to operate. Finally, he proved a master at improving the combat effectiveness of his river craft by mounting new weapons or equipment on them.[54] Wells went out of his way to help and support Fulton in every way possible, whether that meant having one of the shops fabricate a longer bunk for the tall, 6-foot 3-inch Army officer or endorsing Fulton's unconventional concept of mounting field artillery on barges. Wells was also Fulton's "go-to-guy" for just about anything, be it extra barracks ships or beer for the troops. Wells, who never went anywhere without his two beloved Dachshunds, presented one of his dogs to Fulton as a gift.[55]

At lower echelons the command arrangements could be confusing and even vexing at times, but in the end officers in both services worked hard to iron out differences. Lieutenant (j.g.) Stephen T. Dexter, a supply officer with TF 117 who worked very closely with his Army colleagues to keep his barracks ship *APL-30* properly provisioned, described the situation this way: "No one was in overall command. The flotilla commander did not report to the brigade commander and the brigade commander did not report to the flotilla commander. You had to go all the way to MACV to find a common senior for both commands. But the situation worked remarkably well." Dexter always secured what he needed from the 9th Infantry Division Supply and Transportation Department and vice versa without ever having to involve the chain of command. Any issues that arose were resolved at the local level between Dexter and his Army counterparts.[56]

The first elements of the Army's contribution to the MRF began arriving in Vung Tau on 19 December 1966. As initially configured, the 9th Infantry Division MRF component would consist of the 2d Brigade—a force that by the end of February 1967 included three infantry battalions, an artillery battalion, and a cavalry squadron plus various supply, medical, and maintenance detachments.[57] The Navy contribution would be RIVFLOT 1, comprising two river assault squadrons (RAS 9 and RAS 11), each with two river assault divisions under them.[58] By the end of 1967 each river assault squadron contained 26 ATCs, 16 assault support boats (ASPBs), five monitors, two command and control boats (CCBs), and one refueler (a modified LCM). On 7 January 1967 the first Navy units of the MRF arrived at Vung Tau on *Whitfield County* (LST-1169).[59] After June 1968, Squadrons 13 and 15 joined the force. In 1968, Task Force 117 also was reorganized into Mobile Riverine Group Alpha with Squadrons 9 and 11, and Mobile Riverine Group Bravo with Squadrons 13 and 15.[60]

Boats of the Mobile Riverine Force

The basic mission of RIVFLOT 1 was to transport Army troops to battle zones and support them in battle. The craft the Navy acquired for this task was the armored troop carrier, a modified mechanized landing craft known by its crewmembers as the "Tango boat." Like its World War II ancestor, it had a large well deck for transporting troops and a drop-down ramp for landing soldiers on a hostile beach. The VNN had been using LCM variants in its river assault groups for many years, so the craft had a proven track record on the rivers. The U.S. Army, however, wanted more than a simple landing craft; it desired a craft capable of patrolling rivers, providing fire support for troops, and minesweeping. The boat ultimately developed was equal parts assault craft and troop transporter.

The Tango was 56 feet long with a 17-foot 6-inch beam and a 3-foot 4-inch draft. Displacing 66 tons, it could achieve a top speed of eight knots with its twin Gray Marine 225-horsepower diesel engines. At six knots with a full fuel load of 450 gallons of diesel, the Tango could travel 110 miles without refueling. High-hardness XAR-30-type steel and bar armor provided ballistic protection for the crew from rounds up to .50-caliber in size and offered some protection against high explosive antitank (HEAT) rounds up to 57mm. Below-waterline hull blisters provided added hull protection, minimized draft, and increased stability. The Tango's armor, however, generally could not withstand the full force of a B40 rocket. According to Michael Harris, a radioman on Tango 152-1, the outside armor was supposed to stop the first stage of a B40

Armored Troop Carrier 92-2 operating in the Mekong Delta. The flotsam on the starboard side of this "Tango" boat is water hyacinth, which is ubiquitous in the Mekong Delta, November 1967.

rocket from boring a hole into the boat, "but invariably it would burn on inside and explode, and the shrapnel would go off of all the steel and end up wounding many guys."[61] Rockets also could be fired through the gun and coxswain slits and into the well deck through the boat's thin-skinned canopy.

Armament on the Tango usually consisted of one 20mm cannon, two .50-caliber and four .30-caliber machine guns, two M18 grenade launchers, and various personal weapons (M16 rifles, shotguns, and M79 grenade launchers). The ATC carried a Navy crew of seven and could accommodate a platoon of 40 soldiers, an M113 armored personnel carrier, or a 105mm howitzer with a prime mover. "I thought it was invincible until we got to Vietnam," noted Fireman 3rd Class Steve Vitale.[62]

As Vitale implies, sailors who served in Tangos generally had mixed feelings about the boats. They had fond memories of them but often complained about everything from the engines to the guns. Larry D. Rodgers, a 21-year-old engineman fireman from Fort Worth, Texas, lamented the fact that his Tango boat's sea strainers became clogged with river debris during the most inopportune moments. "Sometimes I found myself down in the engine room during the heat of battle switching sea strainers—a job that could take up to 40 minutes to complete."[63] Gunner's Mate 3rd Class Arthur J. Dodd of Tango 91-9 grumbled about the temperamental nature of the 20mm gun. "The 20 was specialized. Everything had to be just right." While some of his shipmates enjoyed a beer on the pontoons after a long mission, Dodd would be diligently cleaning his gun with diesel fuel and a shaving brush. "To me it was a life or death situation and I wanted to keep that gun in the best shape I could." The fuzing on the 20mm also did not make the weapon very effective as a bunker buster because the round had no penetration capability—it exploded on impact with a hard surface.[64]

The .50-caliber machine gun was one of the most reliable weapons on the Tango boat (as well as on numerous other MRF vessels), but even this weapon was not entirely appropriate for the conditions of the delta. It could not destroy or even penetrate most Viet Cong bunkers. Its projectile also traveled long distances, making it difficult to use in populated areas. "Probably the focal point of my discontent was the .50-caliber machine gun," lamented Captain Robert S. Salzer, who served as the commodore of TF 117 from November 1967 to November 1968. "This is an extremely powerful weapon, very high muzzle velocity and long range. It was the commonest weapon available not only on the river assault force but on the patrol boats of Task Force 116 and also the Swift boats and WPBs in the Market Time inshore patrol area, and the muzzle velocity was such that the bullets would ricochet all over the place . . . [and yet] it could not destroy fortifications such as bunkers. . . . We did not come into the delta to destroy it but to attack a finite enemy who was living in masses of people."[65]

The ATC's slow speed was the bane of nearly everyone serving on them. "The boats were originally built to weigh 66 tons, but with all the armor and weaponry added, they weighed much more," explained Boatswain's Mate 2nd Class Robert Franson. "They could only make seven knots on a great day with a tailwind, going downstream with the tide. It was more like four knots under normal conditions. It was terrible."[66] Steven Vitale similarly complained about the ATC, especially when his unit had to transit long distances like the 100-mile journey from Dong Tam to Can Tho endured during Tet in 1968. "We all bitched. We had to leave at 10 p.m. and did not arrive there until 10 a.m. in the next morning." During long transits even simple issues such as going to the head could be fraught with peril. As Vitale explained, "Both the Army and the Navy guys would relieve themselves by peeing over the side. We'd crap in a bucket and throw the contents over the side. We would go as fast as we could in the back of the boat because we never knew when we might get hit. There was a 12-inch catwalk that ran around the boat."[67]

At the end of a dangerous mission, though, the men rarely wanted to leave their boats. Most slept, ate, and bathed on their ATCs. "I learned to curl up and sleep anywhere. I used to curl up in the bottom of my gun mount," explained John Green. Others would sleep on fold-down bunks in the well deck or in the open air on the stern. Bathing often involved tying a lanyard to a bucket and washing one's self with river water. "The corpsman said we could bathe with river water as long as we did not have any open wounds and kept our mouths shut because the water was off the Richter scale when it came to bacteria," said Dodd.[68] For food, sailors mainly ate canned rations, or "C-rats," as they called them. Sailors often heated the C-rat cans with small pieces of C-4 plastic explosive. "If you tore off a 1-inch square of C-4 and lit it," according to Lester Schneider, "it would burn fast and short and heat up a can (it burned for about 30 seconds)." Schneider's favorite C-rat was "beanies and weenies." He also liked the boned chicken and beef. Other sailors enjoyed spaghetti.[69] The ham and lima beans meal was universally despised. Unpopular varieties of C-rats often ended up being donated to the Vietnamese, who readily accepted any addition to their meager, protein-deficient diet.

The battleship of the MRF was the monitor. Another LCM conversion, the monitors were similar in many respects to the Tangos. They had a nearly identical draft, beam, and top speed as the ATCs as well as a 20mm cannon and two .50-caliber machine guns mounted on the superstructure. The chief difference between the boats could be seen in the well deck area. Monitors had a rounded bow as opposed to a drop-down ramp, making them a bit longer than the ATC (60 feet 6 inches vice 56 feet). They also mounted additional weaponry—a 40mm gun turret forward and an 81mm mortar amidships—and carried four additional sailors to help man those weapons and operate the boat. The 81mm mortar was the only indirect-fire weapon fielded by RIVFLOT 1 and, with the assistance of an artillery observer, could hit targets up to 4,000 yards away. Like any mortar, however, this one had a low muzzle velocity, making it ineffective against hardened enemy positions such as bunkers.[70] The monitor's main weapon was the 40mm cannon—a very accurate direct-fire weapon that packed a tremendous punch. The 40mm cannon was the only weapon in the MRF's inventory capable of smashing mud bunkers, but the rounds tended to damage rather than destroy these fortifications, allowing the Viet Cong to quickly repair and reuse them for future ambushes. The 40mm guns also had such great range that monitors' crews had to take great care not to hit friendly forces or civilians when employing them.[71]

Monitor 91-2 on the My Tho River, December 1967.

In summer 1967, when the Viet Cong constructed bunkers capable of withstanding 40mm rounds, RIVFLOT 1 began exploring the idea of deploying flamethrowers on riverboats as a potential bunker buster. On 4 October, the M132A1, an Army flamethrower, was shoehorned into an ATC. Commanders hoped the M132A1's 32-second burst and 150-yard range would not only neutralize enemy bunkers but also deter river ambushes.[72] Tests proved satisfactory, but the M132A1, weighing 23,000 pounds, was too heavy for the Navy's needs. Instead, lighter M10-8 flamethrowers were installed on six monitors delivered in May of 1968. Nicknamed "Zippo" after the popular cigarette lighter, these monitors mounted two M10-8 flamethrowers, each with an effective range of 200–300 yards. With 1,350 gallons of napalm fuel, the M10-8 could lay down a sheet of flame for 225 seconds. Sailors would make napalm by mixing a powder consisting of the coprecipitated aluminum salts of naphthenic and palmitic acids with gasoline. Compressed air propelled the napalm through the flamethrower, and a gasoline lighter acted as the trigger. "You had to be careful to get the right jelly consistency when making it," explained Gunner's Mate 3rd Class Joseph Lacapruccia, "but firing the weapon was not dangerous. No one was ever burned. It was much safer than the 20mm, and napalm was effective against the VC because it could travel into spider holes and deplete oxygen."[73]

The CCBs served as flagships for river squadron and river division commanders as well as command posts for Army battalion commanders. Another LCM conversion, they were similar to monitors except they contained a communications suite amidships rather than an 81mm mortar. The communications suite had five AN/VRC-46, three AN/GRC 106, one AN/PRC-25, and one AN/ARC-27 radios—giving it the ability to communicate with units on land, air, and sea. The CCB also featured Raytheon Pathfinder 1900 radar and a Decca navigation installation.[74]

Zippo monitor in action.

Command and Control Boat 91-1.

    The only MRF boat developed from the keel up was the assault support boat (ASPB), or "Alpha" as it was called by its crews. Designed as the American successor of the French STCAN/FOM, the ASPB was to be the MRF's destroyer—a combination of an escort, a gunboat, a waterway interdiction and surveillance craft, and a minesweeper all in one. MACV wanted this "jack

Assault Support Boats 112-2 and 112-3. Note the nonregulation clothing worn by the sailor on the left of ASPB 112-2.

of all trades" to have a 38-foot length and a higher speed than an LCM, a shallow draft, a hull capable of withstanding a blast from a 55kg (TNT equivalent) mine, and lots of firepower. The ultimate craft designed by the Bureau of Ships (BuShips) incorporated all these demands, but at 50 feet in length it surpassed what MACV planners had envisioned. In some respects it was also over-engineered.

The V-shaped hull, made of 7/32-inch steel with extra steel from the gunwale to two inches above the lower-side longitudinal, provided a degree of mine protection for the boat. Instead of bar armor, the Alpha employed lightweight quarter-inch aluminum trigger plate to protect the crew against 57mm recoilless rifle rounds and armor-piercing bullets up to .50-caliber in size. Powered by two V-8 diesels, the ASPB could achieve speeds of up to 14.8 knots—more than twice that of the Tangos. Alphas also expelled exhaust directly into the water to reduce noise and smoke emissions, making it the stealthiest of all the MRF vessels. Armed with two Mark-48 combination turrets, the ASPB platform could carry a variety of armament, including 20mm cannon, .50-caliber machine guns, and MK-19 grenade launchers. Some also had a .50-caliber machine gun/81mm mortar combination mounted in the fantail. Minesweeping gear consisted of a straight drag chain designed to sever wires of command-detonated water mines. Although not in the original plans for the boat, ASPBs could carry six to eight soldiers or Navy SEALs in addition to its crew of five.[75]

The first two Alpha boats arrived at Vung Tau on 20 September 1967 and were in action ten days later. MRF sailors assigned to the Alphas appreciated the boat's higher speed and firepower but, within months of their deployment, these boats began revealing some shortcomings. Between February and March 1968 four ASPBs sank due to noncombat reasons. In one event, on 2 March two passing Alphas swamped ASPB 91-1, causing the boat to sink in less than a minute and drowning Seaman Michael A. Evenson, who became trapped in a berthing compartment. A Navy investigation of all four sinkings concluded that while human error contributed in some cases, the primary faults were the lack of seaworthiness caused by inadequate compartmentalization and marginal buoyancy, coupled with excessive weight and a low freeboard.[76] As a quick fix, NAVFORV tried to improve the ASPB's seaworthiness by removing engine-compartment armor to reduce top weight. "Even then," noted ship design historian Norman Friedman, "the ASPB had a hair-raising ride, tending to heal outboard rather than inboard in a turn."[77] When Robert Salzer witnessed one of the sea trials of the ASPB in California, he leaned over to an Army colleague and said, "This thing is never going to float."[78]

The armor also never lived up to its promise. Engineers had difficulty developing a hard, lightweight armor that was not brittle. On the first generation boats, a 75mm recoilless rifle round aimed at the cockpit could break off an entire piece of armor and propel it through the cockpit, spelling doom for the boat captain and the coxswain.[79] "They were death traps," lamented Lieutenant (j.g.) Walter Lineberger. "There were two instances I remember distinctly when four out of five of an Alpha's crew had to be medically evacuated after ambushes."[80] As Salzer put it, "what they [BuShips] asked for in this armor was impossible." By 1969, TF 117 was using ASPBs primarily as minesweepers and base defense craft. In the end this jack of all trades became master of just two. "On the whole I disliked the ASPB enormously—there was nothing right about it," Salzer complained.[81]

When compared with the PCF, PBR, or LCM conversions, the ASPB had a rather checkered record in Vietnam, but given how little time BuShips had to develop this truly revolutionary weapon system, it's a small miracle that the boat deployed in the first place. After all, the Navy demanded a riverine boat that offered high-speed, tremendous firepower, and crew protection against shaped RPG rounds, armor-piercing .50-caliber bullets, and water mines. The bureau had to employ some of the most advanced technology of the day (from composite materials to new propulsion systems) to achieve this result. No other riverine platform offered such all-in-one capability. That the ASPB came close in some respects represents a tremendous achievement for the engineers of BuShips.

Moreover, as a minesweeper the ASPB performed better than expected. It was the only boat in TF 117's inventory capable of handling some of the Viet Cong's more clever mining techniques. For example, the enemy would occasionally thread detonating wires through bamboo, causing the drag hooks to slip over the wires. The ASPB's powerful V-8 engines could produce enough torque to rip those bamboo-armored wires from the river-bottom mud.[82] The ASPB hull also performed better than expected during a mine detonation. On 21 December 1967, ASPB 111-4 hit a 75-pound mine two miles northwest of Dong Tam. Although the mine detonated right against the ASPB, the charge failed to puncture the hull, and the ASPB was able to return to base on its own power with only moderate damage (a dished-in hull). If the situation had demanded it, this rugged little boat could have pressed on with the mission.[83]

Afloat and Ashore Bases

In many respects the core capability of the MRF was its mobility in the swamps, jungles, and waterways of the Mekong Delta, and the key enablers of this mobility were the MRF's floating barracks and repair ships, collectively known as the Mobile Riverine Base. By May 1967, floating base elements consisted of two air-conditioned command and control ships (*Benewah* and *Colleton*), an LST converted into a repair ship (*Askari*), a non-self-propelled barracks barge (*APL-26*), and a logistic support LST assigned on a two-month rotational basis by the Seventh Fleet (initially *Kemper County*). Another LST made regular supply runs from Naval Support Activity Saigon to the afloat base and various anchorages. Together these ships provided all the afloat basing capacity necessary to support 1,900 embarked troops of the 2d Brigade, 9th Infantry Division and 1,600 sailors of TF 117 for ten or more days. This support included messing, berthing, boat and weapons repair, medical, and supply. The MRB ships made the MRF a truly self-sufficient force, capable of operating independent of land-based support for long stretches of time.[84]

Aerial view of the Mobile Riverine Base on the My Tho River. The MRB is made up of five mother ships that can support and sustain a strike force of 3,600 sailors and soldiers, and numerous small craft, June 1968.

For much of the history of the MRF, *Benewah* served as its flagship. Originally a 542- class LST, the ship was built by the Boston Naval Shipyard and commissioned on 19 March 1946. During the early Cold War period, she served in noncombatant assignments in Europe, including time as the flagship for Commander, Fleet Air Eastern Atlantic and Mediterranean in the mid 1950s. Before being converted to a self-propelled barracks ship, she had been serving as living quarters for precommissioning crews of new ships being built in Newport News, Virginia.[85]

The conversion, which began in July 1966 at the Philadelphia Naval Shipyard, was completed on 28 January 1967. The newly modernized barracks ship was 328 feet long with a beam of 50 feet and a draft of 14 feet. Her ship's company consisted of 13 officers and 190 sailors. In all, she could berth a total of 115 officers, 25 chief petty officers and master sergeants, and 990 enlisted for a grand total of 1,130 service personnel. Armament included two 3-inch 50- caliber guns, two 40mm cannons, and eight .50-caliber machine guns.[86] A large helicopter landing platform constructed over the superstructure allowed the Army to evacuate casualties straight from the battlefield to the onboard medical facilities, and by February 1968 the ship had registered 5,000 landings (4,948 by Army helicopters). *Benewah* arrived in Vung Tau, Vietnam, on 23 April 1967, where she immediately assumed duties as the flagship of the MRF. To honor the ship's new role and welcome the Army aboard, sailors had painted her hull Army green during a stopover at Pearl Harbor.[87]

On a typical day, *Benewah* served three meals for over 1,000 personnel. Her soda fountain sold 300 cups of ice cream, 20 cases of soda, 150 bags of popcorn, and other assorted "gedunk" to hungry members of the armed forces. The ship's laundry room worked around the clock to supply soldiers and sailors with clean uniforms and bed linens. The barbershop often accounted for over a hundred haircuts per day. Yeomen typed hundreds of messages and transmitted those

The self-propelled barracks ship *Benewah* (APB-35), a floating support base for soldiers, sailors, and assault craft, and the flagship of the Mobile Riverine Force.

messages around the world from the ship's communications facilities. The ship's small hospital treated the wounded directly from the battlefield, Army and Navy staff officers planned and managed the riverine war from the ship's modern Joint Tactical Operations Center, and soldiers cleaned their weapons on a pontoon barge attached to the ship.[88]

Captain James D. Johnson, an Army chaplain attached to the 9th Infantry Division, lived in a stateroom with three other officers and found the ship quite comfortable. "The room is small but . . . quiet and air-conditioned. Dinner is held in the officer's ward room. This is 'high cotton.' There's carpet, tablecloths, overstuffed chairs, and Filipino stewards. My bed is wonderful and cozy. There's no sound of outgoing artillery and mortars such as at Dong Tam. In fact, the only sound is the faint hum of the air conditioner."[89] Ensign Edwin "Larry" Oswald, a Navy supply officer assigned to NSA Saigon, was a bit taken aback by the traditional Navy atmosphere he found on *Benewah* and her sister ship *Colleton* (APB-36) when he visited them in 1968. "In officer's country these damned things had wall-to-wall carpeting, paneled walls. You would have thought you were in a four-star hotel somewhere. The officers wore the kind of khaki uniforms they'd wear on duty at the Pentagon."[90]

As Johnson and Oswald noted, the atmosphere on APBs may have been more formal than on the riverboats, but APBs did serve in combat zones and took fire on numerous occasions. On 9 March 1968, *Benewah* came under mortar fire while anchored near My Tho. One round hit the ship directly, causing a small fire. A few days later on 22 March, the Viet Cong hit the ship twice with 75mm recoilless rifle rounds. One HEAT round penetrated the bulkhead on the forward mess decks, rupturing a steam line and an air vent and spraying the area with shrapnel. A second round opened a 10-inch hole in the hull near the accommodation ladder, rupturing two ballast tanks and causing minor flooding. Fortunately, no personnel were injured in either attack, but a few weeks later on 15 April three rockets fired at *Benewah* at the My Tho anchorage wounded 11 servicemen on the ship.[91]

TF 117 sailors assigned to smaller boats rarely slept on the barracks barges, preferring instead to sleep on their converted LCMs. When Oswald visited *Benewah*, he noticed the riverine sailors sleeping on their boats and asked them if they were on alert. One sailor looked at him straight in the eye and said, "Motherfucker, are you kidding? This is where I've been sleeping since I got here." Oswald thought the man was joking at first until he started asking around. "While the Naval Academy guys were in wall-to-wall carpet, paneled walls, leather sofas, [and] service dress khaki uniforms, these poor bastards were being eaten alive by gnats and mosquitoes, pissing in the river, eating canned food."[92]

What Oswald did not understand is that most TF 117 slept in their boats more out of choice than necessity. They became accustomed to living in their boats during extended missions, and when they returned they found it more convenient to stay in the boats than on barracks ships crowded with Army troops. In the boats sailors could perform maintenance or clean weapons if they couldn't sleep, and they were never far from those same guns in the event of an enemy attack. As Engineman Fireman Larry D. Rodgers put it, "I liked sleeping on the boats rather than on the barracks ship or Dong Tam because I could experience some quiet time by myself, and if something happened at night and we had to make a mad scramble for the boats, I was already there."[93] Some river sailors never adapted to shipboard life. Gunner's Mate Arthur Dodd noted: "That green monster was air-conditioned and had good food, but I preferred life in the boats. The regular Navy sucks. Dress blues, dress whites, regulation haircuts. When you were out there on the boat, you answered to nobody except the boat captain."[94]

As Dodd and Oswald imply, a social chasm of sorts existed between the ships company of *Benewah*, *Colleton*, and the other support ships and the small-boat sailors of the MRF. The sailors on the ship lived in relative comfort and safety in contrast to the "River Rats" who, like their Army comrades, exposed themselves to enemy fire daily on the rivers. Consequently, some tensions occasionally developed between the two groups. "These sailors haven't the slightest idea of what the infantry and River Rats face day after day," complained Army chaplain Johnson. "Their stateside 'regulations' are often interpreted by some of them as permission to harass."[95] First Lieutenant Jack Benedick, a platoon commander with the 4th Battalion, 47th Infantry, recalled being told to change his clothes once when he entered the officer's wardroom dressed in shorts and a tee shirt. Benedick refused, explaining that he had been in the rice fields for the last 24 hours and desperately needed to dry his skin out. A standoff ensued between him and a group of Navy officers in starched khakis that did not end until Colonel Fulton entered the room and convinced the Navy officers to make an exception to policy for reasons of health.[96]

Many River Rats and soldiers found the *Benewah*'s practice of cleaning muddy troops with a fire hose before they were allowed to enter the ship particularly onerous. Embarkation procedures outlined in the TF 117 Operation Order specifically state "if muddy, troops will be hosed off on the inboard side of the pontoon prior to boarding ship using the ship's salt water hoses."[97] However, it did not give ship's company sailors license to abuse incoming troops with a high-powered fire hose. "A bitter experience that many soldiers will take with them from this era of their lives is a mean Navy chief whose job is to man a fire hose when we return from operations,"

A soldier with the 9th Infantry Division wades through mud and water en route to an armored troop carrier in the Mekong Delta, June 1968.

185

Johnson lamented.[98] Gunner's Mate Chester Stanley concurred. "I did not get along well with the shipboard guys. I hated seeing the shipboard guys hose down the Army guys with the fire hoses. Most of them were so damn tired they could barely stand up anyway. These guys had been humping in the woods for four days and the ship guys wanted to play with the fire hose."[99]

Sometimes tensions between the groups led to angry confrontations and even fights. Seaman Lester Schneider once asked the *Benewah* cook to store some Landjäger sausages his mother had sent him from Wisconsin. When he returned from a mission, the sausages were gone. The enterprising chef had apparently used them as toppings for pizza. "I felt like shooting up the boat I was so mad."[100] As his ATC pulled up to the ship, John Green once noticed a rat eating a dead American corpse through an open body bag on the pontoons.

> I went up the gangplank of the troopship, screaming every four-letter word at the top of my lungs. I was furious that a few hours ago these boys were serving their country and now just because they were a piece of dead meat, they could not afford to keep a guard down on the pontoons to keep the rats off the bodies. And I am screaming and demanding to see the senior officer on the troop ship. And a senior officer finally comes down to meet me and says, "hold on, son, what's wrong?" And I just laid into him and said every four-letter word again. He then realized what happened and realized he was wrong and that someone should have been down there to keep the rats away from the bodies. And he said, "I'll take care of it right now. It's done. Thank you."[101]

Most of the time cordial relations prevailed. River Rats utilized the barracks ships for a hot shower, a good meal, and occasionally a card game, but otherwise kept to themselves in their boats. Army troops, similarly, appreciated these ships for the amenities offered and because the ships afforded them the opportunity to dry out after long missions, clean their weapons (done on the pontoons), and get a decent night's rest without having to pull guard duty.[102]

Post-mission "beer bashes" on the pontoons represented a high point of the MRF experience for both soldiers and River Rats alike. Beer could be consumed on the pontoons but not on ship, and as Gunner's Mate 3rd Class Joseph Lacapruccia explained, "The officers never bothered us on the pontoons." Some even participated in the festivities, albeit in a low-key fashion.[103] Card games were another staple of off-duty time. "There were some awesome poker and craps games on the LSTs and barracks ships, recalled Lacapruccia. "I lost a little TV, a camera, and some stereo equipment in these games." For Engineman Fireman Larry D. Rodgers, these games remain one of his fondest memories of the war. "The night before I was supposed to go to Saigon for R&R, I got into a game that was a $100 buy-in and a $10 pot limit. I got real lucky and ended up winning $500 to go on R&R with."[104]

Like drinking and gambling, prostitution occurred in the MRF, albeit in a limited capacity. Unlike PBR and PCF sailors based on towns, TF 117 sailors generally did not have the same sort of opportunities to mix with the local populace, and few long-term relationships ever resulted from these associations. Boatswain's Mate Seaman Thomas A. Dempsey claimed that prostitutes would ply their trade from sampans near the MRB and Dong Tam. Dempsey also stated that prostitutes operated from a hooch just outside the boat basin at Dong Tam. "You'd drop your ramp, and three guys would jump off and use the whorehouse, and the next boat would pick them up."[105] Gunner's Mate 3rd Class Arthur Dodd corroborated these stories. "You could always get some lovin' from the women on the sampans and stuff like that. There was a little whore house outside of Dong Tam as well." Lieutenant Pat Haggerty, a former chief of staff of River Division 111, admitted that prostitution existed but doubted that very many sailors engaged in it. "I think the fear of being captured or having your throat cut and the lack of access made it hard for our men to find prostitutes."[106] As Dodd put it, "All I really wanted after 24 hours on the river was a good meal and some sleep."[107]

In addition to APBs like *Benewah*, the MRF employed *APL-26*, a non-self-propelled barge as berthing ship. Known affectionately as the "Green Apple" or just "Apple" for short, the 226-foot-long barge deployed with the MRF in April 1967 and had enough transient berthing spaces for 39 officers and 290 sailors, and berthing for its permanent crew of five officers and 84 men. Although *APL-26* had no means of self-propulsion, it was equipped with boilers for steam and hot water, evaporators for making 24,000 gallons of fresh drinking water daily, generators for electricity and air-conditioning, and six .50-caliber mounts for self-defense. Commodore Wells liked the ship so much that he secured a whaleboat for the barge's skipper, which was promptly nicknamed, "Apple Seed." The Apple also impressed Vice Admiral Edwin Hooper, COMSERVPAC. "As I waded through the mud and up the brow on my first visit to these craft, in late April [1967], I was greeted with boat gongs, six side boys, and a boatswain's mate piping—just as if I had been boarding a first line combatant ship in some peaceful port."[108]

Repair ships served another vital support function for the MRF. *Askari* (ARL-30) joined the MRF in February 1967 and functioned as an afloat advanced base tender capable of repairing the various small craft of the MRF. At 338 feet in length, the converted LST carried a crew of 12 officers and 178 enlisted men. Its shops provided a broad range of engine, hull, electronics, and other specialized repair for small boats, including engine overhauls. Her mobility and cruising speed of 10.8 knots allowed her to provide repair support almost anywhere along the main rivers. The other major repair vessel was the non-self-propelled *YRBM-17*—a repair, berthing, and messing barge based at Dong Tam. *YRBM-17* was 260 feet long and contained berthing and messing for 97 crewmembers and maintenance personnel. It had the capability to maintain all MRF craft and performed everything from minor hull repairs to complete boat modifications. During the first six months of MRF operations, *YRBM-17* overhauled four boats every eight days in addition to performing emergency battle repairs; by 1968 its repair capability had increased to where it could overhaul seven boats every 12 days. Together, the ARL and YRBM were the unsung heroes of the MRF, working around the clock, often at 150 percent capacity, to keep ATCs and other essential craft functioning. After the big battles of 15 September and 4 December 1967, these repair ships rebuilt some of the most heavily damaged monitors and ATCs—a herculean effort that few outside of TF 117 fully appreciated.[109]

One of the three mobile bases for the Mobile Riverine Force, the landing craft repair ship *Askari* (ARL-30) provides maintenance and support for various craft assigned to the command, May 1967.

The iconic image of the Mobile Riverine Force is that of a flotilla of Tango boats rafted up to a mother ship. In truth, the most important MRF base and logistics provider was not a ship but an Army base called Dong Tam. To build the facility, located eight kilometers from My Tho, engineers had to fill over 600 acres of inundated rice paddies with six feet of landfill—the most massive reclamation project of the war. General Westmoreland decided to create the base from landfill because there were no plots of dry land in the region large enough to accommodate the installation; ultimately, the base would cover an area nearly as big as My Tho, the provincial capital. The only other alternative would have been to seize developed land by imminent domain—something Westmoreland was loath to do because it would have involved displacing a large number of Vietnamese civilians. He also believed that by building a massive military complex on reclaimed land, he would send a powerful message to the Vietnamese—that America would go to great lengths to protect the delta from the communists and that its commitment to the people of the delta was absolute.

Dong Tam meant "united hearts and minds" or "singleness of mind, in thoughts, and actions" depending on how one translates the words.[110] Westmoreland specifically chose the name because it signified the bond between the American and Vietnamese, and it was easy for Americans to pronounce. Seabees, Army Engineers, and civilian contract workers all participated in the construction, which began in mid-1966. Dredging and excavation were the biggest challenges. Some of the largest dredges in the world, including *Jamaica Bay* and *New Jersey*, helped to turn 600 acres of swamp into a base capable of accommodating over 12,000 members of the armed forces.[111]

The 16-inch pipeline cutterhead, *Cho Gao*, the first of five dredges assigned to the project, started work on 4 August 1966. Throughout the construction of the base, the Viet Cong attempted to thwart progress by sabotaging and attacking dredges. Sappers sunk *Jamaica Bay*, a 30-inch pipeline cutterhead dredge, on 9 January 1967, killing three crewmembers (see chapter 3). Fortunately, her sister dredge, *New Jersey*, was in-country and available as a replacement. On 28 July 1968 sappers struck again, sinking *Thu Bon 1*, a 12-inch pipeline cutterhead dredge, and on 28 September 1969, the 27-inch pipeline cutterhead *Sandpumper* sucked up a piece of live ordnance that exploded, destroying the dredge. That same year on 22 November the Viet Cong sank *New Jersey*.[112]

In January 1967 the Army sent the 3d Battalion, 60th Infantry to Dong Tam to provide security for the construction units and the fledgling base. On 10 March the Headquarters, 2d Brigade, moved to Dong Tam, where it too initially devoted most of its attention to base defense. Viet Cong regularly mortared the base during construction. On 11 March 1967, for example, they showered the facility with 80 well-placed rounds, wounding 18 workers. "The fact that only 18 were wounded, and none seriously, seemed remarkable," wrote Vice Admiral Hooper, who visited the facility shortly after the attack. "All hands reached sandbag enclosures with remarkable speed."[113]

The Navy's River Assault Squadron 9 arrived at Dong Tam in April and began supporting riverine assault operations up to a battalion in size. By this time the base had berthing and messing for one river assault squadron, a boat basin to accommodate one river assault squadron, waterfront facilities for unloading the resupply LST, small-craft drydocks, command posts for the Army and Navy commanders, and a repair, berthing, and messing barge (*YRBM-17*).[114]

Aerial view of Dong Tam, a dry land base for the Mobile Riverine Force, August 1967.

By 1 June 1967, Dong Tam occupied 12-square kilometers and contained a cantonment and storage facilities for the entire 2d Brigade, 9th Division, as well as a 500-meter runway and a two-square-kilometer turning basin for boats. The turning basin greatly facilitated the loading and unloading of men and material by allowing boats to move within a few feet of the troop embarkation and debarkation points. With only one entrance, however, the basin did not flush properly. Consequently, sewage pipelines had to be constructed from the MRF support ship anchorage areas in the basin to the My Tho River.[115]

When the MRF officially activated on 1 June, it consisted of 1,900 soldiers and 1,600 sailors. The Army component consisted of the 2d Brigade, 9th Division; and the Navy element, River Assault Squadrons 9 and 11, each containing 26 assault troop carriers, three command and control boats, five monitor fire support ships, and a refueler. Late in the fall with the arrival of the ASPBs, the size of a standard river assault squadron jumped from 35 boats to 51.[116]

When completed, Dong Tam was an island of sand that became "one of the dustiest places on earth during the dry season" and a "mud pit" during the wet season.[117] Still, many soldiers and sailors developed affection for the place. "We had a PX and a bar, and they showed nightly movies on the repair barge. There was a small casino with half a dozen slot machines (penny, nickel, dime). You could even get beer," recalled Larry Rodgers.[118] Lester Schneider liked to buy cases of beer for his boat at the Dong Tam enlisted club on the base. According to Arthur Dodd, "at Dong Tam it was just nice to get off the boat and walk on the ground."[119] Army chaplain Jim Johnson was amazed at how quickly the base improved between June and December 1967. "When I arrived here six months ago, Dong Tam was a muddy camp with a few tropical-sided hootches and tents for tops. The engineers have modernized Dong Tam to the point that it looks more like Bear Cat and Long Binh."[120] Since Dong Tam was usually the last place a sailor stayed before flying home at the end of a tour, it left an indelible impression on many. My best memory of the war," Radioman 3rd Class John L. Miller confessed, "was the night before I left at Dong Tam. It started with a sunset that I had never seen the likes of. It filled the entire sky."[121]

Dong Tam, however, was not without hazards. According to Raybell, "it was constantly being infiltrated by VC, who would sneak in and place a satchel charge somewhere."[122] Mortar attacks were also a perennial problem. "When we were there, I lived in the boats because Dong Tam always got mortared at night," claimed Miller.[123] For Rodgers, a mortar attack welcomed him to the base at the very beginning of his Vietnam tour. "We rolled off the back ramp while the Caribou was still taxiing and took cover under a deuce and a half [truck]. I told a buddy of mine, 'You think we might have gotten ourselves in trouble.'"[124] Being awakened in the middle of the night by a mortar attack could be a jarring experience, even for hardened combat veterans. "I've never heard an incoming mortar round, but I immediately know exactly what it is. My adrenaline kicks into high gear," wrote Jim Johnson.

> We grab out flak vests and steel helmets and make a run out the front door to head for the bunker, about fifteen steps from my hootch. The first two rounds hit just to our left front. As we run, the next round follows and explodes behind us. I hear fragments

hitting the tin roof of the new tropical barracks under construction just behind my hootch. As I slide into the bunker, my heart is pounding. Outside I hear the continual dull thuds of exploding mortars. It's pitch black. I crouch in the bunker with about twenty enlisted men. A few soldiers light cigarettes which offer only a quick glow that reflects controlled fear on each face. The mortar attack is over in five minutes. The only sounds now are the hum of generators, a far away helicopter, and a vehicle some distance away.[125]

Dong Tam may have offered some amenities and comforts that the barracks ships lacked, but its fixed location made it a constant target of Viet Cong attack and harassment. Base defense tied down as much as a third of the MRF at any given time. The dry land base also mitigated two of the most precious advantages of the MRF—its mobility and ability to surprise the enemy by showing up in unexpected areas. Logistically, however, it is doubtful that the 9th Infantry Division could have operated exclusively from barracks ships and LSTs, especially given its increasing reliance on helicopters for hot extractions, medical evacuations (dustoff), and basic transportation of men and supplies. Given its voracious appetite for fuel and ammunition, the MRF also needed a rear area to serve as a supply depot—a role that LSTs and other larger riverine vessels alone could not have fulfilled.

Operational Tactics and Rules of Engagement

When General Westmoreland established the MRF, he envisioned it primarily as a mobile strike force designed to seek out and destroy Viet Cong main force and guerrilla units operating in the Mekong River Delta.[126] To accomplish this end, planners designed the MRF to launch assaults ranging in size from a platoon all the way up to a battalion and sometimes larger in areas where Viet Cong battalions were thought to operate. Since the Viet Cong rarely tried to hold ground, the MRF would attempt to surround an enemy unit by dropping off assault forces at various locations and then drive the defenders against a blocking force in classic hammer and anvil maneuvers.

Army and Navy officers planned and conducted MRF operations based on current intelligence about the disposition of enemy forces in the delta. Much of this intelligence came from U.S. Army and ARVN sources but some was derived from naval intelligence liaison officers as well as from Vietnamese hamlet chiefs, Army advisors, and Regional and Popular forces in the field. Later in the war, air- and ground-based sensors designed to detect formations of enemy soldiers were employed but, in areas teaming with people, these technological methods never proved very reliable. More often than not it was simply a matter of Army and Navy officers poring over maps and estimating where they thought the enemy might be located based on recent operations, intuition, and educated guesswork. "We hit a large number of dry holes, but we had an astonishing number of successes where there was no intelligence report of enemy activity. It might just be some district reports of kidnappings in this area and we haven't been there in a while, and maybe we ought to take a look there. Why not?"

noted Commodore Salzer. He believed that the highest success would be achieved if the MRF roamed far and wide and struck unsuspecting localities. Focusing on a single locale, he reasoned, generally played right into the hands of the local insurgents, who would either temporarily withdraw from the area or quickly learn the MRF's capabilities and limitations and capitalize on this knowledge.[127]

Staff officers from both the Army and Navy composed a single joint MRF operational plan for each operation signed by both the TF 117 and 2d Brigade commanders. The plans usually covered a relatively long period and focused on a broad mission. For example, the "the MRF will conduct operations for three weeks to destroy Viet Cong elements located in Base Area 4670 of Dinh Tuong Province." As time progressed and the tactical situation became more fluid, these operation orders ended up being written more for the benefit of the higher headquarters in Saigon than the Navy river division and Army company commanders in the field, who quickly mastered standard operating procedures and simply needed a handful of specifics about the assault—where to go, what time to get there, and specifics about air and artillery support, etc.[128] "The tactics were not too sophisticated," explained Lieutenant Alan Breininger, the chief staff officer for River Division 91 in 1967. "Shoot your way in. Drop off the troops. Set up blocking stations and then pick the troops up again and move to a new assault zone or back to base."[129] Simple operating procedures and tactics, along with very tight teamwork among Army and Navy junior officers, allowed the MRF to react quickly to rapidly changing tactical situations.

Success in these operations depended on speed—the MRF had to be able to deploy forces rapidly and then assume blocking positions to prevent the Viet Cong from using the rivers and streams as a means of escape. Occasionally, helicopters would insert troops ahead of a riverine assault force, but because Army helicopters were often in short supply, planners could not rely on them for every mission, even though their presence often could mean the difference between success and failure.[130] As Salzer explained, "If you are trying to take on an indigenous force and crush it, you must envelope it.... You can seal off the flanks with river forces, and they do have a great advantage that they can come in *en masse*, much more than a helicopter assault. But to get behind them you have to have airborne or heliborne [insertion] because the paddy island is where they will fade into."[131]

Missions began with the loading of troops onto the ATCs. To facilitate this process, the Navy constructed pontoon barges (often referred to as AMMI barges) alongside the barracks ships. The pontoons obviated the requirement for troops to scramble down the sides of the barracks ships on rope ladders or nets. These pontoons not only prevented injuries (falls, twisted ankles, etc.) but also enabled the MRF to load three ATCs at once (a full company of soldiers) in just 20 minutes.[132] Once each company was loaded, it steamed to a rendezvous point and waited for the remainder of the battalion to join up. After the entire unit was embarked, the ATCs, like sailboats in a regatta, moved at a specified time across a starting line. Throughout this elaborate process, the boats maintained strict radio silence.[133]

An armored troop carrier (ATC) and a monitor rafted together. Another ATC can be seen in the background, May 1967.

Loading and unloading soldiers wearing helmets and flak jackets and laden with supplies, ammunition, and weapons, onto small boats was a difficult and dangerous evolution.[134] Four MRF sailors interviewed for this book discussed drownings that occurred at the mobile riverine base. According to John Green, "Once in a while one of the soldiers would slip and fall into the river, and there was nothing we could do. Soldiers who fell into the river drowned. His weight would pull him right to the bottom, and the next day a diver would go down and retrieve his body from the mud. In the year I was there I saw four people drown. We would try to throw these guys life preservers, but the river just sucked them down."[135] Robert Franson actually saved the life of his radioman, Johnny J. Sauer, who fell into My Tho River near *APL-26*.

> I had just showered and I was coming back to the boat. I heard someone say man overboard and I dove into the water. I saw the person in the water because someone had a battle lantern shining on him. I'm swimming for dear life because the My Tho River has such a strong current, and someone threw a life ring in front of me. I grabbed it and kept going towards the guy. I got it over to the guy and held on and a couple of guys from the 9th Infantry Division soon picked us up in a Boston Whaler. This was my best experience in Vietnam.[136]

Two minesweepers (ATCs initially and then ASPBs) would form the lead boats in a column. These boats would drag a steel cable attached with hooks along the bottom of the river, hoping to sever any electrical lines attached to command-detonated mines. The remainder of the column consisted of sections of three ATCs plus a monitor as the lead boat in the column behind the minesweepers, and a CCB or another monitor bringing up the rear. Each ATC carried a platoon of 40 soldiers and three platoons made an assault company. Army artillery, helicopter gunships, and occasionally close air support from jets prepared assault zones prior to landing. On many missions Army 105mm howitzers operated directly from barges towed near assault areas by Army-crewed LCMs—each barge contained two M102 howitzers, and the LCM functioned as a battery command post as well as a tug boat.[137]

When the lead section of the column got to within a half-kilometer of a landing site, artillery and air bombardment of the area would cease. The minesweepers and monitors would move into position and pepper the beach and the opposite bank with fire. Landing boats then approached the beaches in sections of three, with each boat landing about 5–10 meters apart and sections landing 150–300 meters apart depending on the terrain. Once the troops were disgorged and the boats released by the battalion commander, they moved to positions where they could provide fire support for the troops or to blocking positions or rendezvous sites. While in the blocking mode, riverine boats provided gunfire support for troops and were available to resupply platoons with ammunition and medically evacuate the wounded.

One ATC served as a medical aid station for a column and was often staffed with an Army doctor, Army medics, and Navy hospital corpsmen, along with operating tables, surgical supplies, and refrigerated blood. The presence of an armored aid station in the battle zone allowed medical personnel to rapidly triage and treat casualties, consequently saving many lives. The lightly wounded could be patched up and returned to battle; the more serious casualties could be stabilized and safely moved away from hostile fire for helicopter evacuation to Army hospitals. On 4 July 1967 a helicopter landed on the first ATC equipped with a steel flight deck instead of an awning above the well deck. This concept caught on quickly, and the MRF soon converted several ATCs into the smallest aircraft carriers in the fleet and redesignated them armored troop carriers (helicopter) ATC(H)s. As the war progressed, these small carriers were being used to medically evacuate wounded as well as to leapfrog units by helicopter from one battle area to another.[138]

A battalion commander in a helicopter often controlled battalion-size insertions and extractions because visibility was much better in the air than on the ground. During extractions, soldiers marked exfiltration beaches, often quite some distance from the landing zone, with smoke, making them easier for boat captains to locate. Often ATCs made multiple landings and extractions in a single operation, constantly shifting troops to different areas as battles evolved. Soldiers simply could not move far in the muddy rice paddies and needed constant transportation support during operations, which lasted anywhere from one to three days.

These operations were not limited by the endurance of the Navy boats, which could be resupplied by water during a combat evolution, but by the health of the soldiers, whose feet

A U.S. Army "dustoff" helicopter sets down on the landing pad of a converted armored troop carrier (ATC[H]) serving as a medical aid station to pick up a patient, August 1967.

An ATC with its ramp down.

could only take so many days of exposure in the wet conditions before they needed to dry out. Whenever soldiers remained out in the field more than 48 hours, they would begin to suffer from "paddy foot," a severe fungal infection caused by excessive exposure to moisture and water and characterized by erythema and red lesions. In October 1967, 66 men per day in the 4th Battalion, 47th Infantry were unable to deploy in the field because of paddy foot, and for that month alone the battalion lost 2,000-man days because of this condition. On average, foot infections sidelined 7.9 percent of the 9th Division's combat troops in the delta on any given day, and 95 percent of the soldiers deployed would contract some form of dermatophytosis during their deployment.[139] Troops used silicone ointment to prevent wet skin from chaffing against boots but, as Army historian George MacGarrigle wrote, "The skin problem would never be solved, even with the introduction of special Delta boots made of loose-fitting plastic mesh."[140] The only real cure for paddy foot was air and sunshine, making it imperative for soldiers to have at least 24 hours of dry-out time following each 48 hour operation.[141]

Rashes and skin problems were not limited to feet but plagued the rest of the body as well, since troops often became totally immersed in water during operations. Some soldiers went so far as to stop wearing underwear in a desperate attempt to stave off fungal infections in the genital area, and officers would order their men to remove all clothes and dry out their skin whenever breaks in action occurred.[142] The Viet Cong, by contrast, did not suffer as much from these problems because they wore lightweight, loose fitting clothing; carried very few supplies; often moved around the delta on small sampans rather than by foot; and most importantly, wore rubber sandals on their feet. Many U.S. sailors wore shower flip-flops and sometimes shorts and T-shirts. They also rarely had to exit their boats and slog in the mud—only doing so on rare occasions to carry ammunition to an Army position or to help soldiers evacuate the wounded, so they did not suffer as much from skin problems as their Army comrades. Crew fatigue, however, could be an issue, especially on long missions. Sailors had to be constantly alert for dangers while on operations and rarely got much rest. As one after-action report explained, "The boats are highly visible, concentrated point targets that cannot dig in for protection against fire. Consequently, they must be ready to move at a moment's notice to escape fire from the banks.... After three days of such operations, crew efficiency is drastically reduced."[143] On one mission, Robert Davis actually passed out after manning the helm of a CCB for 14 hours in a helmet and flak jacket. "It was 0200 and I could swear the river was going uphill."[144]

During an assault operation, timing movements appropriately with the tides was critical. In much of the delta, ten-foot tidal differences were the norm and, in some areas, river levels varied as much as 13 feet, so if commanders did not properly schedule landings and extractions, the MRF ran the risk of getting stuck in the mud. Strong tides also created currents up to six knots strong, which could also greatly affect movement of boats.[145] Commodore Salzer always carefully plotted TF 117's movements on a map, giving his units plenty of buffer time for the tides. As he put it, "it meant the poor troops that were riding the boats were there longer [and] complained more ... but it is important that you be completely coordinated as far as your air strikes and artillery and everything is concerned, and that means you've got to be on time. These tides were a major detriment." Even the most careful planning, though, could not prevent boats from occasionally ending up high and dry. The Navy had a good understanding of the tidal cycles of major rivers but, according to Salzer, "what was known about the tidal functions in the narrow rivers and canals was about zero."[146] Many TF 117 veterans have stories about running aground, especially on small patrols and other missions unconnected with major assaults. "I was on Tango 112–13 during monsoon season," recalled Robert Franson, "and we just ran out of water. The tide went out fast and we ended up sitting on a puddle. We just manned our guns and waited for the tide to come in again. That was one of the scariest evolutions that we were involved in."[147] In some cases the Viet Cong used tides to trap or ambush MRF units. On 6 February 1968, John Green's boat was operating near Vinh Long with six other boats as the tide was coming in during the monsoon season. Just after all the boats had run under a low bridge, the Viet Cong started firing recoilless rifles, hitting two of the lead boats. The section tried to reverse course but could not make it back under bridge because the water level had risen a few inches. "We had to maneuver near the ambush zone until the tide reversed itself."[148]

Soldiers disembarking from boats had it even worse. During low tides they might sink in mud up to their armpits as they disembarked from boats or have to scale mud banks 6–12 feet tall to get ashore; during high tides they would on occasion have to wade or swim around half-submerged Nipa palms to get to terra firma. Soldiers carried rope to move across deepwater or pull comrades out of the mud.[149] Tides affected not only water depth but current velocity and direction. For example, traveling 30 kilometers upstream against an ebbing tide could take six hours, whereas the same journey might only take four hours with an incoming tide.[150]

The rules of engagement (ROE) were another critical element that affected nearly every operation. The ROE guiding philosophy as promulgated in the TF 117 Operation Order was restraint and economy of force. The MRF deployed to the delta to destroy Viet Cong main force elements and extend government control in the countryside. It was not there to harm the civilian population, even civilians sympathetic to the Viet Cong. TF 117 Operation Order 201-YR of 10 June 1968, stated unequivocally that the "use of unnecessary force leading to noncombatant battle casualties in areas temporarily controlled by the VC, will embitter the population, drive them into the arms of the VC, and make the long range goal of pacification more difficult and costly to achieve." It goes on to implore commanders to exercise extreme fire-discipline and restraint during operations.

> Commanders at all echelons must strike a balance between the force necessary to accomplish their mission with due regard to the safety of their commands and the high-importance of reducing to a minimum the casualties inflicted on the non-combatant populace. The VC exploit fully incidents of noncombatant casualties and destruction of property of RVNAF and U.S. forces. Their objectives are to foster resentment against GVN and the U.S., and to effect the permanent alienation of the Vietnamese people from their government.[151]

In other words, the ROE were designed to promote a measured and appropriate response to combat situations without infringing on a commander's inherent right to self-defense—a writ that demanded "restraint and mature judgment" among division officers and boat captains. Nothing in the ROE prevented an MRF unit receiving direct fire from returning fire, even if that fire emanated from a town or other populated area, but at the same time it did not allow the MRF to raze a village just to kill a single sniper. Return fire had to be proportional.

In situations where the MRF was not receiving fire directly, commanders could initiate direct fire in uninhabited areas only on targets positively identified as enemy; armed personnel "attempting by hasty or suspicious acts to obviously avoid contact with friendly troops; and suspected enemy targets where no non-combatants are in the area." Against villages, hamlets, or other inhabited territory, the MRF had to exercise more caution. During curfew hours targets had to be seen moving outside the immediate premises of homes, and during noncurfew hours they had to be positively identified as the enemy. In every circumstance, if a civilian was caught in the crossfire, the MRF was to make an effort to render medical assistance to the victim unless providing such aid detracted the unit from "essential support of U.S. Forces."[152]

With regard to property, the ROE demanded that the MRF take great care not to damage or destroy civilian homes and other structures:

> Destruction of houses within inhabited villages, which because of person or items found therein are obviously being used by VC, may cause more harm than good. In such cases local civil authorities should be consulted. If the local authorities state that the house should be destroyed, every effort should be made to have local authorities do the actual destruction. When in doubt, refrain from destroying the buildings.[153]

In theory, these rules gave the MRF commanders enough latitude to protect their men while limiting collateral damage to the civilian populace. In practice, things did not always work out so neatly. Commodore Salzer summed up the dilemma posed by the ROE for him and other commanders:

> The rules of engagement were written by a lawyer. They bore no relationship to what was happening to a man in a river boat in combat. We complied with them as best we could, but I was not going to be a party to hanging someone who complied with the rules but overreacted in his response. You were allowed to respond to fire, as the rules said, but you were supposed to minimize casualties. Well you know that's great to write in Saigon. How do you do it in operational practice?[154]

For example, if nearly every Vietnamese family in the delta constructed a bunker under their homes for protection during battles, how were commanders on the ground to differentiate friendly from unfriendly bunkers, especially when the Viet Cong often used family bunkers during firefights? "What looks good on paper is hard to apply in the heat of battle," lamented Major General George G. O'Connor, who took command of the 9th Division in late 1967.[155]

As commander of TF 117 Salzer's solution was to rely on the best judgment of river division commanders and not punish those who overreacted to hostile fire from the shore unless a massacre ensued, which fortunately for the MRF never occurred. "People got killed," explained Salzer in an oral history after the war, "but there were no My Lais in the sense that I know, no deliberate massacres, and, in fact, we probably lost quite a few of our own men trying not to have those things."[156] Most junior officers studied the ROE carefully and thought through how they would react to each situation they expected to encounter. "My great general fear in the MRF," Lieutenant (j.g.) Walter Lineberger said, "was that the VC would fire at us behind kids or women. Every JO [junior officer] had to decide ahead of time what they would do in that situation."[157]

Unlike officers and boat captains, crewmembers did not generally make decisions about when to fire or cease-fire in an engagement. In the final analysis, though, the ordinary sailor aimed a weapon and pulled the trigger and, in the often-confusing circumstances of counterinsurgency warfare in Vietnam, a few wondered after a firefight if they had killed innocents. "When we were ordered to fire," Steve Vitale said:

> We automatically opened up. It did not matter what side of the riverbank it was, you just fired. You did that until you got through the kill-zone. I know that I personally would get so crazy mad, the adrenaline would pump so much, that I felt indestructible. I get goose bumps when I talk about this. I did not care. I would blow hootches up. I would blow grain storage pots up. I would blow buffalo up. At the time, I was so psyched out that I did not stop firing until they ordered a cease fire. You fire at anything out there, especially when ambushed. When someone fires at you, you can't be selective. With the green Nipa palm coverage, you cannot always tell if there are civilians mixed in with the enemy. After it was over, I wet my pants—other guys did too. It was after you got done that you realized, "Oh my God, I'm alive."[158]

Dave Butler told a story about receiving fire from a village one night and then returning fire with heavy machine guns. "The next day, someone had laid out a bunch of civilian bodies to make us look responsible for the deaths, which we probably were. The following morning we were in what we were told was a free-fire zone."[159]

The dilemma for the sailor was that hesitating to fire when fired upon or ordered to fire could easily result in the death of a shipmate, yet firing blindly into a palm grove or village where fire originated could result in the death of innocent civilians, especially in the crowded confines of the Mekong Delta. Salzer put it this way:

> There were plenty of incidents where innocent civilians were killed; perhaps they weren't so innocent, but as far as we knew, they were, especially the so-called friendly village attack, where you'd get a couple of rocket shots from the center of town. It's very easy for me to say that it will not be responded to by fire, but it's very hard for a boat crew that's been hit and perhaps lost its boat captain and perhaps had one or two other men seriously wounded by, say, two rockets, to remember that when they have

guns in their hands and they can see their friends bloody and dead. It's a very difficult condition and we don't always succeed.[160]

Initial Operations

Advance naval elements of the MRF began arriving in Vietnam in January 1967, but since the first river assault craft were not due for delivery until March, sailors from River Assault Division (RAD) 91 and elements of the 9th Division initially trained on boats borrowed from the Vietnam Navy (seven LCM [6] troop carriers, one monitor, and a commandament).[161] This training, which consisted of river movements, gunnery, and day and night landings, was cut short in mid-February after the Viet Cong launched a series of attacks against U.S. minesweepers on the upper Long Tau River (see chapter 3). RAD 91, along with the 3d Battalion, 47th Infantry, was ordered into immediate action against Viet Cong elements threatening friendly shipping in the RSSZ. Phase I of the operation, called River Raider I, lasted from 16 February to 4 March, and consisted of a series of company- and platoon-size search and destroy operations in areas along the upper Long Tau River. Phase II (5–19 March) included multi-company attacks against VC logistics facilities in the southwestern portion of the RSSZ.[162]

A "Tango" boat steams down the Long Tau River. As the photo suggests, there is very little dry land in the alluvial areas of South Vietnam, July 1967.

This operation had no contacts with large formations of VC troops, but it did capture a significant amount of enemy supplies, including 118 water mines, 3,842 rounds of small arms ammunition, and 196 pounds of explosives. It also destroyed 64 Viet Cong buildings, 356 bunkers, and 87 foxholes, and killed 22 enemy guerillas; eight U.S. Army soldiers were wounded.[163] During Phase I there were no attacks against shipping on the Long Tau channel, but once the Army moved into the southwestern RSSZ, attacks on friendly vessels on the upper Long Tau resumed.[164] This became a typical pattern during MRF operations: troops would move into an area, the enemy would flee and hostile activity would cease but, as soon as the soldiers departed, guerrilla activity would resume.

As the first joint Army-Navy operation on the rivers of Vietnam, River Raider I provided many valuable "lessons learned" for future operations. The MRF's use of boats allowed a relatively small ground force to conduct wide-ranging combat operations across an area over 600-square kilometers in size. By contrast, on foot, soldiers would only have been able to move 300 meters per hour under the best circumstances. LCMs allowed the Army to transport its soldiers nearly anywhere in the RSSZ with ease, and once at an area of operations, they served as floating islands where soldiers could rest, refill their canteens, or dry out their feet. With the extra storage capacity offered by the boats, individual soldiers only needed to carry seven clips for their M16 rifles, 200 rounds of machine-gun ammo, and 12 grenades for M79 grenade launchers.

The boats also greatly facilitated night operations. Before River Raider I began, the Army was unsure if the MRF would be able to maneuver well at night, but the experience of the operation proved beyond a doubt that the MRF could function effectively after dark. Over half of the Army's assaults, ambushes, and movements took place at night during River Raider I—a trend that would continue until the MRF halted operations in June 1969. Under the cover of darkness, a platoon or company would often be withdrawn and transported to another area of operation where it would make a limited penetration into the jungle, set up ambush positions, and be ready for a search and destroy mission at first light.[165]

One of the most innovative adaptations of LCM (6) during River Raider I was the mortar boat, which contained two 81mm mortars installed in the well deck. During operations the mortar boat coxswain would nose the LCM into the riverbank with the engines running, so he could advance or back up the boat quickly depending on tides. Crewmembers used ropes to stabilize the lateral movement of the craft, and troops stationed on the boat would establish a small security perimeter on the bank. According to the 3d Battalion, 47th Infantry after-action report, "The rig permitted a high degree of mobility, rapid positioning for firing, minimum wasted effort by the gun crews, and an ample supply of ammunition close at hand." The boat operated both day and night, providing troops with highly responsive artillery support deep within enemy territory. This boat was a precursor to the artillery barges developed in April 1967, which Colonel Fulton described as "the most important equipment decision made by the Army for the MRF."[166]

Upon the completion of River Raider I, the MRF embarked on a similar follow-on operation in the RSSZ called Spearhead I with the 4th Battalion, 47th Infantry, again using equipment borrowed from the VNN. Spearhead I killed 13 Viet Cong and destroyed 88 water mines.

During April the MRF also began receiving its first modified LCMs from the United States, and by end of the month 18 ATCs, two monitors, and a CCB had deployed to the delta. On 14 April *Kemper County* (LST-854) arrived at Vung Tau and became the first MRF support ship. On 22 April *Benewah* arrived as well.[167]

The first major riverine operation involving heavy contact with the enemy was Coronado I (1 June to 26 July). This operation took place in Can Giuoc, the easternmost district of Long An Province, where an excellent network of waterways made it a good proving ground for the MRF. It was also a base area for the *5th Nha Be Battalion*, a Viet Cong unit that had been active around Saigon and had recently fought against the U.S. Army's 199th Infantry Brigade (Light). Before commencing operations, the MRF moved its afloat base within three kilometers of the *5th Battalion*'s base, and two kilometers south of Can Giuoc, the district capital. Fulton's plan was to land the 4th Battalion, 47th Infantry north and east of the objective, and two companies of the 3d Battalion, 47th Infantry north and west of the area. These units would swing across the northern part of the base area and then reassemble along an east-west waterway that ran across the enemy redoubt, ferry across the stream, and continue south. An ARVN battalion would provide security for the force's western flank while Navy assault craft would cover its eastern flank.[168]

On the evening of 18 June, Army combat units embarked on nearly 80 river assault craft under blackout conditions. They landed in their designated zones without incident and began to sweep their assigned sectors. The Can Giuoc district chief then told Fulton that a large force of Viet Cong was located further to the southeast than the original intelligence had indicated. Unwilling to cancel the operation, Fulton continued sweeping south, but he did order his reaction force, Company C, 3d Battalion, 47th Infantry, to leapfrog by helicopter to the reported new enemy concentration and hit them from the rear. This unit, commanded by Captain Ronald Menner, made no contact with the enemy. Meanwhile, the rest of the Army force continued moving toward their original objective, slogging for over three hours through knee-deep water and thick mud in the sweltering midday heat.[169]

While the Army troops struggled across the difficult terrain toward their objective, the *5th Battalion* lay in wait in a fortified, L-shaped ambush position, resting up during the traditional Vietnamese siesta period. Captain Robert Linton Reeves commanded Company A, 4th Battalion, 47th Infantry. Shortly before noon, his men approached some thatched huts near the elbow of the L-shaped enemy line, and an astute point man in the 2d Platoon noticed a claymore mine suspended from a tree. Just as he sounded the alarm, the Viet Cong opened fire with machine guns and small arms, catching the entire company in the open with little in the way of cover. The enemy machine guns were so well laid that their grazing fire completely sawed off the legs of four soldiers and wounded scores of others. Overall, nearly every man in Company A was killed or wounded that day, with the dead totaling 32 and the wounded, 76.[170] The ambush essentially took the unit out of action before it had time to react.

Nonetheless, Reeves continued to fight. He immediately called in artillery strikes on the bunker line and tried to reorganize an assault on the enemy positions but had trouble communicating with his various elements because many of the radio operators had been killed or wounded. Meanwhile, the 4th Battalion, 47th Infantry commander, Lieutenant Colonel Guy Tutwiler, ordered the remainder of his forces to assist the beleaguered company, with Company B arriving first on the scene, followed by Company C.

The first priority of Company B and the survivors of Company A was to clear the battlefield of wounded—a challenging task given that many casualties were caught in an open kill zone with little or no cover to protect them or potential rescuers. Two medics died trying to reach the wounded. Specialist 4th Class (Sp4c) William L. "Bill" Reynolds, a rifleman with 2d Platoon, Company A remembered being pinned down behind a rice paddy dike for much of the day unable to move out and assist the wounded in the kill zone because of heavy fire and taking sniper fire from the rear. "Our radio operator, Sp4c Bob French got hit in the lower back and let out a blood-curdling scream I will never forget." The sniper then hit Sp4c Ronnie Bryan, a machine gunner, in the buttocks. The 2d Platoon medic, Sp4c William "Bill" Michael Geier, immediately leapt to action and went to treat Bryan, but while bandaging the gunner Geier took a round in his lung. "I did all I could to help Bill," Reynolds later recounted "but he died before we could medevac him."[171]

The first gunfire support craft on the scene was a RAS 9 command boat. Lieutenant Commander Charles L. Horowitz, the squadron commander, stood exposed on the top of the boat directing fire from his column. When he noticed that his 40mm and 81mm rounds were having little effect on the enemy positions, Horowitz, a 1954 Naval Academy graduate from Utica, New York, ordered his command boat to push up a narrow inlet and fire at closer range from a bank. Army Captain Herbert E. Lind, the commander of Company C, was an eyewitness to the action. According to his after-action report, it took 20 well-placed rounds at a distance of just 25 meters to silence one of the bunkers. Horowitz, who received a fragment wound to his left foot during the engagement, later received a Silver Star for his heroism that day.[172] Another naval officer who took great risks to provide gunfire support for the beleaguered Army troops was Commander Dusty Rhodes, the hard-boiled commanding officer of River Assault Squadron 11. Rhodes guided

Lieutenant Commander Francis E. Rhodes, Commander, River Assault Squadron 11.

his monitor down a small stream, beached it, and then unleashed devastating 40mm fire against the Viet Cong, knocking out several bunkers the process. "That helped. Less than the air support but it played a role" explained First Lieutenant Jack Benedick, another eyewitness to the event.[173]

But the title of "most valuable player" for the Navy team that day belonged to neither a line officer nor a sailor, but to a charismatic young chaplain by the name of Raymond Wendell Johnson. Lieutenant Johnson (no relation to the Army chaplain with the same last name) came from Minneapolis where he excelled in high school sports, being named to the all-state football and baseball teams. Upon graduation from high school in 1952, scouts for the Brooklyn Dodgers offered him a generous contract bonus to sign with their organization, but Johnson decided to forego instant fame and fortune and pursue higher education instead. He eventually graduated from Gustavus Adolphus College in St. Peter, Minnesota, in 1956 and then attended seminary at the Augustana Theological Seminary in Rock Island, Illinois.[174] To support himself during seminary, he worked as a medical technician in the emergency room at City Hospital in Moline/Rock Island, Illinois. This training would allow him later to serve a dual role in Vietnam, that of chaplain and lead medical corpsman.

Ordained in 1960 as a Lutheran minister, he served for the first six years of his pastoral career at the Good Shepherd Lutheran Church in Rutland, Vermont, with collateral campus ministry duties at Dartmouth and Middlebury colleges. In 1966 the Navy was looking for chaplains and, with the strong encouragement of a friend, Johnson volunteered for the Navy Chaplain Corps. After sending him to Officer Candidate School at Newport and assigning him briefly as the chaplain at the Charleston Naval Hospital, the Navy transferred him to TF 117, in part because of his athleticism and medical skills. The Navy needed a chaplain who could get through small boat and SERE training and, when necessary, assist corpsmen in the medical aid boat during combat. Johnson fit the bill perfectly.

On 19 June he was on the medical aid boat when he noticed a wounded Army radioman desperately trying to make it to the boat. Johnson left the boat and helped the soldier reach the relative safety of the aid station. The radioman told Johnson about three areas where wounded needed assistance: "They're all bleeding to death,

Lieutenant/Chaplain Raymond Wendell Johnson sitting on an ATC-H.

all the officers and medics have been killed," he told the chaplain. Johnson grabbed a stretcher and in the same movement asked for volunteers. Boatswain's Mate 3rd Class Cecil O. "Swede" Johnson Jr. and Engineman 2nd Class Michael W. "Red" Dolezal from Tango 92-7 immediately agreed to help him. Padre Johnson later compared these two sailors to the Good Samaritans: "These two junkyard dogs would never have been allowed to even enter the maintenance building of the Naval Academy, but at that moment they stood on the summit of Mount Everest."[175]

Under cover of heavy fire from a gunboat, the three men zigzagged their way toward the wounded men and as they approached a dike, Chaplain Johnson felt a sudden sting in his left leg and noticed that he had been wounded from a grenade fragment. He checked the wound, put a compress on it, and decided to keep going. "My emergency room training had taught me a great deal about the endurance of the wounded. If you are mentally positive, you can just about survive the impossible." As he got up to continue, he felt a strong thud in his chest, "like the wallop of a baseball bat," and was thrown into the mud. A .30-caliber bullet sliced into his flak vest and lodged itself into a copy of the New Testament he carried, fracturing three of his ribs but miraculously failing to penetrate his body.

He and the sailors then dashed 75 yards through open terrain to a group of wounded. The three men, with the assistance of a soldier, carried two of the most seriously wounded to the aid boat in two litters under "hypnotic" cover fire from the boats. Johnson then returned alone to the battlefield with his medical bag and administered what he could in the way of first aid to various wounded, running back and forth to different groups. He then carried another wounded man to the aid boat. Exhaustion and dehydration finally overwhelmed him; he threw up and collapsed in the aid boat.

After resting a bit, he ventured out one last time alone with his medical bag, offering limited medical assistance to the wounded and words of prayer and encouragement. On this foray he came across a close friend, Army First Lieutenant Fred Bertolino. "I wanted so deeply to help save Fred's life. I attempted mouth to mouth resuscitation until I could not force another breath." Suddenly in his deepest moment of despair, Johnson observed a lotus flower at the edge of the mangrove, and felt an unexpected moment of peace while placing his dead friend on a muddy patch of ground over 8,000 miles away from his family. As he viewed that flower, the Vietnamese symbol for optimism, Padre Johnson knew that he had the capacity to carry on, and soon found himself running and crawling to another group of three casualties. This time the results were favorable and all three survived. When Johnson finally returned the boat, he refused medical evacuation for himself, arguing that his services as a medical assistant were required on the boat. For his heroism that day, the Navy awarded Lieutenant Johnson a Silver Star—the first such decoration awarded to a Navy chaplain since the Korean War. BM3 Johnson also received the Silver Star, and EN2 Dolezal, a Bronze Star.[176]

As the Johnson story revealed, medical evacuation of the wounded posed one of the biggest command challenges of the engagement. It took over two hours of pounding by artillery fire, naval gunfire support, and air strikes before Army commanders felt the area was safe enough for dustoff helicopters to land. The first Army Huey to attempt a medevac landed in the zone of Company C, picked up five wounded, and then attempted a liftoff. A bullet slammed through the windshield and hit the pilot in the left shoulder, causing the aircraft to spin out of control and crash. "I remember seeing my friend Sp4c Forrest Ramos getting on it and I was thrilled. We were happy that our guys were getting out of there," recalled Bill Reynolds. "When the chopper was 150 feet off the ground, the pilot was hit, and the aircraft came down hard. We were devastated. My friend Forrest fell out of the chopper and died as it was coming down."[177]

A second Army helicopter landed to recover the more seriously wounded from the first helicopter, but as it got 150 feet off the ground, enemy machine-gun bullets knocked it out of the sky. Some of the wounded thrown out of the second aircraft died upon impact with the ground. Another soldier died while pinned beneath the wreck. Realizing that no more landings could be made under such conditions, Colonel Tutwiler ordered a halt to all dustoffs in the ambush area until the rest of the bunkers were destroyed. A third helicopter disregarded this guidance and additional warnings from a radio operator from 2d Platoon, Company C and insisted on coming anyway. The chopper landed but was unable to take off, and both of its machine gunners were wounded in heavy enemy fire. A fourth helicopter came in several hours later to evacuate wounded from 1st Platoon, Company C and was hit as it lifted off. "It did a half back-flip, straightened out, did another one and then came crashing to the ground nose first," wrote the platoon commander, First Lieutenant Lynn J. Hunt, in an after-action report. Hunt's medic and five other men tried to rescue men from the helicopter and saved most of them, but one died under the helicopter wreck and another died later in a hospital.[178] "Special recognition should be given to the dustoff choppers," wrote Captain Reeves in his after-action report. The pilots "were told how the air was filled with .50-caliber and .30-caliber rounds. They said they would give it a try." The ones that "were shot down on the battlefield conducted especially heroic landings and take offs and deserve recognition for their total disregard of their own safety."[179]

Casualties from the battle were taken to an Army evacuation hospital and to *Benewah* and *Colleton*, which together treated 45 patients and received helicopter-evacuated casualties all day and throughout the night despite the fact that neither ship was a hospital vessel equipped to handle mass casualties. Navy ships and small boats also resupplied the Army forces during the battle, with *Kemper County* and later *Vernon County* providing a steady flow of 105mm artillery shells to an Army fire support position located in an old French Fort. A Navy explosive ordinance disposal team destroyed two 105mm shells, two claymore mines, and one water mine during the operation. Finally, as mentioned earlier, river craft offered steady fire support throughout the day. Captain Reeves later defined these efforts in his after-action report as the "second most responsive supporting fire" after Army artillery. On several occasions Navy vessels were hit by rocket fire. ATC 112-4 took two hits from rocket-propelled grenades and a third from a 57mm recoilless rifle. The Tango boat's armor deflected the 57mm round, but one RPG-2 penetrated the ballistic armor plate and hull plating at the waterline, flooding the well deck and forcing the boat to beach. Another RPG penetrated the armor plate at deck level in the .50-caliber turret and pilothouse, injuring four crewmembers. Emergency repairs eventually got the boat up and running on its own power, so salvage was unnecessary.[180]

Lack of transport helicopters meant that Army reinforcements had to travel overland to the ambush site—an agonizingly slow process given the mud and numerous streams in the area. Company C of the 3d Battalion actually had to requisition sampans from villagers to ford a 10-meter stream. By the time that the Army had a significant number of troops stationed on three sides of the enemy, darkness had begun to fall, forcing Fulton to delay a counterattack until morning. During the night most of the enemy escaped through gaps in the lines. "They probed our positions with small patrols looking for an exit," Menner recalled.[181] A significant number of enemy troops might have escaped via sampans on the Rach Nui. During the night of 19–20 June, several naval craft withdrew from the area of the ambush. Had they stayed, these boats might have helped prevent the Viet Cong ambushers from escaping. When he found out about the withdrawal, Fulton angrily confronted Wells, who conceded that it had been a mistake and immediately ordered the boats back out. From that point onwards, he promised that his boats would always be available to support the Army on a 24-hour basis.[182] A significant lesson from this battle, one not originally envisioned by the initial MRF planners, was that the boats could be used independently as floating armor to block an enemy escape route across a major waterway. The ARVN had employed its river assault craft mainly in the transport role, but this June engagement in Can Giuoc district revealed a potentially broader role for the boats.[183]

Army forces swept the area on the 20th, but only achieved contact with small VC elements, and on the 21st, Army units began withdrawing to the Mobile Riverine Base. Overall, Army casualties included 50 killed and another 150 wounded; Navy losses were 15 wounded.[184] Army losses for this battle were so severe that II Field Force Headquarters demanded high VC body counts to justify the investment in American blood. When Fulton informed Major General George G. O'Conner, the 9th Division commander, that he could not produce meaningful numbers because of darkness and the fact that the Viet Cong had evacuated many of their dead and wounded, O'Conner reported that 256 enemy bodies had been discovered. Fulton only found 70 the next day. According to Army historian George MacGarrigle, "The division headquarters had created the spurious statistics out of concern that MACV might relieve Fulton" if a large body count was not produced. Captured documents found later suggest that the Fulton's brigade had killed 170 Viet Cong."[185]

Coronado V: Rach Ba Rai

Coronado I, in many respects, set the pattern for future MRF operations. It demonstrated that the Viet Cong only intended to engage the MRF with large units at times and places of its choosing—usually in well-placed ambushes designed to inflict maximum casualties on the American side. One of the most deadly of these surprise attacks occurred on 15 September 1967 at the Ba Rai Creek, a narrow waterway ten kilometers upstream from My Tho. The day before, ARVN sources reported that the *263d Viet Cong Battalion* was in the area, and the 9th Infantry Division decided to attempt to encircle it with two riverine battalions (3d Battalion, 47th Infantry and 3d

Battalion, 60th Infantry) and a mechanized battalion (5th Battalion, 60th Infantry) operating M113 armored personnel carriers (APCs). The riverine battalions would travel up the Rach Ba Rai and act as blocking forces, with the 3d Battalion, 60th Infantry landing north of the suspected Viet Cong force, and the 3d Battalion, 47th Infantry to the south. Meanwhile, the 5th Battalion, 60th Infantry would travel overland to the target from Route 20 in their APCs in an attempt to pin the enemy battalion against the Ba Rai Creek.[186]

Lieutenant Commander Dusty Rhodes commanded the 23 river assault craft that would carry the 3d Battalion, 60th Infantry. The Navy unit, Task Group 117.2, had the most difficult and dangerous role to play in the operation. It had to pass through an area where the river was only 30 meters-wide—a nearly ideal ambush site. The unit would be broken up into two convoys with the bulk of the force in the 17 boats of the lead convoy, and a small number of troops in a trailing column of five ATCs and two monitors.[187]

A native of Norfolk, Virginia, Rhodes fought as an enlisted quartermaster on a motor gunboat in the Pacific during World War II and took immense pride in his "deckplate" knowledge of small-unit operations and his "mustang" heritage. After the war he earned a degree at the College of William & Mary and later served in Korea as the executive officer of the motor minesweeper *Swallow* (AMS-36). In 1964 he became an advisor to the VNN, and in that capacity worked with three different river assault groups. In December 1966 he became the commanding officer of River Assault Squadron 11 of the Mobile Riverine Force. In this role he quickly gained a reputation for having substantive knowledge of riverine warfare, excellent instincts in combat, and also a rather abrasive personality. Chaplain Raymond Johnson, who worked closely with Rhodes, described him this way: "He was blustery, fun to be around, and a risky old fart. He garnered both respect and disdain."[188]

At 0300 on 15 September, 3d Battalion, 60th Infantry began loading from the barracks ship *Colleton*, which was anchored on the My Tho River near Dong Tam. The loading was complete by 0415, and the Rhodes task unit made its way slowly up the river to the Rach Ba Rai. Most of the Army troops slept during the relatively safe three-hour transit on the My Tho River. These men had been up most of the night preparing for the mission (cleaning weapons, organizing equipment, and being briefed on the operation order) and had had very little rest.[189] As the unit entered the Rach Ba Rai at 0700, the sailors and soldiers became more alert. "When you go up the little ones," explained GMG2 Chester Stanley, the 40mm gunner on Rhodes' CCB, "you put your helmet and flak jacket on. And you batten down hatches because you know it's going to happen."[190]

The boats passed the first eastward bend of the river, known as Snoopy's Nose, without incident and continued north past the two beaches where the 3d Battalion, 47th Infantry, which followed behind this convoy, was to land. At the front of the 3d Battalion, 60th Infantry column were two minesweepers, T 91-4 and T 91-1. Their chain-drag minesweeping slowed the forward movement of the convoy and would double its exposure in the kill zone. A COMNAVFORV after-action report concluded that had the speedier Alpha boat minesweepers been available at the time, they might have spared the task unit casualties.[191]

Armored troop carriers rafted alongside the barracks ship *Colleton* (APB-36), 29 September 1967.

At 0730, the Viet Cong fired two B40 rockets from a concealed bunker at T 91-4. The initial rounds fell short off the starboard bow, but three additional B40 rounds fired at the boat found their mark, hitting the starboard side 20mm mount, the starboard bow, and the port side 20mm mount, and wounding eight sailors. Between 0731 and 0738, five B50 and B40 rounds hit the other minesweeper (T 91-1), wounding another eight. Soon other boats in the column were taking hits. Army Chaplain James Johnson, who was in the medical aid boat, vividly remembers the initial minutes of the ambush.

> I'm standing at the front of the well deck next to the landing ramp munching on the remainder of my C-rats when suddenly explosions begin going off everywhere in the small stream. I'm almost knocked off my feet as the aid boat swerves.... Someone tells me a VC rocket has hit near our fantail and exploded, apparently just below the water level, knocking the rudder loose, but not incapacitating our boat.... Within seconds, both banks of the stream are erupting with fire. The unmistakable rip of enemy AK-47 assault-rifle fire and the staccato sound of machine-gun fire are interrupted time and again by the explosions of rocket-propelled grenades, recoilless rifles, and B40 rockets. This is worse than playing dodge ball; only these balls do not bounce. They kill and maim."[192]

After the minesweepers, the next boats in the column to be hit were two monitors and the CBB. Monitor 111-2 took a B40 round on the port side of the coxswain's flat, killing the coxswain, Seaman Richard Allan Cheek, and causing the monitor to go out of control and beach. Two B40 rounds then hit the port side of the CCB's 40mm mount. These rounds knocked Dusty Rhodes (who was between the two gun tubs in the coxswain's flat) to the deck but caused minimal damage to the boat. GMG2 Stanley continued firing the 40mm gun at the enemy, as if nothing had happened, but complained later that he could not depress the gun far enough to hit the low-lying enemy bunkers.[193] In fact, close quarters combat with these bunkers proved a challenge for just about every weapon in the task unit's inventory; for example, 40mm rounds had to actually penetrate the slits of the bunkers to disable them. Only when Viet Cong troops emerged from spider holes and could be raked with machine-gun fire was naval gunfire effective during the battle. The disappointing performance of TF 117's direct fire weapons during this battle would hasten the development of the Zippo monitor.[194]

Radioman Seaman (RMSN) Dave Raybell experienced the brunt of the initial run through the gauntlet on Monitor 111-3. Raybell, a 22-year-old sailor from Washington State, joined the Navy after attending Grays Harbor Community College in Aberdeen for a year. An intelligent young man, who was also a decent athlete, having lettered in both football and track in high school, Raybell nonetheless lacked the motivation to finish a college program. "I was not mature enough at the time to apply myself to my studies." He joined the Navy to avoid being drafted into the Army and because his Dad had served as a machinist's mate first class on *Botetourt* (APA-136), an amphibious attack transport, during World War II.

Like many new enlisted sailors, Raybell did not have a firm idea of what he wanted to do in the service. He considered becoming an electronics technician, but when he discovered that the rating required a commitment of two additional years of service, he steered clear. He also declined a slot at the U.S. Naval Academy as a midshipman because "I couldn't see four years of boot camp." He finally settled on the radioman rate, which only required four months of specialized training. After attending boot camp and A School in San Diego, he joined the destroyer *Richard B. Anderson* (DD-786) as a radioman seaman, but once again shifted gears when he learned that the Navy was looking for volunteers for the Mobile Riverine Force. When he volunteered for TF 117, he "had no idea what they were or that it would be an overseas assignment. It just sounded interesting."[195]

As the radioman for Monitor 111-3, Raybell had seen some action earlier in the year in the Rung Sat, but nothing had prepared him for what happened on 15 September. In the third minute of the ambush, he witnessed his best friend Seaman Cheek die in Monitor 111-2. Two minutes later at 0735, a B40 round slammed into the slit of Monitor 111-3's 40mm mount, setting off ammunition in the turret and wounding three of his shipmates: Seaman Bryan Girard Craft, Engineman 3rd Class William Harris Little, and Gunner's Mate (Guns) 2nd Class James Ezra Elkins. As the three wounded sailors exited the gun mount, another B40 hit the lip around the mortar pit and exploded, killing Little and wounding Fireman Abraham Cecemski and Lieutenant (j.g.) George Washington Hawkins. Cecemski, a dual American-Israeli citizen and the only Jew in the entire boat division, received a shell fragment in the frontal lobe of his brain but did not die.[196] Hawkins, the executive officer for River Division 111 and a Silverdale, Washington native, had his left kidney sheared off by shrapnel. Raybell later found the kidney after the battle when cleaning the boat. "It was intact and looked to be surgically removed."[197]

Monitor 111-3 took a fourth B40 round at 0745 on the port side. The round went through the port side machine-gun mount. "My boat was basically out of action at that point," Raybell explained. "The 50- and 20-millimeter kept up fire but we had lost our main weapon, the 40-millimeter. All this took place about 15 feet from the riverbank."[198] For the rest of the battle Raybell multitasked between various jobs on the boat, ranging from manning the radios, steering the boat, firing a .30-caliber machine gun, and assisting the wounded in the mortar pit. "I remember having to grab my boat captain a couple of times and tell him to keep his head down. He was very much in shock." Of the original 11 sailors in the boat, five were seriously wounded and one killed in action. Raybell received minor shrapnel in his back, knee, and several other spots but stayed with the boat for the entire battle. "I was running on adrenaline." When he finally did receive medical attention the next day on board *Askari*, Navy doctors removed the shrapnel in his knee and back but kept him in sick bay for three days due to concerns about possible infection.[199]

Shortly after Monitor 111-3 took its third hit, rockets began finding their marks on the troop carriers. By 0749, Viet Cong B40 rockets had hit three ATCs (T 111-13, T 111-11, and T 111-6). ATC 111-13 had a three-man U.S. Marine Corps hydrographic survey team on board, but after the boat took a B40 round in the port .50-caliber mount, the marines reverted to their traditional rifleman role, grabbing weapons from wounded sailors and fighting hard for the remainder of the battle.[200] Army soldiers also lent a helping hand, pulling wounded sailors from gun mounts and manning those guns themselves. Others returned fire with M79 grenade launchers, M60 machine guns, and M16 rifles. In one boat a company commander, Captain Wilbert Davis, took over a Navy gun from a wounded sailor. One of his sergeants then relieved him, only to be to be shot in the chest by a sniper. As soon as the sergeant fell, another soldier jumped up and took his place. On another troop carrier, 1st Lieutenant Peter M. Rogers, the commander of Company B, 3d Battalion, 60th Infantry, saw six of his men hit in the first few seconds. Overall, the Army lost four men, and another 49 were wounded during the battle.[201]

At 0750, Lieutenant Commander Rhodes, who had regained consciousness after having been knocked down to the deck, ordered all units to assemble back at Red Beach Two, one of the beaches south of the gauntlet that had been assigned to the 3d Battalion, 47th Infantry. Rhodes decided that by regrouping south of the area, the unit could safely evacuate wounded and then bring in reinforcements for a second attempt to cross the kill zone.

By this time all boats had stopped moving through the gauntlet except for one: Tango 111-6. Several minutes before the withdrawal order had been issued, two B40 rounds had slammed into the port side of the coxswain's flat, destroying all of the boat's radios and wounding five crewmembers, including the boat captain, Boatswain's Mate 1st Class Carroll E. Dutterer Jr. Unable to receive any communications or observe the movements of the other boats due to intense smoke, Dutterer pressed on through the 1,800-meter kill zone and landed his troops at their assigned beach. When those troops became pinned down by intense enemy fire, Dutterer directed fire from an exposed position topside and then re-beached and picked up 1st Platoon, Bravo Company. During the reembarkation, BM1 Dutterer was seriously wounded by another rocket, which hit the port side .50-caliber mount. Despite his wounds, which by now consisted of shrapnel wounds in both legs and the stomach, he maintained control of his craft until reembarkation was completed. For his courage, the Navy would later award Dutterer, a native of Muskegon, Michigan, the Navy Cross.[202]

Flying above the scene in a helicopter, Lieutenant Colonel Mercer M. Doty, the 3d Battalion, 60th Infantry commander, was encouraged by Tango 111-6's success in making it through the gauntlet and landing troops. He therefore encouraged Rhodes to continue with the mission. Pleased that a large concentration of enemy troops was exactly where intelligence reports had said it would be, Doty wanted to land more troops as quickly as possible and press on with the attack. Rhodes disagreed. Before continuing the attack, he wanted to evacuate casualties and bring in replacement minesweepers. The TF 117 operation orders required minesweepers to precede ATCs at all times, and Rhodes was loath to violate these accepted tactical practices, especially given recent intelligence reports indicating that the Viet Cong might employ water mines on the Rach Ba Rai.[203] When Doty heard the withdrawal order, he had no choice but to comply, since Rhodes was in overall command of the operation during the transit.[204]

By 0758, all the boats, including Tango 111-6, had pulled back to the vicinity of Red Beach Two and began transferring their wounded to the aid boat. Metal fragments produced when B40 and B50 rounds penetrated the assault boats had caused most of the injuries. These rockets typically inflicted many minor wounds, but only a small number of serious wounds. In most cases, the lightly injured were treated and sent back to battle—men like Dave Raybell and Terry Gander, an Army M60 machine gunner from Company B who had helped defend his ATC and caught a piece of shrapnel in his chest. According to Chaplain James Johnson, "Terry was patched up and elected to stay with his buddies. A hero among heroes."[205]

With the more seriously wounded, medical staff attempted to stabilize their wounds and then transport them by boat or helicopter to an evacuation hospital or the MRB. At 0845, the first medevac helicopter arrived and began removing patients from the ATC(H), dubbed the U.S.S. *Scarecrow* by its brave crew of Army medics and Navy hospital corpsmen.[206] In all, 52 battle casualties were treated and medically evacuated from *Scarecrow*—an asset that one after-action report described as "invaluable."[207]

By 0900, replacement minesweepers (T 91-11 and T 91-13) and a monitor (M 91-3) had arrived on scene to replace the boats heavily damaged in the first attack. The new boats also brought ammunition and extra sailors to replace those wounded earlier in the day. During the next hour the convoy reformed for a second attack while F-4C Phantom jets pounded enemy positions with bombs and napalm. Three batteries of artillery and Army helicopter gunships would also support the second run. As Army historian John Albright wrote, "This time no element of surprise existed for either side; the issue would be settled by firepower alone." The convoy began making its way again up the Rach Ba Rai at 1025. Five minutes later the lead unit began taking fire from both sides of the bank. Minesweeper T 91-13 took two B40 rounds in the port side, wounding five men. The other minesweeper, T 91-11, also came under rocket attack and, by the time it reached the objective beaches, it had sustained seven hits from B40 rockets, resulting in three casualties. Viet Cong rockets also found their mark on two ATCs. On board Tango 111-10, a B40 rocket penetrated the bar armor and exploded above the well deck canopy, killing one soldier and wounding another 18 plus two sailors.[208]

Chaplain Jim Johnson was one of the first to arrive at the scene in the aid boat. "Wounded soldiers are lying in several masses, some sprawled on top of others," he wrote. "Some are calm while others are panicky. I quickly assure them in a loud but steady voice that help is on the way.... As I talk, I'm putting on field bandages as quickly as I can." A single rocket had rendered one of Company A's platoons combat ineffective; only five men of the platoon would be healthy enough to continue the fight after the explosion.[209] A lucky shot perhaps, but one the Viet Cong had been training for since the arrival of the first MRF boats earlier in the year.

Huynh Ly commanded one of the Viet Cong *263d Battalion*'s platoons at the Rach Ba Rai battle. Born in 1943 near My Tho, Ly grew up working on his father's rice farm and had no formal education. His only military training consisted of the eight-month basic training that he had received when he became a Bo Doi (guerrilla) in 1962. On 15 September 1967, Ly's platoon of 22 men was stationed along the banks of the Rach Ba Rai. Ly had received information several hours ahead of time from a spotter unit that the Americans were on the way. During the attack Ly fired eight B40 rounds at American boats. "The river was so narrow that whenever I took a shot, I hit a boat. I would aim at the engine spaces." Ly and his men focused most of their efforts on the Tango boats and the minesweepers (which looked like troop carriers in the eyes of the Viet Cong) because their goal was to take out as many American soldiers as possible on the river before they had an opportunity to engage the Viet Cong on land. "I'll never forget the sounds of the wounded screaming and crying in the boats. Personally, I was very sorry and unhappy, but my duty as a soldier was to fight the Americans and I performed my duty."[210]

Throughout the run, Rhodes was an island of calm in turbulent waters. From an exposed position between the stern gun mounts, he issued orders and maintained pressure on his boat captains to continue fighting to their objective beaches. At 1035, his CCB took two near misses from B40s. At 1106, his CCB took a B50 round while providing gunfire support for soldiers, who had just landed at White Beaches One and Two. Although three men had been wounded in the boat, Rhodes stayed topside and continued to maintain an offensive posture. Seeing two Viet Cong with weapons running along the shore, he grabbed an M16 rifle and shot both. In another instance, a Tango boat reported a sniper in a tree and called Rhodes to inform him of the situation. Rhodes said "shoot him" The boat captain called back and said, "But I got to shoot over a monitor." "Well shoot the bastard," Rhodes replied in a completely relaxed tone of voice. The ATC then fired a single 20mm round over Monitor 112-2. The monitor's boat captain made the following report: "That there sniper fell out of the tree."[211] The Navy later awarded Rhodes a Navy Cross for his leadership throughout the four-hour battle.[212]

At 1048, the ATC coxswains nosed their craft into the muddy banks of White Beaches One and Two under automatic weapons fire. Army troops returned fire, mainly with M79 grenade launchers, backed up by F-100 jets and a rolling Army artillery barrage. Having lost a platoon earlier in the day and facing stubborn enemy resistance despite significant air and artillery support, Captain Greg Orth, the Company A commander (3d Battalion, 60th Infantry), asked Colonel Doty if he should continue to press the fight.

Doty replied: "You haven't got much choice; you've got to continue on."

Orth answered, "We're moving out."[213]

Of the three companies involved in the attack, only one had more than two effective platoons, yet these troops slowly gained ground against a determined enemy. The 3d Battalion, 60th Infantry was to serve as a blocking force while other Army units moved in from the south and east to encircle the enemy. Those units were the 5th Battalion, 60th Infantry and the 3d Battalion, 47th Infantry, plus the 2d Battalion, 60th Infantry, a two-company unit that had been moved in to fill a gap between the other two companies. Together the four battalions would form an irregular arch extending clockwise from the White beaches along the east side of the Rach Ba Rai.

Shortly before 1700, the 3d Battalion, 60th Infantry again encountered heavy contact with the enemy. Aware of the losses suffered by the unit earlier in the day, Colonel Bert A. David, the 2d Brigade commander (Fulton had recently been promoted to brigadier general and become the assistant division commander), ordered the battalion back to the northern beach to form a defensive perimeter for the night—a move that ultimately helped the Viet Cong escape the noose slowly forming around it. Under the cover of darkness, the *263d Battalion* escaped in small groups through gaps in the American lines or by swimming the Rach Ba Rai.

The next day, Army soldiers swept through the area and discovered over 250 enemy bunkers and 24 dead Viet Cong, but made only sporadic contacts with active guerrilla fighters. BM1 Robert Edward Davis, whose monitor reinforced Rhodes' column later in the day, recalled seeing a dead VC soldier wearing a pith helmet and a poncho and thinking, "Here were these little guys without even steel helmets and flak jackets holding back the United States Navy. I was impressed."[214] Overall, a single Viet Cong battalion hit 21 MRF boats with a range of weapons, killing seven Americans and wounding another 123.[215] Sixty percent of the American casualties during this battle were U.S. Navy personnel. More ominously, Navy explosive ordnance disposal (EOD) personnel later discovered that the Viet Cong employed a new weapon in this attack—the RPG-7, an antitank rocket significantly more powerful than 57mm recoilless rifle and B40 rounds. Their use might have contributed to the high American casualties in this ambush.

The battle at Snoopy's Nose demonstrated that even the Navy's best-armored craft would not stand up well against a dug-in enemy possessing the latest, lightweight Soviet armor-piercing weaponry. The Army later estimated that 79 Viet Cong lost their lives in this fight and that enemy morale in the province subsequently deteriorated. Nonetheless, the fact that a single Viet Cong battalion stood and fought against the impressive firepower of the MRF and inflicted the casualties it did in such a short amount of time, can hardly be seen as a victory of joint American arms. It was a close call indeed.[216]

Coronado IX: Rach Ruong

The next big engagement for TF 117 occurred on 4 December 1967. Like the 15 September battle, this one involved an ambush on a narrow waterway by dug-in Viet Cong. Like the earlier engagement, the Navy suffered heavy casualties. With that said, TF 117 generally acquitted itself better in this battle for a number of reasons. First, faster and more powerful ASPB minesweepers allowed the convoys to move more rapidly through kill zones and reduced transit times considerably. Second, TF 117 took a "damn the torpedoes, full speed ahead" attitude and pressed forward with the attack despite receiving heavy fire and taking casualties. In this battle the MRF's heavily armored boats finally demonstrated their ability to remain in a battle zone even when taking numerous hits from B40 rockets, recoilless rifle rounds, and automatic weapons. Third, once they committed to the attack, the ground forces involved (in this case a battalion of Vietnamese marines) fought ferociously to neutralize the enemy positions in short order and inflicted the heaviest losses to date by the MRF against Viet Cong. Their resolve and that of Navy boat captains and division officers to remain steadfast in the face of a hurricane of enemy fire saved the day for the MRF.

The 5th Vietnamese Marine Battalion had joined the MRF on 6 November 1967, becoming its third maneuver battalion. The unit possessed four rifle companies and a heavy weapons company, making it the equivalent of two embarked U.S. Army battalions. Moreover, these marines, as Fulton wrote, brought a special esprit de corps to the Mobile Riverine Force. Padre Raymond Johnson described them as "Special Forces-caliber" troops with "a different energy than standard ARVN soldiers." Lester Schneider, whose Tango boat carried a platoon of marines on 4 December, was even blunter: "The marines were mean. I talked to one who was a teenager and he told me he had killed two VC that day [4 December], and he asked me if I wanted to see their ears. I said no, 'I don't want to see no ears.'"[217]

Shortly before the arrival of the marine battalion on 2 November, the MRF had commenced Operation Coronado IX, a series of strike operations against targets in the Dinh Tuong, Go Cong, and northern Kien Hoa provinces. One goal of the operation was to increase security along Route 4 and the Dong Tam base area. Another was to weaken or destroy the Viet Cong's *502d Local Force* and *267th Main Force* battalions. Contact with the enemy was light until 18 November, when the Vietnamese marines and the 4th Battalion, 47th Infantry engaged significant numbers of the enemy in the vicinity of the Rach Ruong Canal, a small stream that extended north of the My Tho River and formed part of the border between Dinh Tuong and

Kien Phong provinces. During this engagement, which lasted two days, allied ground forces, assisted by helicopter gunships, killed 178 Viet Cong and uncovered a large cache of medical supplies. U.S. Army and Vietnamese marine losses were 26 killed and 155 wounded.[218]

On 4 December, the 3d and 4th battalions, 47th Infantry, and the 5th Vietnamese Marine Battalion returned to the Rach Ruong Canal determined to destroy any remaining elements of the *267th Main Force* and the *502d Local Force* battalions. RAD 112 carried the marines; RAD 111, the 3d Battalion, 47th Infantry; and RAD 91, the 4th Battalion, 47th Infantry.[219] The assault force left the Mobile Riverine Base very early in the morning on 4 December and the MRB, in turn, delayed moving to a new anchorage six miles east of Sa Dec in order to confuse the enemy about the intentions of the convoys.[220] "We left the base ships behind where they were," stated TF 117 Commodore Salzer, "and went about forty miles under cover of darkness towards the objective area, just to do something different because they hadn't been doing it that way and they had been moving the big ships first."[221]

RAD 112 departed the MRB at approximately 0300. "We were supposed to drop off troops five miles up a canal and set up blocking stations," explained Lieutenant Norman Wells, the RAD 112 commander. Wells was in the lead monitor just behind two ASPB minesweepers. At 0700, the lead boats entered the Rach Ruong Canal and motored past a small village near a bridge that had been blown up by Vietnamese combat engineers in November (the bridge had been destroyed so that MRF boats could more easily penetrate the canal during high tides). According to Wells,

> We had gone several miles up the canal when the ASPBs reported that there were three big cables blocking the advance up the canal. I told the conn to slow down. We first used the 40mm to try and break the cables. I then asked Chief Lang if we could break them by ramming them. All of a sudden we started hearing noise from the rear [approximately where RAD 111 was sailing at the time]. Crack, boom, bang! And I got on the radio to Lieutenant (j.g.) Richard A. Citarella, the RAD 112 executive officer, and asked him for a report, and I will never forget to my dying day his reply, 'I don't know and I ain't going to look.' All of sudden all hell breaks loose and boats started taking hits. Commander [Lieutenant] Rhodes, in the CCB, got on the radio and said, 'The marines are taking hits on the ATCs, land the troops.' I looked back and immediately gave the order to land the troops. And it was a beautiful site: all ten ATCs at the same time, wheeling to port, dropping their ramps, running up on the left bank, and discharging the Vietnamese marines. Those Vietnamese saved our asses that day. We apparently landed in the middle of a VC battalion that was just resting.[222]

River Assault Division 112 had encountered the *502d Local Force Battalion* in a fortified base area on the west bank of the Rach Ruong. Elements of this force fired at the MRF from point-blank range with antitank rockets, registering 43 total hits against the boats. But the MRF refused to back down. Instead, it returned fire and landed the marines just north of the enemy position while RAD 111 landed the 3d Battalion, 47th Infantry to the south, and RAD

91 disembarked the 4th Battalion, 47th Infantry to the west. The river assault craft, along with helicopters, provided fire support throughout the ensuing battle for the troops.[223] "The Marine major dropped these guys right where the bunkers were," explained GMG2 Stanley, who manned a 40mm gun on the RAD 111 CCB, "I ended up firing 1,072 rounds during that fight."

Another sailor who vividly recalled the events of this day was Gunner's Mate (GM) 3 John Green with RAD 111. Green grew up in a Navy family, attending four different high schools in four different states, and endured a hardscrabble existence as a kid. "My Mom and Dad never had a pot to pee in or a window to throw it out of because military families weren't paid a whole lot then." Green vividly remembers his dad, a Navy master chief and a World War II veteran, having to pump gas at an Atlantic Richfield station at night just so the family could make ends meet. The younger Green entered Southeast Missouri State University at Cape Girardeau in 1965, and immediately tried out and was accepted to the varsity basketball team, but the demands of the team, along with a tendency to drink too much beer and attend too many parties, caused his grades to suffer, and John ended up flunking out of school his freshmen year: "I had an A in Basketball, a B in weight lifting, and three Fs and a D in scholastic courses my freshman year." Mad and ashamed that his father had worked so hard only to see him flunk out of college, John decided to volunteer for the service in Vietnam in February 1966.

Green arrived at the Naval Training Center in San Diego at 0230 and was awakened two and a half hours later for testing. Groggy from the long trip, he failed to qualify for A School and instead ended up as boatswain's mate striker on the submarine tender *Proteus* (AS 19) based in Guam. Wise to Navy ways, Green immediately began talking to chief petty officers about the "best" ratings onboard ship and ended up volunteering to become a fire control technician ballistic striker. "While most of the other unrated sailors were chipping paint, I was working in air-conditioned missile silos on ballistic missile submarines." After qualifying for A School in this rating, however, Green again had a change of heart: he switched to gunner's mate because he wanted to go to Vietnam, and the Navy wasn't allowing fire control technicians (ballistic missile fire control) to serve there at the time.

On 4 December, Green went on his first mission. "I was very scared. I was in the starboard .50-caliber mount of ATC 111-8." Since Green's crew was new to Vietnam, former ATC 111-8 crewmembers accompanied them on this mission to observe and train the sailors. After sailing over four hours, the boat entered the Rach Ruong canal and passed the small village near the blown-up bridge. Green noticed that most of the villagers stood by the banks staring at the boats. "No one smiled or waived." About this time, one of the older hands, Fireman Robert J. Moras of Escanaba, Michigan, came up from the well deck and tapped the rooky coxswain, Boatswain's Mate 3rd Class Joseph V. R. Camara, on the shoulder. "Look, you've been driving for the last four and a half hours let me give you a break." Joe said sure and stepped away from the wheel. As he turned away, a B40 rocket slammed into the coxswain's flat. As Green recalled, "Our flaps were down around the coxswain's flat, and that's when the rocket hit. The rocket blew me, the radioman, and Fireman Robert Moras onto deck on our backs. Moras' face was less than six inches from mine, and he had his hands on his face and blood was gushing out. And he was saying 'help me, help me.'"[224]

The force of the blast blew the ATC 111-8 to the side of the river, perpendicular to the beach. It was now blocking the forward movement of 15 boats. Camara, whose face was peppered with shrapnel and bleeding, turned around and confronted the scene. The fate of 15 boats and the troops they carried was now in the hands of a scared, wounded 24-year-old first generation Portuguese immigrant from Fall River, Massachusetts, who had never attended a day of school past the 8th grade and spoke English in a heavy accent. "I turned around," Joe said, "and Robert Moras was screaming with blood squirting out of his eyes. And it was scary! I wanted to run but did not know where." Joe did not run. Instead he jumped back on the wheel, pulled the boat off the beach, and put it back in the line so the convoy could continue to move through the kill zone to the objective beaches. Camara sailed the boat without the flap—only the bar armor protected him. For his heroism that day, the Navy would award Camara a Navy Commendation Medal with Combat V.[225]

Boastwain's Mate 3rd Class Joseph V. R. Camara receives the Purple Heart from Captain Robert Salzer, Commander, River Assault Flotilla 1, on 22 March 1968.

While Camara steered the boat, Green got back into his turret and started firing the .50-caliber gun after the initial rocket detonation.

> The roar of that blast was deafening. You can't hear anything afterwards. But everyone is screaming and it's mass confusion. You're firing your .50-caliber as fast as you can. Hot shell casings are building up almost to your knees. Every time you empty your weapon, you have to shimmy down and grab another box of rounds, shimmy back up, and then reach over the top of your gun, put it in, feed it into the .50 and start firing again. Every time I did it, I was exposed from my shoulders up on the top of the gun mount because I was so tall. Here I am in-country four days, and I am in one of the biggest firefights in the Mekong Delta. You find out if you are going to function the way you've been trained or roll up into a little ball and cry like a baby. You just don't know until it happens.[226]

Shrapnel from the B40 rocket not only caused damage to the coxswain's flat but also killed and wounded men in the well deck, including a member of the old crew, Fireman Adrian Ealon Howell of Lucedale, Mississippi. "When we opened the ramps to let the troops out," Green explained, "there was no one to come out—everyone had been wounded." Tango 111-8, however, still did not turn back. Instead, it transferred the wounded to the aid boat and continued the fight throughout the day until the next morning. During the evening a Viet Cong sapper threw a grenade into the then empty well deck of the boat, but it did not wound any of the crew. Except to retrieve ammunition, Green did not leave his gun mount for two hours. The next morning he went down to the well deck and found the bodies of his two shipmates covered by a tarp. "That's the first dead body I ever seen in my entire life. You have to force yourself to confront the reality of what you just saw. I forced myself to go down there and I knelt down and said a prayer for the two guys. And I forced myself to uncover the tarp and look at their faces, and then I went back up and got back into my mount." Tango 111-8 lost Firemen Robert Moras and Adrian E. Howell as well as five soldiers on 4 December. Two other sailors from the boat along with 20 soldiers received wounds severe enough to be medevaced from the scene.[227]

Green's unit, RAD 111, had landed its soldiers (3d Battalion, 47th Infantry) south of the main enemy position, but in the face of stubborn opposition, the Army unit was unable to link up with the Vietnamese marines, who had landed to the north. During the afternoon of 4 December, the marines, supported by helicopters and naval gunfire from the assault boats, made a frontal attack against the main enemy bunkers, overrunning the enemy positions and killing over 266 Viet Cong in the process.[228] The Vietnamese marines suffered 41 killed and another 70 wounded; the U.S. Navy, two killed and 68 wounded; and the U.S. Army, nine killed and 89 wounded.[229] Commodore Salzer, who witnessed the marine attack from a helicopter, had nothing but praise for the marines. "They were very aggressive and had a very good commander, excellent fellow. The upshot of the thing was that they effectively destroyed both battalions, including the only frontal assault I've ever seen mounted against prepared positions."[230] The marines essentially decimated a significant number of men from the *267th Main Force* and *502d Local Force* battalions and significantly reduced the guerrilla threat in the area. They succeeded because of the tenacity and bravery of their warriors and also due in no small measure to the ability of the MRF to rapidly relocate a large ground force in the delta, punch through a fortified canal to land this force at the enemy's doorstep, and then support that force with naval gunfire. The marine commander later told Lieutenant Colonel James S. G. Turner, USMC, that he was "impressed" that the MRF boats stayed around after dropping them off and "rendered effective support to his troops during the course of the battle."[231]

But did the large number of allied losses, especially those suffered by the marines, make 4 December a Pyrrhic victory? In an oral history conducted years later, Salzer lamented that Vietnamese and American authorities looked upon the actions of the Vietnamese marines with a jaundiced eye. "They were complimented on this, to be sure," he said, "but the fact that they had taken substantial casualties was made to appear almost unprofessional. American soldiers would never have done that. I believe that because I never saw an American soldier take a fixed position. There was almost an ethical rule; draw back and call in artillery."[232]

Taken in a broader context, the MRF as a whole killed more enemy soldiers than any other brown water unit deployed by the U.S. Navy in the Vietnam War, but it also took some of the heaviest losses—casualty levels not seen by the naval service since the blockade of Wonson during the Korean War. Helicopters might have been a safer means of transporting troops around the delta, but acute shortages of these aircraft compelled General Westmoreland to rely instead on boats. Fortunately, the boats proved rugged enough to assault enemy positions even when confronted by dug-in enemy troops firing armor-piercing rockets. After nearly a year of operations and three significant battles, the MRF had emerged as a force capable of taking on the most effective Viet Cong units in the delta.

It operated in areas that had been VC strongholds for many years and forced the enemy to defend places that it had always considered as its rear. The massive firepower (air, naval gunfire, and artillery) that the MRF brought to bear on the enemy was a new experience for the Viet Cong, and it disrupted numerous main and local force units. Operations in the delta, the Viet Cong rice bowl, also disrupted enemy logistics and loosened its chokehold on the populace. The MRF achieved these goals with a much lower impact on Vietnamese society than a traditional ground force operation. For the most part, the River Force lived aboard ship or on reclaimed land and did not compete with civilians for the limited dry land available in this alluvial area. The floating nature of the MRF also limited negative interactions between Americans and Vietnamese—commercial interactions that could spark inflation or encourage criminal activities, such as black marketeering and prostitution. Finally, barracks ships provided excellent living conditions, including top quality Navy chow and air-conditioning, and allowed troops to dry out their bodies after enduring in the delta's swampy conditions.[233]

The Tet Offensive would demonstrate that the MRF did not come close to defeating the Viet Cong in 1967, but it certainly hurt enemy operations in the delta and put American forces in an excellent position to crush the Viet Cong offensive when it did occur.

CHAPTER 5

War on the Coast, 1967

Lieutenant Commander Max G. Branscomb entered the Naval Reserve in high school and quickly set his sights on becoming a naval aviator. As a child Branscomb caught the flying bug from his father, who had flown Navy patrol planes in the Atlantic during World War II. After graduating from Boise Junior College (now Boise State University) with an associate's degree in 1955, he signed up for Navy flight training. In a little over a year, he was the flying P-2V Neptune patrol planes with VP 2 based at Whidbey Island in Washington State. Early in his career, Branscomb flew surveillance missions along the North Korean and Soviet Union coastlines in the Pacific and rose quickly to command his own aircraft. In 1967 Branscomb was the maintenance officer for VP 1—the fifth most senior officer in the squadron and a seasoned pro when it came to flying the P-2V.

The morning of 11 July 1967 started out as a normal day for Branscomb and his 11-member crew (three other officers and eight enlisted) preparing for a patrol. His aircraft, "Backdoor 10," took off from its base at Cam Ranh Bay at 1200 and began making its way north along the coast of Vietnam, looking for potential Viet Cong supply craft. The aircraft's main tool for

Lieutenant Commander Max G. Branscomb.

U.S. Navy

221

Courtesy Max G. Branscomb

The crew of this P-2V, shown here at Danang on 7 August 1967, identified and tracked a North Vietnamese trawler for four days until allied surface forces captured it on 15 July 1967.

maritime surveillance was the APS-20 radar, a powerful air and surface search radar with an effective range of nearly 200 miles. In the ten missions he had flown in Southeast Asia since deploying in May 1967, Branscomb's crew had detected hundreds of vessels off the coast of Vietnam, but not one had proven to be a hostile infiltrator. This bothered neither him nor his crew. The Navy patrol community tends to be cerebral and stoic about long patrols because they know that patience, thoroughness, and attention to detail are keys to success. As intelligence collectors they also understood implicitly that torture and perhaps death awaited them if they made a mistake and were shot down.

His aircraft generally searched the entire west coast of Vietnam from Cam Ranh Bay to the Chinese border during a single eight-hour patrol, cruising at a speed of 170 knots. It was hot, uncomfortable work flying for hours at a time in a non-air-conditioned aircraft at low levels in Southeast Asia. During patrols the crew generally ate cold, canned rations, and relieved themselves through tubes in the fuselage or in an unenclosed head in the after part of the aircraft. Life back at the Cam Ranh base was not much better. Sailors lived in dilapidated trailers or tents described in the squadron history as "very limited and somewhat crude." Over time VP-1 sailors improved their quarters with sweat equity, using tools and construction materials scrounged from the base, and built a volleyball court and other recreational facilities to turn the bare-bones facility into more of a home. The medical department even established a refreshment mess, dubbed the "Rice Paddy Inn," where sailors could take a break from the extreme Southeast Asian heat and enjoy a cold soft drink or a snack. Sailors could also swim in the clear waters of Cam Ranh Bay. Morale, in short, was high for the 360 members of VP-1

Market Time Base at Cam Ranh Bay, South Vietnam, September 1967.

because they understood absolutely how important their role was in Operation Market Time and that their plight, no matter how arduous compared with civilian life in the United States, was far better than that of servicemen operating in the nearby jungles.

At 1915 near the end of the patrol, Branscomb's radar operator picked up a large contact steaming at 10 knots 55 miles east of Chu Lai. Branscomb immediately ordered his crew to man their "rigging stations." Under this battle-stations-like posture, each crewmember would focus exclusively on gathering a single piece of information as the aircraft passed over the contact. Rigging stations allowed the crew to gather the maximum amount of information possible in a single pass. Branscomb noted the sea state and lighting conditions and then opted to pass the contact on the most favorable side for photography. The Neptune carried a large, box-mounted aviation camera, and it was the photographer's job to take three photos of the contact: a stern quarter, a broadside, and a bow quarter shot. Intelligence analysts back at Cam Ranh would later scrutinize this imagery to determine as much as possible about the contact.

When he finally laid eyes on the 120-foot-long vessel during the pass, Branscomb thought to himself, "Bulls eye, that's a trawler and that's what we're supposed to be looking for." The P-2V passed within 200 feet of the trawler, took pictures, noted other pertinent details, and then moved to a standoff position about 30 miles from the contact. As he passed the vessel, Branscomb noticed that the ship contained fishing nets, but that its hull was not rusty. "She was definitely not a fisherman. Fishing hulls get rusty from nets being constantly dragged against them." After reporting the contact to the Danang Coastal Surveillance Center, Branscomb was ordered to make a second pass to reconfirm that the ship was running with no lights on and double check its course and speed. Backdoor 10 made the pass in the now dark sky and then moved to a position 30 miles away to shadow the trawler until a replacement arrived. Market Time air and surface units would continue to shadow this vessel on the high seas for four days before the trawler finally entered Republic of Vietnam waters where it could be legally searched and seized—a cat-and-mouse game that ultimately resulted in the most significant Market Time seizure of 1967.[1]

By January 1967 Market Time was a mature blockade, capable of preventing 94 percent of North Vietnamese steel-hulled infiltrators and 70 percent of wooden-hulled infiltrators from supplying Viet Cong forces in South Vietnam. General Westmoreland, in assessing Market Time's impact in August 1966, noted that in 1965 "70% of the enemy's resupplies came by sea, but due to the Market Time Operation, only 10% come in by sea now."[2] One of the main reasons for the operation's success was the air patrol, which swept every inch of a 100-nautical-mile-wide, 1,200-mile-long air barrier along the South Vietnam coast with powerful radars. A suspicious contact would then be further inspected by surface units, which by the end of 1966 consisted of 84 PCFs, 26 WPBs, and 11 DERs or other larger vessels. So effective was this integrated system that the North Vietnamese attempted to penetrate it with steel-hulled trawlers only four times in 1966. Of this number, one was sunk, another captured, and the two others fled to the north.[3]

Success in halting large infiltrators allowed the Market Time units to focus more attention on other missions such as search and rescue, psychological operations, and naval gunfire support. During 1967 Market Time also expanded its operations five miles up the major rivers and began turning over some of its coastal patrol sectors to the Vietnam Navy. As effective as the blockade was, it did not make the inshore waters any safer for the Swift boat crews, which frequently received fire from the shore as well as from hostile junks and sampans, nor did it persuade the North Vietnamese to discontinue attempts to penetrate the barrier with steel-hulled ships. In fact, the Military Assistance Command Vietnam concluded in September that while infiltration attempts by steel-hulled trawlers were "infrequent and irregular," the fact that the North Vietnamese continued to attempt these passages indicated that seaborne infiltration was "still preferred by the enemy and that if Market Time forces were withdrawn, infiltration could be successfully carried out."[4] MACV even considered building a land fence along parts of the South Vietnamese coast to bolster the Market Time blockade but concluded that the effectiveness of such a land barrier would be "questionable primarily because the Viet Cong controlled portions of land along the coast that would be the weak links."[5] Consequently Market Time would continue to function exclusively as a sea and air barrier for the remainder of America's involvement in the war. In the end the greatest challenges for Market Time would not be maintaining an effective barrier at sea and in the air but defending its forces against the increasingly hostile threats emanating from shore, and also training and equipping the South Vietnamese to assume more responsibility for the blockade.

Market Time SITREP

By 1967 Market Time consisted of nine patrol sectors covering the 1,200-mile South Vietnamese coast. Within each sector, there were three layers or "barriers" of defense: an inner surface patrol barrier, an outer surface patrol barrier, and an air barrier. Three shore-based radar installations augmented these barriers.[6]

The first surface patrol barrier stretched from the coastline to approximately 12 miles offshore—the territorial waters limit of the Republic of Vietnam. The inner barrier covered 1,200 miles of coastline, including Phu Quoc Island, and was divided into nine major sections, which in turn were divided into smaller subdivisions.[7] Eighty-four Swift boats and over 2,000 personnel of the U.S. Navy's Coastal Squadron 1 patrolled this barrier, assisted by 26 Coast Guard WPBs from Coast Guard Squadron 1 and various units of the Vietnam Navy, ranging from junks to larger patrol vessels. Since trawler intercepts were few and far between, these smaller boats spent much their time searching smaller craft running in the waters 12 miles from shore —an often boring and thankless task. "Like all traffic cops, our work is ninety percent boredom," wrote Lieutenant (j.g.) Virgil Erwin in his memoir about his service as an officer in charge of a PCF. "We check water taxis full of people commuting to work, fishermen coming home from the sea, farmers taking rice to market, women shopping for vegetables, and we look for Viet Cong who are trying to slip by, moving men and supplies, and collecting taxes in their brutal and fanatical way."[8] Additionally, PCFs and WPBs performed naval gunfire support, search and rescue for mariners in distress, surveillance, and other operations as time permitted. PCFs generally operated on 24-hour patrols, and the larger, more seaworthy WPBs patrolled up to six days at a stretch.

Lieutenant (j.g.) Virgil Erwin commanded this Cat Lo-based Swift boat from September 1968 to July 1969.

Beyond the first barrier were nine patrol areas guarded by one or more larger ships such as ocean minesweepers and radar picket escort ships. The outer surface patrol area stretched from the 12-nautical-mile limit to 40 nautical miles from the Vietnamese coastline.[9] The task of the larger ships patrolling this sector was to track and maintain surveillance on potential infiltrators until they crossed the 12-nautical-mile mark. At that point they could search potential suspects for contraband. Usually four or five DERs were actually on patrol stations augmented by minesweepers, but by late December 1966 a shortage of naval gunfire ships along the coast of North Vietnam and a requirement for more assets for the Taiwan Strait patrol compelled Admiral Roy L. Johnson, Commander Pacific Fleet, to reassign Market Time DERs to the interdiction campaign, known as Operation Sea Dragon, against communist vehicles and lines of communication in North Vietnam.[10] To make up for this shortfall, the Navy requested five Coast Guard high endurance cutters (WHECs) to replace the DERs in this barrier, and in March 1967 WHECs began patrolling this sector.[11] The larger ships provided Market Time with platforms capable of reacting to larger infiltrators with speed and firepower in the rougher seas, and their powerful radars provided enhanced search capability. These ships also provided some logistic support (mainly water and fuel) for the smaller vessels and would prove indispensable in Market Time naval gunfire support missions in South Vietnam. The patrol track of these ships was not fixed, but the ships generally operated about 20 miles from the shoreline.[12]

The Coast Guard high endurance cutter *Bering Strait* (WHEC-382) participated in Operation Market Time during 1967–1968 and deployed to Vietnam for a second tour in 1970.

A P-3 Orion flies a Market Time patrol off the coast of South Vietnam, August 1968. This aircraft carried a crew of 12 and had a maximum range of 8,750 miles.

The Market Time air patrol area extended from 20 to 120 miles from the shore. Every inch of this 1,200-mile-long barrier of coastal water was swept by radar from a P-2V (and later a P-3) every four to eight hours around the clock.[13] By 1968, 12 patrol aircraft were assigned to the Market Time air surveillance mission. Two planes remained airborne at all times, and a third provided additional coverage at night. During the day Navy aircraft flew at low altitudes between 300 and 3,000 feet, scanning an area between 50 and 100 miles from the coast with radars capable of identifying targets up 105 miles away. At night the third aircraft flew a higher track to provide additional coverage within and beyond the 50–100-mile belt. Navy patrol aircraft flew at a cruising speed of 170–180 knots during 14–20 hour patrols in all weather conditions and often varied their tracks and altitudes to confuse the enemy. Most aircraft contained 70-million- candlepower searchlights, flares, and special flash cartridges that turned night into day for the purposes of intelligence photography. Commander TF 115 required flight crews to investigate, photograph, and report details on all steel-hulled vessels over 1,000 gross tons or that could not be positively identified. Roughly 50 percent of radar contacts fell into this category. Coastal radars strategically located on three islands (Con Son, Cu Lao Re, and Hon Khoai [Poulo Obi]) to cover prominent landfalls augmented the radar coverage of the air patrol.[14] The primary responsibility of the air barrier and coastal radar network was to initially detect and track targets until surface vessels arrived on scene.

Coastal Surveillance Centers located at Danang, Qui Nhon, Nha Trang, Vung Tau, and on the island of Phu Quoc provided command, control, communications, and intelligence (C3I) for the operation. These centers, manned by both American and Vietnamese naval personnel,

Vung Tau Coastal Surveillance Center.

collected reports from all Market Time units in their respective zones and organized appropriate responses to suspicious contacts. They represented a critical link between the air barrier and the surface patrols, continually relayed information back and forth between units operating in the various barriers, and vectored patrol vessels to contacts deemed suspicious. At times they also provided higher authorization for certain actions (searches of foreign vessels operating outside of Vietnam's territorial waters, for example) and provided real-time guidance for on-scene commanders regarding the rules of engagement.[15]

In 1966 U.S. Market Time units from all three barriers recorded 801,214 waterborne detections. Of this number, allied vessels visually inspected 215,857 at close range and boarded and searched 175,186.[16] For surface ships, the rules of engagement for stopping, visiting, and searching vessels were relatively straightforward. Within the territorial waters of South Vietnam (the area from the low tide mark extending three miles offshore), Market Time vessels could stop and search merchant vessels of any nation not clearly engaged in innocent passage. In the contiguous zone of the Republic of Vietnam (the area of seas from three to 12 miles from the coast), Market Time ships could stop and search any Republic of Vietnam–flagged vessel and demand the identification and a declaration of intent of vessels (less warships) of any nation. Suspicious merchant ships from nations other than South Vietnam traveling within contiguous zone could be searched subject to approval from CTF 115. Beyond the 12-mile mark, U.S. ships could only stop and search vessels believed to be South Vietnamese. If fired upon by another vessel in international waters, Market Time vessels had the authority to pursue a target over international waters or into the territorial seas or air spaces of North Vietnam.[17]

The rules of engagement encouraged local commanders to employ "the minimum force necessary to accomplish surveillance operations . . . up to and including destruction if required" of hostile vessels. If fired upon or in the vicinity of friendly forces under fire, TF 115 units could immediately return fire, but commanders were expected to "display sound judgment" when firing near villages or hamlets, and when possible, employ a spotter (either on the ground or airborne). TF 115 units were also under orders to report all hostile fire incidents to the appropriate Coastal Surveillance Center as soon as possible.[18] Commander Norman C. Venzke, USCG, who commanded Coast Guard Division 11 based at An Thoi, described how the system worked:

> Any time friendly forces were under fire, you could fire back and just report the incident. Now if the MACV advisor wanted you to fire upon a given position, he would normally request right through the unit because normally the unit was in the area. The unit would pass the request up to me and I could make a ruling on it. I could either say go on and fire or under certain conditions I could not and I'd have to ask CTF 115 in Cam Ranh Bay.[19]

For Venzke, and many other division commanders, Market Time's relatively straightforward rules of engagement seemed to work well. Rules of engagement were not nearly as big an encumbrance for the WPB or PCF sailors as they were for sailors of the TFs 116 and 117, who generally operated in much closer proximity to heavily populated villages and hamlets.

Vietnam Navy and Market Time

Between 1965 and 1968, the Vietnam Navy doubled in size—growing from 8,242 personnel, 44 ships, and 200 other vessels to 17,574 personnel, 65 ships, 300 junks, and 290 other craft.[20] Despite meteoric growth, the VNN still suffered from growing pains and a variety of deficiencies. Officer promotions and assignments were still influenced more by politics than merit; the enlisted force still suffered from poor pay, inadequate training, and squalid living conditions; and maintenance problems continued to plague the fleet. The VNN's operational effectiveness, however, began improving in many ways by 1967, especially after its ships began taking over entire Market Time patrol areas from the U.S. Navy. By giving the VNN more responsibility for the in-country naval war, the Military Assistance Command Vietnam not only greatly bolstered morale but improved performance as well.

Before the May 1967 turnover, the Fleet Force, renamed Fleet Command in January 1967, maintained 11 ships on station for coastal patrol, four ships for river patrol, and one ship for convoy escort duty between Vung Tau and Tan Chau on the Mekong.[21] Coastal patrol zones corresponded to the four MACV/ARVN tactical zones in Vietnam. Fleet Force ships assigned to patrol those zones would often cover 90 or more miles of coastline in a single 35–50 day patrol. As advisor Lieutenant Thomas J. Bender observed, such a patrol sector was too large for a single patrol escort (PCE) to cover effectively. When operating with Market Time forces, the Fleet Command patrol vessels were supposed to patrol the seas between the PCFs/WPBs and the DERs/WHECs/MSOs, but in practice they often strayed into the American operational areas.[22] As a consequence many Fleet Force commanders made no effort to perform their duties.[23] "Many ships were anchoring over night, going to Coastal Groups for R&R, running through a fleet of fishing junks without inspecting or boarding any of them, returning to port early in spite of instructions from Coastal Zone commanders and recommendations of ship riders [U.S. Navy advisors], and in general conducting haphazard and indifferent patrol," noted Lieutenant George E. Hays, an advisor stationed on HQ-08.[24] The attitude of most VNN commanders, according to Lieutenant (j.g.) Whitney Goit II, a ship rider with PGM-608, was "U.S. units have better support and organization; they're doing the job, why should we bother."[25]

On 15 May 1967, this situation changed when HQ-08 took over the outer Market Time sea barrier in the Second Coastal Zone from *Gannet* (MSC-290). For the first time in the war, the VNN had sole responsibility for its own Market Time area of operation. Lieutenant Hays thought that working with Market Time "contributed significantly to an increase in patrol effectiveness."[26] Similarly, Lieutenant Elroy A. Soluri noted in his end-of-tour report that "the integration of the VNN into Operation Market Time has made possible a more rigid planning and employment schedule and has eliminated mutual interference. Because the officers and crew now feel they are performing a vital function, there has been an increase in morale and patrol effectiveness."[27] Lieutenant George S. Forrester, an advisor with PGM-600, stated that before the Market Time integration, his ship spent most patrols steaming back and forth between two towns. "The feeling was that if no one cared what the ship was doing, why bother." Once the ship received orders to join in a Market Time blocking force and provide naval gunfire support for the South Korean 2d Marine Brigade, however, the attitude of the Vietnamese commander and crew changed completely. The PGM increased the number of junks checked, volunteered for gunfire missions, and focused operations on areas of suspected infiltration.[28] Market Time participation transformed PGM-600 from a passive bystander to an eager predator. By 1968 the VNN had taken over seven Market Time patrol stations, and the change in morale of the VNN officers and crew was palpable.

The VNN, however, was far from being a world-class navy. Advisors still complained incessantly about maintenance, training, crew pay, morale, and lackluster leadership, but a comparison of 1967–1968 end-of-tour reports with earlier ones shows more optimism and hope, especially as the Fleet Command assumed greater responsibilities in Market Time. Lieutenant Noel M. Allen of PGM-607 at first complained about the lack of aggressiveness of his two counterparts, the poor pay VNN sailors received, and the high turnover rate of the crew he concluded, "as a military organization, I feel, the Vietnamese Navy leaves much to be desired." He then goes on to write that the Fleet Command is nevertheless "progressing as more of their truly capable people are being placed" in command assignments. He also mentioned that if he had to do it all over again, he would choose the very same billet. "I take particular pride in having spent a year in the Fleet Command. There exists an *esprit* and camaraderie that is found nowhere else in the advisory effort."[29] Likewise, Lieutenant Richard J. Robbins of PGM-610 was highly critical of the VNN for its lack of understanding of Market Time procedures, and yet in the same report declared that he "had seen much improvement" and was "particularly pleased to work with my present counterpart [Lieutenant (j.g.)] Trung-Uy On."[30]

The improvement in VNN operational effectiveness during the year was not only evident in advisors' end-of-tour reports but also in the statistics provided by the advisors to TF 115. In January 1967 Fleet Command maintained 13 patrol ships off the coast of South Vietnam and had four ships patrolling the rivers of the Mekong Delta. In one month these ships searched 372 junks and performed nine naval gunfire missions. Twelve months later the Fleet Command stationed 15 ships off the coast of South Vietnam and another five on the major rivers.[31] Together these ships searched 576 junks and engaged in 140 gunfire support missions. By 1968 Fleet Command units manned seven Market Time stations and were poised to take over even more. Summing up the Fleet Command's progress, Lieutenant Commander Lawrence F. De Angelo, the Flotilla One advisor, stated in his end-of-tour report in November 1967 that "patrol effectiveness has increased slowly but steadily and in the not too distant future I foresee that some of the ships will not require advisors."[32]

Market Time Naval Gunfire Support

Although the major mission of Market Time was seaborne interdiction, naval gunfire support (NGFS) emerged as a significant collateral mission in 1967. In February 1967 U.S. Market Time forces only conducted ten such missions; by September that figure had risen to 140 with another 33 provided by the Fleet Command units supporting Market Time. As COMNAVFORV gained more confidence in the ability of air patrols to detect most infiltration from the sea, he began releasing more Market Time assets for NGFS, and by the end of 1968 Market Time forces were supplying over ten percent of all NGFS in South Vietnam and the majority of naval gunfire support missions in IV Corps Tactical Zone.[33] The shallow draft of Market Time vessels allowed them to get within range of many difficult to reach target areas and provide highly accurate fire in support of troops in contact situations.

This was the certainly the case for 12 Green Berets and 120 Regional Forces defending the village of Song Ong Doc located 155 miles southwest of Saigon in An Xuyen Province. In three separate incidents in 1967, the cutter *Half Moon* (WHEC-378) helped beat back Viet Cong attacks against this village, which one coastguardsman described as "huddling nervously on the north bank of a river and surrounded on three sides by the Viet Cong."[34] On 27 August, 120 Viet Cong began attacks on the town. *Half Moon* steamed within two miles of the shoreline and laid down 7,000 pounds of high explosives on the VC position for two and a half hours. The spotter plane reported that the shells demolished two structures sheltering the enemy and damaged 13 others. Three days later on 30 August, *Half Moon* returned and placed 50 rounds of high explosive shells on enemy positions eight miles from the cutter, destroying eight structures.[35] On 12 September over 200 Viet Cong attacked the village, compelling *Half Moon* to once again steam to the rescue. On this day the cutter destroyed three structures, damaged 12, and destroyed a sampan near the Special Forces camp.[36]

To the casual observer, the all-white hulls of Market Time's high endurance cutters looked like angels of mercy, but the 5-inch 38-caliber gun mounts on these ships could let loose significant destructive power upon an unsuspecting enemy up to nine miles away. Nine men worked in the cramped confines of these turrets, enduring extreme heat and the ever-present smell of gun grease and cordite, to place ordnance on targets. In built-up areas like Song On Doc, where the Viet Cong often sheltered in structures, the methodology for dislodging defenders was to set the initial rounds to burst in the air to kill anyone exposed outdoors. Assuming troops will then run for bunkers and slit trenches soon after a bombardment begins, the next shots would be set to hit the ground and explode. Gunners would then walk the rounds across a target area like a checkerboard so as to cover as much of the kill zone as possible. White phosphorus represented the grand finale. Since many Vietnamese structures were made of bamboo, it did not take many well-placed WP rounds to transform a small village or small settlement into smoldering ashes. Shards of white phosphorus extending outwards from an airburst shot literally created a rain of fire, igniting everything in a wide dispersal area.[37] Commander Herbert J. Lynch, who commanded *Winona* (WHEC-65) in early 1968, claims it was "nothing to fire 50 rounds of shoreside support. We did so much shooting we had to rebarrel the gun." During four and a half years of operation, Coast Guard high-speed endurance cutters fired 77,036 rounds of 5-inch 38-caliber ammunition at targets in South Vietnam.[38]

Although many of these rounds consisted of unspotted harassment and interdiction missions that did little more than tear up ground and knock down palm trees, when Coast Guard vessels were allowed to fire at actual targets, the results could be devastating. For instance, on 27 August, *Half Moon* conducted a gunfire mission against Viet Cong troops operating on the Ca Mau Peninsula in An Xuyen Province. Subsequent intelligence reports stated that 5-inch fire destroyed three enemy buildings and killed 11 Viet Cong. On 26 September 1967, *Yakutat* (WHEC-380) destroyed or damaged 27 fortified enemy positions, four sampans, and an enemy canal blockade in a single gunfire support mission off the coast of An Xuyen Province.[39] The high endurance cutters, with their relatively shallow 22-foot draft, were the only ships with 5-inch guns capable of operating in the shallow waters of An Xuyen Province and much of the rest of the IV Corps area.[40] "Sometimes we would go into areas with only one or two feet clearance between the hull and sea floor," recalled Captain Robert W. Durfey, who commanded *Rush* (WHEC-723) in 1970, but "fortunately the bottom was mostly mud."[41]

Of course, the larger barrier patrol ships did not perform all Market Time NGFS missions; PCFs and WPBs often took great risks to provide naval gunfire at extremely close range. In February 1967 smaller Market Time vessels engaged in nine NGFS missions in the Third and Fourth Coastal Zones, destroying 17 structures and damaging another 12. In April, PCFs and

WPBs destroyed 19 structures, six bunkers, and 12 sampans in 18 separate NGFS missions, eight of which occurred in the Third Coastal Zone.[42] While supporting U.S. marines operating 16 miles southeast of Danang, two PCFs received ground fire on four separate occasions. In one those instances on 9 April, PCF-15 returned fire with 500 rounds of .50-caliber machine-gun ammunition, killing eight Viet Cong from a 10–12-man squad. Later that afternoon grenade fire from the same PCF destroyed four enemy bunkers.[43]

Unlike the larger high endurance cutters, which generally engaged targets well away from potential ground fire, PCFs often got close enough to shore to be hit by the smallest caliber bullets and sometimes paid a high price for their intrepid actions. Such was the case on 25 June 1967, when PCF-97 engaged ground targets in the mouth of the Ganh Hao River, 150 miles southwest of Saigon. A brand new crew had just taken over the boat and was investigating a known hostile area when they came under heavy automatic weapons and recoilless rifle fire from the shore. While returning fire, the PCF was hit by a 57mm recoilless rifle round that tore a 2.5- foot hole in the Swift's starboard bow and blew shrapnel into the right shoulder, arm, and leg of the officer in charge, Lieutenant (j.g.) Thomas A. Whithey. The Swift headed seaward but sank minutes later, forcing the crew to abandon ship. Arriving at the scene soon after the attack, PCF-26 picked up all crewmembers and transferred them to the tank landing ship *Sedgwick County* where Whithey was soon medevaced. The Navy later awarded Whithey, a young officer from Kenosha, Wisconsin, a Silver Star for his actions during his first and only patrol on PCF-97.[44] Gunner's Mate (Guns) 3rd Class Randal "Randy" Kenneth Fredricksen, a PCF-97 sailor who had patrolled the area shortly before Whithey's crew arrived on scene to relieve his crew, vividly recalled his interactions with the officer:

> We specifically told him not to go to the Ganh Hao because we had just taken fire from the area and had literally shot everything we had at the Viet Cong there, taking down half the jungle in the process. I knew they were going to go back there because that's what any Swifty would do. I even took their gunner aside while we were resupplying the ammo and went over the twin .50-cal. to make sure he was up to date.[45]

PCF-97 was the second PCF sunk in enemy action during the war. Later that day PCFs-26 and -98 returned to the area with a spotter aircraft and fired into the area, taking out 12 Viet Cong, two bunkers, and two sampans with what the spotter called "outstandingly accurate fire." On 2 July *Oak Hill* (LSD-7), assisted by *Sedgwick County* and Harbor Clearance Unit 1 (Team 5), worked in varying winds and strong currents to salvage PCF-97 from 27 feet of water at the mouth of the Ganh Hao. Commander, Amphibious Force U.S. Seventh Fleet, later praised *Oak Hill* for accomplishing an "unequaled task" for an LSD.[46]

The principal NGFS weapon for both PCFs and WPBs was the 81mm Mark II mortar. One well-placed 81mm high explosive round could accomplish the same destruction as hundreds of .50-caliber bullets. This mortar, which also featured a .50-caliber machine gun mounted over it, was unique to the U.S. Navy and Coast Guard in Vietnam because of its design as both a

The mortar crew of PCF-54, Coastal Division 14, based at Cam Ranh Bay, prepares to fire a Mark II 81mm mortar. A .50-caliber machine gun is mounted on top of the mortar, 6 April 1967.

direct and indirect fire weapon. A conventional mortar is loaded by dropping a round into the upright barrel. The round travels down the tube and is triggered by striking a nail at the base of the tube. By comparison, the Mark II not only could be fired in this traditional, high angle (indirect) manner, but also be trigger fired in a low angle, nearly horizontal (direct) position. This versatility allowed sailors to lay down direct fire against close-in enemy positions or fire indirectly at targets as far as 3,940 yards from the boat. The Mark II could fire high explosive or WP incendiary rounds at a rate of 18 rounds a minute in the drop fire indirect mode and 10 in the direct trigger fire mode. Later in the war, the Navy developed an antipersonnel (AP) round for close-in targets. The AP round transformed the 81mm into a giant shotgun capable of hurdling 1,200 flechette rounds over a broad area up to 600 yards from the boat.[47]

The Mark II was very accurate but not always reliable. On 18 October 1966 PCF-9 was conducting an NGFS mission one-half mile off the east coast of Phu Quoc Island in support of U.S. Special Forces when a high explosive round exploded in the mortar, killing three sailors: Engineman 2nd Class Gale Jackson Hays, Quartermaster 3rd Class Eugene Lawrence Self, and Boatswain's Mate 2nd Class Hubert Tuck Jr. An investigating board found no evidence of malpractice, negligence, or misconduct on the part of the crew.[48] On 11 March of 1967, another incident occurred during a gunfire exercise in Ganh Ria Bay eight miles from Vung Tau. Seaman Gary W. Friedman was trigger firing the mortar on PCF-39 when it exploded, blowing Friedman over the side of the boat and wounding two other crewmembers. It took Market Time forces two days to locate Friedman's body, which had sustained multiple shrapnel wounds in the chest and face.[49] A final incident occurred on 9 August 1969, when the mortar on *Point Arden* (WPB-82309) exploded during a routine harassment and interdiction mission. The blast killed the cutter's executive officer, Lieutenant (j.g.) Michael W. Kirkpatrick, and its engineer, Engineman 1st Class Michael H. Painter. Both the Navy and Coast Guard conducted multiple investigations into the root causes of these explosions, and numerous theories resulted. Some investigators theorized that the practice of firing two rounds at once (double rounds) might have caused at least one of the mishaps. Others believed that carbon buildup in the mortars from excessive firing caused bore constriction, which in turn led to the misfires. One Naval Ordnance System Command study suggested that burning embers in the bore could potentially set off a charge in the trigger-fire mode. Another investigation discovered old, decomposing gunpowder in a 1955 lot of mortar rounds used by PCF-39 and blamed it for the explosions. Whatever the case, these weapons on occasion could be as dangerous to their gunners as the enemy was.[50]

While PCFs took plenty of risks and performed numerous gunfire support missions, Market Time's most effective small gunnery platforms were the WPBs. These 82-foot boats carried similar weapons as the Swift boats but were much more stable, especially in rough seas. With an average age of 26, many of the WPB crewmembers also had years of experience in small boats from peacetime service in the Coast Guard and tended to excel in small arms and gunnery. As for the officers, the Coast Guard sent only its very best to Vietnam. Most WPB commanders had graduated from the Coast Guard Academy and commanded a small boat prior to being sent to Southeast Asia. Detailers carefully screened potential candidates for physical and mental defects because as one Coast Guard headquarters solicitation directive stated, "The arduous duty requirements can bring out the worst aspect of character in socially disoriented individuals, the alcoholic, the authority flaunters and the rebellious."[51] The Coast Guard expected its WPB skippers to spend 70 percent of their time at sea and work at least 12 hours a day, seven days a week. At the time it was one of the most demanding duty assignments in the entire Coast Guard.

The attention the Coast Guard detailers placed on crewing its WPBs paid off. Repeatedly, ground units praised the WPBs for their highly accurate NGFS and willingness to take great risks to lay down ordnance in support of ground troops. On 23 February 1967 *Point Marone* answered an urgent call for gunfire support from the troops of the Civilian Irregular Defense Group and U.S. Special Forces advisors engaged with the Viet Cong 55 miles east of An Thoi. The cutter's fire destroyed two enemy structures and killed three Viet Cong. *Point Marone* then evacuated a wounded CIDG soldier. After the event, the head Special Forces advisor sent a "well done" message to NAVFORV for the cutter's fine shooting.[52] A day later another Coast Guard Division 11 cutter, *Point Clear,* responded to an urgent request from a South Vietnamese L-19 spotter aircraft for fire support against enemy positions 39 miles northeast of An Thoi and destroyed three structures and damaged ten others.[53]

In April *Point Welcome* and a PCF provided cover for a marine helicopter assault just north of Cape Batangan. To suppress sniper and small arms fire, the two boats laid down nearly constant fire with a circular "wagon train" formation—each boat fired when on the beach side of the circle, with both units combined expending 3,500 rounds in the operation. The tactic worked, and the helicopters were able to safely land the troops. According to the Coast Guard Division 12 War Diary, "the Marines were very appreciative."[54] In mid April 1967, *Point Cypress* responded to a call from a U.S. Army spotter plane to shoot up some sampans. Despite being allowed to fire only in the drop-fire mode because of concerns with the 81mm mortar, the cutter still managed to heavily damage the two sampans and destroy three buildings in fire reported by the Army pilot as "very accurate."[55] On occasion the presence of just a single WPB in a gunfire support role could turn the tide of battle. That happened on 17 July 1967 when elements of the ARVN 21st Division operating on the Ca Mau Peninsula requested urgent gunfire support from *Point Banks*, operating 31 miles away. The cutter beat a hasty course to the scene and struck enemy positions with its 81mm mortar, causing 17 secondary explosions and helping to repel enemy forces.[56] So effective was Coast Guard gunfire support that ground forces often explicitly requested help from WPBs. Lieutenant Commander Thomas G. Volke, the commander of Coast Guard Division 12 in 1968, once received a call from a marine air-naval gunfire liaison company (ANGLICO) officer, asking him to attend a planning meeting for a September 1969 operation. Volke recalled the general at one point asking the marine ANGLICO officer what he wanted in the way of gunfire support.

"Sir, I want Coast Guard WPBs," the officer replied.

When asked why, the marine said, "When I say I got guys in trouble and we need gunfire at this point, I get it. I don't get a lot of questions about whether I have permission from the province chief or how deep the water is or how far I can go in? If I can get other resources fine, but I want WPBs."[57]

Fog of War

Market Time forces operated in a highly fluid environment within firing range of a large variety of allied air, ground, and naval forces. For most of the war, the biggest threat of friendly fire came from ground units on the beach. During the month of August 1966 alone, for example, Market Time units received friendly fire from the shore on eight separate occasions.[58] These incidents mainly consisted of small arms fire from South Vietnamese units. The language barrier and poor communications made such episodes a common occurrence, and Market Time boat commanders made it a habit to keep U.S. advisors on the beach informed of their presence whenever operating near friendly Vietnamese forces. Friendly fire incidents between Market Time units and American forces were much rarer due to better coordination, command and control, and communications.

Nevertheless, they did occur on occasion, and two incidents in particular stand out: an Air Force attack against *Point Welcome* (WPB-82329) in August 1966, and several Air Force attacks against Market Time and Seventh Fleet vessels in June 1968. Both episodes took place in a Seventh Air Force operational area near the 17th parallel code-named Tally Ho—a special interdiction zone that extended from the DMZ 30 miles north into North Vietnam. This zone contained several surface arteries and was a major transshipment point for communist supplies heading south. A large number of antiaircraft artillery and automatic weapons defended the zone, making it a dangerous place to fly, especially for slower moving forward air controllers.[59] Air Force planes hit interdiction targets both on land and at sea in Tally Ho, and for much of 1966 there was little or no coordination with Market Time forces operating offshore. The situation improved somewhat after the *Point Welcome* incident, but as the June 1968 friendly fire incidents revealed, Air Force aircraft posed a distinct danger to Market Time forces operating in I Corps, even after recognition procedures and rules engagement became more streamlined and efficient.

Point Welcome Incident

In the early morning hours of 11 August 1966, an Air Force (FAC), call sign Blind Bat-2, was working in the Tally Ho area near the DMZ from the shoreline to three miles offshore looking for waterborne targets of opportunity. Blind Bat-2 was a specially outfitted C-130 used for night forward air control missions. At 0300 a U.S. Army OV-1B Mohawk spotter plane, call sign Spud-13, spotted a watercraft at the mouth of the Cua Tung River with SLAR and reported the sighting to his relief, Spud-14, and Blind Bat-2.[60] Twenty minutes later, Spud-14 painted multiple targets in the area of the Cua Tung River with its SLAR and reported those targets to Blind Bat-2.[61] During the next 15 minutes, Blind Bat-2 made four passes over *Point Welcome*, dropping three to four flares per pass at altitudes between 4,500 and 5,000 feet.[62]

These flares illuminated *Point Welcome* "well," according to the Blind Bat-2 commander, Captain Charles B. Chism, United States Air Force (USAF), but not well enough for either the aircraft commander or any of his crew to discern U.S. markings on the boat, including an American flag on the mast and large international call-sign letters painted on the roof of the pilothouse.[63] Captain Chism had flown only one other mission in the area prior to this one and was unaware of any Market Time units in the sector.[64] Procedures outlined by the Seventh Air Force demanded that the C-130 fly a recognition pass over any vessel illuminated and display mission lights (a rotating beacon/anticollision light). In response, allied vessels were supposed to display running lights, attempt to contact the aircraft via the radio and, if necessary, ignite a red flare or attempt to signal with an Aldis lamp.[65] Fearing hostile fire from the shore, Chism chose not to fly a recognition pass with his mission lights on.[66] After *Point Welcome* sped up, began making evasive turns, and failed to issue any recognition signals, Chism authorized a B-57, code-named Yellow Bird-18, to attack.[67] The B-57, flown by Captain John S. Lynch, USAF, had been loitering in the area waiting for targets of opportunity to arise.[68] On the night of the 11th, both Lynch and his copilot had trouble acquiring the target, so they circled the area four times before picking out what Lynch thought was the "classic silhouette" of a Chinese junk with a "high stern and big sail."[69]

When she was illuminated, *Point Welcome* was in Market Time Patrol Area 1A1 within her assigned area, approximately three-quarters to one mile offshore at or slightly south of the 17th parallel. The boat was on the second day of a three-day patrol, had just come about at the DMZ, and was steaming south at five knots. The cutter contained a crew of 11 plus Lieutenant (j.g.) Do Viet Vien, a Vietnamese liaison officer, and Timothy R. Page, a freelance photographer on assignment with *Life Magazine*.[70] Coast Guard Lieutenant (j.g.) Ross Bell, the executive officer, was standing watch on the bridge as officer of the deck, and Gunner's Mate 3rd Class Mark D. McKenney, USCG, manned the helm.[71] Both men saw Blind Bat-2 dropping flares, but they believed that its targets were some nearby junks and not the WBP since the C-130 never once made a recognition pass over *Point Welcome* with its mission lights on.[72] After the third pass by Blind Bat-2, Bell began getting concerned and ordered McKenney to wake the skipper, Lieutenant (j.g.) David C. Brostrom, USCG, sleeping in his cabin.[73] Seconds later at 0340, Yellow Bird-18 began its first strafing run from the stern to the bow.[74] Lynch fired 800 rounds of 20mm on this run, hitting the pilothouse and the stern of the vessel. One of these rounds sheared off two of Bell's toes and took off a chunk of flesh from his arm. Other rounds shattered the bridge's windshield and set fire to gas cans at the stern (used for an outboard motor). Before collapsing on the deck, Bell sounded general quarters.[75]

During the attack Brostrom ran to the bridge and placed an emergency call to the Coastal Surveillance Center (CSC) in Danang.[76] Navy Lieutenant Arthur J. Cote, the watch officer in charge of the CSC that morning, received Brostrom's dispatch and began making urgent calls to III MAF Command Operations Center and the I Corps Tactical Operations Center in an attempt to stop the attack. He also ordered three WPBs and *Haverfield* into the area to assist *Point Welcome*. A former enlisted quartermaster who had served in shipboard assignments both in World War II and Korea, Cote understood implicitly *Point Welcome*'s situation and worked furiously during the next 60 minutes to halt the attacks.[77]

Meanwhile, on the cutter the ranking petty officer on the boat, Chief Boatswain's Mate Richard H. Patterson, organized a damage control party to extinguish the fire on the fantail. Using a portable fire pump, the crew put out the flames in minutes. On the bridge, Brostrom stepped out onto a narrow platform with either the Aldis lamp or the Very pistol just as Yellow Bird-18 was making its second pass on the boat.[78] A 20mm round cut Brostrom's body in half, killing him instantly. He was the first coastguardsman to die in the Vietnam War.[79] Engineman 2nd Class Jerry Phillips, who was topside during the strafing, was hit in the back by a round and later died. Nearly everyone else on the boat suffered shrapnel wounds.[80]

Chief Patterson temporarily disregarded the mayhem around him, scrambled up to the bridge, which was covered with broken glass and blood from the wounded CO and XO, and began steering the boat at full speed toward the Coastal Group 2 base located near the mouth of the Cua Viet River. He also ordered all men to take cover below decks and attend to the wounded. Patterson thought about turning on the navigation lights but "thought better of it" because it would have made the boat a "much better target." Instead, he opted to make evasive maneuvers whenever the boat came under attack.[81]

On its third attack run against the ship, Yellow Dog-18 ran out of ammunition and returned to base, but the attack was not over. Two F-4 Phantoms had arrived on station, ready to resume the strike. The leader of the two-plane "Coyote" section, Major Richard F. Gibbs, USAF, asked Blind Bat-2 if recognition passes had been flown. Although Blind Bat-2 responded affirmative, Gibbs' wingman, Captain Stanley P. Franks Jr., USAF, opted to make his own recognition pass over *Point Welcome*, blinking his navigation lights during the run. After the cutter failed to respond, Franks initiated an attack run with a cluster bomb unit (CBU).[82] Franks' aircraft made the first runs over the target because his aircraft had CBU munitions, and Gibbs' did not. Miraculously, no cluster bomblets found their mark on the first run, and only a few struck the stern during his second attack. Gibbs then made three passes over the cutter, dropping 250-pound bombs on the first and third runs. All bombs missed. In all of these attacks Chief Patterson's evasive maneuvering made the boat a difficult target to hit and almost certainly spared the cutter from significant additional damage.[83]

At 0415, thirty minutes after the first attack, *Point Welcome* went dead in the water (probably from a loss of forced draft air to the engine). To protect his men from possible follow-on attacks, Chief Patterson ordered all hands to abandon ship. The wounded were placed in rubber and balsa rafts, and the more able bodied swam beside the rafts, pushing them toward the Coastal Group 2 base about three-quarters of a mile away. During the transit EN2 Phillips expired while GM3 McKenney, swimming alongside him, tried to comfort him with his free arm.[84] About half way to the beach, small arms and machine guns opened up on the survivors from two locations near the junk force base. Some of the crew led by SN O'Connor attempted to get back to *Point Welcome* to provide cover fire for their shipmates, but by the time they reached the cutter, *Point Caution* (WPB-82301) had arrived on scene and all shooting ceased.[85]

Between 0430 and 0445, the I Corps Tactical Operations Center informed Lieutenant Cote that the planes attacking *Point Welcome* were not Vietnamese Air Force aircraft and suggested that he call Panama, the Air Force's 620th Tactical Control Squadron located at Son Tra (Monkey Mountain), to inquire about the aircraft. Cote immediately called Panama control, which quickly confirmed that U.S. planes were in the area and then relayed a cease-fire order to Blind Bat-2 via Waterboy, a U.S. Air Force control and reporting post located at Dong Ha. Cote's testimony to the Board of Investigation shortly after the attack best reveals the confusion and chaos of that moment: "During this time, I had probably six calls between me and my assistant. I was also trying to monitor our radio circuit in the CSC office. I had two or three calls with the Air Force. I don't know whether they called me or I called them; it happened that fast."[86]

By 0545, all the seriously wounded had been transferred by *Point Caution* and Coastal Group 2 craft to the junk base for medical evacuation to the Marine Corps field hospital at Phu Bai.[87] These included Mr. Page, Lieutenant (j.g.) Bell, GM3 McKenney, Fireman Apprentice (FA) Davidson, and Culinary Specialist 2nd Class Donald L. Austin. All other crewmembers had shrapnel wounds but returned to duty the same day after receiving first aid from hospital corpsmen.[88] The entire crew of *Point Welcome* eventually received Purple Hearts for wounds sustained in the attack. Tim

Page received treatment for numerous shrapnel wounds at Phu Bai and later at the U.S. Army 17th Evacuation Hospital in Saigon before being released from medical treatment three weeks later. It would take him over a year to recover from the wounds suffered in the attack.[89]

COMUSMACV convened a board of investigation on 13 August to ascertain what happened and offer suggestions for preventing similar incidents.[90] After interviewing most of the witnesses, the board concluded that there had been no coordination between Market Time forces and Tally Ho operations near the DMZ. When those forces came into contact, neither the Air Force nor the Coast Guard followed proper identification procedures. Blind Bat-2 failed to make a proper recognition pass before authorizing strikes, and *Point Welcome*, once illuminated, failed to display running lights, signal with the Aldis light, or shoot flares, although Brostrom was attempting to signal when he was killed, and Chief Engineman William H. Wolf, USCG, made a sustained attempt to contact the Air Force on the radio after the attacks began.[91] During the attack, "all participants performed in a manner consistent with their assigned duties," and Chief Patterson should "be commended for his action in the incident." A subsequent Navy report on the incident concluded that his performance "probably saved the WPB." Patterson ultimately received a Bronze Star with Combat V for his role in the attack.[92]

To preclude further friendly fire incidents, the board recommended that allied aircraft not attack a surface craft on the water unless they had either certified that the target was unfriendly with the local coastal surveillance center or witnessed the craft conducting offensive operations against friendly craft. The board also recommended that all services be thoroughly trained in identification of recognition procedures for both friendly and nonfriendly surface craft. Finally, and much to the dismay of the *Point Welcome* survivors, the board stated that no disciplinary action should be taken against any personnel involved in the incident.[93]

More Friendly Fire Attacks

On the night of 15–16 June 1968, U.S. marine aircraft spotters on the ground began reporting unidentified helicopters near the DMZ. The first report stated that four helicopters had been detected and were proceeding toward Tiger Island at an altitude of 700–1,000 feet. These spotters observed the aircraft visually, using Starlight Scopes, and by radar.[94] Over the course of the night, Air Force pilots reported 19 additional helicopter sightings.[95]

On this same evening the guided missile heavy cruiser *Boston* (CAG-1), operating near the DMZ, also began reporting helicopter activity in the vicinity of Ben Hai, Cap Lay, and Tiger Island.[96] At 0010 on the 16th, an unidentified aircraft fired three rockets or missiles at the ship, but none hit the vessel.[97] Fifty minutes later two rockets slammed into the hull of PCF-19, also in the area.[98] Most of the PCF-19 crew was asleep in the cabin when the rockets hit. One of the rockets struck the cabin just below the pilothouse on the port side, killing Engineman 2nd Class Edward Cruz and Gunner's Mate (Guns) 2nd Class Billy Armstrong instantly. The other rocket slammed into the engine room, killing the boat's Vietnamese Navy liaison and interpreter, Bui Quang Thi. PCF-19 sank four minutes after the attack. Another sailor, Boatswain's Mate 2nd

Class Anthony Chandler went missing and presumably drowned. Quartermaster 2nd Class Frank Bowman managed to escape the boat but was never rescued and was later presumed dead.[99] The remaining crew managed somehow to swim free from the sinking craft and cling to a life raft until *Point Dume* (WPB-82325) arrived on scene at 0130, approximately 30 minutes after the attack. One of the survivors, Gunner's Mate (Guns)/Seaman John Anderegg, would later receive a Silver Star for risking his life during and immediately after the attack to save his shipmates.[100]

As soon as the survivors were on board, *Point Dume* departed the scene to drop them off at the Cua Viet Clearwater Dock for a medevac to Danang. In the meantime, the crew of PCF-12, which had arrived on scene at 0150 to continue the search for survivors, noticed illumination rounds being fired that were not their own.[101] Opting to investigate, Lieutenant (j.g.) Peter Snyder, the officer in charge, ordered the boat to speed to the Cua Viet River. When PCF-12 was three miles from the river mouth, crewmembers observed two sets of aircraft lights off the port and starboard beam, about 300 yards away and 100 feet above the water.[102] Snyder immediately got on the radio and requested permission to engage the aircraft. At 0225, PCF-12 received a single rocket from seaward at a low trajectory. The rocket passed a couple feet over the main cabin and exploded in the water ten feet from the boat.[103] PCF-12 came about, increased speed, and moved away from the kill zone while bringing its .50-caliber guns to bear against an aerial target hovering at 1,000 feet with lights blinking. The aircraft decreased altitude and turned off its lights. After a short time, PCF-12 stopped to observe the scene. "At first there was nothing to see, but then the two aircraft appeared off our beams again with lights on," explained Engineman 3rd Class James Steffes, one of the crew. Lieutenant (j.g.) Snyder contacted the marine observer and inquired about their status. The marines told him that they could not identify the aircraft because they did not have their identification, friend or foe (IFF) transponders turned on. At 0235, the aircraft near the beach fired 40–50 rounds of .50-caliber tracer fire at the PCF. All rounds landed astern. PCF-12 responded with machine-gun and mortar fire.[104]

The next 75 minutes are among the most confusing of the entire set of engagements occurring during this period. At 0240, *Point Dume*, now back on scene after evacuating the patients from PCF-19, was attacked by a fixed-wing aircraft, which made two attack runs against the vessel. Both Lieutenant (j.g.) Ronald E. Fritz, USCG, the commanding officer of *Point Dume*, and Snyder on PCF-12 positively identified the aircraft as a "jet."[105] The crews of *Point Dume* and PCF-12 then observed numerous lighted aircraft that appeared to be helicopters in the northern part of the area. These aircraft approached the U.S. vessels and made firing runs with their lights off. *Point Dume* received heavy caliber automatic weapons fire from these aircraft and returned fire. PCF-12 also returned fire intermittently for approximately 75 minutes.[106] Neither vessel was damaged in the engagement; there were no personnel injured. Fritz credits strong suppressive fire from both boats for keeping the aircraft at a distance and minimizing the effects of their attacks.[107]

On the afternoon of 16 June, Task Unit 77.1.0 ordered *Edson* (DD-946), *Theodore E. Chandler* (DD-717), and the Royal Australian Navy guided missile destroyer *Hobart* (DD-39) to conduct a surveillance mission in the vicinity of Tiger Island in attempt to flush out any enemy helicopters or waterborne craft operating from there.[108] At 0118 on the 17th, *Boston*, which was engaged in a naval gunfire support mission in the same general area, came under attack from an unidentified jet aircraft. The jet fired two missiles at the ship: one exploded 200 yards off the port beam; and the other close aboard to port, showering the ship with fragments. No sailors were injured, and the missiles caused only minor structural damage to the ship.[109]

Less than two hours later, another unidentified jet aircraft attacked *Hobart*. In the early morning hours of the 17th, *Hobart* was searching a 5-mile radius area between the coast and Tiger Island with its radar when, at 0309, it detected a single aircraft tracking east. The aircraft was not squawking IFF. An attempt was made to identify the aircraft by visual gun direction personnel on the bridge. Five minutes later a missile slammed into the chief petty officers' mess and nearby spaces, killing Ordinary Seaman R. J. Butterworth and wounding two other sailors. The ship took evasive action but temporarily lost radar contact with the aircraft.[110]

At 0316, two more missiles hit the ship, destroying the gunners' store and damaging other spaces, including the engineers' workshop, the seamen's mess, the missile director room, the Tartar checkout room, and the chiefs' mess (again). This second attack killed Chief Petty Officer R. H. Hunt and wounded other sailors. As the aircraft turned to make a third pass, one of the ship's gun turrets fired five rounds, and the aircraft turned and retreated.[111] Fourteen minutes later *Edson*, now at general quarters due to reports from *Hobart* about hostile aircraft in the area, came under attack by an unidentified aircraft. Lookouts and sonar confirmed a near miss astern by a missile.[112]

The next day Vice Admiral William F. Bringle, Commander Seventh Fleet, appointed Rear Admiral S. H. Moore, Commander Task Group 77.1/70.8, to conduct an informal JAG investigation into the various firing incidents occurring between 15 and 17 June. The board determined that Air Force F-4s launched two AIM-7E Sparrow missiles on 17 June at 0115, and one at 0315 that same day. Fragments of Sparrow missiles complete with serial numbers found on *Boston* and *Hobart* confirmed these findings.[113] The case was therefore quite clear with regard to these two attacks on 17 June—*Hobart* and *Boston* had been the victims of friendly fire.[114]

The board also investigated the 16 June attacks on *Boston* and PCF-19, and the attack on *Edson* on the 17th. From the positions of American vessels and attacking aircraft, the board concluded that Air Force aircraft attacked *Boston* and PCF-19 on the 16th, and that American aircraft also attacked *Edson* on the 17th. Unlike the case of the *Boston* and *Hobart* attacks on the 17th, however, no physical evidence supported these findings.[115] Steffes later researched the incident with surviving veterans and wrote a book on PCF-19, *Swift Boat Down*. Looking at salvage reports from *Acme* (MSO-508), the ship that recovered the bodies and code books from PCF-19 shortly after the attack, Steffes noted that the rocket entry holes in the hull of PCF-19 were 76.2mm in size—the size of a standard helicopter rocket carried by a Soviet-manufactured MI-4 Hound helicopter and not Sparrow or Sidewinder holes, which would have been larger.[116]

A National Military Command Center Operational Summary reported 14 visual sightings of helicopters and three radar sightings for 17 June and stated that COMUSMACV "believes there are enemy helicopters operating in the DMZ/Tiger Island areas."[117] Messages sent by COMUSMACV on 16 and 18 June to Commander in Chief, Pacific list 35 separate visual and radar sightings of enemy helicopters operating near the DMZ between 16 and 18 June 1968.[118] Air Force pilots in the air, marine spotters on the ground, and Navy vessels at sea made these observations. The fact that so many separate observers reported seeing enemy helicopters around the time of the PCF-19 attack, and that forensic evidence seen on the sunken hull of the boat suggested a rocket as opposed to an air-to-air missile attack, calls into question the official findings of the investigation with regard to PCF-19. The language of the official investigation best encapsulates the confusing situation of that evening:

> The presence of many combat units, both air and surface, in the area created a highly intense and sensitive atmosphere lending itself to potential confusion. Additionally, the many reported helicopter sightings and reports from Navy units that they were being attacked by enemy helicopters and fixed wing aircraft contributed to an environment in which all forces were keyed for quick reaction to potential enemy targets.[119]

Perhaps in all the confusion, enemy helicopters did indeed attack PCF-19. After-action reports written by the officers in charge of both *Point Dume* and PCF-12, along with oral histories of veterans of those vessels, suggest that enemy helicopters were flying and attacking American units in the early morning hours of 16 June, but more research is needed before the case on this mysterious episode can be closed.

Air Force leadership, to its credit, worked extremely hard to lower the rate of such incidents, known as miscues or short rounds, both before and after the 16–17 June 1967 incidents. The Air Force reported 14 short rounds for 1965 (out of 45,709 sorties flown); 21 incidents in 1966 (out of 105,745 sorties); and 24 incidents in 1967 (out of 157,000 sorties). Statistically, this meant that the rate of miscues dropped from 0.031 percent in 1965 to 0.015 percent by 1967—hardly a zero-defect result but a significant improvement in a war featuring supersonic aircraft, broad area dispersal munitions, a severe paucity of precision-guided munitions, no global positioning system, and ground and sea units often unable to communicate directly with air units.[120]

Asheville-class Patrol Gunboats

The U.S. Navy first contemplated developing a class of fast patrol boats in the 1950s after senior leadership began noticing a sharp uptick in the number of fast missile and torpedo boats being deployed by the Soviet Fleet. These boats posed a serious threat to large warships operating close to Soviet shoreline.[121] The Navy originally developed the *Asheville* (PGM-84)-class motor gunboat to defend its amphibious forces from these fast Soviet patrol boats, and to participate in the coastal patrol off Vietnam. On 5 March 1962, the Chief of Naval Operations ordered the Bureau of Ships to develop gunboat prototypes with "good sea keeping abilities and an adequate endurance suitable for patrol, blockade or surveillance missions."[122] The *Asheville* class, in short, was to be tailor-made for Market Time—one that demanded speed, low draft, high endurance,

Asheville (PGM-84) is 156 feet long and armed with a radar-controlled 3-inch 50-caliber mount, a 40mm mount, and two twin .50-caliber machine gun mounts, 16 January 1967.

and significant hitting power. Unfortunately for the Market Time leadership, the boat lacked one crucial ingredient necessary for success in the waters of Southeast Asia—mechanical reliability.

The *Asheville*-class gunboat represented a radical departure from past designs for small combatants. The Bureau of Ships specifically designed it to move quickly in very shallow waters yet carry enough firepower to engage a well-armed adversary. To achieve this end, the boat possessed a lightweight, 165-foot-long aluminum hull that drew only 8.5 feet of water and was powered by two Cummins diesel engines for cruising and a GE LM1500 gas turbine engine for high-speed propulsion. This revolutionary hybrid power plant allowed *Asheville* to sprint at speeds of up to 37 knots. At the time of its commissioning, it was the first Navy warship to possess a turbojet propulsion system and the first to make extensive use of fiberglass, which designers employed to create a deckhouse with an extremely low radar profile. Armament consisted of a 3-inch 50-caliber single mount in the bow of the boat and a 40mm single mount at the stern plus two twin .50-caliber machine-gun mounts for close-in combat. These weapons, though perfect for trawler engagements and naval gunfire support in Vietnam, were deemed inadequate by planners for potential confrontations with Soviet gunboats armed with Styx missiles. Consequently, later versions of the vessel were equipped with Standard ARM missiles. Tacoma Boatbuilding Company constructed *Asheville* and *Gallup* (PGM-85) in 1966 at a cost of $3 million per vessel ($22 million in 2014 dollars) and, following sea trials and shakedowns, both boats headed to Vietnam in early 1967 to augment the Coast Guard high endurance cutters on the outer sea barrier.[123] On 1 April *Asheville* and other vessels in her class were redesignated patrol gunboats, or PGs.

Both ships would suffer from mechanical problems during their next two years in combat, but *Asheville*'s problems were so numerous and frequent that they deserve special mention. Launched on 1 May 1966, *Asheville* underwent sea trials and then spent approximately a month in the shipyard in early 1967 to correct deficiencies found in the propulsion system, the generators, various pumps, and other systems. On the morning of 28 March, she set sail on the first leg of a Pacific crossing with *Gallup* and *Catamount* (LSD-17) and quickly ran into rough seas, experiencing 45-degree rolls. While the patrol gunboat (PG) was designed to transit oceans and ride out severe storms, it tended to pitch and roll ferociously in seas above eight feet, causing severe fatigue for the 24 crewmembers.[124]

Asheville arrived at Pearl Harbor on 5 April and departed on the 21st en route to Subic Bay, Philippines. Just a few hours out, she lost her main diesel engine because of a con-rod bearing failure and had to leave her convoy for repairs in Guam. After receiving a new engine, emergency airlifted from the United States by the Cummins Diesel Engine Company, *Asheville* steamed out of Guam and arrived at Cam Ranh Bay, Vietnam, on 7 May. She then headed to Vung Tau in preparation for her initial patrols in the Mekong Delta but broke a blade on her port propeller while traveling at high speed, forcing her to return to Cam Ranh. As the boat's 1967 Command History lamented, "It was but a sample of the difficulties that were to plague her for the remainder of her first year in Vietnam." *Asheville* spent four days in drydock having her titanium propeller blades replaced with standard steel blades and was back under way again on 25 May. She spent the next 33 days operating on Market Time's outer sea barrier, mainly querying merchant ships about their cargo, nationality, and destination. She also boarded several larger cargo junks and some fishing vessels in search of contraband goods.

On 17 June while on patrol, she lost her main port engine again due to another con-rod bearing failure and had to return to Danang for an engine change. During this repair, workers modified the lube-oil system for both main engines by installing a 50-gallon tank and dry sump system. Upon completion of the work on 23 July, the boat underwent additional sea trials, but the engines failed to pass tests and workers later found metallic flakes in the reduction gear lube-oil strainer. Two days later the boat went out on another sea trial. Once again one of the engines failed completely, and *Asheville* had to be towed back to port. That same day the boat's commanding officer, Lieutenant Henry Dale, checked himself into the U.S. Naval Hospital at Danang with an ailing back, and the executive officer, Lieutenant C. J. Baker, became the acting commander. Dale, a 39-year-old former enlisted man from Flint, Michigan, was a qualified Navy parachutist, which might explain his back problems. Nevertheless, the timing of his medical problems also may have related to the stress of the deployment.[125]

Representatives from Tacoma Boatbuilding flew to Danang to inspect the ship and speculated that the engine overload problem related to the transmission system. They recommended that she go into restricted availability at the U.S. Naval Ship Repair Facility at Yokosuka, Japan. On 24 August *Asheville* suffered a steering casualty en route to Japan and had to be towed to Subic Bay, Philippines, for repairs. She stayed in the Philippines on restricted availability until the transmission system and numerous other repairs were made. As the boat's 1967 command history noted, however, a basic question remained unanswered: "Why had this ship since 23 July been unable to duplicate her [engine] performance as demonstrated during trials in Tacoma and San Diego?" An answer never emerged. The mechanical problems did not end at Subic Bay. The command history stated "problems were continually encountered with the main-propulsion diesels, the overrunning clutches, the power-take-off gear boxes, and the ship's service generator. The number and frequency of these casualties made Market Time patrolling very difficult." The last week of 1967 found *Asheville* in Cam Ranh Bay awaiting the arrival of yet another part, in this case a friction clutch.[126]

Although *Asheville*'s mechanical tribulations in 1967 were the most severe among all of the PGs, every one of them suffered from a one form of ailment or another when deployed in Southeast Asia. *Gallup*'s problems during 1967–1968 ranged from a broken blade on the port screw to a failure of both hydraulic clutches to intermittent main engine failures.[127] Even *Crocket* (PG-88), which had one of the best maintenance records of all the PGs deployed to Vietnam, only achieved a 60 percent on-station time during Market Time, a percentage lower than the 70 percent times achieved by many of the lower endurance Coast Guard WPBs.[128]

Maintenance issues unquestionably reduced the effectiveness of the *Asheville*-class patrol gunboats during their first few years of operations in Southeast Asia, but it should be stressed that when these platforms functioned smoothly, their speed, weapon systems, and shallow draft made them ideal for Market Time as the following examples illustrate.

On 20 December 1968, a PCF under fire from the beach radioed *Asheville* ten miles from the scene for gunfire support. Firing up her turbine, *Asheville* managed to reach the Swift in just 11 minutes. Her shallow draft then allowed her to get within 1,000 yards of the beach and silence the enemy positions, using all of her weapons, including small caliber M60 machine guns.[129] On 13 February 1970 *Antelope* (PG-86) provided fire support for three PCFs ambushed on the Cua Lon River 12 miles east of Sea Float, the Navy's floating base during that period. UDT personnel operating in the area credited *Antelope* with destroying 19 bunkers, 11 houses, and 26 cisterns.[130]

Antelope's tour with Sea Float in 1970 displayed the PG as an exceptional gunfire platform, demonstrating that these robust little ships were capable of operating even in the most dangerous combat environments. During 1970 alone *Antelope* survived four well-laid ambushes without suffering serious material damage or losing a single crewmember. On 5 April an enemy patrol on the Cua Lon River fired six B40 rockets at the boat, causing minimal damage to the ship. *Antelope* responded with immediate counterbattery fire and drove the enemy away. On 25 April a guerrilla hiding along the bank of the Cua Long catapulted a satchel charge at the ship while she lay at anchor. The charge blew a 5-inch hole through the main deck but did not damage the interior or hurt any of the crew. Five days later enemy again ambushed her on the Cua Lon, firing six B40s from the north bank. *Antelope* began returning fire while some of the rockets were still airborne. No hits resulted from the attack. On 11 May the ship was transiting the Bo De River when it again was ambushed. *Antelope* returned fire. Ground forces later recovered a variety of ordnance from the area, including B50 rockets. During its 1970 deployment, *Antelope* was underway 80 percent of the time with no serious maintenance problems reported in her monthly summaries.[131]

Another hero of Sea Float was *Canon* (PG-90) and her commanding officer, Lieutenant Commander David B. Robinson. In August 1970, PG-90 was engaged in "harassment and interdiction" fire against suspected enemy positions on the shore. Suddenly, a Viet Cong platoon opened fire from both banks of the river on *Canon*. An exploding RPG round hit the gunboat's bridge, breaking Robinson's leg and lacerating his body with shrapnel. The badly wounded officer ordered his men to strap him to a stretcher and prop it upright so he could continue directing the battle. Only when *Canon* drove off the ambushers and steamed to a safe anchorage at Sea Float did the commanding officer consent to medical evacuation. Robinson received the Navy Cross for his heroism that day.[132]

Historian Norman Friedman claims that PGs "were subject to damage," especially when used on rivers, because of the lightweight material used to build them, and he cites the *Antelope*'s experiences as evidence. The gunboat's command history and monthly summaries, however, tell a very different story—a story not of a ship "badly mauled" as Friedman argues but a scrappy boat capable of surviving numerous attacks and offering Sea Float unprecedented firepower for gunfire support missions.[133]

Gallup (PGM-85).

No Market Time mission was more important than interdiction and in this role, too, PGs excelled. A good example of their prowess as a seaborne interdiction platform occurred in July 1967. Following Max Branscomb's radar intercept of a large steel-hulled trawler on 11 July, *Wilhoite* (DER-397) had covertly trailed the vessel in international waters until the evening of 13 July, when *Gallup* arrived on the scene to support the effort. As the Navy prepared to pounce on the trawler as soon as she crossed into Vietnam's territorial waters, Commander Charles R. Stephan, the commander of Market Time's Northern Surveillance Group (NSG), found *Gallup*'s presence "most welcome" for a variety of reasons. "Her 3-inch and 40mm guns would provide important firepower, her speed might be extremely useful in some unpredicted emergency.... [A]nd finally the men of this new class of ship wanted, and deserved a chance to prove their worth."[134] True to his predictions, the ship proved its worth just three days later.

Trawler Intercepts

Lieutenant (j.g.) Edward J. Bergin was a fisherman at heart. The son of an Air Force officer, Bergin spent a great amount of time as a child fishing the waters near Ramey Air Force Base in Aguadilla, Puerto Rico, where his father worked. "I learned just enough Spanish to talk to the fishermen," he explained. In college at Florida State in Tallahassee, Bergin enjoyed fishing along coast of the Florida panhandle. After college he joined the Navy, hoping to fly, but injuries sustained from a scuba diving accident prevented him from passing the flight physical. Instead, he attended Officer Candidate School at Newport and entered the surface Navy as an ensign in 1964. In the Navy, Bergin continued to fish when time permitted and has fond memories of fishing the waters of Chile and Peru during a South American cruise with escort ship *Van Voorhis* (DE-1028) in 1966. In Vietnam as the officer in charge of PCF-79, Bergin had little time to fish, but for the "heck of it" he used to keep an old Calcutta rod in the boat. Toward the end of his tour during an uneventful patrol, he decided to do a little trolling. "You probably won't believe it, but I hooked a Marlin," he recounted in an oral history. "I told the helmsman to stop the boat, but he did not hear me and the fish got away."[135] In Operation Market Time, intercepting a steel-hulled trawler was the equivalent of hooking a Marlin, and PCF-79 and several other Swift boats and WPBs would be instrumental in catching one of these big fish in 1967.

The first significant sea infiltration effort detected since June 1966 and the fourth steel-hull infiltrator incident since Market Time began occurred on 23 December 1966. An aircraft from Patrol Squadron 16 achieved a contact with a steel-hulled trawler traveling low in the water 80 miles off the coast of Qui Nhon and followed the ship for four hours until being relieved by another aircraft. The Navy maintained covert air surveillance above the ship until 25 December, when *Hissem* (DER-400) started tracking her. The DER, commanded by Lieutenant Commander James Alden Barber Jr., covertly followed the ship for three days, preparing to intercept her if she entered South Vietnamese waters. The trawler instead sailed into Chinese waters in the Hainan Strait on the 27th, compelling *Hissem* to break off pursuit.[136]

Market Time forces finally engaged an enemy trawler in combat during the night of 1–2 January 1967. PCF 71, operating 165 miles off Vung Tau in torrential rain and three-foot seas, made the initial radar contact at 2115.[137] Under the command of Lieutenant (j.g.) Richard Wesley Dawson, the PCF closed on the trawler and ordered it to stop. The trawler, traveling at 10–12 knots, ignored the order and instead fired on the Swift boat at close range with small arms and machine guns. Although hit by shrapnel, Dawson ordered the Swift to return fire and pull back to a safer position. Rounds from the PCF struck the trawler's hull and cargo deck as the PCF moved back to care for Dawson, a 1964 Naval Academy graduate, and several other crewmembers who were lightly wounded in the attack.[138]

Point Gammon was tied up alongside PCF-68 helping to repair the Swift boat's broken fathometer when she first learned of the intercept at 2130. Both units then proceeded at full speed to contact and while en route received a Mayday call from PCF-71, informing them that she had been hit and was pulling back. By 2140, *Point Gammon* had closed within six miles of the trawler and began issuing challenges with a signal light. Operating in heavy rain and pitch darkness, Lieutenant Richard W Hassard, USCG, the WPB commander, wanted to be sure the contact was the trawler and not a friendly unit before opening fire. "I thought it probably was a VNN PGM, which, as usual, was slow in answering the flashing light," Hassard wrote in his after-action report. At 2,000 yards from the target, Hassard ordered his mortar crew to fire an illumination round, but it was not bright enough to identify the trawler. He moved his WPB closer to the stern quarter of the trawler and lit up the night skies again with an 81mm illumination flare. This time he positively identified the trawler and prepared for action just as PCF-68 arrived on scene at 0123 on 2 January.

Hassard asked PCF-68 to get ahead of the trawler and fire warning shots across the bow. Under the command of Lieutenant (j.g.) Alexander Bass, the PCF crew fired a few shots ahead of the trawler, which replied with machine-gun fire. *Point Gammon* fired another illumination and began laying down machine-gun fire on the trawler while the PCF-68 fired white phosphorus rounds with its mortar. One "Willy Peter" round scored a direct hit on the pilothouse, which burned for the remainder of the action. Throughout the engagement the trawler kept changing courses between north and west at a constant speed of 15 knots. With the trawler burning, Hassard no longer needed his mortar for illumination fire so he ordered a high explosive round with proximity fuze to be lobbed at the enemy ship. After one miss, Hassard decided to secure the 81mm mount and rely solely on his .50-caliber guns to return fire against the high-speed, maneuvering contact.[139]

At 0200, the trawler stopped dead in the water 200 yards from the beach with a fire still blazing in the pilothouse. Fifteen seconds later, Hassard observed three large explosions on the trawler, and then the fire went out, indicating that the trawler had sunk.[140] By 0245, the trawler could no longer be detected visually or by radar. Divers sent to the scene at daybreak found no debris from the trawler in the area, but adverse weather and muddy water may have hindered their salvage efforts.[141] A subsequent aerial search of the area and nearby coastline and rivers using a magnetic anomaly detection system also found no evidence of the ship.[142] A message later sent by Commander in Chief, Pacific Fleet stated that its analysis of all available data on the incident indicated "the trawler may not have sunk and possibly could have escaped into one of the nearby streams. The result of the incident is therefore reassessed to one trawler possibly sunk."[143] In all, three sailors from PCF-71 and three from PCF-68 received minor wounds in the engagement. PCF-71 returned from the incident with 30 bullet holes in its hull, one 3-inch hole on the port side, and three holes in the windshield; PCF-68 suffered two .50-caliber holes in its hull.[144] Hassard, a 1963 Coast Academy graduate, would later receive a Bronze Star with Combat V for his leadership during the engagement; a copy of the citation is displayed in the Hall of Heroes in Chase Hall at the United States Coast Guard Academy in New London, Connecticut.[145]

The next major Market Time trawler intercept occurred on 14 March 1967. At 0114 local time, a P-3B aircraft from Patrol Squadron 46 reported an unlit steel-hulled contact 67 miles southeast of Danang and 14 miles from the mainland heading east northeast. The night was clear and the seas calm. The aircraft tracked the suspect vessel until *Brister* achieved radar contact at 0403 and joined the hunt. Seventeen minutes later the contact changed course and headed for the mainland. A P-3B illuminated the ship at 0430 and positively identified it as an 80-foot-long steel-hulled trawler, traveling at ten knots. Minutes later *Brister* challenged the vessel with its signal lamp. After being ignored, *Brister* fired several warning shots and directed PCF-78 and *Point Ellis* to intercept the ship.

PCF-78 made a close-in pass at the ship at 0540 and came under heavy small arms fire, forcing her to back off. *Brister*, now also under fire from the trawler, responded with 3-inch 50- and .50-caliber fire. At 0617, the trawler grounded on the beach 60 miles southeast of Danang near the village of Phuoc Thien. By this time *Point Ellis* had joined the two Navy units in the area, and all three craft began laying down suppressing fire on the trawler and nearby beach areas to prevent Viet Cong from offloading the vessel. At one point in the melee, *Point Ellis* received machine-gun fire as she closed to approximately 500 yards of the trawler in a zigzag attack.[146] Fireman Richard Picard, who was firing an M16 on the bow of *Point Ellis*, vividly remembered the scene. "We were told not to fire below the waterline, but when you have all that firepower coming back at you, all you want to do is let go. We opened up with three .50-calibers plus small arms."[147]

At 0655, two minutes after sunrise, the trawler exploded in a huge mushroom cloud of smoke. *Point Ellis* was so close to the explosion that *Point Arden*, which arrived shortly after the explosion, thought her sister ship had exploded with the trawler. "Guys on *Point Arden* were crying when they finally pulled up alongside us and realized we were still intact," recalled Picard, who strongly believed fire from his WPB caused the explosion. "Every fifth round our 50s fired was an armor-piercing incendiary; we were really pounding them." Official reports from the Navy and Coast Guard, however, claim that trawler's crew blew the ship up with some type of charge.[148]

After the explosion *Brister, Point Ellis,* PCF-78, and *Point Arden* then formed a semicircular perimeter around the trawler's position and laid down more suppressive fire for 35 minutes or so before *Arden* was released to resume her patrol. An AC-47 Spooky gunship on scene observed possible enemy personnel running across a nearby wooded area and fired at them with unknown results. *Point Ellis* used its Boston Whaler to collect debris and other evidence from the water. "We collected Chicom rifles wrapped in burlap and even located the ship's bell," explained Picard. At 1700, a Marine Corps landing party arrived and established a defensive perimeter around the area of the explosion. Salvage operations the next day discovered a variety of machine guns, small arms, ammunition, and other war supplies.[149]

During the engagement PCF-78 received 11 bullet holes but no personnel casualties. *Point Ellis* took no hits, which Coast Guard Division 12 attributed to the "excellent manner in which the CO, Lieutenant (j.g.) Morris Dean Helton, maneuvered the *Ellis* during her attack runs."[150] Helton was another hard-charging Coast Guard Academy graduate, hand-picked by the Coast Guard to command a WPB—a man described by one of his crew, Engineman 3rd Class Anthony J. Trackerman, as "one of the best officers I ever served under during my 20 year career in the Coast Guard."[151] In a cable written two days after the attack, General Westmoreland himself specifically mentioned Helton's WPB, along with PCF-78 and *Brister*, in his Bravo Zulu:

> Market Time scored another big success on 14 March. The enemy, forced to destroy a precious cargo of mortars, small arms, uniforms, and other contraband, has been deprived of large quantities of much needed war material. Please pass on my hearty congratulations to the USS *Brister*, USCG *Point Ellis*, PCF-78, and all other units involved in this brilliant operation.[152]

Picard was more candid: "Everything happened so quickly. We just reacted the way we had been trained. We felt we were the cream of the crop and indestructible. It was the best experience of my life even though it was war."[153]

As in the case of Picard, Seaman Raul Herrera's life would be changed by a 1967 trawler intercept, but that's where the similarities end. The son of a railroad engineer, Picard grew up in Natick, Massachusetts, a middle-class, white suburb of Boston. He joined the service not out of financial necessity but to avoid getting drafted into the Army. Herrera, by contrast, came from what he described as the "lowest rung of the economic ladder." The son of a Mexican-American housepainter, he grew up in a poor immigrant neighborhood of San Antonio and worked as a custodian at his parochial high school to help pay the modest tuition. "I wanted to go into architecture, but my parents could not afford to pay for college so I decided to join the Navy because it had a good drafting program."[154]

Herrera volunteered for the Navy in 1965 and, after attending boot camp, he worked for a year as a draftsman at the Naval Training Center, San Diego. Things were going well for him for a year until he learned that the Navy was phasing out the drafting rating and that he soon would be transferred to Swift boats. Herrera had no idea what a Swift boat was, but when told by his chief that it was a combat assignment in Vietnam, he knew he was "in trouble." After attending PCF training at Coronado, Herrera flew to Vietnam and arrived at Danang in April 1967. On his first patrol with PCF-79 a grizzled, tattoo-festooned Boatswain Mate 2nd Class from Leesville, Louisiana, named Bobby Don "Boats" Carver approached him and told him from that moment on he would be called "Bean." When Herrera asked why, Carver replied, "Because all compadres go by that nickname in the Navy." Rather than being offended by this racist remark, Herrera accepted his nickname as the price to be paid for being part of the crew. "I did not even realize it was derogatory until long after I left the Navy. My Navy friends still call me Bean and I am honored by the nickname because it was personally chosen by Carver." He and Boats would later form a deep bond during the many hours they spent working on the boat together. "We painted, shellacked, and varnished every inch of that boat until she shone. She looked so nice that she could have served as a flagship." On patrol, Herrera quickly settled into his job as a radioman and cook. He would pick out stores for the boat from cold storage and strive to cook restaurant quality food for his shipmates. Occasionally on slow patrols, the PCF would pull into a quiet cove, and Herrera would barbecue food on the fantail. Although he never volunteered for service on Swifts, Herrera adapted well to the duty and mastered every job on the boat. He especially enjoyed taking his turn at the helm. Driving the boat at high-speeds was exhilarating for him and similar in many respects to a speedboat ride on a lake in Texas. The boring part of his job involved searching junks and sampans for contraband. "In the time we spent doing this in Vietnam, we never found any contraband." That would change on 15 July 1967.[155]

Wilhoite first made contact with the steel trawler during the night of 11–12 July. The trawler was 45 miles from the coast on a southwest heading. Lieutenant Commander Estel Wilbur Hays, the ship's commanding officer, kept the DER eight to ten miles behind the trawler. On the morning of the 12th, he ordered the ship to move within visual range of the trawler and challenged her. The trawler did not reply. He noted that it was fully loaded and running darkened with no sign of nationality. *Wilhoite* then fell back out of visual range and continued surveillance for the next three days, always keeping eight to ten miles behind the contact. The trawler headed north to the Paracel Islands, then came about and headed south for over 50 miles before finally heading west towards the coast just before midnight on the 13th.[156]

Once the *Wilhoite* crew was certain that the trawler was about to make a run for the beach, it informed the Danang-based Northern Surveillance Group. Commander Charles R. Stephan, the NSG commander, assembled his staff late on the evening of the 13th to prepare for an intercept. The eventual plan called for a task unit that would ultimately include *Wilhoite*, *Gallup*, PCF-79, and *Point Orient* (WPB-83319) to position themselves in an extended line astern of the contact. That way, if the trawler tried to escape either to the port or starboard, it would be trapped by one of the wing units. Stephan would command Task Unit (TU) 115.1, which contained a PSYOP (psychological operations) speaker-team that would try to convince the trawler to surrender just prior to intercept.[157]

Commander Stephan, a former enlisted radarman for six years, was intimately familiar with the art of tracking a hostile contact over large expanses of open ocean. At 1715 on the 14th, he left Danang on board *Gallup*, which sprinted to the rendezvous point with *Wilhoite* in less

Wilhoite (DER-397) was one of the Navy units that participated in the 15 July 1967 trawler intercept.

than three hours. After transferring to the DER and assuming formal command of TU 115.1, Stephan was immediately impressed by Commander Hays' ship and its 160 crewmembers. "Hays had fully prepared the ship for boarding and hand-to-hand combat," he later wrote. "If required, *Wilhoite* could have made the intercept alone."[158]

Wilhoite and *Gallup* assumed positions astern of the trawler and waited for other units to arrive. Ninety minutes later at 2130, *Point Orient* rendezvoused with the two units, and the three ships continued tracking the trawler which, after making a few minor course corrections, headed directly for the coastline south of Cape Batangan. The sky was overcast, the seas were eight to ten feet, and the wind was gusting up to 30 knots. To offload cargo in these conditions, the trawler would need to sail to the protected waters of a harbor or river inlet. Stephan therefore was not surprised when he received an intelligence message from CTF 115 informing him that a group of Viet Cong had just assembled up the Sa Ky River ready to offload the trawler. "This bit of intelligence cinched the trawler's destination. Now it would be possible to select the Swift boat which would be closest to the track of the trawler. . . . It was the PCF-79." Stephan sent out an encrypted message finalizing station assignments for the three units of TU 115.1.[159]

253

The enemy steel-hulled trawler steams in international waters toward the South Vietnamese coastline while under Operation Market Time surveillance, 14 July 1967. The next day, Market Time forces engaged the 120-foot trawler and ultimately captured it.

Herrera was manning the PRC-25 radio when the message came through but in all the excitement of the evening failed to properly decrypt the shackle codes. Rather than telling his officer in charge, Lieutenant Bergin, to head for the starboard quarter as ordered, he told him to head directly behind the trawler's stern—the position *Wilhoite* and *Gallup* were supposed to cover.[160] Bergin claimed that trying to fully decrypt a shackle code in rough seas by flashlight "was damn near impossible . . . and consequently never completed. But Bean did get enough of it decoded to indicate the bare essentials."[161]

As PCF-79 gunned its engines to rendezvous with the other units, the trawler got closer and closer to the 12-mile territorial waters of the Republic of Vietnam, and the "excitement built up rapidly within the quiet, darkened CIC" of *Wilhoite*. Stephan asked *Wilhoite*'s navigator to plot the line one more time for accuracy and then ordered several Chu Lai-based helicopter gunships to prepare to attack the Viet Cong ground positions as soon as the intercept occurred. At 11 minutes after midnight on 15 July, the trawler crossed the 12-mile line. On order, the PSYOP team on *Point Orient* transmitted in Vietnamese the following message: "You must stop and don't shoot because you are surrounded! We knew clearly that you were coming here and we have been waiting for you for three days. You must quickly wake up to the fact and surrender. The government will be merciful." After the tape had been played several times, a Vietnamese liaison officer got on the loudspeaker and attempted to communicate directly with the trawler.[162]

When the trawler failed to heed orders, *Point Orient*, now only 1,000 yards from the ship, fired an illumination round from the 81mm mortar. As Stephan later described it, "There, big as life, before our eyes was the enemy trawler."[163] Stephan ordered PCF-79 to fire a second illumination round. Bergin, manning the PCF's helm, grabbed the radio from Herrera and responded: "Negative *Wilhoite*. We're traveling too fast. All we would do is illuminate ourselves."[164] Stephan instead asked PCF-79 and *Point Orient* to fire across the trawler's bow, which they did, but the trawler still made no attempt to reduce speed. Bergin then asked for permission to fire. Stephan acceded because, as he later wrote in a 1968 *Proceedings* article, "All criteria had been met to establish the trawler as the enemy and as an evading, hostile unit, even though she had not opened fire on the task unit."[165]

No sooner had Bergin secured permission to fire than the trawler fired on the PCF with a 12.7mm machine gun located near the stern of the ship. To suppress the gun, Bergin told Torpedoman's Mate 3rd Class Robert J. Middleton, his topside twin .50-caliber gunner, to walk the tracers up and down the ship's stern area and until he killed the trawler's rear gunner.[166] *Point Orient* also fired from the port side, as did *Gallup* with 40mm and 3-inch fragmentation shells. *Wilhoite* had to maneuver to avoid shallow water but soon joined in with her 3-inch and 40mm guns.[167] Salvage parties later determined that the trawler was equipped with three 12.7mm machine guns and at least one 57mm recoilless rifle.[168]

Seeing that the trawler was heading for the mouth of the Sa Ky River, Bergin followed her in PCF-79 and told his mortarman, Bobby Carver, to try to set a fire on the trawler with a white phosphorus round. The lieutenant hoped that by creating a fire, he would make the contact more visible. The PCF moved to the port side of the trawler. This maneuver gave the fantail mortar a clear field of fire, but it also gave the trawler's gunner a good target. "All hell broke loose from both vessels," claims Bergin. "Splashes from what could have been recoilless rifle shells were seen close by." Making matters more dangerous, Carver's first round missed. Thinking that the mortar had been double loaded, Carver then tried to remove the round. Bergin handed the helm to Herrera and went down to assist. "Carver wasn't just gently tapping the tube as recommended in the manual. He was banging it down as hard as he could to get the round out as quickly as possible." Confident that his boatswain's mate had the situation under control, Bergin returned to the pilothouse, arriving just in time to see surf cresting a few yards head on a rock formation. He grabbed the wheel from Herrera and turned hard port, and the PCF narrowly averted grounding on the rocks.[169]

Bergin placed the PCF behind the silenced 12.7mm gun on the trawler's stern—a zone of safety created in the first moments of the battle by the Middleton's skillful shooting on the topside 50s. As the PCF got within 50 yards of the trawler, Carver let loose a second "Willy Peter" round. This one did not miss. It went through the door of the pilothouse, causing a massive explosion and fire. A salvage crew later discovered the charred remains of a crewmember holding a Type 56 assault rifle (a Chinese version of the AK-47).[170] Carver released one more round into the stricken vessel while the rest of the crew admired his handiwork. "We just watched in awe as the flaming vessel careened out of control and struck hard near a small islet inside the calm waters of the Sa Ky," explained Bergin. "We had done it! There was no more gunfire from the trawler.... She looked like a burning pig over a spitfire."[171]

With the trawler grounded and burning, Stephan ordered the helicopter gunships to attack, and soon rockets and red M60 tracer fire could be seen flowing from the aircraft to the stricken trawler. At 0115, elements of the 2d Korean Marine Brigade called to let Stephan know that the trawler was in their tactical area of responsibility (TAOR) and that they would soon begin bombarding the area. Reluctantly, Stephan ordered PCF-79 and other units to back off but to continue firing while Korean howitzers pulverized the area for a solid hour. At 0200, the destroyer *Walker* (DD-517) joined the group and added her gunfire to the mix. One and a half hours later PCF-20 arrived to relieve *Point Orient*, which, according to Stephan, had been "firing slowly, deliberately, and accurately for over an hour," and by 0415, PCF-79 ran out of ammunition and returned to base after being relieved by PCF-54.[172]

For the rest of the night, five Navy units continued illuminating the trawler and making occasional firing runs. At dawn on the 15th, Stephan transferred from *Wilhoite* to PCF-20 to take a closer look at the trawler. By the time the PCF had carefully made its way through the rocky river mouth to reach the trawler, Korean marines had assumed control of the vessel. They "politely" informed Stephan to back away because this was their booty, having grounded in their TAOR. For the next few hours, all Stephan could do was watch as the marines removed much of the trawler's cargo, including caches of weapons. TF 115 eventually secured permission to assist the marines in salvaging the boat and sent two LCM (8)s from Chu Lai to commence work on the project.[173]

The first American to board the vessel was Gunner's Mate 2nd Class Eddie A. Knaup, an EOD specialist, who immediately disarmed a self-destruction system rigged to detonate 2,000 pounds of TNT.[174] Stephan then came on board to examine his capture. Expecting to find only charred remains, he was surprised to find most of the trawler intact with only the pilothouse and after section of the ship burned. "The paint forward had not even blistered." Many tons of ammunition were still on the ship, and Stephan noted that spent brass from the 12.7mm machine guns littered the decks. The LCMs from Chu Lai arrived and began working to free the stuck trawler. By 1630, the two LCMs had the trawler in between them and set course for Chu Lai. During the transit Knaup noticed the trawler beginning to smoke. The quick thinking sailor ran into the main hold of the trawler and saw a fire burning in the storeroom. He immediately ordered the LCMs to stop in order to minimize wind draft. He then threaded a hose from PCF-20 down to the hold and quickly extinguished the flames. Had the fire continued, it might have ignited defused TNT charges as well tons of ammunition in the hull.[175]

The trawler arrived at Chu La at 2000 and was later transferred to Danang where officials began inventorying her cargo. In all, they found 90 tons of supplies, including 1,200 weapons

North Vietnamese trawler captured on 15 July 1967 being towed by LCM (652). In the background is PCF-79, which participated in the capture of the trawler.

of various types, and over 700,000 rounds of ammunition—enough to equip a Viet Cong regiment for several months. It was one of Market Time's biggest successes of the war. In a Bravo Zulu message to units participating in the intercept, Rear Admiral Kenneth L. Veth praised the tenacity and patience of the Market Time units in trapping their prey. "Through your shrewd tactical planning, distribution and utilization of air and surface units," he wrote in a message to CTF 115, "you and your units have again proved that the coast of Vietnam is inviolable to steel hull infiltration, and by your actions have undoubtedly saved lives of your comrades in arms." This capture marked the eighth time Market Time forces had intercepted an enemy steel-hulled trawler since the 1965 Vung Ro Bay incident.[176]

Demise of Coastal Group 16

Not long after the trawler episode, the Viet Cong regained the initiative along the coast of I Corps through a daring attack on a VNN coastal group base. Located in isolated areas, these small bases lacked adequate defenses and were highly vulnerable to attack. By 1967 the Coastal Force consisted of 27 coastal groups located at 22 sites spread out along the coast of South Vietnam. Each base consisted of approximately 10 junks and 148 sailors. The men, most of whom had just a few years of grade school education, lived in primitive conditions far from the comforts of larger towns or cities.[177]

Coastal Group 16 was one such forgotten outpost. Located at the mouth of the Tra Khuc River 70 miles south of Danang at the southernmost tip of I Corps and surrounded by an estimated 1,200–1,500 Viet Cong, the base consisted of a triangular perimeter with one side to the water and fencing on the other sides. The base's low-lying position made it prone to flooding

AK-47 assault rifles captured by Market Time forces on 15 July 1967.

Coastal Group 16 base located 70 miles south of Danang. Viet Cong forces overran the base on 7 August 1967. The rooftop slogan, "To Quoc Tren Het," means "Country Above All," 6 March 1966.

and complicated efforts to construct defenses. During the May–September monsoon, very little could be shipped by sea to the base, and local roads were often washed out or vulnerable to Viet Cong ambushes. This meant that the facility was short on everything from food to ammunition on 7 August 1967.[178]

Just before 0300, a mortar round hit the inside perimeter of the compound. Chief Engineman Harold N. Guinn bolted up from his sleep and made his way into the command shack, where he found the other three Americans attached to the facility: Lieutenant William C. Fitzgerald, the chief advisor; his deputy, Lieutenant (j.g.) Anthony C. Williams; and Boatswain's Mate 1st Class Leo E. Pearman, an enlisted advisor.[179] After the first round exploded, mortar rounds began hitting the base at a rate of one every 10 to 15 seconds. The two officers immediately entered the command bunker to call for help while the two enlisted sailors ran to prepared fighting positions behind the command house to return fire.[180]

Unbeknown to the group, a multi-battalion-size force was in the process of attacking the small compound from several directions at once. It only took the Viet Cong 15 minutes to penetrate the perimeter, but Guinn and Pearman did their best during those first crucial minutes of the battle to defend the place, firing over 600 rounds from various small arms in the process. By 0325, Guinn and Pearman were the only ones defending the rear perimeter of the base.[181] As he was firing an M60 light machine gun, a bullet grazed Guinn in the arm, but he ignored the pain and continued to fight. At 0328, he ran into the command house, retrieved a 57mm recoilless

259

rifle, and returned to the fighting position accompanied by Lieutenant (j.g.) Williams. Noticing automatic weapons fire coming from three different places across the river, Guinn laid down fire on those points while Pearman served as his loader. During one shot the hot exhaust gas from the recoilless rifle struck Williams in the face. In pain, he crawled back into the command bunker, and in a few minutes the skin around his eyes swelled, causing him to lose most of his vision. In the bunker Williams heard Fitzgerald requesting fire support from the Army or Air Force. A few minutes later, all communications went dead, and no artillery fire was received. VNN junks, though, continued to support the base by firing on targets across the river.[182]

Outside the command bunker, Guinn fired four or five rounds from the recoilless rifle before Pearman informed him that the VC had breached the compound. The two sailors retreated to the command bunker where Guinn could not believe what he saw as he peered through the gun slit. "The VC were all over the base, running around just shooting and looting. The base was theirs. They were dancing, war hooping, and yelling."[183] Fitzgerald instructed everyone to lay low in the bunker while he continued trying to secure help on the radio. A 1963 Naval Academy graduate, Fitzgerald had served on destroyers before deploying to Vietnam in 1967 as an advisor.[184] Well respected by the group, Lieutenant Fitzgerald told the men to man different spots in the bunker while they waited for help to arrive. At 0345, Chief Guinn noticed two Viet Cong sneak behind the bunker and try to enter it through the left door, which was guarded by Williams. As one of the Viet Cong raised his weapon to shoot Williams, Guinn felled the man with his automatic rifle and then killed the second soldier with another burst of automatic fire. After the shootings Fitzgerald turned to the group and told them to make for the river.[185] While Pearman and Williams headed for the fence line behind the base, Guinn remained behind with Fitzgerald to provide additional cover fire. "I couldn't see very well," Williams later wrote in an eyewitness statement. "The only way I could tell which way I was going was to keep the flames from the base on my left."[186]

Guinn finally made a run for it by following a ditch behind the bunker to a hole in the fence that the Vietnamese cleaning women often used to access the river to wash clothes. Shrapnel hit Guinn's leg as he struggled to get through the fence, but he made it and found Pearman just beyond the perimeter. The two men began looking for Williams and Fitzgerald, but did not find either. They would later learn that Williams had made it to the river and was in the water trying to swim for the junks. Fitzgerald remained in the command bunker, stoically trying to coordinate a rescue with Swift boats en route to the area.[187]

By this point, PCFs-15, -20, -54, and -75 were making their way to the scene under the tactical control of *Camp* (DER-251). Boatswain's Mate 2nd Class Michael "Boats" Turley was on PCF-15 and remembered seeing the explosions from the ammunition dump blowing up. "We wanted to go up the river and try to cut the enemy off, but authorities in Cam Ranh Bay wouldn't let us." Instead, they ordered PCF-15 to focus on evacuating survivors, including women and children. According to Turley, two women gave birth on the PCF. "I assisted my radio operator Quartermaster/Seaman Scott in delivering two babies that night."[188]

Guinn and Pearman waded out to the middle of the river and climbed aboard a VNN junk. The junk transferred the two sailors plus a group of wounded Vietnamese to PCF-75, which was holding station at the river's mouth. Once on the Swift boat, Guinn requested that the boat take them back to the junk base so they could look for the other Americans. When the PCF arrived at the post, Guinn and Pearman with an Army enlisted advisor carefully made their way to the command bunker. At 0440, Guinn entered and found Fitzgerald lying dead with a bullet wound to the head. He also found a severely wounded VNN second class petty officer. The three men evacuated the petty officer and some wounded dependents to *Camp* for treatment.[189]

Around 0600, Guinn transferred to another PCF to resume the search for Williams and eventually found the officer on a small sampan. Reunited, the advisors evacuated Williams to *Camp* for medical treatment. For their actions on the 7th, Guinn later received a Silver Star, and Pearman and Williams, Bronze Stars with Combat V. Fitzgerald was later awarded a posthumous Navy Cross, and the Navy eventually named the guided missile destroyer *Fitzgerald* (DDG-62) in his honor.[190]

Two infantry companies of the ARVN 2d Division and a company of U.S. Army troops from Task Force Oregon secured the Coastal Group 16 base at 0700 on the 7th. Using classic guerrilla tactics, the Viet Cong never intended to hold the base. As soon as they captured it, they drifted back into the jungle. In addition to Fitzgerald, Coastal Group 16 lost 13 Vietnamese sailors and 20 Navy civilian dependents during the attack.[191] The Viet Cong also destroyed all but one building on the base and freed 35 detainees while losing 11 men in the assault.[192] The VC attack once again revealed the extreme vulnerability of the junk force bases, causing some skeptical American officers to question again the efficacy of the VNN Coastal Force program. "Coastal groups are aware of the U.S. ability to react more quickly to intelligence due to better communications and vessels," noted a 1967 Naval Advisory Group study, "and as a result, there is an increasing tendency to 'Let George do it.'" The same study stated that "the coastal groups are physically incapable of countering infiltration or transshipment" due to the technical limitations of the junks, which by 1967 were generally slower, less seaworthy, and less well armed than infiltrators. Rather than employing them in a Market Time role, the study recommended that coastal groups instead be devoted to other missions such as psychological operations, amphibious raids with South Vietnamese forces, fisheries protection, and patrols at river mouths and lagoons.[193]

PSYOP and Civic Action

By summer 1967 psychological warfare had emerged as one of the most important secondary missions for Market Time forces. NAVFORV defined psychological operations as "the planned use of propaganda and other measures to influence the opinions, emotions, attitudes, and behavior of hostile, neutral, or friendly groups to support achievement of national objectives." It defined "propaganda" as any "information, ideas, doctrines, or special persuasion in support of national objectives, designed to influence the opinions, emotions, attitudes, or behavior of any specified group in order to benefit the sponsor directly or indirectly."[194] Civic action in Vietnam mainly consisted of public health, medical, and charitable efforts designed to build support for the government among the civilian populace—operations that today's Navy generally defines as "humanitarian operations." In Vietnam, PSYOP and civic action were intimately linked and often performed at the same time by the same personnel.

PSYOP officers conveyed propaganda and other information to civilians by various media, including television, radio, loudspeaker broadcasts, and face-to-face encounters. In September alone, crewmembers of PBRs, PCFs, and WPBs distributed 334,000 leaflets, 111,000 newspapers, 33,000 magazines, and 20,000 posters. Navy boats and aircraft broadcast over 400 hours of propaganda from speakers, and U.S. aircraft dropped 11 million leaflets on Viet Cong areas. Navy units also distributed additional propaganda materials during the course of boarding and inspecting 82,462 junks and sampans.[195] In the words of Navy PSYOP advisor Lieutenant Victor G. Reiling Jr., the "USN/VNN have the best consistent face-to-face communications capabilities of any force in Vietnam."[196] By 1967 U.S. Navy and VNN personnel had become instrumental to the overall allied PSYOP campaign in the country.

But did PSYOP actually have an impact on the local populace? One measure of the effectiveness of these operations was the Chieu Hoi program. Chieu Hoi, which translates to "open arms," sought to persuade Viet Cong to switch to the government side by promising potential defectors literacy and vocational training and help with resettlement and job placement. The program attempted not only to peel away soldiers from the other side and bring them into the government fold, but also to exploit these turncoats for military purposes. In many cases the government deployed defectors as "Kit Carson Scouts" in military units. Founded in 1966 by the U.S. marines in I Corps, the Kit Carson Scouts led U.S. forces to enemy units and assisted in pacification efforts. By 1968 more than 700 former Viet Cong were serving with U.S. forces, often in long-range reconnaissance patrols or in civic action efforts designed to convince more enemy villagers to defect.[197] By August 1967 the overall Chieu Hoi program had deprived the Communist forces of 66,000 members. More than 20,000 Viet Cong rallied to the government side during the first seven months of 1967 alone—more than the entire total for 1966, and an 82 percent increase over 1965.[198]

Some of these defections may have resulted more from the difficult living conditions in Viet Cong areas than from allied psychological operations. In addition to constant allied bombing, enemy soldiers suffered from food shortages as the war dragged on. In 1965 the rice ration for a Viet Cong soldier was 2.5 cans per day; by 1967 it was down to 1.5 cans. There were also reports that as many as 50 percent of the soldiers in some units suffered from malaria.[199] For many, the prospect of a good meal and rest in a Chieu Hoi resettlement center was all it took for them to abandon their posts and defect. For the allies, every rallier represented one less enemy combatant in the field. Some estimates placed the cost of killing one Viet Cong to be $9,000 alone just in ammunition expended; the cost of maintaining a Hoi Chanh [returnee] at a center and then reintegrating him in to South Vietnamese society, by comparison, was only $150.[200]

Every U.S. Navy boat and VNN junk was a Chieu Hoi rallying point but, given the logistical difficulties of escaping to the allied side by sea, most participants in the program defected on land, usually to South Vietnamese forces or bases in the countryside. Sea craft were more instrumental in spreading the word of the program in enemy territory than accepting defectors. Coastal Force bases, because of their remote locations, were particularly convenient rally points—yet another reason why the Viet Cong targeted Coastal Division 16 for attack in August. The VNN also mentioned the 15 July trawler intercept in many propaganda broadcasts around that time, which also may have antagonized the Viet Cong operating near Coastal Division 16.[201]

U.S. Navy PSYOP advisors generally authored the scripts for propaganda leaflets and broadcasts. All attended a six-week course in psychological operations taught by the Army at Fort Bragg, North Carolina, and received language, weapons, and counterintelligence training. Three advisors graduated from a 47-week Vietnamese language course administered by the Defense Language Institute in Washington, D.C., and many others completed courses lasting 12 weeks or longer. Lieutenant Commander Lawrence L. Combs, a Second Coastal Zone PSYOP advisor during the 1967–1968, wrote in his end-of-tour report that though the language course did not make him fluent, he still considered it of great value. "The value lies not so much in the practicalness as in the rapport that has usually developed between myself and the Vietnamese [with whom] I have come into contact."[202]

By October 1967 NAVFORV possessed 13 officers and 10 enlisted personnel with PSYOP schooling. All but two were advisors to the VNN, and most of these advisors were colocated with U.S. Navy units to provide guidance and assistance for U.S. Navy psychological operations.[203] Although the naval service had a long tradition of humanitarian operations and civic action, PSYOP was a relatively new field of warfare for the Navy in Vietnam. Before 1966, Navy psychological efforts had been limited to showing the flag, goodwill visits to foreign ports, and joint exercises. There was no clear-cut career path for PSYOP officers in the 1960s, and all took great professional risks to enter the field. Lieutenant Reiling, a 1962 Naval Academy graduate with command experience on minesweepers, had to invest nearly one and a half years of his career in specialized training (one year of language training at the Defense Language Institute plus six weeks of insurgency training at Coronado and another six weeks of PSYOP training at Fort Bragg) before he could deploy as a PSYOP advisor for the First Coastal Zone. Once in Vietnam, he faced all the usual hardships of being a Navy advisor at a VNN facility. The NAVFORV Psychological Operations Manual warned incoming officers that "living conditions at most Vietnamese Naval bases are unsatisfactory.... The water supply is inadequate in the dry season and non-potable all the time. Personal hygiene is totally lacking in some areas." Despite these hardships and others, most officers enjoyed the job and believed firmly that PSYOP could make a real difference in Southeast Asia. "I have never had a more productive or rewarding tour" Reiling wrote in his end-of-tour report.[204]

PSYOP advisors strove to write succinct broadcast messages that provided clear instructions on the mechanics of rallying to the allied forces or surrendering in combat. They also tried to reassure a potential Hoi Chanh that he would be treated well after defection, and that America intended to stay in Vietnam until the Communists were defeated. The messages also sought to exploit vulnerabilities without resorting to derogatory language, divisive techniques, or outright lies. Partial truths could be employed only "in the interest of security and the exigencies of tactical situations."[205]

Good intelligence could be critical in devising an effective broadcast. As one manual noted, "Knowledge of the audience and its personalities is very important. If a soldier hears his unit addressed correctly, his platoon officers called by name, and his casualty figures given accurately, he will react favorably to a loudspeaker message."[206] The best appeals often came directly from the Vietnamese themselves. For example, Lieutenant Ah, the commander of Coastal Group 46 at An Thoi in 1967, would stop at Ham Ninh village on the east coast of Phu Quoc Island on each patrol. He would discuss government policies, the Chieu Hoi program, and the need for no-fishing zones. Twenty-three military defections resulted directly from his efforts, and 90 civilians relocated from VC-controlled areas to Ham Ninh to be under the protection of Coastal Group 46 and Regional Forces based there.[207]

Because VNN coastal forces lived close to the local populace and spoke Vietnamese, they were in many respects the most suitable personnel for psychological operations. Every Coastal Force base painted Chieu Hoi rallying point signs in prominent places and on their junks. In I Corps, four out of six coastal groups conducted weekly waterborne speaker operations. According to Lieutenant Reilly, "Reaction from the VNN personnel has been most favorable. The VC are not quite as happy."[208] VNN hospital ships often participated in psychological operations concurrently with civic action. In July 1967, HQ-401 treated over 2,000 Vietnamese in need of medical or dental care in the Third Coastal Zone. During these humanitarian operations the ship's crew also distributed printed propaganda materials, and embarked government PSYOP teams conducted loudspeaker broadcasts. Sometimes "cultural platoons" riding on the ships would entertain the villagers, and at the conclusion of the performance a Hoi Chanh would give a brief address, extolling the virtues of the Open Arms program.[209]

Overall, during the second half of 1967, VNN coastal groups distributed 38,376 pyswar kits, 200 pounds of commodities and leaflets, and 750 gifts. These groups constructed schools, playgrounds, fresh water wells, a Buddhist pagoda, and a shrimp-drying pad and donated much of the building materials for these projects and others.[210] While many coastal force units made huge contributions to the PSYOP effort, it should be mentioned that some resisted. In a service where the average enlisted man barely made enough money to support himself, let alone a family, it seemed senseless to some to give away scarce commodities to civilians other than military dependents. "Civic action to my counterparts is first and foremost assistance to the sailors and their families in the first coastal zone," wrote LTJG Ross N. Driver, Assistant Psychological Operations/Civic Action Advisor for the First Coastal Zone in 1968. "I cannot recall one instance where my counterparts expressed a genuine interest in civic action directed toward the civilian population." Reiling concurred, "Military Civic Action is at present executed for instead of by the

VNN." If a coastal group was not authorized to use civic action materials for its own purposes, they often resorted to theft. "One reason for a shortage of civic action materials, such as wood or cement," wrote Driver, "was that such materials, according to my counterpart, were apt to be pilfered, no matter whether a special storage area was erected or not."[211]

The tremendous generosity of many American units made up for these shortcomings. In November 1967 alone, U.S. Navy units distributed 217,000 pounds of food stuffs, 373,000 pounds of lumber, and 57,300 pounds of cement to Vietnamese civilians in various civic action programs. In no area of civic action was the U.S. Navy more influential than in medicine and public health. Navy medical personnel ranging from enlisted hospital corpsmen to surgeons performed 36,514 medical exams, 3,428 dental treatments, and 1,254 immunizations in November 1967 alone, for example.[212] Navy medical personnel volunteered for this work, often during time off, and took great risks traveling with PSYOP officers to remote villages. According Lieutenant James R. Adams, the Fourth Coastal Zone PSYOP officer from June 1968 to June 1969, there were never any shortages of volunteers. Doctors eagerly volunteered because they wanted to get out of the base, see the country, and help people. For many, it was among the most rewarding work during their tours in Vietnam."[213]

Many Navy personnel performed these missions under the auspices of the Military Provincial Health Assistance Program (MILPHAP). Navy MILPHAP teams generally consisted of three doctors, a Medical Service Corps officer, and 12 corpsmen. In 1967 the Navy had seven teams stationed in the following provinces: Quang Tri, Quang Nam, Quang Tin, Lam Dong, Chau Doc, Ba Xuyen, and Kien Giang. The teams worked in provincial hospitals and often traveled to remote villages and even hamlets to provide care and wage preventative medicine campaigns. Working in overcrowded hospitals frequently in disrepair and lacking essential equipment and basic medical supplies, these teams quickly made their presence known, not only assisting local doctors with procedures but improving hygiene and sanitation as well. They also risked their lives on a daily basis. On 27 August 1967 the enemy attempted to overrun the compound of Navy MILPHAP Team Two in Quang Nam Province, seriously wounding three. On 27 September a sniper round wounded a member of MILHAP Team 5 ten miles southwest of Chau Doc.[214]

For all Navy medical personnel, whether participating in a MILHAP mission or a basic MEDCAP, the biggest challenge was not security or even the work environment, but the huge number of patients who would show up at village MEDCAPs for treatment. Demand always exceeded supply when it came to medicine in rural Vietnam. So as not to disappoint peasants who often waited hours in line for an evaluation, the Navy psywar manual advised Navy medical personnel to treat as many people as possible in as short a time as possible and refer complicated cases to the provincial hospitals. "Never, never tell a villager who says he is sick that he is not sick," it advised. "Give him sympathy and sugar pills."[215] Lieutenant James Adams, the PSYOP advisor to the Fourth Coastal Zone from June 1968 to June 1969, participated in many MECAPs and claimed that his team treated a lot of skin rashes and colds but also ran across the occasional gunshot wound. "We knew that these gunshot cases were probably Viet Cong, but we

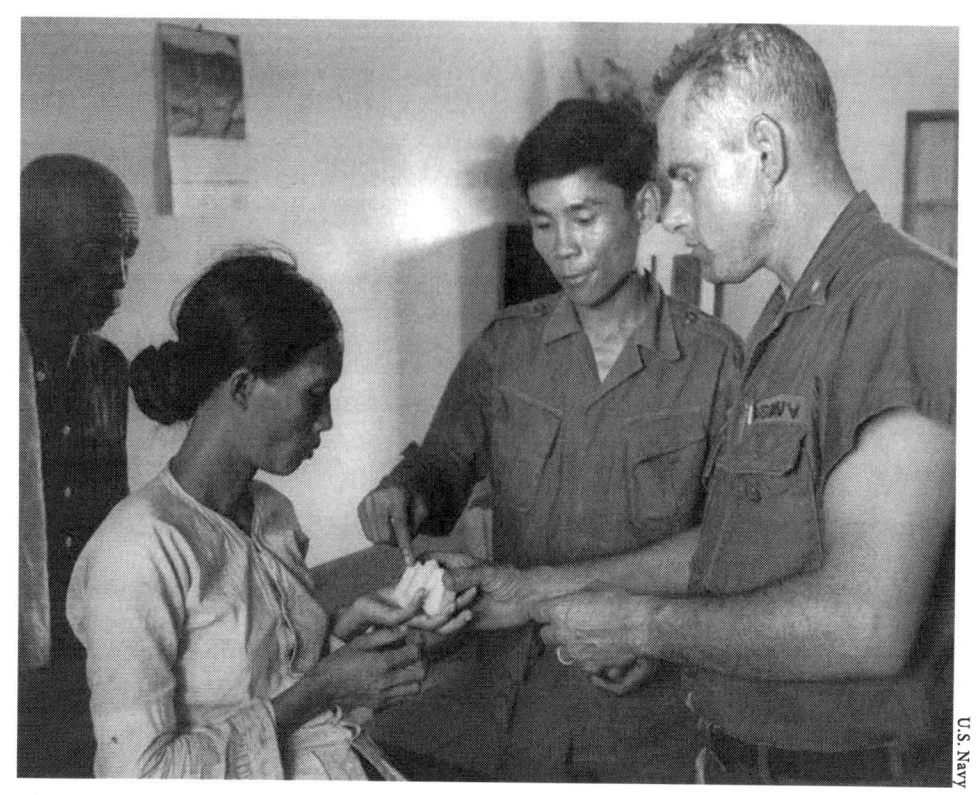

A hospital corpsman second class and a patient during a MEDCAP visit.

treated them nonetheless, cleaning their wounds and referring them to the provincial hospital for more comprehensive treatment." According to Adams, the purpose of the civic action was to convince the enemy that "we were the good guys," even if that occasionally meant providing limited medical treatment to enemy combatants or handing out food in Viet Cong villages. For him, humanitarian missions represented a much more effective form of psychological warfare than speaker operations or leaflet drops.[216]

Other advisors disagreed. Lieutenant (j.g.) John Francis Miller, the assistant Fourth Riverine PSYOP advisor in 1967, obtained fluency in Vietnamese from his language training and time spent in Vietnam, and therefore developed unique insights into the Navy's PSYOP programs. He believed that humanitarian aid often caused more harm than good. Villages that do not receive aid often developed strong resentment toward those who do, he observed. "The Vietnamese particularly resented seeing their children begging for candy from Americans. Schools and other facilities constructed by Americans often became targets of Viet Cong attack."[217] The COMNAVFORV Psychological Operations Manual advised officers to involve local communities as much as possible in these projects. Local Vietnamese should decide what should be constructed, and projects should be accomplished mainly with local labor. "The Viet Cong won't make much of an impression if they blow up a school which has been constructed wholly by the villagers for their children." Civic action's goal was to build mutual respect between the military and civil populations, and the only way to accomplish this end was to involve civilians in all aspects of these programs.[218]

Credibility also lay at the core of effective PSYOP broadcasts and leafleting. If a broadcast urged civilians to relocate from a Viet Cong area to a government-controlled area, the PSYOP officer, the manual warned, should be absolutely sure that the government area was properly secured. Similarly, a potential Chieu Hoi needed assurances that he would be well received by the government, and that his family would be taken care of after defection. Unfortunately for PSYOP officers, many Viet Cong were better off than average peasants. They generally lived at home with their families and had more to eat than their noncommunist neighbors. According to Miller, this type of Viet Cong

> ... laughs at the leaflets dropped on him, telling him how miserable he and his family are for he is not miserable. He laughs that he would be better off in a government controlled area, for he would not be. He laughs when he reads that the government is winning the war, because in his area, it is not. In short, he is relatively immune from the type of propaganda that is effective in much of the rest of the country. Only two things might persuade him to give up his cause; the belief that he and his family are in mortal danger, and the belief that the government really can offer him a brighter future.[219]

Psychological operations, no matter how effective, were no substitute for victory on the battlefield.

PSYOP Mission: 6 December 1967

Lieutenant (j.g.) Ed Bergin was not new to the Navy when he took command of PCF-79. His experience as the first lieutenant on the destroyer escort *Van Voorhis* (DE-1028) had given him a good introduction to the service and the many issues that boat commanders confronted at sea. Still, when he first met his future boatswain's mate Bobby Carver at Coronado, he knew that Carver would be a challenge to command. Carver possessed many years of seafaring experience and first-rate boatswain's mate skills but also an attitude that matched his service record. On the commercial flight over to Vietnam, Carver and Engineman 1st Class Ronald J. "Porky" Rinehart got so drunk and boisterous that the stewardesses nearly had them arrested in Alaska. "Look, I need these guys," Bergin pleaded with the captain of the Northwest Orient flight, "I won't be able to run my boat without them." The airline captain reluctantly agreed to allow the men to stay, and the flight proceeded to Saigon without further incident.

Once in Vietnam, Bergin and Carver immediately clashed. "He was a very knowledgeable boatswain's mate and I thought I was a very knowledgeable j.g., and I could feel this undercurrent of tension between us on each patrol." It all came to a head a month after the tour began when Carver referred to PCF-79 as "his boat." Bergin immediately corrected him, "It's my boat. But I'll tell you what. It's your boat when we're in port. That's when it needs fuel, ammunition, and stores.

Boatswain's Mate 2nd Class Bobby Don "Boats" Carver, right, at an awards ceremony in Vietnam.

Then, when I step aboard, it's my boat and stays my boat until I get off and then it's your boat." That cleared the air for a while, but after the two men had their next spat, Bergin threw down the gauntlet. He stared into Carver's steely blue eyes and said, "We can either duke it out or arm wrestle." Carver chose to arm wrestle. Fearless in the face of Carver's bulging bicep and the naked girl tattooed on his forearm, Bergin soundly defeated his boatswain's mate and then, according to Bergin, the two men bonded as friends. They both shared a love of the sea and had an aggressive attitude towards the Vietnamese. Combat on 15 July solidified this bond. "The intercept, according to Herrera, "bolstered Bergin's reputation for being an aggressive commander and I think Carver took great pride in serving under him."[220]

On 6 December 1967, PCF-79 was conducting a speaker broadcast mission south of Cape Batangan and not far from Coastal Division 16. Many TF 115 sailors resented these missions because it meant traveling close to the shore and broadcasting their position to the enemy.[221] "The speakers were so loud and cacophonous," noted one sailor, "that you often could not hear the discharge from a sniper rifle."[222] Bergin, however, was not one to shy away from a dangerous mission and agreed to take on the assignment. The boat ran along the coast most of the morning playing a pre-taped message urging the Viet Cong to surrender under the Chieu Hoi mandate. Around noon the boat pulled in a mile offshore for lunch, and while the men silently munched on their sandwiches, an albatross circled the boat and landed. Carver said it was a bad-luck omen.[223] The crew finished lunch and headed back to the beach to resume its PSYOP mission. Bergin told the coxswain to start the first run 50 yards from the beach and then back off 25–50 yards for each additional run. At 1400, Bergin received a call from an Army Piper Cub forward air controller, asking if he wanted to take four to five black-clad males on the beach under fire. Since the area was a free-fire zone, no higher authorization was required, but Bergin still hesitated. "Since they did not have any weapons on them, I thought they might just be fishermen and said no."[224] Carver then grabbed a pair of binoculars and closely examined the beach. "I think there may be bunkers there," he told Bergin. As he laid the binoculars on the aft .50-caliber/81mm mortar for Bergin to use, the Vietnamese opened fire. Carver shoved Bergin to the deck to get him out of the line of fire and began firing the .50-caliber.[225]

Raul Herrera, who was manning the radios during the attack, vividly recalled seeing water spouts from the Vietnamese fire coming towards the boat. One round hit the bottom part of the front windshield near where Herrera was standing. "We saw water spouts from the line of fire coming at us. That shocked me because if the boat had dipped, I would have been hit in the face or chest. I hit the ground when the glass shattered. I started making emergency calls to other boats, indicating that we were in a firefight."[226] Bergin, who by this time had gotten back on his feet and was firing a .30-caliber mounted on one of the stanchions, noted that the forward .50-caliber had jammed, and then he saw Carver lying on the deck. "I ran to the stern controls and hit the throttles just as Engineman 1st Class James Schneider, who was in the pilothouse, did the same thing, causing the engines to flood. Bergin restarted the engines and told Herrera to call for a medevac and alert the nearby destroyer about the situation. He then went to check on Carver, who was sprawled on the deck with a bullet hole in his head. The round had entered Carver's head just above the eyeball and exited from the rear of his skull, leaving a large, ugly exit wound.[227]

Herrera followed Bergin aft to help with first aid, but Bergin told him to back off. "I did not want Raul to see his boatswain's mate in this condition," Bergin later said. Herrera is still grateful to Bergin for his thoughtfulness. "Bergin really took care of me. I was so taken by what had happened and was so overwhelmed with anger that I took an M79 grenade launcher and fired a couple of rounds over the fantail. I don't know where those rounds went."[228] Bergin soon ordered him to cease fire and return to the radios while he began returning fire with Carver's .50- caliber. "They were dug-in to the sand dune and I just kept spraying the beach" until the boat was out of range. During the short ride to the destroyer, Schneider cradled Carver in his arms and tried to hold his head together with a compress bandage. Once on the destroyer, Carver, who still had a pulse, was immediately flown to Danang for additional treatment. After evacuating Carver, the destroyer commenced fire on the beach. "They pretty much tore up a quarter-mile of the beach with 5-inch guns."[229]

Ten minutes later as PCF-79 was transiting to Chu Lai, it received a radio call informing them that their boatswain's mate had died. In that moment Bergin felt more relief than remorse. "I was sick to my stomach that he was going to be blind and have all sorts of serious problems. I felt sort of guilty that I was relieved after he had expired because the wound was so horrendous." It was at that moment as well that the trajectory of Bergin's life completely changed. Before Carver's death, the lieutenant saw a bright future for himself in Navy. With the trawler victory under his belt and a chest full of combat medals, he had envisioned staying in the service for at least 20 years. Carver's death shattered these dreams. "Everything was so hazy after the boatswain's mate's death. It had such an impact on me. I became disenchanted with the war and decided not to pursue a career in the Navy even though the Navy had offered me a slot in flight school." Bergin left Vietnam in February 1968 and got out of the Navy shortly thereafter. He eventually became a salesman for IBM but stayed in the Reserves, later retiring as a captain. Herrera also left the Navy soon after returning from Vietnam in May 1968. He earned an associate's degree from San Antonio College and worked in land development and civil engineering.[230]

By July 1968 the Coastal Surveillance Force included over 5,300 American personnel and 126 vessels of various sizes. From 1 January 1967 to 31 March 1968, these forces detected 1,069,016 junks and steel hull ships; inspected 415,525 of these contacts; boarded and searched 253,804; and detained 1,192 junks and 10,920 people. So effective had this blockade become by July 1967 that the North Vietnamese did not attempt to infiltrate it with a steel-hulled trawler until early 1968, when it made four intercept attempts in two days.[231]

Desperate to resupply its forces during the Tet Offensive, the North Vietnamese gambled that they could overwhelm the barrier by making multiple infiltration attempts in a short period. On 29 February a Market Time aircraft reported a trawler 103 miles east of Cape Batangan on a course of 270 degrees at 12 knots. The Coast Guard cutter *Androscoggin* (WHEC-68) made radar contact with the infiltrator at 2047 local time and began maintaining covert surveillance. Early in the morning of 1 March, the trawler crossed into the 12-mile contiguous zone 22 miles from Cape Batangan, and *Androscoggin* soon challenged it by firing an illumination round. The trawler responded with machine gun fire, and *Androscoggin* returned fire with her 5-inch 38-caliber guns, hitting the trawler in the starboard quarter. Army helicopter gunships, *Point Welcome*, *Point Grey*, and PCFs -18 and -20 joined the attack as the trawler headed toward the beach. At 0210, the trawler beached itself and blew itself up in two attempts. During the battle, machine-gun rounds hit *Androscoggin* and other units but caused no casualties. Salvage crews later recovered a variety of military cargo from the scene, including 600 rifles, 41 submachine guns, and 11 light machine guns along with ammunition. Of the North Vietnamese crew, all that was recovered was a head and a full set of teeth.[232]

While this activity was taking place, *Winona* acquired a radar contact on a second trawler at 0105 on 1 March and headed to its location near Con Son Island in the IV Corps area of South Vietnam. The cutter followed the trawler as it steamed toward the mouth of the Cau Bo De River. At 0151, *Winona*'s commanding officer, Captain Herbert J. Lynch, USCG, calculated that he had 18 minutes to intercept the boat before he would have to share his prey with smaller inshore craft, now steaming towards the contact at flank speed. According to historian Paul Scotti, Lynch's strategy was to "crowd" the trawler and "give her little room in which to evade." Nine miles from the shore, *Winona* steamed within 1,100 yards of her quarry and signaled for it to stop. After lookouts reported seeing its crew jettisoning boxes over the side, Lynch ordered the 5-inch mount crew to fire a round across the bow. The trawler again failed to heed the warning and continued toward the beach. At 0202, *Winona* turned off her spotlight and opened fire at a distance of 550 yards from the vessel with 5-inch and 50-caliber guns. The trawler returned fire with .50- and .30-caliber machine guns. At 0207 the trawler exploded and disintegrated. The entire engagement lasted just five minutes. Lynch dispatched the trawler just two minutes before other units arrived. Thirteen machine-gun rounds hit the cutter, causing minor structural damage to the ship. There were three personnel casualties: one man's arm was grazed by a bullet, another was struck by shrapnel in the forehead, and a third was hit in the helmet by a 6-inch chunk of steel plate.[233]

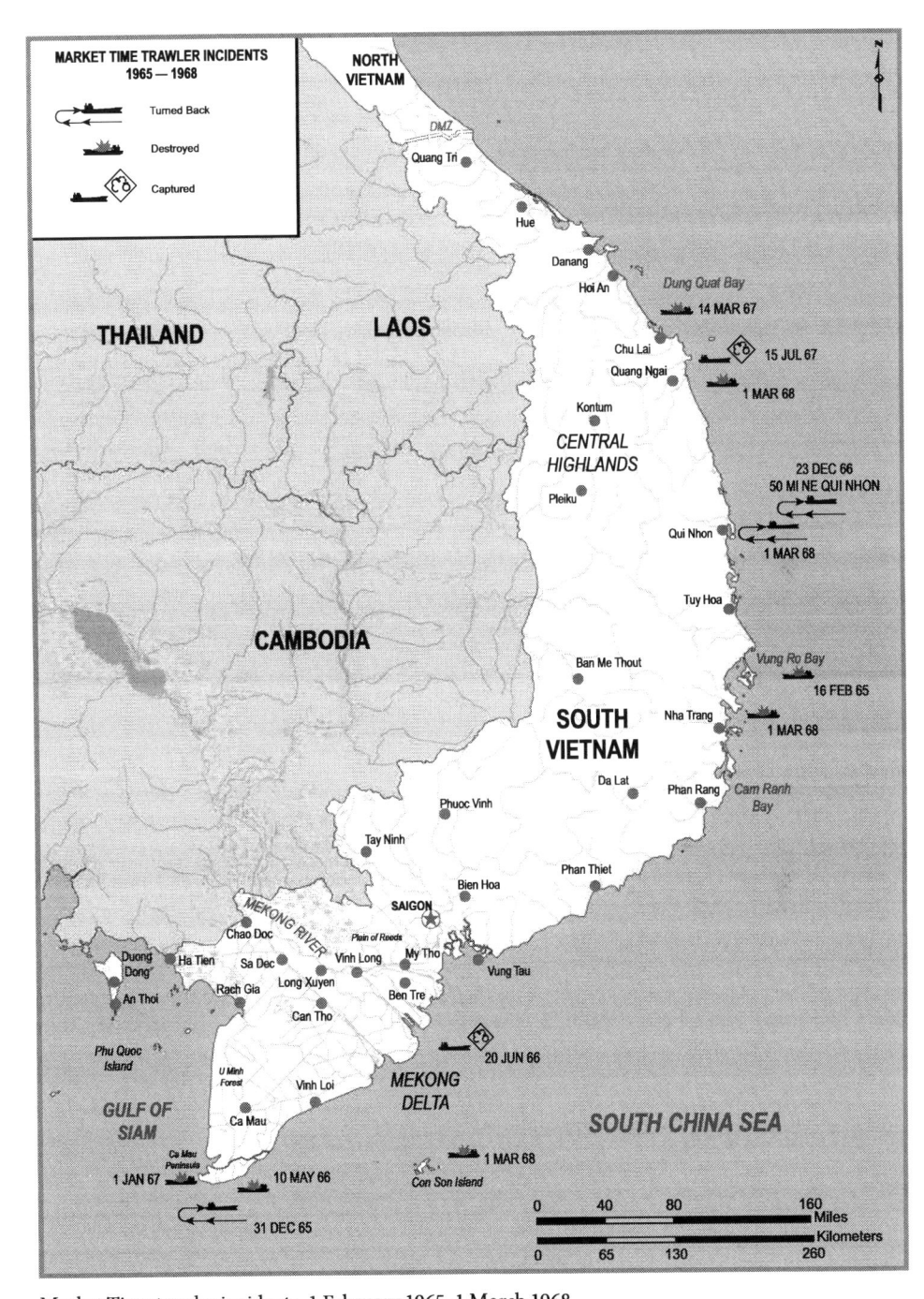

Market Time trawler incidents, 1 February 1965–1 March 1968.

A Market Time patrol aircraft had spotted a third trawler 91 miles east northeast of Nha Trang at 1714 on 29 February. Navy and VNN surface units kept the boat under surveillance until she crossed the 12-mile contiguous zone 28 miles northeast of Nha Trang. As she made her final approach to the beach, PCFs, VNN vessels, and an Air Force C-47 took her under fire. At 0200 on 1 March, the trawler beached 11 miles northeast of Nha Trang. PCFs and the AC-47 continued attacking while patrol escort HQ-12 and motor gunboat HQ-617 of the VNN hit Viet Cong positions on the beach with higher caliber guns. At 0230, the trawler exploded. U.S. and Vietnamese diving teams later recovered 14 enemy dead and a variety of contraband, including close to 150 rifles and submachine guns, 68 cases of 14.5mm ammunition, and 745 82mm mortar rounds.[234]

A fourth trawler had been discovered north of Qui Nhon on the afternoon of 29 February in international waters and trailed by *Minnetonka* (WHEC-67). At 0212 on 1 March, while the trawler was still in international waters, CTF 115 directed the cutter to "turn the trawler using any method short of taking it under direct fire." *Minnetonka* flashed its lights and fired illumination rounds and warning shots with her 5-inch guns but the trawler failed to stop. When it was 32 miles from the coast, the trawler suddenly changed course and headed toward mainland China. Market Time units trailed the ship until she entered Chinese territorial waters.[235]

Taken together, the three trawler sinkings and the one turn-away in 1968 represented the biggest Market Time victory to date.[236] They also represented a high water mark for the trawler interdiction campaign. By March 1968 infiltration attempts by the North Vietnamese tapered off considerably. "As time progressed," noted a 1969 Navy Market Time study, "tangible results slackened as a result of either more covert attempts by infiltrators or partial to complete abandonment of the inshore coastal route as a means of contraband infiltration." With a 94 percent success rate in stopping steel-hulled infiltrators and a 70 percent success rate in interdicting large wooden junks, it's no wonder that the North Vietnamese avoided coastal routes for infiltration and focused instead on the less well-defended border regions with Laos and Cambodia.[237]

As infiltration activity waned, Market Time assets were devoted to other missions—especially NGFS and PSYOP. Between January and March 1967, Market Time units conducted 1,345 NGFS missions, killing an estimated 300 Viet Cong and destroying over 305 structures, 99 bunkers, and 280 sampans. Market Time's 53 loudspeaker units also bombarded the coast with propaganda, and Coastal Surveillance aircraft dropped over 29 million leaflets. By 1968 Market Time units were traveling up to five larger rivers to conduct PSYOP, NGFS, and other missions. In 1968 they began raiding Viet Cong sanctuaries on rivers. In the first of these river raider missions on 20 August 1968, Market Time and VNN coastal group units hit Viet Cong bases seven miles up the Ong Doc River, destroying 62 structures and 16 sampans.[238]

Riskier missions along the river and close to the shoreline did not come without a cost. Between January 1967 and March 1968, 51 Market Time sailors received battle wounds serious enough to receive the Purple Heart, and five paid the ultimate price. They included BM1 Carver and the following men: Seaman Gary Wayne Friedman, Engineman 2nd Class Carl Raymond Goodfellow, Lieutenant (j.g.) William Henry Murphy III, and Seaman Dennis Ray Puckett.

Other sailors, like Lieutenant Fitzgerald, lost their lives as advisors serving heroically with the VNN under the worst conditions imaginable.[239]

By the end of 1967 the Viet Cong realized that it was often easier to attack scattered VNN and Market Time shore facilities along the coast than the surface units themselves. In addition to the Coastal Division 16 raid, the Viet Cong attacked Coastal Group 14, a VNN base 15 miles south of Danang on 20 April 1967, and Coastal Group 35 in the Mekong Delta on 10 October.[240] In these latter two cases, Coastal Force sailors repelled the assaults without any losses. The Viet Cong concluded 1967 with a daring attack on the Market Time and Coastal Group 22 base and adjacent VNN repair facility at Qui Nhon. An estimated platoon of enemy sappers blew up a command junk anchored off shore and then struck the bases. During the course of the night, U.S. and VNN sailors fought off the attack, killing seven Viet Cong, including two frogmen. The Viet Cong continued to lob mortar rounds into the facility for the next five days.[241] Two American sailors died in the attack: EN2 Goodfellow and Seaman Michael Joseph Di Napoli.[242]

TF 115's quest for greater involvement in the war effort would ultimately lead to SEALORDS, when Market Time units would begin taking over some of the river patrol areas from TF 116, thereby freeing up PBRs for upriver operations closer to the Cambodian border.[243] SEALORDS, with its emphasis on halting the flow of supplies from Cambodia to South Vietnam, appeared to accomplish what Market Time failed to do—prevent a major Communist offensive in the III and IV Corps Tactical Zones, at least until the operation was turned over to the VNN in 1971. Despite Market Time's success in stopping seaborne infiltrators in 1967, the Viet Cong still managed to lay siege to nearly every major city in South Vietnam during the 1968 Tet Offensive. Areas on the Mekong Delta previously thought to be secure "rear" areas would become battle zones. As hermetically tight as the naval blockade was in 1967, Market Time was not effective in and of itself at halting the flow of supplies to the Viet Cong as long as land and river avenues to infiltration remained porous. It wasn't until after the Tet Offensive that some planners in MACV began to understand this fact, and a more comprehensive strategy known as SEALORDs emerged.

CHAPTER 6

Tet, 1968

In the weeks and days leading up to the Tet Offensive, General Westmoreland was fixated not on the Mekong Delta or Saigon but on battles taking place around Khe Sanh, a base camp in northern South Vietnam not far from the DMZ and just six miles from Laos. Between April and May 1967, the 3d Marine Regiment had been fighting a series of engagements with communist forces located in hills above the camp. These battles convinced him that the North Vietnamese were trying to seize control of the area, thus setting the stage for the Battle of Khe Sanh. In January 1968 Westmoreland assigned half of all U.S. maneuver battalions in South Vietnam to I Corps—the tactical zone adjacent to the DMZ—and by mid-January 6,000 marines defended the Khe Sanh area and its surrounding hills. Forces of the People's Army of Vietnam (PAVN) launched their attack on Khe Sanh on 20 January, soon surrounding the marine base, and seemed poised to deliver a crushing defeat to American arms, something akin to the French loss at Dien Bien Phu. Fortunately, America's firepower and ability to supply the base by an air and river "bridge" would allow the marines to survive 77 intense days of fighting and bombardment.[1]

While Khe Sanh did not end up being a major defeat for the United States, it did draw attention and resources away from other areas of the country and left General Westmoreland with little in the way of reserves for many areas of the country, including the Mekong Delta. On 31 January 1968 Viet Cong units attacked nearly every major city and town in the region, including My Tho, Ben Tre, Vinh Long, Chau Doc, and Can Tho. In early 1968 the delta was defended by three ARVN divisions, the U.S. Army 9th Division, naval forces from Task Forces 116 and 117, various South Vietnamese Regional and Popular forces units, Civilian Irregular Defense Group forces, Vietnamese National Police, and Special Forces. However, over 50 percent of the ARVN troops were on leave for the Tet holiday, leaving only skeleton units in place to repel the offensive. In short, the initial communist attacks created a potentially disastrous situation. "My God, it's Pearl Harbor all over again," Brigadier General William A. Knowlton, the assistant commander of the 9th Infantry Division, remarked as he flew into the area on the second day of the offensive.[2] Fortunately for MACV, some very competent, battle-hardened soldiers, sailors, and Special Forces from the Mobile Riverine Force and Game Warden were on hand to prop up the South Vietnamese forces and help transform a potential defeat into a devastating blow for the Viet Cong.

On the eve of the Tet Offensive, the MRF consisted of a brigade of U.S. Army troops transported and protected by a collection of approximately 100 armored landing craft and other vessels organized into two river assault squadrons. The River Patrol Force (TF 116) comprised thirteen 10-boat PBR sections spread across the delta and the Rung Sat, plus five SEAL detachments and six light helicopter detachments.[3] How these men and their South Vietnamese and U.S. Army comrades in other units defended the delta's major cities and towns during the course of simultaneous attacks by seven VC battalions and numerous local force units remains one of the greatest triumphs of the war.

The Man at the Center of the Storm

At the helm of Task Force 117 during the Tet Offensive was Commodore Robert Salzer, who had led the unit since 25 August 1967. Salzer possessed skills often not found in a naval surface warfare officer—a superb grasp of land warfare and a highly flexible mind capable of adapting to the dynamic nature of the Tet attacks. Salzer's intellect, derived from an elite education and a propensity for lifelong learning, was the product of a social background distinctly different from many naval officers. Salzer neither came from a military family nor graduated from the Naval Academy. He joined the Navy during World War II out of patriotism and rose through the ranks, mainly because of his skills as a leader, securing a handful of prestigious ship commands as well as some unorthodox assignments in the mine warfare community, the intelligence field, and in the amphibious force. Through it all, Salzer managed to keep his naval career afloat by focusing on achieving what he believed should be the primary goal of every officer—wartime operational command.

The son of a medical doctor from Hungary, Salzer was born in 1919 and grew up in Far Rockaway, New York. His father, Dr. Benjamin Salzer, ran a successful Park Avenue medical practice catering to wealthy New Yorkers. When young Robert reached the 9th grade, Dr. Salzer shipped him off to boarding school at Phillips Exeter Academy. At Exeter, Salzer received one of the finest secondary educations available in the United States. He later praised the school for its emphasis on the Socratic Method and critical thinking. Prep school is also where Salzer learned to box—a sport he would continue to pursue during his first two years at Yale University. Boxing helped nurture his warrior soul and taught him a range of skills he would later draw upon as a naval officer in battle.

After graduating Phi Beta Kappa from Yale in 1940, Salzer had intended to pursue a graduate degree in economics at Columbia University, but the war intervened, and he applied for a direct commission in the U.S. Naval Reserve. Commissioned as a Reserve ensign in 1940, Salzer initially worked for the Office of the Chief of Naval Operations in the area of export controls before being assigned in 1942 to *Fulmar* (AMS-47), a motor minesweeper operating mainly in the North Atlantic.

The motto of the Navy's mine warfare community at the time was "Wooden Ships, Iron Men," and the 32 crewmembers of the 136-foot long *Fulmar* lived up to this reputation. "They were tough as nails and hard cases from the old Navy," explained Salzer. These men, most of whom had never graduated from high school, and the cruel winter seas of the North Atlantic transformed him from a landlubber to a sailor worthy of his own command. "I got seasick a lot initially, lost 20–30 pounds, but learned a lot about seafaring."[4]

In March 1943 he became officer in charge of coastal minesweeper *Summit* (AMC-106), an *Accentor*-class coastal minesweeper used to remove minefields laid by the Navy to protect ports and sea lanes. In July he took command of auxiliary motor minesweeper YMS-347, a "Yard"-class auxiliary motor minesweeper. With that vessel, he experienced his first combat—a sonar contact with a German submarine that may have resulted in a probable kill. "The thing about the YMS was that it solidified in my mind that probably the finest thing about the Navy was command."[5]

The high point of his World War II service was a tour as the commanding officer of LST-624 between June 1944 and December 1945. During this period the ship participated in the invasion of the Philippines and Okinawa and also survived the Okinawa typhoon of 1945. In April 1945 a kamikaze exploded 25 feet from the ship, showering the vessel with shrapnel and causing severe casualties among some Army troops who had come up to the deck to watch the attack.[6] In addition to this attack, Salzer also survived the epic Okinawa typhoon of October 1945, which sank 12 ships and grounded or damaged 254. LST-624 battled the storm at sea for three long days. "I got a very keen appreciation of how bad the sea can get when it can really get mad."[7]

After the war Salzer had planned to hang up the uniform. He began work with an investment bank in New York and found the work interesting, but it did not compare with the Navy. "I kept wondering is this all there is to life. Do I want to do this for the rest of my life? I missed the Navy." Salzer applied for a regular commission in 1946 and soon found himself in command of *Guadalupe* (AO-32), an oiler operating in the Western Pacific. He stayed with that ship for two years before returning to the Atlantic coast for shore assignments, including one at the Naval Intelligence School in Washington, D.C.[8]

From 1954 to 1956 he commanded the destroyer *Abbot* (DD-629). Under his command, the ship operated with the Seventh Fleet in the South China Sea and the Taiwan Strait. It also circumnavigated the globe, passing through both the Panama and Suez canals.[9] During the late 1950s Salzer served in the J-2 (Intelligence) Directorate of the Joint Chiefs of Staff and then attended the Industrial College of the Armed Forces (ICAF). Attending night classes, he earned a master's degree in business administration at The George Washington University (GW).

Time spent at ICAF and GW helped him with his next assignment as commander of *Bryce Canyon* (AD-36) based in Long Beach. On that ship he employed managerial innovations learned in his graduate programs to enhance efficiency, earning an excellence award in the process. From *Bryce Canyon*, Salzer went on to command two different destroyer divisions (132 and 192) followed by another stint in Washington, this time as head of the CNO's Analytical Support Group.

Yearning for an assignment that might allow him to participate in war operations, he accepted an assignment with the amphibious forces as Commander, Amphibious Squadron (PHIBRON) 4, rather than pursuing a more prestigious cruiser or destroyer squadron command. But PHIBRON 4 deployed to the Mediterranean and did not see any combat. Still, his experience in amphibs did put him in the running to become commander of Task Force 117, a job eventually offered to him in the fall of 1967.

He arrived in Vietnam with a view of the war quite different from General Westmoreland's. Salzer believed that the riverine forces should be employed to halt infiltration, not to search out and destroy the enemy's main units. He planned to establish multiple, integrated interdiction barriers with small units, which would include both ground and naval forces. He wanted to make the enemy come out and fight, and he reasoned the best method for achieving that end was to choke off supplies. When the enemy got desperate enough, it would come out of hiding and attack one of the barriers, thus allowing him to counterattack with rapid reaction forces. Westmoreland, who favored big-unit operations, dismissed Salzer's ideas, but later in the war General Creighton Abrams, Westmoreland's replacement, adopted them as part of Vice Admiral Zumwalt's new SEALORDS campaign.

As the commodore of TF 117, Salzer quickly developed a reputation as an officer who led from the front. Rather than monitoring big battles from the relative safety of *Colleton* or *Benewah*, he often accompanied his men to battle, either flying in a light aircraft or riding on a Mike boat or a CCB. Engineman 2nd Class Dwayne L. Parsons of Zippo Monitor 111-1 had fond memories of the man. "He impressed me for being hands on and riding the boats on every mission between the mounts. He was quite educated and all that, but he wasn't afraid to get in the mud with the GIs. He had a commanding personality. I liked him."[10]

Salzer also had an excellent relationship with his subordinate officers. "He gave me a lot of latitude to lead my unit as I saw fit," claimed Lieutenant (j.g.) Peter B. Rankin, the chief of staff for River Division 111. Rankin was especially grateful to Salzer for allowing him to give several battlefield promotions to his top enlisted men. "Medals are great but what these men really appreciated was the authority and increase in pay that came with advancement in rate." According to Rankin, Salzer was one of the few higher-ranking officers who understood the stresses of being a junior officer in TF 117. After a particularly tough mission, Rankin was once confronted in the bar by a TF 117 staff officer who demanded that he leave the bar immediately and complete his paperwork. Rankin told the officer off in not very polite language. When the senior officer complained to Salzer, the commodore simply advised him to avoid Rankin and took no further action. "I really appreciated him overlooking this unfortunate event. I was under a lot of strain then."[11]

Rankin was not the only officer under strain in Vietnam. Salzer himself nearly worked himself to death during his first tour there. Soon after his return to the States in 1969, he suffered a heart attack while playing tennis with a fellow naval officer. Unwilling to retire for health reasons, Salzer spent three months convalescing and then resumed work as a destroyer flotilla commander. In April 1971 he reported as Commander, U.S. Naval Forces Vietnam and once again plowed into his work. "He worked 18 hours a day, 7 days a week, and wrote many of his own messages," recalled Lieutenant Commander Paul E. Tobin, who served under Salzer during this tour as his aide. Salzer also read a lot about counterinsurgency and conferred with all the top experts in the field. While not a people person per se, he invested all of his energy into his job, and almost everyone who worked under him left their assignments duly impressed with their CO.[12]

On the eve of Tet, Salzer had a good idea that something big was about to occur. He had sensed a Viet Cong buildup in the weeks prior to the offensive and had even remarked to Rear Admiral Veth, COMNAVFORV, that "every little old lady in tennis shoes in the Delta seems to have her own personal B40 rocket launcher." When the attack came on 31 January, Salzer was with his Army counterpart, Colonel Bert David, in the Dong Tam command center. Reports began filtering in from one city after another that they were under attack. In all, the Viet Cong attacked 13 of the delta's 16 major cities, and it soon became clear to Salzer that the principal city in the northern delta, My Tho, was on the verge of falling. Rather than waiting for instructions from Saigon, also under attack, Salzer decided to act. "We didn't have any time or the slightest inclination to ask anybody. It was sort of like the cavalry coming to the rescue of the fort besieged by Indians or rather with the Indians already in it."

At My Tho, approximately 50 percent of the city's ARVN defenders had gone home for the holiday when three Viet Cong battalions entered the city. To prevent the city from falling before reinforcements arrived, Salzer and David flew in to meet with the 7th ARVN Division commander there. What Salzer found shocked him. "That son of a bitch was about to bug out. All he was doing was packing his car and wailing, 'My city is gone, my city is gone.' He had let his troops go on Tet leave and was totally unprepared for the attack. We just buoyed him up and he finally came to understand that an hour away the river cavalry was coming to the rescue. All of a

Colonel Bert David, USA, right, and Captain Robert S. Salzer, USN, the commanding officers of the Mobile Riverine Force during Tet 1968.

sudden he says: 'An hour? An hour?' " Salzer nodded and told him where to position his men in expectation of the rapid arrival of the MRF. According the Salzer, the general later became a corps commander. "He had just the right attributes to be a Vietnamese Corps commander."[13]

Storm Clouds

In the months leading up to Tet, the delta was far from quiet. On 4 December the MRF fought one of its biggest battles to date at the Rach Ruong Canal in western Dinh Tuong and eastern Kien Phong provinces (see chapter 4 for details). On 7–8 January, the 3d Battalion, 60th Infantry achieved heavy contact in the Don Nhon district of Vinh Long Province, killing over 30 Viet Cong.[14] Two days later on the 10th, the MRF again engaged the enemy during a two-battalion search and destroy in the Cai Be district of Dinh Tuong Province. During this latter engagement the Viet Cong killed 19 Americans and wounded another 54 while losing an estimated 47 of their own troops.[15]

In the days and weeks before Tet, Game Warden forces were also quite active, engaging in 61 firefights and suffering their highest casualty rates to date with one sailor killed and another 81 wounded; 120 Viet Cong were killed, 36 wounded, and 51 captured. The most significant engagements of the period occurred on the following dates:

- 2 January 1968: A Viet Cong 75mm recoilless-rifle attack against the Game Warden base at Nha Be wounded two sailors and scored a direct hit on an minesweeping boat, which burned for an hour and had to be stricken from the Naval Vessel Register following the attack.

- 4 January 1968: A Viet Cong company ambushed three PBRs from River Section 534 on the Mang Thit River, 13 miles southeast of Vinh Long. The enemy opened fire simultaneously from both sides of the river, wounding all three forward gunners in the opening seconds of the fight, and a fourth sailor in one of the coxswain's flats. The PBRs returned fire as best they could but had to leave the area shortly after the attack to medically evacuate the wounded. One sailor, Gunner's Mate 3rd Class Dell R. Claiborne, died four days later from a bullet wound to the head.

- 8 January 1968: A B40 rocket struck the after .50-caliber gun shield of PBR-738 on the upper Dong Tranh River. Shrapnel from the explosion wounded eight sailors and a Navy civilian from Navy Research and Development Unit 3. The River Section 524 PBR was a new Mark II variant on a test fire mission when the attack occurred.

- 18 January 1968: While chasing two sampans on the My Tho River, PBR-153 was ambushed by a VC platoon, which opened fire from the riverbank with 57mm recoilless rifles and automatic weapons. One rocket hit the coxswain's flat and another, the radar dome. Though seriously wounded, the boat captain, Boatswain's Mate 1st Class William R. Goldman, managed to maneuver the boat to the center of the river, where he and the other wounded could be evacuated by another PBR. In all, four sailors and one Vietnamese national policeman were wounded in the attack.[16]

Hostile actions such as these, especially the uptick in attacks with rockets and recoilless rifles, represented one indication that the situation in the delta was beginning to heat up. Another

Gunner's Mate 3rd Class Earnest McGowan sits in the gun tub of the twin .50-caliber gun mount on a new Mark II PBR, 13 January 1968. Many of these newer PBRs saw action during the Tet Offensive. On the Mark II, the ".50s" are electronically fired and sit low into the deck.

was the increase in suspected Viet Cong detained by Game Warden forces. In November 1967, PBRs arrested only 356 suspected civilians of military age lacking proper documentation on water taxis, sampans, and other river craft. By the end of December, that number jumped to 774; and by the end of January, to 1,257.[17]

Clearly, Viet Cong were infiltrating men and material via the rivers in the days leading up to Tet. One sailor who experienced this effort firsthand was Quartermaster 1st Class Ray Verhasselt, a boat captain with River Section 531. A soft-spoken westerner from Billings, Montana, Verhasselt had dreamed of having a warrior experience from the day he enlisted in the Navy in September 1962. His first ship *Pritchett* (DD-561) deployed to South Vietnam in 1964 and participated in naval gunfire support missions off the coast of South Vietnam, giving Verhasselt his first taste of combat and making him eager for more. With DD-561, Ray also found his place in the Navy, rising quickly from seaman to quartermaster second class. In the Navy, quartermasters assist in navigation and ship movement, and Verhasselt would prove exceptionally competent in this rating, becoming assistant navigator of the ship. Before his discharge in 1966 he passed the test for quartermaster first class (E-6) but opted to leave the Navy in an attempt to save a failing marriage. After 60 days out, he realized that his marriage was doomed and he reenlisted. "Once the recruiter guaranteed me my E-6, a $7,000 reenlistment bonus, and an assignment to Vietnam in PBRs, I signed on the dotted line. I wanted excitement, and I also knew that Vietnam would get me way, way away from my wife."[18]

On the night of 3 January 1968, Verhasselt's boat, PBR-103, was on the Ham Luong River about six miles from the South China Sea. At 2300 hours, Verhasselt shut down the engines and let the boat drift silently down the middle of the river. While his men took a break and tried to catch a brief nap, he stood watch at the helm, scanning the radarscope for activity. Because of the recent monsoons the river was high and filled with flotsam—tree branches, garbage, dead animals, and even the occasional corpse. This debris caused a lot of radar reflection, making it difficult to pick out targets. At one point Ray noticed a blip going across the river as opposed to downstream with the current. "That ain't right," he remarked to no one in particular, and then roused his men, alerted the cover boat two miles away, and took off at an angle for an intercept.

When the 103 boat got within a few yards of the contact, Verhasselt turned on the spotlight, and then "all hell broke loose." PBR-103 had just surprised a 20-foot-long motorized sampan filled with arms destined for use during the Tet Offensive. One of the occupants immediately jumped overboard. The other one followed as Verhasselt's engineman, ENFN Larry Burnett, attempted to take him down with his M16. Soon, Viet Cong on the western shore of the river were firing at the PBR with automatic weapons and a machine gun, but boat did not back down. Verhasselt maneuvered next to the sampan, which had its engine on and was running in circles, and hooked on to it with a grapnel. Without being asked, Burnett jumped off the boat into the sampan and pulled the sparkplug cable loose from the engine, thereby shutting it down. Meanwhile, the cover boat, PBR-101, made a close-in gun run against the enemy position on the beach. Under the command of Boatswain's Mate 1st Class Ivan Moon, PBR-101 lit up the beach with guns blazing and silenced the Viet Cong machine gun. The two boats departed the area with the sampan in tow. A search of the boat back at *Harnett County* uncovered 60 bangalore mines, 40 claymore mines, 200 electric primers, and 150 rounds of ammunition. The commander of the ARVN 7th Division, Brigadier General Nguyen Viet Than, later awarded Verhasselt a Vietnamese Cross of Gallantry for his role in thwarting this crossing.[19]

Despite this engagement and many others fought by Game Warden patrols and the MRF in January 1968, many senior officers in MACV headquarters believed that allied forces had essentially pacified the delta. On 9 January 1968, over two weeks prior to Tet, Army Brigadier General William R. Desobry, the outgoing senior U.S. advisor in the delta, proclaimed that the Viet Cong in his region were "poorly motivated and poorly trained" and that "ARVN now has the upper hand completely."[20]

Other officers saw the impending Tet holiday as an opportunity to lure Viet Cong deserters going on leave into the Chieu Hoi program. According the Brigadier General Knowlton, "We had more deserters from the Viet Cong forces come to our side during the Tet period than the entire rest of the year, each year. So we were quite delighted with the cease-fire." Knowlton and others hoped that while at home, away from the influence of political officers, many Viet Cong would "see the light" and convert to the government side. Knowlton also viewed Tet as an excellent opportunity to thwart infiltration along the Cambodian border, which often took place during these truce periods. What he and many others did not understand at the time was that most of the communist forces who fought in the Tet Offensive were either local Viet Cong already living in or near the major cities or troops who had infiltrated the delta during the months leading up to the offensive. The offensive was not a conventional cross-border invasion but an internal uprising of embedded forces.[21]

There were a few skeptics, however. Commodore Salzer believed that Desobry's claim about the delta being pacified was "self-intoxication, self-delusion, of the worst kind."[22] Another skeptic was Lieutenant General Frederick C. Weyand, the commander of II Field Force (the 9th Infantry Division's parent unit and a corps-level formation). Concerned about how quiet the Cambodian border appeared in mid-January, Weyand, with Westmoreland's permission, ordered a redeployment of U.S. forces from border areas closer to the national capital. By 29 January only 22 of II Field Force's battalions remained outside of the base area, while 27 were within helicopter-reinforcing distance of Saigon.[23] This last minute repositioning of forces arguably saved Saigon from complete disaster and allowed Salzer and David to focus attention on the delta rather than having to employ the MRF to reinforce Saigon.[24]

As mentioned earlier, most of the attention of the Saigon headquarters during the weeks leading up to the Tet Offensive focused on I Corps and Khe Sanh, not on the delta or Saigon. By 21 January the marines were completely surrounded and low on ammunition due to the loss of their ammunition depot early in the battle.[25] The U.S. Air Force began a focused effort to resupply the base by air, and allied aircraft commenced Operation Niagara II, an intensive bombing campaign against the North Vietnamese troops besieging Khe Sanh. On 25 January, General Westmoreland reported to Washington that the situation at Khe Sanh was critical and might represent the turning point of the war. To better support the besieged marines at Khe Sanh, General Creighton Abrams, the deputy commander of MACV, requested a greater naval presence in I Corps. Since the summer of 1967, PBRs had been providing river security on the Cua Viet, but Khe Sanh compelled NAVFORV to beef up this security force to better protect supply convoys moving along the Cua Viet to Dong Ha, a major air transshipment hub for Khe Sanh.[26] This naval force in I Corps was designated Task Force Clearwater in February 1967.

On 27 January 1968, the official seven-day Tet cease-fire began. That same day the MRF shifted its anchorage east of My Tho to Vinh Long in support of Coronado X, an operation designed to interdict VC resupply efforts in the western Dinh Tuong and eastern Kien Phong provinces. Three days later the Viet Cong launched surprise attacks against eight towns and cities in the I and II Corps tactical areas, prompting Westmoreland to rescind the Tet truce.[27]

On 31 January the Tet Offensive began in earnest with simultaneous attacks throughout the country, including a dramatic assault against the U.S. embassy in Saigon. Enemy artillery, mortars, or ground troops hit 29 of South Vietnam's 44 provincial capitals from the northernmost

Quang Tri Province to the southernmost An Xuyen. Sixteen were penetrated by communist troops, and eight were partially or completely captured.[28]

For the Navy, one of the most spectacular initial attacks occurred at the Vietnam Navy headquarters in Saigon. At 0300 on the 31 January, twelve Viet Cong sappers drove up to the compound in civilian cars, killed two guards at a barricade at Me Linh Square, and assumed control of the checkpoint. The majority of the unit then sped forward to the main gate of the base, but a quick-thinking VNN sentry, having heard the fire at the barricade, secured the gate and rang the alarm before they arrived. Lieutenant Commander Giam, the VNN command duty officer, ordered his gate sentries to withdraw in order to clear a field of fire for a .30-caliber machine gun positioned on the second floor of the headquarters. Fire from this gun disabled both vehicles (a Simca and a taxi) and killed or wounded several sappers. Meanwhile, another duty officer, Lieutenant Dinh, organized a counterattack with a small force of guards while a U.S. Navy advisor, Lieutenant (j.g.) Robert W. Ledoux, ran to the second floor of the advisor building to contact the U.S. Army military police. From an exposed window, Ledoux directed MP firepower against Viet Cong positions just outside the gate of the compound while Dinh's force attacked the Viet Cong from within facility. The combined hail of fire from the U.S. MPs and Vietnam Navy sentries effectively ended the assault. In all, the allies killed eight sappers and captured two.[29]

With a small group of sailors, Do Kiem witnessed the battle from just outside the headquarters facility. At one point, he ordered one of his men to fire an M79 grenade at some Viet Cong near the Tran Hung Dao statue just a stone's throw from the headquarters. He worried about damaging this monument to the famous Vietnamese general who repelled two Mongolian invasions in the 13th century, but circumstances left him with little choice. The grenade killed two enemy soldiers and only slightly damaged the statue. Do Kiem later examined the bodies and discovered that one was just a 16-year-old "simpleton" with his mouth "gaping stupidly open." In ten years of war as an officer with the VNN, this was the first time he had seen a dead enemy's face close-up. "I felt nothing inside, nothing. . . . I deserve a better class of enemy" was all he could think.[30]

In the delta, the Viet Cong attacked 13 of the 16 provincial capitals and captured large sections of Ben Tre, Can Tho, Chau Doc, My Tho, and Vinh Long on the first day of the offensive.[31] On the afternoon of the 31st, the MRF was conducting a sweep in the area along the Rach Ruong when it was ordered to airlift a company to Vinh Long to assist in the defense of the airfield there and another company to Dong Tam to reinforce the base. The MRF then withdrew from the Rach Ruong but was ambushed on the way out from both sides of the 30-meter-wide canal. The column, firing available weapons at point-blank range, ran the gauntlet for 25-minutes, suffering one killed, Boatswain's Mate 2nd Class William M. Comer Jr., the boat captain of ASPB 91-2. During the early hours of 1 February, the MRF assembled at the Mobile Riverine Base, refueled, resupplied, and rested for a few hours awaiting orders. At daybreak the MRF was ordered to head to Cai Be but at the last minute the orders were changed, and the elements of two battalions (3d Battalion, 60th Infantry and 3d Battalion, 47th Infantry) were instead diverted to My Tho, where they would arrive at 1515 on 1 February.[32] GMG3 John Green, with the MRF at the time, vividly recalled the scene:

> Everybody silently went to their boats, put on their flak jackets, and checked their weapons. No one said a word. We automatically got in a column, loaded the troops up, and headed to My Tho. We were going to take back a city and we felt really proud about it. One of the ammo barges took a direct hit and the sky lit up just like the scene in the film *Apocalypse Now*. No one said a word. We just kept sailing.[33]

From that day until 10 February, the MRF was involved in nearly continuous movements, maneuvering and fighting over a large part of the delta. Orders were usually verbal, and operational planning had to be completed in utmost haste, usually on the fly. Through it all, however, the MRF, as the 3d of the 47th Infantry action report noted, performed "magnificently."[34]

My Tho

At My Tho, an estimated 1,200 Viet Cong fighters from three battalions (261st, 263rd, and 514th), plus a sapper company (207th), entered the city while another battalion stood in reserve on the outskirts. The only defenders in the city were a squadron of the 6th ARVN Armored Cavalry, and one battalion of the 11th ARVN Infantry Regiment, supplemented by Vietnamese RAG units and U.S. Navy personnel based in the city. As in most other Tet attacks, this one began with mortar and rocket fire followed by a ground assault led by the sapper company. Once inside My Tho, the Viet Cong vanguard linked up with guerrillas who had infiltrated the city in the days leading to Tet. These infiltrators served as guides for the main force units, pointing out predetermined targets and fighting positions. Propaganda teams then came in and attempted to win over the local populace to the Communist cause.[35] It took the allied forces three days to take back the city in a battle that featured intense urban warfare—a type of combat never before experienced by the Mobile Riverine Force.

Lieutenant Robert Fuscaldo, the officer in charge of River Section 532 was having dinner with the family of his Vietnamese interpreter in My Tho on the night of 30–31 January. "They served a deboned roasted chicken filled with meat. I had never seen that before—these perfect looking chickens with no bones, and I was just about to cut into one when I heard a mortar round land." At first, Fuscaldo assumed it was just another mortar attack. "We used to get mortared a lot and you got to the point where you could almost sleep through a mortar attack because you knew they weren't close." However, on that night more rounds than usual seemed to be falling on the city, so Fuscaldo excused himself, went back to his base, and ordered several PBRs to go up the canal near the base, hoping to catch some of the enemy in the open. The PBRs, along with troops from the 32nd ARVN Ranger Battalion, made contact, killing a large number of the enemy. According to Fuscaldo, "There were so many bodies in the semi-circular canal surrounding the base there that you could almost walk across."[36]

Lieutenant Richard J. Cragg, the outgoing senior patrol officer of River Section 532, was awaiting transportation to Saigon when Tet occurred. "I woke up that night to explosions. I went out and found much of My Tho on fire because of the Viet Cong attack. I did not have a weapon anymore, and was completely by myself." Rather than hunker down in the Carter Hotel, Cragg decided to volunteer to help a group of SEALs and Army advisors defend the city. They gave him a helmet, flak jacket, and a sawed-off shotgun with flechette rounds. For the next two days, he helped evacuate Vietnamese wounded and even went on a few patrols.[37]

Quartermaster 3rd Class Ken Delfino, a Filipino-American sailor with River Section 533, was sleeping in the Carter Hotel at 0400 on the 31st, when the Viet Cong attacked. Earlier in the evening, he had celebrated the Vietnamese New Year with members of the Philippine Civic Action Group (PHILCAG) unit housed in a villa near downtown My Tho and was trying to sleep off the effects of one too many San Miguel beers. Still buzzed from the alcohol, he almost slept through the initial mortar attack but was eventually awakened by the staccato sound of machine-gun fire and his boat captain, Boatswain's Mate 1st Class Jim Hicken, urging him to wake up. He dressed quickly in fatigues, choosing to wear his black beret rather than a helmet for easier recognition and grabbed his sawed-off M1 carbine, some extra ammunition, and headed for the Tactical Operations Center housed in the Victory Hotel nearby on Avenue Le Loi. He took two steps across the street and then froze when he heard the unmistakable sound of a .50-caliber machine gun being loaded. "Delfino coming over," he yelled. The response was "Who won the 1967 World Series?" to which he replied "St. Louis!"

At the TOC, he learned that the PHILCAG team was trapped in the villa, located about a mile away near the point where Highway 4 enters My Tho from the east—the so-called "Y" intersection. Delfino asked Commander Sam Steed, the commander of River Division 53, if he could round up some volunteers to rescue the team, which included several female Philippine army medical officers. Steed agreed, and Delfino quickly found several willing sailors, who armed themselves with Winchester pump-action shotguns and M16s, and loaded onto a truck for a quick ride to the villa. When the truck neared the Y, it dropped off Delfino, Gunner's Mate (Guns) 2nd Class Rich Wies and Gunner's Mate (Guns) 3rd Class Dennis Keefe, who made their way cautiously to the villa, hugging the building as they moved down the deserted street. "Bodies and debris were everywhere ... in the streets, on the sidewalks and in the blasted buildings. The smell of burning flesh was thick in the heavy air ... a smell I've never forgotten." The sailors retrieved the PHILCAG personnel and drove them to the hospital, where they could begin work assisting the medical staff with the wounded. Delfino's group of volunteers then patrolled American facilities in My Tho in a blue USAID (United States Agency for International Development) jeep for the rest of the day, at one point firing on a suspected Viet Cong position near the soccer field.[38]

Fire Control Technician G (Gun Fire Control) 3rd Class Stephen Sumrall does not remember exactly where he was in My Tho when the attack transpired, but he remembers vividly what happened next. Because he was scheduled to rotate home, his parent unit, River Section 532, left him and five other sailors in My Tho a day after the attack began. "As the PBRs were leaving the pier, I yelled out to an officer, 'What are we supposed to do?' He replied, 'Just wait there until an Army convoy picks you up and takes you to Saigon.'" That never happened, and Sumrall wound up being stranded in My Tho for the next three weeks. "We survived because the SEALs had set up a perimeter around our billet, and I really feel the reason that the enemy soldiers didn't try to take the compound was because of the fierce resistance put up by the SEAL team."[39]

One day he escorted an Army officer to a communications facility a few blocks from town. "At one point we got pinned down by snipers behind some trash cans, and fortunately a Korean force came running up the street and took out the snipers." On another day a Navy maintenance officer told him and the other sailors to report to the civilian hospital two blocks away near the soccer field. The hospital only had two doctors and three to four nurses, and desperately needed orderlies. When Sumrall arrived there, he found the main hallway of the hospital filled with civilian and military casualties. "Our job was to hold down patients while doctors amputated limbs. It was a horrific environment, and after two days I could not go back. I couldn't take it anymore." Eventually, Sumrall and several of his transient shipmates were transported to Saigon in an Army helicopter. "We were very appreciative to the pilot. We told him thanks for not leaving us there a moment more."[40]

Harry Constance was one of the SEALs whose actions saved Sumrall and many others trapped in the Carter and Victory hotels. The Quartermaster 1st Class Terrel E. Carter Billet was named after a sailor who was killed in action in 1967 (see chapter 3). Built by the Navy in 1967 to house an additional river section and a SEAL contingent, the billet was located half a block from the other Navy housing facility, the Victory Hotel. Sailors in the Carter billet had to walk to the Victory for chow and to receive briefings. By 1968 the Victory Hotel not only contained billeting but a kitchen, a mess, a cold storage facility, and a sandbagged rooftop Tactical Operations Center equipped with encrypted high-frequency radios capable of communicating with other PBR bases and LSTs in the delta. In January 1968 the Victory had enough food, water, ammunition, and diesel fuel to last three to five days or even longer in the event of a siege, but those living in the Carter Hotel had to subsist mainly on C-rations during the early days of Tet.

On the first night of the attack, Constance and his SEAL Team 2 comrades were relaxing on the roof of the Carter Billet drinking beer and watching tracer rounds that they thought were being fired in the air in celebration of the Tet holiday. A team member informed the group that My Tho was under attack and that they should take up positions to defend the hotel. Several days earlier Senior Chief Interior Communications Electrician Robert Gallagher, the highest ranking enlisted SEAL in the group, had told the team to begin moving weapons and ammunition from the SEAL compound on the waterfront to the Carter Hotel in the event it was attacked. On 31 January, Senior Chief Gallagher's foresight paid off. Team 2 had stocked their rooms on the third deck with plenty of assault rifle rounds, M79 grenades, and ammunition for Stoner light machine guns—enough ammunition to defend the building during the first tense hours of the attack.[41] Gallagher would later receive a Navy Cross for his heroism in a night action on 13 March 1968.[42]

When enemy troops began nearing the Carter Billet, Constance and several of his SEAL Team 2 teammates took up fighting positions on the third deck of the billet. At one point, he remarked to Aviation Electrician's Mate 2nd Class Curtis Ashton, "Can you believe this?" Ashton smiled and replied, "I think it's great. All of our trips into the jungle and now they are coming to us!"[43] During the first night of the attack, several SEALs armed with sniper rifles[44] kept enemy troops at bay by dropping any enemy soldier foolish enough to get near the billet.[45]

A respite in the fighting at 0715 on the 31st allowed the SEALs to retrieve more weapons and ammunition from the SEAL compound and fortify their hotel fighting positions with more sandbags. Along the roof the SEALs established multiple sniper positions. They also drafted many of the resident sailors as riflemen. According to Constance, the sailors "were excited about getting hardware and ammunition to effectively fight. They appreciated us, realizing we weren't going to abandon them." This effort was worthwhile because the enemy made no concerted effort to capture the hotel. Viet Cong, armed mainly with light arms, could not get near the hotel without suffering from a barrage of deadly fire from SEAL marksmen stationed on the roof. "We wanted to give them the impression that we were loaded for bear and good to go," Constance later wrote. "The more time we had, the better our strategic viability. If we could stay alive, it bought time for reinforcements and relief."[46]

SEALs Terry Sullivan, left, and Curtis Ashton with a captured Viet Cong in the My Tho area, 1969.

The ruse worked. Whenever the SEALs saw a Viet Cong making his way toward their perimeter, one of the SEALs would kill him with a well-placed round.[47]

Constance described one such experience as follows:

> I ran my scope up on 12 power and scanned the outlying streets. Approximately six hundred yards to the north of us was a group of seven NVA [more likely Viet Cong] soldiers discussing something. I placed my crosshairs on them. At this distance, they had no idea I was there. I put a round in the chamber. Next, I laid the rifle on sandbags and took a deep breath. Sigh. Squeeze. *Bam!* One of the NVA soldiers did a backwards cartwheel. Animatedly, the remaining soldiers looked around in alarm. They searched the surrounding buildings and touched off a few rounds for good measure. There was so much shooting going on all around us that they couldn't figure out where my solitary shot came from. *Bam!* Another soldier hit. They went crazy. They couldn't think to look 600 yards away. Fifty to one hundred yards away, but not any farther. Jesse and I had a ball.[48]

In the end the spirited defense by the SEALs prevented the Carter Hotel from being overrun. "We never suffered a serious assault," recalled HMC Erasmus "Doc" Riojas, the SEAL Team 2 hospital corpsman, "We took mainly rocket and mortar rounds, most hit near the hotel but not on the hotel."[49]

One of the pervasive memories for Constance, Riojas, and others of Tet was the smell of decaying bodies. Hundreds of bodies, mostly civilians killed by the Viet Cong, were stacked in a courtyard near the Carter Billet until relatives could retrieve them. The civilian hospital, inundated with casualties, could not properly handle the carnage, and many innocents died from lack of adequate medical care. During the battle at one point, the SEALs on patrol began taking fire from the hospital. Although they could have easily destroyed these positions with light antitank weapons (LAW) rockets, the team risked taking counterfire to acquire targets visually and take them out surgically with M16 rifles.[50]

One civilian who vividly recalled the events in My Tho during Tet was Nguyen Thi Lung, a 10-year-old girl housed in a Catholic orphanage. During the evening of the 31st, the sound of explosions and the acrid smell of smoke rudely awakened this young amputee from her slumber. She and a schoolmate tried to escape from the dorm but instead ended up hiding under a stairwell when she caught sight of Viet Cong running past the open gates of the orphanage. "They had slim bodies, carried long weapons, and did not wear uniforms," she wrote in her memoir. The Viet Cong took over the orphanage and used it as a fighting position until an ARVN armored tank counterattacked. "I saw two of the black figures fly through the air, their arms outstretched, and land like rag dolls on the ground. The heat and shock of the blast took my breath away." Soon after the tank arrived, the Viet Cong abandoned the orphanage, and as one of the fighters near her left the building, she noticed that he looked like a frightened teenager. Lung stayed in her hiding place until dark before she dared venture outside. In the courtyard, she found several of her classmates and a priest huddled over the lifeless mass of one of her best friends, Phuong. "Phuong's face was an unrecognizable mass of blood."[51]

The priest told Lung and a classmate to find a water taxi, escape to her former village, and try to take shelter with a relative. Because Lung had a prosthetic leg, the journey to the river was not easy, and she found herself tripping frequently over debris in the roads. She passed dead bodies and smoking buildings, and heard frequent gunfire, but eventually made it to the river where she ended up traveling to her village in a water taxi seated next to an ARVN soldier bleeding from a wound to his side. When she reached her destination and departed the boat, the soldier slumped dead to the bottom of the boat, his eyes staring blankly at the sky.[52]

The tide of the battle of My Tho changed dramatically with the arrival of MRF units. Beginning at 1518 on 1 February, three companies of the 3d Battalion, 47th Infantry landed unopposed on the southwestern edge of the city and then swept north, initiating clearing operations. These units were soon joined by elements of the 3d Battalion, 60th Infantry and two additional companies from the 3d Battalion, 47th Infantry. "The city had to be cleared slowly and systematically," wrote Brigadier General William Fulton, at the time the assistant 9th Infantry Division commander. "Pockets of enemy resistance had to be wiped out to prevent the Viet Cong from closing in behind the allied troops." Air support and artillery were often used to dislodge stubborn defenders from buildings, but the Army soon found itself taking casualties. At 1630, Company A, 3d Battalion, 47th Infantry requested a dustoff for five wounded and at 1634, requested a helicopter light fire team to support its point element, which was pinned down by strong enemy fire. The fire team arrived at 1825 and immediately began placing fire just 25 meters from American positions. Desperate to evacuate his wounded, the commander of the 1st Platoon, an Army lieutenant, sprinted through a hail of bullets to an abandoned ARVN jeep parked in the street. Ignoring intense enemy machine-gun fire, he drove the jeep to his wounded, loaded the men on board, and then drove to a safe area behind company lines where a dustoff flight could get in and evacuate them to an Army hospital. After completing the evacuation of the wounded, Company A moved to the rear and assumed the role of battalion reserve.[53]

In the meantime, the 3d Battalion, 60th Infantry also continued moving north under heavy fire. Battalion movement was slow, but effective, as troops moved from house to house, clearing enemy defenders as they were discovered. Artillery strikes were called in on Viet Cong fleeing the area. At 1955, a group of Viet Cong engaged Company B, 3d Battalion, 60th Infantry, and an intense firefight resulted. By 2020, the company had killed 15 Viet Cong, suffering only two wounded in the process.[54]

American forces continued receiving sporadic fire until 2100, when many of the Viet Cong defenders, under the cover of darkness, began withdrawing from positions. Throughout the night American units received sniper fire but fought no major engagements. At dawn the next day the U.S. battalions resumed their attack against the remaining enemy strongholds in the city and along with Vietnamese units tried to prevent any remaining Viet Cong from escaping the noose slowly tightening around enemy positions. Resistance was light, and the last pockets of resistance north of the city were cleared by 1000. "By this time," wrote Fulton, "the Viet Cong offensive had lost much of its original intensity in Dinh Tuong Province and the enemy appeared to be withdrawing north and west." Hoping to cut the Viet Cong off as they egressed from the My Tho area, the MRF departed on armored troop carriers at 1201 for redeployment to Cai Lay.[55]

The success of the Mobile Riverine Force at My Tho can be measured by how rapidly the Viet Cong defense collapsed after the MRF landed at the edge of the city and by the relative casualties incurred by both sides. Within hours of the assault, the Viet Cong were abandoning their hard-fought-for positions and moving out of the provincial capital. Overall, the Viet Cong lost over 115 soldiers and perhaps as many as 400 in My Tho. By comparison, the MRF lost three soldiers and the ARVN, 25. Fifty-seven Americans and an undetermined number of ARVN troops were wounded in the battle.[56]

American soldiers searching bodies after the battle were sometimes shocked at what they discovered. Many of the enemy dead were youths between 14 and 16 years old. Interrogations of captured Viet Cong revealed that many of these child soldiers had been inducted only days prior to the offensive and had received only rudimentary training.[57] Huynh Ly was a 25-year-old platoon commander in VC Battalion 263 during the battle of My Tho, and his experience was typical of some of the enemy defenders. During Tet his small unit fought mainly against ARVN forces from a single, fixed battle position located in a private house. "I fought in that house for two and a half days. When the house was blown up, we left and walked out of My Tho late in the afternoon." During the battle, eight of Ly's soldiers were killed and another 20 wounded. Ly survived Tet unscathed but later in the war was wounded by a .50-caliber bullet fired from an M113 armored personnel carrier.[58]

If the MRF was the biggest winner at My Tho, those who lost the most were civilians. In all, 64 of them died in the attack on city and another 638 were wounded.[59] In the Dinh Tuong Province as a whole, the MACV advisor in the IV Corps Tactical Zone estimated conservatively that 528 civilians were killed and another 1,219 wounded. As Stephen Sumrall's experience revealed, casualties quickly overwhelmed local hospitals, and many of the wounded later perished from the lack of proper medical care and infection. Overall, civilian hospitals in the IV CTZ admitted 7,000 casualties during the Tet Offensive, and all but the most critically ill were either discharged or turned away. Making matters worse, over 190 key civilian medical personnel in the zone were on leave for the Tet holiday and could not return to their posts after the attack began.[60] Rod Davis could not believe the conditions he witnessed at one hospital. "I went down to the province hospital where we would medevac people, and it looked like the railroad station scene from *Gone with the Wind*. The whole yard of the hospital was full of people on stretchers. There was a 60mm mortar round that hadn't exploded in the middle of the yard with sandbags around it. It had not been disarmed."[61]

Because the attack shattered My Tho's fragile public works system, sailors were enlisted after the attack to collect bodies scattered around the town. Harry Constance and several other members of SEAL Team 2 drove around town in a deuce-and-a-half truck in 90 degree heat, first delivering food to civilians who either worked at the Navy compound or were SEAL informants, and then picking up bodies, mostly civilians and Viet Cong. "The bodies were rank, bloated, and horribly disfigured." Constance remembered seeing a lot of charred human flesh and struggling to place decomposing bodies, which were literally falling apart, into the truck. Having nowhere to properly dispose of the bodies, they dumped them in the river.[62]

Civilians who did survive were often left homeless. Over 4,939 homes were destroyed, mainly from allied artillery and air strikes, but also from VC mortar rounds and rockets, as well as by fires started by tracer rounds used by both sides.[63] This destruction displaced 5,674 families and created over 39,000 refugees in a district of 129,922 people. Provincial officials were only able to house 8,569 of these refugees in temporary camps, leaving most to fend for themselves.[64] When QM1 Verhasselt returned to the city after spending four long nights on his PBR, he found it heavily damaged. "I have pictures of a bus turn-around station with five or six burned busses. Two of our utility vehicles had bullets all over them. I remember an M113 with a rocket hit in the front of it." Back at the Carter Billet, a Vietnamese maintenance manager told Verhasselt that the Viet Cong had entered his home and shot his daughter in the foot after he refused to give him information about the Americans. Other Vietnamese told him about how the Viet Cong had taken over schools, orphanages, churches, and medical facilities, hoping that the Americans would not bomb them. They also killed some of the occupants of those places, including wounded ARVN soldiers and even children.[65] Quartermaster 1st Class Robert W. Smith, a boat captain with River Section 532, remembered returning to the Victory Hotel after Tet only to learn that his Vietnamese best friends, the bartender and his wife, had lost their home. "Before the battle, they had invited me to their home on numerous occasions. I only went twice. They had two or three kids, and always served me a very good meal. I felt so sorry for them." Although homeless, the couple continued to work at the Victory Hotel for the remainder of Smith's tour.[66]

Ben Tre

Wedged between two branches of the Mekong River and crisscrossed by several smaller canals and rivers, Ben Tre lies 13.3 kilometers south of My Tho. In 1967 it had a population of approximately 74,544 and was the capital of Kien Hoa, an island province surrounded by water with no bridge links to any of its four neighboring provinces.[67] In January 1960, one of the very few high-ranking Communist women, Nguyen Thi Dinh, led the first large-scale armed rebellion against the South Vietnamese government at Ben Tre. Nguyen Thi Dinh's insurgents captured ten government buildings and assassinated 43 individuals before an ARVN force retook the city ten days later.[68] Although Nguyen Thi Dinh was unable to establish a permanent liberated zone for the Communists, the rebellion provided great inspiration for insurgents in the south.

Because of Ben Tre's significance as the cradle of the southern insurgency, and also because the rural area surrounding it provided excellent terrain for guerrilla operations, the Viet Cong utilized this area as an important base for much of the 1960s. Army Brigadier General William Desobry, the IV Corps advisor, noted in a 1968 debriefing report: "The population is fractured, is dissident and in general has little if any history of loyalty to Saigon. The 7th ARVN Division has had little success in operating here in the past two years."[69]

Despite the heavy VC presence in the Kien Hoa Province countryside, Ben Tre itself was relatively peaceful just months before Tet. Lieutenant Wynn Goldsmith, a patrol officer with River Section 534, found the town very pleasant when he first visited the place in the fall of 1967. He had expected "mud huts" but discovered a medium city with well-maintained houses undamaged by war and many buildings with stucco facades and aesthetically pleasing red-tile roofs.[70] The situation would change dramatically on 31 January, when the Viet Cong decided to seize this symbolically important city.

At 0415 in the morning of the 31st, a force of approximately 800 Viet Cong from the 518th Main Force and the 516th Local Force battalions began their attack on Ben Tre.[71] On that day the city was defended by two battalions of the 1st Brigade, 7th ARVN Division, and about 70 American advisors and Central Intelligence Agency (CIA) personnel housed in the MACV compound—a full city block of military buildings surrounded by a 10-foot-tall masonry wall in downtown Ben Tre. Within 16 hours of the first attack, the Viet Cong controlled virtually the entire city. The only territory still in allied hands was a four-square-block area surrounding the MACV compound. With the MRF focused on saving My Tho, Ben Tre's defenders had to rely mainly on airpower and naval gunfire support from PBRs to keep the enemy from completely overrunning their positions.[72]

Wynn Goldsmith was drifting in the PBR-721 along the Ham Luong River not far from Ben Tre when he heard fire from city. Like many others, he first thought that Vietnamese soldiers might be celebrating the Tet but soon noticed the telltale VC green tracer rounds and decided to run his boat and PBR-720 down the Ben Tre Canal to investigate. About a mile into the canal he came across six South Vietnamese LCVPs along the north bank firing at targets on the south bank. Goldsmith alerted the MACV compound, which in turn told him, "Stay close. We might need you."[73]

Shortly thereafter, the compound requested gunfire support from Goldsmith's section, and his boats headed up the canal to assist. As they passed the Vietnamese Coastal Force junks, Goldsmith turned on his sirens and ordered all lights on the recognition masts of the PBRs switched on to alert the South Vietnamese forces of their presence. The warning worked, and the junk force sailors ceased firing as the PBRs approached. Wearing nothing but underwear, the junk sailors cheered when the PBRs passed by, but Goldsmith had little time to savor the moment because the enemy was soon firing on his section. Low tide and high riverbanks made it difficult for the enemy gunners to hit the PBRs, and most of the rounds passed harmlessly over the boats.

When the firefight began, Goldsmith, a recent NROTC graduate from the University of Virginia, worried that his men, who had been eagerly awaiting the fight for over an hour, would show poor fire discipline and waste ammunition. "I believed that they would hose down that south bank with no end until their gun barrels melted or the ammo was exhausted." To his surprise, his sailors demonstrated excellent poise under fire and expended their rounds judiciously. The .50-caliber gunners on his boat fired a combination of full-metal jacket, red tracer, and armor-piercing incendiary (API) rounds. Designed to destroy thin-skinned armored vehicles, the API rounds also proved effective in burning down buildings containing Viet Cong fighters.[74] "The bullets appeared to shut down enemy machine guns one after another," noted Goldsmith, "Maybe the explosions and fires, trees being knocked down over their heads, and other mayhem put the fear of God into those Cong gunners."[75]

Less than a minute after the firefight began the enemy guns went silent and the shooting subsided. The two PBRs then idled offshore from the MACV compound while his gunners replenished their trays. In the dim light, Goldsmith could see friendly troops manning machine guns in front of the MACV compound. After lingering for a while, Goldsmith's section was relieved by the 7-13 and 7-14 boats, and Goldsmith headed to *Harnett County*, anchored on the Ham Luong River, for more fuel and ammunition.[76]

PBRs 7-13 and 7-14 got as far as the Ben Tre Bridge when they were hit by fire from the south bank of the canal. A rocket or mortar round hit the 7-14 boat, lightly wounding several men including Gunner's Mate (Guns)/Seaman Apprentice David Lee Copenhaver.[77] Other PBRs, some from other river sections, soon began arriving on-scene, and their gunfire began killing Viet Cong trying to cross the bridge from the south to the north bank. The 7-18 boat from River Section 534, a Mark II PBR outfitted with a 60mm mortar, shelled targets near the MACV compound with white phosphorous and high explosive rounds. Sailors equipped with M72 LAW rockets fired on Viet Cong hiding in buildings, setting them on fire.[78] Other hootches and dwellings were burned down with API and tracer rounds.

Gunner's Mate 3rd Class Paul W. Cagle, an aggressive young sailor from Florence, South Carolina, was one of the first members of River Section 532 to see action at Ben Tre during Tet. In the early morning hours Cagle's boat, PBR-124, and PBR-126 were idling at the mouth of the confluence of the Ben Tre Canal and the Ham Luong River when Cagle and the other sailors began hearing mortar round explosions and seeing tracers. According to Cagle, "We asked the LST what to do and they said not to go up the canal. They finally told us to go up the canal at about daybreak, but under no circumstances go beyond the bridge."[79]

Like many who ended up in PBRs, Cagle joined the Navy in 1964 to avoid being drafted into the Army, but once in the Navy found that he loved it. On his first assignment on *Braine* (DD-630), Cagle served as a powder man on a 5-inch gun mount and participated in naval gunfire support missions along the coasts of both North and South Vietnam.[80] Excited by his first combat experience and hoping to get closer to the action, Cagle volunteered in late 1966 for the riverine force. By January 1968, Cagle had been fired upon on numerous patrols and considered himself to be a "combat hardened, C-Rat eating, crap from the stern, *dinky dau* [crazy] PBR river rat."[81]

Aerial view of the Ben Tre Bridge, showing a downed span, October 1968.

Gunner's Mate (Guns) 3rd Class Paul W. Cagle next to a ladder on *Hunterdon County* (LST-838), left, and sitting in the forward mount of a PBR, circa 1968.

By the time his PBR reached the bridge in Ben Tre, Cagle was champing at the bit to fire his guns. The boat had been taking small arms fire, mainly from the south bank, and Cagle began aiming at Viet Cong moving across the 12-foot-high bridge and along the south bank, where he was able to put rounds into the enemy at knee level. "It takes their legs off and spins them around.... The first mission could have been two hours, it could have been 30 minutes, I can't really say. You lose track of time." At one point in the battle, he began firing from only one gun of the twin-.50 to save ammunition. During the first days of Tet, Cagle's PBR made multiple sorties into Ben Tre, sometimes rearming and refueling from *Harnett County* and sometimes by an LCM. On 1 February, Cagle's boat received its first cans of API ammunition. "When I opened up with those rounds (I had never fired them before), my lord, it just lit up everything I shot. Next thing I know buildings were on fire. The place was already on fire anyhow but these rounds caused even more fires."[82]

Until units from the 9th Infantry Division arrived late in the day on 1 February, the PBRs and close air support from allied aircraft were the only outside help the beleaguered defenders of Ben Tre received. Without their assistance, the MACV compound may not have survived the initial onslaught. Goldsmith argued that attacks by PBRs on Viet Cong crossing the bridge and in the nearby marketplace were critical in blunting the attack. In particular, he cites the actions of PBRs 7-16, 7-17, and 7-18, which put intensive fire on the marketplace with their machine guns, grenade launchers, 60mm mortars, and M72 LAW rockets. The M72s destroyed buildings being used by the Viet Cong for protection and API rounds set fire to the marketplace. One LAW set off a secondary explosion that tore off the roof of the main marketplace building and looked "like special effects from a Hollywood movie."[83] Aviation Boatswain's Mate Chief David W. Clouse, a River Section 532 patrol officer who made four runs up the Ben Tre during the first 24 hours of the battle, noted that the Viet Cong "completely underestimated the firepower of the PBRs." According to Clouse, they kept trying to cross the bridge into the city despite the fusillade of .50-caliber fire pouring forth from the PBRs.[84]

In addition to taking many rounds of automatic weapons fire, Goldsmith claims that the Viet Cong fired over 20 rockets at PBRs near the marketplace on the 31st.[85] One of those rockets hit the starboard cowling of the 7-18 boat just inches above the head of the forward gunner, Gunner's Mate (Guns)/Seaman Apprentice Wayne Forbes. The blast blew out the controls of the boat and knocked the patrol officer, Lieutenant Ronald M. Wolin, and the coxswain, Boatswain's Mate 1st Class Charles R. Carvander, to the deck. The boat veered out of control toward the south bank as Carvander and Wolin, both of whom had sustained minor wounds during the initial attack, struggled to steer it with just the cables attached to the water pumps.[86] Meanwhile, Forbes, whose turret control system had been knocked out by the blast, grabbed an M16 and started firing at targets on the south bank. PBRs 7-17 and 7-16 soon rushed to the aid of the crippled boat, expending nearly all of their machine-gun ammunition trying to neutralize fire from the south bank. All boats were hit by small arms fire, and the 7-18 took over 40 hits before it was finally towed to safety by the 7-16 boat.[87]

Air support began arriving just after the marketplace attack. Among the first to reach the scene were Navy helicopters from HAL-3, which immediately began blasting VC positions near the MACV compound. Other aircraft soon followed, including U.S. Air Force AC-47 Spooky gunships.[88] *Harnett County*, likewise, lent firepower to the effort by attacking targets near the confluence of the Ben Tre Canal and Ham Luong River. During the course of Tet, the LST's 40mm mounts delivered over 20,000 rounds of API shells in the Ben Tre area, destroying 30 structures, three bunkers, a sampan, and a brick factory.[89] The brick factory, near the mouth of the Ben Tre Canal, was one of the last structures destroyed. A group of Viet Cong holdouts had retreated to the beehive-shaped structure after the Army reinforcements arrived in the city. The Army tried to negotiate surrender, but the Viet Cong steadfastly refused. Rather than sending troops into the building, the Army requested 40mm gunfire support from the LST. According to Cagle, who witnessed the bombardment, "they busted the place to pieces and buried the Viet Cong alive."[90]

A 40mm mount on *Harnett County* (LST-821). During the Tet Offensive, this weapon provided valuable gunfire support for allied ground units at Ben Tre, May 1969.

At 1810 on 1 February, reinforcements from the 9th Infantry Division began arriving at Ben Tre. Elements of the 3d Battalion, 39th Infantry landed by helicopter in the area of Ben Tre near the MACV compound to bolster its defensive perimeter. The following day troops from the 2d Battalion, 39th Infantry landed east of the city and moved west in an attempt to link up with the 3d Battalion, which was supposed to break out from its defensive position and begin moving east. Both units encountered fierce opposition. Unfamiliar with urban warfare, the 3d Battalion fought a slow, house-by-house advance, until it stalled near the main highway on the eastern edge of the city unable to advance further and link up with its sister battalion. The 2d Battalion encountered a battalion-size force of Viet Cong, forcing it to move from its landing zones to the northern edge of the city.[91]

By this point the two battalions had lost 16 soldiers and were completely pinned down, unable to advance. Air support was called in on the eastern portion of the city with seven sorties going into one eight-block area. These strikes broke up enemy formations and forced the Viet Cong to flee across open rice fields, where they were attacked by helicopter gunships, artillery, and fixed-wing strikes. Essentially, airpower corralled the enemy into convenient kill zones whereupon American firepower could be brought to bear in the most effective manner possible.[92]

With the logjam opened up by airpower, the 2d and 3d Battalions, 39th Infantry began making significant progress. After three days of relatively light fighting, these units cleared the area of Viet Cong and recaptured areas of the city lost during Tet. Overall, during the month of February 1968, U.S. forces killed 328 Viet Cong, mostly during the battle of Ben Tre, in what proved a very tough fight. As the 3d Brigade's after-action report stated, "With the enemy in control of virtually the entire city, it became a matter of door-to-door, street-by-street advance under constant sniper fire to drive him [the Viet Cong] out in the open."[93] The job would have been even tougher had it not been for the support provided by the PBRs, artillery, and especially airpower.

Many of the PBRs that fought at Ben Tre did so for almost four straight days with few breaks—just short trips to the LST anchored on the Ham Luong for fuel, supplies, and ammunition. Cagle recalled eating baloney sandwiches and drinking coffee supplied by an LCM during one of those breaks. He gazed at his surroundings and what he saw shocked him. His shipmates were covered in cordite and gun grease, and the boat was littered with brass shell casings, food scraps, cigarette butts, empty ammo cans, and other detritus of war. "We were a dirty, nasty bunch of people. And our boat was the dirtiest boat. And I am thinking who cares?" And he was right. Cagle's boat and the other PBRs in the area had helped stem one the Viet Cong's biggest offensives in the delta during the crucial first day of what was arguably the most important battle of the war, the Tet Offensive. As one Army advisor remarked to journalist Lee Lescaze of the *Washington Post*, "They [the PBRs] saved our tails that first day."[94]

The Ben Tre battle will be remembered not for the service and sacrifice of men like Cagle but for an alleged comment made by an Army officer to journalist Peter Arnett, an Australian reporter working for the Associated Press. Arnett claimed that in describing the battle, the Army officer said to him that "it became necessary to destroy the town to save it." The quote was

View of Ben Tre from the Ben Tre Canal during the Tet Offensive, February 1968.

rapidly disseminated throughout the American media and, according to William H. Hammond, a historian with the U.S. Army Center of Military History, soon "passed into the lore of the war to become one of the most serviceable icons of the anti-war movement."[95]

Like any great quotation propagated by the media, there were more than a few grains of truth to it. As Army official reports stated, the city of Ben Tre "suffered major damage" during Tet. The attack destroyed over 5,000 homes and generated over 30,000 refugees in the Ben Tre and neighboring Mo Cay districts.[96] However, Brigadier General Knowlton claims that tracer rounds from both sides, but mainly from the Viet Cong, caused most of the damage:

> It was the kind of weather where the fire just swept through that little tarpaper town . . . . The thing that destroyed Ben Tre was the fire that got started from the tracers. There was no fire department and no way in the middle of the fight that that could be put out. And as you know, the Vietnamese houses are built very flimsily because the weather is such and they don't have to be built strongly. And they all went up pretty well in the fire and that's what really destroyed big parts of the city.[97]

Air Force Major James K. Gibson, a forward air control pilot who fought at Ben Tre, blames the Viet Cong for choosing Ben Tre as the battleground: "The way we selected these targets was determined by the VC. They chose the battleground and we really had no choice where we put the target. There were American soldiers lying dead on the road and there were going to be a lot more if we did not put ordnance (air) into the town."[98] GMG3 Cagle and Chief Clouse both claim that the town was "pretty much destroyed when we got there," but admitted that the API rounds fired by some of the PBRs contributed to the destruction.[99] In the end both sides burned Ben Tre, perhaps not equally but with the same results—death and destruction for the Vietnamese people. In all, civilian casualties in Kien Hoa Province included 528 killed and 1,219 wounded.[100]

Cagle recalled that after the battle there were so many bodies in the streets that the Vietnamese resorted to throwing them in the water to dispose of them. Lack of potable water forced many local civilians to drink contaminated river water, which caused illnesses and additional deaths.[101] Cagle and his shipmates were so short of water that they often drank syrup from fruit cocktail cans. "*Hunterdon County* was trying to purify water as best they could, but purification chemicals in it would still burn our eyes and mouth." To help prevent a cholera outbreak, Cagle and other PBR crews lashed the Vietnamese bodies into bundles and pulled them out to the Ham Luong, hoping the tide would carry them out to the South China Sea. "This is what happened to some of the dead people. The Army also buried a bunch of them. People have pictures of these bundles but no one will show them to anyone."[102]

For Chief Clouse, one of his most vivid memories of Ben Tre was not the destruction of the city or the bodies left on the streets but a simple humanitarian mission. Rather than sleeping, or playing cards, after the battle ended, he and another sailor volunteered to spend one of their few days off helping an old man rebuild his simple house. "The Vietnamese man taught us how to weave foliage together and build a small but sturdy shelter. It was very rewarding."[103]

Vinh Long

Ensign Robert A. Pinion was in some ways typical of many "rear echelon" sailors who found themselves in a serious combat situation during the Tet Offensive. A native of Muncie, Indiana, Pinion graduated from Ball State University in 1966 and joined the Navy partly to avoid being drafted into the Army and partly because in his words, "I had no plan for my life."[104] Pinion attended Officer Candidate School at Newport and chose to become a supply officer because poor vision disqualified him from line officer duty. After receiving his Supply Corps badge, a gold oak leaf that corps members irreverently refer to as the "pork chop," Pinion volunteered for duty in Vietnam out of pure patriotism and the fact that he was "single and care free."[105] After attending SERE and the short riverine course at Coronado, Pinion shipped out to Vietnam and reported to his first duty station, Naval Support Activity Saigon, Detachment Vinh Long—a small unit consisting of 22 enlisted men and three officers commanded by a lieutenant.

Located three hours from Saigon on Route 4, Vinh Long was the capital of Vinh Long Province. With a population of 110,000,[106] the city was larger than Ben Tre and contained more military facilities, including a joint USN PBR/VNN RAG base along the Co Chien River and an airfield with a 3,000-foot-long asphalt runway located two miles east of town.[107] Like many of the larger delta towns, Vinh Long city was surrounded by rivers and canals with the Co Chien, the main river, passing to the north side of the city. From the Co Chien ferry to Vinh Long, one had to cross three bridges to get to the city and another four to reach the NSA detachment villa located approximately six miles south of town just off Route 4.[108]

Since the main function of the detachment was to manage the logistic operations for the 144 personnel at the Vinh Long PBR base, most of the NSA sailors had to commute every day from the villa to the base along a rutted, pot-holed road. Lieutenant Edwin "Larry" Oswald, a supply officer assigned to the facility after Tet, speculated that the Navy purchased the facility because it was "ready-made and comfortable," and not because it made much sense from a security perspective. Although the facility had clear fields of fire for over 500 meters on every side and was protected with a chain link fence topped with concertina wire, several sandbagged emplacements, a .50-caliber machine gun, and a couple of 60mm mortars, it could not survive a frontal assault by anything larger than a platoon, and its isolated location would complicate an evacuation.[109] The villa's security situation did not raise too many eyebrows. "This place was very comfortable," claimed Oswald. "It wasn't air-conditioned, but it was comfortable."[110]

Pinion concurred. "Life before Tet was pretty easy duty. You put in long hours but there were no attacks or threats." Pinion's primary duties entailed managing a 64-person Vietnamese civilian workforce that cooked and cleaned for the sailors stationed at Vinh Long. Before Tet, his biggest concerns were making sure his Vietnamese staff adhered to proper standards of hygiene such as using hot water to wash dishes and throwing garbage in trashcans rather than on the ground.[111]

At 0300 on 31 January, an estimated force of 1,200 Viet Cong from two main force battalions (306th and 308th) and several other units, including the D857th Provincial Main Force Battalion and two district consolidated units, launched attacks against Vinh Long and several surrounding military installations. Defending the city was a squadron of the 2d ARVN Armored Cavalry, the 43d ARVN Ranger Battalion, sailors from the PBR/RAG base, and a small contingent of MACV advisors, U.S. Army military police, and U.S. Army combat engineers.[112] According to Pinion, "It was mass confusion that night. They attacked all over the place. They pretty much took over the city of Vinh Long. We had something called a sector net—radio communications with various posts, and everyone was on it at once. How anyone had a clue what was going on was beyond me."[113]

Fortunately for the support activity detachment, their villa was not an initial priority for the Viet Cong whose forces fired at the billet mainly with small arms, reserving heavier B40 fire for the nearby Chau Thanh ARVN artillery compound. At 1700 the next day, everyone in the villa retreated to the PBR base.[114] "I'd like to say that the evacuation was all executed in a well-timed, well-led, well-coordinated effort but it wasn't," claimed Pinion. "It was sort of like we're evacuating, everyone get in the trucks and let's go. We lost a lot of equipment including a classified starlight scope. I had to write off a lot of equipment."[115] Pinion had so much trouble destroying the classified Moser safe with a thermite grenade that he and a fellow officer decided to stuff the documents in pillowcases and carry them to Vinh Long. The situation was no more organized at the PBR base. At the supply department building on base, another officer again tried to destroy classified documents with thermite grenades, but this time the grenades worked so well that they burned down the entire building, including the NSA detachment's operations center, supply storerooms, and communications facility.[116]

Just hours after Pinion's group reached the base, the entire U.S. Navy contingent evacuated on PBRs to *Garrett County*, anchored at the junction of the Co Chien and Tien Giang Rivers about two miles from the city.[117] As the Americans started to evacuate, a VNN officer turned to Pinion and said, "Where are you going?" To which Pinion replied, "I don't know; I really don't know." Pinion personally did not understand why the Navy had decided to abandon Vinh Long—the only major U.S. base in the delta evacuated during Tet. "There was no reason for the evacuation based on what I saw. We had complete confidence in the VNN river assault group. They would stand and fight with you."[118]

And stand and fight they did. As the American sailors bugged out, a skeleton force of 40 VNN sailors successfully defended the perimeter of the base supported by naval gunfire from RAGs 23 and 31 on the river. The Vietnam Navy also temporarily relocated over 2,500 dependents and other civilians from Vinh Long to an island in the center of the river—an auspicious move because during the ensuing battle, VNN monitors and LSSLs would destroy nearly every building and house within 300 meters of the river, including almost all dependent housing, in its attempt to keep the Viet Cong from overrunning the base.[119] Barracks and other buildings built along the riverfront were burned down to the concrete slabs.[120]

While most U.S. Navy personnel in Vinh Long retreated from the city to the comparative safety of *Garrett County*, 11 pilots and 22 maintenance personnel from HAL-3, Detachment 3, based at Vinh Long airfield, opted to remain on station and fight. Lieutenant Tom Anzalone, a pilot, remembered the Viet Cong breaching a section of the perimeter early in the fight and taking over one end of the runway. "The airfield was under attack by mortars and everything else the Viet Cong could throw at it."[121] Despite heavy fire, the detachment's two armed UH-1B light attack helicopters, which were on a mission at Tra Vinh when Tet started, chose to return to the airfield to refuel and rearm rather than head to *Garrett County*. Once landed, the door gunners removed their M60 machine guns and formed a defensive perimeter around the helicopters while maintenance personnel prepped the birds for action. The helicopters were soon back in the air en route to targets at Tra Vinh.[122]

Lieutenant Commander Allen Weseleskey, a Detachment 3 pilot, vividly remembered the situation. At the beginning of the attack, he counted the mortar rounds as he ran to the bunker. After the tenth round fell, he told the guys in the bunker, "This is more than a harassment attack. This is something big." As he surveyed the situation from the bunker, he noticed that there were no ARVN guards to be seen, and that sappers had already breached security. Weseleskey and the others knew they had to do something. With just side arms and M16s, pilots and aircrew joined Army maintenance personnel and technicians and made their way to the southern end of the runway to help repel the attack. Weseleskey's copilot, Ensign Richard A. Martz took a bullet in the upper arm and suffered shrapnel wounds to wrist and knee. His M16 absorbed a second bullet, probably saving his life. After helping evacuate Martz to the dispensary, Weseleskey continued to fight with his Army comrades. He moved from one aircraft revetment to another, helping to clear Viet Cong and assisting wounded Americans. He ran through heavy fire to forward positions to ensure they were secure and continued fighting until he had to pull alert as a helicopter pilot. Once in his helicopter, he put ordnance on the very same positions he had been fighting near on the ground. "I made multiple rocket and machine-gun runs on enemy positions just outside the wire. In some cases, I was only in the air less than six minutes before I had to land again and rearm. The action was that close!"[123]

A small group of Navy maintenance personnel led by Lieutenant Commander Joseph S. Bouchard, an aviation maintenance limited duty officer with the unit, also helped defend the Seawolves' section of the air base. "Our fighting bunkers were manned when the Viet Cong made their initial assault. We killed a batch of them."[124] Bouchard made sure his men held their positions until reinforcements arrived later that morning. The 3d Squadron of the ARVN 2d Armored Cavalry Regiment arrived first and immediately worked to clear the outer perimeter of the airfield with M 113 armored personnel carriers and M-41 A3 light tanks. The ARVN unit then departed later that day to engage the enemy in the center of Vinh Long.[125] At 1802 on the 31st, the U.S. Army's Company C, 3d Battalion, 47th Infantry inserted by helicopter into Vinh Long airfield to shore up base defenses for the evening and then airlifted to My Tho at 0905 on 1 February.[126]

While the situation at the airfield remained tense for most of 31 January, it was by no means as dire as what was transpiring in the city of Vinh Long which, except for a few small pockets of allied resistance, had essentially fallen to the Viet Cong by midday. One pocket of resistance that survived the initial attack was a villa housing a squad from the 148th Military Police Platoon, a U.S. Army unit tasked with escorting convoys and performing road reconnaissance along Route 4. The villa, situated 100 yards from the MACV compound near the river, was more heavily fortified than the NSA villa and defended by well-armed, combat-hardened soldiers as opposed to a miscellaneous group of yeomen, storekeepers, and other NSA sailors. Between them, the ten military policemen of the unit had four M60 machine guns, three 60mm mortars, M79 grenade launchers, LAW rockets, and numerous small arms. Sandbagged bunkers and a fenced-in perimeter protected their villa, and various living spaces within the facility had been "hardened" with sandbags. But it wasn't these defensive measures or their armament that saved the MPs but their attitude. Accustomed to operating alone and heavily outnumbered along the roadways, their members easily adapted to the situation they confronted during Tet and ably defended their position against a sustained frontal assault.[127]

The next day the MPs evacuated the villa and headed to the airfield to provide backup for the security force there. They performed that duty for a day and then fought their way back to the villa, which survived the battle pretty much intact. To better secure the area immediately surrounding the villa, the MPs searched local houses for arms caches and Viet Cong but found none. They also threw lime on dead bodies to cut down on odor and keep the bugs off. "The town had taken a beating," recalled Sergeant Eldon Banegas, one the MPs. "There were civilian and Viet Cong bodies all over the place, and I never saw one body in a uniform." After Tet, Banegas' attitude about Vinh Long and its populace completely changed. "Before Tet, most people did not carry weapons while off duty. We affectionately called it the 'eight to five war.' You went to war at 0800 and got off at 1700. Off duty, we dressed in civies." But after Tet, the MPs always wore green fatigues in the town and carried their M14s. "It was no longer papasan with his pedal bike selling Coca Cola. Everyone I looked at sort of slipped into black pajamas at night and that was it. Things were not as comfortable."[128]

The Viet Cong held many positions in the Vinh Long area until 7 February. Some of the heaviest fighting occurred within the city between 31 January and 2 February. On the 31st, the 3d Squadron, 2d ARVN Armored Cavalry attempted to clear Vinh Long's main street but was stalled by machine-gun fire and rocket propelled grenades. By evening it was forced to pull

View of a Vinh Long neighborhood after Tet 1968.

back to more secure areas. The next morning the 3d Squadron again tried to recapture the main street but made no progress due to lack of infantry support. That evening the 3d Battalion, 15th ARVN Infantry arrived on boats to reinforce the 3d Squadron, and the next morning, 2 February, the two units again attempted to dislodge the Viet Cong defenders from the city's main thoroughfare, battling the enemy house-to-house and through piles of rubble. Fighting continued until 4 February, when the combined efforts of these two units plus the 43rd Rangers and reinforcements from the MRF finally cleared the western section of the city and compelled the remaining Viet Cong to retreat from the city to the outskirts of town.[129]

During the first two days of February, the Seawolves were the only Navy elements still operating on land in Vinh Long. In fact, during this period HAL-3 Detachment 4 actually left the comparative safety of *Garrett County* and joined Detachment 3 at the airfield to make room on the ship for Vinh Long–based PBR crews and over 150 American, Vietnamese, and Korean civilians sheltering on the LST.[130] The bravery demonstrated by the Seawolves is perhaps best embodied in Lieutenant Commander Bouchard, who earlier in his career had performed evacuation missions during the Chinese Civil War as an enlisted aircrewman on seaplanes. Bouchard not only led the Seawolves' maintenance personnel in a spirited defense of their sector of the airfield but took two volunteers, Chief Aviation Machinist Mate J (jet engine mechanic) Francis Smith and Aviation Ordnanceman 1st Class Charles "Chuck" Fields, to rescue 130 orphans trapped in a small orphanage 400 yards beyond the perimeter of the airfield. On the night of the 1 February, the sailors made their way to the compound and established a defensive position on the roof. The next day Bouchard made contact with Captain Robin Miller, an Army Huey pilot who made repeated flights into the compound to evacuate the orphans and 12 nuns to the airfield.[131]

On the morning of 2 February, River Section 535 units returned to Vinh Long and joined the Vietnam Navy in defending the combined base while Navy SEALs and an advance party of NSA personnel reoccupied the NSA villa. No damage had been done to the structure and the Viet Cong had not attempted to occupy it.[132] The Viet Cong lobbed mortar rounds at the facility during the next six days but did not attempt an assault. During one of those bombardments, Pinion was told to get up and man the villa's command post (CP) on the roof. "I was really tired that night and getting a bit lax, but I finally made it to the CP 15 minutes later, just in time for a mortar round to smash right through my rack. The good news is that no transients ever wanted to borrow my rack again when I wasn't using it."[133] In October 1968 the Navy finally abandoned the villa and PBR base at Vinh Long for good, opting instead to base the PBRs on a specially configured floating base, barracks craft *APL-46*. As Vice Admiral Edwin Hooper, the commander of Service Force Pacific, later wrote, it wasn't the security situation that finally convinced the Navy to abandon Vinh Long but the "inadequate facilities."[134]

On 4 February 1968, the tide of battle finally turned in favor of the allies. A major reason for this shift was the MRF, which was finally able to leave Dinh Tuong Province and relieve Viet Cong pressure on Vinh Long. Helicopters and boats transported two battalions of the 9th Infantry Division (the 3d Battalion, 60th Infantry and the 3d Battalion, 47th Infantry) to the south and, together with ARVN units already in the area, established a cordon around the city.

The first unit to encounter serious opposition was Company E, 3d Battalion, 60th Infantry. As soon as its troops alighted from helicopters at 1733 hours, the company began taking fire and was soon pinned down in a horseshoe-shaped position. Company E, along with Companies A and C, engaged the enemy for the remainder of the day and throughout the night. During a nighttime resupply mission, an Army Huey was shot down.[135] At dawn U.S. Army units searched the battlefield and discovered 29 Viet Cong bodies. Friendly casualties included 38 American soldiers wounded and one killed.[136]

While all this was taking place, elements of 3d Battalion, 47th Infantry leapfrogged around the southern perimeter of Vinh Long, trying to trap Viet Cong units fleeing the area. RADs 111 and 92 assisted in these efforts, conducted patrols, and suppressed fire along the banks of waterways in the area. The Navy units took some automatic weapons and rocket fire, but there were no casualties.[137]

On 5 February elements of the 3d Battalion, 60th Infantry conducted airmobile-search operations and also cleared an area near the airfield. The 3d Battalion, 47th Infantry operated east of the Rach Cai Cam, making several landings southeast from ATCs operated by RAD 91.

River assault craft established waterblocks and provided fire support as the 3d Battalion, 47th Infantry units engaged small pockets of enemy resistance in the area. Late in the afternoon, infantry from both the 3d of the 60th and the 3d of the 47th loaded onto ATCs and returned to *Colleton* for their first night's rest after eight straight days and nights of operations. On 6 February elements of the 3d of the 60th departed the Mobile Riverine Base in an attempt to cut off a large force of Viet Cong moving southwest of Vinh Long.[138]

Engineman 3rd Class William "Tex" Donham had just arrived in-country on 31 January and was a replacement engineman on Tango 111-8 on the morning of the 6th. Donham dropped out of high school at 17 and joined the Navy. He had hoped to become a Navy diver but failed to qualify for the program. After serving for two years on the combat store ship *Mars* (AFS-1) chipping paint on the deck, cleaning boilers, and working in the mess deck, he volunteered for what he thought would be more interesting service in Vietnam. He would not be disappointed. When his plane touched down at Tan Son Nhut air base near Saigon, he had to walk between two rows of body bags to get to the terminal. "I had never seen a body bag or smelled a dead person, but I did not have too much time to look because they told us to hurry up because there might be a mortar attack." From his hotel room that night, he watched fires burning in Saigon and then flew out the next day to join up with RAD 111 at Dong Tam where he enjoyed a heartfelt reunion with two sailors he had trained with at Vallejo: GMG3 John Green and BM3 Joseph Camara.

Green, now a combat veteran, "was mister information," and Donham listened closely to what he had to say. Despite the advice received, Donham forgot everything he was told to do on his first mission the next day. On a canal near Dong Tam, Donham was manning one of the 20mm guns and thought he spotted some movement near a bunker. Instinctually, he poured fire into the bunker until his barrel burned. "BM1 John Brabston was yelling and screaming at me to cease fire until I got authorization, but it was too late by then." Donham committed two serious errors his first day of action. He fired his weapon in anger without permission from the boat captain, and he failed to maintain fire discipline (shooting ten rounds at a time, pausing to let the barrel cool, and then resuming fire).[139] After that incident Donham knew he had to improve his performance to redeem himself with his shipmates.

On 6 February 1968, intelligence sources indicated that the Viet Cong had moved large forces southwest of Vinh Long straight through the allied cordon. In an attempt to engage this force, RAD 111 participated in a reconnaissance-in-force operation with Company B, 3d Battalion, 60th Infantry. The river assault division departed the MRB early in the morning and at 0810 made its first landing south of the Highway 4 bridge on the Rach Cai Cam, a narrow waterway that flowed due south of Vinh Long. The old French-built bridge had elegant Romanesque arches, but Green, Donham, and others had little time to marvel at the architecture. They worried about being trapped on the wrong side of the arches during high tide. The first landing was made without making contact with the enemy. The force reembarked in the boats and moved to an assault position 500 meters south where Popular Force units reported a large VC unit in some woods along the river.[140]

At 1100, Viet Cong forces on both banks fired automatic weapons and RPGs at the lead ATCs, causing minor damage and wounding one sailor. Donham's gun mount was pointed southeast when the ambush occurred. "I saw a mound and a gun pointing out of it and opened up with my 20mm. I could see a water buffalo standing behind the mound and my fire hit the animal and a nearby shack, setting it on fire." Unable to retreat back under the bridge because of the high tide, the column, supported by artillery, helicopter gunships, and naval gunfire, proceeded to the landing zone on the west bank of the river to drop off Company B, which swept south toward the ambush zone. No contact was made and the troops reembarked on the ATCs. For the next few hours, probing patrols were landed on the west bank, but none made any contact.[141] At 1430, another RAD 111 convoy arrived with reinforcements from Company E, 3d Battalion, 60th Infantry, and both companies landed on opposite sides of the river near the original 1100 ambush site. "No sooner did we open our ramp than they opened up on us," explained John Green. The troops fought their way off the boats into the jungles. One of those soldiers was Specialist 4th Class Thomas James Kinsman, a 22-year-old from Washington State. During the course of the fight, Kinsman and eight others from Company B became separated from the main body of troops in the dense jungle. A grenade was thrown at the group and Kinsman shouted a warning to his squad and then dove on the grenade, shielding his comrades from the worst effects of the blast.

Seeing wounded emerging from the jungle, John Green and Engineman 2nd Class David Allen left the boat to administer first aid and get the men back into the ATC. One of the men told John that others were in need of help. Green grabbed a canvas and metal bunk frame to use as a stretcher, jumped off the boat with no weapon, and headed into the jungle looking for the wounded. Passing dead Viet Cong as he moved further and further away from the relative safety of his ATC, Green marched toward the sound of gunfire until 150 meters into the jungle where he found a small group of soldiers engaged in a fierce firefight. The fight suddenly ended when he reached them. While administering first aid, Green learned that one of the men had jumped on a grenade to save the lives of the squad. That man, Sp4c Kinsman, had wounds to his head, chest, and leg. Green knew that if they did not move Kinsman immediately, he probably would not survive, so he told two soldiers to load him onto a stretcher and move out. Green grabbed a rifle and led the group back to the river. The soldiers were disoriented, and several of them had minor wounds. Carrying Kinsman through the marsh and mud was exhausting, and the soldiers had to stop several times to rest. It took the men close to 20 minutes to reach the ATC. According to Donham, who tended to Kinsman on the ATC, "We applied battle dressings to his wounds, tied him to the litter, and put him up on a helo deck and whoosh, he was gone—dustoff." Thanks to the actions of Green and other members of Tango 111-8, Kinsman survived the battle and later received the Medal of Honor for his heroism on 6 February.

Seeing Kinsman's shattered body up close affected different people in different ways. Immediately after the evacuation, Green went back to his starboard .50-caliber gun mount and spent a few moments alone, trying to collect himself and summon the energy to keep fighting.

Donham took out his fear and aggression directly on the enemy. When he spotted a Viet Cong trying to remove a dead comrade from a trench, he grabbed an M14 and shot him. "The bullet went straight through the dead guy, and his comrade went down in the trench."[142]

By 1510, the enemy pulled back to the southwest. Company A leapfrogged by boat to try to block the retreat while the other companies pushed southwest in pursuit of the fleeing Viet Cong. Contact was made in a wooded area between the two groups of American soldiers, but by nightfall the Viet Cong managed to escape the impending encirclement. The 3d Battalion, 60th Infantry returned to the Mobile Riverine Base on the afternoon of the 7th and departed Vinh Long for Dong Tam the next day. During the fighting between 4 and 6 February 1968, the U.S. Army suffered four killed and 62 wounded, and the Navy, one killed (Radioman 3rd Class Samuel Boyce) and 14 wounded. Cumulative Viet Cong losses were 138 killed and numerous wounded. In addition, 121 Viet Cong suspects were detained, 43 weapons captured, and 45 bunkers destroyed. Civilian losses in the province as a whole included 230 killed and 283 wounded. Fighting in Vinh Long Province also created over 30,000 civilian refugees.[143]

Counteroffensive operations designed to relieve pressure on My Tho and Vinh Long, two of the delta's most important cities, ended on 12 February. In both cases the MRF was able to defeat large enemy formations and exact severe casualties. From 29 January to 7 February, the Viet Cong lost 269 troops compared to 12 killed in action sustained by the MRF (9 soldiers and 2 sailors).[144] More significantly, the defeat of the Viet Cong at My Tho, Ben Tre, and Vinh Long and in much of Saigon by the second week of February allowed the allies to focus more resources on the north in general, and Hue and Khe Sanh in particular. As historian James Willbanks described the situation, "The Communist offensive seemed to run out of steam by the end of the first week of February."[145]

Can Tho

Fighting in the delta, however, was far from over on 7 February. Tet related mop-up operations would continue throughout the summer and beyond. In mid-February one of the biggest such operations occurred at Can Tho. Near this city of approximately 166,000, the capital of Phong Dinh Province, the Communists had assembled a force of 2,500 soldiers, many of whom were hastily recruited teenage boys, and appeared poised to attack.[146] To relieve pressure on the area, the senior IV Corps advisor ordered the MRF to make a 110-mile journey from Dong Tam to Phong Dinh Province. One of the longest transits of the war for the force, it took the MRF far from its normal supply lines.[147]

Operations began on 14 February when RADs 92 and 111 landed the 3d Battalion, 47th Infantry and the 3d Battalion, 60th Infantry south of Can Tho. Only light contact was achieved, but ground troops did discover a large cache of enemy weapons and ammunition, including 460 B40 rocket rounds. At 1600, elements of the 3d of the 47th made contact with an estimated two to three companies of Viet Cong southwest of the city and after over seven hours of often fierce fighting, forced the enemy to withdraw.[148]

During the next several days 9th Infantry Division units made additional beach and air mobile assaults west of Can Tho and near the airfield. Contact was sporadic, but soldiers did manage to destroy 273 bunkers and kill 52 Viet Cong. U.S. losses as of 17 February were eight soldiers killed and 38 wounded. On 19 February, two B40 rockets struck Monitor 91-1 on the Can Tho River south of city. The rockets penetrated the 40mm turret, wounding seven crewmembers and a Vietnamese interpreter. Although four of the wounded received wounds serious enough to require evacuation, the rugged monitor and its crew immediately returned fire after the attack until all fire from three enemy gun emplacements was suppressed. A day later a recoilless-rifle round hit M 92-2 but caused no damage or casualties.[149]

On 22 February, MRF soldiers and South Vietnamese troops from the ARVN 21st Division launched an operation in the Phung Hiep district not far from Can Tho to locate and destroy the VC Military Region III headquarters. Army combat engineers raised a bridge span over the Cai Con Canal with jacks so that MRF boats could pass underneath and surprise the Viet Cong in an area 14 miles from the Bassac River that they thought could not be penetrated by river boats. The MRF encountered no defenses designed to counter such an assault and took the enemy by complete surprise. When elements of the 3d Battalion, 47th Infantry landed along the Kinh Lai Hieu Canal, the Viet Cong retreated into open fields away from the canal, where artillery and helicopter gunships could kill them with ease. In all, American firepower killed 60 Viet Cong in the brief engagement.[150]

More fighting occurred on the 26th, when Company B, 3d Battalion, 60th Infantry met a large force of Viet Cong during an air mobile assault northwest of Can Tho. Twelve helicopters were damaged and the unit suffered many wounded. TF 117 units also encountered action this day while patrolling on the Bassac (Song Can Tho). A couple of B40 rockets hit ASPB 112-4, wounding several sailors and flooding the boat. A battle ensued as other units attempted to rescue the crew and the sinking vessel. The ASPB crewmembers were saved, but the assault support boat sank as it was being towed by Monitor 112-1. During this same period, a recoilless rifle round killed Boatswain's Mate 1st Class Jeider J. Warren and Boatswain's Mate 3rd Class James L. Lien, and wounded three others on another ASPB. The stricken, out-of-control boat beached itself and was later towed back to the fire support base.[151] "At Can Tho, Charlie realized that if you hit an Alpha boat in the cockpit, you could knock it out," explained Boatswain's Mate 2nd Class Robert E. Davis, who fought at Can Tho on Monitor 112-2. "A blast from a rocket would cause pieces of the cockpit's armor to break off and kill the crew."[152]

On the 27th, fleeing insurgents attempted to escape from Can Tho, but the naval blockade, which had grown to over 44 river assault boats augmented by over ten PBRs, and pincer movements from ground forces, impeded their attempts. TF 117 units raked the banks of the Bassac in the Can Tho area with fire in an attempt to deny the enemy an egress. In all, gunfire from MRF vessels killed 68 Viet Cong during the two-day blockade. The MRF also uncovered a large cache of weapons, including 280 mortar, rocket, and recoilless rifle rounds. American losses in the action included 19 soldiers and two sailors killed and 97 servicemen wounded.[153]

Can Tho PBR base, February 1967.

On 3 March the MRF left Can Tho and returned to Dong Tam. Can Tho was the last major delta city to face a significant Viet Cong threat during the Tet Offensive. After this battle the MRF shifted attention from the cities back to the countryside where units continued to hunt down and destroy the remnants of the VC's Tet Offensive units. Although these mop-up operations would extend into the summer, the Viet Cong lost the initiative after Can Tho which, for all intents and purposes, was the last major urban battle in the delta during the Tet Offensive of 1968.

The key to the success of American arms at Can Tho and throughout the delta during Tet was the MRF's ability to move significant forces to battle areas before the Viet Cong could consolidate their initial gains. The MRF transported forces to battlefields in eight provinces in February and sustained them once the battle was joined by providing gunfire support—a significant asset during Tet when aviation and artillery assets were almost always in short supply—and ammunition, food, water, and medical aid. The logistic support provided to the Army by the MRF cannot be understated. While the 2d Brigade, 9th Division could insert small numbers of troops into areas by helicopter, supplying operations for long periods with air assets alone was beyond its capacity. Again, riverine mobility was instrumental. So too was the joint effect of naval, surface, and airpower in the delta environment. As Salzer later put it, "I felt very strongly that the lesson on the Tet Offensive was that we could not afford to tie down the MRF to one location. We had to pursue enemy units to the limits of the draft of our boats and then take to the air, the helicopters. We had to have a truly integrated water/land, air mobile, air supported operation going after main force units wherever they were."[154]

Furthermore, unlike in 1967 when the MRF often had to fight the Viet Cong in rural areas only accessible by narrow canals, the most significant delta battle sites of the Tet Offensive were cities accessible by major rivers. Here, the MRF was not only less vulnerable to ambushes but less dependent on tides. Finally, many cities (namely My Tho, Ben Tre, and Vinh Long) were within short steaming distance of the MRF's land base at Dong Tam, and those that were not (such as Can Tho) could easily be supported by the MRB, again because of the close proximity to major rivers.

Did the MRF save the delta as General Westmoreland claimed? Salzer, in an oral history, noted that Westmoreland

> ... did say to me at that time, that there was one thing that he was confident of and that was the MRF that [sic] saved the Delta. I agree with him, it was true. The loss of the Delta would have meant the loss of South Vietnam because that was where all the food and supply was and the largest percentage of the population. If Saigon was the heart and brains of the country (or its cancer, as I once said) South Vietnam was hopeless without the Delta. The Delta was the stomach and legs.[155]

Although Salzer was correct to emphasize the importance of the delta as the breadbasket of South Vietnam and the MRF's role in saving it during Tet, he failed to credit other players in the drama. ARVN and VNN forces fought extremely hard in certain areas, especially My Tho and Vinh Long. PBRs and airpower also played a significant role in providing fire support for defenders early on in the struggle. Arguably at Ben Tre, if it were not for the combined effect of airpower and naval gunfire support, the MACV compound might not have survived the first 16 hours of the attack. "Who dares, wins" is the motto of the British Special Air Service, but the same could be said of the SEAL defenders at My Tho or of HAL-3 and the Army MPs at Vinh Long. Their spirited defense of their facilities reveals how a determined defense, even by the smallest numbers of allied defenders, often held back attacks by much larger numbers of enemy troops for long periods.

Monitor 92-1 leads a formation of armored troop carriers in the Mekong Delta, June 1968.

In the end, the Viet Cong had only a few advantages in the delta during Tet—namely mass and surprise. The MRF and the allies held most of the other cards, including superior firepower, mobility, and logistics, as well as better trained and more disciplined troops. Once the MRF identified the key cities under attack, it was only a matter of time before it would prevail against a lightly armed, nonmechanized foe with no long-term plan to reinforce, supply, and consolidate initial gains made during Tet.

Postscript: Task Force Clearwater during Tet

In the fall of 1967, the People's Army of Vietnam began a campaign of attacks against allied forces operating near the DMZ in the I Corps Tactical Zone.[156] These attacks, noted Tet historian James Willbanks, "served to screen the infiltration of troops and equipment in South Vietnam" in preparation for the Tet Offensive.[157] Many of the allied positions near the DMZ could be supplied by air, but waterborne craft also played a critical logistics role. Naval Support Activity Danang operated a small fleet of LCMs and LCUs that supplied two of the most significant of these positions, Hue on the Perfume River and Dong Ha on the Cua Viet. Hue was the scene of the longest and bloodiest battle of the Tet Offensive—one in which the allies lost over 600 men and the North Vietnamese over 5,000. It was also the eastern anchor of a chain of fortified positions in the northern part of I Corps running from the South China Sea to the Cambodian border. Khe Sanh formed the western anchor of that chain and emerged as another major flashpoint of the Tet Offensive and a test of wills between Generals William Westmoreland and Vo Nguyen Giap. The siege of Khe Sanh, which began on 21 January, lasted 77 days and resulted in 205 American deaths and over 1,600 PAVN killed. Nearly all supplies flown into Khe Sanh during the siege came from Dong Ha on the Cua Viet. Providing security for supplies moved on this river, and also on the Perfume to Hue, would become the raison d'être for a new river patrol force in I Corps, which eventually became Task Force Clearwater.

Recognizing the importance of these waterways to the defense of I Corps, Marine Lieutenant General Louis W. Walt, the commander of III Marine Amphibious Force and the senior U.S. advisor in I Corps, first requested 30 to 40 PBRs from the Military Assistance Command Vietnam in early in 1967.[158] Fearing that such a force would drain precious resources from the Mekong Delta, the Navy leadership in South Vietnam was initially reluctant to contribute to the mission, but as the fighting in I Corps intensified, a compromise was eventually struck, and COMNAVFORV agreed to assign one river section of PBRs to I Corps. On 18 September 1967, ten PBRs from River Section 521 arrived on *Hunterdon County* at the mouth of Cua Hai Bay, 17 miles northwest of Danang, to participate in a river security operation code-named Green Wave.[159]

Unfamiliar with the area, several PBRs ran aground on the first day of operations. Large swells in the bay also made launching and recovering PBRs from the LST particularly hazardous. A week after commencing operations, *Hunterdon County* relocated its anchorage to the Cau Dai River 18 miles southeast of Danang. On 28 September, the Green Wave force achieved its first contact with the enemy when five rounds of heavy automatic weapons fire hit PBR-118.[160] The next day PBRs engaged the enemy in 15 separate incidents during what one officer described as "a day-long running gun battle." In one of those engagements near Hoi An in Quang Nam Province, small arms fire killed one sailor and wounded another.[161] Three hours later, PBRs 53 and 84, accompanied by an Army helicopter, returned to the area and destroyed 15 shore structures, sank three sampans, and killed seven Viet Cong soldiers.[162]

On 30 September, COMNAVFORV terminated Green Wave, and *Hunterdon County* with River Section 521 embarked departed I Corps for the Mekong Delta. Fifty percent of the PBRs in the unit had sustained damage from groundings and combat in just 12 days of operations, but the main factor that convinced Vice Admiral Elmo Zumwalt, the new COMNAVFORV at the time, to withdraw his forces was rough seas. High swells in the various bays and inlets of the northern I Corps area had made operating PBRs from an LST virtually impossible.[163] NAVFORV would have to find other basing solutions.

Less than two months after *Hunterdon County*'s departure, Game Warden forces returned to the area, supported by a new land base at Tan My on the Perfume River and a floating base called Mobile Support Base 1. The base consisted of several pontoon AMMI barges rafted together and contained enough repair, berthing, messing, and command and control facilities to support ten PBRs in sustained riverine operations. Mobile Support Base 1, which arrived in Danang on 2 December, eventually supported PBR operations on the Cua Viet as well.[164]

River Section 521 deployed to Tan My soon after Green Wave ended and started patrolling the Perfume River on 9 January.[165] These patrols were relatively uneventful until 31 January, when the PAVN and the VC forces attacked Hue and held it for 25 days. During the nascent hours of the attack, eight PBRs made firing runs on enemy positions on the northern bank of

A Task Force Clearwater PBR crew searches a sampan on the Perfume River in I Corps, 20 August 1968.

the Huong River opposite the LCU ramp until marines secured the area that same evening.[166] During the next few weeks River Section 521 PBRs were heavily involved in fighting around the old imperial city, securing landing zones for medevac and resupply helicopters, and evacuating isolated groups of marines as well as Vietnamese refugees. For its actions during Tet, the unit received a Presidential Unit Citation.[167]

During the month of February, VC and PAVN forces made a concerted effort to sever Hue's logistics lifeline by launching multiple attacks on the Hue boat ramp and attacking 44 allied logistics craft on the Perfume River. During these attacks, enemy fire hit 32 NSA Danang logistics craft and two PBRs, killing five American servicemen and wounding 37. B40 rockets and rocket-propelled grenades completely destroyed a self-propelled harbor utility craft and a utility landing craft and severely damaged several other small boats. On 1 February an enemy rocket or mortar round set a newly constructed 3,000-barrel JP-4 tank near the Hue ramp on fire, forcing NSA personnel to evacuate the ramp and quickly set up Tan My as an alternative refueling point for marine helicopters. The Hue boat ramp was not manned in early February, so little or no cargo moved on the Perfume River during the first ten days of the month. However, NSA sailors did not rest during this period; instead, they used their boats to evacuate over 1,300 refugees from Hue to Danang in the largest humanitarian operation of the war involving riverine forces.[168]

Another hive of enemy activity in I Corps during Tet was the ten-mile stretch of the Cua Viet River running from the coast to Dong Ha. Knowing that the Dong Ha supply hub was critical to Khe Sanh's survival, Communist forces made a concerted effort during January-February 1968 to sever its water link to the sea. Mining and ambushes of resupply craft in January resulted in one boat sunk, eight damaged and two sailors killed and 18 wounded.[169] The most tragic incident of the month occurred on 24 January when an LCM (8) carrying a load of cement and B rations hit a mine on the Cua Viet and sank, taking down two sailors with her.[170] In February, PAVN and Viet Cong Forces attacked 27 craft on the Cua Viet, killing seven sailors and wounding 42 others. There also were 26 separate artillery attacks on the Dong Ha and Cua Viet ramp areas.[171]

Concerned that water access to Dong Ha would become cut off, General Creighton Abrams, the deputy commander of MACV, requested that the Navy stand up a patrol force for the Cua Viet River. In response, the Navy activated Task Force Clearwater on 24 February under the command of Captain Gerald W. Smith.[172] An initial force consisting of PBRs from River Section 521 arrived at Cua Viet at the end of the month and was soon augmented by Army helicopters, an Army signal detachment, and elements of a marine searchlight battery.[173] Eventually, Clearwater would grow to over 20 riverine warfare craft of various types and would oversee river security forces on both the Cua Viet and Perfume Rivers.[174]

The town of Cua Viet, situated five miles from the DMZ at the mouth of the river, formed the terminus of the riverine supply route stretching ten miles up the Cua Viet to Dong Ha. Fuel from Navy tankers was offloaded at Cua Viet to a large bladder farm and then transported by LCM (8) bladder boats to Dong Ha, where it was consumed mainly by C-130s and other aircraft shuttling supplies from Dong Ha to Khe Sanh. NSA watercraft also supplied Dong Ha (and by extension Khe Sanh) with most other supplies, ranging from ammunition to food. Keeping this supply line running smoothly proved difficult even under relatively peaceful conditions because of the dredging work required to keep the Cua Viet River and harbor operational. In February the situation became more tenuous after PAVN forces began a sustained artillery attack on the Cua Viet base.[175]

On 24 February, PAVN artillery shelled the base on seven separate occasions, killing one American and causing minor property damage.[176] On 11 March another attack destroyed more than a third of the base, including the maintenance, messing, and berthing facilities.[177] By the end of March most remaining buildings on base were completely fortified with sandbags, including the chapel, which sailors had ingenuously built using the remains of a shelled marine amphibious tractor. The sandy ground absorbed much of the impact of rounds, limiting personnel casualties, but also turned the place into a desert-like sandbox. Sailors eventually constructed boardwalks between buildings and bunkers to make the transit easier. Cua Viet was the only facility that Commander Sayre Swartztrauber, who commanded TF Clearwater from November 1968 to February 1969, ever inhabited in Vietnam that had neither cleaning women nor adequate supplies of fresh water. "It was really austere," he recalled.[178]

In March, River Assault Division 112, less its ASPBs, deployed to the Cua Viet base to provide additional security there.[179] With the arrival of this unit, Task Force Clearwater assumed an offensive posture. ATCs guarded convoys, served as mine countermeasures vessels, and were used for troop insertions and gunfire support.[180] The biggest loss of the month for the task force occurred on 14 March when ATC 112-7, sweeping close to the west bank of the Cua Viet River two miles southeast of Dong Ha, hit an estimated 900-pound water mine. The force of the explosion flipped the 72-ton ATC upside down, causing extensive damage and killing six crewmembers and wounding a seventh.[181] To thwart future mining attempts and ambushes, the task force initiated a 1630–0830 curfew against sampan traffic on the waterway.[182]

March saw a continuation of attacks on river traffic and on the Cua Viet base, which sustained seven rocket/artillery attacks during the course of the month. On 10 March, incoming rounds ignited 150 short tons of staged ammunition, causing fires and secondary explosions throughout the facility and destroying staged cargo, housing, the mess hall, the communications facility, and 47 of the base's 64 10,000-gallon fuel bladders. One sailor was killed and 22 wounded in the attack.[183] Undaunted, the stalwart sailors of the NSA Danang detachment went to work rebuilding their facility immediately after the fire subsided. Aided by sailors from Clearwater, NSA personnel restored cargo operations within 30 hours of the attack and had 60 percent of the base repaired and reconstructed by month's end.[184]

While enemy activity along the Perfume River generally decreased in March, the waterway was not entirely exempt from action. A satchel charge partially destroyed an AMMI fuel barge in Tan My Cove on 1 March and, on the 25th, the enemy fired 30 to 50 mortar rounds at the base's boat cove, fuel farm, and cantonment area. In addition to wounding six sailors, the rounds damaged three LCM (8)s, several petroleum, oil, and lubricant (POL) pipes, and a JP-4 tank.[185]

In April enemy activity on the Perfume declined, but combat action continued on the Cua Viet, where mining, small arms, and rocket/artillery attacks damaged three LCUs, two LCM (8)s, and the gasoline tanker *Genesee* (AOG-8). Personnel casualties included four Navy men killed and 15 wounded.[186] *Genesee* was moored at Cua Viet, offloading motor gas when on 22 April the ship received hostile mortar fire from the shore. One round hit the ship's O-2 level, igniting two gasoline drums; another set the AMMI barge moored alongside her on fire. Intensive damage control efforts extinguished the fires within five minutes, and the ship soon returned to delivering fuel to Cua Viet. Two *Genesee* sailors received shrapnel wounds during the attack.[187]

At the end of the month, PAVN made yet another concerted attempt to halt the flow of supplies to Dong Ha. On 30 April enemy forces entrenched along the banks of the Song Bo Dieu, the access river running from Dong Ha to the Cua Viet River, opened fire with rocket propelled grenades, recoilless rifles, and machine guns on a Clearwater patrol and a logistics convoy. The attacks damaged several craft, wounded six sailors, and killed three.[188] Following the ambushes the Navy suspended all supply operations in that area while two companies of U.S. Marine Battalion Landing Team 2/4 launched a counterattack. The marines encountered fierce resistance from what was thought to be a battalion-size element of the 320th PAVN Division and, during a daylong battle, killed 90 enemy troops, while suffering 16 dead and 107 wounded of its own.[189] Marine Colonel William Weise, the BLT 2/4 commander, directed much of the engagement from a Task Force Clearwater monitor, which he described as "an ideal command post with good communications and significant fire power."[190] Evidently, units from the 320th had deployed to the area in an effort to cut off and shut down the Dong Ha logistics hub; U.S. marines would spend much of May dislodging these forces.

During the early morning hours of 2 May, a PBR, using an infrared illumination device, observed 25 PAVN troops and five others in what looked to be wet suits on the north bank of the river just south of the 30 April ambush area. The patrol boat, joined by two other PBRs, engaged the enemy force with M79 grenade launchers until they fled to the northwest. Navy EOD personnel called to the scene later discovered one magnetic influence mine and part of another. By 5 May six such mines had been located. RAD 112 ATCs went to work immediately to sweep these mines and others from the area.

Elements of the 320th Division continued harassing logistics traffic on the Cua Viet throughout the month. Between 1 and 7 May, PAVN forces fired upon river patrols and logistics craft with rockets and mortars 13 times. Fortunately for the Navy, no casualties and only minor damage resulted. The Cua Viet base also came under sustained enemy pressure. On the 1st, the base received 60 incoming rounds that damaged five craft and wounded six. The next day, 69 incoming artillery bracketed a YOG in the turning basin. The largest attack of the month occurred on 25 May, when the enemy fired 111 artillery rounds at the base. There was no noteworthy damage to Navy installations, but destruction among marine facilities was significant.[191]

In all, there were 12 separate artillery/rocket attacks on Cua Viet and two on the Dong Ha ramp in May, and seven and two, respectively, in June. These attacks killed three sailors, wounded 13, and damaged six LCMs and a significant number of facilities at both installations. In spite of this destruction, the attacks only had a minor impact on the flow of supplies to Dong Ha—no small victory for the sailors of Task Force Clearwater and NSA Danang, Detachment Cua Viet. In no case was this truer than with respect to POL. Daily river transit capability from Cua Viet to Dong Ha remained steady at 340,000 gallons in May despite the destruction of 17 fuel bladders at Cua Viet and resultant loss of 170,000 gallons of POL. While replacement bladders were under order, AMMI barges and an AOG on station near the base provided ready fuel storage, thereby minimizing supply disruption.[192]

Attacks on traffic on the Cua Viet River itself actually declined during May and June—so much so that RAD 12 was allowed to return to IV Corps on 29 May. Its patrol duties were assumed by PBRs from River Section 543 which, according to Swarztrauber, "were better suited for convoy protection than TF 117 craft because of their enhanced speed and maneuverability."[193] On the Perfume, Viet Cong and PAVN forces made one last concerted effort to challenge the Navy's supremacy before ending its campaign to shut down this lifeline. Early in the morning of 7 May, an ambush wounded eight sailors and damaged three PBRs from River Section 521 in the bloodiest action to date for the unit. Logistics craft had to be held at Tan My until Army airborne units completed a sweep of the area at first light.[194] Three days later the Viet Cong again ambushed a River Section 521 patrol. Troops of the 101st Airborne Division began aggressive ground operations, supported by River Section 521, which drove the enemy from the area.[195] By 1 June the Perfume River had been fully pacified, and Task Force Clearwater began shifting resources to interdiction and population control missions, such as sampan searches, curfew enforcement, amphibious insertions, and psychological warfare.[196]

Overall, Task Force Clearwater and its antecedents along with NSA Danang succeeded for all but a few brief periods in keeping supplies flowing to allied forces fighting in two of the most significant battles of the Tet Offensive period: Hue and Khe Sanh. "With the interdiction of much of Route 1 during and after Tet," noted the official marine history, "the lifeline of the marine forces in the north depended more and more upon the sea," and by extension, the rivers. During February, for example, Dong Ha received over 475,000 short tons of material by river and only 342 by air.[197] That naval forces accomplished this herculean riverine supply effort, despite frequent minings, ambushes, and artillery shelling, was a testament to the competence of the boat crews and the sailors who supported them on land and afloat. The I Corps experience demonstrated the significance of waterborne logistics during the Tet Offensive and the ability of the Navy's riverine forces to operate under constant attack for months on end without relief.

CONCLUSION

When Vice Admiral Elmo Zumwalt became Commander, Naval Force Vietnam in the fall of 1968, he found that the interdiction mission "had pretty much been accomplished as far as the coast and the main branches of the Mekong were concerned."[1] Market Time represented the most successful of the Navy's interdiction programs, all but eliminating infiltration by North Vietnamese steel-hulled freighters and curtailing oceangoing junk infiltration by 70 percent. Overall, Market Time reduced North Vietnamese resupply by sea of its forces in the South by 90 percent—a far more successful and less resource-intensive allied interdiction program than the air campaigns to interdict communist supplies along land routes through North Vietnam, Laos, and Cambodia. One of the main reasons Market Time succeeded so well was that powerful Navy radar (based on land, sea, and air) could easily detect large vessels attempting to break the blockade. Maritime patrol aircraft were one of the most effective links in the chain, allowing the Navy to identify and track steel-hulled blockade-runners over vast distances of water. The effectiveness of the Market Time air blockade eventually allowed COMNAVFORV to devote Task Force 115 surface vessels to other missions. By 1967 Market Time units were providing allied forces with naval gunfire support along the coast and actively engaging in civic action and psychological operations. In addition, PCFs had begun patrolling up to five miles inland along major rivers.

The riverine interdiction by Game Warden forces was less successful as a static interdiction barrier but more than made up for this shortcoming by providing a strong naval presence on the main rivers of the Mekong Delta and the RSSZ. This naval inshore presence often hindered large-scale Viet Cong operations and secured the rivers for commerce. PBRs offered a rapid strike force capable of seeking out and engaging enemy combat units wherever they might be found in the watery worlds of the delta and the RSSZ. Their patrols made large enemy movements risky. For much of the war Game Warden's biggest successes involved attacks against VC troops crossing the large rivers and other types of attacks against VC combat troops, so much so that direct action emerged as a significant Game Warden mission by the end of 1968. In no case was this shift more apparent than in the Tet Offensive where Game Warden forces proved instrumental in defending My Tho, Chau Doc, Ben Tre, Vinh Long, and many other places in the Mekong Delta. As James Williams, Paul Cagle, and many others learned firsthand, the PBRs had an uncanny ability to surprise, engage, and kill large numbers of Viet Cong whenever the enemy exposed himself.

The Mobile Riverine Force performed a similar direct combat role, albeit with the able assistance of soldiers of the 9th Infantry Division. As Zumwalt noted when he became COMNAVFORV, the MRF "could carry perhaps 500 9th Division troops to remote locations, give them heavy artillery support as they landed and withdrew, and provide them with far better command, control, and communications than they could possibly have carried on their own backs."[2] Task Force 117 also provided organic medical and logistic support for troops in the field. Modern infantry combat demands a lot of kit, and the capability of the armored troop transports to carry extra gear for the infantry (much more than could be carried in a helicopter) often spelled the difference between victory and defeat, especially when soldiers had to overnight in hostile areas. The ability of soldiers to get comprehensive medical treatment, dry out their wet bodies, eat a hot meal, and sleep in an air-conditioned rack on a barracks ship or LST allowed for sustained combat far from a land base. Of course, barracks ships and LSTs also represented large targets for the enemy. Two of the biggest disasters that befell the shallow water Navy in Vietnam involved the mining of floating mobile bases: *YRBM-16* in November 1967 (seven sailors killed), and *Westchester County* (LST-1167) in November 1968 (18 sailors killed).

Still, the 15 to 1 kill ratio achieved by the MRF probably justified the risks inherent in conducting riverine assault operations deep within enemy territory, especially given General Westmoreland's attritional warfare approach. Even when ambushed, the MRF generally suffered far fewer casualties than the Viet Cong as the high kill ratios achieved by the MRF in the 1967 Rach Ba Rai and Rach Roung battles revealed.[3] When the enemy exposed itself in large numbers, as was the case during Tet 1968, the MRF's ability to project a massive force nearly anywhere in the delta proved instrumental in recapturing cities and inflicting a severe blow on the enemy in the process. As General Westmoreland later commented, the MRF, with the valuable assistance of Vietnamese allies and a handful of American units not attached to the 9th Infantry Division, did indeed save the delta during Tet.

After Tet, the Navy's strategic emphasis shifted back to interdiction. In particular, Zumwalt wanted to stem the flow of enemy supplies along the Cambodian border from Tay Ninh to the Gulf of Thailand. His eventual strategy, known as SEALORDS (Southeast Asia Lake, Ocean, River, and Delta Strategy) established a string of small bases and barrier patrols along the waterways near the border designed to disrupt enemy resupply there. In October 1968 when Zumwalt initiated the operation, the strength of the in-country Navy peaked with 144 vessels deployed with the Coastal Surveillance Force (TF 115); 258 with the River Patrol Force (TF 116); and 184 with the River Assault Force (TF 117) augmented by a Vietnam Navy comprising 655 vessels of various types.[4] By spring 1969 these forces had seized over 200 tons of supplies near the border and, according to the then MACV commander, General Creighton Abrams, greatly reduced Viet Cong activity in the delta.[5]

As is the case of many of America's overseas military endeavors, just when the allied interdiction campaign in the delta was finally achieving some tangible successes, the order to withdraw sounded. Beginning in early 1969, President Nixon made good on his promise to begin pulling American forces out of Southeast Asia. For the Navy, this meant turning over most of its riverine and coastal vessels to the VNN and, by April 1971, the American role in the SEALORDS campaign ended. During this period, the VNN grew from 18,000 personnel in the fall of 1968 to 32,000 by the end of 1970. Vice Admiral Zumwalt did his best to train and prepare the VNN for its new responsibilities, and some significant improvements were achieved. Once America departed the scene, the war was not lost on the waterways of the delta or the coast but in the mountains and flatlands of I, II, and III Corps.

Some of the core problems with the VNN were never fully solved during the course of the war. These included a poorly paid, inadequately trained enlisted force and a young officer corps racked with corruption and graft. With a few significant exceptions, the officers and enlisted personnel together generally lacked the motivation to fight a sustained insurgency by a more determined foe. Sadly, many problems and frustrations encountered by Captain Joseph Drachnik as the MACV naval component commander in 1964 were still present in 1972 when NAVFORV closed shop. Simply providing large amounts of money and equipment to the VNN could not solve their problems—many of which were deeply rooted in Vietnamese political culture.

Paternalism was also to blame. The U.S. Navy's paternalistic attitude toward the VNN manifested itself at every level from COMNAVFORV down to the lowest enlisted advisor and undermined the relationship at every turn. Advisors like Dale Meyerkord, who treated their counterparts with respect and could motivate them to take operational risks, were a rarity. More common were advisors who had great difficulty adapting to the Vietnamese culture and had

New recruits march into the receiving area at the Vietnam Navy headquarters in Saigon, 10 June 1968.

little or no rapport with their counterparts. The language barrier was part of the problem but so too was the profound lack of understanding of the Vietnamese culture. Improved language and culture training and the more widespread use of bilingual VNN liaison officers, sailors, and police partly solved the problem as the war progressed, but in the early years, the yawning cultural gulf between Americans and Vietnamese resulted in misunderstandings and much friction. An even greater form of paternalism during 1965–1968 was the U.S. Navy's tendency to strip away VNN responsibility and give it to the newly formed U.S. Navy in-country task forces. The Americanization of the war retarded the development of the Vietnam Navy and made matters more difficult later on, when the Navy had to return operational responsibilities to the VNN. If the Navy had attempted to better integrate the two forces from 1965 onward, the overall interdiction program arguably might have been more successful, especially with regard to smaller coastal junks and river craft. The presence of more Vietnamese speakers would have improved the visit, board, search, and seizure activities of both TFs 115 and 116 and would have helped naval forces make better informed decisions about which boats to search and which ones to let pass through the net unimpeded.

The technology deployed to Vietnam for inshore operations proved a mixed bag. Nearly every boat sent to Southeast Asia suffered some maintenance problems in the cruel climate of Southeast Asia, but certain platforms were operationally superior to others. Of the vessels deployed there in a large-scale, nonexperimental basis, the WPBs, PBRs, and LCM (6) conversions (ATCs and monitors) performed best, while the Alpha boats and *Asheville*-class PGs suffered the most problems. Comparing these boats to one another, it is ironic that modified off-the-shelf technology generally performed better in Southeast Asia than purpose-built, formally programmed naval weapons. Furthermore, the less an off-the-shelf piece of technology had to be modified for the war, the better its combat performance. ATCs and monitors functioned better than the more heavily modified commercial boats such as the PBRs and PCFs, and the boat with the best combat record was the Coast Guard WPB, which was barely modified at all for use in Southeast Asia.

However, both the PCF and PBR offered shallow-draft capabilities unavailable in the naval weapons inventory at the time and, more important, could be produced in large numbers rapidly and cheaply. The PCF, in the end, functioned well as a coastal patrol craft in fair seas during the dry season, but it was never seaworthy enough to endure the high seas of the monsoon season. The PBR, on the other hand, was in many respects an ideal craft for the River Patrol Force. Its speed allowed crews to surprise the enemy, especially at night when these craft often accelerated from 0 to 25 knots to thwart enemy troop crossings; its water jets and extremely shallow draft allowed it to maneuver easily in even the narrowest channels, and its twin-mount and single-mount .50-caliber guns gave it enough firepower to engage light infantry fighting from crude bunkers and behind earthen levies. It also proved useful for missions not originally envisioned by its creators, such as gunfire support against shore positions, Special Forces insertions, and civic action.

No amount of speed or firepower, however, offered PBRs much in the way of protection against rocket propelled grenades, antitank rockets, or even an accurate rifle round but, if employed in a hit-and-run fashion, similar to how BM1 Williams used the boat, the PBR could inflict devastating damage on an enemy and then flee the scene before the enemy could recover and offer serious resistance. Like PBRs, unarmored PCFs were highly vulnerable to shore fire and had to rely mainly on speed and surprise to prevail in engagements against dug-in ground forces. Monitors and ATCs offered much more protection against small arms, but the Vietnamese quickly developed tactics to damage them. Rocket propelled grenades aimed to explode over well decks with no topside armor and armor-penetrating rockets were especially devastating to the craft of the Mobile Riverine Force.

Mine warfare was another "surprise" of sorts for the Navy. Fortunately, the service possessed enough smaller minesweepers to keep the Long Tau channel open and relatively safe for commercial shipping for all but a few brief periods in the war. Mines also became a problem for the MRF, compelling it to adapt preexisting technology to use in minesweeping and to assign ATCs and Alpha boats to a minesweeping role. Swimmer mine attacks against larger vessels such as LSTs and berthing ships were harder to thwart, but by 1969 extensive use of netting, defensive patrols, and sentries reduced the threat considerably. None of the large floating bases employed in SEALORDS, including Sea Float, were successfully mined by the Viet Cong.

Platforms developed hastily from the keel up and programmed specifically for riverine and coastal warfare were the most problematic craft of the inshore fleet in Vietnam. Although it later performed well as a minesweeper, the Alpha boat represented the biggest disappointment of the war.[6] Nothing about this boat lived up to its promises. It was neither seaworthy nor armored enough to operate effectively with the other MRF armored craft. The *Asheville*-class patrol gunboat, with its higher speed and shallower draft, offered Market Time a potentially superior outer barrier patrol boat to the DER but was plagued by engineering and maintenance problems. However, when the PG worked as promised, it emerged as a fearsome weapon—fast, able to withstand punishing enemy fire, and capable of projecting a massive amount of firepower against the enemy. The performance of these boats in ambushes on rivers later in war, in particular, represented a testament of their potential in the inshore environment. The *Asheville*-class PG, the Alpha, and the PBR did improve over time as modifications and other fixes were made. In the case of the PG, these modifications often required significant periods in the yard, but for smaller boats like the PBR and Alpha most modifications could be made on the spot, either at land bases or on floating bases. The simpler the technology, the easier it was for deckplate-level sailors to modify it for the unique operational needs of the theater.

For the Navy's personnel, Vietnam was a watershed in many ways. It represented the first time since the Civil War that large numbers of sailors experienced riverine warfare in small boats—a combat experience more akin to that of an infantry soldier than a sailor on a large oceangoing surface combatant. For the most part, the sailors who fought in the shallow water Navy were volunteers eager to serve and were excited to participate in this nontraditional type of warfare. Consequently, discipline problems were rare and morale generally high. Drugs were not much of an issue in these units, nor were incidents of racial unrest. Even alcoholism did not undermine the force in a meaningful way prior to 1968. Sailors certainly drank (some even on patrol), but most of those interviewed claimed that it did not affect operational performance. Except in a few isolated cases, fraternization with local civilians also did not cause too many problems. The language barrier and constant movement of forces between afloat and ashore bases did not encourage romantic involvement with locals. Prostitution represented the main form of sexual relations between civilian women and sailors and even this type of interaction was severely limited due to the operational demands of the war and the isolated basing arrangements of many units. Many sailors interviewed for this book refrained from seeing prostitutes for moral or health reasons or out of loyalty to a girlfriend or spouse at home.

The most significant sea change for the Navy that resulted from Vietnam was the enlisted leadership. In the blue water Navy, petty officers supervised teams of sailors and had other responsibilities on a ship but did not generally make decisions with regard to use of force—those decisions were reserved for senior officers (generally ship commanders but sometimes even higher echelon commanders). The fact that most boat captains and many patrol officers in the riverine force were petty officers turned the Navy's traditional sense of what defined command upside down. On these vessels enlisted personnel decided whether or not to employ lethal force in combat situations, and their decisions more often than not shaped the course of the many small engagements that together defined the riverine war.

Junior officers, similarly, had vastly more authority over life and death issues than similar ranking officers on larger ships. The lieutenants who commanded PCFs and WPBs often proved instrumental in some of the most significant Market Time intercepts of the war. With a few tragic exceptions (such as the PCF-4 incident), their leadership and thoughtfulness under fire showed maturity beyond their years. Unfortunately, Vietnam service pulled them away from traditional blue water assignments (such as division officer duties on a destroyer) and precluded many from receiving promotions to high ranks after the war; the Navy personnel system, with its traditional mindset, did not recognize the talent nascent in this pool of junior officers coming home from Vietnam. Few officers interviewed for this book, especially those with Reserve backgrounds, ended up making the Navy a career. Most either separated from the Navy soon after returning home or served in one or two more assignments before leaving the service.

The Navy may never again fight a shallow water war as extensive as Vietnam, but littoral combat, coastal surveillance and interdiction, and riverine operations have all occurred in more recent maritime operations and will probably continue in the future. This form of warfare has never been popular with officials interested in the acquisition of big decks, but the Vietnam experience revealed that the U.S. Navy, when pressed, can adapt rapidly to a shallow water environment and prevail. In the Vietnam context, the Navy's human beings often proved more adaptable than the technology deployed or the tactics employed. Any success achieved had as much to do with the sailors and junior officers who volunteered for this arduous duty than with all other factors combined. It was truly a sailor's war like no other in the Navy's recent history.

ACRONYMS AND ABBREVIATIONS

AD	destroyer tender
AFHRA	Air Force Historical Research Agency
AFS	combat store ship
AGMR	major communications relay ship
AK	cargo ship
AKA	attack cargo ship
AMC	coastal minesweeper
AMS	motor minesweeper
ANGLICO	air-naval gunfire liaison company
AO	oiler
AOG	gasoline tanker
APA	attack transport
APB	self-propelled barracks ship
API	armor-piercing incendiary
APL	barracks craft (non-self-propelled)
AR	repair ship
AR	Archives, Naval History and Heritage Command (NHHC)
ARL	landing craft repair ship
ARVN	Army of the Republic of Vietnam
ASPB	assault support boat
ATC(H)	armored troop carrier (helicopter)
ATC	armored troop carrier
AV	seaplane tender
BB	battleship
BLT	battalion landing team
BM	boatswain's mate
BuShips	Bureau of Ships
CA	heavy cruiser
CAG	guided missile heavy cruiser

CBU	cluster bomb unit
CCB	command and control boat
CDR	commander
CIA	Central Intelligence Agency
CIDG	Civilian Irregular Defense Group
CINCPAC	Commander in Chief, Pacific
CINCPACFLT	Commander in Chief, Pacific Fleet
CL	light cruiser
CLG	guided missile light cruiser
CMH	Center of Military History
CNA	Center for Naval Analyses
CNO	Chief of Naval Operations
CO	commanding officer
COMNAVFORV	Commander, Naval Forces Vietnam
CONEX	Container Express
CP	command post
C-rat	canned ration
CSC	Coastal Surveillance Center
CTF	commander, task force
CTZ	corps tactical zone
CV	aircraft carrier
CVA	attack aircraft carrier
CYN	communications yeoman
DANFS	Dictionary of American Naval Fighting Ships
DD	destroyer
DDG	guided missile destroyer
DDR	radar picket destroyer
DE	escort ship
DER	radar picket escort ship
DLG	guided missile frigate
DMS	high-speed minesweeper, or destroyer minesweeper
DMZ	demilitarized zone (the border between North and South Vietnam)
EN	engineman
ENFN	engineman fireman
EOD	explosive ordnance disposal
ET	electronics technician
ETR	electronics technician radar
FA	fireman apprentice
FAC	forward air controller

FTL	flight team lead
GM	gunner's mate
GMG	gunner's mate (guns)
GMGSA	gunner's mate (guns)/seaman apprentice
GMGSN	gunner's mate (guns)/seaman
GVN	Government of Vietnam
GW	The George Washington University
HACS	House Committee on Armed Services
HAL	helicopter attack (light) squadron
HC	helicopter combat support squadron
HEAT	high explosive antitank
HM	hospital corpsman
HQ	*Hai Quan* (Vietnam Navy)
ICAF	Industrial College of the Armed Forces
IFF	identification, friend or foe
JAG	judge advocate general
JGS	Joint General Staff
LAW	light antitank weapon
LCDR	Lieutenant Commander
LCM	landing craft, mechanized
LCPL	landing craft personnel (large)
LCU	landing craft, utility
LCVP	landing craft, vehicle, personnel
LDNN	*Lien Doc Nguoi Nhia* (South Vietnamese frogmen)
LPH	amphibious assault ship
LSD	dock landing ship
LSIL	landing ship, infantry (large)
LSM	medium landing ship
LSSL	support landing ship (large)
LST	tank landing ship
LT	lieutenant
LTJG	lieutenant junior grade
MAAG	Military Assistance Advisory Group
MACV	Military Assistance Command, Vietnam
MDMAF	Mekong Delta Mobile Afloat Force
MEDCAP	Medical Civic Action Program
MILPHAP	Military Provincial Health Assistance Program
MINRON	mine squadron
MLMS	motor launch minesweeper

MP	military police
MRB	Mobile Riverine Base
MRF	Mobile Riverine Force
MSB	minesweeping boat
MSC	minesweeper, coastal (nonmagnetic)
MSF	minesweeper, fleet (steel hull)
MSO	minesweeper, ocean (nonmagnetic)
NAG	Naval Advisory Group
NAVFORV	Naval Forces Vietnam
NDL	Navy Department Library
NGFS	naval gunfire support
NILO	naval intelligence liaison officer
NIOTC	Naval Inshore Operations Training Center
NROTC	Naval Reserve Officer Training Corps
NSA	naval support activity
NSG	Northern Surveillance Group
NFV	Naval Forces Vietnam (abbreviated version)
OEG	Operations Evaluation Group
OINC	officer in charge
OPNAV	Office of the Chief of Naval Operations
PAVN	People's Army of Vietnam
PBR	river patrol boat
PC	submarine chaser (Vietnam Navy designation)
PCE	patrol escort
PCF	patrol craft, fast
PG	patrol gunboat
PGM	motor patrol gunboat motor
PHIBRON	amphibious squadron
PHILCAG	Philippine Civic Action Group
PRU	provincial reconnaissance unit
PTSD	posttraumatic stress disorder
PSYOP	psychological operations
QM	quartermaster
R&R	rest and relaxation
RAD	River Assault Division
RAG	River Assault Group
RAS	river assault squadron
RF	Regional Forces
RIVFLOT	River Assault Flotilla

RMSN	radioman seaman
RM	radioman
ROE	rules of engagement
ROTC	Reserve Officer Training Corps
RPG	rocket-propelled grenade
RSSZ	Rung Sat Special Zone
RVN	Republic of Vietnam
RVNAF	Republic of Vietnam Armed Forces
SEAL	military member
SEALORDS	Southeast Asia Lake, Ocean, River, and Delta Strategy
SERE	survival, evasion, resistance, and escape
SERVPAC	Service Force, U.S. Pacific Fleet
SH	Ships Histories
SLAR	side-looking airborne radar
SLED	South Carolina Law Enforcement Division
SN	seaman
Sp	specialist (U.S. Army)
SS	submarine (USN); steamship (Merchant Marine)
SSBN	ballistic-missile submarine
STCAN/FOM	*Services Techniques des Construction et Armes Navales/France Outre Mer* [Technical Services and Construction of Naval Weapons/Overseas France]
SVN	South Vietnam
TAOR	tactical area of responsibility
TF	task force
TG	task group
TOC	Tactical Operations Center
TRIM	Training Relations Instruction Mission
TU	task unit
UDT	underwater demolition team
USA	United States Army
USAF	United States Air Force
USAID	United States Agency for International Development
USCG	United States Coast Guard
USNI	U.S. Naval Institute
USNR	United States Naval Reserve
VA(AW)	attack squadron (all-weather)
VC	Viet Cong
VCF	Vietnam Command File
VF	fighter squadron

VFMA	Valley Forge Military Academy
VNAF	(South) Vietnamese Air Force
VNN	(South) Vietnam Navy
VP	patrol squadron
WHEC	high-endurance cutter (USCG)
WP	white phosphorus
WPB	patrol boat (USCG)
XO	executive officer
YFNB	large covered lighter (non-self-propelled)
YFU	harbor utility craft (self-propelled)
YMS	auxiliary motor minesweeper
YOG	gasoline barge (self-propelled)
YRBM	repair, berthing, and messing barge (non-self-propelled)

BIBLIOGRAPHY

Archival Records
Air Force Historical Research Institute, Maxwell Air Force Base, Montgomery, AL.
Army Center of Military History, Washington, DC:
> Central Files.
> Files of Dr. Eric Villard.
> General Officer Bio Files.
> Oral History Collection.

Coast Guard History Office, Washington, DC:
> Central Files.
> Oral History Collection.
> Photography Collection.

Helm, Glenn. Personal Papers. Private Collection.
Mahon Library, Lubbock, TX:
> Special Collections.

National Archives and Records Administration. College Park, MD:
> Records of the United States Forces in Southeast Asia, 1950–1975, Record Group 472.
> U.S. Navy Deck Logs.
> Vietnam Photos. Still Pictures Branch.

Naval History and Heritage Command, Archives Branch. Washington Navy Yard, DC:
> CINCPACFLT Message Traffic.
> CNO Flag Plot Files.
> Commander Naval Forces Vietnam (COMNAVFORV) Files.
> Immediate Office Files of the Chief of Naval Operations (Double Zero Files).
> Ismay, Arthur. Papers.
> Marolda, Edward J. Papers.
> National Military Command Center (NMCC) Operation Summaries (OPSUM) Files.
> Naval Advisory Group Vietnam Records.
> Officer Bio Files.
> Operation Orders.

Bibliography

    Oral History Collection.
    PACFLT Message Traffic.
    Photography Collection.
    Post–1946 Command Files.
    Rare Books and Manuscripts, Navy Department Library.
    Salvage Reports.
    Seventh Fleet Provenance.
    Sheehan, Neil. Personal Papers.
    Sherwood, John Darrell. Personal Papers.
    Ships History Collection.
    Studies Collection. Center for Naval Analyses (CNA).
    Vietnam Command Files.
    Vietnam Awards Cards.
    Vietnam War Casualty Cards.
Navy Department Board of Decorations, Washington, DC.
Olds, Frederick A. Personal Papers. Private Collection.
Oswald, Edwin "Larry." Personal Papers. Private Collection.
Sheboygan County Historical Research Center, Sheboygan Falls, WI:
    Freund, Terrence "Terry" J., File.
United States Marine Corps History Division, Grey Research Center, Quantico, VA:
    After Action Reports.
    Operation Orders.
Vietnam War Archive, Texas Tech University, Lubbock, TX:
    "A Review of U.S. Navy Experience in Establishment and Conduct of South Vietnam Inshore Coastal Patrol: Operation Market Time." Westwood Research, Inc., Project WR-119-B, May 1969.
    Oral History Collection.
    Photography Collection.

Oral Histories

Author Interviews. Digital Files held by Archives Branch, Naval History and Heritage Command:
    Ismay, Arthur. McLean, VA, 19 June 2008.
    Lloyd, Charles. Washington Navy Yard, DC, 22 May 2008.
    Ly, Huynh. My Tho, Vietnam, 21 September 2009.
    Mosher, Charles. Falling Waters, WV, 9 April 2008.
    Vi, Nguyen Huu. Ben Tre, Vietnam, 18 September 2009.
Author Telephone Interviews:
    Adams, James R. 17 May 2011.
    Balian, Alexander. 10 September 2008.

Banegas, Eldon. 9 November 2010.
Barney, Eugene. 24 July 2008; 6 February 2009.
Beery, Jere. 24 November 2008.
Benedick, Jack. 14 May 2010.
Bergin, Edward J. 4 June 2008.
Billings, Al. 23 October 2008.
Bolduc, Lucien "Blackie." 12 February 2010.
Branscomb, Max G. 24 June 2008.
Breininger, Alan. 8 June 2008.
Butler, David K. 19 November 2009.
Cagle, Paul W. 15 September 2010.
Carlstrom, Ken. 6 May 2009.
Clouse, David W. 1 November 2010.
Cox, Charlie. 21 October 2009
Cragg, Richard J. 29 October 2008.
Davis, Robert E. 11 August 2009.
Davis, Roderick. 5 November 2008.
Dempsey, Thomas A. 6 August 2009.
Devlin, Mike. 5 November 2008.
Dexter, Stephen T. 19 August 2009.
Do, Kiem. 1–7 November 2007.
Dodd, Arthur J. 21 August 2009.
Donham William B., II. 15 November 2010.
Donovan, John J., Jr. 3 November 2008.
Franson, Robert. 14 August 2009.
Fredricksen, Randal "Randy" Kenneth. 21 December 2010.
Fuscaldo, Robert P. 13 February 2009.
Goins, Timothy S. 5 November 2010.
Green, John L., Jr. 31 July 2009.
Haggerty, Pat. 21 August 2009.
Hammel, Jerry M. 4 March 2009.
Hendrickson, John. 22 June 2011.
Herrera, Raul. 29 May 2008.
Johnson, James D. 25 June 2009.
Johnson, Raymond W. 8 March 2010.
Johnson, Robert R. 7 January 2009.
Kiem, Do. See Do, Kiem.
Lacapruccia, Joseph. 3 September 2009.
Lineberger III, Walter F. 12–13 January 2010.

Bibliography

    McDavitt, Fred M. 22 October 2008.
    Menner, Ronald R. 18 February 2010.
    Miller, John L. 20 August 2009.
    Olds, Frederick A. 6 April 2009.
    O'Leary, Dennis Boe John. 20 May 2009.
    Oswald, Edwin "Larry." 28 June 2001.
    Parsons, Dwayne L. 3 November 2010.
    Picard, Richard. 29 March 2011.
    Pinion, Robert A. 5 November 2010.
    Rankin, Peter B. 31 March 2011.
    Raybell, David. 25 June 2009.
    Reynolds, William L. "Bill." 29 April 2010.
    Riojas, Erasmo "Doc." 18 October 2010.
    Rodgers, Larry D. 4 August 2009.
    Schlosser, Jim. 29 April 2009.
    Schneider, Lester. 5 August 2009.
    Smith, Chester B. 6 March 2009.
    Smith, Robert W. 20 August 2010.
    Spatt, Frank R. 3 June 2009.
    Stanley, Chester C., Jr. 26 June 2009.
    Sumrall, Stephen. 13 August 2010.
    Thorell, James C. 18 March 2009.
    Trackerman, Anthony J. 25 Mar 2011.
    Turley, Michael. 28 May 2008.
    Ulmer, Stephen T. 19 September 2008.
    Verhasselt, Ray J. 24 August 2010.
    Vitale, Steven J. 18 August 2009.
    Wasmund, Thomas. 7 May 2009.
    Watson, Stephan "Steve." 18 November 2008.
    Weatherall, James L. "Larry." 28 April 2010.
    Webb, Lowell Elliott. 13 November 2008.
    Wells, Norman. 2 November 2009.
    Weseleskey, Allen E. 9 March 2012.
    Williams, Michael. 25 March 2009.
    Wojciechowski, Jerome "Jerry." 27 June 2011.
Coast Guard History Office, Coast Guard Headquarters, Washington, DC:
    Nelson, Robert T. Interview by Alex Larzelere, undated.
Frank, Timothy. Private Collection:
    Williams, James E. Interview by Tim Frank. Medal of Honor Society, Patriots Point, SC, 25 September 1997.

Naval History and Heritage Command, Archives Branch, Washington Navy Yard, DC:
    Oral History Collection:
    Blackburn, Paul P. Interview by Oscar Fitzgerald, undated.
    Bucklew, Phillip H. Interview by Oscar Fitzgerald, undated.
    Cang, Chun Tan. Interview by Oscar P. Fitzgerald, 8 October 1976.
    Chidsey, John W. Interview by Dean C. Allard, Oscar P. Fitzgerald, and Michael Kelly, 1 December 1966.
    Doyle, Robert C. Interview by Edward J. Marolda, 28 September 1978.
    Drachnik, Joseph B. Interview by Oscar Fitzgerald, undated.
    Drachnik, Joseph B. Interview by William W. Moss, Norfolk, VA, 27 July 1970.
    Friedman, Malcolm C. Interview by Oscar P. Fitzgerald, undated.
    Gray, Paul N. Interview by Edward J. Marolda, 10 September 1983.
    Hardcastle, William H. Interview by Oscar Fitzgerald, 15 July 1978.
    Ismay, Arthur. Interview by Dean C. Allard, Oscar P. Fitzgerald, and Michael Kelly, 6 June 1967.
    Swartztrauber, Sayre A. Interview by Oscar P. Fitzgerald, 3 June 1969.
    Thang, Bang Cao. Interview by Oscar P. Fitzgerald, 21 August 1975.
    Thoai, Ho Van Ky. Interview by Oscar P. Fitzgerald, 20 September 1975.
    Venzke, Norman C. Naval History Division Staff, 28 February 1969.
U.S. Army Center of Military History. Washington, DC:
    Vietnam Interview Collection:
    Turner, James S. G. Interview by MAJ Phillip J. Thomas, USA, 2 March 1968.
U.S. Army Military History Institute, Carlisle Barracks, Carlisle, PA.
    DePuy, William E. Interviewer unknown, 1988.
    Knowlton, William A. Interview by LTC David W. Hazen, 1982.
U.S. Naval Institute, Annapolis, MD:
    Oral History Collection:
        Bucklew, Phillip H. Interview by John T. Mason Jr., 19 March 1980.
        Salzer, Robert S. Interview by John T. Mason Jr., November 1981.
        Ward, Norvell G. Interview by Edward G. Marolda, 6 September 1983.
        Ward, Norvell G. Interviews by Paul Stillwell. Interview Numbers 1, 4, 5, 7; 14 May 1985, 11 September 1986, 15 September 1986, and 30 June 1987, respectively.
        Vietnam Archive. Texas Tech University, Lubbock, TX:
        Harris, Michael. Interview by Stephen Maxner, 22 August 2000.
        Oswald, Edwin "Larry." Interviews by Laura Calkins, 1, 27, 30 April 2004; 13, 27 May 2004.
        Rectanus, Earl F. Interview by Paul Stillwell, 19 November 1982.

Published Books

Billings, Al. *Seawolf 28: A True Story*. Charleston, SC: BookSurge, 2004.

Blair, Clay, Jr. *Silent Victory: The U.S. Submarine War Against Japan*. New York: J.B. Lippincott Company, 1975.

Blinn, Gary R. *Confession to a Deaf God: Memoir of a Mekong River Rat*. Philadelphia, Pennsylvania: Xlibris, 2002.

Bruhn, David R. *Wooden Ships and Iron Men*. Vol. 3, *The U.S. Navy's Coastal and Inshore Minesweepers and the Minecraft that Served in Vietnam, 1953–1976*. Westminster, MD: Heritage Books, 2011.

Cash, John A., John Albright, and Allan W. Sandstrum. *Seven Firefights in Vietnam*. Washington, DC: Office of the Chief of Military History, 1985.

Christopher, Ralph. *Duty, Honor, Sacrifice: Brown Water Sailors and Army River Raiders*. Bloomington, IN: AuthorHouse, 2007.

Constance, Harry, and Randall Fuerst. *Good to Go: The Life and Times of a Decorated Member of the U.S. Navy's Elite SEAL Team Two*. New York: William & Morrow, 1997.

Croizat, Victor J. *Journey among Warriors: The Memoir of a Marine*. Shippensburg, PA: White Mane Publishing Company, 1997.

Cutler, Thomas J. *Brown Water, Black Berets: Coastal and Riverine Warfare in Vietnam*. Annapolis, MD: Naval Institute Press, 1988.

Dix, Drew. *The Rescue of River City*. Fairbanks, AK: Drew Dix Publishing, 2000.

Do, Kiem, and Julie Kane. *Counterpart: A South Vietnamese Naval Officer's War*. Annapolis, MD: Naval Institute Press, 1998.

Dockery, Kevin. *Navy SEALS: A History Part II: The Vietnam Years*. New York: Berkley, 2002.

Dunn, Carroll H. *Base Development in South Vietnam, 1965–1970*. Washington, DC: Department of the Army, 1991.

Erwin, Virg. *Cat Lo: A Memoir of Invincible Youth*. Indianapolis, IN: Dog Ear Publishing, 2009.

Fall, Bernard B. *Street without Joy*. Harrisburg, PA: Stackpole, 1964.

Friedman, Norman. *U.S. Small Combatants, Including PT-Boats, Subchasers, and the Brown Water Navy: An Illustrated Design History*. Annapolis, MD: Naval Institute Press, 1987.

Fulton, William B. *Riverine Operations 1966–1969*. Washington, DC: Department of the Army, 1973.

Goldsmith, Wynn. *Papa Bravo Romeo: U.S. Navy Patrol Boats at War in Vietnam*. New York: Ballantine Books, 2001.

Grey, Jeffrey. *Up Top: The Royal Australian Navy and Southeast Asian Conflicts, 1955–72*. Canberra, AUS: Australian War Memorial, 1998.

Hammond, William H. *Reporting Vietnam: Media & Military at War*. Lawrence: University Press of Kansas, 1998.

Herring, George C. *America's Longest War: The United States and Vietnam, 1950–1975*, 2d ed. New York: Alfred A. Knopf, 1979.

Hooper, Edwin B. *Mobility, Support, Endurance: A Story of Naval Operational Logistics in the*

Vietnam War, 1965–1968. Washington, DC: Naval History Division, 1972.

Hooper, Edwin Bickford, Dean C. Allard, and Oscar P. Fitzgerald. *The United States Navy and the Vietnam Conflict.* Vol. 1, *Setting the Stage to 1959.* Washington, DC: Naval History Division, 1976.

Huchthausen, Peter A., and Nguyen Thi Lung. *Echoes of the Mekong.* Baltimore, MD: Nautical & Aviation Publishing Co., 1996.

Jane, Fred, and Dennis H. R. Archer. *Jane's Infantry Weapons, 1976.* New York: Franklin Watts, 1976.

Jane's Fighting Ships. New York: McGraw-Hill, 1963–1964.

Johnson, James D. *Combat Chaplain: A Thirty-Year Vietnam Battle.* Denton: University of North Texas Press, 2001.

Johnson, Raymond W. *Postmark: Mekong Delta.* Westwood, NJ: Fleming H. Revell Co., 1968.

Kelly, Daniel E. *Seawolves: First Choice.* New York: Ivy Books, 1998.

Kelly, Orr. *Brave Men—Dark Waters: The Untold Story of the Navy Seals.* Novato, CA: Presidio, 1992.

Knott, Richard. *Fire from the Sky: Seawolf Gunships in the Mekong Delta.* Annapolis, MD: Naval Institute Press, 2005.

Koburger, Charles W., Jr. *The French Navy in Indochina: Riverine and Coastal Forces, 1945–1954.* Westport, CT: Praeger, 1991.

Larzelere, Alex. *The Coast Guard at War: Vietnam, 1965–1975.* Annapolis, MD: Naval Institute Press, 1997.

Lloyd's Register of Shipping. 1966–1967. Annual Periodical. London: Lloyds, 1967.

MacGarrigle, George L. *Taking the Offensive: October 1966 to October 1967.* Washington, DC: Center of Military History, 1998.

Marolda, Edward J. *The Approaching Storm: Conflict in Asia, 1945–1965.* Washington, DC: Naval History and Heritage Command, 2009.

———. *By Sea, Air, and Land: An Illustrated History of the U.S. Navy and the War in Southeast Asia.* Washington, DC: Naval Historical Center, 1994.

———. *Ready Seapower: A History of the U.S. Seventh Fleet.* Washington, DC: Naval History and Heritage Command, 2012.

Marolda, Edward J., and Oscar P. Fitzgerald. *The United States Navy and the Vietnam Conflict.* Vol. 2, *From Military Assistance to Combat, 1959–1965.* Washington, DC: Naval Historical Center, 1986.

Marolda, Edward J., and R. Blake Dunnavent. *Combat at Close Quarters.* Washington, DC: Naval History and Heritage Command, forthcoming.

Mercogliano, Robert. "Sealift: The Evolution of American Military Sea Transportation." Ph.D. diss., University of Alabama. Tuscaloosa, AL, 2004.

Moyar, Mark. *Triumph Forsaken: The Vietnam War, 1954–1965.* Cambridge: Cambridge University Press, 2006.

Nalty, Bernard C. *Air Power over South Vietnam, 1968–1975.* Washington, DC: Air Force History and Museums Program, 2000.

Naval History Division, Navy Department. *Riverine Warfare: The U.S. Navy's Operations on Inland Waters*. Washington, DC: Government Printing Office, 1969.

Naval Training Command. *Rate Training Manual: Boatswain's Mate 1&C*. NAVTRA 10122-D. Washington, DC: Government Printing Office, 1973.

Nyc III, Frederick F. *Blind Bat: C-130 Night Forward Air Controller Ho Chi Minh Trail*. Austin, TX: Eakin Press, 2000.

Office of the Prime Minister, Directorate General of Planning. *Vietnam Statistical Yearbook 1967–1968*. Vol. 14. Saigon, VN: National Institute of Statistics, 1968.

Page, Tim. *Page After Page*. New York: Atheneum, 1989.

Schlight, John. *The War in South Vietnam: The Years of the Offensive, 1965–1968*. Washington, DC: Office of Air Force History, 1988.

Schreadley, Richard L. *From the Rivers to the Sea: The U.S. Navy in Vietnam*. Annapolis, MD: Naval Institute Press, 1992.

Scotti, Paul C. *Coast Guard Action in Vietnam: Stories of Those Who Served*. Central Point, OR: Hellgate Press: 2000.

Sheehan, Neil. *The Arnheiter Affair*. New York: Random House, 1971.

Sheppard, Don. *Riverine: A Brown-Water Sailor in the Delta, 1967*. San Francisco, CA: Presidio, 1992.

Shulimson, Jack, Leonard A. Blasiol, Charles R. Smith, and David Dawson. *U.S. Marines in Vietnam: The Defining Year: 1968*. Washington, DC: History and Museums Program, Headquarters, U.S Marine Corps, 1997.

Spector, Ronald H. *Advice and Support: The Early Years of the U.S. Army in Vietnam, 1941–1960*. New York: Free Press, 1985.

Starry, Donn A. *Mounted Combat in Vietnam*. Washington, DC: Department of the Army, 1989.

Steffes, James. *Swift Boat Down: The Real Story of the Sinking of PCF-19*. Bloomington, IN: Xlibris, 2006.

Symmes, Weymouth D. *This is Latch: The Story of Rear Admiral Roy F. Hoffmann*. Missoula, MT: Pictorial Histories Publishing Company, 2007.

Tucker, Spencer C., ed. *Encyclopedia of the Vietnam War: A Political, Social, and Military History*. New York: Oxford University Press, 1998.

Uhlig, Frank, Jr., ed. *Vietnam: The Naval Story 1950–1970*. Annapolis, MD: Naval Institute Press, 1986.

Willbanks, James H. *The Tet Offensive: A Concise History*. New York: Columbia, 2007.

Zumwalt, Elmo R., Jr. *On Watch: A Memoir*. New York: Quadrangle, 1976.

Articles

Anderson, Jack. "Navy Clams Up on Arnheiter Case." *Washington Post*, 24 April 1967, B11.

———. "U.S. Navy Suffering Leadership Crisis." *Washington Post*, 9 October 1969, G15.

"The Arnheiter Case." *Virginian-Pilot*, 14 May 1968, 16.

"Arnheiter Case Needs Review." *Denver Post*, 7 June 1968, 12.

Chapelle, Dickey. "Water War in Viet Nam." *National Geographic* 129 (February 1966): 272–296.

Cobb, Broughton. "River Patrol Boat for Vietnam." *Yachting,* December 1966, 101–103.

Cutts, Bob. "Swift Boat Crew Survive Horror." *Pacific Stars and Stripes,* 13 June 1966.

Davidow, Julie. "Proud but haunted, ex-Vietnam riverboat gunner is remembered." *Seattle Post-Intelligencer,* 16 July 2006. www.seattlepi.com/local/277800_riverboat17.html, accessed 16 April 2009.

Faram, Mark D. "Father of Naval Special Warfare Dies at 78." *Navy Times,* 18 January 1993, 22.

"First Silver Star Presented to a Sailor." *The Jackstaff News,* 4 November 1966.

"Game Warden Patrol Takes Heavy Casualties." *The Jackstaff News,* 16 June 1967, 1.

Ginter, Barry. "Victim of Vietnam Honored: Navy Building Named for Sheboygan Man." *Sheboygan Press,* undated copy, 11.

Gray, Paul N. "We Will Remain Until the Conflict Is Won." *The Jackstaff News,* 30 June 1967, 1.

Harvey, Frank. "Clean Sweep for the River Jets." *Argosy,* February 1967, 42–43, 80–85.

Herrera, Raul. "Swift Boats in Operation Market Time." *Vietnam,* February 1966, 37–9.

Hodgman, James A. "Market Time in the Gulf of Thailand." *United States Naval Institute Naval Review* 94 (May 1968): 38–49.

Hymoff, Edward, "Sea Raiders: U.S. Navy's Silver Star Commandos," *Saga: The Magazine for Men,* March 1967, 64.

Jensen, Dean. "Honors for a Hero: Navy Cross Awarded Posthumously to Local GI." *Sheboygan Press,* 18 May 1967, 1.

Kasperick, Dan. "What Makes a Hero?" *All Hands,* June 1968, 2–6.

Kay, Robert. "VN Navy Headquarters Attacked." *The Jackstaff News,* 16 March 1968.

Kilpatrick, James Jackson. "He Might Have Been Another Halsey." *National Review,* 26 March 1968, 288–296.

Lescaze, Lee. "Bentre: Only Part of the City Was Saved." *Washington Post,* 8 February 1968, A-10.

"Lt. Charles Don Witt Is Killed in Vietnam Clash." *Lubbock Avalanche-Journal,* 25 May 1967, 1, 14.

Maffre, John. "How the Hell Could This Happen?" *Washington Post,* 19 November 1967, B1.

McClintock, Robert. "The River War in Indochina." *U.S. Naval Institute Proceedings* 80 (December 1954): 1305.

McDougal, Lee and Mary K. Rice. "Johnson is his Name, Versatility is his Game." *Navy Recruiter,* October 1969, 14.

Menzoff, J. A. "SEAL (Sea, Air, Land) Teams." In *Encyclopedia of the Vietnam War: A Political, Social, and Military History,* edited by Spencer C. Tucker, 370–371. New York: Oxford University Press, 1998.

Michener, James A. "Essex Skipper Clips Wings of Death." *Washington Times–Herald,* 6 February 1952.

Mumford, Robert E., Jr. "Jackstay: New Dimensions in Amphibious Warfare." *U.S. Naval Institute Naval Review* 94 (1968): 68ff.

"Navy Swift Boat Sunk But Revenge Exacted." *The Jackstaff News.* 14 Jul 1967.

Bibliography

"New Gunboat to Join Fleet Soon." *Navy Magazine,* February 1966.
Oladeinde, Patricia. "Riverboat Gambler." *All Hands,* July 1998, 14–17.
Popowitz, A.G. "Repair Support for the MRF." *The Jackstaff News,* 18 May 1968.
Randal, Jonathan. "Enemy Sinks U.S. Dredge; 3 Other Vessels Damaged." *New York Times,* 10 January 1967, 1, 3.
Reiling, Victor G., Jr., and G. W. Scott. "Psychological Operations in Vietnam. *U.S. Naval Institute Proceedings* 94 (Jul 1968): 124.
Rose, Dick. "Seawolves of the Delta." *The Jackstaff News,* 16 March 1968, 10.
Shea, Dan. "SADJ Identification Series: The RPG ID Guide." *Small Arms Defense Journal.* www.sadefensejournal.com/. Accessed 21 April 2012.
Sheehan, Neil. "The 99 Days of Captain Arnheiter." *New York Times Magazine.* August 1968.
Sprinkle, James D. "Helatkltron Three: The Seawolves." *Journal of the American Aviation Historical Society* 33 (Winter 1988): 290–310.
Stephan, Charles R. "Trawler!" *U.S. Naval Institute Proceedings* 94 (September 1968): 60–71.
Sullivan, Bob. "Helping Vietnamese SOP for Long Xuyen Sailors." *The Jackstaff News,* 10 March 1967.
Sullivan, Bob. "Long Xuyen is Biggest PBR Base." *The Jackstaff News,* 24 March 1967.
Swartztrauber, Sayre A. "River Patrol Relearned." *United States Naval Institute Proceedings Naval Review* 96 (May 1970): 120ff.
"SWO Training Facility Names [sic] for Vietnam Hero." *Surface Warfare,* November 1980, 31–33.
Travnicek, Ivan. "A Short Savage Ambush." *Naval History,* October 2006, 25–27.
"Viet Cong Fire Kills City Man." *Lubbock Avalanche-Journal,* 26 May 1967, 1, 7.
Wainwright, Loudon. "In Search of a Vietnam Hero." *Life Magazine,* 28 May 1965, 23–26.
Wunderlin, Jr., Clarence E. "Paradox of Power: Infiltration, Coastal Surveillance, and the United States Navy in Vietnam, 1965–1968." *The Journal of Military History* 53 (July 1989): 275–289.

Internet Resources

Defense Prisoner of War/Missing Personnel Office. www.dtic.mil/dpmo
Defense Technical Information Center (DTIC). www.dtic.mil/dtic
The Gamewardens of Vietnam Association. www.tf116.org
Home of Heroes. www.homeofheroes.com
Military Times. www.militarytimes.com
Mobile Riverine Force Association. www.mrfa.org
Naval History and Heritage Command. www.history.navy.mil
Patrol Craft Fast. www.pcf45.com
Seawolf Association. www.seawolf.org
United States Coast Guard Academy. www.uscga.edu
United States Coast Guard Parents Association. www.uscgaparents.org
United States Department of Veterans Affairs, Public Health. www.publichealth.va.gov

Vietnam Veterans Memorial. thewall-usa.com
Virtual Vietnam Archives, www.vietnam.ttu.edu/virtualarchive
The Virtual Wall, Vietnam Veterans Memorial. www.virtualwall.org

ENDNOTES

Preface

1. Military Assistance Command Vietnam, Directorate for Information Operations, Enemy and Free World Forces, South Vietnam, 1960–72, Operational Archives (AR), Naval History and Heritage Command (NHHC).

2. These were the sailors who worked for Commander, Naval Forces Vietnam (COMNAVFORV), the Navy's operational commander and chief naval advisor in South Vietnam.

3. For a list of individuals killed in Task Forces 115, 116, and 117, see http://mrfa.org/, accessed 1 February 2012.

4. For examples of memoirs written by sailors who fought in South Vietnam, see Wynn Goldsmith, *Papa Bravo Romeo: U.S. Navy Patrol Boats at War in Vietnam* (New York: Ballantine Books, 2001); Peter A. Huchthausen and Nguyen Thi Lung, *Echoes of the Mekong* (Baltimore, MD: Nautical & Aviation Publishing Company, 1996); Daniel E. Kelly, *Seawolves: First Choice* (New York: Ivy Books, 1998); and Don Sheppard, *Riverine: A Brown-Water Sailor in the Delta, 1967* (San Francisco, CA: Presidio, 1992).

5. Edward J. Marolda, *By Sea, Air, and Land: An Illustrated History of the U.S. Navy and the War in Southeast Asia* (Washington: Naval Historical Center, 1994), 310–318.

1. Early Years

1. Lieutenant (LT) Harold Dale Meyerkord, Personal Diary, 8 Aug 1964, 13 Aug 1964, Individual Persons, Post-1946 Command Files, AR; excerpts from Meyercord, Aug 1964 Action Reports, 23rd RAG Advisor, Box 223, Records of Chief, Naval Advisory Group [hereafter NAG Records], AR; Edward J. Marolda, *The Approaching Storm: Conflict in Asia, 1945–1965* (Washington, DC: Naval History and Heritage Command, 2009), 44–45.

2. Thomas J. Cutler, *Brown Water, Black Berets: Coastal and Riverine Warfare in Vietnam* (Annapolis, MD: Naval Institute Press, 1988), 48.

3. Meyerkord as cited in Cutler, *Brown Water*, 48; LT Harold D. Meyerkord, USNR, Officer Bio File, AR, NHHC.

4. Chief Eugene Barney as cited in Cutler, 52; Dickey Chapelle, "Water War in Viet Nam," *National Geographic* (Feb 1966): 272–296. Barney confirmed quoted material in a telephone interview with the author on 24 July 2008.

5. Meyerkord diary, 13 Aug 1964.

6. Ibid.

7. Where possible I have used the units of measurement found in the original sources; consequently, Imperial and metric units are depicted throughout this book.

8. Norman Friedman, *U.S. Small Combatants: An Illustrated Design History* (Annapolis, MD: Naval Institute Press, 1987), 283; Cutler, *Brown Water*, 45.

9. Meyerkord diary, 13 Aug 1964.

10. Excerpts from Meyerkord, Aug 1964 Action Reports.

11. Loudon Wainwright, "In Search of a Vietnam Hero," *Life Magazine*, 28 May 1965, 23.

12. See Mark Moyar, *Triumph Forsaken: The Vietnam War, 1954–1965* (Cambridge: Cambridge University Press, 2006), 335.

13. Marolda, *Approaching Storm*, 17.

14. Edwin Bickford Hooper, Dean C. Allard, and Oscar P. Fitzgerald, *The United States Navy and the Vietnam Conflict*, vol. 1, *Setting the Stage to 1959* (Washington, DC: Naval History Division, 1976), 197; Charles W. Koburger Jr., *The French Navy in Indochina: Riverine and Coastal Forces, 1945–1954* (Westport, CT: Praeger, 1991), 101.

15. Hooper et al., *Setting the Stage to 1959*, 187; Koburger, *French Navy in Indochina*, 102.

16. Koburger, *French Navy in Indochina*, 8.

17. Robert McClintock, "The River War in Indochina," *United States Naval Institute Proceedings* (Dec 1954): 1305.

18. Cutler, *Brown Water*, 44; Koburger, *French Navy in Indochina*, 44.

19. Bernard B. Fall, *Street without Joy* (Harrisburg, PA: 1964), 44.

20. Victor J. Croizat, "The Origins of Vietnamese Naval Forces," 9, Box 205, NAG Records.

21. Hooper et al., *Setting the Stage to 1959*, 200.

22. Croizat, "The Origins of Vietnamese Naval Forces," 8, 10–11.

23. Ibid, 12.

24. Hooper et al., *Setting the Stage to 1959*, 317.

25. Victor J. Croizat, *Journey among Warriors: The Memoir of a Marine* (Shippensburg, PA: White Mane Publishing, 1997), 118; Hooper et al., *Setting the Stage to 1959*, 265–666.

26. Croizat, *Journey among Warriors*, 118; Hooper et al., *Setting the Stage to 1959*, 323.

27. George C. Herring, *America's Longest War: The United States and Vietnam, 1950–1975*, 2d ed. (New York: Alfred A. Knopf, 1979), 52.

28. Hooper et al., *Setting the Stage to 1959*, 322; Herring, *America's Longest War*, 54–55.

29. Croizat, *Journey among Warriors*, 114.

30. Naval History Division, Navy Department, *Riverine Warfare: The U.S. Navy's Operations on Inland Waters* (Washington, DC: Government Printing Office, 1969), 43.

31. Kiem Do, interview with author, 2 Nov 2007; Kiem Do and Julie Kane, *Counterpart: A South Vietnamese Naval Officer's War* (Annapolis, MD: Naval Institute Press, 1998), 79–80;

Hooper et al., *Setting the Stage to 1959*, 327–328. Note: Vietnamese surnames commonly precede given names. I have used this convention in the text of this history but not in bibliographic entries, which conform to the Library of Congress catalog entries.

32. Hooper et al., *Setting the Stage to 1959*, 373–374.

33. The North Vietnamese Central Committee authorized an armed struggle against the Republic of Vietnam in January 1959 and created the National Liberation Front (Viet Cong) in December 1960. Cutler, *Brown Water*, 19.

34. Memo, Lieutenant Junior Grade (LTJG) Harold V. Smith, USNR, to Chief, Navy Section, Military Assistance Advisory Group (MAAG) Vietnam, subj: After Action Report on Completion of Tour, 31 Dec 1962, Box 192, NAG Records.

35. Memo, LTJG Charles G. Stowers, 26th River Assault Group Advisor to Chief, Navy Section MAAG Vietnam, subj: After Action Report on Completion of Tour, 26 Nov 1963, Box 192, NAG Records.

36. Do and Kane, *Counterpart*, 102–103.

37. Ho Van Ky Thoai, interview by Oscar P. Fitzgerald, 20 Sep 1975, transcript, 32, NHHC Oral History Collection, AR.

38. MAAG Indochina became Military Assistance Command, Vietnam (MACV) on 8 February 1962 in recognition of the increase in U.S. military aid to Vietnam.

39. Memo, CAPT Joseph B. Drachnik to ADM Claude V. Ricketts (Vice Chief of Naval Operations), subj: Experience as Chief, Navy Section MAAG Vietnam, Dec 1961–Jan 1964, 13 Mar 1964, 6, Box 575, NAG Records.

40. Due to wartime expediency, his course of instruction was reduced to three years. Thus, Drachnik graduated in 1942 but is technically a member of the Class of 1943. CAPT Joseph B. Drachnik, Officer Bio File.

41. Ibid.; Joseph B. Drachnik, interview by Oscar Fitzgerald, undated, NHHC Oral History Collection; Edward J. Marolda and Oscar P. Fitzgerald, *The United States Navy and the Vietnam Conflict*, vol. 2, *From Military Assistance to Combat, 1959–1965* (Washington: Naval Historical Center, 1986), 266.

42. Joseph B. Drachnik, interview by William W. Moss, Norfolk, VA, 27 Jul 1970, Box 192, Vietnam Command File (VCF), AR.

43. CAPT Phillip Bucklew, interview by Oscar Fitzgerald, undated, NHHC Oral History Collection.

44. Marolda and Fitzgerald, *From Military Assistance to Combat*, 135–137.

45. Commander, Naval Forces Vietnam (COMNAVFORV), "The Naval War in Vietnam," 30 Jun 1970, 16–17, Box 137, VCF.

46. Marolda and Fitzgerald, *From Military Assistance to Combat*, 228–239, 158–159; Marolda, *By Sea, Air, and Land*, www.history.navy.mil/seairland/chap2.htm, accessed 13 May 2014.

47. Drachnik interview, undated.

48. Naval Advisory Group, "Vietnamese Navy's Role in the Counterinsurgency," 12 Jun 1964, 6, Box 205, NAG Records.

49. Lieutenant Commander (LCDR) Wesley A. Hoch, USN, subj: After Action Report on Completion of Tour, 1 Jul 1964, Box 192, NAG Records.

50. Naval Advisory Group, MAAG, subj: Coastal Force Problems in Personnel and Support, 25 Sep 1964, Box 241, NAG Records.

51. LT P. E. Byron, "Medical Survey of Junk Division 33," 31 Oct 1963, Box 192, NAG Records.

52. NAG, "Vietnamese Navy's Role in the Counterinsurgency," 6.

53. Hoch, After Action Report, 1 Jul 1964.

54. Marolda and Fitzgerald, *From Military Assistance to Combat*, 234.

55. Croizat, "The Origins of Vietnamese Naval Forces," 7–8.

56. LT Billy D. Graham, "Junk Force Operation, Vinh Hy Bay, 19 Aug 1963," After Action Report No. 719-63, undated, Edward J. Marolda Papers, AR.

57. Ibid.; LCDR Dallas W. Shawkey, Officer Bio File; Dallas W. Shawkey, Bronze Star with V Citation, Award Cards Vietnam, AR; Msg, COMUSMACV to CINCPAC, 190805H Aug 1963, Marolda Papers; Marolda and Fitzgerald, *From Military Assistance to Combat*, 234.

58. NAG, "Vietnamese Navy's Role in the Counterinsurgency," 7.

59. Marolda and Fitzgerald, *From Military Assistance to Combat*, 234.

60. Moyar, *Triumph Forsaken*, 194.

61. Marolda and Fitzgerald, *From Military Assistance to Combat*, 237.

62. Ibid., 219–250; Navy Section MAAG Vietnam, Advisory Plan 01-63, 10 Sep 1963, Virtual Vietnam War Archive, Texas Tech University, www.vietnam.ttu.edu/star/images/075/0750102001a.pdf, accessed 4 May 2007.

63. Hoch, After Action Report, 1 Jul 1964.

64. LT Charles Patrick Ragan, After Action Report on Completion of Tour, 17 Apr 1964, Box 192, NAG Records; Navy Section MAAG Vietnam, Advisory Plan 001-62, Jan 1962, Marolda Papers.

65. Marolda and Fitzgerald, *From Military Assistance to Combat*, 248.

66. Ragan, After Action Report, 17 Apr 1964; Navy Section MAAG Vietnam, Advisory Plan 001-62, 10 Sep 1962.

67. Joseph Drachnick, River Boat Incident Log, Mar to Oct 1962, Virtual Vietnam Archive, Texas Tech University, http://www.vietnam.ttu.edu/star/images/075/0750110004.pdf, accessed 4 May 2007.

68. LCDR Richard Chesebrough, Senior River Force Advisor, "Problem Areas of the VNN River Force," 21 Dec 1962, Virtual Vietnam Archive, Texas Tech University, accessed 4 May 2007, http://www.vietnam.ttu.edu/star/images/075/0750107012.pdf.

69. Ragan, After Action Report, 17 Apr 1964.

70. LCDR Ray C. Nieman, "Vietnamese River Forces—Are We Winning the War?" 6 May 1962, encl in Joseph Drachnik, Command Briefing, 6 May 1962, Virtual Vietnam Archive, Texas Tech University, http://www.vietnam.ttu.edu/star/images/075/0750103008.pdf, accessed 4 May 2007.

71. Chesebrough, "Problem Areas of the VNN River Force, 21 Dec 1962.

72. Ragan, After Action Report, 17 Apr 1964.

73. Marolda and Fitzgerald, *From Military Assistance to Combat*, 247.

74. The Sea Force included 5 PCs, 4 LSMs, 7 LSILs, 3 YMSs, and 1 AKL. See Marolda and Fitzgerald, *From Military Assistance to Combat*, 153.

75. Friedman, *U.S. Small Combatants*, 237; *Jane's Fighting Ships*, 1963–1964, "Vietnam," s.v., 449–451; Marolda and Fitzgerald, *From Military Assistance to Combat*, 153–157, 239–243; Naval History Division, Office of the Chief of Naval Operations (OPNAV), "History of Naval Operations Vietnam," vol. 2, 1946–1963, Jun 1964, 220–221, Box 85, VCF.

76. Ibid., 222–229; Marolda and Fitzgerald, *From Military Assistance to Combat*, 239–243.

77. Report as cited in Marolda and Fitzgerald, *From Military Assistance to Combat*, 157.

78. Ibid., 239–243.

79. LT J. O. Richter Jr., USNR, After Action Report on Completion of Tour, 23 Apr 1964, Box 192, NAG Records.

80. LT Charles W. Long, USNR, After Action Report on Completion of Tour, 29 May 1964, Box 192, NAG Records.

81. Commander (CDR) Aaron A. Levine, USN, End of Tour Report for Period 7 August 1963 to 1 July 1964, 1 Jul 1964, Box 192, NAG Records.

82. Do interview, 2 Nov 2007.

83. Long, After Action Report, 29 May 1964.

84. Eugene Barney, telephone interview with author, 24 Jul 2008.

85. Levine, End of Tour Report, 1 Jul 1964.

86. Do and Kane, *Counterpart*, 103.

87. Marolda and Fitzgerald, *From Military Assistance to Combat*, 272; translation of article on Captain Quyen's death from the newspaper, *Don Nai*, 11/11/1963, Box 192, Drachnik File, VCF.

88. Moyar, *Triumph Forsaken*, 157.

89. Luc later retrieved the body and delivered it to Cong Hoa Military Hospital. CAPT Ho Tan Quyen was buried on 6 November in a simple Buddhist ceremony. He received no military honors, and only three very junior VNN officers attended. A group of U.S. Navy officers raised money to help Quyen's wife immigrate to Japan and train to become a hairdresser. Msg, American Legation United States Naval Attaché (ALUSNA) to Director Naval Intelligence (DNI), 061219Z Nov 1963, Box 177, CNO Flag Plot, AR; *Don Nai*, 11/11/1963; Drachnik interview, 27 Jul 1970, 12; Marolda and Fitzgerald, *From Military Assistance to Combat*, 273; CAPT Malcolm C. Friedman, USN, interview by Oscar P. Fitzgerald, undated, transcript, 16, NHHC Oral History Collection, AR; Do interview, 2 Nov 2007.

90. Msg, ALUSNA to DNI, subj: Resume of VNN Participation in the Coup d'État of 1–2 Nov 1963, 050834Z Nov 1963, Box 177, CNO Flag Plot.

91. Drachnik interview, 27 Jul 1970, 13; *Don Nai*, 11/11/1963.

92. Thoai interview, 20 Sep 1975, 17; Drachnik interview, 27 Jul 1970, 13; Joseph Drachnik, Command Briefing, 6 May 1962, Virtual Vietnam Archive, Texas Tech University, www.vietnam.ttu.edu/star/images/075/0750103008.pdf, accessed 4 May 2007; Bang Cao Thang,

interview by Oscar P. Fitzgerald, 21 Aug 1975, transcript, 9, NHHC Oral History Collection; Do interview, 2 Nov 2007.

93. Do interview, 2 Nov 2007; Do and Kane, *Counterpart*, 119–120.

94. Msgs, ALUSNA to DNI, 050834Z Nov 1963; ALUSNA to DNI, subj: Resume As of 1515H, 010943Z Nov 1963, Box 177, CNO Flag Plot.

95. Do interview, 2 Nov 2007.

96. Do and Kane, *Counterpart*, 120.

97. Msg, ALUSNA to DNI, 050834Z Nov 1963.

98. Drachnik interview, undated.

99. Herring, *America's Longest War*, 136.

100. Thoai interview, 20 Sep 1975, transcript, 19.

101. LT F. T. Lazarchick, USN, After Action Report on Completion of Tour, 1 Jun 1964, Box 192, NAG Records.

102. Marolda and Fitzgerald, *From Military Assistance to Combat*, 169–171; Cutler, *Brown Water, Black Berets*, 72; Marolda, *By Sea, Air, and Land*, 36–37.

103. Marolda and Fitzgerald, *From Military Assistance to Combat*, 171–174.

104. Msg, COMSEVENTHFLT to CINCPACFLT, 291038Z Mar 1962, Marolda Papers.

105. Msg, CTG 72.7 to COMSEVENTHFLT, 120615Z Mar 1962, Marolda Papers.

106. Commander Task Group 72.7, Report Analyzing and Making Recommendations on Problems Concerning Participation in Patrols off the Coast of Vietnam, 18 May 1962, Marolda Papers.

107. Moyar, *Triumph Forsaken*, 300.

108. Marolda and Fitzgerald, *From Military Assistance to Combat*, 303.

109. CAPT Phillip H. Bucklew, interview by John T. Mason Jr., 19 Mar 1980, 1–61, U.S. Naval Institute (USNI) Oral History Collection, Annapolis, MD; Mark D. Faram, "Father of Naval Special Warfare Dies at 78," *Navy Times*, 18 Jan 1993, 22; Bucklew, Officer Bio File.

110. Bucklew interview, 19 Mar 1980, 62–125; Bucklew, Officer Bio File.

111. Faram, "Father of Naval Special Warfare Dies at 78," 22; Bucklew, interview by Mason, 19 Mar 1980, 25–138.

112. Bucklew interview, 19 Mar 1980, 25–138.

113. Ibid., 239.

114. Bucklew interview, 19 Mar 1980, 239, 241–241, 254.

115. This command included Underwater Demolition Teams 11 and 12, Beach Jumper Unit 1, SEAL Team 1, and Boat Support Unit 1.

116. Bucklew interview, undated (1975).

117. Ibid.

118. Bucklew interview, 19 Mar 1980, 333.

119. Senior Member, Vietnam Delta Infiltration Study Group, "Report of Recommendations Pertaining to Infiltration into South Vietnam of Viet Cong Personnel, Supporting Materials,

Weapons and Ammunition," 15 Feb 1964, Box 73, COMNAVFORV Files, AR [hereafter cited as Bucklew Report].

120. Bucklew Report, "Infiltration Counter-measures," App. II and III.

121. Bucklew interview, 19 Mar 1980, 338.

122. Nearly all of the original SEALs came out of the 1960s UDT community, but the SEAL organization itself traces its legacy back to the scouts and raiders, naval combat demolition units, Office of Strategic Services operational swimmers, underwater demolition teams, and motor torpedo boat squadrons of World War II.

123. *From Military Assistance to Combat, 1959–1965*, 189; Seal Team 2, Command History, 1966, Post-1946 Command File.

124. Much of the current SEAL training for the U.S. Navy is now conducted at the United States Phil Bucklew Naval Special Warfare Center at Coronado, California.

125. *From Military Assistance to Combat, 1959–1965*, 191; J. A. Menzoff, "SEAL (Sea, Air, Land) Teams," in Spencer C. Tucker, ed., *Encyclopedia of the Vietnam War: A Political, Social, and Military History* (New York: Oxford University Press, 1998), 370–371.

126. RADM Allan L. Reed, Assistant Chief of Naval Operations (Fleet Operations and Readiness), "SEAL Teams in Naval Warfare," Naval Warfare Information Publication 29-1 as cited by Marolda and Fitzgerald, *From Military Assistance to Combat*, 191–192.

127. LCDR Carmine Tortora, "An Analysis of SEAL Operations and Effectiveness in the Mekong Delta, June 1969–April 1970," U.S. Naval Postgraduate School, Research Note RN-24, Box 137, VCF.

128. Victor Daniels and Judith Erdheim, "Game Warden," Center for Naval Analyses Operations Evaluation Group, CRC 284, Jan 1976, www.dtic.mil/dtic/tr/fulltext/u2/a034269.pdf, accessed 28 Mar 2012.

129. Marolda, *By Sea, Air, and Land*, 170.

130. SEAL Team 1, Command History Updated to 1966; Navy Medal of Honor: Vietnam War, 1964–75, http://www.history.navy.mil/faqs/moh/moh20.htm, accessed 28 Mar 2012; Vietnam War Recipients of the Navy Cross, www.homeofheroes.com/members/02_NX/indexes/ncross_rvn_list.html, accessed 28 Mar 2012.

131. SEAL Team 1, Command History, Updated to 1966.

132. SEAL Team 1, Command History, 1967, Post-1946 Command File.

133. SEAL Team 2, Command History, 1967, ibid.

134. SEAL Team 2, Command History, 1968; and Operational Summary Report Detachment Alpha, annex to SEAL Team 1, Command History, 1968, ibid.

135. Drew Dix, *The Rescue of River City* (Fairbanks, AK: Drew Dix Publishing, 2000), 57–69; See also the "High Drama in the Delta" sidebar in Edward J. Marolda and R. Blake Dunnavent's manuscript, "Combat at Close Quarters: Warfare on the Rivers and Canals of Vietnam," forthcoming from Naval History and Heritage Command.

136. Menzoff, "SEAL (Sea, Air, Land) Teams," 371.

137. Tortora, "An Analysis of SEAL Operations and Effectiveness in the Mekong Delta, June 1969–April 1970."

Endnotes

138. DM1 Harry Humphries, interview by Kevin Dockery, in Kevin Dockery, *Navy SEALS: A History Part II: The Vietnam Years* (New York: Berkley, 2002), 189.

139. Commander in Chief Pacific (CINCPAC), Command History, 1965, Annex A, United States Military Assistance Command Vietnam (MACV), 1965, 58, Post 1 Jan 1946 Command Files; Armed Forces Information and Education, Department of Defense, "The Evidence at Vung Ro Bay," 1965, Box 23, VCF.

140. Second Naval Zone Intelligence Advisor, Combat Operations After Action Report: Vung Ro Bay and Bai Coc Operations, 17–24 Feb 1965, 27 Feb 1965, Box 222, NAG Records; Moyar, *Triumph Forsaken*, 357; CINCPACFLT, "The United States Navy in the Pacific 1965," 26, Post 1 Jan 1946 Command Files.

141. Chief, Naval Advisory Group, Historical Review, Feb 1965, dated 26 Mar 1965, Annex Alfa, The Vung Ro Incident, 1–3, based on the After Action Report of LCDR Harvey P. Rodgers, USN, Vung Ro folder, Author Files (see also Amphibious Support Battalion Advisor, Phuc Yen Operation, 16 Feb–20 Feb 1965 attached to Annex Alfa); CINCPACFLT, "The United States Navy in the Pacific, 1965," 27; Harvey P. Rodgers, Officer Bio File; Msg, MACV to CINCPAC, 010325Z Mar 1965, Marolda Papers; Cutler, *Brown Water*, 76.

142. NAG Historical Review, Feb 1965, 3.

143. Moyar, *Triumph Forsaken*, 357.

144. NAG Historical Review, Feb 1965, Annex Alfa, 2–3.

145. GEN William E. DePuy, Oral History, United States Military History Institute, 1988; NAG Historical Review, Feb 1965, v; and Annex Alfa, 3; CINCPACFLT, "The United States Navy in the Pacific 1965," 27; Marolda and Fitzgerald, *From Military Assistance to Combat*, 513; Naval History Division, OPNAV "History of U.S. Naval Operations in the Vietnam Conflict," vol. 3, "1965–1967," 230–231, Box 85, VCF; CINCPAC Command History, 1965, Annex A, 54.

146. NAG Historical Review, Feb 1965, v; Annex Alfa, 4.

147. Ibid., v, and Annex Alfa, 1–8; Second Naval Zone Intelligence Advisor, After Action Report: Vung Ro Bay and Bai Coc Operations, 17–24 Feb 1965, 27 Feb 1965, Vung Ro Folder, Author Files.

148. Thoai interview, 20 Sep 1975, 27.

149. NAG Historical Review, Feb 1965, v, and Annex Alfa, 1–8; Second Naval Zone Intelligence Advisor, After Action Report: Vung Ro Bay and Bai Coc Operations, 17–24 Feb 1965.

150. NAG Historical Review, Feb 1965, v, and Annex Alfa, 4, 6.

151. Thoai, interview by Fitzgerald, 25.

152. NAG Historical Review, Feb 1965, v, and Annex Alfa, 5, 7.

153. Department of Defense, "The Evidence at Vung Ro Bay," 1965.

154. The flotilla included LSMs (HQs 405 and 406), PC/patrol escorts (PCEs) (HQs 04, 08, and 09); NAG Historical Review, Feb 1965, Annex Alfa, 8.

155. Ibid.

156. Paul P. Blackburn, interview by Oscar Fitzgerald, undated, audio CD, NHHC Oral History Collection.

157. Bucklew Report, Appendix IV.

158. Marolda and Fitzgerald, *From Military Assistance to Combat*, 515.

159. Msg, CINCPACFLT to CINCPAC, 100023Z Mar 1965, Marolda Papers.

160. Eventually an agreement was reached that permitted U.S. Navy ships to stop and search suspicious vessels within the three-mile Republic of Vietnam (RVN) territorial limit.

161. The patrol areas varied in length, but each averaged 35–40 nautical miles in depth. See Concept for the Interdiction of Communist Infiltration of RVN from the Sea, Conference at Saigon 3–10 Mar 1965, Records of the Immediate Office of the Chief of Naval Operations [hereafter Double Zero Files], 1965, AR; Marolda and Fitzgerald, *From Military Assistance to Combat*, 517.

162. Naval Advisory Group, Historical Review, Mar 1965, 30 Apr 1965, 4, Box 69, VCF.

163. Cutler, *Brown Water*, 81.

164. LT M. L. McGuire, Third Naval Zone Advisor, End of Tour Report, Oct 1965, Box 192, NAG Records.

165. See the preface to the Free Press edition of Ronald H. Spector, *Advice and Support: The Early Years of the U.S. Army in Vietnam, 1941–1960* (New York: Free Press, 1985), x.

166. Memo, CAPT William H. Hardcastle to Secretary of the Navy, subj: Posthumous Award of the Navy Cross to LT Harold Dale Meyerkord, 30 Mar 1965, serial 1650, Meyerkord folder, Author Files.

167. The action was reconstructed from these sources: LT Harold Dale Meyerkord, 23d RAG Advisor, After Action Report, 13 Jan 1965; memo, Hardcastle to SECNAV, 30 Mar 1965; Meyerkord diary, 13 Jan 1965.

168. Ltr, MAJ Oscar H. Padgett, United States Army (USA), to Chief Naval Advisor Group, MACV, undated, serial 1650, Meyerkord folder, Author Files.

169. The action was reconstructed from these sources: Meyerkord, After Action Report, 24 Jan 1965; Hardcastle to SECNAV, 30 Mar 1965; Meyerkord diary, 24 Jan 1965; Naval Speed Ltr, Chief Naval Advisory Group to Chief of Naval Personnel, 8 Feb 1965, serial 1650, Meyerkord folder, Author Files.

170. ENC Ralph J. Gentile, Engineer Advisor 23rd RAG, Statement on H. D. Meyerkord, undated, serial 1650, Meyerkord folder, Author Files.

171. William H. Hardcastle, interview by Oscar P. Fitzgerald, 15 Jul 1978, NHHC Oral History Collection.

172. Barney telephone interview, 24 Jul 2008; Cutler, *Brown Water, Black Berets*, 65; Memo, Chief Naval Advisory Group to SECNAV, subj: Posthumous Award of Navy Cross to Lt. Harold Dale Meyerkord, 30 Mar 1965, Awards Files.

173. Gentile, Statement on H. D. Meyerkord.

174. MAJ Oscar Padgett Jr., USA, as cited by Loudon Wainwright, "In Search of a Vietnam Hero," *Life Magazine*, 28 May 1965, 24.

175. Hardcastle interview, 15 Jul 1978.

2. Coastal Warfare, 1965–1966

1. In a 9 April 2008 interview about the incident, Charles Mosher could not recall the Army officer's first name.

2. *Point Grey* trawler intercept was reconstructed from the following sources: Charles B. Mosher, interview with author, Falling Waters, WV, 9 Apr 2008; Coastal Surveillance Force, Market Time, Monthly Historical Summary, May 1966, Box 852, Post-1946 Command File; *Brister* (DER-327), Command History, 1966; *Tortuga* (LSD-26), Command History, 1966, Ships Histories (SH), AR; Msgs, COMCOGARRON One to COMCOGARDIV Thirteen, undated, *Point Grey* Attack; COMNAVFORV to USCGC *Point Grey*, 110408Z May 1966; COMCOGARDRON One to COMCOGARDIV Eleven, 121022Z May 1966; and COMCOGARDRON One Diary, 1–15 May 1966, OGACT Ops May 1966: all in Box 224, VCF; Harbor Clearance Unit One, Command History, 1966, Box 1250, Post-1946 Command File; Flag Plot, 11–12 May 1966, Box 8, Flag Plot Chronology File, AR; NMCC Operational Summary (Opsum), 11–12 May 1966, Box 104, NMCC OPSUMS, Post-1946 Command File; Alex Larzelere, *The Coast Guard at War: Vietnam, 1965–1975* (Annapolis, MD: Naval Institute Press, 1997), 61–67; Paul C. Scotti, *Coast Guard Action in Vietnam: Stories of Those Who Served* (Central Point, OR: Hellgate Press, 2000), 41–56.

3. These flaws were originally described by Clarence E. Wunderlin Jr., "Paradox of Power: Infiltration, Coastal Surveillance, and the United States Navy in Vietnam, 1965–1968," *The Journal of Military History* 53 (Jul 1989): 275–289.

4. CINCPACFLT, Command History, 1965, 26, Box 38, Post-1946 Command File. For other descriptions of the Vietnam coastline, see CAPT James A. Hodgman, USCG, "Market Time in the Gulf of Thailand," in Frank Uhlig Jr., ed., *Naval Review 1968* (Annapolis, MD: USNI, 1968), 39; and CDR E. N. Fenno, USN, Naval Advisory Group, MACV, Staff Study, Vietnamese Navy Coastal Force, 20 Feb 1965, Box 74, VCF.

5. Edward J. Marolda, *Ready Seapower: A History of the U.S. Seventh Fleet* (Washington: Naval History and Heritage Command, 2012), 65, 123, 147–148.

6. Naval History Division, OPNAV, "History of U.S. Naval Operations in Vietnam," vol. 3, "1965–1967," 234–236, Box 85, VCF; M. A. Nerenstone and D. D. Culbertson, Operations Evaluation Group (OEG) Study No. 706, "Market Time: Countering Sea-borne Infiltration in South Viet Nam," Center for Naval Analyses (CNA), 20 Dec 1966, 1, CNA Studies, AR; MACV, Market Time Study Group Report, 5 Sep 1967, 10, Box 64, VCF; Naval Advisory Group, Monthly Historical Review, Mar 1965, Box 69, VCF.

7. *Higbee* (DD-806), Command History, 1965; *Black* (DD-666), Command History, 1965, SH.

8. CDR Max Branscomb, USN (Ret.), interview with author, 24 Jun 2008.

9. Msgs, COMSEVENTHFLT to CINCPACFLT, Market Time Utilization of EC121K/DER, 170952Z Apr 1965; and COMSEVENTHFLT to CINCPACFLT, 271058Z Apr 1965, Box 9, Seventh Fleet Provenance, AR; Naval History Division, OPNAV, "History of U.S. Naval Operations in Vietnam," 3:249; CINCPACFLT, Command History, 1965, 35.

10. The "Junk Blue Book," Market Time's ready reference on the subject, was unable to define a junk more specifically than "any civilian or paramilitary surface craft of South Vietnam whose length

is less than 100 feet. The junks described in the guide represent more of a sampling of Vietnamese junks than a comprehensive source on the subject. See CINCPACFLT and Combat Development and Test Center, Army of the Republic of Vietnam, "Junk Blue Book: A Handbook of Junks of South Vietnam," 6 Aug 1962, DTIC, http://handle.dtic.mil/100.2/AD356185, accessed 15 Jul 2008; and Msg, COMSEVENTHFLT to CINCPACFLT, 170954Z Apr 1965, Box 9, Seventh Fleet Provenance.

11. CINCPACFLT, Command History, 1965, 30–33, Box 38, Post-1946 Command File.

12. Msg, CINCPAC to RUEKDA/JCS, 212256Z Apr 1965, Box 9, Seventh Fleet Provenance.

13. COMSEVENTHFLT Report as cited by CINCPAC to RUEKDA/JCS, 212256Z Apr 1965.

14. LT John W. Chidsey, interview by Dean C. Allard, Oscar P. Fitzgerald, and Michael Kelly, 1 Dec 1966, transcript, 15–21, NHHC Oral History Collection; John W. Chidsey, Officer Bio File; Notebook of LT John W. Chidsey, Mar 1965–Jan 1966, Box 192, VCF.

15. LT John W. Chidsey, After Action Report of Patrol on PGM-601 for Dates 13 Jun 1965–7 Jul 1965, Box 192, VCF.

16. Chidsey interview, 1 Dec 1966, 36.

17. Memo, Chief, Naval Advisory Group, MACV to CINCPACFLT, subj: Bronze Star Medal with Combat "V" in the case of LT John Warren Chidsey, USN, serial 212, 24 Jan 1966, Box 57, NAG Records.

18. LT Gordon E. Abercrombie, Deck Advisor and Operations Advisor to Sea Force, Apr 1964–Apr 1965, End of Tour Report, 8 Apr 1965, Box 192, NAG Records.

19. Naval History Division, OPNAV, "History of U.S. Naval Operations in Vietnam," 3:1083.

20. See Chief, Naval Advisory Group, Monthly Evaluation Reports for the Vietnam Navy, Jan 1965, Box 246, NAG Records [hereafter NAG Monthly Evaluation Report for VNN].

21. LT D. M. Bennett, Logistics Advisor to the Vietnamese N-4 from July 1964 to March 1965, and as a Sea Force ship rider for the Remainder of the Tour, End of Tour Report, 6 Jul 1965, Box 192, NAG Records.

22. NAG Monthly Evaluation Report for VNN, 1965; NAG Staff Study, Vietnamese Navy Coastal Force, 20 Feb 1965.

23. Naval History Division, OPNAV, "History of U.S. Naval Operations in Vietnam," 3: 1137, 1151–1152.

24. LT James Vincent as cited in Cutler, *Brown Water, Black Berets*, 35.

25. Naval History Division, OPNAV, "History of U.S. Naval Operations in Vietnam," 3: 1050–1052.

26. Hardcastle as cited in Marolda and Fitzgerald, *From Military Assistance to Combat*, 313.

27. Naval History Division, OPNAV, "History of U.S. Naval Operations in Vietnam," 3: 1050–1052.

28. LT Norman G. Mosher, After Action Report on the Completion of Tour, 1 Aug 1965, Box 192, NAG Records; Norman G. Mosher, Officer Bio File.

29. Memo, Chief, Naval Advisory Group MACV to CINCPACFLT, Re: Legion of Merit with Combat V in the case of LT Norman G. Mosher, USN, serial 2046, 19 Oct 1965, Box 53,

Endnotes

Unclassified Serials, NAG Records.

30. LT Robert K. Reilly, After Action Report on the Completion of Tour, 25 Jun 1965, Box 192, VCF.

31. NAG Staff Study, Vietnamese Navy Coastal Force, 20 Feb 1965.

32. VADM Chun Tan Cang, interview by Oscar P. Fitzgerald, 8 Oct 1976, NHHC Oral History Collection.

33. Msg, COMUSMACV to COMSEVENTHFLT, 201618Z Apr 1965, Coastal Force Folder, Author Files.

34. Kiem Do interview, 1–6 Nov 2007; Do and Kane, *Counterpart*, 124–126.

35. NAG Analysis Sheet, subj: VNN Political Problems, 17 Jun 1965, Box 71, VCF.

36. Bang Cao Thang, interview by Oscar P. Fitzgerald, 21 Aug 1975, NHHC Oral History Collection.

37. NAG Analysis Sheet, subj: VNN Political Problems, 17 Jun 1965; Do and Kane, *Counterpart*, 125.

38. NAG Analysis Sheet, subj: VNN Political Problems, 17 Jun 1965; NAG Historical Review, Naval Advisory Group Activities, Apr 1965, 25 May 1965; CNO Flag Plot, 11 Apr 1965; Kiem Do interview, 1–6 Nov 2007.

39. NAG Analysis Sheet, subj: VNN Deficiency: Supervisory Action, 18 Jun 1965, Box 71, VCF.

40. Msg, COMUSMACV to COMSEVENTHFLT, 201618Z Apr 1965.

41. The original order for 20 boats was expanded to 54 boats on 23 April. For more on the Swifts, see JO2 June M. Trotter, Market Time Summary for Apr 1965, Naval History Division, U.S. Naval Operations in Vietnam, Monthly Report, Oct 1967, Box 86, VCF; Westwood Research, Inc., A Review of U.S. Navy Experience in Establishment and Conduct of South Vietnam Inshore Coastal Patrol: Operation Market Time, Project Number WR-119-B, May 1969, A-1, Post-1946 Command File; CTF 115, Monthly Historical Summary, Apr 1965, 11–12, Box 852, Post-1946 Command File; NAG, Use of Swift-type boats in the Vietnam Coastal Patrol, 1 Apr 1965, Box 69, VCF.

42. Larzelere, *The Coast Guard at War*, 52–54; Westwood Research, Inc., A Review of U.S. Navy Experience in Establishment and Conduct of South Vietnam Inshore Coastal Patrol: Operation Market Time, A-1; Scotti, *Coast Guard Action in Vietnam*, 165–166.

43. Naval History Division, OPNAV, "History of U.S. Naval Operations in Vietnam," 3:238.

44. Cutler, *Brown Water, Black Berets*, 81.

45. Msgs, CINCPACFLT to COMDT COAST GUARD, 160247Z Apr 1965; COMSEVENTHFLT to CINCPACFLT, 271058Z Apr 1965, Box 9, Seventh Fleet Provenance; Market Time Monthly Historical Summary, Apr 1965, Box 882, Post-1946 Command Files.

46. RADM Norvell G. Ward, interview by Paul Stillwell, No. 1, 14 May 1985, 1–47, No. 4, 11 Sep 1986, 149, 198, USNI Oral History Collection; Clay Blair Jr., *Silent Victory: The U.S. Submarine War Against Japan* (New York: J.B. Lippincott Company, 1975), 134, 567.

47. Ward interview, No. 5, 15 Sep 1986, 269, 314–316, 357–400, 433, 441.

48. Ibid., No. 7, 30 Jun 1987, 441, 447; RADM Norvell G. Ward, attachment to ltr to RADM Tom F. Connolly, 11 Aug 1965, Box 201, VCF.

49. NAG Historical Review, Naval Advisory Group Activities, Jul 1965, 21 Aug 1965, Box 69, VCF; Msg, HEDSUPPACT SAIGON to SECNAV, 91330Z Jul 1965, Marolda Papers, AR, NHHC; memo, Senior Naval Advisor, First Coastal District to Senior Coastal Force Advisor, subj: SITREP for week ending 2400, Thursday, 15 Jul 1965, 15 Jul 1965, Box 207, NAG Records; Casualty Cards for LT William L. Brown and BM1 Leon C. Stein, AR; William Lennington Brown, Database Page, www.virtualwall.org/brownWL01a.htm, accessed 15 Jul 2008.

50. Chidsey interview, 1 Dec 1966, 27–28.

51. Naval History Division, OPNAV, "History of U.S. Naval Operations in Vietnam," 3: 1040; NAG Historical Review, Naval Advisory Group Activities, Jul 1965, 21 Aug 1965.

52. Ward interview, No. 7, 30 Jun 1987, 441.

53. Ultimately, CAPT Tran Van Chon, who had served as the VNN CNO from 1957 to 1959, became the new chief on 1 November 1966. See ltr, Tran Van Chon to ADM Elmo Zumwalt, 25 Feb 1993, Vietnam Archive, Texas Tech University, Lubbock, TX; Ward interview, No. 7, 30 Jun 1987, 452–453; Norvell G. Ward, interview by Edward G. Marolda, 6 Sep 1983, NHHC Oral History Collection.

54. OEG Study No. 706, "Market Time," 20 Dec 1966; COMNAVFORV, "The Naval War in Vietnam," 30 Jun 1970, 43, Box 138, VCF.

55. OEG Study No. 706, "Market Time," 20 Dec 1966, 7.

56. Martin J. Kelleher as cited in Scotti, *Coast Guard Action in Vietnam*, 15.

57. Hodgman commanded Coast Guard Squadron 1. See COGARDRON One, Diary, 29 Jul 1965.

58. One WPB did suffer minor engine trouble and had to drop back and make repairs, but the boat nevertheless made it to Vietnam without having to turn around. See Larzelere, *Coast Guard at War*, 47.

59. Ward interview, No. 7, 30 Jun 1987, 438.

60. Hodgman, "Market Time in the Gulf of Thailand," 47; Larzelere, *Coast Guard at War*, 46–54; *Kirshna* (ARL-38), Command History, 1966, SH.

61. VADM Robert T. Nelson, Biography, U.S. Coast Guard Academy Parents Association, www.uscgaparents.org/chapter/RobertTNelson/Nelson.htm, accessed 21 Aug 2008.

62. Robert T. Nelson, interview by Alex Larzelere, undated, Coast Guard History Office, Washington, DC.

63. Naval Advisory Group, Monthly Historical Review, Sep 1965, Box 65; and COGARDRON One, Diary, 19 Sep 1965; Larzelere, *Coast Guard at War*, 44–45.

64. Most written accounts of the incident, including official reports, claimed that the junk intentionally rammed *Point Glover*, but Nelson disagrees. "Ramming is an overstatement." Nelson interview, undated.

65. Again, some written accounts claim that Viet Cong on the junk returned fire, but Nelson strongly disagrees. "I don't ever remember them opening fire." Nelson interview, undated.

66. NAG Monthly Historical Review, Sep 1965; NMCC Operational Summary, 24 Sep 1965, Box 99, NMCC OPSUMs; Msgs, CTU 115.1.9 to CTF 115, 190115Z Sep 1965, CTU 115.1.9 to CTF 155, 181825Z Sep 1965; CTU 115.1.9 to CTF 115, 181850Z Sep 1965; CTU 115.1.9 to PT GARNET, 182045Z Sep 1965; CTU 115.1.9 to CTF 115, 182100Z Sep 1965; CTU 115.1.9 to CTF 115, 182335Z Sep 1965; CTU 115.1.9 to CTF 115, 190115Z Sep 1965; CTU 115.1.9 to PT GARNET et al., 190146Z Sep 1965; CTU 115.1.9 to CTF 115, 211400Z Sep 1965; CTU 115.1.9 to CTF 115, 201430Z Sep 1965: all in Box 223, VCF.

67. COGARDRON One, Diary, 19–21 Sep 1965, Box 23; 19 Sep Incidents in the Gulf of Thailand, Annex to COGARDRON One, Diary; Naval Advisory Group, Monthly Historical Review, Sep 1965; Msg, CTU 115.1.9 to CTF 115 191745Z Sep 1965, Box 223, VCF.

68. COGARDRON One, Diary, 26 Sep 1965; Msgs, CTU 115.1.9 to CTF 115, 270755Z Sep 1965; CTU 115.1.9 to COMUSMACV, 271345Z Sep 1965, Box 223, VCF.

69. COGARDRON One, Diary, 20 Oct 1965.

70. Larzelere, *Coast Guard at War*, 59.

71. COMNAVFORV Monthly Summary, Jun 1966, 1–2.

72. Patrol Squadron 2, Post Deployment Intelligence Report, 1 Oct 1966, SH.

73. Scotti, *Coast Guard Action in Vietnam*, 50; COMNAVFORV Monthly Summary, Jun 1966, 3.

74. Stephen T. Ulmer, interview with author, 19 Sep 2008; Scotti, *Coast Guard Action in Vietnam*, 48–49.

75. Ulmer interview, 19 Sep 2008; COMNAVFORV Monthly Summary, Jun 1966, 3.

76. Ulmer interview, 19 Sep 2008.

77. COMNAVFORV Monthly Summary, Jun 1966, 4; Debriefing Report of LTJG Stephen T. Ulmer, commanding officer, USCG *Point League*, covering 20D2 incident of 20 Jun 1966, 24 Jun 1966, annex to COGARDRON One, Diary, Box 224, VCF.

78. Ulmer interview, 19 Sep 2008.

79. Ulmer Debriefing Report, 24 Jun 1966.

80. Debriefing Report of LTJG B. Foster Thomson III, commanding officer, USCG *Point Slocum*, covering 20D2 incident of 20 Jun 1966, 25 Jun 1966, annex to COGARDRON One, Diary, Jun 1966; COMNAVFORV Monthly Summary, Jun 1966, 5.

81. *Haverfield* (DER-393), Command History, 1966; COMNAVFORV Monthly Summary, Jun 1966, 5.

82. Ulmer interview, 19 Sep 2008.

83. Debriefing Report of LTJG Stephen T. Ulmer, 24 Jun 1966; Ulmer, interview with author, 19 Sep 2008.

84. Ulmer Debriefing Report, 24 Jun 1966.

85. COMNAVFORV Monthly Summary, Jun 1966, 9.

86. Ibid., Appendix III; Scotti, *Coast Guard Action in Vietnam*, 53; Ward interview, No. 7, 30 Jun 1987, 440.

87. Ulmer Debriefing Report, 24 Jun 1966; Ulmer interview, 19 Sep 2008.

88. CAPT Carey E. Landis, Long Range Plan for the U.S. Naval Effort in Vietnam [hereafter Landis Study], 4 Oct 1965, 1, Box 135, VCF.

89. Ibid., A-2.

90. Before Vietnam, the Navy's most significant brown and green water experiences consisted of operations against North Korean small-boat infiltrators, commando raids during the Korean War, and the Rhine River Patrol in the early Cold War period.

91. CDR Arthur P. Ismay, interview by Dean C. Allard, Oscar P. Fitzgerald, and Michael Kelly, 6 Jun 1967, NHHC Oral History Collection; Cutler, *Brown Water, Black Berrets*, 86.

92. Landis Study, D-2.

93. Ismay interview, 6 Jun 1967, 24.

94. Ismay interview, 24–25.

95. OEG Study No. 706, "Market Time," 7; Cutler, *Brown Water, Black Berrets*, 88.

96. Contrary to popular belief, Marilyn Monroe did not attend that party according to Ismay. Arthur P. Ismay, interview with author, 19 Jun 2008, McLean, VA.

97. Ibid.; CAPT Arthur P. Ismay, Officer Bio File.

98. Ismay interview, 6 Jun 1967, 16–17.

99. Ltr, CDR Arthur P. Ismay to RADM H. S. Monroe, 29 Jan 1966, Ismay Papers, AR.

100. Ismay interview, 19 Jun 2008.

101. Friedman, *U.S. Small Combatants*, 304–305.

102. Ltr, LT F. P. Hamilton to CDR Arthur P. Ismay, 24 May 1966, Ismay Papers.

103. Gary R. Blinn, *Confession to a Deaf God: Memoir of a Mekong River Rat* (Philadelphia, PA: Xlibris, 2002), 266.

104. In November 1967 two PCFs capsized in the Cua Viet channel. All crewmen were rescued, but PCF-76 was lost. See Naval History Division, OPNAV, "History of U.S. Naval Operations in Vietnam," 3:322–323; and Coastal Division 12, Command History, 1967, 6.

105. COMNAVFORV Monthly Historical Summary, Nov 1966, 40–41; Cutler, *Brown Water, Black Berrets*, 116–117; Casualty Cards for RM3 Bruce A. Timmons and MRC Willy S. Baker; Navy and Marine Corps Medal Citation, Willie S. Baker, 20 Mar 1967, AR. Several days later, a salvage team tried to locate the wreckage but could find only small pieces of the boat. For more on the salvage, see LTJG Anthony R. Taylor, "The Loss of PCF-77," http://swiftboats.net/stories/pcf77.htm, accessed 3 Sep 2008.

106. Edwin B. Hooper, *Mobility, Support, Endurance: A Story of Naval Operational Logistics in the Vietnam War, 1965–1968* (Washington: Naval History Division, 1972), 163–164; Ismay interview, 6 Jun 1967, 29.

107. LT Charles Lloyd, interview with author, 22 May 2008, NHHC, Washington, DC.

108. Ismay interview, 6 Jun 1967, 29.

109. Hooper, *Mobility, Support, Endurance*, 162–163.

110. Lloyd interview, 22 May 2008.

111. Blinn, *Confession to a Deaf God*, 135, 181, 144, 271.

112. Lloyd interview, 22 May 2008.

113. Robert R. Johnson, telephone interview with author, 7 Jan 2009; RM3 Robert R. Johnson, Narrative of the PCF-4 Attack, 14 Feb 1966, enclosure in letter to author, 29 Dec 2008.

114. CTF 115, Monthly Historical Summary, Feb 1966, Box 333; NAG Monthly Summary, Feb 1966, 10–12, Box 69: both in VCF; Msg, CTF 115 to AIG 7040, 150658Z Feb 19 66, PCF-4 folder, Author Files; Cutler, *Brown Water, Black Berets*, 96; Casualty Cards for EN2 Jack Charles Rodriguez, BM2 Tommy Edward Hill, and GMG2 Class Dayton Luther Rudisill; Johnson telephone interview, 7 Jan 2009; RM3 Robert R. Johnson, Diagram of the Position of the Crew at Time of Explosion, enclosure in letter to author, 29 Dec 2008.

115. Lloyd interview, 22 May 2008; Johnson telephone interview, 7 Jan 2009.

116. Chief, Naval Advisory Group, Vietnam to SECNAV, Bronze Star Medal With Combat "V" in the Case of PO1 Sam Mu Tong, 22 Mar 1966, serial 912, Box 57, Unclassified Serials, NAG Records.

117. Chief, Naval Advisory Group, Vietnam to SECNAV, Navy Commendation Medal with Combat V in the case of PO3 Duong Thuong, PO3 Lam Van Phat, PO3 Nguyen Quang Hoang, SN Huynh Hong Son, SN Huynh Van Ly, and SN Nguyen Duong, 21 Mar 1966, serial 913, Box 57, Unclassified Serials, NAG Records.

118. Johnson telephone interview, 7 Jan 2009; U.S. Naval Hospital, San Francisco, Medical Board Report for RM2 Robert R. Johnson, 14 Jul 1966, enclosure in ltr, Robert R. Johnson to author, 29 Dec 2008.

119. Lloyd received a Ph.D. in history from Georgetown University in 1975 and worked as a historian for the Air Force from 1976 to 1995; Lloyd interview, 22 May 2008; Casualty Card, Charles Lloyd, AR.

120. Johnson retired as a chief warrant officer 4 after 24 years of service. Johnson telephone interview, 7 Jan 2009; ltr, Kathleen M. Lloyd to CWO4 Robert R. Johnson, serial AR/00617, 15 May 2008, TRIM Database, AR.

121. NAG Monthly Summary, Feb 1966, 12; Cutler, *Brown Water, Black Berets*, 99.

122. While he did not blame Lloyd for his ignorance of Viet Cong mining techniques, Ismay did criticize him for demonstrating "very bad judgment" that day. "The thinking was not there." Ismay interview, 19 Jun 2008.

123. Blinn, *Confession to a Deaf God*, 92–93.

124. Naval History Division, OPNAV, "History of U.S. Naval Operations in Vietnam," 3: 271; Naval History Division, *Riverine Warfare*, 42–43.

125. COMNAVFORV Monthly Summary, May 1966, 25–26.

126. CAPT Charles P. Muckenhaler Jr., Fitness Report for ENS Alexander Balian, 15 Sep 1964, courtesy of Balian.

127. Arthur Ismay also took a liking to Balian, finding him to be an officer who worked hard and could be relied upon to volunteer for tough assignments. Biography of CAPT Alexander G. Balian, courtesy of Balian; CDR Arthur P. Ismay, Fitness Report for Alexander Balian, 6 Dec 1966, courtesy of Balian.

128. Bob Cutts, "Swift Boat Crew Survive Horror," *Pacific Stars and Stripes*, 13 Jun 1966.

129. Some early reports suggested that the round might have been a 57mm, but a later salvage team determined that it was a 105mm fin-stabilized round fired from a Chinese B-50 launcher. Author email correspondence with Alexander Balian also confirmed that it was a 105mm round. See Msg, COMNAVFORV to CNO et al., 261036Z May 1966, Box 585, COMNAVFORV File; Alexander Balian, email to author, 10 Sep 2008.

130. Not every account of the episode mentioned the mine blast, but the later salvage report confirmed the explosion. See COMNAVFORV Monthly Summary, May 1966, 21, 23.

131. In analyzing the event after the fact, Kiem believed that Godley may have shoved the throttles forward just before dying. See Edward Hymoff, "Sea Raiders: U.S. Navy's Silver Star Commandos," *Saga: The Magazine for Men*, Mar 1967, 64; Casualty Card for RM3 Robert Lee Kiem, AR; Cutts, "Swift Boat Crew Survive Horror."

132. JO2 R. F. Tills, "PCF Boat Crew Member is Awarded the Silver Star," *Jackstaff News*, 24 Mar 1967, 3.

133. "Swift Boat Crew Survive Horror," *Pacific Stars and Stripes*.

134. COMNAVFORV Monthly Summary, May 1966, 21–24; NMCC Opsum, 24 May 1966, Box 107, NMCC OPSUMS; Market Time Historical Summary, May 1966, Box 517, COMNAVFORV File; memo, Public Affairs Officer, COMNAVFORV to MACOI, 23 May 1966, Attack on Swift, Ismay Papers; Tills, "PCF Boat Crew Member is Awarded the Silver Star," 3; Hymoff, "Sea Raiders: U.S. Navy's Silver Star Commandos," 64; Msgs, CTG 116.2 to ZEN/CTF 116, 221534Z May 1966; CTG 116.2 to ZEN/CTF 116, 221510Z May 1966; ADMINO CTG 116.2 to ZEN/CTF 116, 221612Z May 1966; CTG 116.2 to CTG 116, NO DTG May 1966; ADMINO COMBATRON ONE to SECNAV, 230204Z May 1966; ADMINO COMBATRON ONE to SECNAV, 230225Z May 1966; COMNAVFORV to CINCPAC/NMCC, 230700Z May 1966: all in Box 585, COMNAVFORV File; Alexander Balian, Silver Star Citation, Awards Cards, AR.

135. COMNAVFORV Monthly Summary, May 1966, 23–24; Msgs, COMNAVFORV to CNO et al., 261036Z May 1966; USS *Tortuga* to RUMSBB/CTF 116, 250556Z May 1966, Box 585, COMNAVFORV File.

136. Westwood Research, Inc., A Review of U.S. Navy Experience in Establishment and Conduct of South Vietnam Inshore Coastal Patrol: Operation Market Time, Project WR-119-B, 28.

137. Ibid., 12.

138. Ward interview, No. 7, 433, 30 June 1987.

139. Friedman, *U.S. Small Combatants*, 299.

140. Moyar, *Triumph without Victory*, 358. Moyar's figures support earlier studies by the Center for Naval Analyses and MACV indicating that over 90 percent of steel-hulled infiltrators were being detected by Market Time forces, see MACV, Market Time Study Report, 5 Sep 1967, 4; OEG Study No. 706, "Market Time," 3.

141. OEG Study No. 706, "Market Time," 6.

142. Neil Sheehan, The Arnheiter Affair: Chronology of Events, 3–4, 11, Box 24, Neil Sheehan Personal Papers, AR; memo, Department of the Navy, Office of the Judge Advocate General to SECNAV, subj: LCDR Marcus A. Arnheiter, 21 Nov 1967, 8, Arnheiter Flap, 1967–1968, Uncat-

alogued File, 1968 Double Zero Files; CAPT Ward W. Witter, Investigation to Inquire into the Circumstances Connected with the Relief of LCDR Marcus A. Arnheiter from command of *Vance* (DER-387), which occurred on or about 1 April 1966, Findings of Fact #2, #11, #23, #37, Box 20, Sheehan Papers; Neil Sheehan, *The Arnheiter Affair* (New York: Random House, 1971), 62.

143. Neil Sheehan, Arnheiter Affair: Chronology, 4–5, 10; Witter, Arnheiter Investigation, Findings of Fact #6; John Maffre, "How the Hell Could This Happen?" *Washington Post*, 19 Nov 1967, B1; memo, JAG to SECNAV, 21 Nov 1967, 8–9.

144. In the "Revolt of the Admirals," several high-ranking admirals led by CNO Louis E. Denfield publicly disagreed with the Secretary of Defense and the President over the cancellation of the *United States* super-carrier program. The debate resulted in the firing of Denfield and several other officers in 1949 and sparked congressional hearings that proved embarrassing for the defense establishment. See Jeffrey G. Barlow, *Revolt of the Admirals: The Fight for Naval Aviation, 1945–1950* (Washington: Naval Historical Center, 1995).

The Rickover promotion scandal brought unwanted attention to Navy leadership, delayed the promotion of 39 other Navy captains, and nearly resulted in the complete revamping of the Navy's promotion board system. Often outspoken in his criticism of Navy leadership, Hyman Rickover, the head of the Navy reactor program, was twice passed over for promotion to flag rank before enlisting the support of Congress, the White House, and the Secretary of the Navy to finally advance in rank. See Francis Duncan, *Hyman Rickover: The Struggle for Excellence* (Annapolis: Naval Institute Press, 2012).

145. LCDR Marcus A. Arnheiter, Officer Bio File. Sheehan, Arnheiter Affair: Chronology, 1; Department of the Navy, Office of the JAG to SECNAV, 21 Nov 1967, 1; Sheehan, *Arnheiter Affair*, 31, 39–41; memos, CAPT F. S. Johnson to SECNAV, subj: LCDR Marcus A. Arnheiter, 15 Sep 1967; U.S. House of Representatives, Committee on Armed Services [hereafter HCAS] to Honorable L. Mendel Rivers, Chairman, Armed Services Committee, Mar 1968; Charles K. Duncan, Bureau of Naval Personnel to CNO, subj: LCDR Marcus A. Arnheiter, 16 May 1968: all in Arnheiter Flap, 1967–1968, Uncatalogued File.

146. Arnheiter, Officer Bio File; Sheehan, Arnheiter Affair: Chronology, 1; Sheehan, *Arnheiter Affair*, 43–44; Department of the Navy, Office of the JAG to SECNAV, 21 Nov 1967, 2.

147. Arnheiter, Officer Bio File; Sheehan, Arnheiter Affair: Chronology, 2; Department of the Navy, Office of the JAG to SECNAV, 21 Nov 1967, 2; HCAS to Rivers, Mar 1968.

148. Sheehan, Arnheiter Affair: Chronology, 9, 17; Witter, Arnheiter Investigation, Findings of Fact #2, #39; Sheehan, *Arnheiter Affair*, 89–91; Maffre, "How the Hell Could This Happen?" B1.

149. Witter, Arnheiter Investigation, Findings of Fact #12, 6; Sheehan, Arnheiter Affair: Chronology, 13.

150. Statement of CAPT A. M. Hazen (commanding officer (CO) of *Mason* at the time), 19 Jan 1968, Appendix A in Sheehan, *Arnheiter Affair*, 273–274; Sheehan, Arnheiter Affair: Chronology, 13–14; *Vance* (DER-387), Deck Log, 29–30 Jan 1966; Witter, Arnheiter Investigation, Findings of Facts #6, #8, #13, #28.

151. Sheehan, Arnheiter Affair: Chronology, 17; Witter, Arnheiter Investigation, Findings of Fact #1, #7, #10, #15, #39.

152. Chaplain G. W. Dando, LT, USNR to Commander Escort Squadron Seven, subj: *USS Vance*; Morale Situation, 26 Mar 1966, 4, Arnheiter Flap, 1967–1968, Uncatalogued File; Sheehan, Arnheiter Affair: Chronology, 19–21; memo, JAG to SECNAV, 21 Nov 1967, 11–12; Sheehan, *Arnheiter Affair*, 219–220.

153. Memo, ADM B. J. Semmes Jr. to SECNAV, 9 Feb 1967, Arnheiter Flap, 1967–1968, Uncatalogued File; Witter, Arnheiter Investigation, Findings of Fact #10, 13; Sheehan, Arnheiter Affair: Chronology, 21.

154. Navy Department, Office of Information, Summary of Salient Matters with Respect to the Case of LCDR Marcus A. Arnheiter, USN, 10 May 1968, 3, Arnheiter Flap, 1967–1968, Uncatalogued File; Sheehan, Arnheiter Affair: Chronology, 22.

155. Semmes to SECNAV, 9 Feb 1967.

156. Navy Department, Office of Information, Summary of Salient Matters with Respect to the Case of LCDR Marcus A. Arnheiter, USN, 10 May 1968.

157. Sheehan, Arnheiter Affair: Chronology, 23; Navy Department, Office of Information, Summary of Salient Matters with Respect to the Case of LCDR Marcus A. Arnheiter, USN, 10 May 1968, 4.

158. Sheehan, Arnheiter Affair: Chronology, 25.

159. For an article defending Arnheiter's actions, see James Jackson Kilpatrick, "He Might Have Been Another Halsey, *National Review,* 26 Mar 1968, 288–296.

160. Memos, JAG to SECNAV, 21 Nov 1967, 6, 19–21; SECNAV to LCDR Marcus A. Arnheiter via Commander Western Sea Frontier, 24 Nov 1967: both in Arnheiter Flap, 1967–1968, Uncatalogued File; Sheehan, Arnheiter Affair: Chronology, 27.

161. Ltr, ADM Thomas H. Moorer to Rivers, 30 Dec 1967, Arnheiter Flap, 1967–1968, Uncatalogued File.

162. Congressional Information Division, Office of Legislative Liaison, Report No. 88, 22 May 1968, ibid.

163. CAPT T. J. Ball, Director, Congressional Investigations Division, Memo for Record, 7 May 1968, ibid.

164. "Arnheiter Case Needs Review," *Denver Post*, 7 Jun 1968, 12.

165. "The Arnheiter Case," *Virginian-Pilot*, 14 May 1968, 16.

166. See Jack Anderson, "Navy Clams Up on Arnheiter Case," *Washington Post*, 24 Apr 1967, B-11.

167. Anderson, "U.S. Navy Suffering Leadership Crisis," *Washington Post*, 9 Oct 1969, G-15.

168. Sheehan, "The 99 Days of Captain Arnheiter," *New York Times Magazine*, Aug 1968.

169. See Sheehan, *Arnheiter Affair*.

170. Jack Anderson and James J. Kilpatrick were among the Arnheiter defenders.

Endnotes

3. War on the Rivers: Game Warden, 1966–1967

1. Fred M. McDavitt, meeting with author, 23 Nov 2011, NHHC.

2. McDavitt, interview with author, 22 Oct 2008; CTF 116, Operation Order 11-66, Mar 1966, Operations Orders, AR.

3. McDavitt, "Origin of the Black Beret," The Gamewardens of Vietnam Association, Inc., www.tf116.org/blackberet2.html, accessed 31 Dec 2008; McDavitt meeting, 23 Nov 2011.

4. Naval Advisors and VNN River Assault Group sailors also wore the black beret. According to McDavitt, "we just emulated them." McDavitt meeting, 23 Nov 2011.

5. McDavitt interview, 22 Oct 2008.

6. Memo, COMNAVFORV to CINCPACFLT, subj: Bronze Star Medal with Combat "V" in the case of LT Frederick Harry McDavitt, serial 3352, 28 Dec 1966, Box 86, Naval Forces Vietnam (NFV) Records; memo, COMNAVFORV to CINCPACFLT, subj: Bronze Star Medal with Combat "V" in the case of Chief Radioman Donald Ray Williams, 28 Dec 1966, serial 3356, Box 86, NFV Records; COMNAVFORV Monthly Historical Summary, Jul 1966, 15–16; McDavitt, interview with author, 22 Oct 2008.

7. McDavitt interview, 22 Oct 2008.

8. CDR Sayre A. Swartztrauber, "River Patrol Relearned," USNI *Naval Review* 96 (May 1970): 123; Victory Daniels and Judith C. Erdheim, OEG Study CRC 284, "Game Warden," CNA, Jan 1976, 7, Box 254, VCF.

9. NAG Monthly Evaluation Report for VNN, Feb 1965, Box 70, VCF; Naval Ordnance Test Station China Lake, Revolutionary Warfare on Island Waterways, Box 169, VCF.

10. Naval Ordnance Test Station China Lake, Revolutionary Warfare on Island Waterways; Friedman, U.S. Small Combatants, 331–337.

11. Marolda and Fitzgerald, *From Military Assistance to Combat*, 330.

12. NAG Monthly Evaluation Report for VNN, Jan 1965, Box 70, VCF.

13. Ibid.; Naval History Division, OPNAV, "History of U.S. Naval Operations in the Vietnam Conflict," 3:1214, 1221.

14. NAG Analysis Sheet, VNN Political Problems, 17 Jun 1965, Box 71, VCF; NAG Monthly Evaluation Report for VNN, May 1965, Box 70, VCF.

15. He shared 5,000 piasters of the total with his crew. CDR Charles Z. Hanus, End of Tour Report, Jun 1965, Box 192, NAG Records.

16. Hanus, End of Tour Report; Naval Historical Division, OPNAV, "History of Naval Operations in Vietnam," 3: 1211–1218.

17. LT Liles W. Creighton, End of Tour Reports (Debriefings), undated, serial 5213, Box 192, NAG Records.

18. Memo, MAJ Ardath C. Smith Jr., USMC, Senior Advisor RSSZ to Chief, Naval Advisory Group, subj: Expansion of Market Time Activities, 10 Aug 1965, Box 232, NAG Records.

19. LT Robert J. Powers, Staff Study on VNN Force Structure Requirements, 16 Jan 1966, Box 74, VCF.

20. NAG Staff Study, VNN Personnel Situation, 25 Oct 1965, Box 74, VCF.

21. NAG Monthly Historical Review, Nov 1965, Box 69, VCF; Senior River Force Advisor, SITREP for Period 12–18 Nov 1965, 19 Nov 1965, Box 206, NAG Records.

22. NAG Vietnam Position Paper, Expansion of U.S. Participation in River Patrol Throughout the Delta, 23 Aug 1965, Box 79, VCF.

23. COMNAVFORV, "The Naval War in Vietnam," 30 Jun 1970, 45, Box 137, VCF; Cutler, Brown Water, Black Berets, 159; Naval Historical Division, OPNAV, "History of Naval Operations in Vietnam," 3:332–333.

24. TF 116, Operation Order 11-66; Naval Historical Division, OPNAV, "History of Naval Operations in Vietnam," 3:333–334; Swartztrauber, "River Patrol Relearned," 124–125; Daniels and Erdheim, "Game Warden," 4.

25. In April 1964, for example, Communist forces captured a district capital in Chuong Thien Province, killing over 300 Vietnamese troops. See Marolda and Fitzgerald, *From Military Assistance to Combat,* 332, and memo, Advisory Board to Survey Critical Operations, subj: Report of Advisory Board Concerning Long Tau–Soirap River Area Security, 30 Nov 1964, Box 71, VCF.

26. LCDR Richard P. Multer, NAG, MACV Fact Sheet-6, subj: Rung Sat Special Zone, 20 Nov 1965, Box 71, VCF; Swartztrauber, "River Patrol Relearned," 142; Robert E. Mumford Jr., "Jackstay: New Dimensions in Amphibious Warfare," *U.S. Naval Institute Naval Review* 94 (1968): 70.

27. LT Kenneth Logan MacLeod III, Officer Bio File; Cutler, *Brown Water, Black Berets*, 143; Swartztrauber, "River Patrol Relearned," 145.

28. MacLeod as cited by Cutler, *Brown Water, Black Berets*, 146.

29. Swartztrauber, "River Patrol Relearned," 145.

30. GMCM Chester C. Stanley Jr., interview with author, 26 Jun 2009.

31. NMCC Opsum, 28 Feb 1966, Box 102, NMCC OPSUMS; Flag Plot Chronology, 27 Feb 1966, Box 13, Flag Plot; Mumford, "Jackstay," 70–72; Lloyd's Register of Shipping, 1966–1967 (London: Lloyds, 1967), A-L, SS *Lorinda*.

32. Battalion landing team (BLT) 1/5, Combat After Action Report for Operation Jackstay, 12 Apr 1966; BLT 1/5, Operation Order 328–366, 19 Mar 1966: both in U.S. Marine Corps History Division, Grey Research Center; Mumford, "Jackstay," 83.

33. BLT 1/5, Combat After Action Report for Operation Jackstay, 12 Apr 1966; Mumford, "Jackstay," 75.

34. COMSEVENTHFLT, Detachment Charlie-PAO, "Operation Jackstay," Release 53-66, 26 Mar 1966, Box 535, NFV Records; BLT 1/5, Combat After Action Report for Operation Jackstay, 12 Apr 1966; Mumford, "Jackstay," 77.

35. BLT 1/5, Combat After Action Report for Operation Jackstay, 12 Apr 1966.

36. The PCF-31 ambush was reconstructed from the following sources: LT James C. Thorell, interview with author, 18 Mar 2009; Msg, CTF 115 Rep., Belle Grove to CTF 115, subj: PCF-26 Incident SITREP, 270638Z Mar 1966, Box 603, NFV Records; Thorell as cited in COMSEVENTHFLT, "Instant Responses," Release 59-66; COMNAVFORV Monthly Summary, Mar

1966; LTJG James Carl Thorell, Officer Bio File; Casualty Cards for EN2 Alton R. Gunter and BM2 Robert Peter Heinz Jr.; "First Silver Star Presented to a Sailor," *Jackstaff News*, 4 Nov 1966.

37. COMSEVENTHFLT, Detachment Charlie-PAO, Release 66-66, 1 Apr 1966, Box 535, NFV Records; Richard J. Cragg, interview with author, 29 Oct 2008; Mumford, "Jackstay," 78. Cragg was the boat group commander and the assistant gunnery officer on *Merrick* (AKA-97), and directly participated in the Jackstay operation.

38. Cragg interview, 29 Oct 2008; COMSEVENTHFLT, Detachment Charlie-PAO, Release 71-66, 31 Mar 1966; and Release 74-66, 1 Apr 1966, Box 535, NFV Records; Naval History Division, *Riverine Warfare*, 43; Mumford, "Jackstay," 78.

39. BLT 1/5, Combat After Action Report for Operation Jackstay, 12 Apr 1966. For a breakdown of casualties, see also NMCC Opsum, 7 Apr 1966, Box 103, NMCC OPSUMS.

40. COMSEVENTHFLT, Detachment Charlie-PAO, Release 90-66, 4 Apr 1966, Box 535, NFV Records.

41. COMSEVENTHFLT, Release 84-66.

42. According to Mayo Clinic, cellulitis "is a common, potentially serious bacterial skin infection. Cellulitis appears as a swollen, red area of skin that feels hot and tender, and it may spread rapidly." See www.mayoclinic.com/health/cellulitis/DS00450, accessed 1 Sep 2011.

43. BLT 1/5, Combat After Action Report for Operation Jackstay, 12 Apr 1966.

44. Daniels and Erdheim, "Game Warden," 5.

45. Thomas Glickman, unpublished memoir, 13–15, Author Files; Department of the Navy, Naval Ship Systems Command, "Boats of the United States Navy," NAVSHIPS 250–452, May 1967, NDL; Broughton Cobb, "River Patrol Boat for Vietnam," *Yachting*, Dec 1966, 101–103; Cutler, *Brown Water, Black Berets*, 151–154; Friedman, *U.S. Small Combatants*, 312–314.

46. The cabin cruiser version of the boat cost only $12,000, and it came with features not found on the PBR, such as a galley, a head, and teak trim. Art Nortveldt, former president of United Boatbuilders, interview with author, 29 Oct 2008; Friedman, *U.S. Small Combatants*, 312–314; "The Navy Sends Plastic Boats to Vietnam," *U.S. Naval Institute Proceedings* 92 (Mar 1966): 152. Inflation adjusted using the U.S. government Consumer Price Index Inflation Calculator, data.bls.gov/cgi-bin/cpicalc.pl, accessed 9 Jun 2011.

47. Thomas Glickman, Unpublished Memoir, 13–15; Friedman, *U.S. Small Combatants*, 313.

48. Friedman, *U.S. Small Combatants*, 313.

49. Peter A. Huchthausen and Nguyen Thi Lung, *Echoes of the Mekong*, 23–24.

50. Jerry M. Hammel, interview with author, 4 Mar 2009.

51. Naval Ship Systems Command, Performance of River Patrol Boat (PBR), 31 Jul 1966, serial 529B-0216, Box 188, VCF.

52. Email, McDavitt to author, 31 Mar 2009.

53. Chester B. Smith, interview with author, 6 Mar 2009; Roderick Davis claims that River Patrol Sections 531 and 532 employed that technique (email, Davis to author, 27 Mar 2009); email, McDavitt to author, 31 Mar 2009; James L. "Larry" Weatherall said that the practice of shimming the governors continued long after Williams left Vietnam. Weatherall, interview with author, 28 Apr 2010.

54. Email, Roderick Davis to author, 27 Mar 2009.

55. Email, McDavitt to author, 31 Mar 2009.

56. The hulls were eventually replaced with ones more suitable to the climate. CDR Sayre A. Swartztrauber, interview by Oscar P. Fitzgerald, 3 Jun 1969, 19, NHHC Oral History Collection.

57. Holes had to be drilled in the hulls to get the water out. Email, McDavitt to author, 31 Mar 2009.

58. Weatherall interview, 28 Apr 2010.

59. Swartztrauber interview, 3 Jun 1969, 18; Huchthausen, *Echoes of the Mekong*, 24.

60. Jere Beery, interview with author, 24 Nov 2008; Robert P. Fuscaldo, interview with author, 13 Feb 2009. Other PBR sailors who complained about the issue in interviews with the author include Fred McDavitt, Steve Watson, and John Donovan.

61. Naval Ship Systems Command, Performance PBR.

62. Cutler, *Brown Water, Black Berets*, 158.

63. Beery interview, 24 Nov 2008.

64. McDavitt interview, 22 Oct 2008.

65. Jere Beery, interview with author, 6 Feb 2009.

66. Email, Davis to author, 6 Feb 2009; McDavitt, meeting with author, 23 Nov 2011.

67. CTF 116, Operation Order 11-66; Daniels and Erdheim, "Game Warden," 20–24.

68. CTF 116, Operation Order 11-66; LCDR William W. Elpers, Staff Study: USN River Patrol Planning, 25 Dec 1965, Box 74, VCF.

69. Huchthausen, *Echoes of the Mekong*, 24.

70. Smith interview, 6 Mar 2009.

71. *Jennings County* (LST-846), Command History, 1965–1967, 7 Jan 1967, SH; Swartztrauber, "River Patrol Relearned," 146.

72. Don Sheppard, *Riverine: A Brown-Water Sailor in the Delta, 1967* (San Francisco, CA: Presidio, 1992), 275.

73. *Tortuga* (LSD-26), Command History, 1966, SH.

74. *Hunterdon County* (LST-838), Command History, 1967, SH.

75. The LSTs involved were *Garrett County* (LST-786), *Harnett County* (LST-821), *Hunterdon County* (LST-838), and *Jennings County* (LST-846). See Navy Unit Citation, Task Unit 76.8.3, 8 Apr 1969, *Garrett County* Files, SH.

76. Swartztrauber interview, 3 Jun 1969; Naval Support Activity Saigon, Command History, 1966, Box 1526, Post-1946 Command File; Daniels and Erdheim, "Game Warden," 15; Swartztrauber, "River Patrol Relearned," 146.

77. Hammel interview, 4 Mar 2009.

78. Swartztrauber, "River Patrol Relearned," 147.

79. COMSERVPAC, Pacific Area Naval Operations Review, Mar 1967, Box 163, VCF; JO1 Bob Sullivan, "Long Xuyen is Biggest PBR Base," *Jackstaff News*, 24 Mar 1967, 10.

Endnotes

80. Hooper, *Mobility, Support, Endurance*, 175.

81. Fuscaldo interview, 13 Feb 2009.

82. COMSERVPAC, Pacific Area Naval Operations Review, Mar 1967, Box 163, VCF; Hooper, *Mobility, Support, Endurance*, 175.

83. COMSERVPAC, Pacific Area Naval Operations Review, Mar 1967; COMSERVPAC, Weekly Summary, 19 Feb 1967 to 4 Mar 1967, Box 163, VCF.

84. John J. Donovan Jr., interview with author, 3 Nov 2008.

85. Hammel interview, 4 Mar 2009.

86. Email, McDavitt to author, 12 Feb 2013.

87. Fuscaldo interview, 13 Feb 2009.

88. Roderick Davis, interview with author, 5 Nov 2008.

89. Hammel interview, 4 Mar 2009.

90. Fuscaldo interview, 13 Feb 2009.

91. Donovan interview, 3 Nov 2008.

92. Rodney Dean "Weazel" Morgan, interview with author, 20 Mar 2010.

93. Beery never had a problem with alcohol during the war, but when he returned to the United States severely wounded, he turned to alcohol to alleviate depression and post-traumatic stress. "I was 21 years old, badly scarred, and disfigured. I had gotten addicted to pain meds in the hospital and when I got out, I went about drinking and drugging, trying to forget." Beery interview, 24 Nov 2008.

94. Steve Watson, interview with author, 18 Nov 2008.

95. Lowell Elliott Webb, interview with author, 13 Nov 2008.

96. Frank R. Spatt, interview with author, 3 Jun 2009.

97. *YRBM-16*, Command History, 1967, SH.

98. Edwin "Larry" Oswald, interview by Laura Calkins, Apr–May 2004, Vietnam Archive, Texas Tech University, 53–54.

99. YRBM Interior Layout, courtesy of Edwin "Larry" Oswald.

100. Wynn Goldsmith, *Papa, Bravo, Romeo: U.S. Navy Patrol Boats at War*, 55–56.

101. John Hendrickson, interview with author, 22 Jun 2011.

102. Ibid, 175; LCDR Villard Blevins Jr., Officer Bio File.

103. Oswald interview, Apr–May 2004, 54. Wynn Goldsmith speculated that the sapper who attacked the boat was one of eight VNN UDT swimmers trained by the Navy at Coronado who later defected to the Viet Cong. See Goldsmith, *Papa, Bravo, Romeo*, 93.

104. Msg, NILO Ben Tre to ZEN/COMNAVFORV, 050400Z Dec 1967, YRBM-16 folder, AR.

105. Jerome "Jerry" Wojciechowski, interview with author, 27 Jun 2011.

106. Hendrickson interview, 22 Jun 2011; email, GMG3 Joseph M Slavish to Mobile Riverine Force Association, brownwater-navy.com/vietnam/YRBM16b.htm, accessed 28 Jun 2011.

107. 231815 Greenwich Mean Time (GMT) or "Zulu" time in military parlance (local

"Hotel" time was GMT plus seven hours). See Msg, COMNAVFORV to CINCPACFLT, YRBM-16 Explosion and Fire, 241157Z Nov 1967, YRBM-16 Salvage folder, AR.

108. Msgs, COMNAVFORV to CINCPACFLT, YRBM-16 Explosion and Fire, 241157Z Nov 1967; CTF 116.1.3.6 to ZENI/CTF 116, 240103Z Nov 1967; COMNAVFORV Saigon to ZEN/COMNAVFORV, 240542Z Nov 1967; COMNAVFORV Saigon to ZEN/COMNAVFORV, 240922Z Nov 1967, YRBM-16 Salvage File; COMSERVPAC, Pacific Area Naval Operations Review, Nov 1967, Box 164, VCF; COMNAVFORV Monthly Historical Summary, 1967; Naval History Division, OPNAV, "History of U.S. Naval Operations in Vietnam," 3:404; Brownwater Navy Vietnam, YRBM-16, http://brownwater-navy.com/vietnam/YRBM16c.htm, accessed 13 Jun 2011.

109. Wojciechowski interview, 27 Jun 2011.

110. John Hendrickson, Account of the Mining of YRBM-16, http://brownwater-navy.com/vietnam/YRBM16jh.htm, accessed 14 Jun 2011.

111. Wojciechowski interview, 27 Jun 2011.

112. PBR crew killed in the attack included SN George R. Ycoco, BM1 Joseph J. Simon, GMG3 Lonnie B. Evans, SN Dale E. Egbert, and GMG3 Ronald E. Crose. Also killed were ETN3 Robert Lyndon Gray and EN2 Wilson Nathaniel Flowers from the ship's company.

113. Email, John Hendrickson to author, 24 Jun 2011.

114. Email, Slavish to Mobile Riverine Force Association, http://brownwater-navy.com/vietnam/YRBM16b.htm, accessed 28 Jun 2011.

115. Email, Hendrickson to author, 24 Jun 2011.

116. Edwin "Larry" Oswald, interview with author, 28 Jun 2001; Oswald interview, Apr–May 2004, 81.

117. Wojciechowski interview, 27 Jun 2011.

118. Goldsmith, *Papa, Bravo, Romeo*, 92.

119. *Hunterdon County*, Command History, 1967; Dick Strandberg, Account of the Mining of YRBM-16, brownwater-navy.com/vietnam/YRBM16ds.htm, accessed 14 Jun 2011.

120. *Abnaki* (ATF 96), Command History, 1967, SH; *Abnaki* (ATF 96), Dictionary of American Naval Fighting Ships (DANFS) entry, www.history.navy.mil/danfs/a1/abnaki.htm, accessed 28 Jun 2011.

121. Oswald interview, Apr–May 2004, 53–54.

122. The Sasebo overhaul incorporated many changes, including the addition of a topside superstructure and a helicopter flight deck. See YRBM-16, Command History, 1967, AR.

123. Ibid.; COMNAVFORV Monthly Summary, Nov 1967.

124. Richard Knott, *Fire from the Sky: Seawolf Gunships in the Mekong Delta* (Annapolis, MD: Naval Institute Press, 2005), 20–21.

125. HAL-3, "History of Helicopter Attack (Light) Squadron Three," Fleet Aviation Commands Pre-1998, HAL-3, Box 25A, Aviation History Branch [hereafter AVH], NHHC; Seawolf Association, "Navy Seawolves: Early History," www.seawolf.org/history/hal3_history.asp, accessed 8 Mar 2012.

126. Knott, *Fire from the Sky,* 24–25.

127. James D. Sprinkle, "Helatkltron Three: The Seawolves," *Journal of the American Aviation Historical Society* 33 (Winter 1988): 293.

128. HAL-3, "History of Helicopter Attack (Light) Squadron Three."

129. Sprinkle, "Helatkltron Three: The Seawolves," 294.

130. Knott, *Fire from the Sky,* 34–35, 61–62.

131. Al Billings, *Seawolf 28: A True Story* (Charleston, SC: BookSurge, 2004), 157; Knott, *Fire from the Sky,* 28–29.

132. "Navy UH-1B 'Huey' Helicopter," *U.S. Naval Institute Proceedings* 94 (May 1968): 104.

133. Sprinkle, "Helatkltron Three: The Seawolves," 296; Knott, *Fire from the Sky,* 32.

134. Billings, *Seawolf 28,* 195.

135. Knott, *Fire from the Sky,* 68.

136. HAL-3 Monthly Strength Report, 28 May 1968, Fleet Aviation Commands Pre-1998, HAL-3, Box 48, AVH.

137. For a list of HAL-3 squadron COs, see www.seawolf.org/history/co_s.asp, accessed 23 Mar 2012.

138. Alan Billings, interview with author, 23 Oct 2008; Billings, *Seawolf 28,* 140.

139. Seawolf Association, "Navy Seawolves: Early History," www.seawolf.org/history/hal3_history.asp, accessed 8 Mar 2012; Sprinkle, "Helatkltron Three: The Seawolves," 294.

140. Daniel E. Kelly, *Seawolves: First Choice,* 48–85.

141. Billings, *Seawolf 28,* 187.

142. Email, Allen E. Weseleskey to author, 20 Mar 2012.

143. Billings, *Seawolf 28,* 169.

144. Kelly, *Seawolves: First Choice,* 48–85.

145. Allen E. Weseleskey, interview with author, 9 Mar 2012.

146. Knott, *Fire from the Sky,* 4.

147. Billings, *Seawolf,* 28, 184.

148. Weseleskey interview, 9 Mar 2012.

149. Ibid.; CDR Allen E. Weseleskey, Officer Bio File.

150. Knott, *Fire from the Sky,* 98–101; Jack H. Jacobs, "If Not Now, When?" www.seawolf.org/history/jack_jacobs.pdf, accessed 21 Mar 2012.

151. Weseleskey interview, 9 Mar 2012; Knott, *Fire from the Sky,* 98–101; CDR Allen E. Weseleskey, Navy Cross Citation, 9 Mar 1968, www.seawolf.org/history/navycross.asp#allen, accessed 21 Mar 2012; Casualty card for LTJG Harold W. Guinn Jr.

152. Delta River Group, Presidential Unit Citation for the period 31 Jan to 9 Apr 1968, courtesy of Allen E. Weseleskey.

153. COMNAVFORV, "Staff Organization and Regulations Manual," 15 Oct 1966, D-12 of enclosure 1 of NAVFORV Instruction 05400.1; and COMNAVFORV Operation Order No. 201-68,

23 Sep 1967, C-V-2 of Appendix V to Annex C, "Intelligence Collection Guide," both courtesy of Glenn Helm; After Action Report, NILO Conference, Vietnam Archive, Texas Tech University.

154. CDR Nicholas Carbone, USN (Ret.), NILO Lam Son, May 1969 to May 1970, courtesy of the Vietnam Center, Texas Tech University.

155. VADM Earl F. Rectanus, interview by Paul Stillwell, 19 Nov 1982, courtesy of the Vietnam Archive, Texas Tech University.

156. According to Rectanus, "defectors and documents were obviously important and SEALs played a major role there." Rectanus interview, 19 Nov 1982.

157. LT Fred McDavitt, "My Tho Intel Situation," undated, courtesy of Fred McDavitt.

158. LT Albert G. Hallowell, Information Page, Vietnam Veterans Memorial, http://thewall-usa.com/info.asp?recid=20900, accessed 10 Apr 2012.

159. COMNAVFORV Monthly Summary, Nov 1969, 55; Defense Prisoner of War/Missing Personnel Office (DPMO) Case Summary, LCDR John G. Graf, courtesy of the Vietnam Archive, Texas Tech University; DPMO, U.S. Unaccounted-For from the Vietnam War Prisoners of War, Missing in Action and Killed in Action/Body not Recovered, www.dtic.mil/dpmo/vietnam/reports/documents/pmsea_una_p_name.pdf, accessed 10 Apr 2012.

160. CDR Peter B. Decker and CAPT John E. Vinson, "Bad Things Happen When You Take a War Too Littorialy [sic] (A Tale of two NILOs)," courtesy of the Vietnam Archive, Texas Tech University.

161. Frederick A. Olds, interview with author, 6 Apr 2009.

162. Memo, Chief Naval Advisory Group to CINCPACFLT, subj: Bronze Star Medal with Combat "V" in the case of LT Frederick A. Olds, 15 Mar 1967, courtesy of Frederick A. Olds.

163. The mission of the provincial reconnaissance units was to capture VC leaders and other cadre, which were good sources of intelligence but, as Olds mentioned, access to PRU prisoners often required NILOs to cultivate good relations with other U.S. and RVN agencies. See Olds interview, 6 Apr 2009.

164. Rectanus interview, 19 Nov 1982.

165. LT Kenneth W. Tapscott died on 6 August 1970 when the PBR patrol he was accompanying was ambushed on the Song Ong Doc. A B-40 rocket struck the NILO in the chest and shoulder, mortally wounding him. For details on the event, see COMNAVFORV Monthly Summary, Aug 1970, 24.

166. LT Robert C. Doyle, interview by Edward J. Marolda, 28 Sep 1978, 6, AR.

167. Memo, COMNAVFORV to COMUSMACV, Military Civic Action Report for September 1967, Box 525, NFV Records.

168. Seabee Teams, Civic Action, Jun 1967, Box 525, NFV Records.

169. JOCS Dick Rose, "The Navy's Peace Corps in the Delta," COMNAVFORV Navy News Release, 47F-67, Box 525, NFV Records.

170. Fourth Riverine Area Advisor/Commander Delta River Patrol, Military Civic Action/Psyops Activities conducted during May 1967, 7 Jun 1967, Monthly Civic Action Reports, Box 526, NFV Records.

171. *Jennings County* (LST-846), Civic Action Report for August 1967, Box 425; NAVFORV,

Psyop Newsletter, undated, Box 525, NFV Records.

172. LT Ken Anderson as quoted in JO1 Bob Sullivan, "Helping Vietnamese SOP for Long Xuyen Sailors," *Jackstaff News,* 10 Mar 1967, 3.

173. Under this program, any refugee who has a relative in the United States or some other tie to the U.S. government can officially apply to leave his country and enter the U.S.

174. For the complete story of Lung and Huchthausen, see their *Echoes of the Mekong.*

175. Donovan interview, 3 Nov 2008.

176. Fuscaldo interview, 13 Feb 2009.

177. Watson interview, 18 Nov 2008; Dean Jensen, "Honors for a Hero: Navy Cross Awarded Posthumously to Local GI," *Sheboygan Press,* 18 May 1967, 1; Barry Ginter, "Victim of Vietnam Honored: Navy Building Named for Sheboygan Man," *Sheboygan Press,* undated, 11; both in Terrence J. Freund File, Sheboygan County Historical Research Center.

178. Watson interview, 18 Nov 2008; email, Steve Watson to author, 25 Feb 2009; COMNAVFORV Monthly Summary, Oct 1966, 22.

179. Memos, COMNAVFORV to SECNAV, Re: Navy Cross (Posthumously) in the case of RM2 Terrence Jay Freund, 28 Dec 1966, 1650 Files, serial 3347; COMNAVFORV to SECNAV, Re: Bronze Star Medal with Combat "V" in the case of GMG3 William Alan Ratliff, 23 Dec 1966, 1650 Files, serial 3295: both in Box 86, NFV Records; Watson interview, 18 Nov 2008.

180. Memo, COMNAVFORV to SECNAV, Re: Navy Cross (Posthumously) in the case of RM2 Terrence Jay Freund; Watson interview, 18 Nov 2008; COMNAVFORV Monthly Summary, Oct 1966, 22.

181. Smith interview, 6 Mar 2009.

182. Ibid; USS *Timmerman* (AG-152), DANFS, www.history.navy.mil/danfs/t6/timmerman.htm, accessed 20 Sep 2012.

183. USS Hugh Purvis (DD-709), DANFS, www.history.navy.mil/danfs/h9/hugh_purvis.htm, accessed 20 Sep 2012.

184. Smith interview, 6 Mar 2009; *Sunnadin* (ATA-197), Command Operational Report, 1963, Post-1946 Command File; USS *Sunnadin* (ATA-197), DANFS, www.history.navy.mil/danfs/s20/sunnadin-ii.htm, accessed 21 Sep 2012.

185. Smith interview, 6 Mar 2009.

186. Fred McDavitt, "Comments about SM1 Chester B. Smith, USN, for the time period 1966–1967," 24 Sep 2012, courtesy Fred McDavitt.

187. Casualty Card for SN1 Chester B. Smith, 2 Dec 1966.

188. McDavitt, telephone conversation with author, 21 Sep 2012.

189. McDavitt, telephone conversation with author, 26 Sep 2012.

190. Smith interview, 6 Mar 2009.

191. SM1 Chester Smith, Hostile Fire Incident, 11 Dec 1966, Approx 0730 to 1145, Units Involved: PBR-98A, PBR-106, PBR-103, PBR-110, After Action Report, courtesy of Chester Smith; Smith interview, 6 Mar 2009; COMNAVFORV Monthly Summary, Dec 1966, 16–20.

192. As cited in COMNAVFORV Monthly Summary, Dec 1966, 20.

193. SM1 Chester Smith, Navy Cross Citation, Vietnam Awards Cards.

194. Smith interview, 6 Mar 2009.

195. According to the Navy Department Board of Decorations, BM1 Williams' medals include, by order precedence: Medal of Honor, Navy Cross, Silver Star Medal, Legion of Merit with Combat "V," Bronze Star Medal with Combat "V" (two awards), Navy Commendation Medal with Combat "V," Purple Heart (two awards), Combat Action Ribbon, Presidential Unit Citation, Good Conduct Medal with 4 Bronze Stars, Navy Expedition Medal (Cuba), National Defense Service Medal, Korean Service Medal with two Bronze Stars, Armed Forces Expeditionary Medal (Dominican Republic), Republic of Vietnam Gallantry Cross with Bronze Star, Korean Presidential Unit Citation, Republic of Vietnam Meritorious Unit Citation (Gallantry Cross), Republic of Vietnam Meritorious Unit Citation (Civil Actions), United Nations Service Medal, Republic of Vietnam Campaign Medal. See BM1 James E. Williams File, Navy Department Board of Decorations and Medals Files, Building 36, Washington Navy Yard, DC. A Navy Marine Corps Medal was also found in his files.

196. DDG-95 was commissioned in 2003.

197. BM1 James E. Williams, Bio File, AR.

198. James E. Williams, interview by Tim Frank, 25 Sep 1997.

199. Although his official Navy biography states that he was 17 when he joined the Navy, James Williams claimed in later interviews that he joined the Navy at 16 with the help of his father, who had his birth certificate altered to indicate that he was 17. See Williams interview, 25 Sep 1997; Michael Williams, interview with author, 25 Mar 2009; Patricia Oladeinde, "Riverboat Gambler," *All Hands,* Jul 1998, 14–17.

200. USS *Sedgwick County* (LST-1123), DANFS, www.history.navy.mil/danfs/s9/sedgwiek_county.htm, accessed 7 Apr 2009.

201. Williams Bio File; Williams interview, 25 Sep 1967.

202. *Douglas H. Fox* (DD-779), Command History, 1952, SH; E. Andrew Wilde Jr., "The U.S.S. Douglas H. Fox (DD-779) in Korea: 1952 and 1954," 1991, unpublished manuscript, NDL.

203. Wilde, "The U.S.S. Douglas H. Fox (DD-779) in Korea."

204. Williams as quoted in Oladeinde, "Riverboat Gambler," 15.

205. Williams, interview by Frank, 25 Sep 1997.

206. Ltr, James E. Williams to Rubin Binder, 22 Jul 1997, courtesy Fred H. McDavitt.

207. JOC Dan Kasperick, "What Makes a Hero?" *All Hands,* Jun 1968, 2–6.

208. For more on the skills needed to advance to chief boatswain's mate during the Vietnam era, see Naval Training Command, Rate Training Manual: Boatswain's Mate 1 & C, NAVTRA 10122-D (Washington, DC: Government Printing Office, 1973). Michael Williams, interview with author, 25 Mar 2009; James E. Williams, Bio File; email, McDavitt to author, 3 May 2009; Alfred Jensen, telephone conversation with author, 3 May 2009.

209. McDavitt interview, 22 Oct 2008.

210. According to Fred McDavitt, when Williams became a U.S. Marshall, he later asked

his colleagues to call him Elliot after Eliot Ness, the famous prohibition agent popularized by the TV series, "The Untouchables." McDavitt meeting, 23 Nov 2011.

211. McDavitt interview, 22 Oct 2008.

212. Smith interview, 6 Mar 2009.

213. Email, McDavitt to author, 8 Apr 2009.

214. Ibid.

215. Crew list of PBRs 105 and 107, 31 Oct 1966, BM1 Williams File, Navy Department Board of Decorations and Medals Files; email, McDavitt to author, 21 Sep 2010.

216. Email, McDavitt to author, 21 Oct 2012; memo, COMRIVRON 5 to SECNAV, subj: Medal of Honor; Recommendation for in [sic] the case of Boatswain's Mate 1st Class James Elliot Williams, 31 Jul 1967, 1650, serial 1163, BM1 Williams File, Navy Department Board of Decorations and Medals Files.

217. Ibid.

218. Memo, LCDR Joseph B. Howard to Commander Task Unit 116.1.3, subj: Eye Witness Account of Action from 311758H to 312045H Oct 1966 at coordinates 305403, BM1 Williams File, Navy Department Board of Decorations and Medals Files.

219. Always proud of his Jewish heritage, Binder later ordered a vanity plate for his Porsche after the war that read, "Oy Vey."

220. The main source in reconstructing the 31 October episode was memo, COMRIVRON 5 to SECNAV, subj: Medal of Honor, James Elliot Williams, 31 Jul 1967. Other sources consulted include COMNAVFORV Monthly Historical Summary, Oct 1966; Msgs, COMUSMACV to NMCC, 012233Z Nov 1966; CTE 116.1.3.1 My Tho to RUMSBB/CTG 116.1 Saigon, 311855Z Oct 1966; memo, COMRIVPATFOR to SECNAV, subj: Presidential Unit Citation in the case of the Delta River Patrol Group (TG 116.1), 3 Oct 1967, 1650, serial 084, Box 600, NFV Records; Chester Smith, Michael Williams, and Fred McDavitt interviews; email correspondence with Fred McDavitt; Frank Harvey, "Clean Sweep for the River Jets," Argosy, Feb 1967, 42–43, 80–85; Cutler, *Brown Water, Black Berets*, 199–204; Julie Davidow, "Proud but haunted, ex-Vietnam river boat gunner is remembered," Seattlepi.com, www.seattlepi.com/local/277800_riverboat17.html, accessed 16 Apr 2009.

221. SN Rubin G. Binder and SM2 Thomas A. Poling each received a Bronze Star with Combat V for the action; Williams also received a Purple Heart for the 31 October 1966 action. See Awards Approved for 31 Oct 1966 action, BM1 Williams File, Navy Department Board of Decorations and Medals Files. See also endnote 195 for a complete list of awards received by James E. Williams during his Navy career.

222. Overall, out of a crew of 25 aboard *Jamaica Bay*, two were killed, another went missing, 21 received superficial wounds, and one survived unscathed. See Msg, CTF 116 to RUEKDA/JCS, 110500Z Jan 1967, Box 241, NFV Records; NMCC Opsum, 10 Jan 1967, Box 111, NMCC OPSUMS.

223. Sources of the *Jamaica Bay* incident include COMNAVFORV Monthly Summaries, Jan and Mar 1967; NMCC Opsums, 9–10 Jan 1967, Box 111, NMCC OPSUMS; Salvage Operations,

Mar 1967, Box 520, NFV Records; Msg, CTF 116 to RUEKDA/JCS, 110500Z Jan 1967, Box 241, NFV Records; Msgs, OINC JAMAICA BAY SALVOPS MY THO to RUMSBB/COMNAVFORV, 010923Z Feb 1967, 020932Z Feb 1967, 030911Z Feb 1967, 041000Z Feb 1967, 051200Z Feb 1967, 070930Z Feb 1967, 081315Z Feb 1967, 081850Z Feb 1967, and 010923Z Feb 1967: all in Box 393, NFV Records; BM1 James E. Williams, Navy and Marine Corps Medal Citation, 5 Sep 1967, BM1 Williams File, Navy Department Board of Decorations and Medals Files; McDavitt interview, 22 Oct 2008; "Base in the Swamps," *Newsweek,* 13 Feb 1967; Jonathan Randal, "Enemy Sinks U.S. Dredge; 3 Other Vessels Damaged," *New York Times,* 10 Jan 1967, 1, 3; Kasperick, "What Makes a Hero?" 4–5; Hooper, *Mobility, Support, Endurance,* 211–213, 172–174.

224. Sources for the description of the 15 January 1967 incident include COMNAVFORV Monthly Summary, Jan 1967; Msg, CTF 116 to RUEPJS/JCS, 180230Z Jan 1967, Box 241, NFV Records; River Patrol Section 531, Combat After Action Report, (RCS:MACVJ 3-32), 151548H Jan 1967, 20 Jan 67, serial 018, Box 226, NFV Files; James E. Williams, Navy Cross Citation, from Bio File; Fred McDavitt, Chester Smith, Frank Spatt, and Michael Williams interviews; Casualty Cards for Quartermaster (QM) 1 Terrel E. Carter, 15 Jan 1967, BM1 James E. Williams, 15 Jan 1967; Patricia Oladeinde, "Riverboat Gambler," 17; JOC Dan Kasperick, "What Makes a Hero?" 2–6.

225. See TF 116, Operation Order 11-66.

226. Michael Williams, McDavitt, and Donovan interviews; email, McDavitt to author, 20 Apr 2009.

227. Paul N. Gray, interview by Edward J. Marolda, 10 Sep 1983, 30, NHHC.

228. Email, McDavitt to author, 6 May 2009.

229. See TF 116, Operation Order 11-66.

230. Ivan Travnicek, interview with author, 6 May 2014.

231. Mike Devlin, interview with author, 5 Nov 2008.

232. Ibid.

233. LT Don Witt ultimately received a posthumous Silver Star for a separate action that occurred on 19 May 1967. During this action, Witt's patrol received shore fire while pursuing an evading sampan on the Ham Luong River. The PBRs returned fire, destroying the sampan and killing four Viet Cong on the shore, including an officer from the 261st Battalion. See COMNAVFORV Monthly Summary, May 1967; Awards Cards for LT Donald Witt, Silver Star, 19 May 1967, Navy Commendation Medal with V, 4 Mar–24 May 1967.

234. According to the Vietnam Awards Cards at NHHC, the following also received decorations for the action: EN3 Warren G. Bolen, Bronze Star with Combat V; Gunner's Mate (Guns)/Seaman (GMGSN) Charles A. Davidson, Navy Commendation with Combat V; and GMG3 Daniel P. Artman, Bronze Star with Combat V.

235. Sources on the 24 May 1967 ambush include COMNAVFORV Monthly Summary, May 1967; COMRIVRON 5, River Squadron Five Command History from March 1967 to December 1967, 26 Apr 1968, Box 521; LT Earl L. Langenberg, After Action Report for 240540Z May 1967, 27 May 1967, Box 221; Msgs, CTF 116 to JCS, 300200Z May 1967, Box 335; CTF 116 to RUEPJS/JCS, 300200Z May 1967, Box 241; CTF 116.1.3.1 to ZEN1/CTF 116, 241629Z May

1967, Box 221: all in NFV Records; Msg, COMNAVSURPACT SAIGON to SECNAV, 241241Z May 1967, in Charles D. Witt, Bio File; Casualty Cards for EN3 Warren G. Bowlen, GMGSN Charles A. Davidson Jr., GMSN Daniel P. Artman, SN Michael C. Quinn, ENFN Terry F. Leazer, and LT Charles D. Witt; Awards Cards for SN Michael J. Devlin (Silver Star), SN Michael C. Quinn (Bronze Star with V Citation), ETR2 Roy L. Castleberry (Bronze Star with V citation), LT Charles D. Witt (Navy Commendation with Combat V), GMGSN Charles A. Davidson (Navy Commendation with Combat V), GMG3 Daniel P. Artman (Bronze Star with Combat V), EN3 Warren G. Bolen (Bronze Star with Combat V); emails, McDavitt to author, 21 Apr 2009; Donovan to author, 7 and 12 Nov 2008 (include several messages forwarded from RADM Morton E. Toole); author interviews with Mike Devlin, Jim Schlosser, John Donovan, and Fred McDavitt; "Viet Cong Fire Kills City Man," *Lubbock Avalanche-Journal*, 26 May 1967, 1, 7; "Lt. Charles Don Witt is Killed in Vietnam Clash," *Lubbock Avalanche-Journal*, 25 May 1967, 1, 14, newspaper clippings courtesy Special Collections, Mahon Library, Lubbock, TX; "Game Warden Patrol Takes Heavy Casualties," *Jackstaff News*, 16 Jun 1967, 1; Ivan Travnicek, "A Short Savage Ambush," Naval History, Oct 2006, 25–27.

236. COMNAVFORV Monthly Summary, Sep 1966.

237. Ibid., Dec 1966.

238. Ibid., Aug 1966; Salvatore Robert Mercogliano, "Sealift: The Evolution of American Military Sea Transportation" (Ph.D. diss., University of Alabama, Tuscaloosa, AL, 2004), 292.

239. For a brief description of the MSB and its capabilities, see COMNAVFORV Monthly Summary, Dec 1967, III-8.

240. BM3 Ken Carlstrom, interview with author, 6 May 2009.

241. For more on the history of Mine Warfare in Vietnam, see David R. Bruhn, *Wooden Ships and Iron Men*, vol. 3, *The U.S. Navy's Coastal and Inshore Minesweepers and the Minecraft That Served in Vietnam, 1953–1976* (Westminster, MD: Heritage Books, 2011).

242. Memo, COMNAVFORV to SECNAV, subj: Presidential Unit Citation in the Case of Mine Squadron 11, Detachment Alpha, 9 Mar 1967, serial 988, enclosure in MINERON 11 Command History, 1967; "Bronze Star Awarded," Mine Squadron Eleven Newsletter, vol. 12, no. 2, Feb 1967, enclosure in Mine Squadron 11 Command History, 1967: both filed in Box 904, Post-1946 Command File; COMNAVFORV Monthly Summary, Aug 1966; Marolda, By *Sea, Air, and Land*, 170.

243. Memo, COMNAVFORV to SECNAV, Presidential Unit Citation in the Case of Mine Squadron 11, Detachment Alpha, 6 Mar 1967, serial 988, Box 23, NFV Records; COMNAVFORV Monthly Summary, Nov 1966.

244. Mine Squadron 11, Command History, 1967; COMNAVFORV Monthly Summary, Feb 1967; memo, COMNAVFORV to SECNAV, subj: Presidential Unit Citation in the Case of Mine Squadron 11, Detachment Alpha, 9 Mar 1967; Casualty Cards for SN Rodney H. Rickli, DC3 Gary C. Paddock, SN Kenneth M Carlstrom, BM3 Thomas J. Crain, BM2 Patrick T. Welch, and EN2 Lonnie J. I. Treat; author interviews with Carlstrom, 6 May 2009, and SM2 Thomas Wasmund, 7 May 2009; Naval History Division, OPNAV, "History of U.S. Naval Operations in the Vietnam Conflict," 3:376.

245. Naval History Division, OPNAV, "History of U.S. Naval Operations in the Vietnam Conflict," 3:376.

246. See Edward J. Marolda and Blake Dunnavent, "Combat at Close Quarter," unpublished manuscript, NHHC.

247. The main sources on the March 1967 sniper incidents come from the Sniper File, Box 586, NFV Records and include "Viet Cong Sniper Activity," undated report; CAPT Robert A. Dowd, Game Warden Weekly Intsum, 2-67/120001H to 182400H MAR 1967, 200112Z Mar 1967; Msgs, SA RSSZ to COMNAVFORV, 050130Z Apr 1967; CTF 116 to COMNAVFORV, 070135Z Apr 1967; COMNAVSUPPACT SAIGON to RUCIJDA/SECNAV, Personnel Casualty Report, 111516Z Mar 1967; CTF 116 to RUMSHS/COMNAVSUPPACT SAIGON, 120020Z Mar 1967; COMNAVSUPPACT SAIGON to RUCIJDA/SECNAV, Personnel Casualty Report LTJG David George Kearney, USNR, 120206Z Mar 1967; COMNAVSUPPACT SAIGON to RUCIJDA/SECNAV, Personnel Casualty Report LTJG David George Kearney, USNR, 111518Z Mar 1967; CTG 116.2 to ZEN/CTF 116, 181529 Mar 1967; CTG 116.2 to ZEN/CTF 116, Game Warden Spotrep 03-18/4/RSSZ/2, 180700Z Mar 1967; CTE 116.1.3.1 to ZEN1/CTF 116, Game Warden Spotrep 3-11/1/116.1.3.1/1, 110440Z Mar 1967; COMNAVSUPPACT SAIGON to RUCIJDA/SECNAV, Personnel Casualty Report, 181827Z Mar 1967; 182132Z Mar 1967; COMNAVSUPPACT SAIGON to RUCIJDA/SECNAV, Personnel Casualty Report; RIVSECT 511 to ZEN/COMRIVRON 5, Personnel Casualty Report, 030235Z Mar 1967. Other sources include Msg, COMNAVSUPPACT SAIGON to SECNAV, Personnel Casualty Report, 111518Z Mar 1967, LTJG David George Kearney, Officer Bio File; CAPT Robert A. Dowd, Officer Bio File; Casualty Cards for ENFN Charles M. Dunn, SN Rene Garcia, and LTJG David George Kearney; Spatt interview, 3 Jun 2009.

248. CAPT Paul N. Gray, Officer Bio File; James A. Michener, "Essex Skipper Clips Wings of Death," *Washington Times-Herald*, 6 Feb 1952; and Thomas Glickman, unpublished memoir, 10–11.

249. Gray interview, 10 Sep 1983, 21.

250. Sheppard, Riverine: *A Brownwater Sailor in the Delta*, 87–88.

251. Goldsmith, *Papa, Bravo, Romeo*, 177.

252. Gray interview, 10 Sep 1983, 21.

253. Memo, COMNAVFORV to CINCPACFLT, Silver Star Medal in the case of CAPT Paul N. Gray, 6 Sep 1967, serial 4500, 1650 Files, Box 24, NFV Records; COMNAVFORV Monthly Summary, May 1967, 6–7.

254. CAPT Paul N. Gray, "We Will Remain Until the Conflict Is Won," *Jackstaff News*, 30 Jun 1967, 1.

255. Gray, End of Tour Report, 28 Jun 1968, Box 99, VCF.

256. BG William R. Desobry, IV Corps Advisor, Debriefing Report, Aug 1965–Jan 1968, Annex H, Villard Files, U.S. Army Center of Military History (CMH).

257. See Gray interview, 10 Sep 1983, 5, 10.

258. Daniels and Erdheim, "Game Warden," 5.

259. COMNAVFORV Monthly Summaries, Nov 1966, Nov 1967.

4. Mobile Riverine Force

1. According to the United States Department of Veterans Affairs, Veterans who develop Parkinson's disease and were exposed to Agent Orange or other herbicides during military service *do not have to prove a connection* between their disease and military service to be eligible to receive VA disability compensation. See www.publichealth.va.gov/exposures/agentorange/conditions/parkinsonsdisease.asp, accessed 6 Apr 2012; David K. Butler, interview with author, 19 Nov 2009.

2. In navy parlance, "striking" for a rating means earning it through on the job training as opposed to A school.

3. Butler interview, 19 Nov 2009.

4. COMNAVFORV Monthly Summary, Jul 1967.

5. Of the seven USN wounded in action, two required dustoff, three were treated on the scene, and two returned to *Benewah* by boat. See CTF 117 to ZEN/COMNAVFORV, Daily Opsum, 7-11, Box 283, NFV Records.

6. Butler interview, 19 Nov 2009.

7. CTF 117 to ZEN/COMNAVFORV, Daily Opsum, 7-11; COMNAVFORV Monthly Summary, 11 Jul 1967, 39.

8. Norman Wells, interview with author, 2 Nov 2009.

9. Note: Wells does not recall making this announcement, but Butler claims he did. Ibid; Butler interview, 19 Nov 2009.

10. Msgs, COMRIVFLOT ONE to RUENAA/CNO, Personnel Casualty Report, 120625Z Jul 1967; COMRIVFLOT ONE to RUENAA/CNO, 111450Z Jul 1967, Daily Opsum, Box 283, NFV Records; Butler interview, 19 Nov 2009.

11. Wells interview, 2 Nov 2009.

12. Only Butler recalls this second round hitting the boat. None of the official reports mentions this second round.

13. Butler interview, 19 Nov 2009.

14. Robert E. Davis, interview with author, 11 Aug 2009.

15. Casualty Card for BM2 David K. Butler; email, David K. Butler to author, 4 May 2012.

16. This number includes sailors killed on TF 117 support ships. For a full list of names, see Mobile Riverine Force Association, CTF 117, Personnel Killed in Action/Missing In Action, Southeast Asia Theater of the Vietnam War, 1960–1975, www.mrfa.org/navykia.htm, accessed 15 Dec 2009. For a list of 9th Infantry Division soldiers killed, see http://mrfa.org, accessed 6 Apr 2012.

17. Nguyen Huu Vi, interview with author, 18 Sep 2009. General Vi operated out of Ben Tre and commanded 1,000 Viet Cong. He was personally responsible for forming special Viet Cong boat-hunting units in the Ben Tre and My Tho areas.

18. The weapons were also greatly feared by TF 116. James D. Johnson, interview with author, 25 Jun 2009; V. Nadin, Shoulder-fired Antitank Weapons, Army Foreign Science and Technology Center, Charlottesville, VA, AD-783 955, 9 Aug1973, www.dtic.mil/dtic/tr/fulltext/u2/783955.pdf, accessed 21 Apr 2012; Dan Shea, "SADJ Identification Series: The RPG ID Guide," *Small Arms Defense Journal*, sadefensejournal.com/wp/?p=1042, accessed 13 Apr 2012;

Janes Infantry Weapons 1976, 570, 589–590; James D. Johnson, *Combat Chaplain: A Thirty-Year Vietnam Battle* (Denton, TX: University of North Texas Press, 2001), 47–48; Donn A. Starry, *Mounted Combat in Vietnam* (Washington, DC: Department of the Army, 1989), 47.

19. George L. MacGarrigle, *Taking the Offensive: October 1966 to October 1967* (Washington, DC: Center of Military History, 1998), 430.

20. Westmoreland apparently made the statement to Rear Admiral Kenneth A. Veth, COMNAVFORV. See Schreadley, *From the Rivers to the Sea*, 139.

21. Ibid, 394–395; MACV Command History, 1966, 45–48, Box 44, VCF; William B. Fulton, *Riverine Operations 1966–1969* (Washington, DC: Department of the Army, 1973), 24–25.

22. Naval History Division, OPNAV, "History of U.S. Naval Operations in the Vietnam Conflict," 3:425–426.

23. General William C. Westmoreland as cited in HQ PACAF, Riverine Operations in the Delta, May 1968–June 1969, CHECO 67, 31 Aug 1969, Air Force Historical Research Institute, Maxwell AFB, Montgomery, AL, 1, Author Files.

24. Naval History Division, OPNAV, "History of U.S. Naval Operations in the Vietnam Conflict," 3:425–426; MacGarrigle, *Taking the Offensive*, 396; Fulton, *Riverine Operations*, 47.

25. TF 117, Operation Order 201-YR, 10 Jun 1968, Box 858, Operation Orders Collection, AR.

26. Even officers who trained in 1967 noted that their men received no small boat training in the United States prior to deploying to Vietnam. Email, Courtney Frobenius to author 12 Feb 2010; Naval History Division, OPNAV, "History of U.S. Naval Operations in the Vietnam Conflict," 3:430; Fulton, *Riverine Operations*, 43–44.

27. Bolduc also complained about having to prepare for a command management inspection and attend command and staff training sessions at night. Lucien "Blackie" Bolduc, interview with author, 12 Feb 2010.

28. RIVFLOT 1 Briefing Book, May 1967, Box 161, VCF; NIOTC Command History, 1966, Box 1338, Post-1946 Command File.

29. Alan Breininger, interview with author, 8 Jun 2008.

30. Lester Schneider, interview with author, 5 Aug 2009.

31. David Raybell, interview with author, 25 Jun 2009.

32. Butler interview, 19 Nov 2009.

33. Larry D. Rodgers, interview with author, 4 Aug 2009.

34. Michael Harris, interview by Stephen Maxner, 22 Aug 2000, 13, Vietnam Archive.

35. Ibid., 10.

36. Walter F. Lineberger III, interview with author, 12–13 Jan 2010.

37. Harris interview, 22 Aug 2000, 12.

38. John L. Green Jr., interview with author, 31 Jul 2009.

39. Harris interview, 22 Aug 2000, 12.

40. Raymond W. Johnson, interview with author, 8 Mar 2010.

41. Chester C. Stanley Jr., interview with author, 26 Jun 2009.

42. Oswald interviews, Apr–May 2004, 37–40.

43. Wells interview, 2 Nov 2009.

44. Breininger interview, 8 Jun 2008.

45. Stanley interview, 26 Jun 2009.

46. USS *Tingey* (DD-539), DANFS, www.history.navy.mil/DANFS/t6/tingey-iii.htm, accessed 18 Dec 2009; CAPT Wade C. Wells, Bio File.

47. VADM Robert S. Salzer, interview by John T. Mason, Nov 1981, 349, USNI Oral History Collection.

48. Raymond Johnson interview, 8 Mar 2010.

49. MacGarrigle, *Taking the Offensive*, 415–416.

50. RIVFLOT 1 Briefing Book, May 1967; MacGarrigle, *Taking the Offensive*, 415–416.

51. RIVFLOT 1 Briefing Book, May 1967; LTC James S. G. Turner, USMC, interview by MAJ Phillip J. Thomas, USA, 2 Mar 1968, 8–9, Vietnam Interview Collection, (CMH); MACV Command History, 1966, 138–144; Fulton, *Riverine Operations*, 85–88.

52. LTJG William B. Fulton, Bio File, CMH.

53. Turner interview, 2 Mar 1968, 38.

54. For more on Wells' accomplishments as the Navy component commander of the MRF, see memo, COMNAVFORV to SECNAV, subj: Distinguished Service Medal in the case of CAPT Wade Cantrell Wells, 5 Nov 1967, NFV Records.

55. The dogs were named Linus and Lucy after the characters in the *Peanuts* cartoon strip. Wells gave Lucy to Fulton as a gift. Bolduc interview, 12 Feb 2010; Raymond Johnson interview, 8 Mar 2010.

56. Generally speaking, the Army provided Class I (food), Class III (POL), and Class V (ammo) supplies to *APL-30*. The barracks ship, in turn, secured its Class II (personal support items), Class IV (organizational support items), and Class IX (repair parts) from Naval Support Activity Saigon. If Dexter could not obtain an item from the NSA, he would often resort to cumshaw. For example, he traded Navy office supplies for green fatigues. Stephen T. Dexter, interview with author, 19 Aug 2009.

57. Naval History Division, OPNAV, "History of U.S. Naval Operations in the Vietnam Conflict," 3:431; Fulton, *Riverine Operations*, 59.

58. Originally, these units were to be called river assault groups, but the Navy later changed their names to river assault squadrons so they would not be confused with Vietnam Navy river assault groups.

59. RIVFLOT 1 Briefing Book, May 1967; Fulton, *Riverine Operations*, 61; COMNAVFORV Monthly Summary, Jan 1967, 43–44.

60. Marolda, *By, Sea, Air, and Land*, 205.

61. Harris interview, 22 Aug 2000.

62. RIVFLOT 1 Briefing Book, May 1967; Steven J. Vitale, interview with author, 18 Aug 2009; NAVSHIPS, "Boats of the United States Navy," May 1967, NDL; Cutler, *Brown Water Black Berets*, 240–241; Friedman, *U.S. Small Combatants*, 330–331.

63. Rodgers interview, 4 Aug 2009.

64. Arthur J. Dodd, interview with author, 21 Aug 2009.

65. Salzer interview, Nov 1981, 364, 451–453.

66. Robert Franson, interview with author, 14 Aug 2009.

67. Vitale interview, 18 Aug 2009.

68. Dodd interview, 21 Aug 2009.

69. Schneider interview, 5 Aug 2009.

70. Salzer interview, Nov 1981, 452; Cutler, *Brown Water, Black Berets*, 243.

71. Stanley interview, 26 Jun 2009; Friedman, *U.S. Small Combatants*, 336.

72. This was the same weapon the Army employed on the flamethrower version of the M113 armored personnel carrier (the M132).

73. RIVFLOT 1 Briefing Book, May 1967; Joseph Lacapruccia, interview with author, 3 Sep 2009; Cutler, *Brown Water, Black Berets*, 243; Friedman, *U.S. Small Combatants*, 339–340; Flamethrower Monitors Specifications, Naval Inshore Operations Training Center in Vallejo, www.rivervet.com/miscboatinfo.htm, accessed 30 Dec 2009.

74. Cutler, *Brown Water, Black Berets*, 243; RIVFLOT 1 Briefing Book, May 1967.

75. RIVFLOT 1 Briefing Book, May 1967; Friedman, *U.S. Small Combatants*, 348–357; Cutler, *Brown Water, Black Berets*, 247–248.

76. COMNAVFORV Monthly Summary, Mar 1968, 53.

77. Friedman, *U.S. Small Combatants*, 355.

78. Salzer interview, Nov 1981, 414.

79. Ibid., 415.

80. Lineberger interview, 12–13 Jan 2010.

81. Salzer interview, Nov 1981, 418.

82. Ibid., 415.

83. It should be noted, however, that three crewmen were wounded in the attack, and RMSN Frederic P. Webb was knocked off the boat by the force of the blast and drowned. COMNAVFORV Monthly Summary, Dec 1967, 54.

84. Naval History Division, OPNAV, "History of U.S. Naval Operations in the Vietnam Conflict," 3:430; Turner interview, 2 Mar 1968, 27; Naval History Division, *Riverine Warfare*, 54.

85. USS *Benewah* (APB-35), DANFS, www.history.navy.mil/danfs/b5/benewah-i.htm, accessed 6 Jan 2010; Albert Moore, "History of the USS *Benewah* (APB-35)," 6 Dec1998, mrfa.org/apb35.htm, accessed 6 Jan 2010.

86. On 3 March 1968, for instance, *Benewah* destroyed four Viet Cong bunkers with its 3-inch 50-caliber and 40mm guns during a 12-hour, 106-mile transit from Can Tho to Dong Tam. See *Benewah* (AP- 35), Command History, 1968.

87. RIVFLOT 1 Briefing Book, May 1967; "Welcome Aboard U.S.S. *Benewah* APB-35," *Benewah* File, SH; *Benewah* (APB-35), DANFS; Moore, "History of the USS *Benewah*"; *Jackstaff News*, 1 Apr 1968, Box 184, VCF.

88. *Benewah* Bulletin, September–October 1967, www.ussbenewah.com/pdfs/Benewah-Bulletin1967.pdf, accessed 6 Jan 2010.

89. Johnson, *Combat Chaplain*, 26.

90. Oswald interview, Apr–May 2004, 126.

91. *Benewah* (APB-35), Command History, 1968.

92. Oswald interview, Apr–May 2004, 126–127.

93. Rodgers interview, 4 Aug 2009.

94. Dodd interview, 21 Aug 2009.

95. Johnson, *Combat Chaplain*, 42–43.

96. Jack Benedick, interview with author, 14 May 2010.

97. TF 117 Operation Order 201-YR, 10 Jun 1968.

98. Johnson, *Combat Chaplain*, 42–43.

99. Stanley interview, 26 Jun 2009.

100. Schneider interview, 5 Aug 2009.

101. Green interview, 31 Jul 2009.

102. Benedick interview with author, 14 May 2010.

103. Lacapruccia interview, 3 Sep 2009.

104. Rodgers interview, 4 Aug 2009.

105. Thomas A. Dempsey, interview with author, 6 Aug 2009.

106. Pat Haggerty, interview with author, 21 Aug 2009.

107. Dodd interview, 21 Aug 2009.

108. COMNAVFORV Monthly Summary, Dec 1967; LCDR Charles W. Lynch, "*APL 26*: Barracks Barge with a Combat Role," http://mrfa.org/apl26.htm, accessed 9 Apr 2010; Edwin B. Hooper, *Mobility, Support, Endurance*, 173.

109. Msg, CTF 117 to COMNAVFORV, Increased Tempo of Operations, 081618Z Dec 1967, Spotreps/Opsums, Box 281, NFV; Raybell interview, 25 Jun 2009; COMNAVFORV Monthly Summary, Dec 1967; JO3 A. G. Popowitz, "Repair Support for the MRF," *Jackstaff News*, 18 May 1968, 7–8, Box 184, VCF; Edwin B. Hooper, *Mobility, Support, Endurance*, 174; Doug Lindsey, "History of the *YRBM-17* (Vietnam)," www.mrfa.org/yrbm17.htm, accessed 9 Apr 2010; Mobile Riverine Force Association, "History of the USS *Askari* (ARL-30)," www.mrfa.org/arl30.htm, accessed 9 Apr 2010.

110. MACV tended to translate it as "united hearts and minds" whereas contemporary Vietnamese speakers interpret the phrase to mean "singleness of mind, in thoughts and actions." The MACV translation can be found in Fulton, *Riverine Operations*, 47; Phuc Minh and Serena Le Whitener helped the author with the modern translation of the phrase.

111. Msg, COMUSMACV to CINCPAC, 250420Z Mar 1967, subj: Enlargement of Dong Tam, Box 377, NFV; Fulton, *Riverine Operations*, 47.

112. The dredge *New Jersey* was ultimately salvaged by Harbor Clearance Team 1 and returned to service in Vietnam in 1970. See Carroll H. Dunn, *Base Development in South Vietnam 1965–1970* (Washington, DC: Department of the Army, 1991), 53–54.

113. Hooper, *Mobility, Support, Endurance*, 173.

114. Naval History Division, OPNAV, "History of U.S. Naval Operations in the Vietnam Conflict," 3:439.

115. Hooper, *Mobility, Support, Endurance*, 173–174.

116. RIVFLOT I, "Informal Resume of Operations of TF 117 from Commencement of Operations 16 February 1967 to 16 February 1968," Box 161, VCF; MacGarrigle, *Taking the Offensive*, 411, 414.

117. Dave Raybell, interview with author, 25 Jun 2009. Westmoreland as cited by Cutler, *Brown Water, Black Berets*, 237.

118. Rodgers interview, 4 Aug 2009.

119. Dodd interview, 21 Aug 2009.

120. Johnson, *Combat Chaplain*, 142.

121. John L. Miller, interview with author, 20 Aug 2009.

122. Raybell interview, 25 Jun 2009.

123. Miller interview, 20 Aug 2009.

124. Raybell interview, 25 Jun 2009.

125. Johnson, *Combat Chaplain*, 18.

126. Turner interview, 2 Mar 1968, 6–7.

127. Salzer interview, Nov 1981, 324.

128. Ibid.; Turner interview, 2 Mar 1968, 14–15.

129. Breininger interview, 8 Jun 2008.

130. RIVFLOT 1 Briefing Book, May 1967; Fulton, *Riverine Operations*, 94.

131. Salzer interview, Nov 1981, 326.

132. COL Burt David, USA, interview by MAJ Philip Thomas, USA, Jun 1968, 12, Vietnam Interview Collection, CMH.

133. Fulton, *Riverine Operations*, 96.

134. An MRF soldier typically carried 7 magazines for his M16, 200 rounds of machine-gun bullets, and 12 40mm grenade launcher rounds. See Fulton, *Riverine Operations*, 62.

135. Green interview, 31 Jul 2009.

136. Most men who fell overboard were not so lucky. The high velocity current of the Mekong combined with the low visibility of the water made recovering men from the rivers very difficult, and many were lost. See Salzer interview, Nov 1981, 463; Robert Franson, interview with author, 14 Aug 2009.

137. Fulton, *Riverine Operations*, 73, 96–98.

138. Turner interview, 2 Mar 1968, 29; Cutler, *Brown Water, Black Berets*, 214–215.

139. See LTC Foster H. Taft, Jr., "The Impact of Skin Diseases on Military Operations in the Delta Region RVN," undated, Eric Villard Files, CMH; and MAJ George G. O'Conner, Debriefing, 22 Feb 1968, HRC 314.82, 7, CMH.

140. O'Conner, Debriefing, 98–101; MacGarrigle, *Taking the Offensive*, 400, 424–425.

141. Taft, "The Impact of Skin Diseases."

142. Breininger interview, 8 Jun 2008; 3d Battalion, 47th Infantry, After Action Report, River Raider I, Operations in the RSSZ, 16 Feb–20 Mar 1967, 3, RG 472, National Archives and Records Administration (NARA II), College Park, MD.

143. Msg, CTF 117 to COMNAVFORV, Increased Tempo of Operations, 081618Z Dec 1967, Spotreps/Opsums, Box 281, NFV.

144. Davis interview, 11 Aug 2009.

145. Fulton, *Riverine Operations*, 20; 3d Battalion, 47th Infantry, After Action Report, 16 Feb–20 Mar 1967, 4.

146. Salzer interview, Nov 1981, 363–395.

147. Franson interview, 14 Aug 2009.

148. Green interview, 31 Jul 2009.

149. Email, Frobenius to author, 12 Feb 2010; Bolduc interview, 12 Feb 2010; Ronald R. Menner, interview with author, 18 Feb 2010.

150. Fulton, *Riverine Operations*, 100–101.

151. TF 117, Operation Order 201-YR, 10 Jun 1968.

152. Ibid.

153. See TF 117, Operation Order 201-YR, 10 Jun 1968.

154. Salzer interview, Nov 1981, 392–393.

155. O'Connor, Debriefing, 22 Feb 1968, 5.

156. Salzer interview, Nov 1981, 391.

157. Lineberger interview, 12–13 Jan 2010.

158. Vitale interview, 18 Aug 2009.

159. Butler interview, 19 Nov 2009.

160. Salzer interview, Nov 1981, 386–387.

161. COMNAVFORV Monthly Summary, Apr 1967.

162. 3dBattalion, 47th Infantry, After Action Report, 16 Feb–20 Mar 1967, 1–2, 16; COMNAVFORV Monthly Summary, Feb 1967, 14; RAS 9, Command History, 1967, Author Files; Naval History Division, OPNAV, "History of U.S. Naval Operations in the Vietnam Conflict," 3:433.

163. 3dBattalion, 47th Infantry, After Action Report, 16 Feb–20 Mar 1967, 1–2, 16; COMNAVFORV Monthly Summary, Feb 1967, 12–14.

164. On 16 March there were three attacks against PBRs and one against a merchant ship. Ibid., 21.

165. Ibid., 24.

166. Ibid., C-6; Fulton, *Riverine Operations*, 72–73.

167. COMNAVFORV Monthly Summary, Apr 1967.

168. COMNAVFORV Monthly Summary, Jun 1967; Fulton, *Riverine Operations*, 104–106; MacGarrigle, *Taking the Offensive*, 416–418.

169. MacGarrigle, *Taking the Offensive*, 418–420.

170. According to Captain Ronald A. Menner, 9th Infantry Division companies were authorized 160 men but rarely fielded more than 110. Email, Menner to author, 24 Feb 2010; Ralph Christopher, *Duty, Honor, Sacrifice: Brown Water Sailors and Army River Raiders* (Bloomington, IN: AuthorHouse, 2007), 195.

171. Reeves, After Action Statement, 30 June 1967, 17–19; William L. "Bill" Reynolds, interview with author, 29 Apr 2010.

172. CDR Charles L. Horowitz, Bio File; Casualty Card for CDR Charles L. Horowitz; Silver Star Award Card for CDR Charles L. Horowitz; Reeves, After Action Statement, 30 Jun 1967, 22; Christopher, *Duty, Honor, Sacrifice*, 180.

173. Benedick interview, 14 May 2010; Christopher, *Duty, Honor, Sacrifice*, 180.

174. It should be noted that Johnson was a star football and baseball player in college. Raymond Johnson interview, 14 May 2010.

175. Ibid.

176. Ibid.; JOC Lee McDougal and JOSN Mary K. Rice, "Johnson is his Name, Versatility is his Game," *Navy Recruiter*, Oct 1969, 14; Commander Amphibious Force United States Pacific Fleet, Navy News Release 14-68, "Amphibious Padre Receives First Silver Star Awarded to Navy Chaplain Since Korean War," 18 Jan 1968, Raymond W. Johnson Bio File; Casualty Card for LT Raymond W. Johnson, 19 Jun 1967; Silver Star Award Card for BM3 Cecil O. Johnson, Jr.; Bronze Star Award Card for EN2 Michael W. "Red" Dolezal; Raymond W. Johnson, *Postmark: Mekong Delta* (Westwood, New Jersey: Fleming H. Revell Co., 1968), 81–86; Christopher, *Duty, Honor, Sacrifice*, 180–181.

177. Reynolds interview, 29 April 2010.

178. Reeves, After Action Statement, 30 June 1967, 23–24; Christopher, *Duty, Honor, Sacrifice*, 185–186.

179. Reeves, After Action Statement, 30 June 1967, 20.

180. CTF 117, Opsum 6-19, CTF 117 OPSUMS, Box 283, NFV.

181. Menner interview, 18 Feb 2010.

182. Christopher, *Duty, Honor, Sacrifice*, 195; MacGarrigle, *Taking the Offensive*, 419.

183. Turner interview, 2 Mar 1968, 17.

184. Ibid.; RIVFLOT I, Informal Resume of Operations of TF 117, 16 Feb 1967–16 Feb 1968.

185. MacGarrigle, *Taking the Offensive*, 420.

186. 3d Battalion, 60th Infantry, OPORD 27-67, Coronado V, 29 September 1967, Box 824, RG 472, NARA II; COMNAVFORV Monthly Summary, Sep 1967, 49; MacGarrigle, *Taking the Offensive*, 426–429.

187. CDR Frances E. Rhodes, RAS 11 After Action Report (MACVJ 3-32), 22 Sep 1967, TF 117 General Msgs, July 1966–Dec 1967, Box 279, NFV.

188. LCDR Francis E. Rhodes, Bio File; Charlie Cox, interview with author, 21 Oct 2009; Raymond Johnson interview, 8 Mar 2010; Rhodes, RAS 11 After Action Report, 22 Sep 1967.

189. Rhodes, RAS 11 After Action Report, 22 Sep 1967; John Albright, "Fight Along the Rach Ba Rai," in John A. Cash, John Albright, and Allan W. Sandstrum, *Seven Firefights in Vietnam* (Washington, DC: Office of the Chief of Military History, 1985), 6.

190. Stanley interview, 26 Jun 2009.

191. See COMNAVFORV Monthly Summary, Sep 1967.

192. James D. Johnson, interview with author, 25 June 2009; Johnson, *Combat Chaplain*, 47–48

193. Stanley interview, 26 Jun 2009; Rhodes, RAS 11 After Action Report, 22 Sep 1967; COMNAVFORV Monthly Summary, Sep 1967.

194. Specifically, he recommended that the 40mm turret on some of the monitors be replaced with an M7A 1-6 Flame Turret. Wells reasoned that streams of flame would be effective in entering bunker slits and spider-hole openings and that even if the flame did not burn the enemy soldiers to death, it would kill them through asphyxiation. See CAPT Wade C. Wells, First Endorsement on COMRIVRON 11 ltr 3000 serial 08 of 22 Sep 1967, 7 Oct 1967, TF 117 General Messages, Jul 1966–Dec 1967, Box 279, NFV; msgs, COMRIVLOT ONE to RUWJMSA/COMPHIBPAC, 220230Z Sep 1967; COMRIVLOT ONE to RUHHKUT/COMPHIBPAC, 212345 Oct 1967, TF 117 General Messages, Jul 1966–Dec 1967, Box 279, NFV; COMNAVFORV Monthly Summary, Sep 1967; Albright, "Fight Along the Rach Ba Rai," 75–76.

195. Raybell interview, 25 Jun 2009.

196. Complications from that injury, however, later killed him in 1999.

197. Raybell interview, 25 Jun 2009.

198. Ibid.; Casualty Cards for FN Abraham Cecemski, SN Bryan Girard Craft, GMG2 James Ezra Elkins, LTJG George Washington Hawkins, and EN3 William Harris Little; Rhodes, RAS 11 After Action Report, 22 Sep 1967; email, Raybell to author, 6 Nov 2009.

199. Raybell interview, 25 Jun 2009; Casualty Card for RM/SN David Raybell.

200. Two of these marines were also wounded in the battle.

201. Rhodes, RAS 11 After Action Report, 22 Sep 1967; Raybell interview, 25 Jun 2009; Albright, "Fight Along the Rach Ba Rai," 73–76; MacGarrigle, *Taking the Offensive*, 426–429.

202. BM1 Carroll E. Dutterer Jr., Navy Cross Citation, Awards Files, AR; Casualty Card for BM1 Carroll E. Dutterer Jr.

203. For more on the threat of water mines on the Rach Ba Rai, see Annex A, Intelligence, Coronado OPORD 32-67, 10 Sep 1967, RIVFLOT 1 Summaries, Box 153, VFC.

204. Albright, "Fight Along the Rach Ba Rai," 73–76; MacGarrigle, *Taking the Offensive*, 426–429; Fulton, *Riverine Operations*, 132.

205. Johnson, *Combat Chaplain*, 52.

206. It should be mentioned that some of the dustoff pilots landed under fire and took hits evacuating the wounded. "If anyone deserves a medal, it was those chopper pilots," claimed Chester Stanley, "they had brass balls." Stanley interview, 26 Jun 2009.

207. See COMNAVFORV Monthly Summary, Sep 1967. Another report stated that had it not been for the presence of the ATC(H), the on-scene commanders "would have been faced with the time-consuming task of clearing and securing landing zones from which to evacuate the wounded." See COMRIVFLOT ONE, Informal Summary 30, 24 Sep 1967, RIVFLOT One Summaries, Box 154, VCF. Also, for a more complete breakdown of casualties in the 15 September battle, see Msg, COMRIVFLOT ONE to ZEN/COMNAVFORV, 030900 Oct 1967, TF 117 General Messages, Jul 1966–Dec 1967, Box 279, NFV.

208. Albright, "Fight Along the Rach Ba Rai," 79–81.

209. Ibid.; Rhodes, RAS 11 After Action Report, 22 Sep 1967; Johnson, *Combat Chaplain*, 55.

210. Huynh Ly, interview with author, People's Committee Building, My Tho, Vietnam, 21 Sep 2009. Ly's unit was later decimated in the 1968 Tet Offensive, suffering eight killed and 20 wounded, but Ly survived, eventually retiring from the People's Army of Vietnam in 2006 as a colonel.

211. Davis interview, 11 Aug 2009.

212. Msg, COMRIVFLOT ONE/CTF 117 to RUHHBRA/CINCPACFLT, Recommendation for Individual Award: LCDR Francis E. Rhodes, 051329Z Oct 1967, TF 117 General Messages, Jul 1966–Dec 1967, Box 279, NFV.

213. Albright, "Fight Along the Rach Ba Rai," 80.

214. Davis interview, 11 Aug 2009.

215. For details on the boat damage incurred during the attack, see COMRIVFLOT ONE, Informal Summary 30, 24 Sep 1967, RIVFLOT One Summaries, Box 154, VCF.

216. Ibid.; Davis interview, 11 Aug 2009; MacGarrigle, *Taking the Offensive*, 426–429.

217. Raymond Johnson interview, 8 Mar 2010; Schneider interview, 5 Aug 2009; MACV Command History, 1967, vol. 1, 397, Box 45, VCF; Fulton, *Riverine Operations*, 136

218. COMNAVFORV Monthly Summary, Nov 1967; Fulton, *Riverine Operations*, 138.

219. RAD 91's parent unit was River Assault Squadron 9 and RADs 111 and 112, River Assault Squadron 11.

220. COMRIVFLOT ONE, Informal Summary 41, 10 Dec 1967, Box 154, VCF.

221. Salzer interview, Nov 1981, 351.

222. Wells interview, 2 Nov 2009.

223. COMRIVFLOT ONE, Informal Summary 41, 10 December 1967; CTF 117 to COMNAVFORV, Daily Opsum 12-4, 041540Z Dec 1967, Box 281, NFV.

224. Green interview, 31 Jul 2009.

225. Joseph V. R. Camara, interview with author, 19 Aug 2009.

226. Green interview, 31 Jul 2009.

227. Ibid.; COMRIVFLOT ONE, Informal Summary 41, 10 Dec 1967; email, John Green to author, 12 Jun 2011.

228. A group of reporters from Saigon who toured the battlefield on the 5th were impressed by the fact that they could actually go through the area and count the bodies themselves. Turner interview, 2 Mar 1968, 22; Fulton, *Riverine Operations*, 139.

229. RIVFLOT ONE, Command History, 1967, Box 516, NFV; COMNAVFORV Monthly Summary, Dec 1967.

230. Salzer interview, Nov 1981, 352.

231. Turner interview, 2 Mar 1968, 23.

232. Salzer interview, Nov 1981, 357.

233. O'Connor, Debriefing, 22 Feb 1968, 8.

5. War on the Coast, 1967

1. Max G. Branscomb, interview with author, 24 Jun 2008; CDR Max G. Branscomb, Officer Bio File; VP-1 Command History, 1967; COMNAVFORV Monthly Summary, Jul 1967; Charles R. Stephan, "Trawler!" *U.S. Naval Institute Proceedings* 94 (Sep 1968): 60–71.

2. GEN William C. Westmoreland as cited in Naval History Division, OPNAV, "History of U.S. Naval Operations in Vietnam," 3:286.

3. MACV Market Time Study Group Report, Sep 1967, 15–16, Box 64, VCF; H. D. Cluck, OEG Study No. 738, "Market Time Effectiveness," May 1970, Box 65, CNA Studies, AR.

4. MACV Market Time Study Group Report, Sep 1967, 15–16.

5. Memo, F. A. Parker to R. A. Gessert, subj: Effectiveness of Market Time Operations, 24 May 1968, Box 64, VCF.

6. COMNAVFORV Market Time II, Feb 1970, 6, Box 136, VFC; Marolda, *By Sea, Air, and Land*, 143–144.

7. COMNAVFORV Market Time II, Feb 1970, 6.

8. Virg Erwin, *Cat Lo: A Memoir of Invincible Youth* (Indianapolis, IN: Dog Ear Publishing, 2009), 111.

9. COMNAVFORV Market Time II, Feb 1970, 6.

10. Naval History Division, OPNAV, "History of U.S. Naval Operations in Vietnam," 3:297.

11. The U.S. Coast Guard eventually sent the following WHECs to Vietnam: *Half Moon* (WHEC-382), *Yakutat* (WHEC-380), *Barataria* (WHEC-381), *Bering Strait* (WHEC-378), and *Gresham* (WHEC-387). Naval History Division, OPNAV, "History of U.S. Naval Operations in Vietnam," 3:290; Larzelere, *Coast Guard at War*, 124.

12. John Webb, COMNAVFORV Staff, Market Time Barrier Documentation and Analysis, Market Time Studies folder, Author Files.

13. VP-1, Command History, 1967; Webb, Market Time Barrier Documentation and Analysis, Feb 1970.

14. NAG Staff, Vietnamese Navy Optimum Force Structure Study FY-68-70, Jul 1968, 30–31, Box 75, VCF; VP-1, Command History, 1967; Webb, Market Time Barrier Documentation and Analysis, Feb 1970.

15. Webb, Market Time Barrier Documentation and Analysis, Feb 1970.

16. MACV Market Time Study Group Report, Sep 1967, 15–16.

17. Webb, Market Time Barrier Documentation and Analysis, Feb 1970; MACV Market

Time Study Group Report, Sep 1967, 15–16.

18. MACV Market Time Study Group Report, Sep 1967, Appendix A, 29–33.

19. CDR Norman C. Venzke, USCG, interview by Naval History Division staff, 28 Feb 1969, 10, NHHC Oral History Collection.

20. Marolda, *By Sea, Air, and Land*, 216–222.

21. COMNAVFORV Monthly Summary, Apr 1967, 35.

22. They usually strayed into the inner barrier patrolled by PCFs and WPBs.

23. LT Thomas J. Bender, End of Tour Report, Fleet Command End of Tour Reports, 1967–1968, Box 194, NAG Records.

24. LT George E. Hays, End of Tour Report, Fleet Command End of Tour Reports, 1967–1968, ibid.

25. LTJG Whitney Goit II, End of Tour Report, Fleet Command End of Tour Reports, 1967–1968, ibid.

26. Hays, End of Tour Report, ibid.

27. LT Elroy A. Soluri, End of Tour Report, Fleet Command End of Tour Reports, 1967–1968, ibid.

28. LT George S. Forrester, End of Tour Report, Fleet Command End of Tour Reports, 1967–1968, ibid.

29. LT Noel M. Allen, End of Tour Report, Fleet Command End of Tour Reports 1967–1968, ibid.

30. LT Richard J. Robbins, End of Tour Report, Fleet Command End of Tour Reports 1967–1968, ibid.

31. COMNAVFORV Monthly Reports, Jan, Dec, 1967.

32. LCDR Lawrence F. De Angelo, End of Tour Report, Fleet Command End of Tour Reports, 1967–1968, Box 194, NAG Records.

33. Cruisers and destroyers of the Naval Gunfire Support Unit of Task Group 70.8 provided the other 90 percent of NGFS. See JCS, Combat Analysis Group, Review and Appraisal of Naval Gunfire Support Operations, 1 Aug 1968, 22 Box 33, VCF; Venzke interview, 28 Feb 1969, 8–10.

34. Scotti, *Coast Guard Action in Vietnam*, 70.

35. Msg, *Half Moon* to COMNAVFORV, 300800Z Aug 1967, USCG Squadron 3, Jul–Aug 1967 folder, Box 229, VCF.

36. COMNAVFORV Monthly Summary, Sep 1967; Scotti, *Coast Guard Action in Vietnam*, 70.

37. Scotti, *Coast Guard Action in Vietnam*, 60; Blinn, *Confession to a Deaf God*, 53–54.

38. CDR Herbert J. Lynch as cited in Larzelere, *Coast Guard at War*, 131–132.

39. COMNAVFORV Monthly Summary, Aug, Sep 1967.

40. Destroyer and cruiser gunfire support was of limited utility in IV Corps Tactical Zone not only because mud flats were so prevalent but because replenishment for these large ships of TF 70.8 was conducted in I and II Corps tactical zones (CTZs) far to the north. Venzke interview, 28 Feb 1969, 10; JCS, Review and Appraisal of Naval Gunfire Support Operations, 1 Aug 1968, 43.

41. CAPT Robert W. Durfey as cited in Alex Larzelere, *Coast Guard at War*, 132.

42. COMNAVFORV Monthly Summary, Feb, Apr 1967.

43. Msg, CTF 115 to COMNAVFORV, 110334Z Apr 1967, VN Report, Message Traffic, Jan–Jun 1967 folder, Box 333, VCF; COMNAVFORV Monthly Summary, Apr 1967.

44. After recovering from his wounds in Japan, Withey ended up working as a liaison officer to the Vietnamese at Cat Lo. See *Sedgwick County* (LST-1123), Command History, 1967; Casualty Card for LTJG Thomas A. Withey; Silver Star Award Card for LTJG Thomas A. Withey.

45. Randal "Randy" Kenneth Fredricksen, interview with author, 21 Dec 2010.

46. Msg, CTF 115 to AIG 495, 270028Z Jun 1967, VN Report, Message Traffic, Jan–Jun 1967 folder, Box 333, VCF; COMNAVFORV Monthly Summary, Apr, Jun 1967; *Oak Hill* (LSD-7), Command History, 1967; *Sedgwick County*, Command History, 1967; Market Time Historical Summary, Jun 1967, Box 517, NFV; "Navy Swift Boat Sunk But Revenge Exacted," *Jackstaff News*, 14 Jul 1967.

47. Scotti, *Coast Guard Action in Vietnam*, 163–164; Bob Stoner, "Mk 2 Mod 0 and Mod 1 .50 Caliber MG/81mm Mortar," www.pcf45.com/misfire/mortar.html, accessed 9 Mar 2011.

48. COMNAVFORV Monthly Summary, Oct 1966; "Mortar Explosion Aboard PCF-9," Coastal Squadron One Directory, www.swiftboats.net/stories/pcf9mortar.htm, accessed 9 Mar 2011.

49. COMNAVFORV Monthly Summary, Mar 1967.

50. COGARDIV 11, War Diary, 17–23 Apr 1967; COGARDIV 13 Diary, 3–9 Apr 1967: both in Box 226, VCF; Scotti, *Coast Guard Action in Vietnam*, 164.

51. Coast Guard solicitation directive for Vietnam WPB commanders as cited by Scotti, *Coast Guard Action in Vietnam*, 166.

52. Webb, Market Time Barrier Documentation and Analysis, Feb 1970; COGARDIV 11, War Diary, 23 Feb 1967, Box 226, VCF; COMNAFORV Monthly Summary, Feb 1967.

53. COGARDIV 11, War Diary, 24 Feb 1967, Box 226, VCF; COMNAFORV Monthly Summary, Feb 1967.

54. COGARDIV 12, War Diary, 3–9 Apr 1967, Box 226, VCF.

55. COGARDIV 13, War Diary, 17–23 Apr 1967.

56. COMNAFORV Monthly Summary, Jul 1967.

57. Larzelere, *Coast Guard at War*, 43.

58. COMNAVFORV Monthly Summary, Aug 1966.

59. John Schlight, *The War in South Vietnam: The Years of the Offensive, 1965–1968* (Washington, DC: Office of Air Force History, 1988), 206–211.

60. The Cua Tung is the mouth of the Song Bin Hai. Testimony of Capt Robert D. Lufburrow, USAF, in Reid et al., Report of the Board of Investigation, 15 Aug 1966, 85; William R. Wells II, USCG *Point Welcome*: A Target of Opportunity, www.aug.edu/~libwrw/ptwelcome/PointWelcome2.html, accessed 21 Dec 2011.

61. Testimony of 2Lt Jimmy N. Brasher, USA, Reid et al., Report of the Board of Investiga-

tion, 15 Aug 1966, 88–89.

62. Testimony of Capt Charles B. Chism, USAF, in Col Samuel L. Reid, USAF, et al., Report of the Board of Investigation, 15 Aug 1966, 63, Box 232, VCF. For more on the Blind Bat program, see Frederick F. Nyc III, *Blind Bat: C-130 Night Forward Air Controller Ho Chi Minh Trail* (Austin, TX: Eakin Press, 2000).

63. Scotti, *Coast Guard Action in Vietnam: Stories of those Who Served*, 104.

64. Memo, Chief, Operational Readiness Division to Chief, Office of Operations, subj: *Point Welcome* Attack, 11 Aug 1966, 22 Nov 1966, Box 232, VCF.

65. 7th AF WSN RVN, Tally Ho Frag Order 22 for TR 510-33, 091240Z Jul 1966, ibid.

66. Testimony of Chism, Reid et al., Report of the Board of Investigation, 15 Aug 1966, 63–64.

67. Ibid.; memo, Chief, Operational Readiness Division to Chief, Office of Operations, 11 Aug 1966, 22 Nov 1966.

68. Testimony of Capt John S. Lynch, USAF, Reid et al., Report of the Board of Investigation, 15 Aug 1966, 91; CTF 115, *Point Welcome* Incident, Preliminary Investigation Report, 111542Z Aug 1966, Box 578, NFV.

69. Testimony of Lynch, Reid et al., Report of the Board of Investigation, 15 Aug 1966, 91.

70. The crew included LTJG Ross Bell, the executive officer; Culinary Specialist (CS)2 Donald L. Austin, a cook; FA Houston J. Davidson, a fireman apprentice; GM2 Mark D. McKenney, a gunner's mate; SN David E. O'Connor, an unrated seaman; BMC Richard Patterson, the ranking petty officer on the boat; BM1 Billy R. Russell, a boatswain's mate; ET2 Virgil G. Williams, an electronics technician; ENC William H. Wolf, the chief engineman; and EN2 Jerry Phillips.

71. Note: McKenney was wearing one chevron on his uniform during the attack but made GM2 shortly thereafter (he was a gunner's mate second class by the time he was interviewed by the Board of Inquiry between 13 and 15 August). Paul Scotti, email to author, 29 Dec 2011; Findings of Fact, Reid et al., Report of the Board of Investigation, 15 Aug 1966; Wells, USCG *Point Welcome*: A Target of Opportunity.

72. Testimony of GM2 Mark D. McKenney, Reid et al., Report of the Board of Investigation, 15 Aug 1966, 2; Scotti, *Coast Guard Action in Vietnam*, 102–103.

73. Testimony of McKenney, Reid et al., Report of the Board of Investigation, 15 Aug 1966, 2.

74. Testimony of Lynch, Reid et al., Report of the Board of Investigation, 15 Aug 1966, 91.

75. Ibid.; Wells, USCG *Point Welcome*: A Target of Opportunity; Scotti, *Coast Guard Action in Vietnam*, 104–105.

76. According to Paul Scotti, "it is arguable that Brostrom thought that they were South Vietnamese and not North Vietnamese aircraft, but in his radio call he did not specify South or North. He simply said Vietnamese." Email, Scotti to author, 29 Dec 2011. See also Scotti, *Coast Guard Action in Vietnam*, 104–105.

77. Testimony of 2d Lt Arthur J. Cote, USAF, Reid et al., Report of the Board of Investigation, 15 Aug 1966, 36.

78. Lynch had delayed his second pass for several minutes to survey the damage inflicted by his first pass. See Testimony of Lynch, Reid et al., Report of the Board of Investigation, 15

Endnotes

Aug 1966, 91.

79. Testimony of BMC Richard H. Patterson, USCG, Reid et al., Report of the Board of Investigation, 15 Aug 1966, 11–17; Msg, COMCOGARDRON ONE to TF 115, 120745Z Aug 66, Box 578, NFV; Wells, USCG *Point Welcome*: A Target of Opportunity; Larzelere, *The Coast Guard in Vietnam*, 24–27; Scotti, *Coast Guard Action in Vietnam*, 111.

80. Msgs, COMNAVFORV to CINCPAC, 120855Z Aug 1966; CTF 115 to COMNAVFORV, 110839Z Aug 1966: both in Box 578, NFV; Testimony of McKenney and LTJG Stanley E. Bork, USCG, Reid et al., Report of the Board of Investigation, 15 Aug 1966, 2–8, 80–81; Wells, USCG *Point Welcome*: A Target of Opportunity; Larzelere, *Coast Guard in Vietnam*, 24–25; Scotti, *Coast Guard Action in Vietnam*, 104–105; Tim Page, *Page After Page* (New York: Atheneum, 1989), 128–129.

81. Msg, COMCOGARDRON ONE to CTF 115, 120745Z Aug 1966; Testimony of Patterson, Reid et al., Report of the Board of Investigation, 15 Aug 1966, 11–17; Wells, USCG *Point Welcome*: A Target of Opportunity; Larzelere, *Coast Guard in Vietnam*, 24–27; Scotti, *Coast Guard Action in Vietnam*, 104–107.

82. Schlight, *War in South Vietnam*, 231.

83. Testimony of Maj Richard F. Gibbs, USAF, and Capt Stanley P. Franks Jr., USAF, Report of the Board of Investigation, 15 Aug 1966, 54–56, 59–61.

84. Testimony of McKenney, Reid et al., Report of the Board of Investigation, 15 Aug 1966, 2–3; *Point Welcome*, Decklog Entry, 11 Aug 1966, Box 232, VCF; Scotti, *Coast Guard Action in Vietnam*, 107, 109.

85. Testimony of SN David E. O'Connor, USCG, Reid et al., Report of the Board of Investigation, 15 Aug 1966, 25.

86. Testimony of LT Arthur J. Cote, USN, and Capt Charles B. Chism, USAF, Reid et al., Report of the Board of Investigation, 15 Aug 1966, 36, 65; Scotti, *Coast Guard Action in Vietnam*, 109.

87. Commanding Officer, USCGC *Point Caution*, Summary of Events, 11 Aug 1966, Box 232, VCF; Wells, USCG *Point Welcome*: A Target of Opportunity.

88. Msgs, CTF 115 to MACV COC, 110849Z Aug 1966, Attack on USCGC *Point Welcome*, 111540Z Aug 1966, *Point Welcome* Incident, Personnel Status, Box 578, NFV; COMNAVFORV Monthly Summary, Aug 1966.

89. Page, *Page After Page*, 131–132.

90. The other members were Captain John C. McDonnel, USN, and Lieutenant Colonel Richard B. Peterson, USAF; Major Thomas E. Bradley, USMC, served as a recorder. See Reid et al., Report of the Board of Investigation, 15 Aug 1966.

91. The other members were Captain John C. McDonnel, USN, and Lieutenant Colonel Richard B. Peterson, USAF; Major Thomas E. Bradley, USMC, served as a recorder. See Reid et al., Report of the Board of Investigation, 15 Aug 1966.

92. Reid et al., Report of the Board of Investigation, 15 Aug 1966, Opinions; memo, Chief, Operational Readiness Division to Chief. Office of Operations, 22 Nov 1966; Msgs, CTF 115 to MACV COC, 110849Z Aug 1966, and 111540Z Aug 1966; COMNAVFORV Monthly Summary,

Aug 1966; Scotti, *Coast Guard Action in Vietnam*, 111.

93. See Reid et al., Report of the Board of Investigation, 15 Aug 1966, Recommendations.

94. Msg, COMUSMACV to CINCPAC, 182205Z Jun 1968, CINCPAC Message Traffic, AR; Headquarters 1st Amphibian Tractor Battalion, 3d Marine Division FMF, Command Chronology, 1–30 Jun 1968, PCF-19 folder, Author Files; Seventh Fleet, Monthly Historical Summary, Jun 1968, 51–53, Box 117, VCF.

95. PACAF Command Center Chronological Log, 3–29 Jun 1968, Air Force Historical Research Agency, Maxwell AFB, AL.

96. Seventh Fleet, Monthly Historical Summary, Jun 1968, 51–53.

97. *Boston* (CAG-1), Deck Log, 16 Jun 1968; *Boston*, Command History, 1968.

98. Msg, CINCPAC to NMCC, 200223Z Jul 68, PACOM Message Traffic; PACAF Command Center Chronological Log, 3–29 Jun 1968; memo, Commanding Officer, USCG *Point Dume* to Commander Task Group 115.1, subj: Hostile Aircraft Incident, area 1A1, early morning of 16 Jun 1968, Chronological Narrative, 16 Jun 1968, Box 228, VCF.

99. Salvage divers never found Bowman's body, and the remains of this 32-year-old African American from Walterboro, S.C., are missing to this day.

100. See Msg, CINCPAC to NMCC, 200223Z Jul 1968; Casualty Cards for GMGSN John Anderegg, and LTJG John D. Davis, 16 Jun 1968; COMNAVFORV Monthly Summary, Jun 1968; James Steffes, *Swift Boat Down: The Real Story of the Sinking of PCF-19* (Xlibris, 2006), 53–54.

101. Memo, *Point Dume* to CTG 115.1, 16 Jun 1968.

102. Steffes, *Swift Boat Down*, 47–48.

103. LTJG Peter B. Snyder, OIC, PCF-12, Combat After Action Report, 151130H Jun to 161130H Jun 1968, PCF-19 folder, Author Files.

104. Ibid.

105. Ibid.; memo, *Point Dume* to CTG 115.1, 16 Jun 1968.

106. Steffes, *Swift Boat Down*, 48–49.

107. Memo, *Point Dume* to CTG 115.1, 16 Jun 1968; Snyder, Combat After Action Report, 151130H Jun to 161130H Jun 1968.

108. *Edson* (DD-946), Command History, 1968; Jeffrey Grey, *Up Top: The Royal Australian Navy and Southeast Asian Conflicts, 1955–72* (Canberra, Australia: Australian War Memorial, 1998), 175–176.

109. *Boston* (CAG-1), Deck Log, 17 Jun 1968; *Boston*, Command History, 1968; PACAF Command Center Chronological Log, 3–29 Jun 1968; Msg, CINCPAC to NMCC, 200223Z Jul 1968.

110. PACAF Command Center Chronological Log, 3–29 Jun 1968; PACFLT, Command Historical Summary, Jun 1968, Post-1946 Command File; Msg, CINCPAC to NMCC, 200223Z Jul 1968; Grey, *Up Top*, 176.

111. NMCC Opsum, 17 Jun 1968, Box 112, NMCC OPSUMs; PACAF Command Center Chronological Log, 3–29 Jun 1968; PACFLT, Command Historical Summary, Jun 1968; Grey,

Up Top, 177–180.

112. *Edson*, Command History, 1968; NMCC Opsum, 17 Jun 1968; CINCPAC to NMCC, 200223Z Jul 1968; PACAF Command Center Chron Log, 3–29 Jun 1968.

113. Seventh Fleet, Monthly Historical Summary, Jun 1968, 51–53; CINCPAC to NMCC, 200223Z Jul 1968.

114. *Hobart*'s Navigating Officer, Lieutenant Commander M. B. Rayment, made the following remarks about the event in a later oral history: "[The] great shock initially combined with some surprise that a mistake between allies could occur [together with] the utter disbelief that we could be fired upon in a friendly air environment and were unable to retaliate was frustrating." See Jeffrey Grey, *Up Top*, 180–183.

115. Seventh Fleet, Monthly Historical Summary, Jun 1968, 51–53; CINCPAC to NMCC, 200223Z Jul 1968; CINCPAC to NMCC, 200223Z Jul 1968; *Boston* Deck Log, 16 Jun 1968; *Boston*, Command History, 1968.

116. Steffes, *Swift Boat Down*, 77–79.

117. NMCC Opsum, 18 Jun 1968, Box 112, NMCC OPSUMs.

118. Msg, COMUSMACV to CINCPAC, 182205Z Jun 1968, PACOM Message Traffic.

119. CINCPAC to NMCC, 200223Z Jul 1968.

120. Schlight, *War in South Vietnam*, 260–261.

121. Friedman, *U.S. Small Combatants*, 243.

122. Marolda and Fitzgerald, *From Military Assistance to Combat*, 289.

123. *Asheville* (PG-84), Brochure, *Asheville* (PG-84), Command History File, SH; "New Gunboat to Join Fleet Soon," *Navy Magazine*, Feb 1966; Friedman, *U.S. Small Combatants*, 268–271.

124. *Asheville*, Command History, 1967; Friedman, *U.S. Small Combatants*, 268–271.

125. Lieutenant Henry Dale, Officer Bio File; *Asheville*, Command History, 1967.

126. *Asheville*, Command History, 1967.

127. *Gallup* (PG-85), Command History, 1967, 1968.

128. *Crockett* (PG-88), Command History, 1969.

129. *Asheville*, Command History, 1968.

130. *Antelope* (PG-86), Informal Monthly Summary 099 for Feb 1970, 26 Feb 1970, Post-1946 Command File; *Antelope* (PG-86), Command History, 1970.

131. The only maintenance items noted were a problem with the power supply of its 2502 radar, a Freon and water link on the S/S/ air conditioning unit, and a loose nut on the 31 gun mount. See *Antelope* (PG-86), Informal Monthly Summary 012 for May 1970, 28 May 1970, Post-1946 Command File.

132. Marolda and Dunnavent, "Combat at Close Quarters," unpublished manuscript.

133. Friedman, *U.S. Small Combatants*, 271.

134. Stephan, "Trawler!" Sep 1968, 62.

135. Edward J. Bergin, interview with author, 4 Jun 2008.

136. MACV Market Time Study Group Report, Sep 1967.

137. Msg, CTF 115 to NMCC, 011828Z Jan 1967, Vietnam Reports, Market Time, Box 333, VFC; COMNAVFORV Monthly Summary, Jan 1967.

138. Msg, CTF 115 to NMCC, 020959Z Jan 1967, Vietnam Reports, Market Time, Box 333, VCF; Christopher, *Duty, Honor, Sacrifice*, 129; CDR Richard W. Dawson, Bio File; CDR Richard W. Dawson, Casualty Card, 1 Jan 1967.

139. Memo, LT Roger W. Hassard to Commander USCG Division 13, Summary of 01D6 Incident, 10 Jan 1967, CGATV OPS, Jan 1967, Box 225, VCF; Msg, CTF 115 to NMCC, 020959Z Jan 1967; COMNAVFORV Monthly Summary, Jan 1967.

140. Memo, Hassard to USCG Division 13, 10 Jan 1967.

141. Memo, COMNAVFORV to SECNAV, subj: Presidential Unit Citation in the Case of the United States Navy Coastal Surveillance Force, 21 Jul 1968, 5, Box 62, NFV; COMNAVFORV Monthly Summary, Jan 1967.

142. Webb, Market Time Barrier Documentation and Analysis, Feb 1970.

143. Msg, ADMINO CINPAC to RUMSA/COMUSMACV, 082335Z Mar 1967, subj: 1 Jan 1967 Trawler Incident, Vietnam Reports, Market Time, Box 333, VCF.

144. Memo, COMNAVFORV to SECNAV, 21 Jul 1968, 5.

145. Roger W. Hassard, Bronze Star Citation, http://www.uscga.edu/uploadedFiles/Campus/Landmarks/Hall_of_Heroes/Hall_of_Heroes_Subs/2010_WoG_Plaques/WOG2010-Hassard.pdf, accessed 22 Mar 2011.

146. VP-46, Command History, 1967; memo, COMNAVFORV to SECNAV, 21 Jul 1968, 6–7; *Brister* (DER-327), Command History, 1967; COGARDIV 12, War Diary 3–19 Mar 1967, Box 226, VCF.

147. Richard Picard, interview with author, 29 Mar 2011.

148. Ibid.; COGARDIV 12, War Diary 3–19 Mar 1967.

149. Picard interview, 29 Mar 2011; COGARDIV 12, War Diary 3–19 Mar 1967; memo, COMNAVFORV to SECNAV, 21 Jul 1968, 6–7; *Brister* (DER-327), Command History, 1967.

150. COGARDIV 12, War Diary 3–19 Mar 1967; memo, COMNAVFORV to SECNAV, 21 Jul 1968, 6–7; *Brister,* Command History, 1967.

151. Helton was later wounded on 24 August 1967 while on patrol near of the Cua Viet River. Anthony J. Trackerman, interview with author, 25 Mar 2011; CDR Armand L. (Toby) Chapeau, USCG (Ret.), "Only a Purple Heart," Draft Article, 1967 Trawler Intercepts folder, Author Files.

152. Westmoreland as cited in Msg, COMNAVFORV to CTF 115, 1610020Z Mar 1967, Box 226, NFV.

153. Picard interview, 29 Mar 2011.

154. Ibid.; Raul Herrera, interview with author, 29 May 2008.

155. Herrera interview, 29 May 2008; Raul Herrera, "Swift Boats in Operation Market Time," *Vietnam*, Feb 1966, 37–39.

156. Msg, *Wilhoite* (DER-387) to CTG 115.1, 150736Z Jul 67, Subj: SITREP Summary,

Wilhoite (DER-397) File, Box 712, Post-1946 Reports; *Wilhoite* (DER-397), Command History, 1967; CDR Estel Wilbur Hays, Officer Bio File.

157. COMNAVFORV Monthly Summary, Jul 1967; Stephan, "Trawler!" Sep 1968, 60–71.

158. Ibid.; Msg, *Wilhoite* to CTG 115.1, 150736Z Jul 1967; *Wilhoite,* Command History, 1967.

159. Stephan, "Trawler!" Sep 1968, 60–71.

160. Bergin interview, 4 Jun 2008.

161. Edward Bergin, "Sa Ky River Victory, Southern River Mouth – Mui Batangan," pcf45.com/trawler/trawler.html, accessed 31 Mar 2011.

162. Stephan, "Trawler!" Sep 1968, 65–66.

163. Ibid.

164. Bergin interview, 4 Jun 2008.

165. Ibid.; NMCC Opsum, 15 Jul 1967, Box 115, NMCC OPSUMS. For alternative perspective on the issue, see *Wilhoite* to CTG 115.1, 150736Z Jul 1967; COMNAVFORV Monthly Summary, Jul 1967.

166. Bergin interview, 4 Jun 2008.

167. *Gallup* (PG-85), Command History, 1967; *Wilhoite* to CTG 115.1, 150736Z Jul 1967; Stephan, "Trawler!" Sep 1968, 65.

168. COMNAVFORV Monthly Summary, Jul 1967.

169. Bergin interview, 4 Jun 2008; Bergin, "Sa Ky River Victory."

170. Ibid.; Stephan, "Trawler!" Sep 1968, 67.

171. Bergin, "Sa Ky River Victory."

172. COGARDIV 12, War Diary, 10–16 Jul 1967, Box 227, VCF; Stephan, "Trawler!" Sep 1968, 67.

173. Stephan, "Trawler!" Sep 1968, 68–69.

174. COMNAVFORV Monthly Summary, Jul 1967.

175. Ibid.; Stephan, "Trawler!" Sep 1968, 71.

176. RADM Kenneth L. Veth as cited in COMNAVFORV Monthly Summary, Jul 1967.

177. A survey of coastal group personnel in 1967 revealed that 35 percent had no formal education, 45 percent had some grade school education, and 20 percent had completed elementary school. The study estimated that only 20–25 percent of coastal group personnel were capable in being trained in technical skills. See NAG, "A Study of the Vietnamese Navy's Coastal Forces," Jun 1968, xvi, Box 75, VCF.

178. Ibid., 88; LTJG Arthur B. Barrena, Assistant Advisor, Coastal Group 16, Debrief, undated, Box 199, NAG Records.

179. Dennis Boe John O'Leary claimed he was also at the base during the attack, but he is not mentioned in any of the official documents on the attack, including witness statements for various awards given to Guinn, Williams, and Fitzgerald. There were too many inconstancies in his story during a 20 May 2009 interview with the author to include it in this section.

180. ENC Harold Norman Guinn, Eyewitness Statement, annex to memo, Chief, NAG to CINCPACFLT, subj: Silver Star Medal in the case of LTJG Anthony C. Williams, USNR,

undated, Box 64, NAG Records; COMNAVFORV Monthly Summary, Aug 1967.

181. LTJG Anthony C. Williams Statement in memo, First Coastal Zone Advisor to Chief, NAG, subj: Recommendation for the Award of the Silver Star with Combat Distinguished Device in the case of ENC Harold N. Guinn, 4 Sep 1967, Coastal Group 16 folder, Author Files.

182. Ibid.

183. Guinn statement.

184. "SWO Training Facility Names for Vietnam Hero," *Surface Warfare*, Nov 1980, 31–33.

185. Williams statement.

186. BM1 Leo E. Pearman, Eyewitness Statement, annex to memo, Chief, NAG to CINCPACFLT, subj: Silver Star Medal in the case of LTJG Anthony C. Williams.

187. Williams statement; Guinn statement.

188. Michael "Boats" Turley, interview with author, 28 May 2008.

189. Guinn statement; Pearman statement.

190. Awards Cards for LTJG William C. Fitzgerald, BM1 Leo E. Pearman, and LTJG Anthony C. Williams, AR.

191. Fitzgerald later received a posthumous Navy Cross for his actions on 7 August, and the Navy later named a guided missile destroyer in his honor, USS *Fitzgerald* (DDG-662). Guinn would later receive a Silver Star; and Pearman and Williams, Bronze Stars with Combat V Devices. See awards citations for Fitzgerald, Pearman, and Williams; https//awards.navy.mil, accessed 21 Apr 2011.

192. COMNAVFORV Monthly Summary, Aug 1967.

193. NAG, "Study of the Vietnamese Navy's Coastal Forces," Jun 1968, xxvi, 30.

194. COMNAVFORV, Psychological Operations Manual, undated, Box 597, NFV.

195. COMNAVFORV, PSYOP Monthly Summary, Sep 1967, Box 520, NFV.

196. Lieutenant Victor G. Reiling Jr. was a PSYOP advisor attached to the VNN Headquarters in 1967. See LT Victor G. Reiling Jr., End of Tour Report, Box 196, NAG Records.

197. Clayton D. Laurie, "Kit Carson Scouts," in Spencer Tucker, ed., *The Encyclopedia of the Vietnam War* (New York: Oxford University Press, 1998), 212.

198. In addition to these military defections, there were more than a half-million civilian refugees from Viet Cong–controlled areas living in temporary shelters or resettlement camps at more than 300 locations. See COMNAVFORV, Psychological Operations Manual.

199. Ibid.

200. LT Victor G. Reiling Jr., and LTJG G. W. Scott, "Psychological Operations in Vietnam," *U.S. Naval Institute Proceedings* 94 (Jul 1968): 124.

201. Reiling, End of Tour Report.

202. LCDR Lawrence L. Combs, End of Tour Report, Box 196, NAG Records.

203. COMNAVFORV, PSYOPs Monthly Summary, Oct 1967, Box 520, NFV.

204. Reiling, End of Tour Report; COMNAVFORV, Psychological Operations Manual; LT Victor G. Reiling, Officer Bio File; Reiling and Scott, "Psychological Operations in Viet-

Endnotes

nam," 122–123.

205. NAVFORV, Psychological Operations Loudspeaker Broadcasts Manual, Box 597, NFV.

206. Ibid.

207. LT William W. Pippenger, Fourth Coastal Zone Psychological Warfare Advisor, End of Tour Report, Nov 1967, Box 597, NFV.

208. Reiling, End of Tour Report.

209. COMNAVFORV Monthly Summary, Jul, Nov 1967.

210. NAG, "Study of the Vietnamese Navy's Coastal Forces," Jun 1968, 29.

211. LTJG Ross N. Driver, USNR, End of Tour Report, Box 597, NFV; Reiling, End of Tour Report.

212. COMNAVFORV Monthly Summary, Nov 1967.

213. James R. Adams, interview with author, 17 May 2011.

214. COMNAVFORV, PSYOPs Monthly Summary, Sep 1967.

215. COMNAVFORV, Psychological Operations Manual.

216. Adams interview, 17 May 2011.

217. LTJG John Francis Miller, End of Tour Report, undated, Box 597, NFV.

218. COMNAVFORV, Psychological Operations Manual.

219. Miller, End of Tour Report.

220. Bergin interview, 4 Jun 2008.

221. Adams interview, 17 May 2011.

222. Rod Davis, interview with author, 18 May 2011.

223. There are numerous superstitions about the albatross, but seeing an albatross is not necessarily a bad luck omen as Carver suggests. When a sailor dies, the albatross carries the soul of the sailor. Hence, an albatross following a ship may offer good luck because the soul of the dead sailor may be looking out for the ship. Killing an albatross, however, always brings bad luck because it is akin to killing a guardian angel. See "Albatross," *Encyclopedia Britannica*, www.britannica.com/EBchecked/topic/12596/albatross, accessed 3 Apr 2011.

224. Bergin admitted that in retrospect the decision not to take these men under fire was a mistake. Bergin interview, 4 Jun 2008.

225. Ibid.; COMNAVFORV Monthly Summary, Dec 1967.

226. Herrera interview, 29 May 2008.

227. Bergin interview, 4 Jun 2008; COMNAVFORV Monthly Summary, Dec 1967.

228. Herrera interview, 29 May 2008.

229. Bergin interview, 4 Jun 2008.

230. Ibid.; Herrera interview, 29 May 2008.

231. Memo, COMNAVFORV to SECNAV, subj: Presidential Unit Citation in the Case of the United States Navy Coastal Surveillance Force, 21 Jul 1968.

232. *Androscoggin* (WHEC-68), OPREP-3, Trawler Incident, 1 Mar 1967, *Androscoggin*

(WHEC68), Monthly Summary Report, Feb 1968, Box 230, VCF; COMNAVFORV Monthly Summary, Mar 1968, Appendix I, Trawler Incidents; Scotti, *Coast Guard Action in Vietnam*, 74–76.

233. *Winona* (WHEC-65), Summary of Trawler Incident, annex to *Winona*, Monthly Summary Report, Feb 1968, Box 230, VCF; COMNAVFORV Summary, Mar 1968, Appendix I, Trawler Incidents; Scotti, *Coast Guard Action in Vietnam*, 76–77.

234. COMNAVFORV Monthly Summaries, Mar and Feb 1968; memo, COMNAVFORV to SECNAV, 21 Jul 1968; Scotti, *Coast Guard Action in Vietnam*, 73–78.

235. *Minnetonka* (WHEC-67), Monthly Summary Report, 1 Feb–3 Mar 1968, Box 230, VCF; COMNAVFORV Monthly Summary, Mar 1968, Appendix I, Trawler Incidents; Scotti, *Coast Guard in Vietnam*, 77–79.

236. The four infiltrators thwarted on 1 March 1968 brought the total number of such incidents since February 1965 to 13. See COMNAVFORV Monthly Summary, Mar 1968, Appendix I, Trawler Incidents.

237. MACV, Market Time Study Group Report, 5 Sep 1967.

238. Memo, COMNAVFORV to SECNAV, 21 Jul 1968; COMNAVFORV Monthly Summary, Aug 1968; Weymouth D. Symmes, *This is Latch: The Story of Rear Admiral Roy F. Hoffman* (Missoula, MT: Pictorial Histories Publishing, 2007), 186–188.

239. Memo, COMNAVFORV to SECNAV, 21 Jul 1968; Coastal Squadron One Casualty List, http:swiftboats.net/extras/casualties.htm, accessed 5 May 2011.

240. Naval History Division, OPNAV, "History of U.S. Naval Operations in Vietnam," 3: 1183–1184; COMNAVFORV Monthly Summary, Oct 1967.

241. Ibid.; COMNAVFORV Monthly Summary, Dec 1967.

242. Di Napoli, a young sailor attached to the Naval Support Activity detachment at Qui Nhon, was killed manning the base fire truck. See Dana R. Ruff note, http://thewall-usa.com/guest.asp?recid=13347, accessed 6 May 2011.

243. The additional risks of riverine operations during SEALORDS also pushed casualties upward. Coastal Squadron lost another 22 men between November 1968 and December 1969. Coastal Squadron One Casualty List, http://swiftboats.net/extras/casualties.htm, accessed 5 May 2011.

6. Tet, 1968

1. In all, Army and marine artillery units fired over 158,000 rounds during the siege, and aircraft from all the services launched over 22,000 air strikes. See James H. Willbanks, *The Tet Offensive: A Concise History* (New York: Columbia, 2007), 64.

2. Knowlton as cited in Schreadley, *From the Rivers to the Sea*, 137.

3. See COMNAVFORV Monthly Summary, Jan 1968; RIVFLOT One Briefing Book, May 1967; Marolda, *By Sea, Air, and Land*, 204–205.

4. Ibid., 14, 27, 40.

5. Ibid.

6. At least twenty-five soldiers were killed and many others wounded. See LST-624, Command History, Mar 1944–Oct 1945; Salzer, interview by Mason, Nov 1981, 71–74; and Robert

S. Salzer, Officer Bio File.

7. Salzer interview, Nov 1981, 90. For more on the typhoon, see "Typhoons and Hurricanes: Pacific Typhoon at Okinawa, October 1945," www.history.navy.mil/faqs/faq102-6.htm, accessed 24 Aug 2010.

8. Salzer interview, Nov 1981, 98–99.

9. *Abbot* (DD-629), Command History, 1954–1955.

10. Dwayne L. Parsons, interview with author, 3 Nov 2010.

11. Peter B. Rankin, interview with author, 31 Mar 2011.

12. Paul Tobin ultimately retired from the service as a rear admiral. Emails, Paul Tobin to author, 12, 13 May 2010.

13. Salzer interview, Nov 1981, 399–408.

14. American casualties during this engagement consisted of two sailors and eight soldiers wounded. COMNAVFORV Monthly Summary, Jan 1968.

15. Army Center of Military History (CMH), Washington, DC; COMNAVFORV Monthly Summary, Jan 1968; RIVFLOT I, Informal Resume of Operations of TF 117, 16 Feb 1967–16 Feb 1968.

16. COMNAVFORV Monthly Summary, Jan 1968, 21–34.

17. Game Warden Statistical Summaries in COMNAVFORV Monthly Summary, Nov 1967, Dec 1967, and Jan 1968.

18. Ray J. Verhasselt, interview by author, 24 Aug 2010; LCDR Ray J. Verhasselt, Officer Bio File.

19. Email, Verhasselt to author, 14 Apr 2011; Verhasselt interview, 24 Aug 2010; COMNAVFORV Monthly Summary, Jan 1968, 40; R. J. Verhasselt Vietnamese Gallantry Cross Citation, http://spg.navylog.org/individual.aspx?&navy_log_id=294685, accessed 25 Aug 2010.

20. BG William R. Desobry, as cited in Willbanks, *Tet Offensive*, 150.

21. GEN William A. Knowlton, interview by LTC David W. Hazen, 1982, 399, Senior Officer Oral History Program, Military History Institute, Carlisle Barracks, PA; Eric Villard Files, CMH.

22. Salzer interview, Nov 1981, 400.

23. II Field Force, Combat Operations After Action Report, 310001 Jan to 182400 Feb 1968, Villard File, CMH; Willbanks, *Tet Offensive*, 150.

24. It should be noted that moving the MRF from the delta to Saigon would have been very difficult logistically.

25. One of the first targets hit by the Viet Cong was the base ammo dump, which contained 1,500 tons of ammunition—90 percent of Marine supplies! See Willbanks, *Tet Offensive*, 64.

26. S. A. Swarztrauber, "River Patrol Relearned," in Frank Uhlig Jr., ed., *Vietnam: The Naval Story. 1950-1970* (Annapolis: Naval Institute Press, 1986); Cutler, *Brownwater, Black Berets*, 273–281; Schreadley, *From the Rivers to the Sea*, 140–141.

27. According to historian James Willbanks, these early attacks resulted from a calendar mix-up by the Viet Cong. See Willbanks, *The Tet Offensive*, 29.

28. Memo, Thomas L. Hughes, INR, to Secretary of State, 1 Feb 1968, Declassified by State, 21 Mar 1979, By IP, NARS, 3-21-79, LBJ Library, Austin, TX.

29. LT Robert Kay, "VN Navy Headquarters Attacked," *Jackstaff News*, 16 Mar 1968, NFV; COMNAVFORV Monthly Summary, Jan 1968.

30. Kiem Do, *Counterpart*, 141–143; Kiem Do interview, 1–7 Nov 2007.

31. MACV Monthly Summary, Feb 1968, 7, author files.

32. CTF 117, Daily Opsum 2-1, 011300Z Feb 1968, Daily OPSUMs, Jan–Apr 68, Box 281, NFV; TF 117, Command History, 1968, Box 516, NFV; COMNAVFORV Monthly Summary, Jan 1968, 69; Fulton, *Riverine Operations*, 150.

33. John Green, interview with author, 31 Jul 2009.

34. 3d Battalion, 47th Infantry, 9th Infantry Division, Combat After Action Report, 290400 Jan to 091445 Feb 68, Villard Files, CMH.

35. COMNAVFORV Monthly Summary, Jan 1968, 70; Willbanks, *Tet Offensive*, 31–37, 41.

36. Fuscaldo interview, 13 Feb 2009.

37. Cragg interview, 29 Oct 2008; email, Cragg to author, 27 Aug 2010.

38. Ken Delfino, "As If It Were Yesterday!" unpublished article courtesy of Richard J. Cragg, Author Files.

39. Stephen Sumrall, interview with author, 13 Aug 2010.

40. Ibid.

41. Emails, McDavitt to author, 18, 19 Oct 2010.

42. When his patrol was ambushed and the patrol leader seriously wounded, Gallagher took command of the unit, rallied his troops, and exposed himself to heavy enemy fire to evacuate his men. According to his citation, he was "directly responsible for the safe withdrawal of his patrol and for killing a large number of the enemy in their own base area." A full text of the citation is at www.militarytimes.com/citations-medals-awards/recipient.php?recipientid=4405, accessed 24 Apr 2012.

43. Harry Constance and Randall Fuerst, *Good to Go: The Life and Times of a Decorated Member of the U.S. Navy's Elite SEAL Team Two* (New York: William & Morrow, 1997), 159.

44. A mix of Winchester Model 70, .30-06, rifles with Unertl 10-power scopes and .762-caliber Remington Heavy Barrel Model 700 rifles with Redfield scopes. Erasmo "Doc" Riojas, interview with author, 18 Oct 2010.

45. Riojas interview, 18 Oct 2010. Chief Riojas served with SEAL Team 2 as a hospital corpsman and was at the Carter Billet during the first few days of the Tet Offensive. Email, A. D. Clark to Erasmo "Doc" Riojas, 18 Oct 2010.

46. Ibid., 163, 165.

47. Orr Kelly, *Brave Men—Dark Waters*, 130–131.

48. Constance and Fuerst, *Good to Go*, 175.

Endnotes

49. Riojas interview, 18 Oct 2010.

50. Constance and Fuerst, *Good to Go*, 164, 175–176.

51. Nguyen Thi Lung, as cited in Huchthausen and Lung, *Echoes of the Mekong*, 77–78.

52. Ibid., 79–80.

53. 2d Brigade, 9th Infantry Division, After Action Report, 18 Jan 1968–12 Feb1968; 3d Battalion, 47th, Infantry, Combat After Action Report, 290400 Jan to 091445 Feb 1968; 3d Battalion, 60th Infantry, Combat After Action Report, 18 Jan–13 Feb 1968, Villard Files, CMH; TF 117, Command History, 1968, Box 516, NFV; Fulton, *Riverine Operations*, 150–151.

54. 2d Brigade, 9th Infantry Division, After Action Report, 18 Jan–12 Feb 1968.

55. 3d Battalion, 47th Infantry, Combat After Action Report, 290400 Jan to 091445 Feb 1968; 3d Battalion, 60th Infantry, Combat After Action Report, 18 Jan–13 Feb 1968; 2d Brigade, 9th Infantry Division, After Action Report, 18 Jan–12 Feb 1968; TF 117, Command History, 1968; Fulton, *Riverine Operations*, 150–151.

56. 3d Battalion, 47th Infantry, Combat After Action Report, 290400 Jan to 091445 Feb 1968; 3d Battalion, 60th Infantry, Combat After Action Report, 18 Jan–13 Feb 1968; TF 117 Command History, 1968; COMNAVFORV Summary, Feb 1968.

57. MACV Monthly Summary, Feb 1968.

58. Huynh Ly interview, 21 Sep 2009.

59. COMNAVFORV Monthly Summary, Feb 1968.

60. U.S. Army Advisory Group, IV CTZ, Historical Summary of Viet Cong Tet Offensive, Mar 1968, Villard Files, CMH.

61. Rod Davis interview, 5 Nov 2008.

62. Constance and Fuerst, *Good to Go*, 179.

63. COMNAVFORV Monthly Summary, Feb 1968.

64. U.S. Army Advisory Group, IV CTZ, Historical Summary of Viet Cong Tet Offensive, Mar 1968.

65. Verhasselt interview, 24 Aug 2010.

66. Robert W. Smith, interview with author, 20 Aug 2010.

67. This number also includes the rural population who lived in Ben Tre district. See Office of the Prime Minister, Directorate General of Planning, *Vietnam Statistical Yearbook 1967–1968*, vol. 14 (Saigon, Vietnam: The National Institute of Statistics, 1968), 14:388.

68. The reaction to the uprising by the South Vietnamese military was allegedly so brutal that thousands of women from Ben Tre surrounded the district headquarters after the town's re-capture and defecated on the ground in protest against the brutal behavior of the South Vietnamese troops. Moyar, *Triumph Forsaken*, 88.

69. Desobry, IV Corps Advisor, Debriefing Report, Aug 1965–Jan 1968, 3–4, Villard Files, CMH.

70. Wynn Goldsmith, *Papa, Bravo, Romeo*, 38–40.

71. II Field Force, Combat Operations After Action Report, 310001 Jan to 182400 Feb 1968; RIVFLOT I, Informal Resume of Operations of TF 117, 16 Feb 1967–16 Feb 1968.

Endnotes

72. CIA, Intelligence Memorandum: Situation in South Vietnam No. 11, 3 Feb 1968, LBJ Library; Mandatory Review, Case # NLJ 82-230, Document 94, Sanitized, Authority NLS 82-230, by NARS, 10-06-83, Approved for Release, 15 Sep 1983, Author Files; Goldsmith, *Papa, Bravo, Romeo,* 39–40.

73. Goldsmith, *Papa, Bravo, Romeo,* 39–40.

74. Emails, Cragg to author, 21 Oct 2010; Paul Cagle to author, 21 Oct 2010; Sumrall interview, 13 Aug 2010; Joseph Vitale, interview with author, 17 Sep 2010.

75. Goldsmith, *Papa, Bravo, Romeo,* 141–142.

76. Ibid., 145

77. Ibid, 148–149; Casualty Card for Gunner's Mate (Guns)/Seaman Apprentice David Lee Copenhaver.

78. Goldsmith, *Papa, Bravo, Romeo,* 151–152.

79. Cagle interview, 15 Sep 2010.

80. USS *Braine* (DD-630), Command History, 1966.

81. PBR sailors had to defecate off the stern of the boat—hence "crap from the stern." Email, Cagle to author, 21 Oct 2010.

82. Cagle interview, 15 Sep 2010.

83. Goldsmith, *Papa, Bravo, Romeo,* 156.

84. David W. Clouse, interview with author, 1 Nov 2010.

85. Goldsmith, *Papa, Bravo, Romeo,* 155–156.

86. Lieutenant Wolin suffered cuts in the neck and right arms from broken windshield glass, and BM1 Carvander sustained a light wound to his index finger. See Msgs, HELATKLTRON THREE to RUENAAA/SECNAV, 020535Z Feb 1968; and COMNAVSUPPACT SGN to RUENAAA/SECNAV, 020620Z Feb 1968, CTF 116 Casualty Reports, Box 225, NFV.

87. Casualty Card for LT Ronald M. Wolin; Goldsmith, *Papa, Bravo, Romeo,* 156–157.

88. Goldsmith, *Papa, Bravo, Romeo,* 157.

89. *Harnett County* (LST-821), Command History, 1968.

90. Cagle interview, 15 Sep 2010.

91. 3d Brigade, 9th Infantry Division, Operational Report-Lessons Learned Period Ending 30 Apr 1968, 30 Apr 1968, Villard Files, CMH.

92. Bernard C. Nalty, *Air Power over South Vietnam 1968–1975* (Washington, DC: Air Force History and Museums Program, 2000), 21.

93. 3d Brigade, 9th Infantry Division, Operational Report—Lessons Learned Period Ending 30 Apr 1968.

94. Lee Lescaze, "Bentre: Only Part of the City Was Saved," *Washington Post,* 8 Feb 1968, A-10.

95. For a further discussion of this quotation and its impact, see William H. Hammond, *Reporting Vietnam: Media & Military at War* (Lawrence: University Press of Kansas, 1998), 115; and Willbanks, *Tet Offensive,* 41.

96. Desobry, IV Corps Advisor, Debriefing Report, Aug 1965–Jan 1968.

97. Knowlton interview, 1982, 423.

98. MAJ A. W. Thompson, and Mr. C. Richard Thorndale, Project CHECO, "Air Response to the Tet Offensive," HQ PACAF, Directorate, Tactical Evaluation, CHECO Division, 40, Air Force Historical Research Institute, Maxwell AFB, AL.

99. Clouse interview, 1 Nov 2010; Cagle interview, 15 Sep 2010.

100. To handle these casualties, Ben Tre only had five Vietnamese doctors and 35 nurses and medical technicians. See Desobry, IV Corps Advisor, Historical Summary of the Tet Offensive, Aug 1965–Jan 1968, 8, 16, Villard Files, CMH; Lescaze, "Bentre: Only Part of the City Was Saved."

101. Cagle interview, 15 Sep 2010; Clouse corroborated this story; Clouse interview, 1 Nov 2010.

102. Ibid.

103. Clouse interview, 1 Nov 2010.

104. Robert A. Pinion, interview with author, 5 Nov 2010; LTJG Robert A. Pinion, Officer Bio File.

105. Pinion interview, 5 Nov 2010.

106. This number also includes the rural population who lived in Ben Tre district. See *Vietnam Statistical Yearbook 1967–1968*, 14:390.

107. Hooper, *Mobility, Support, Endurance*, 174.

108. Email, Edwin "Larry" Oswald to author, 18 Nov 2010.

109. Oswald, interview with author, 3 Nov 2010; Edwin "Larry" Oswald, interview with Laura Calkins, Vietnam Archive, Texas Tech University, Apr–May 2004, 47.

110. Oswald interview, Apr–May 2004, 47.

111. Pinion interview, 5 Nov 2010.

112. RIVFLOT I, Informal Resume of Operations of TF 117, 16 Feb 1967–16 Feb 1968; GEN Donn A. Starry, *Mounted Combat in Vietnam*, 127.

113. Pinion interview, 5 Nov 2010.

114. Commander, U.S. Naval Support Activity, Saigon, Monthly Historical Report, Feb 1968, Box 523, NFV.

115. Pinion interview, 5 Nov 2010.

116. COMNAVFORV Monthly Historical Summary, Jan 1968.

117. *Garrett County* (LST-786), Command History, 1968, AR.

118. Pinion interview, 5 Nov 2010.

119. COMNAVFORV Monthly Summary, Feb 1968.

120. Oswald interview, Apr–May 2004, 47.

121. LT Tom Anzalone, Diary, as cited in Knott, *Fire from the Sky*, 90.

122. Knott, *Fire from the Sky*, 90–91; JOC Dick Rose, "Seawolves of the Delta," *Jackstaff News*, 16 Mar 1968, 10, NDL.

123. Weseleskey interview, 9 Mar 2012; Casualty Card for ENS Richard G. Martz, 31 Jan 1968; Department of the Army, General Orders Number 5273, Award of the Bronze Star Medal

for Heroism to LCDR Allen Weseleskey, 14 Nov 1968, Author Files.

124. LCDR Joseph S. Bouchard as cited in Knott, *Fire from the Sky*, 90; CDR Joseph S. Bouchard, Officer Bio File.

125. Starry, *Mounted Combat in Vietnam*, 128.

126. 3d Battalion, 47th Infantry, Combat After Action Report, 290400 Jan to 091445 Feb 1968.

127. Eldon Banegas, interview with author, 9 Nov 2010.

128. Ibid.

129. Starry, *Mounted Combat in Vietnam*, 128.

130. *Garrett County*, Command History, 1968; Knott, *Fire from the Sky*, 91.

131. Knott, *Fire from the Sky*, 92.

132. Commander, U.S. Naval Support Activity, Saigon, Monthly Historical Report, Feb 1968.

133. Pinion interview, 5 Nov 2010.

134. Hooper, *Mobility, Support, Endurance*, 174.

135. Fulton, *Riverine Operations*, 151–153; 3-47th Infantry, Combat After Action Report, 290400 Jan to 091445 Feb 1968; SGT Timothy S. Goins, interview with author, 5 Nov 2010. Note: Although Goins arrived in Vietnam after the Vinh Long operation, he interviewed most of the survivors after the battle and assembled a history of the battle based on those conversations.

136. Forty-three enemy soldiers were also captured in the vicinity. See 3d Battalion, 60th Infantry, Combat After Action Report, 18 Jan–13 Feb 1968.

137. 3d Battalion, 47th Infantry, Combat After Action Report, 290400 Jan to 091445 Feb 1968; COMNAVFORV Monthly Summary, Feb 1968; Fulton, *Riverine Operations*, 153.

138. Ibid.; COMNAVFORV Monthly Summary, Feb 1968; Fulton, *Riverine Operations*, 153-54.

139. William B. Donham II, interview with author, 15 Nov 2010.

140. 3d Battalion, 60th Infantry, Combat After Action Report, 18 Jan–13 Feb 1968, 17 Mar 1968; COMNAVFORV Monthly Summary, Feb 1968; Fulton, *Riverine Operations*, 153–154.

141. 3d Battalion, 60th Infantry, Combat After Action Report, 18 Jan–13 Feb 1968; COMNAVFORV Monthly Summary, Feb 1968; Donham interview, 15 Nov 2010; Fulton, *Riverine Operations*, 153–154.

142. Donham interview, 15 Nov 2010.

143. 3d Battalion, 60th Infantry, Combat After Action Report, 18 Jan–13 Feb 1968; Desobry, IV Corps Advisor, Historical Summary of the Tet Offensive, Aug 1965–Jan 1968; COMNAVFORV Monthly Summary, Feb 1968; Fulton, *Riverine Operations*, 154.

144. Desobry, IV Corps Advisor, Historical Summary of the Tet Offensive, Aug 1965–Jan 1968.

145. Willbanks, *Tet Offensive*, 42.

146. This number also includes the rural population who lived in the Chau Thanh district. See *Vietnam Statistical Yearbook 1967–1968*, 14:389.

147. Fulton, *Riverine Operations*, 154, 159.

148. 3d Battalion, 47th Infantry, After Action Report, 140410 to 201635 Feb 1968.

Endnotes

149. COMNAVFORV Monthly Summary, Feb 1968.

150. Ibid.; Fulton, *Riverine Operations*, 157–158.

151. COMNAVFORV Monthly Summary, Feb 1968, 158–159.

152. Davis interview, 11 Aug 2009.

153. COMNAVFORV Monthly Summary, Feb 1968; Fulton, *Riverine Operations*, 159–160.

154. Salzer interview, 410.

155. Ibid., 411.

156. I Corps was the northernmost tactical zone in South Vietnam. Its area consisted of all the Vietnamese territory from the border of Kontum and Binh Dinh provinces to the DMZ.

157. Willbanks, *Tet Offenive*, 15.

158. Swarztrauber, "River Patrol Relearned," 130.

159. Cutler, *Brown Water, Black Berets*, 273.

160. COMNAVFORV Monthly Summary, Sep 1967.

161. Fire Control Technician G (Gun Fire Control) 3rd Class David M. Agazzi was the sailor killed. Casualty Card for FTG3 David M. Agazzi.

162. COMNAVFORV Monthly Summary, Sep 1967.

163. *Hunterdon County* (LST), Command History, 1967; COMNAVFORV Monthly Summary, Sep 1967; Cutler, *Brown Water, Black Berets*, 274.

164. Swarztrauber, "River Patrol Relearned," 130.

165. Ibid., 130; Cutler, *Brown Water, Black Berets*, 275.

166. COMNAVFORV Monthly Summary, Jan 1968.

167. Task Force Clearwater, Command History, 1968–1970, Box 519, NFV; Cutler, *Brown Water, Black Berets*, 275.

168. SERVPAC Operations Review, Feb 1968, Box 165, VCF; COMNAVFORV Monthly Summary, Feb 1968; COMNAVFORV Monthly Summary, Feb 1968.

169. SERVPAC Operations Review, Jan 1968, Box 165, VCF.

170. BM3 Charles M. White Sr. of Lathrap, California, and Engineman (EN)3 Michael E. Stephens of Huntington, West Virginia, both perished in the attack. See Casualty Cards for each in AR. SERVPAC Operations Review, Jan 1968; Mobile Riverine Force Association, NSA Danang KIA List, mrfa.org/NSADanang.KIA.htm, accessed 28 Feb 2012.

171. Hooper, *Mobility, Support, Endurance*, 126; COMNAVFORV Monthly Summary, Feb 1968; SERVPAC Operations Review, Feb 1968.

172. Task Force Clearwater Command History, 1968–1970; Swarztaruber, "River Patrol Relearned," 130–131.

173. The Marines manned 24-inch xenon gas infrared searchlights mounted on seven LCPLs for night surveillance patrols. Task Force Clearwater Command History, 1968–1970; Cutler, *Brown Water, Black Berets*, 279; COMNAVFORV Monthly Summary, Feb 1968.

174. Edward J. Marolda, *By Sea, Air, and Land*, 188.

175. Hooper, *Mobility, Support, Endurance*, 119–122.

176. Task Force Clearwater, Feb–Jun 1968, Box 520, NFV.

177. COMNAVFORV Monthly Summary, Mar 1968; Swarztrauber, "River Patrol Relearned," 131.

178. CDR S. A. Swarztrauber, interview by Oscar Fitzgerald, 3 Jun 1969, 86–89, NHHC Oral History Collection.

179. Swarztrauber, "River Patrol Relearned," 130.

180. Commander, Naval Forces Vietnam, "The Naval War in Vietnam," 30 Jun 1970, 96, Box 138, VCF; COMNAVFORV Monthly Summary, Mar 1968.

181. The dead included SN Robert W. Cawley, BM1 Edward J. Hagl, EN3 Frankie R. Johnson, FN Eugene Nelson, SN Joseph S. Perysian, and BM3 Ernest W. Wiglesworth. See Casualty Cards for each in AR. COMNAVFORV Monthly Summary, Mar 1968; CTF 117, Mobile Riverine Force, Personnel Killed In Action/Missing In Action, Southeast Asia Theater of the Vietnam War, 1960–1975, http://mrfa.org/navykia.htm, accessed 7 Feb 2011.

182. COMNAVFORV Monthly Summary, Mar 1968.

183. Shrapnel from the initial explosion in the staging area struck SN James Wesley Williams in the right arm and chest, killing him. Casualty Card for SN James Wesley Williams, AR.

184. SERVPAC Operations Review, Mar 1968, Box 165, VCF; Williams, Casualty Card.

185. COMNAVFORV Monthly Summary, Mar 1968; SERVPAC Operations Review, Mar 1968.

186. "Task Force Clearwater," Feb–Jun 1968; SERVPAC Operations Review, Mar 1968.

187. See Casualty Cards for SF3 Arthur W. Ball and SN Theodore V. Perkins; *Genesee* (AOG-8), Deck Log, 22–23 Apr 1968, AR; SERVPAC Operations Review, Apr 1968, Box 165, VCF.

188. FN Michael A. Burns, RM3 Dale L. Kruse, and SN Larry J. Leindecker were killed in the attack. See Casualty Cards for each in "Task Force Clearwater," Feb–Jun 1968; Naval Support Activity Danang. Killed in Action List, http://mrfa.org/NSADanang.KIA.htm, accessed 10 Feb 2012.

189. "Task Force Clearwater," Feb–Jun 1968.

190. Jack Shulimson et al., *U.S. Marines in Vietnam: the Defining Year: 1968* (Washington, DC: History and Museums Program, Headquarters, U.S Marine Corps, 1997), 296–297.

191. Ibid.

192. SERVPAC Operations Review, May, Jun 1968.

193. Swarztrauber, "River Patrol Relearned," 131.

194. "Task Force Clearwater," Feb–Jun 1968.

195. Task Force Clearwater Command History, 1968–1970.

196. Swarztrauber, "River Patrol Relearned," 132.

197. Shulimson et al., *U.S. Marines in Vietnam: The Defining Year: 1968*, 231.

Conclusion

1. Elmo R. Zumwalt Jr., *On Watch: A Memoir* (New York: Quadrangle, 1976), 36.

2. Ibid., 37–38.

Endnotes

3. In the 15 September 1967 Rach Ba Rai battle, the MRF lost seven personnel; 79 enemy were killed (11.29:1 kill ratio); at Rach Ruong, the numbers were 52 and 266, respectively (5.12:1 kill ratio).

4. These numbers come from Marolda, *By Sea, Air, and Land*, 268–269.

5. See Zumwalt, *On Watch*, 39.

6. Another candidate would be the PACV hovercraft, but it was never deployed in large numbers and its use was more experimental. As historian Edward Marolda noted, "The PACVs proved to be too noisy and too mechanically sophisticated for riverine war in South Vietnam. After the Tet emergency, the craft were shipped back to the United States for reevaluation." See *By Sea, Air, and Land*, 167–168.

INDEX

Abercrombie, Gordon E., 46
Abrams, Creighton W. Jr, 278, 283, 314, 320
Adams, James R., 265–66
advisors, U.S. Navy: 1–3, 9–12, 14–20, 22–24, 27, 28–29, 31, 32–33, 36–38, 45–52, 258–61. *See* also advisors by individual name, SEALsafloat bases. *See also* LSD; LST; Mobile Base 1; Mobile Riverine Base; Sea Float; YRBM
AIM-7E Sparrow missiles, 242
Aircraft
    A-1/AD-5N/AD-6 Skyraider, 21, 23, 32, 128, 129
    A-4, 162–63
    AC-47, 64, 251, 272, 297
    B-52, 98, 102
    B-57, 237–239
    C-130, 237–238, 314
    EC-121, 44
    F-4, 213, 239, 242
    F-100, 40, 63, 214
    L-19, 130, 146, 235
    O-1, 130, 132
    OV-1, 131, 237
    P-2/P-2V Neptune, 44, 221–24, 222
    SP-2H, 34, *61*
    P-3, 44, *227*, 250
    SP-5B Marlin, 24
    UH-1, 30, 31, 103, 112, 123–130, *124*, 206, 302
Albright, John, 213
Alderson, John W. "Clem," 107, 143
Alexander, Richard G., 83, 85–86
Allen, David, 307

Allen, Noel M., 230
alpha boat. *See* ASPB
American Bridge Company, 111
Americanization (of the war), 5, 80, 322
amphibious base
    Coronado, 28, 69, 72, 120, 160, 169, 173, 251
    Little Creek, 26, 28, 161
amphibious operations, 7, 33, 98–103. *See also* Jackstay; Mobile Riverine Force
Amphibious Training Command, 25, 27
An Duc, 133
An Lac Thon, 135
An Thoi, 13, 40, 57, 67, 69, 70, 72, 229, 235, 264
An Xuyen Province, 19, 231, 232
Anderegg, John, 241
Anderson, Carl, 135
Anderson, Franklin W., 32
Anderson, George W. Jr., 12
Anderson, Jack, 86
Anderson, Ken, 134
Angel, William E., 61
ANGLICO (air-naval gunfire liaison company), 236
Annamite Mountains, 43
antitank rockets. *See also* Viet Cong heavy weaponry
Ap Bac, 16
API. *See* armor-piercing incendiary ammunition
armor-piercing incendiary (API) ammunition, 294–300
Armstrong, Billy, 240

407

Army of the Republic of Vietnam. *See* ARVN
Arnett, Peter, 298
Arnheiter, Marcus Aurelius, 80–87
　affair, 80–87
Artman, Daniel Paul, 151
ARVN, 5, 10, 16, 17, 22–23, 34, 94, 98, 127, 129, 152, 165, 275, 289, 290, 293, 302, 311
　2d Division, 261
　2nd Armored Cavalry Regiment, 3d Squadron, 301, 303–4
　5th Division, 130
　6th Armored Cavalry Regiment, 285
　7th Division, 120, 131, 146, 279, 282, 292–93
　9th Division, 158
　11th Infantry Regiment, 285
　13th Regiment, 37
　15th Infantry Regiment, 304
　21st Division, 65, 236, 309
　23d Division, 32
　32nd Ranger Battalion, 285
　43d Ranger Battalion, 301, 304
　11th Infantry Regiment, 285
　13th Regiment, 37
　15th Infantry Regiment, 304
Armed Forces Staff College, Da Lat, 52
Ashton, Curtis, 288
Austin, Donald L., 239

B40/50. *See* Viet Cong heavy weaponry
Ba Giong River, 101
Ba Xuyen, 265
　province, 135
Baird, Orlie G., 64
Baker, C. J., 245
Baker, Charles A., 153
Baker, Willy S., 70
Balboa Naval Hospital, 38
Balian, Alexander, 75–77, *77*
Banegas, Eldon, 303
Bannister, Howard M., 164–65, 171
Barney, Eugene, 2, 20, 37–38
Barham, Charles "Charlie," 76, *77*
Bass, Alexander, 249

Bassac River, 28, 36, 113, 126, 135, 153, 159, 309
Baumberger, Walter H., 85
Bear Cat, 190
Beery, Jere, 108, 109, 118
Bell Helicopter Company, 126. *See also* aircraft, UH–1
Bell, Ross, 238–39
Belmonte, Louis A., 81
Ben Tre, 121, 123, 133, 151–52, 275, 284, *295*, *299*
　bridge, 294–96, *295*
　canal, 120, 293–300, *295*, *299*
　during Tet, 292–300, 308, 311, 319
　hospital, 152
Bender, Thomas J., 230
Benedick, Jack, 185, 204
Bennett, D. M., 47
Bergin, Edward J., 248, 254–56, 267–69
Bertolino, Fred, 205
Bien Hoa, 125
Biet Hai (sea commandos), 29
Binder, Rubin G., 143–44, 146
Binh Thuy, 103, 111, 113, 118, 126. *See also* Can Tho
Binh Xuyen, 8, 21, 94
Blackburn, Paul P., 34, 45
Blevins, Villard Jr., 120, 122–23
Blinn, Gary R., 70, 72, 74–75
blockade. *See* counterinfiltration
Bo De River, 246
Bo Dieu River, 316
boats. *See* ships, boats, and auxiliaries
Bolduc, Lucien "Blackie," 168
Bolen, Warren G., 151
Bouchard, Joseph S., 302–3, 304
Bowers, James S., 31
Bowman, Frank, 241
Boyle, David J., 73
Brabston, John, 306
Bragg, Leroy G., 143
Branscomb, Max G., 221–24, *221*, 248
Breininger, Alan, 169, 171, 192
Brevie Line, 57
Bringle, William F., 242
Brisbane, Thomas E., 133
Brock, Harry G., 70

Brostrom, David C., 238, 240
Brown, William L., 56
Bucklew, Phillip H., 12
    and SEALs, 29
    biography, 25–26
    report, 24–28, 34, 36, 42
Bureau of Ships, 104, 180–81, 243, 244
Burnett, J. R., 99
Burnett, Larry, 282
Butler, David K., 161–65, 199
Butterworth, R. J., 242

C-4 plastic explosive, 177
Ca Mau, 113
Ca Mau Peninsula, 8, 39, 41, 43, 61, 113, 232, 236
Cagle, Paul W., 294, 296–300, *296*, 319
Cai Be, 284
    district, 280
Cam Ranh Bay, 15, 67, 71, 95, 221, 222, 245, 246, 260
    Market Time base, 223
Camara, Joseph V. R., 217–18, *218*, 306
Cambodia, 24, 28–29, 42–43, 79, 129, 132, 159, 273, 320
Can Gio, 100
Can Giuoc, 162, 202, 207
Can Tho, 2, 6, 103, 111, 113, 132, 135, 177, *310*
    during Tet, 308–10
Cang, Chung Tan, 22–23, 51–52, 94
Cao Lanh, 129
Cao, Nguyen Van, 51
Cap Varella, 31, 34
Cape Batangan, 236, 253, 268
Carbone, Nicholas, 130, 132
Carlstrom, Kenneth M., 153, 155
Carter Hotel (billet), 286, 287–89, 292
Carter, Terrel E., *142*, 146–47. *See also* Carter Hotel
Carvander, Charles R., 297
Carver, Bobby Don "Boats," 252, 255–56, 267–69, *268*, 272
Castleberry, Roy L., 150
casualties
    ARVN, 16, 19, 291, 292, 312
    civilian, 199, 287, 291–92, 299–300, 308

U.S. Army, 129, 165, 186, 201, 202, 205, 206, 207, 211–14, 219, 280, 291, 305, 308, 309
U.S. Coast Guard, 238–40
U.S. Marine Corps, 312
U.S. Navy: 30, 31, 38, 73, 76, 92, 100–101, 103, 122–23, 136, 150–52, 153, 160, 164–65, 210, 211, 212, 214, 219, 234–35, 261, 269, 272–73, 280, 284, 308, 309, 312, 313, 314, 315, 316–17, 320
Viet Cong/PAVN, 16, 19, 30, 31, 33, 37, 60, 73, 78, 94, 101, 102, 131, 139, 145, 159, 160, 201, 207, 214, 215, 216, 219, 233, 272, 273, 280, 284, 285, 289, 290, 291, 298, 305, 308, 309, 312, 313, 316
Vietnam Marines, 216, 219
VNN, 32, 33, 37, 95, 151–52
Cat Lo, 67, *71*, 101, 103, 111, 113
Cau Bo De River, 270
CBU. *See* Cluster Bomb
Center for Naval Analyses (CNA), 29, 79, 159
Chandler, Anthony, 241
Chau Doc, 31, 111, 265, 275, 284, 319
Chau Fu. *See* Chau Doc
Chau Thanh, 301
Chau, Troung Huong, 151–52
Cheek, Richard Allan, 210
Chesebrough, Richard, 18
Chidsey, John Warren, 45–47, 56
Chief of Naval Operations, 243
Chieu Hoi, 130, 262–64, 267, 268, 282
China, 16, 41, 222
Chism, Charles B, 237
Cho Gao Canal, 124
Chu Lai, 254, 256, 269
CINCPAC, 66–67, 95, 168
CINCPACFLT, 66, 95
Citarella, Richard A., 164, 216
civic action, 133–35, 262–67
Civil Defense Corps, 13
Civil Guard, 1, 13
Civilian Irregular Defense Group (CIDG), 60, 235, 275
Claiborne, Dell R., 280
Claymore mine, 162, 202, 282

Clearwater (Task Force), 283
Clouse, David W., 296, 299–300
Cluster Bomb (CBU), 239
Co Chien, 113, 126
 river, 36, 62, 153, 300, 301
coastal districts (VNN), 13
 First (Zone), 264
 Second (Zone), 11, 15, 23, 32, 230, 263
 Third (Zone), 36, 49, 50, 131, 232–33, 263, 264
 Fourth (Zone), 14, 17, 58, 131, 232, 265
Coastal Divisions (VNN), 13, 14
 Coastal Division (Group) 2, 238–39
 Coastal Division (Group) 14, 273
 Coastal Division (Group) 15, 56–57, *56*
 Coastal Division (Group) 16, 258–61, *259*, 263, 268, 273
 Coastal Division (Group) 22, 273
 Coastal Division (Group) 35, 64, 134, 273
 Coastal Division (Group) 43, 73
 Coastal Division (Group) 46, 264
 Coastal Division (Group) 104, 71
Coastal Force (VNN), 13–17, 28, 34–35, 45, 61, 80, 264, 293
 Coastal Group 16 attack, 258–61, 263
 force structure, 13, 16, 47, 258
 operations, 15–16
 problems, 14–15, 17, 47–52
Coastal Group. *See* Coastal Divisions
coastal interdiction, 24, 34, 79, 231, 319
coastal surveillance centers, 13, 35, 57, 62, 83, 227, 229
 Danang, 224, 227, 233, 238
 Nha Trang, 227
 Phu Quoc Island, 227
 Qui Nhon, 227
 Vung Tau, 227, *228*
Coastal Surveillance Force. *See* Market Time
coastal zones. *See* coastal districts
Combs, Lawrence L., 263
Comer, William M. Jr., 284
Communist supply system, 27
COMNAVFORV, 42, 131, 133, 157, 172–73, 181, 208, 231, 235, 261, 263, 266, 279, 283, 312, 313, 319, 320, 321, 312–13, 319, 320

Con Son Island, 44, 61, 227, 270
Constance, Harry, 287–92
Copenhaver, David Lee, 294
Coronado. *See* Amphibious Base; Coronado I; Coronado V; Coronado IX; operations
Cote, Arthur J., 238–39
counterinfiltration, 5, 35, 42, 51, 270–73. *See also* infiltration
Cragg, Richard J., 286
Crain, Thomas J., 155
Crawford, Michael D., 100
Croizat, Victor J., 7, 8
Cruz, Edward, 240
Cu Lao Re Island, 227
Cua Dai River, 36
Cua Lon River, 246
Cua Tung River, 237
Cua Viet
 base and ramp, 314–17
 river, 238, 241, 283, 312, 313, 314, 316
Curtis Bay Shipyard, 53–54
Cutler, Thomas J., 108

Dale, Henry, 245
Danang, 13, 29, 45, 46, 56, 57, 62, 67, 71, 222, 224, 227, 233, 238, 245, 251, 258, 269
Dando, George W., 84
David, Bert A., 214, *279*
Davidson, Charles A. Jr., 151
Davidson, Houston J., 239
Davis, Bruce D., 64
Davis, Robert E., 164, 196, 214 309
Davis, Roderick, 109, *117*, 134, 291
Dawson, Richard Wesley, 249
De Angelo, Lawrence F., 231
de Tassigny, Jean de Lattre, 5
Dean, Paul, 98
Decca, 45, 178
Decker, Peter B., 131–32
Defense Language Institute, 130, 263
Delfino, Ken, 286
Demilitarized Zone (DMZ), 44, 237, 238, 240, 243, 275, 312, 314
Dempsey, Thomas A., 186–87

Dennis, William R. III, 157
Depuy, William E., 32
Desobry, William R., 282, 293
Devlin, Mike, 148–52, *150*
Dexter, Stephen T., 174
Di Napoli, Michael Joseph, 273
Ngo Dinh, 5, 21
Dien Bien Phu, 275
Dinassaut, 5–7, 8, 93
Dinh Bah River, 75, 76
Dinh Tuong Province, 131, 139, 192, 215, 280, 283, 291, 305
Dinh, Nguyen Thi, 292
Dix, Drew, 31
Do, Khanh Quang, 94
Do, Kiem, 10–11, 20, 22–24, 51–52, 284
Dodd, Arthur J., 176–77, 185, 186, 187
Dohn Nhon District, 280
Dolezal, Michael W. "Red," 205
Don, Tran Van, 8, 21
Dong Ha, 239, 283, 314
    base and ramp, 314–17
    river, 312, 316
Dong Hoa, 134
Dong Tam, 123, 126, 145, 168, 176, 184, 185, 188–91, *189*, 208, 279, 306, 308
Dong Tranh River, 100, 280
Donham, William "Tex" II, 306–8
Donovan, John J. Jr., 115, *116*, 148, 151, 152
Doty, Mercer M., 212
Doung Don, 15
Doung Le, 163
Dowd, Robert A., 157
Doyle, Robert C., 133
Drachnik, Joseph B., 11, *12*, 18, 22–23, 320
dredging, 115
Driver, Ross N., 264
Duc Hoa, 131
Dunn, Charles M., 157
Dunn, Gilliam, 73
Duong, Nguyen, 73
Durfey, Robert W., 232
dustoff (helicopter), *195*, 206
Dutterer, Carroll E. Jr., 212
Dykes, Jim, 123

Eckhardt, George S., 173
Eichner, Andrew J., 143
Elkins, James Ezra, 210
Erwin, Virgil, 225
Evenson, Michael A., 181

Fall, Bernard, 6
Felt, Harry D., 13, 24, 27
Fenlin, George, 76
Fields, Charles "Chuck," 305
First Indochina War, 5, 7
Fitzgerald, William C., 259–61, 273
Forbes, Wayne, 297
force levels (U.S. Navy in Vietnam), 320
Forrester, George S., 230
Fort Benning, GA, 126
Fort Rucker, AL, 126–27
France, 5, 7, 8, 9
Franks, Stanley P. Jr., 239
Franson, Robert, 176–77, 193, 197
Fredricksen, Randal "Randy" Kenneth, 233
freighters (steel-hulled). *See* trawlers
French, Bob, 203
Freund, Terrence Jay, 92, 135–36
Friedman, Gary Wayne, 234–35, 272
Friedman, Norman, 181, 247
friendly fire, 236–43
Fritz, Ronlad E., 241
Fulton, William B., 167, 172–74, 185, 201, 202, 207, 290–91
Fuscaldo, Robert P., 108, 114, 116–17, 135, 285

Gallagher, Robert, 287
Game Warden (TF 116), 19, 29–31, 42, 54, 89–92, 98, 104–11, 153–60, 275, 276, 280–82, 285–89, 293–300, 319–20, 322–23
    River Section 511, 118, 135, 157
    River Section 512, 109, 112
    River Section 513, 134
    River Section 521, 313–14, 317
    River Section 522, 121–23, 143
    River Section 524, 280

Index

River Section 531, 89, 107, 110, 118, 131, 135, 137–39, 143–49, 148–49, 157
River Section 532, 116, 285–86, 294, 296
River Section 533, 286
River Section 534, 120, 280, 293–94
River Section 535, 305
HC-1, 124–27
HAL-3, 103, 107, 123, 126–28, 130, 139, 297, 302, 304, 305, 311. *See* Seawolves
River Division 53, 148, 151, 286
River Squadron 5, 93
Mine Squadron 11, 153–56
Delta River Patrol Group (TG 116.1), 96, 134, 151
Rung Sat Patrol Group (TG 116.2), 96, 151
basing, 111–18
civic action, 133–35
combat experiences, 135–52
helicopter support for, 155, 123–30, 159, 297
operation order, 109–11, 136, 151
origins and development, 92–96
rules of engagement, 110
searches, 109–110, *110*
Gander, Terry, 212
Ganh Hao River, 233
Ganh Ria Bay, 234
Garcia, Rene, 157
Geier, William "Bill" Michael, 203
General Motors (GM), 105
Generous, William T., 82, 85
Geneva Agreement (1954), 7
Gentile, Ralph J., 38
Giang, Nguyen Kim, 21–22
Giap, Vo Nguyen, 312
Gibbs, Richard F., 239
Gibson, James K., 299
Go Cong Province, 215
Godley, Raleigh, 76
Goit, Whitney II, 230
Goldman, William R., 280
Goldsmith, Wynn A., 120, 158, 293–94, 296
Goodfellow, William Henry Murphy III, 272, 273
Graf, John "Jack," 131–33

Graham, Billy D., 16
Grall Hospital, Saigon, 134
Gray, Paul N., 147, 157–60, 158
Gray, Robert Lyndon, 122
Green, John L. Jr., 170, 177, 186, 193, 197, 217, 219, 285, 306–07
Greene, Glenn, 76
Group 125, 31
Guinn, Harold W. Jr., 129, 259–61
Gulf of Siam Patrol, 24–25
Gulf of Thailand, 24, 43, 58–59, 320
Gulf of Tonkin Incident, 42
Gunter, Alton R., 100–101

Ha Tien, 60, 72
Haggerty, Pat, 187
Hallowell, Albert G., 131, 132
Ham Luong River, 120, 126, 150, 282, 293, 294, 297, 298
Ham Ninh, 264
Hamilton, Frank P., 70
Hammel, Jerry M., 107, 113, 116, 118
Handclasp (project), 112
Hanus, Charles Z., 94
harassment and interdiction fire, 232, 235, 247
Harbor Clearance Team
    Team 1, 41, 65
    Team 3, 65
Hardcastle, William H., *12*, 36, 48, 53, 54
Hardy, Ray S. Jr., 83, 85–86
Harris, Michael, 169, 170, 171, 175
Hassard, Richard W., 249–50
Hatteras Yacht Company, 104
Hawkins, George Washington, 211
Hays, Gale Jackson, 234
Hays, George E., 230
Heinz, Robert P. Jr., 100
helicopter support, 124, 143. *See also* aircraft, UH-1; Game Warden, HC-1; Game Warden, HAL-3; Seawolves
Helton, Morris Dean, 251
Hendrickson, John, 12, 120, 121, 122
Herrera, Raul, 251–52, 254–55, 268, 269
Hicken, Jim, 286
High Endurance Cutter. *See* WHEC

412

High Explosive Antitank (HEAT) round, 175, 184
Hill, Tommy Edward, 73
Ho Chi Minh Trail, 25, 28
Hoang, Nguyen Quang, 73
Hoch, Wesley A., *12*, 14, 15
Hodgman, James A., 57, 60, 61
Hoi An, 46, 313
Hon Khoai Island, 227
Hon Mot Island, 60
Hon Mot River, 60
Hooper, Edwin B., 114, 187, 189, 305
Hop, Do Quy, 94
Hopwood, Herbert G., 9
Horowitz, Charles L., 203
Howard, Joseph B., 145
Howell, Adrian Ealon, 219
Howell, Jim, 116
Howell, Norman B., 135–36
Huchthausen, Peter A., 105, 110, 134
Hue, 308, 312, 313, 314, 317
    ramp, 314
    humanitarian operations, 314
Humphries, Harry, 31
Hung My, 134
Hung, Dinh Manh, 22
Hunt, Lynn J., 206
Hunt, R. H., 242
Huong River, 314
hyacinth, water, 103, 107, *175*
hygiene, 11, 45–46, 109, 133, 263, 265, 301,

Ignatius, Paul R., 85–86
infiltration barrier, 24–25, 57, 224, 225, 270–73
infiltration, 5, 16, 18, 19, 24, 25, 26, 27, 28, 31, 34, 36, 38, 42, 57, 59, 61, 66, 79, 80, 89, 92, 95, 111, 129, 224, 230, 231, 248, 258, 261, 270, 272, 273, 283, 312, 319
intelligence, 26, 27, 29, 30, 31, 32, 33, 40, 66, 91, 116, 117, 118, 120, 130, 131, 132, 133, 136, 143, 145, 157, 158, 160, 191, 202, 212, 222, 223, 227, 232, 253, 261, 263, 264, 276, 277, 293, 306

interdiction, 13, 18, 19, 31, 34, 36, 42, 87, 92, 109, 156, 159, 179, 226, 231, 235, 237, 247, 248, 272, 278, 317, 319, 320, 322, 324,
International Control Commission, 33
Isles des Pirates, 60
Ismay, Arthur P., 67, 69, 70, 74, *77*, 101

Johnson, Cecil O. "Swede," 205
Johnson, James D., 184, 185, 186, 190, 209, 212–13
Johnson, Lyndon B., 42, *158*
Johnson, Raymond Wendell, 171, 172, 204–05, *204*, 215
Johnson, Robert R., 72, 73, 74
Johnson, Roy L., 226
Johnson, William W., 154
Joint General Staff (JGS), 22–23
Junk Division. *See* Coastal Division
Junk Force. *See* Coastal Force; ships, boats, and auxiliaries

Kearney, David George, 157
Keefe, Dennis, 286
Kelleher, Martin J., 40, 57
Kelly, Daniel E., 127
Kepler, William N., 40, *41*
Khanh, Nguyen, 23, 51, 52
Khe Sanh, 275, 283, 308, 312, 314, 315, 317
Kiem, Do. *See* Do, Kiem
Kiem, Robert Lee, 76–77
Kien Giang. *See* Rach Gia
Kien Hoa, 1
    province, 50, 131, 215, 292, 293, 299
Kien Phong Province, 216, 280, 283
Kin Tinh Hotel, 113
King, Thomas S., 84–85
Kinh Dong River, 163
Kinsman, Thomas James, 307
Kirkpatrick, Michael W., 235
Kit Carson Scouts, 262
Klein, Henry I., 153
Knaup, Eddie A., 256
Knott, Richard, 127

Knowlton, William A., 276, 282–83, 299
Koral, Gene, 131
Ky, Nguyen Cao, 23, 51, 55

Lacapruccia, Joseph, 178, 186
Lam Dong, 265
Lam Son, 130
Landis Study, 66–67
Landis, Carey E., 67
LAW (light antitank weapon), 289, 294, 296, 303.
Le, Thom Thi, *20*
leaflets, *See* PSYOP
Leazer, Terry F., 150–51
Ledoux, Robert W., 284
Lescaze, Lee, 298
Lien, James L., 309
Lind, Herbert E., 203
Lineberger, Walter F. III, 170, 181, 199
Little Creek. *See* Amphibious Base, Little Creek
Little, William Harris, 210
Lloyd, Charles, 72–74
logistics, 1, 6, 7, 17, 19, 49, 58, 80, 83, 111, 113, 168, 174, 182, 188, 200, 220, 226, 300, 310, 312–17, 320
Long An Province, 94, 162, 172, 202
Long Binh, 165, 190
Long Ho Canal, 37
Long Range Plan for the U.S. Naval Effort in Vietnam. *See* Landis Study
Long Son Island, 50
Long Tau River (and shipping channel), 30, 71, 76, 96, 97, 98, 100, 102, 103, 114, 153–56, *156*, *200*, 201, 323
Long Thanh Peninsula, 99, 100
Long Xuyen, 111, 113, 134
Luc, Thuong Ngoc, 21–23, 52
Lung, Nguyen Thi, 134-35, 289–90
Ly, Huynh, 213, 291
Lynch, Herbert J., 232, 270
Lynch, John S., 237-38

M10-8 (flamethrower), 178
M113 (armored personnel carrier), 16, 176, 208, 291, 292

M132A1 (flamethrower), 178
M1891 (rifle), 157
M39 (automatic cannon), 63
M-41 A3 (tank), 303
M72 (LAW rocket), 294, 296
M79 (grenade launcher), 76, 163, 176, 201, 211, 214, 269, 284, 287, 303, 316
MacGarrigle, George L., 167, 196, 207
MacLeod, Kenneth Logan III, 97–98
MacLeod's Navy, 97–98
Machen, Billy, 30
MACV. *See* Military Assistance Command Vietnam
Mang Thit River, 1, 280
Manh, Nguyen Van, 166–67
Mare Island, CA, 105, 148, 169
Market Time (TF 115), 35, 38, 39–47, 57, 61–72, 80–87, 96, 98, 160, 176, 221–29, 261–73, 270–73, 319, 322, 324. *See also* PCF; WPB
  Task Unit 115.1, 252–53
  Boat Squadron 1, 67, 75
  Division 101, 67, *69*
  Division 102, 67
  Division 103, 67
  Division 104, 67
  Division 105, 67
  Coastal Squadron 1, 74, 225
  Patrol Squadrons (VP)
    VP-1, 221–22
    VP-2, 61
    VP-16, 248
    VP-46, 250
  aerial patrol, 221–24, 227
  Coast Guard Support for, 57–66, 225
  coastal radars, 227
  establishment, 52–57
  evaluation of, 79–80
  force structure, 57, 270, 320
  friendly fire incidents, 236–43
  units in Operation Jackstay, 98–103
  naval gunfire support, 231–36
  patrol gunboats (PGs) in, 243–48
  patrol sectors, *68*
  rules of engagement, 54, 229
  trawler intercepts, 39–42, 43, 61–66, 79,

Index

221–23, 248–58, 270–73, 271
    and Vietnam Navy, 229–31
    waterborne detections, 228
Markle, Neil, 62
Marolda, Edward J., 156
Martz, Richard A., 302
McDavitt, Fred M., 89–91, *90*, 107, 109, 116, 131, 137, 138, *142*, 143, 144, 148, 149
McGowan, Earnest, *281*
McGuire, M. L., 36
McKenney, Mark D., 238–39
McNamara, Robert S., 24, 52, 54
medical support, 1, 133–35, 194, 310, 320
    MEDCAP, 131, 134, 135, 265–66, *266*
Mekong Delta Mobile Afloat Force (MDMAF), 168
Mekong Delta, 29–31, 41–43, 75, 80, 92–96, *93*, *96*, 103, 112, 124, 125, 126, 137, 160, 165, 166–67, 169, 182, 199, 218, 231, 245, 273, 275, 312, 313, 319
    provinces, 1, *167*, 273, 275
Mekong River, 19, 28, 42, 89, 143, 145, 150, 229, 292
Menner, Ronald R., 202, 207
Metropole Hotel, 55
Meyerkord, Harold "Dale," 1, 2, 3, 5, 36–38, 321
    Navy Cross action, 37–38
Middendorf, J. William II, 147
Middleton, Robert J., 255
Military Assistance Advisory Group (MAAG), Vietnam, 5, 7, 9, 11
Military Assistance Command Vietnam (MACV), 11, 18, 31, 66, 75, 80, 95, 97, 98, 165, 172, 179, 180, 224, 229, 282–83, 291, 293, 294, 296, 297, 298, 312, 314, 320
Planning Directive 12–66, 173
Military Provincial Health Assistance Program (MILPHAP), 265
Military Sea Transportation Service (MSTS), 156
Miller, John Francis, 266, 267
Miller, John L., 190
Miller, Robin, 305
Milligan, Donald F., 82, 84
mines and minings, 72–74, 120–23, 145, 153–56, *154*, 179–80, 182, 201, 206, 282, 314, 315, 316, 323
Minesweeper Division, 24
minesweeping, 7, 19, 96, 156, 175, 181, 194, 208, 323 *See also* YMS
Minh, Doung Van, 21–23
Minh, Nguyen, 116
MK-19 (grenade launcher), 180
MLMS (motor launch minesweeper), 19
Mo Cay District, 299
Mobile Riverine Base (MRB), 168, *182*, 216, 284, 306, 311
Mobile Support Base 1, 313
Mobile Riverine Force (MRF), 28, 54, 103, 127, 155, 161–21, 215–20, 275, 278–80, 283, 284–85, 290–91, 293, 298–99, 304, 305–12, 320. *See also* Mobile Riverine Base, Coronado I; Coronado V; Coronado IX; Tet Offensive
    bases, 182–91
    boats, 175–82
    casualties, 165, 186, 201, 202, 205, 206, 207, 210–12, 213, 214, 216, 219, 220, 280, 291, 305, 308, 309
Mobile Riverine Group Alpha, 174
operations, 200–220
River Assault Division 91, 170, 200, 216–17, 305
River Assault Division 92, 308
River Assault Division 111, 187, 211, 216–19, 278, 305–8
River Assault Division 112, 163, 216, 316–17
River Assault Squadron 9, 174, 189, 190, 203
River Assault Squadron 11, 172, 174
River Assault Squadron 13, 174
River Assault Squadron 15, 174
rules of engagement, 197–200
tactics, 191–97
Task Force 117 Operation Order, 185, 197, 212
Task Group 117.2, 208
training, 168–72
monsoon, 54, 70, 79, 197, 282, 322

415

Moon, Ivan, 282
Moore, S. H., 242
Moore, Thomas M., 155
Moorer, Thomas H., 86
Moras, Robert J., 217–19
Morgan, Rodney Dean "Weasel," 118
Mosher, Charles B., 39–41
Mosher, Norman G., 48–50, *50*
Moyar, Mark, 79
My Canh Cafe, 55
My Loi, 94
My Tho, 31, 89, *90*, 94, 103, 105, 111, 113, 115–18, 131, 134, 137–38, 143, 144, 145, 148–50, 152, 157, 184, 188, 207, 279, 283, 284, 285–93, 308
    river, 113, 178, 182, 190, 193, 208, 215, 280
    during Tet, 285–92, 311, 319
My, Le Quang, 8

Nam Thon River, 144
napalm, 32, 40, 162–63, 178, 213
Naval Advisory Group, 3, 5–12, 14, 34–38, 51, 54, 56, 66, 94–95
Naval gunfire support (NGFS), 7, 113
    in Market Time, 231–36, 272
    during Tet, 310–11
naval guns
    20mm cannon, 2, 6, 19, 22, 41, 101, 162, 169–70, 176, 177, 178, 211, 306–7
    40mm cannon, 2, 3, 6, 19, 101–2, 112–13, 136, 162, 164, 169–70, 183, 204, 208, 210, 211, 216, 244, 248, 255, *297*
    81mm mortar, 2, 40, 41, 53, 54, 60, 61, 65, 70, 76, 100, 120, 121, 162, 177, 180, 233–35, 234, 236, 249
    3-inch gun, *244*, 248, 255
    5-inch gun, 232, 270, 272, 294
Naval Inshore Operations Training Center (NIOTC), 169–70
Naval Intelligence Liaison Officers (NILOs), 130–33
Naval Ordnance System Command, 235
Naval Postgraduate School, 128
Naval Ship Systems Command, 108
Naval Support Activities (NSA), 89, 113, 119, 300–301, 305, 312–17
Naval Zones (VNN), 13
    Third, 36
NAVFORV. *See* COMNAVFORV
Navy Research and Development Unit 3, 280
Nelson, Robert T., 59
NGFS. *See* Naval Gunfire Support
Ngo Hiep Island, 144, 146
Nha Be, 30, 78, 103, 111, 113, 114, *115*, 126, 155, 280
    river, 127
Nha Trang, 13, 16, 34, 227, 272
Nha Trang Naval Academy, 22, 95
Nieman, Ray C., 18
NILO. *See* Naval Intelligence Liaison Officers
NIOTC. *See* Naval Inshore Operations Training Center
Nitz, Paul, 52–53
Nixon, Richard M., 321
North Vietnam, 7, 9, 24
North Vietnamese Army (NVA). *See* PAVN
Northern Surveillance Group, 248, 252
Nui Bai, 59

O'Connor, David E., 239
O'Connor, George G., 198, 207
Olds, Frederick A., 132
On, Trung-Uy, 231
Ong Doc River, 272
Ontos, 101
Operations
    Attelboro, 156
    Cedar Falls, 156
    Cleft Lip, 135
    Coronado I, 202–07
    Coronado V, 207–15
    Coronado IX, 215–20
    Green Wave, 312–13
    Jackstay, 75, 98–103, 124
    Junction City, 156
    Niagara II, 283
    Sea Dragon, 226. *See also* naval gunfire support
    River Raider, 200–201
OPNAV, 66, 95

Orth, Greg, 214
Ortoli, Paul, 5
Oswald, Edwin "Larry," 119, 120, 122, 123, 171, 184, 185, 300–301

Pacific Repair Shop, 111
Padgett, Oscar H., 37
Page, Timothy R., 238–40
Painter, Michael H., 235
Parsons, Dwayne L., 278
Patrol Gunboat. *See* PG
Patrol Squadrons (VP). *See* Market Time
Patterson, Richard H., 238–40
Pearman, Leo E., 259–61
People's Army of Vietnam (PAVN), 275, 289, 312, 313–17
    125th Sea Transportation Unit, 16
    320th Division, 316
Perfume River, 312, 313, 314, 315, 316, 317
Phan, Tran Van, 52, 57
Phat, Lam Van, 73
Philadelphia Naval Shipyard, 183
Philippine Civic Action Group (PHILCAG), 286
Philippines, 21, 44, 57, 245, 277. *See also* Subic Bay; Philippine Civic Action Group
Phillips, Jerry, 238–39
Phong Dinh Province, 308
Phu Bai, 239
Phu Quoc Island, 58, 60, 69, 225, 227, 234, 264
Phu Vinh, 131
Phung Hiep District, 309
Phuoc Thien, 250
Phuoc Tuy Province, 50
Picard, Richard, 250–51
Pinion, Robert A., 300–301, 305
Plain of Reeds, 132
police (Republic of Vietnam), 107, 135, 151–52, 275
Poling, Thomas A., 143
Popular Force. *See* Regional and Popular Forces
Portsmouth Naval Hospital, 165
Powers, Ralph E., 76, 77

Powers, Robert J., 95
prostitution, 8, 117–18, 186–87, 220, 324
Pruit, James Elmer, 60
PSYOP, 252, 254, 261–67
    leaflets, 262–64, 266–67, 272
    mission, 6 December 1967, 267–72
Puckett, Dennis Ray, 272

Quang Nam, 265
    province, 313
Quang Tin, 265
Quang Tri Province, 265, 284
Qui Nhon, 31, 57, 67, 83, 227, 248, 272, 273
Quigley, Michael P., 123
Quimby, Jack, 10–11
Quinn, Michael C., 150–51
Quyen, Ho Tan, 12, 13, 21, 22, 23, 52

Rach Ba Rai (battle), 207–15, 320
Rach Cai Cam, 305–6
Rach Gia, 15, 70, 72, 73, 74
Rach Nui, 207
Rach Ruong Canal, 215–20, 280, 284. *See also* Coronado IX
radar
    APS-20, 222
    Pathfinder 1900N, 105, 178
    SLAR, 132, 237
RAG (Vietnam Navy River Assault Group), 1, 36, 75, 93–94, 98, 101, 109, 114, 115, 136, 285, 300–302
    RAG 21, 9, 302
    RAG 22, 18, 19, 78, 94, 95
    RAG 23, 1–3, 37, 64, 302
    RAG 27, 94, 131, 147
    RAG 31, 302
Ragan, Charles Patrick, 18
Ramos, Forrest, 206
Rankin, Peter B., 278–79
Raytheon, 105
Ratliff, William A., 135–36
Raybell, David, 169, 190, 210–12
recoilless rifle. *See* Viet Cong heavy weaponry
Rectanus, Earl "Rex," 131

Index

Reeves, Robert Linton, 202–3, 206
Regional and Popular Forces, 13, 50, 60, 78, 94, 97, 166, 191, 231, 275, 306
Reiling, Victor G., 262–64
Reilly, Robert K., 51
Research and Development Unit, Vietnam, 156
Resnick, Paul Y., 86
Reynolds, William L. "Bill," 203, 206
Rhodes, Francis E. "Dusty," 171, 203, 208, 210–16
Rickli, Rodney H., 155
Rickover, Hyman, 82
Rinehart, Ronald J. "Porky," 267
Riojas, Erasmus "Doc," 289
River Assault Force (TF 117). *See* Mobile Riverine Force
River Force (VNN), 13, 17–19, 20, 22, 37, 92–95
River Patrol Force. *See* Game Warden
Riverine interdiction, 159, 319–20
RIVFLOT 1, 173–75, 177, 178
Robinson, David B., 247
Robbins, Richard J., 231
Rodgers, Harvey P., 11, 31, 32–33
Rodgers, Larry D., 169, 176, 184, 186, 190
Rodriguez, Jack Charles, 73
Rogers, Peter M., 211
Route 4, 167, 215, 300, 303
Rudisill, Dayton Luther, 73
Rung Sat Special Zone (RSSZ). *See* Rung Sat Swamp
Rung Sat Swamp, 8, 9, 29–30, 75, 92, 95, 96, 97–103, *99*, 114, 124, 159, 160, 172, 200–201, 276, 319. *See also* Operation Jackstay

Sa Dec, 111, 113, *114*, 134, 216
Sa Ky River, 253, 255, 256
Saigon Naval Headquarters, 51
Saigon Naval Shipyard, 7, 45, 47, 48, 52, 155
Saigon, 8, 22, 75, 97, 135, 267, 275, 300, 306, 308
 river, 23, 97, 130
Salzer, Robert S., 176, 181, 192, 196–200, 216, *218*, 219, 276–80, *279*, 283, 310–11
 background and early military career, 276–77
San Clemente Island, CA, 169–70

San Francisco Bay Naval Shipyard, 169
Sang, Tran Binh, 14, 17, 33
Sangley Field, 44
sappers (Viet Cong), 30, 120, 155, 189, 273, 284, 302
Sauer, Johnny J., 193
Savage, Paul, 25
Schaeffer, Ted, 134
Schlosser, Jim, 150, 152
Schneider, James, 269
Schneider, Lester, 170, 177, 186, 190, 215
Schoech, William A. Jr., 24
Scotti, Paul C., 66, 270
Sea Float, 246–47, 323
Sea Force (VNN), 13, 16, 19–24, 28, 34–35, 45–47, 57. *See also* LSIL under ships, boats, and auxiliaries
 HQ-04, 32
 HQ-06 (*Van Don*), 22
 HQ-08, 32, 33, 230
 HQ-12, 272
 HQ-231 (*Nguyen Doc Bong*), 35
 HQ-401, 264
 HQ-404 (*Huong Giang*), 21
 HQ-405 (*Tien Giang*), 32–33
 HQ-500 (*Cam Ranh*), 22–23
 HQ-601 (*Tien Moi*), 45–46
 HQ-607 (*Nam Du*), 16
 HQ-617, 272
 HQ-9612, 123
seabees, 114, 133, 188
SEALORDS (Southeast Asia Lake, Ocean, River, and Delta Strategy), 42, 273, 278, 320, 321, 323
SEALs, 28–31, 72, 78, 92, 124, 127, 131, 132, 159, 169, 276, 286, 287–89, 291–92, 305, 311
 SEAL Team 1, 28–30
 SEAL Team 2, 28–31, 287–89, 291
 Basic Underwater Demolition/SEAL Course (BUDS), 29
 body snatch operations, 29
Seawolves, 123–30, 143, 144–45, 302, 305. *See also* Game Warden, HAL-3
sectarian conflict, 51
Self, Eugene Lawrence, 234

418

Semmes, Benedict Joseph, 85
SERE, 125, 170–71, 204, 300
Service Force Pacific (SERVPAC), 113, 114
17th Parallel, 7, 24, 28, 34, 43, 45, 57–58, 237, 238
Seventh Fleet, 24, 35, 43, 54, 55, 182, 237, 242, 277
    Task Group 72.7, 25
    Task Unit 77.1.0, 241
Shawkey, Dallas Walton, 15–16
Sheehan, Neil, 86–87
Shepherd, John T., 99
Sheppard, Donald D., 111, 158
Sheppard, Leonard Lee, 143
Sherman, Harold, 109
ships, boats, and auxiliaries (types)
    AMMI barges, 120, 192, 313, 315, 316–17. *See also* pontoon
    AN/GRC-106, 89
    AOG-8 (Genesee), 178
    APB
        Benewah (APB-35), 162, 182–83, *183*, 184, 185, 186, 187, 202, 206, 278
        Colleton (APB-36), 182, 184, 185, 206, 208, *209*, 278, 306
    ARL
        Askari (ARL-30), 182, 187, *188*
        Krishna (ARL-38), 55, 58–59, 60, 70, 74
    ASPB, 156, 174, 179–82, 315
        91-1, 181
        91-2, 284
        111-4, 182
        112-2, 163, 164, *180*, 214, 309
        112-3, *180*
    ATC, 174–77, *175*, 192–94, *193*, *195*, 305–7, 315, 322–23
        91-1, 208–9
        91-3, 212
        91-4, 208–9
        91-11, 212–13
        91-13, 212–13
        92-7, 205
        111-6, 211–12
        111-8, 217–19, 306–7
        111-10, 213
        111-11, 211
        111-13, 211
        112-4, 162, 206, 309
        112-7, 315
        152-1, 175
    ATC(H), 194, *195*, *204*, 212
    Baton Rouge Victory, 153
    BB
        New Jersey (BB-62), 85
    Boston (CAG-1), 240, 242
    Boston Whaler, 60, 131, 193, 251
    Cho Gao, 189
    Command and Control Boat (CCB), 174, 178, 194, 196, 202, 208, 210, 213, 216, 217, 278
        91-1, *179*CV
        Kitty Hawk (CV-63), 102
        Hancock (CVA-19), 98, 100, 101, 102, 128
    DD
        Black (DD-666), 43
        Edson (DD-946), 241–42
        Higbee (DD-806), 43
        Hobart (DD-39), 241–42
        Jenkins (DD-447), 44
        Mason (DD-852), 83
        Pritchett (DD-561), 281
        Theodore E. Chandler (DD-717), 241
        Walker (DD-517), 256
    DDG
        Robison (DDG-12), 98, 100, 102, 103
    DE
        DE-361, 24
        Edmonds (DE-406), 24
        Van Voorhis (DE-1028), 248, 267
    DER, 57, 58, 61, 80–84, 226, 230, 323
        Brister (DER-327), 40–41, 250
        Camp (DER-251), 260–61
        Finch (DER-328), 83
        Haverfield (DER-393), 64, 66, 238
        Hissem (DER-400), 248
        Otterstetter (DER-244), 67
        Vance (DER-387), 80–86, *81*. *See also* Arnheiter Affair
        Wilhoite (DER-397), 248, 252–56, *253*
    Eastern Mariner (Panamanian), 153
    Jamaica Bay, 145–46, 153, 188–89

Index

junks, Viet Cong, 5, 13, 42, 44, 59, 60, 62, 79–80, 84, 144–45, 160, 237
    VNN, 12, 14, 15, 48, 61, 258, 260, 263, 293
    Yabuta junks, 47–48, *49*
LCM, 2, 3, *6*, 17, 18, 37, 65, 74, 101, *102*, 122, 159, 175, 177, 180, 181, 184, 194, 202, 296, 298, 312, 317, 322. *See also* ATC; CCB; Monitor
    LCM (3)
    LCM (6), 2, *90*, 93, 95, 102, 169, 200, 201, 322
    LCM (8), 74, 94, 256, 314, 315, 316
    LCM 652, 257
LCPL, 97–98, *97*, 103
LCU, 7, 312, 316
LCVP, 3, 6, 18, 23, 37, 65, 94, 95, 293
Lien Doc Nguoi Nhia (LDNN), 29, 32–33, 120
Lorinda, 98
LSD, 104, 125
    Alamo (LSD-33), 98
    Belle Grove (LSD-2), 98, 103, *104*, 112, 124
    Catamount (LSD-17), 245
    Comstock (LSD-19), 112
    Oak Hill (LSD-7), 233
    Thomaston (LSD-28), 141
    Tortuga (LSD-26), 65, 66, 112
LSIL, 21, 65
    HQ-331, 10
    LSIL-225, 65
LSM, 7, 19, 32–33, 34
LSSL, 6, 7, 302
    LSSL-129, 35
    LSSL-226, 66
    LSSL-228, 46
LST, 19, 22, 111, 125, 126, 191, 287, 298, 313, 320, 323
    Cam Rahn (HQ-500), 22
    Floyd County (LST-762), 45, 46, 57, 58, 61
    Garrett County (LST-786), 111, *125*, 301, 302, 304
    Harnett County (LST-821), 111, 112, 282, 294, 297
    Henry County (LST-824), 101, 102
    Hunterdon County (LST-838), 111, 112, 113, 123, 296, 299, 312, 313
    Jennings County (LST-846), 111, 134
    Kemper County (LST-854), 182, 202, 206

    Sedgwick County (LST-1123), 140, 233
    Vernon County (LST-1161), 206
    Washoe County (LST-1165), 101, 102
    Westchester County (LST-1167), 320
    Whitfield County (LST-1169), 174
LSVP, 123
Monitor, 6. *See also* Zippo Monitor
    91-2, *178*
    92-1, *311*
    111-1, 278
    111-2, 210
    111-3, 210–11, 302
    112-1, 161–63, 309
    112-2, 163, 164, 178, 214, 309
MSB, 153–56, 156
    MSB-21, *156*
    MSB-22, 155
    MSB-32, 155
    MSB-45, 153, 155
    MSB-49, 154, 155
    MSB-51, 155
    MSB-54, 154, 155
MSC, 57, 61
MSC-116, 22
    Gannet (MSC-290), 230
    Spoonbill (MSC-202), 67
    Vireo (MSC-205), 40–41
MSF, 19
MSO, 24, 57, 58, 61, 230
    Acme (MSO-508), 242
    Esteem (MSO-438), 25
MSR, 156
PBR, 30, 31, 89–92, *90*, 103, 104–15, *105*, *106*, *108*, *110*, *112*, *114*, *124*, *125*, 155, 280, 285, 286, 293–300, 311–14, 313, 314, 319, 322–23
    basing, 111–18, 122, 134, 186, 300–301, 30
    combat experiences, 135–52
    crewing, 109
    early development, 104–5
    jet propulsion system 105–7, *106*
    Mark I model, *106*, 107
    Mark II, 280, *281*, 294
    patrols, 109
    PBR 7-13, 294
    PBR 7-14, 294

Index

PBR 7-16, 296–97
PBR 7-17, 296–97
PBR 7-18, 294, 296–97
PBR-34, 135
PBR-40, 135–36
PBR-53, 313
PBR-84, 313
PBR-96, 146, 157
PBR-98, 137–39
PBR-101, 149–51, 282
PBR-103, 91, 139, 146, 282
PBR-104, 151
PBR-105, 91, 143–44, 146, 150
PBR-106, 138–39, 150–51
PBR-107, 143–44
PBR-110, 51, 91, 139, 151
PBR-116, 121
PBR-118, 312
PBR-124, 294
PBR-126, 294
PBR-130, *106*
PBR-144, 118
PBR-153, 280
PBR-720, 293
PBR-721, 293
PBR-738, 280
PC, 24
PCE, 32, 49, 230
    HQ-08, 32–33, 230
    HQ-12, 272
PCF (Swift Boat), 52, 54, 61, 66, 67–72, *69*, 79, 83, 98, 103, 181, 224, 225, 230, 232–33, 235, 246, 272, 319, 322–24
    bases, 70–71, 186
    general description 52–53
    PCF-3, 67, 73
    PCF-4, 67, 72–75, *74*, 324
    PCF-9, 69, 234
    PCF-10, 69
    PCF-12, 69, 241, 243
    PCF-14, 79
    PCF-15, 233, 260
    PCF-18, 270
    PCF-19, 240–43
    PCF-20, 256, 260, 270
    PCF-22, 70

    PCF-26, 233
    PCF-31, 100–101
    PCF-37, 77
    PCF-38, 53
    PCF-39, 234
    PCF-41, 75–78
    PCF-54, *234*, 256, 260
    PCF-68, 249–50
    PCF-71, 249–50
    PCF-75, 261
    PCF-76, 79
    PCF-77, 70, 79
    PCF-78, 250–51
    PCF-79, 248, 252–57, *257*, 267–69
    PCF-97, 70, 233
    PCF-98, 233
    seaworthiness, 70, 79
PGM/PG (*Asheville* class), 243–48, 322, 323
    Antelope (PG-86), 246–47
    Asheville (PGM/PG-84), 243–46, 244
    Canon (PG-90), 247
    Crockett (PG-88), 246
    Gallup (PGM/PG-85), 244–46, 247, 248, 252–55
PGM (VNN motor patrol gunboat motor), 19, 45–46
    PGM-600, 230
    PGM-607, 230
    PGM-608, 230
pontoon barges, 120, 174, 184, 186, 192–93, 313. *See also* AMMI barges
PRC
    PRC-10, 73
    PRC-25, 178, 254
Princeton (LPH-5), 98
PT-109, 89
sampans, 15, 19, 30, 35, 36, 42, 71, 89, 91, 93, 94, 97, 98, 110, 135–139, 144–45, 160, 207, 232–33
Sandpumper, 189
STCAN/FOM, 1, 2, 3, 18, 179
trawlers, 31 34, 36, 39–42, 61, 62–66, 63, 64, 65, 79–80, 223, 224, 248–58, 254, 257, 270–72, *271*, 317. *See also* Vung Ro Incident; *Point Grey*; *Point League*

421

Index

United 31-foot cruiser, 105. *See also* PBR
WHEC, 226, 230–33
    Androscoggin (WHEC-68), 270
    Bearing Strait (WHEC-382), *226*
    Half Moon (WHEC-378), 231–32
    Ingham (WHEC-35), 62
    Minnetonka (WHEC-67), 272
    Rush (WHEC-723), 232
    Winona (WHEC-65), 232, 270
    Yakutat (WHEC-380), 232
WPB, 57–58, 60, 66, 67, 83, 98, 100, 176, 224, 225, 230, 232–33, 235, 246, 322
    Point Arden (WPB-82309), 235, 250–51
    Point Caution (WPB-82301), 239
    Point Clear (WPB-82315), 60–61, 235
    Point Comfort (WPB-82317), 60, 67
    Point Cypress (WPB-82326), 41, 236
    Point Dume (WPB-82325), 241, 243
    Point Ellis (WPB-82330), 250–51
    Point Gammon (WPB-82328), 62, 249
    Point Garnet (WPB-82310), 67
    Point Glover (WPB-82307), 59, 60
    Point Grey (WBP-82324), 39–42, 57, 60, 61, 270
    Point Hudson (WPB-82322), 64
    Point League (WPB-82304), 61
        trawler intercept (June 1966), 62–66, *63*
    Point Marone (WPB-82331), *58*, 60, 235
    Point Orient (WPB-83319), 252–56
    Point Slocum (WPB-82313), *64*, 65
    Point Welcome (WPB-82329), 236, 270
        friendly fire incident, 237–40
        general description, 53–54
YMS, 5, 7
    YMS-347, 277
YOG, 19, 316
YFNB-21, 71, 119
YR-71, 71
YRBM, 125
    YRBM-16, 119–23, 320
    YRBM-17, 187, 189
    YRBM-21, 119
Zippo monitor, 178, 179, 210, 278. *See* monitor
Sihanoukville, 42, 159
Skyraider. *See* aircraft

Slane, Willis, 104
SLAR. *See* radar
Slavish, Joseph, 121–22
Smith, Ardath C. Jr., 95
Smith, Chester B., 110, 136–39, 143
Smith, Francis, 305
Smith, Gerald W., 314
Smith, Harold V., 9–10
Smith, Margaret Chase, 27
Smith, Robert W., 292
Snipers, 139, 157, 198, 287, 288–89, 290
Snoopy's nose, 208, 214
Snyder, Peter B., 241
Soc Trang, 125
Soirap River, 94, 100, 101, 114
Soluri, Elroy A., 230
Son, Huynh Hong, 73
Song On Doc, 232
South Korea, 26, 172, 230, 256
Spatt, Frank R., 118, 157
Special Forces, 29, 31, 32, 33, 60, 92, 126, 127, 231–32, 234, 235, 275, 276. *See also* SEALs
Spector, Ronald H., 36
Spencer, Robert W., 128
Stanley, Chester C Jr.., 98, 171–72, 186, 208, 210, 217
Steed, Sam, 286
steel-hulled trawlers. *See* trawlers
Steffes, James, 241–42
Stein, Leon C., 56
Stephan, Charles R., 248, 252–56
Stewart Seacraft, 53
Stouffer, Gary, 151
Stover, Thomas E., 164
Stowers, Charles G., 10
Strandberg, Dick, 121
Stump, Harry L., 143
Subic Bay Naval Base, *58*, 245
Sullivan, Terry, *288*
Sumrall, Stephen, 286–87, 290
Supply Corps (USN), 300
Swartztrauber, Sayre A., 92–93, 113, 315
Swift Boat. *See* PCF
swimmers (Viet Cong), 60, 73, 120, 145. *See also* sappers

Tacoma Boat Building Company, 244
Tactical Operation Center (TOC), 286–87
Tactical Zones (MACV)
    I Corps, 237, 238, 239, 258, 262, 275, 283, 312–17, 321
    II Corps, 283, 320
    III Corps, 173, 273, 321
    IV Corps, 172, 173, 270, 273, 291, 293, 308
Taiwan Strait patrol, 226
Tan Chau, 111, 114, 120, 229
Tan Dinh Island, 159
Tan My, 313, 314, 317
    Cove, 315
Tan Son Nhut, 44, 125, 306
Tango boat. *See* ATC
Tapscott, Kenneth W., 133
Task Force 71, 43–45, 54
Task Force 115. *See* Market Time
Task Force 116. *See* Game Warden
Task Force 117. *See* Mobile Riverine Force
Task Force Clearwater, 283, 312–17. *See also* Game Warden; Naval Support Activities; Mobile Riverine Force
Tay Ninh, 320
taxation (Viet Cong), 1, 3, 50, 91, 92, 96, 167
Tet Offensive (1968), 30, 80, 92, 116, 125, 128, 130, 134, 166, 177, 220, 270, 273, 275–317, 320
Than, Nguyen Viet, 282
Thang, Bang Cao, 23, 52
Thi, Bui Quang, 240
Thien, Do Van, 135–36
Thieu, Nguyen Van, 23, 51, 66
Thoai, Ho Van Ky, 11, 32–33
Thoi Son Island, 138
Thompson, B. Foster III, 64
Thorell, James C., 100–101
Thuong, Duong, 73
Thurmond, Strom, 142
tides, 196–97
Tien Giang River, 301
Tiger Island, 240–43
Timmons, Bruce A., 70
Tobin, Paul E., 279
Tong, Sam Mu, 73
Toole, Morton E., 148

Tra Khuc, 258
Tra On, 2
Tra Vinh, 302
Trackerman, Anthony J., 251
Training Relations Instruction Mission (TRIM), 7
Travnicek, Ivan, 149
Treat, Lonnie J. I., 155
Triet, Tran Van, 32
Tuck, Hubert Jr., 234
Turley, Michael "Boats," 260
Turner, James S. G., 173, 219
Tutwiler, Guy, 203, 206
12-mile limit, 43, 54, 226, 228, 254

U.S. Air Force, 91, 98, 102, 130, 132, 240–43, 297, 299. *See also* aircraft
    in *Point Welcome* incident, 237–40
U.S. Army, 91, 101, 123, 132, 183, 191, 194, 287, 302
    1st Division, 75
    II Field Force, 173, 207, 283
    9th Infantry Division, 162, 165, 168, 172–74, 184, 190, 193, 198, 207, 275, 276, 283, 296, 297, 305, 308, 320
    2nd Brigade, 172–74, 182, 190, 214, 310
    36th Evacuation Hospital, 77, 78
    39th Infantry
        2nd Battalion, 298
        3rd Battalion, 298
    47th Infantry
        3rd Battalion, 168, 200–202, 207–8, 211, 214, 216, 219, 285, 290, 303, 305–6, 308–9
    4th Battalion, 163, 185, 201–3, 215–17
    60th Infantry
        2nd Battalion, 214
        3rd Battalion, 208, 211–12, 214, 280, 285, 290, 305–9
        5th Battalion, 208, 214
    93rd Evacuation Hospital, 165
    101st Airborne Division, 317
    145th Aviation Battalion, 112
    197th Armed Helicopter Company, 125

Index

199th Infantry Brigade (Light), 202
advisors, 285
engineers, 188, 301
helicopter support for Game Warden, 124–26, 136, 305, 313
military police, 284, 301, 303, 311
U.S. Coast Guard Academy, 39, 59, 62, 235, 250, 251
U.S. Coast Guard, 39–41
    Division 11, 57, 58, 59, 229
    Division 12, 57, 62, 71, 236, 251
    Division 13, 62
    Squadron 1, 57, 225
    in Market Time, 57–66, 225–26, 231–32
U.S. Marine Corps, 75, 98–103, 211, 233, 239, 240–41, 251
    III Marine Amphibious Force (MAF), 238, 312
    5th Marines, 1st Battalion, 98–103
    Battalion Landing Team 2/4, 316
Ulmer, Stephen T., 62, 63, 65–66
Underwater Demolition Team (UDT), 27–28, 120, 246. *See also* LDNN; SEALs
United Boatbuilders, 104–5
USAID (United States Agency for International Development), 131, 286

Valin, Wayne, 10
Valley Forge Military Academy (VFMA), 128
Vam Co Dong River, 132
Vam Sat River, 101
Van, Huynh, 73
Varelas, Constantine "Charlie," 91, 116
Vaughn, Daniel R., 62
Venzke, Norman C., 229
Verhasselt, Ray, 281–82, 292
Veth, Kenneth L., 258, 279
Victory Hotel, 89, 286
Vien, Do Viet, 238
Viet Cong units. *See also* People's Army of Vietnam (PAVN)
    5th Nha Be Battalion, 202
    261st Main Force Battalion, 285, 373
    263rd Main Force Battalion, 139, 207, 213, 214, 285, 291

267th Main Force Battalion, 215–16, 219
306th Main Force Battalion, 158, 301
502d Local Force Battalion, 215–16, 219
514th Main Force Battalion, 285
516th Local Force Battalion, 293
518th Main Force Battalion, 293
D857th Main Force Battalion, 301
Viet Cong heavy weaponry
    57mm, 33, 79, 98, 154, 175, 180, 206, 214, 233, 280
    B40, 164–66, 175, 209, 210, 211, 212, 213, 215, 219, 246, 279, 280, 301, 308, 309, 314
    B50, *78*, 166, 209, 212, 213, 247
    recoilless rifle, 33, 64, 98, 150, 154, 155, 180, 181, 184, 206, 214, 280
    rocket propelled grenades (RPG), 165, 206, 247, 307
Vietnam Marines, 19, 28, 50, 215
    5th Battalion, 215–216, 219
Vietnam Navy (VNN), 1, 3, 20, 27, 34, 38, 42–52, 54–58, 64–66, 73, 75, 79, 92–96, 98, 132, 175, 200, 224, 227, 263, 264, 272–73, 284, 300–302, 310, 321. *See also* Coastal Divisions; Coastal
    Force; *dinassauts*; River Force; Sea Force
    1963 coup, 21–24
    1965 mutiny, 51–52, 94
    and Market Time, 229–31
    Coastal Group 16 attack, 258–61, 263, 273
    cultural gap between VNN and USN, 10–11, 322
    during Vung Ro Bay incident, 31–33
    force structure, 7, 13, 16–17, 21, 52, 95, 229, 321
    origins of, 5–24
    problems, 9–12, 14–15, 36, 45–52, 320
Vietnam Air Force (VNAF), 21, 32, 34, 129, 197
Vinh Binh, 1
    province, 50, 158
Vinh Hy, 15
Vinh Long, 2, 7, 125, 126, 127, 128, 133, 275, 280, 283, 284
    during Tet, 300–308, *304*, 311, 319
    province, 1, 37, 111, 158, 280

424